DATE DUE

Mach 20, 2013	
Nov. 3, 2013	

BRODART, CO.   Cat. No. 23-221

ALSO BY HEDRICK SMITH

The Russians

The Power Game: How Washington Works

The New Russians

Rethinking America

The Pentagon Papers (coauthor)

Reagan the Man, the President (coauthor)

Beyond Reagan: The Politics of Upheaval (coauthor)

WHO STOLE THE
AMERICAN DREAM?

WHO STOLE

the

AMERICAN
DREAM?

Hedrick Smith

RANDOM HOUSE

NEW YORK

Published in the United States by Random House, an imprint of
The Random House Publishing Group, a division of Random House, Inc., New York.

RANDOM HOUSE and colophon are registered trademarks of Random House, Inc.

Grateful acknowledgment is made to the WGBH Educational Foundation for permission
to reprint previously broadcast material and excerpts from *Frontline* interviews as follows:
Frontline's "Poisoned Waters" © 2009 WGBH Educational Foundation, www.pbs.org/
frontline, *Frontline*'s "The Card Game" © 2009 WGBH Educational Foundation,
www.pbs.org/frontline, *Frontline*'s "Can You Afford to Retire?" © 2006 WGBH
Educational Foundation, www.pbs.org/frontline, *Frontline*'s "The Wall Street Fix"
© 2003 WGBH Educational Foundation, www.pbs.org/frontline, *Frontline*'s "Is Wal-Mart
Good for America?" © 2004 WGBH Educational Foundation, www.pbs.org/frontline.
Used by permission.

Library of Congress Cataloging-in-Publication Data
Smith, Hedrick.
Who stole the American dream? / by Hedrick Smith.
p. cm.
ISBN 978-1-4000-6966-8
eISBN 978-0-679-60464-8
1. United States—Politics and government—1945–1989.   2. United States—
Politics and government—1989–   3. Political culture—United States—History—
20th century.   4. Political culture—United States—History—21st
century.   5. Polarization (Social sciences)—United States.   6. Middle class—
United States—Economic conditions.   7. Middle class—Political activity—
United States.   8. Public interest—United States.   9. Income distribution—
United States.   10. Divided government—United States.   I. Title.
E839.5.S59 2012   973.91—dc23   2012005865

Printed in the United States of America on acid-free paper

www.atrandom.com

68975

To Susan,
and
to a better future
for our children and grandchildren
and
their generations

We must make our choice. We may have democracy, or we may have wealth concentrated in the hands of a few, but we can't have both.

—LOUIS D. BRANDEIS,
adviser to President Woodrow Wilson

THE CHALLENGE FROM WITHIN

> We are treading the edge of a precipice here. Civilizations die of disenchantment. If enough people doubt their society, the whole venture falls apart. We must never let anger, fashionable cynicism, or political partisanship blur our vision on that point. We must not despair of the Republic.
>
> — JOHN W. GARDNER,
> *cabinet secretary to President Lyndon Johnson*

> Thus, it is manifest that the best political community is formed by citizens of the middle class, and that those states are likely to be well-administered in which the middle class is large, and stronger if possible than both other classes. . . .
>
> — ARISTOTLE,
> *Politics*

IN HIS MAGISTERIAL WORK *A Study of History,* British historian Arnold J. Toynbee tells the story of how civilizations rise and fall through the dynamics of challenge and response. After studying twenty-one civilizations across six thousand years, Toynbee found that the fate of each civilization was determined by its response to the challenges it faced.

Ancient Egypt rose to enduring greatness, Toynbee reported, by overcoming the challenge of a hostile climate with a sophisticated system of agriculture. In South America, the Mayan and Andean civilizations overcame similar environmental hardships but perished before the challenge of more powerful invaders. Other civilizations collapsed from within. The city-states of ancient Greece fell into fierce competition among themselves over trade and spiraled into decline from fratricidal warfare. Ancient Rome fell victim to what Toynbee called a "schism in the body social" and a "schism in the soul"—internal divisions that undermined Rome's unity at the core.

In the twentieth century, America met and overcame the military challenge of mortal enemies—Hitler's Germany and then the prolonged global challenge of Soviet communism.

Today we face a more complicated and potentially more dangerous challenge—a challenge from within. Like ancient Rome, we are in danger of causing or contributing to our own downfall by having spawned the schisms that Toynbee talked about—schisms in the body politic and in the soul of our society.

A House Divided: Two Americas

Over the past three decades, we have become Two Americas. We are no longer one large American family with shared prosperity and shared political and economic power, as we were in the decades following World War II. Today, no common enemy unites us as a nation. No common enterprise like settling the West or rocketing to the moon inspires us as a people.

We are today a sharply divided country—divided by power, money, and ideology. Our politics have become rancorous and polarized, our political leaders unable to resolve the most basic problems. Constant conflict has replaced a sense of common purpose and the pursuit of the common welfare. Not just in Washington, but across the nation, the fault lines that divide us run deep, and they are profoundly self-destructive, unless we can find our way to some new unity and consensus.

Abraham Lincoln gave us fair warning. "A house divided against itself," Lincoln said, "cannot stand."

Americans sense that something is profoundly wrong—that we have gone off track as a nation. Many skilled observers write about this, but it is hard to grasp exactly how we arrived at our present predicament or how to respond—how to go about healing America's dangerous divide. The causes do not lie in the last election or the one before that. They predate the financial collapse of 2008. The timeline to our modern national quagmire lies embedded in the longer arc of our history, and that history, from 1971 to the present, is the focus of this book.

Hidden Beginnings

History often has hidden beginnings. There is no blinding flash of light in the sky to mark a turning point, no distinctive mushroom cloud signifying an atomic explosion that will forever alter human destiny. Often a watershed is crossed in some gradual and obscure way so that most people do not realize that an unseen shift has moved them into a new era, reshaping their lives, the lives of their generation, and the lives of their children, too. Only decades later do historians, like detectives, sift through the confusing strands of the past and discover a hitherto unknown pregnant beginning.

One such hidden beginning, with powerful impact on our lives today, occurred in 1971 with "the Powell Memorandum." The memo, first unearthed by others many years ago, was written by Lewis Powell, then one of America's most respected and influential corporate attorneys, two months before he was named to the Supreme Court. But it remains a discovery for many people today to learn that the Powell memo sparked a business and corporate rebellion that would forever change the landscape of power in

Washington and would influence our policies and economy even now.

The Powell memo was a business manifesto, a call to arms to Corporate America, and it triggered a powerful response. The seismic shift of power that it set in motion marked a fault line in our history. Political revolt had been brewing on the right since the presidential candidacy in 1964 of Senator Barry Goldwater, the anti-union, free market conservative from Arizona, but it was the Powell memo that lit the spark of change. It ignited a long period of sweeping transformations both in Washington's policies and in the mind-set and practices of American business leaders—transformations that reversed the politics and policies of the postwar era and the "virtuous circle" philosophy that had created the broad prosperity of America's middle class.

The newly awakened power of business helped propel America into a New Economy and a New Power Game in politics, which largely determine how we live today. Both were strongly tilted in favor of the business, financial, and corporate elites. Trillions were added to the wealth of America's super-rich at the expense of the middle class, and the country was left with an unhealthy concentration of political and economic power.

This book will take you inside that decades-long story of change and show how we have unwittingly dismantled the political and economic infrastructures that underpinned the great era of middle-class prosperity in the 1950s, '60s, and '70s.

The Economic Divide:
The 1 Percent and the 99 Percent

Today, the gravest challenge and the most corrosive fault line in our society is the gross inequality of income and wealth in America.

Not only political liberals but conservative thinkers as well emphasize the danger to American democracy of this great divide. "America is coming apart at the seams—not seams of race or ethnicity, but of class," writes conservative sociologist Charles Murray of the American Enterprise Institute. Murray voices alarm at what he describes as "the formation of classes that are different in kind and in their degree of separation from anything that the nation has ever known. . . . The divergence into these separate classes, if it continues, will end what has made America America."

Since the era of middle-class prosperity from the mid-1940s to the mid-1970s, the past three decades have produced the third wave of great private wealth in American history, a new Gilded Age comparable to the era of the robber barons in the 1890s, which led to the financial Panic of 1893 and the trust-busting presidency of Theodore Roosevelt; and to the era of great fortunes in the Roaring Twenties, which ended in the stock market crash of 1929 and the Great Depression.

In our New Economy, America's super-rich have accumulated trillions in new wealth, far beyond anything in other nations, while the American middle class has stagnated. What separates the Two Americas is far more than a wealth gap. It is a wealth chasm— "mind-boggling" in its magnitude, says Princeton economist Alan Krueger. Wealth has flowed so massively to the top that during the nation's growth spurt from 2002 to 2007, America's super-rich, the top 1 percent (3 million people), reaped two-thirds of the nation's entire economic gains. The other 99 percent were left with only one-third of the gains to divide among 310 million people. In 2010, the first full year of the economic recovery, the top 1 percent captured 93 percent of the nation's gains.

Americans, more than people in other countries, accept some inequality as part of our way of life, as inevitable and even desirable—a reward for talent and hard work, an incentive to produce and excel. But wealth begets wealth, especially when reinforced through the influence of money in politics. Then the hyperconcentration of wealth aggravates the political cleavages in our society.

The danger is that if the extremes become too great, the wealth dichotomy tears the social fabric of the country, undermines our ideal of equal opportunity, and puts the whole economy at risk—and more than the economy, our nation itself. A solid majority of Americans say openly that we have reached that point—that our economy is unfairly tilted in favor of the wealthy, that government should take action to make the economy fairer, and that they're frustrated that Congress continually blocks such action.

What's more, contrary to political arguments put forward for not taxing the rich, an economy of large personal fortunes does not deliver the best economic performance for the country. In fact, concentrated wealth works against economic growth. Several recent studies have shown that America's wealth gap is a drag on today's economy. Harvard economist Philippe Aghion cites an accumulation of "impressively unambiguous" evidence from multiple economic studies documenting that "greater inequality reduces the rate of growth." A recent International Monetary Fund study came to a similar conclusion—that a high level of income inequality can be "destructive" to sustained growth and that the best condition for long-term growth is "more equality in the income distribution."

The Unraveling

The opposite has happened in America since the late 1970s. The soaring wealth of the super-rich has brought the unraveling of the American Dream for the middle class—the dream of a steady job with decent pay and health benefits, rising living standards, a home of your own, a secure retirement, and the hope that your children would enjoy a better future.

As a country, we have declined from an era of middle-class prosperity and middle-class power from the 1940s to the 1970s to an era of vast fortunes and mass economic insecurity. We have fallen from being the envy of the world, with the most widely shared economic prosperity and the most affluent middle class of any place on earth, to losing our title as "the land of opportunity." It is now easier, in fact, to climb the economic and social ladder in several Western European countries than it is in the United States.

Globalization has hit us all, of course, but the way we have responded with our New Economy has put the American middle class in an ever-tightening financial squeeze, raising protests from both left and right.

"The middle class is the key to greatness in this country," right-wing radio commentator Rush Limbaugh told his audience of millions one sunny fall afternoon in October 2011. "We had the largest middle class in the world, and it's under assault from practically every direction. Look at the destruction of home values. The family home was the largest asset most people in the middle class have, and it's being destroyed, and it's being destroyed after being talked up for generation after generation after generation. The American dream equals owning your own house."

"It was the middle class that made America great," AFL-CIO president Rich Trumka said in a television appearance a few weeks earlier. "We were very, very competitive when the unions were at their heydays. We spread the wealth around to everybody so that the main driver of our economy [was] consumer spending, people [had] money in their pockets to spend." Now, Trumka went on, the question "is whether we'll restore the middle class, which is the heart and the soul of the American dream."

When such normally clashing political voices as Limbaugh and Trumka sound a common theme, it is worth listening. They are highlighting a critical national problem.

The Political Divide: Unequal Democracy

In our political life, too, we have left behind one of the most expansive periods of American democracy, the populist era of the 1960s and 1970s, where much of the dynamism and energy that drove sweeping changes in our laws and policies arose from the belly of the nation. Since then, we have moved from a broad populism to a narrow plutocracy. Instead of a high-visibility, outside political power game of mass movements and public participation, we now have a low-visibility, inside power game dominated by the lobbyists for the American financial and political elite.

In the middle-class democracy of the 1950s, '60s, and '70s, ordinary Americans felt confident of their political power and its impact. They believed that by engaging personally in civic activism, they could help set the nation's agenda—and they succeeded. They forced action by Congress and the White House. Through grassroots power—the civil rights movement, the environmental movement, the peace movement, the consumer movement, the labor movement, and the women's movement—citizen power won important political victories that altered the face of our society and enlarged the American Dream. Seeing their own impact on public policy, people felt connected to government instead of feeling powerless and alienated as they do today.

In the last three decades, except for the organized activism of the Tea Party and the inchoate protests of Occupy Wall Street, Americans at the grass roots have largely retreated from direct citizen action. Our idealism has given way to a sense of futility. That has prompted Ernie Cortes, one of America's most effective grassroots organizers, to amend Lord Acton's famous dictum that power corrupts. Cortes notes: "Powerlessness also corrupts."

Powerlessness breeds cynicism and passivism, especially between elections, which is the crucial time when policies are forged, the time when the organized money of special interests exerts commanding influence. As Senator John McCain, the conservative Republican presidential nominee in 2008, put it, the flow of money into lobbying and into election campaigns is "nothing less than an elaborate influence-peddling scheme in which both parties conspire to stay in office by selling the country to the highest bidder."

Political insiders have always had extra power—more at some times in our history, less at other times. Since the late 1970s, the insiders' advantage has grown exponentially. Today, the New Power Game in Washington is dominated by well-financed professional lobbyists, many of them former members of Congress and government officials with an inside track, working for special interests like

Wall Street banks; the oil, defense, and pharmaceutical industries; and business trade associations.

Our once healthy clash of interests has become precariously one-sided. In the past decade, business has employed thirty times as many Washington lobbyists as trade unions and sixteen times as many lobbyists as labor, consumer, and public interest lobbyists combined. Spending has been even more lopsided in favor of Corporate America. From 1998 through 2010, business interests and trade groups spent $28.6 billion on lobbying compared with $492 million for labor, nearly a 60-to-1 business advantage.

Today, no countervailing power matches the political clout of business. Our democracy has become starkly unequal.

The Interaction of Politics and Economics

This book sets out to describe how, over the past four decades, we came to this point—how we became two such polarized and dissimilar Americas, how the great economic and political divide affects the lives of individual Americans, and how we might, through changed policies and a revival of citizen action, restore our unity and reclaim the American Dream for average people.

In my first book, *The Russians,* I sought to give American readers an intimate human picture of what Russians were like beneath the veneer of Soviet communism and why they behaved the way they did. In *The Power Game: How Washington Works,* I went inside the American political system and the games politicians played in the era of Ronald Reagan and Jimmy Carter to describe how power really works in Washington and why some leaders succeed and others fail.

In this book, I provide a reporter's CAT scan of the Two Americas today, examining the interplay of economics and politics to disclose how the shifts of power and of wealth have led to the unraveling of the American Dream for the middle class. I tell the story, too, of how we evolved into such an unequal democracy—how we lost the moderate political middle and how today's polarized politics reinforce economic inequality and a pervasive sense of economic insecurity.

This is a reporter's book full of stories of Americans high and low. It portrays the impact of the New Economy and the New Power Game on the rich and the middle—on jobs, incomes, homes, retirement—and on people's hopes and dreams. Among these people are many Americans I came to know reporting for *The New York Times,* for PBS investigative documentaries, and for this book— leaders like Bill Clinton, Newt Gingrich, and Martin Luther King, Jr.; CEOs like Al Dunlap, Bob Galvin, or Andy Grove; and middle-class people like jet airline mechanic Steve O'Neill, loan officer Bre Heller, computer plant technician Winson Crabb, contractor Eliseo Guardado, and small-business owner John Terboss.

Most still voice a plucky personal confidence. Yet their faith in the American Dream has been sorely shaken. Like others, they want to know what happened to them and to America—what changed the way our economy and our politics work.

Technology and Globalization

The standard explanation offered by business leaders and political and economic conservatives is that these harsh realities of the New Economy are the unavoidable product of impersonal and irresistible market forces.

America, they point out, was an unchallenged economic colossus at the end of World War II. It was easier then for the United States to generate middle-class prosperity. But as Europe, Japan, and Russia recovered, America's share of world trade shrank from nearly 20 percent in 1950 to less than 10 percent in 1980. In the early 1970s, we began running trade deficits, and as Asia boomed, we imported much more than we sold abroad. As historian Charles Maier put it, the United States morphed from the "empire of production" into the "empire of consumption." Today, we benefit as consumers, but we pay a heavy price in lost jobs, American jobs lost to foreign imports or because U.S. companies have moved them overseas.

Business leaders and free market economists tell us that this economic hemorrhaging is an unavoidable cost of progress. It is the price of the inexorable march of technology and free trade. But that seductive half-truth doesn't fully square with the facts. It ignores the political and economic story that this book tells—the impact of public policy and corporate strategy on how we became Two Americas. It fails to explain why such an overwhelming share of the fruits of technological change and globalization went to a privileged few while the majority of ordinary Americans got left out.

Few would dispute that technological change and the digital age have shaken up the U.S. economy, forcing change, creating new winners and losers, and disrupting many industries and millions of lives. But if technological change and globalization were the primary causes of America's problems today, then we would see the same yawning income inequalities and middle-class losses in other advanced countries. But we don't.

A Comparison—and a Fork in the Road

Germany took a different fork in the road in the 1980s and it has fared far better than America in the global marketplace. While the United States piled up multitrillion-dollar trade deficits in the 2000s, Germany had large export surpluses. In the midst of Western Europe's economic turmoil, Germany is a bastion of strength. Its economy grew faster than the U.S. economy from 1995 to 2010, with the gains more widely shared. Since 1985, the hourly pay of middle-class workers in Germany has risen five times as fast as in the United States, with the result that the German middle class is now paid better on average than Americans.

German leaders worked hard to keep their high-wage, high-skilled jobs at home. While U.S. multinational corporations aggressively moved production offshore, Germany, too, lost some of its production workforce, but it retained a larger share of its manufacturing base at home than America did. Today, 21 percent of Germans work in production; in the United States, it's 9 percent.

The difference is not in technology but in our government policies and our corporate strategies. Germany has maintained strong trade unions and a strong social contract between business and labor, even reducing unemployment during the Great Recession, while America's jobless rate shot up.

America Chose a Different Fork

America chose a different path, driven by the pro-business power shift in politics and a new corporate mind-set, both of which lie at the root of the economic rift in America today. The New Economy laissez-faire philosophy of the past three decades promised that deregulation, lower taxes, and free trade would lift all boats. It argued that sharply reduced taxes for the rich would generate the capital for America's economic growth. Its disciples asserted that the free market would spread the wealth.

But that is not what has happened. The middle class was left behind—the 150 million people whose family incomes range from nearly $30,000 to $100,000 a year—as well as 90 million more low-income Americans living in poverty or just above. Even the 60 million upper-middle-class Americans and the nation's wealthiest 5 percent have been falling steadily further behind America's financial elite, the super-rich 1 percent.

The New Economy mind-set marked a sharp break with the corporate philosophy of the postwar era. Then, the mantra of business leaders was to share the wealth—to distribute to their employees a sizable share of the profits from growth and from gains in productivity. Since the 1970s, business leaders have largely abandoned that share-the-wealth ethic. With some exceptions, CEOs have practiced "wedge economics"—splitting apart the pay of rank-and-file employees from company revenues and profits. In fact, according to the Census Bureau, the pay of a typical male worker was lower in 2010 than in 1978, adjusted for inflation. Three decades of getting nowhere or slipping backward.

Such a dichotomy has developed in America's New Economy that last April, while more than twenty-five million Americans were unemployed, were working part-time against their will, or had dropped out of the labor force and the economy was still struggling to recover, *The Wall Street Journal* ran a front-page story trumpeting that major U.S. companies "have emerged from the deepest recession since World War II more productive, more profitable, flush with cash and less burdened by debt" than in 2007, before the U.S. economy collapsed. Many of the 1.1 million jobs added by American multinationals since 2007 and much of the $1.2 trillion cash added to their corporate treasuries came from overseas. At home, the *Journal* noted, "the performance hasn't translated into significant gains in U.S. employment."

The financial cleavage created by wedge economics has provoked popular discontent. Today, two-thirds of Americans—far more than just a couple of years earlier—say they see "strong" conflicts between rich and poor, and they see economics as more divisive than race, age, or ethnic grouping.

"The Virtuous Circle" of the 1950s–1970s vs. the New Economy of the 1980s–2000s

The New Economy is not smart. It hurts our capacity to grow, as we have seen from America's painfully slow recovery from the financial collapse of 2008. The job losses and stagnant pay of the New Economy have broken what economists call "the virtuous circle of growth"—long the engine of America's economic growth and middle-class prosperity.

In the heyday of the middle class, for thirty years after World War II, America's great companies paid high wages and good benefits.

Tens of millions of families had steady income, and they spent it, generating high consumer demand. Robust consumer demand is the main driving force of the U.S. economy. It propels businesses to invest in new technology, new plants and equipment, and more employees. Corporate expansion contributes to full employment, fueling "the virtuous circle of growth" to another round of expansion and higher living standards.

But in our New Economy, the dynamic thrust of "the virtuous circle" has been disrupted by job losses and the lid on average pay scales. Flat pay is bad not only for individuals, but for the whole economy. Weak pay leads to weak consumer demand. Companies don't expand and hire, and as a country, we bog down in long, painful "jobless recoveries." That has happened several times in the past two decades.

In short, downsizing, offshoring, and wedge economics have backfired. For the economy, they don't work. For the nation, they don't work. Individual corporations may profit, especially multinationals that have moved production overseas. But by sharing so little of their gains with their U.S. employees, they have put a crimp on middle-class spending, and without big consumer demand, the nation's economy can't move well.

Crisis Politics

Washington can't move either—because it is frozen in dysfunctional partisan gridlock.

Certainly, genuine differences divide us as a people. That has always been true. America's political pendulum has swung back and forth as parties battled over policy. But there was an accepted center of gravity. Work got done. Political rivals like Democrat Lyndon Johnson and Republican Richard Nixon would differ, but there was some consensus. Both expanded Social Security; neither tried to privatize it. Republicans might cut specific government programs or trim the budget more than Democrats, but they were not out to dismantle government and shut down entire cabinet departments.

Today, everything is in dispute. Political Washington has lost the habit of compromise and belief in compromise. No issue is ever settled. One Congress passes a law, the next tries to repeal it. The hallmark of the New Power Game is crisis politics—political ultimatums and a partisan blame game. But the stakes are too high for perpetual brinkmanship. It is time to heed Lincoln: "A house divided . . . cannot stand."

Challenge and Response: a New Mind-Set, a Domestic Marshall Plan

It will take a political metamorphosis, a populist renaissance, in America to reverse the political and economic tides of the past three decades and to make our country strong and whole again. The Toynbeean challenge we face requires a response from all of us, a rebirth of civic activism from average people at the grass roots as well as from America's political and economic leaders. Millions of Americans will have to come off the sidelines and reengage in direct citizen action in order to reestablish "government of the people, by the people, for the people" and to achieve a genuine people's agenda in Washington.

It is not hard to conceive of the measures needed to restore a fairer, more level economic playing field—action on jobs, homes, taxes, and fairness, plus a reset in long-term economic thinking. It took decades for us to get into our current national predicament; it will take time—and tenacity—to build our way back to a more just, secure, and vibrant society.

To regenerate widely shared prosperity over the long term, we must get "the virtuous circle" working again. That challenge requires our business leadership to share more of their companies' profits with workers. It requires our political leaders to do more of what past presidents such as Washington, Lincoln, Theodore Roosevelt, and Dwight Eisenhower have done: Use government resources to modernize our aging highways, ports, and airports, to stimulate research and development, to retrain workers who have fallen behind, and to provide incentives to the private sector in order to make America—and Americans—more globally competitive in the years ahead.

There are some hopeful omens. One problem is that we have become so fearful about our economy and so jaded about government that we overlook the good news in our midst. Business leaders have begun to speak out against the New Economy notion that the United States can survive on a service economy. What we need now, insists General Electric CEO Jeffrey Immelt, is a renaissance in manufacturing and production jobs. *Make It in America* is the title theme of Dow Chemical CEO Andrew Liveris's latest book. Other top corporate executives call for a domestic Marshall Plan—a mix of tax incentives, aid for research, public-private investment pools, and a skills alliance to modernize the training of American workers displaced by foreign trade.

General Motors and Chrysler went to the brink of extinction in 2009, but they have come back. The auto industry bailout was brutal, but it signaled some significant changes: business and government working together, management and labor doing give-and-take to save companies and jobs. Both GM's CEO, Dan Akerson, and the United Auto Workers union scrapped their "us vs. them" rhetoric. The union agreed to keep wages steady. GM and Ford pledged to reopen plants in the United States and not to shift production to Mexico as they had planned. By early 2012, the Big Three carmakers planned to invest several billion dollars to retool multiple plants in the United States.

More broadly, manufacturing employment edged up in both 2010 and 2011, adding more than three hundred thousand jobs, and U.S. manufacturing exports began to rise. And by 2012, the once irresistible cost advantages of China were looking less attractive to some U.S. employers. With labor unrest and wage inflation in China and stagnant or falling wages in America, a few companies such as General Electric, Otis Elevator, and Master Lock of Milwaukee have begun to bring jobs back from China to the United States—and smart government policies could foster that trend. In all, some

25,000 manufacturing jobs have returned to the United States in the past few years, according to Harry Moser, president of the nonprofit Reshoring Initiative.

Personal Involvement

But for the long-term effort to level the economic playing field and to reclaim the American Dream, what is needed is a modern political crusade by average Americans on the model of the civil rights and environmental movements of the 1960s and '70s.

Inevitably, people ask for leadership: Where is the great new Lincoln to heal the fissures of our divided nation and set our nation on an upward path? In the past, civic leaders such as Martin Luther King, Jr., have emerged from below, from mass movements. The starting point is populist civic action. The vital ingredient is personal involvement.

As Toynbee observed, a grave danger arises when many people living *in* a mature civilization no longer feel part *of* that society—that is, no longer feel they matter. Mass alienation and serious schisms emerge when people come to believe that they are *not significant participants* with a role and a voice in determining the nation's destiny.

"Americans have reason for negative attitudes," the late John Gardner, head of the public advocacy group Common Cause, observed a few years ago. "But the sad, hard truth is that at this juncture the American people themselves are part of the problem. Cynicism, alienation and disaffection will not move us forward. We have major tasks ahead."

The techniques of the Tea Party have shown one way to press a political agenda in Washington. But instead of pushing a middle-class agenda, the Tea Party freshmen in Congress have pushed tax cuts and policies that protect vested corporate and financial interests. Their strategy has been to cut aid to college education for middle-class kids, retirement funds and health care for middle-class seniors, and programs designed to keep middle-class families in their homes.

The Tea Party agenda is not a middle-class agenda. Perhaps not a surprise, since more than half of the sixty Tea Party members in the House of Representatives are themselves millionaires, with an average net worth of $1.8 million.

But what can be learned from the Tea Party is that a fresh surge of civic energy at the grass roots can change the political debate in Washington—and the balance of power.

Another fresh surge of energy came last fall from Occupy Wall Street demonstrators in New York City and thousands more from Boston to Portland, Oregon, and St. Louis to Los Angeles. They gave voice to a populist protest against concentrated power and wealth in America, and much of the public responded positively to their message. In a few short weeks, the Occupy movement, inchoate as it was, not only changed the public dialogue on economic issues, but implanted in America's political lexicon a vivid, Twitter-easy slogan—"We are the 99 percent"—opposing the richest 1 percent—a slogan that frames a central issue for election-year politics and policy makers in Washington.

But lasting change in America will require a broader movement that is more deeply rooted, better organized, and more politically clear about a short list of policy goals. Still, the first shoots of an American political spring have appeared, and our history teaches that, once mobilized, a peaceful but insistent, broad-based grassroots rebellion can regain the power initiative and expand the American Dream.

What's needed, John Gardner declared, is "a powerful thrust of energy" from grassroots Americans: "We the People" demanding that Washington carry out an authentic middle-class agenda.

CONTENTS

PROLOGUE: THE CHALLENGE FROM WITHIN   xi

PART I: POWER SHIFT   I

CHAPTER I. THE BUSINESS REBELLION:
THE POWER SHIFT THAT CHANGED AMERICAN HISTORY   5

CHAPTER 2. THE PIVOTAL CONGRESS:
JIMMY CARTER AND 1977–78 DEMOCRATS   13

CHAPTER 3. MIDDLE-CLASS POWER: HOW
CITIZEN ACTION WORKED BEFORE THE POWER SHIFT   23

CHAPTER 4. MIDDLE-CLASS PROSPERITY: HOW
"THE VIRTUOUS CIRCLE" WORKED BEFORE
THE NEW ECONOMY   35

PART 2: DISMANTLING THE DREAM   43

CHAPTER 5. THE NEW ECONOMY OF THE 1990S:
THE WEDGE ECONOMICS THAT SPLIT AMERICA   47

CHAPTER 6. THE STOLEN DREAM:
FROM MIDDLE-CLASS TO THE NEW POOR   65

CHAPTER 7. THE GREAT BURDEN SHIFT: FUNDING
YOUR OWN SAFETY NET; CRIPPLED BY DEBT   81

CHAPTER 8. THE WEALTH GAP:
THE ECONOMICS "OF THE 1%, BY THE 1%, FOR THE 1%"   98

PART 3: UNEQUAL DEMOCRACY   121

CHAPTER 9. THE NEW 2000S POWER GAME:
WHY CONGRESS OFTEN IGNORES PUBLIC OPINION   125

CHAPTER 10. THE WASHINGTON–WALL STREET SYMBIOSIS:
THE INSIDE TRACK OF "THE MONEY MONOPOLY"   141

PART 4: MIDDLE-CLASS SQUEEZE   153

CHAPTER 11. BROKEN PROMISES:
BANKRUPTING MIDDLE-CLASS PENSIONS   157

CHAPTER 12. 401(K)'S: DO-IT-YOURSELF:
CAN YOU REALLY AFFORD TO RETIRE?   170

CHAPTER 13. HOUSING HEIST: PRIME TARGETS:
THE SOLID MIDDLE CLASS   192

CHAPTER 14. THE GREAT WEALTH SHIFT:
HOW THE BANKS ERODED MIDDLE-CLASS SAVINGS   216

CHAPTER 15. OFFSHORING THE DREAM:
THE WAL-MART TRAIL TO CHINA   242

CHAPTER 16. HOLLOWING OUT HIGH-END JOBS:
IBM: SHIFTING THE KNOWLEDGE ECONOMY TO INDIA   269

CHAPTER 17. THE SKILLS GAP MYTH: IMPORTING IT WORKERS
COSTS MASSES OF U.S. JOBS   290

PART 5: OBSTACLES TO A FIX   305

CHAPTER 18. THE MISSING MIDDLE:
HOW GRIDLOCK ADDS TO THE WEALTH GAP   309

CHAPTER 19. THE RISE OF THE RADICAL RIGHT, 1964–2010:
ASSAULT ON THE MIDDLE-CLASS SAFETY NET   328

CHAPTER 20. THE HIGH COST OF IMPERIAL OVERSTRETCH:
HOW THE U.S. GLOBAL FOOTPRINT HURTS THE MIDDLE CLASS   353

PART 6: CHALLENGE AND RESPONSE   375

CHAPTER 21. RECLAIMING THE DREAM:
A DOMESTIC MARSHALL PLAN: A TEN-STEP STRATEGY   379

CHAPTER 22. POLITICS: A GRASSROOTS RESPONSE:
REVIVING THE MODERATE CENTER AND
MIDDLE-CLASS POWER   410

ACKNOWLEDGMENTS   427
APPENDIX: *Stolen Dream Timeline: Key Events,*
    Trends, and Turning Points, 1948–2012   431
NOTES   445
BIBLIOGRAPHY   527
INDEX   539

PART I

POWER SHIFT

LEWIS POWELL WAS an unlikely Paul Revere to sound an alarm. He personified the Establishment, the aristocracy of post-Reconstruction Virginia, where he had deep family roots.

By the 1960s, practicing law in Richmond, Powell had become one of America's leading corporate attorneys—in fact, he was president of the American Bar Association from 1964 to 1965. He had been shocked by the Supreme Court's 1954 school desegregation decision but thoughtfully counseled Virginians against what was then known in the South as hard-line "massive resistance" to school desegregation.

Much later, during his tenure on the Supreme Court from 1972 to 1987, Powell often voted with the conservatives, but he also played a moderating role, gaining a reputation as the balancer, the compromiser, in a Supreme Court buffeted by sharp ideological divisions.

Powell's personal manner was unassuming. His questions from the bench were often barely more than whispers. As Linda Greenhouse, long the Supreme Court reporter for *The New York Times,* observed, "His courtly demeanor and soft Tidewater drawl made him the image of the classic Southern gentleman." He would pad around the neoclassical Greek marble temple that houses the high court in crepe-soled shoes, a slender, modest, ascetic figure unrecognized by tourists.

But Powell had a sharp, penetrating mind. He could at times be flinty and assertive, and he had powerful, uncompromising views on the American free enterprise system that gave him enduring influence well into our times.

So perhaps it is not so surprising that Lewis Powell chose to issue a political call to arms to America's business leaders in August 1971.

CHAPTER I

THE BUSINESS REBELLION

THE POWER SHIFT THAT
CHANGED AMERICAN HISTORY

The danger had suddenly escalated. We had to prevent business from being rolled up and put in the
trash can by that Congress.

— BRYCE HARLOW,
business strategist

There has been a significant erosion of the power . . .
of those in the working and middle classes. At the
same time, there has been a sharp increase in the
power of economic elites. . . .

— THOMAS BYRNE EDSALL,
The New Politics of Inequality

IT IS ONE OF THOSE INTRIGUING ironies of history that the
immediate provocation for Lewis Powell's political manifesto to Corporate America—his powerful private memorandum of 1971—came
not from a liberal Democrat in the White House, but from Republican Richard Nixon, the very president who was about to name Lewis
Powell to the Supreme Court.

Powell's intention was to spark a full-scale political rebellion by

America's corporate leaders—what one writer called "the Revolt of the Bosses"—to change the political and policy mainstream in Washington and to put the nation on a new track, a track more favorable to business. And he succeeded, probably far beyond his expectations.

In his memo, Powell never mentioned Nixon or his administration by name. But writing in 1971 on the heels of Nixon's new regulatory initiatives and his new tax law that was hard on business and the wealthy, Powell warned the corporate community that antibusiness sentiment in Washington had reached a dangerous new high, and it was threatening to "fatally weaken or destroy" America's free enterprise system. Business was being victimized, he said, by government regulations, consumer activism, and politically powerful trade unions. The political influence of the business community had become so weak, Powell contended, that the business executive had become "truly the 'forgotten man.' "

In a tone of exasperation, he chided America's corporate leaders for bowing to mainstream middle-of-the-road policies and for adopting a strategy of "appeasement, ineptitude and ignoring the problem." The time has come, he insisted, for Corporate America to adopt "a more aggressive attitude" and to change Washington's policies through "confrontation politics."

Political mutiny had been brewing for some time. By the early 1970s, the free market fundamentalism of economist Milton Friedman, a Nobel laureate from the University of Chicago, was giving new legitimacy to pro-business laissez-faire economics in academic circles. William Buckley's *National Review* and Irving Kristol's *Public Interest* were challenging the long-accepted governmental activism of the welfare state, as it was then called. The "movement conservatism" spawned by the 1964 presidential candidacy of Senator Barry Goldwater, with its ardent anti-union, anti-government ideology, had growing appeal in Sun Belt business circles.

But it was Powell's rallying cry and corporate manifesto, infused into the political bloodstream of the business community by the U.S. Chamber of Commerce, that generated broad tremors of change in Corporate America and set off a seismic transformation of our political system. Forty years later, we still feel the aftershocks.

The Powell Blueprint

Powell was like a commanding general gearing up an army for battle. "Business must learn the lesson . . . that political power is necessary," he asserted; "that such power must be assiduously [*sic*] cultivated; and that when necessary, it must be used aggressively and with determination—without embarrassment and without the reluctance which has been so characteristic of American business."

Powell provided a blueprint, a long-term game plan that would leverage the enormous advantages of corporate money and organized business power to do battle with their critics, with the U.S. Chamber of Commerce in the lead. "Strength lies in organization," he advised, "in careful long-range planning and implementation, in consistency of action over an indefinite period of years, in the scale of financing available only through joint effort, and in the political power available only through united action and national organizations."

And in the clinch, business should not hesitate to take the gloves off. "There should not be the slightest hesitation to press vigorously in all political arenas . . . ," Powell urged. "Nor should there be reluctance to penalize politically those who oppose it."

The Problem: Nixon's Action Agenda

The timing of Powell's 1971 memo, in the midst of a Republican administration, might have seemed strange. Richard Nixon, a self-styled conservative who had won the White House in 1968 with business support, was a great admirer of the captains of American industry. He considered himself "extremely pro-business." In a private session with top auto industry leaders in April 1971, Nixon excoriated consumer advocates and environmentalists in language that Lewis Powell would have heartily applauded. Nixon derided them as "a group of people that aren't really one damn bit interested in safety or clean air. What they're interested in is *destroying the system* [*sic*]. They're enemies of the system." By "the system," Nixon meant free enterprise—the very system that Powell sought to defend.

But Nixon was a political pragmatist who reflected the politics of his time. He took a different line in public and in legislation from what he conveyed in his private talks with business leaders. On policy, he zigzagged. On the one hand, he enacted measures to support business and he watered down bills pushed by liberal Democrats. On the other hand, he launched his own array of regulatory initiatives in response to grassroots pressures from the powerful consumer and environmental movements. So that however much his private diatribes against the political Left appealed to business leaders, Nixon's action agenda—what he actually did—deeply rankled them.

The Bipartisan Consensus: Hallmark of the 1950s to the Mid-1970s

In today's bitterly partisan political climate, people often forget that one hallmark of the 1950s through the mid-1970s was the bipartisan consensus. Republicans as well as Democrats favored stronger regulation of business and industry to protect consumers and workers from the excesses of American capitalism. Often the impetus came from Congress, reacting to demands from the burgeoning consumer movement.

The Nixon administration was swept along by the popular tide. Even more than Democrat Lyndon Johnson, Nixon presided over major expansions of federal regulatory powers, creating several new regulatory agencies and commissions. The most high-profile was the Environmental Protection Agency (EPA), with its laws on clean air, clean water, safe drinking water, and control of pesticides and other toxic substances. Nixon created other agencies as well, such as the

Occupational Safety and Health Administration (OSHA), charged with ensuring safety in the workplace; the Consumer Product Safety Commission; the National Highway Traffic Safety Administration; and the Mining Enforcement and Safety Administration. In addition, Nixon expanded the powers of the Federal Trade Commission and launched an important initiative to protect worker pensions, the Employee Retirement Income Security Act, ultimately enacted under Gerald Ford after Nixon had resigned in 1974.

William Ruckelshaus, a Justice Department lawyer with an impeccable Republican pedigree who was tapped by Nixon as the first administrator of the EPA, confided that Nixon's motivation on environmental policy was purely political. He did not want to be outflanked by pro-environment Democrats, especially Senator Edmund Muskie of Maine, a strong contender for the Democratic presidential nomination in 1972. "He didn't know much about the environment, and frankly he wasn't very curious about it," Ruckelshaus told me. "He never asked me the whole time I was at EPA: 'Is the air really dirty? Is something wrong with the water? What are we worried about here?' He would warn me, 'You've got to be worried about that'—Ehpa, he called it. He was the one person in the country that called it Ehpa. The E-P-A, he'd call it Ehpa, and he said, 'Those people over there, now don't get captured by that bureaucracy.' "

Nixon was pushed along by popular pressure. Facing reelection in 1972 and expecting that his opponent would be the pro-environment senator Ed Muskie, Nixon felt he had to respond to the public's demands. In his memoirs, Nixon later claimed credit for enactment of the Clean Water Act, but in fact he vetoed that legislation. Muskie had been eliminated in the Democratic primaries, and once Nixon saw that he could easily beat the Democratic nominee, Senator George McGovern, he no longer worried about the environmental vote. He felt free to veto the Clean Water Act. After the election, Congress with its strong bipartisan majority on green issues passed the bill over his veto and then armed Ruckelshaus with a raft of new laws imposing strict pollution limits and specifying penalties for violators.

As a firm believer in law enforcement, Ruckelshaus felt he had to go after some high-profile polluters—cities infamous for dumping waste into the air and local rivers, or industrial giants indifferently fouling the skies and the waters. He felt he had to show polluters as well as the public that the EPA took the new laws seriously. Ruckelshaus took strong action. He banned DDT. He imposed a tight deadline for reducing auto emissions. He sued cities like Atlanta, Cleveland, and Detroit, and he took companies like Dow Chemical and U.S. Steel to court. His tough approach made enemies, especially in Corporate America.

"Most of the people running big American manufacturing facilities in those days believed this was all a fad," he recalled. "They figured all they had to do was sort of hunker down until public opinion subsided, public concern subsided, and it would go away." When Ruckelshaus made clear that he was going to enforce the new environmental laws, corporate leaders got angry. "I was the epicenter of hell," Ruckelshaus recalled with a laugh. "I remember going up to see Ed Gott, who was the CEO of U.S. Steel, and he told me, 'You know, we don't like your agency, and we don't like you.' And I said, 'Well, okay, get in line, a lot of people don't like me. But you've got to comply with these laws. We can discuss timelines of compliance, but not whether or not you're going to comply. And if that's your attitude, then we are probably going to get in a fight over it.' In the end, we sued U.S. Steel and they came into compliance."

Perhaps most surprising for Nixon, given his philosophical sympathies for business interests, was his proposal for a tax bill that hit high-end taxpayers and helped low-wage workers. Moving to bring budgets more into balance, Nixon called in 1969 for repeal of the business investment tax credit granted by Democrat John F. Kennedy, thus raising corporate taxes by nearly $3 billion. His package also included an increase in the capital gains tax rate; restrictions on the use of tax shelters by the wealthy; and a new "low-income allowance" that removed two million of the working poor from the tax rolls. As Ed Dale wrote in *The New Republic,* the Nixon tax package was "far and away the most 'anti-rich' tax reform proposal *ever* [*sic*] proposed by a Republican President in the 56 years of the existence of the income tax."

Business Mobilizes

In this political climate, Lewis Powell's corporate manifesto hit a responsive chord. Business sprang to life politically. After having kept government at arm's length, the business community massively expanded its physical presence in the nation's capital. In a few short years, more than 2,000 companies set up Washington offices. The number leapt from 175 in 1971 to 2,445 a decade later. Previously, business politicking had been fragmented, each company operating on its own. Now, business made a concerted effort to organize a broad coalition. Corporations founded new think tanks like the Heritage Foundation and the Cato Institute and vastly stepped up funding for the previously modest American Enterprise Institute, to generate policy analysis from a business perspective.

The chief executives of some of America's blue ribbon corporations—Irving Shapiro of DuPont, Reginald Jones of General Electric, Thomas Murphy of General Motors, and Walter Wriston of Citibank—banded together to form the Business Roundtable to leverage the personal clout of the nation's most powerful CEOs in face-to-face meetings with congressional leaders.

As the core of a new management movement in politics, the Roundtable recruited 180 CEOs from the corporate elite—CEOs with the stature to call anyone in Washington and get their call answered. "If you don't know your senators on a first-name basis, you are not doing an adequate job for your stockholders," GM's Tom Murphy told them bluntly.

The Roundtable quickly became, and remains today, the main political arm of big business in Washington, with a large, professional, full-time staff. Initially, what united these powerful CEOs was a resolve to curb the power of labor unions, but they quickly expanded their agenda to cover the full spectrum of economic policy issues, not only labor law, but taxes, antitrust regulation, banking, and employment.

Small business, too, became a major political player. From 1970 to 1979, the National Federation of Independent Business, the major trade group for small business, leapt from 300 members to 600,000. To connect with this sprawling network, the organization had 600 full-time employees at its California headquarters and a Washington office of 20.

The National Association of Manufacturers moved its national headquarters to Washington and mobilized its business network nationwide. The U.S. Chamber of Commerce, which had been slumbering politically, woke up. Its membership doubled to 80,000 companies in 1974, its budget tripled, and by 1980 it employed 45 full-time lobbyists. Trade associations mushroomed, representing nearly every sector of the U.S. economy. By 1978, nearly 2,000 different trade associations were operating in Washington, with a combined staff of 50,000 employees. Amply funded by their business members, the national organizations and trade groups hired an army of professionals—9,000 lobbyists and 8,000 public relations specialists—to work the corridors of power.

In fact, by the late 1970s, business interests had mustered such a huge force that they outnumbered Congress 130 to 1: They had 130 lobbyists and advocates for each of the 535 members of Congress.

With all that corporate muscle, business shifted the political balance of power in Washington, and that caused a huge swing of the policy pendulum in favor of the corporate elite—at the expense of the middle class.

A parallel transformation was coming in economics with the onset in the 1980s of the New Economy and a business mind-set focused on corporate downsizing, offshoring production, and rewriting the social contract that had been an important foundation of middle-class prosperity in the long postwar period.

But the first bend in the path of American history came in the late 1970s—while the Democrats were firmly in control of Congress and the White House.

CHAPTER 2

THE PIVOTAL CONGRESS

JIMMY CARTER AND 1977–78 DEMOCRATS

Fifteen years ago, the businessman was told that politics is dirty, you shouldn't get involved. Now they
know if you want to have a say, you've got to get in
the pit.

— ALBERT ABRAHAMS, LOBBYIST,
National Association of Realtors

Business's new lobbying weapon combines the power
of new coalitions in Washington with grassroots
organizations that reach into virtually every congressman's home district.

—*Business Week,*
May 1978

1978 IS A YEAR LARGELY FORGOTTEN or overlooked by
many political commentators, but the legislative session of the
Ninety-fifth Congress that year was one of the most pivotal in our
modern political history.

The power shift in favor of pro-business policies began not under
Ronald Reagan and the Republicans in the 1980s, but earlier—under
Jimmy Carter, in the Democratic-controlled Congress of the late 1970s.

In part, that was because Jimmy Carter came to Washington in 1976 with a reform agenda to help the middle class, but as a one-term governor of Georgia, he was unprepared for the rough-and-tumble of the Washington power game. But Carter was also confronting a hidden new reality: The newly organized legions of business, energized by the Powell memo, were ready to play hardball.

As Thomas Edsall wrote in *The New Politics of Inequality,* the anti-business Congress of the early 1970s became the pro-business Congress of the late 1970s.

Time magazine commented that in 1978 the decisive force blocking much of the Carter and liberal agenda was "the startling increase in the influence of special-interest lobbies. . . . Partly because of this influence, Congress itself is becoming increasingly balky and unmanageable."

Target #1—Ralph Nader

Consumer activist Ralph Nader was the first target to feel the potent new challenge of the corporate mutiny against the political status quo. For several years, Nader's chief ambition, and the primary goal of the consumer movement, was to have Congress create a consumer protection agency that would give average American consumers an advocate within the federal bureaucracy and that would consolidate pro-consumer rule making in one place.

Several efforts had been mounted in the early 1970s, but each time a consumer bill would pass in one house, it would fail in the other chamber, or it would be vetoed by Republican president Gerald Ford. With a Democrat in the White House, Nader and other consumer advocates saw their opportunity.

But they were ambushed by the new business lobbying army. Taking House Democratic leaders and Nader's supporters by surprise, corporate forces simply overwhelmed the consumer movement with an unprecedented lobbying blitz that House Speaker Tip O'Neill described as the most potent he had ever seen. "I have been around here for 25 years," O'Neill remarked. "I have never seen such extensive lobbying." The corporate forces, charging that a new $15 million consumer protection agency would mark a massive expansion of the federal bureaucracy, mobilized small business and other supporters across the nation to inundate Congress with mail and phone calls.

Shrewdly, the business lobbying campaign targeted moderate Democratic congressmen who had ridden Nixon's Watergate scandal to victory in 1974 and 1976 in traditionally Republican districts. Their surprise victories left them feeling vulnerable as they faced the 1978 elections. Business played heavily on their fears of a voter backlash against them. When Speaker O'Neill pushed the Carter consumer agency bill to a vote, most of the newly elected Democrats bolted against party discipline and rejected the bill.

The business strategy worked. What the White House and Ralph Nader had expected to be an easy win turned into a disastrous defeat in the House. The idea of a powerful consumer agency was buried for the next three decades.

Target #2—Organized Labor

Having beaten President Carter and Ralph Nader on their first big showdown, the business forces were ready for a test of strength against a politically more organized and more formidable foe, organized labor.

Since the early 1960s, the AFL-CIO labor federation had been itching to roll back the tough anti-union provisions of the Taft-Hartley Act of 1947 and the Landrum-Griffin Act of 1959, with little success, and to win more favorable conditions for union organizing. With a Democrat in the White House for the first time in eight years, the union movement saw a chance finally to achieve victory on three top union priorities—"labor law reform," to make it easier for unions to organize and to curb the most aggressive anti-union activities of business; "common situs picketing," to allow multiple unions to picket a construction site on a grievance from a single union; and legislation to generate automatic increases in the minimum wage, tied to inflation and rising wage scales generally.

Previously, American business had been divided on such issues. Major corporations, which were used to dealing with unions, were inclined to go along with some labor demands to keep peace in their own backyards. But there was a growing sentiment among medium-sized corporations, small businesses, and retailers that labor had gone too far and had gotten too strong. Anti-union feeling was particularly on the rise among the Sun Belt business community, some of it stirred up by the blazingly anti-union rhetoric of Barry Goldwater, the right-wing Republican presidential candidate in 1964, and by Ronald Reagan's run for the presidency in 1976.

With employee health and pension costs rising sharply and a growing gap between union and non-union wages, even employers accustomed to unions were taking a harder line. Some business leaders were determined to roll back union power. The National Association of Manufacturers, with thirteen thousand member companies, set up its own Council on Union-Free Environment to try to get rid of unions as the go-between for management's dealings with employees. So in 1977, the business community was responsive to Powell's call for confrontation politics against organized labor.

With a heavy mail campaign, business lobbying killed the picketing bill in the House. But AFL-CIO president George Meany vowed a tougher fight for the labor law reform bill, and it passed the House by a solid 257–163 vote margin. It was in the Senate, where the rules made it easier to block legislation, that business lobbying paid off. Major corporate leaders from the Business Roundtable joined the lobbying campaign of the U.S. Chamber of Commerce and the National Association of Manufacturers.

A Senate filibuster, led by Utah's junior Republican senator, Orrin Hatch, tied up the labor bill for five weeks. "What the filibuster does is give the right wing and business groups enormous power," complained Ray Marshall, Carter's secretary of labor. "What it does is make it possible for senators who represent about 10 percent of the population to block the will of 90 percent of the population." To try to eke out enough votes, pro-labor Democrats offered some compromises to exempt small businesses from the bill's provisions. But the best they could do was to muster fifty-eight votes, two short of the sixty votes needed to end the filibuster. The bill died without getting a vote—a major triumph for business and a grievous setback for labor.

In frustration over the solid business opposition to the labor bill and what he saw as the political ineptitude of the Carter White House, Douglas Fraser, president of the United Auto Workers union, resigned from Carter's labor-management advisory council. "I believe leaders of the business community, with few exceptions, have chosen to wage a one-sided class war today in this country," Fraser declared, "a war against working people, the unemployed, the poor . . . and even many in the middle class of our society."

Carter did manage some wins for labor, including a good job-training bill and an increase of the minimum wage from $2.30 to $3.35 an hour in four annual steps. But small and independent business interests lobbied hard to block labor's appeal for automatic future increases in the minimum wage. Carter, Marshall, and labor's allies in Congress argued that the minimum wage should be treated the same as Social Security—that is, either indexing it to inflation or pegging it to the nation's average wage. If the average wage went up, they reasoned, the minimum should rise, too.

Business lobbies were adamantly opposed to that, and they successfully bottled up the proposal in Congress. Once again, the political success of business had major long-term impact. In the 1970s, the minimum wage was about 46 percent of the average wage. By 2006, without any legally fixed ratio between the minimum wage and average wages, the federal minimum wage fell to under 31 percent of the average hourly wage in 2006 and recovered to 37 percent in 2009. This wider gap has sharpened income inequality at the lower rungs of the economic ladder.

The Pivotal Year—1978

But the corporate political rebellion was intent on more than block-ing its opponents. Business was bent on gains of its own.

In 1978, the corporate political machine went on the offensive and achieved a legislative agenda that would have profound and far-reaching impact. Over the next couple of decades, it would dra-matically affect the standard of living of tens of millions of middle-class Americans and the American middle-class dream of winning a fair share of the prosperity generated by the nation's economic growth. Virtually every economic bill that passed in 1978 had a pol-icy tilt in favor of business and the wealthy, often at the expense of the middle class, even if that impact was not immediately apparent.

The first priority for the new corporate lobbying army was to re-peal the regulatory regime instituted by Richard Nixon and his pre-decessors. Business lobbies pushed Congress in 1978 to pass bills deregulating the trucking, railroad, and airline industries. Congress was more than willing. Even liberal Democrats like Senator Edward Kennedy of Massachusetts shared the fervor of Republicans for de-regulating various industries to get the economy moving better. They anticipated, correctly, that deregulation would add to business bottom-line profits, and they assumed, incorrectly, that bigger earn-ings would be shared with rank-and-file employees as they had been in the past and not used just to fatten the bonuses of corporate CEOs and to increase the stock market returns of wealthy investors in the New Economy of the 1980s and 1990s.

A New Bankruptcy Law

Another piece of legislation that came to have broad practical impact on the economic balance of power between corporations and their employees was the little-noticed bankruptcy law passed in 1978 by the pivotal Ninety-fifth Congress.

That law, the first major bankruptcy reform in forty years, put corporate management in solid control of restructuring a company during bankruptcy. Instead of ousting the old CEO and replacing the old corporate leadership with an outside bankruptcy trustee, as in the past, the new law not only left the old management in place, but let it mastermind the whole process. Also, by making bankruptcy courts more efficient and financing easier, and by allowing much more handsome pay for a new generation of bankruptcy lawyers, the 1978 law made bankruptcy more attractive for big companies. Instead of facing the old stigma of failure, corporate leaders increasingly saw that the new bankruptcy law, as interpreted by the courts, offered them a legal way to shed old debts and to abrogate long-standing labor union contracts that had guaranteed wages, health benefits, and lifetime pensions. As in the past, banks got top priority for repayment, and management was empowered to deprive rank-and-file employees of billions of dollars in hard-won economic gains.

But that is not how the bill was sold to the public.

"A big part of the selling point on this bankruptcy law was it will preserve jobs, and it will preserve assets for employees—go back and read the legislative history," Elizabeth Warren, then a bankruptcy law professor at Harvard, told me in 2006. "But what happened was that the text of the law clearly gives a priority to the banks and the other creditors who protect themselves by contract. They come ahead of all of the employees and all the pensioners. . . . The sophisticated guys will walk out with everything and the employees and pensioners will be left with nothing."

The 401(k)

That same 1978 Congress tucked into the omnibus tax bill a small-print provision with enormous consequences for the overwhelming majority of American families. It was the antiseptically titled 401(k) subparagraph that eventually became a vehicle for many corporations to off-load hundreds of billions of dollars in pension expenditures onto their employees, a major step that increased company profits and CEO bonuses and left most of the middle class with the job of financing their own retirement.

The 401(k) provision was originally introduced as a tax break for deferred compensation for corporate executives at Xerox and Kodak by Representative Barber Conable of New York, the ranking Republican on the tax-writing House Ways and Means Committee, whose district included head offices of both Kodak and Xerox. Then in 1981, the Reagan Treasury Department, under some ingenious prodding from corporate tax consultants, decided that the 401(k) clause could also apply to rank-and-file employees. Suddenly, visions of a vast new market attracted mutual fund managers and they rolled out the 401(k) red carpet at company after company, promoting the virtues of the new tax shelter to millions of middle-class Americans.

The result was a financial upheaval that revamped most of the old corporate system of providing lifetime pensions to rank-and-file employees and left the middle and lower middle class constantly scrambling to scrape together enough savings for their supposedly golden years. Under the old lifetime pension system, companies guaranteed monthly retirement checks to employees for as long as they lived. Under the new 401(k) system, those monthly company checks were gone. It was now up to employees to provide for their own retirement savings and to manage their money for long-term security, a task beyond the capability of millions, as the record now shows.

Rolling Carter on Taxes

Finally, business felt powerful enough to challenge President Carter on taxes. In his 1976 campaign, Carter had derided the U.S. tax code as "a disgrace to the human race" because it had so many loopholes for the wealthy and for corporations, enabling them to reduce or escape taxes. So Carter sent Congress a tax bill that would close many of these loopholes and end tax breaks for the affluent while cutting taxes for lower-income families.

Congress, by now under the sway of the strong business lobby, balked at Carter's bill and then started rewriting it to tilt it—not against, but in favor of business and the wealthy.

Instead of tax increases, the bill came out with $18.7 billion in tax cuts, including a deep cut in the maximum capital gains tax rate for investors from 49 to 28 percent, a cut in the top corporate tax rate from 48 to 46 percent, and even more generous write-offs for small businesses. Although the size of the tax cuts was relatively small, it marked a watershed in Washington's tax and economic policies. Instead of following the traditional pattern of using the tax system to redistribute income from the affluent and from corporations to the less well-off, the 1978 tax bill charted the opposite course, a course that would be pursued by Ronald Reagan and George W. Bush. It gave the economic benefits of tax law primarily to the economic elites that were now exercising increased political power.

For business, the successful mutiny against Carter's tax bill was a political turning point. It had an electrifying effect in the corporate world, according to Arthur Levitt, who was then chairman of the American Stock Exchange.

"After that," Levitt told me, "business began to see they could get . . . the things they wanted."

With that victory, coming on the heels of the earlier triumphs over labor and consumer groups, Corporate America tasted its own political power and warmed to the Washington power game. Corporate leaders suddenly saw the multibillion-dollar benefits they could reap, both for their companies and for themselves personally, by investing mere millions in the high-stakes competition for political influence. With their string of victories, especially on the tax bill, they sharpened their focus on Washington and how it eases or tightens or tilts the rules for the American economy.

The tax victory was one of those pivotal moments in politics, just as in sports, when the lead changes hands and the dynamics of the game change—not just in terms of power, but substantively as well. For the victories that business won in the Carter Congress dramatically shifted the thrust and direction of America's economic policies to suit the agenda of the business elite. Those victories set a pattern pursued to this day.

Years later, economists and historians would identify the late 1970s as the watershed period when an economic wedge started to be driven into the American workforce, beginning to divide the nation into Two Americas—corporate CEOs and the financial elite put on a sharp upswing, and average Americans left stuck in a rut.

CHAPTER 3

MIDDLE-CLASS POWER

HOW CITIZEN ACTION WORKED
BEFORE THE POWER SHIFT

We have also come to this hallowed spot to remind
America of the fierce urgency of now. This is no time
to engage in the luxury of cooling off or to take the
tranquilizing drug of gradualism. Now is the time
to make real the promise of democracy.

— MARTIN LUTHER KING, JR.,
March on Washington

There was deep public concern [about the environ-
ment]—so deep that the president felt forced to deal
with it. It's the way democracy is supposed to work.
The public says there's some terrible problem out
there and the government responds.

— WILLIAM RUCKELSHAUS,
first administrator of the EPA

MANY OLDER AMERICANS have largely forgotten, and so many
young Americans have never known, what American politics was
like before the late 1970s. The dynamics of that earlier era offer important lessons for solutions to our current predicament.

Unlike most Americans today, who feel ignored by the powers-that-be in Washington and politically powerless to alter that situation, millions of Americans in the 1960s and 1970s believed in the power of ordinary people. They believed that by acting together, they could shape the nation's agenda and influence government policy. Average Americans felt confident that they counted politically. They acted on that confidence, and they generated a period of unprecedented citizen activism from the late 1950s through the early 1970s. It was the political as well as the economic heyday of the middle class.

Ordinary Americans fought for change—and they won change—through the demands of the civil rights movement and the women's movement for equal rights; through the environmental movement and its fight for clean air and water; through the push of the consumer movement for a better quality of life and more honesty in the marketplace; through the battle of the trade union movement for a solid middle-class standard of living; and through the peace movement and its mass protests to end the war in Vietnam.

The gains didn't come easily. But ordinary people could see over time that Congress and the White House, in Republican as well as Democratic administrations, did respond to popular pressures. They came to understand that by putting themselves physically on the line through direct citizen action, they could exercise real political clout in the halls of power.

People could see, through a series of successes, that the middle class could have a clear impact on policy. They saw that they could enlarge the American Dream for average Americans.

The Power of a "Gentle Army"

One balmy August morning in 1963, in the pink-orange light of daybreak that silhouetted the Washington Monument, the buses rolled into the nation's capital. Greyhounds and Trailways arrived from New York and Connecticut and Pennsylvania. More came from

Ohio and Michigan and Illinois. Many had been traveling through the night, and now at their destination, the bus drivers parked along Constitution Avenue and disgorged throngs of ordinary people onto the massive green Washington Mall. People made their way on foot toward the Lincoln Memorial. The day was not yet hot, but the people moved slowly, quietly, talking among themselves expectantly.

Soon, the pilgrimage was joined by civil rights activists who had driven from Alabama, Mississippi, and Tennessee. Others flew or took the train from Georgia, Virginia, or the Carolinas. There were Freedom Riders, black and white, who had been savagely bludgeoned by a white mob in Montgomery or whose Greyhound bus had been torched by a Molotov cocktail outside Anniston. There were college students such as John Lewis, whom I had seen beaten and burned with lit cigarettes while trying to desegregate lunch counters in Nashville; preachers such as Reverend Fred Shuttlesworth from Birmingham, who had been slammed against a church wall by a high-powered police fire hose, and youngsters who had braved nightsticks and snarling police dogs. There were doctors and lawyers and business proprietors who had used their homes or stores as collateral for bond to free thousands of civil rights marchers across the Old Confederacy. And there were professors, ministers, schoolteachers, and ordinary people from the nation's heartland, moved by conscience to bear witness in the March on Washington.

The powers-that-be were braced for the worst. They feared an emotional crowd worked into a volatile fever by its leaders or provoked into a wild rampage by racist troublemakers. But instead, on August 28, 1963, the huge middle-class throng, mostly Negroes but many whites, too, were peaceful, calm, and dignified. As Russell Baker wrote for *The New York Times,* "No one could remember an invading army quite as gentle as the 200,000 civil rights marchers who occupied Washington today."

Fresh from reporting in the Deep South, I was struck by the relaxed and cheerful mood. Parents played with children or lolled under the low trees. Others sauntered on the Mall or spread their blankets beneath the rising sun, fathers dozing off with newspapers folded over their eyes. The event had the sunny air of a mass picnic. But it was no picnic. This was history in the making, the largest peaceful demonstration for a social cause that Washington had ever seen. It was a festival of democracy—a mass celebration of people power and a citizens' call for action by the government to mend the injustice of racist discrimination. As the Reverend Martin Luther King, Jr., said, to resounding cheers, this gentle but expectant crowd felt "the fierce urgency of now."

Few people in America knew better than King how to move a nation and how to shake the power structure out of its reluctance and inertia by dramatizing social and economic injustice. In nearly a decade since the Supreme Court's 1954 decision ordered school desegregation, civil rights legislation had been bottled up in Congress. It was the power of ordinary middle-class Americans, the exercise of grassroots democracy, that broke the logjam. It was the lunch counter sit-ins, the brave Freedom Riders, and the students marching through cities like Birmingham that were altering the attitudes of a nation and the political climate in Washington, by exposing the ugly face of racism and the harsh wages of social and economic injustice in America.

Martin Luther King, Jr., and the Power of the Street

To highlight their cause, Martin Luther King, Jr., and his Southern Christian Leadership Conference had targeted Birmingham in 1963 because of the city's mentality of massive resistance and the no-holds-barred enforcement of segregation by Birmingham's public safety commissioner, Eugene (Bull) Connor.

By then, most southern cities had begun desegregating, but Birmingham remained what King called "probably the most thoroughly segregated city" in America, with an "ugly record of police brutality." There had been twenty-two unsolved bombings of Negro homes and churches. Jewish temples were floodlit and under guard at night. People, fearing informers, were cowed into silence. Veteran *New York*

Times correspondent Harrison Salisbury had called Birmingham "a community of fear." One of the first people I met in Birmingham was an outspoken lawyer named Chuck Morgan, who admitted his fear and showed me the loaded .38-caliber pistol that he carried in his briefcase for self-defense.

King banked on the psychological leverage of people power to prick the conscience of hidden moderates in Birmingham by confronting the city's police with an army of students, calling for the desegregation of department store facilities and for better job opportunities for qualified Negroes. Led by their pastors, teenagers would march through downtown Birmingham day after day, singing "We Shall Overcome" in the face of billy clubs, jet-stream fire hoses, and snarling police dogs. What segregationist diehards failed to grasp was that the images of cops brutally beating peaceful students— beamed nightly to the nation on TV—were King's trump card, his direct channel of influence on political Washington.

When the city got a local court injunction to stop the protests, King put on his coveralls and personally joined the march. And he got arrested. From jail, he chastised white moderates for defending law and order, which, he said, was tantamount to protecting the racist status quo. By his personal involvement, he had upped the ante to try to break the racist stone wall in Birmingham.

Economic Leverage: A Citizen Boycott

But the dynamics of citizen direct action were already having an effect. Even before he landed in jail, King and his lieutenant Andrew Young had opened a secret dialogue with white merchants and moderates through the Episcopal bishop of Alabama. Young understood that Bull Connor, who proudly flaunted that nickname to play up his tough-guy image, was only a front man for "the Big Mules," the city's white power structure.

What would turn around the Big Mules, Young reasoned, was economic leverage—a black shopping boycott. "Money is color-blind," Young reasoned. "It was simple. We had one hundred thousand people, the black population around Birmingham. Nobody was buying anything but food or medicine for ninety days. Businessmen understand that." They also understood that daily images of snapping police dogs were ruining Birmingham's reputation. In private, a deal slowly emerged. The merchants and a newly elected mayor, Albert Boutwell, agreed to meet all the Negro demands for desegregation and job promotions and to dismiss charges against the protesters.

The March on Washington

Now, with the Birmingham victory in hand but a long agenda ahead, Martin Luther King, Jr., and other leaders had brought their civil rights crusade to Washington. At the feet of Abraham Lincoln, they were leveraging the mass support their movement had generated, and they were reminding politicians that the people were now watching—impatient with government inaction.

Martin Luther King's soaring "dream" refrain echoes even now in people's memories. But first, targeting fence-sitters in Congress, he called on the nation to live up to its highest ideals. "In a sense we've come to our nation's capital to cash a check," King declared. "When the architects of our republic wrote the magnificent words of the Constitution and the Declaration of Independence, they were signing a promissory note to which every American was to fall heir. This note was a promise that all men, yes, black men as well as white men, would be guaranteed the 'Unalienable Rights of Life, Liberty, and the pursuit of Happiness.' It is obvious today that America has defaulted on this promissory note. . . . Instead of honoring this sacred obligation, America has given the Negro people a bad check, a check which has come back marked 'insufficient funds.' But we refuse to believe that the bank of justice is bankrupt. . . . And so we've come to cash this check, a check that will give us upon demand the riches of freedom and the security of justice."

Then came those soaring, anguished cadences of King's peroration: "I have a dream. . . ." Again and again, he cried out: "I have a dream that one day this nation will rise up and live out the true meaning of its creed. . . . I have a dream that my four little children will one day live in a nation where they will not be judged by the color of their skin but by the content of their character."

Afterward, the march leaders met with President Kennedy and Vice President Johnson. John Lewis remembers Kennedy standing at the door of the Oval Office. "He was just beaming. He was so pleased everything turned out so well—there was no violence," Lewis recalled. "He shook hands with each of us and said, 'You did a good job. . . . You did a good job.' And then to Dr. King, 'You had a dream.' There was so much optimism, so much hope. He just said, 'We will work to get a civil rights bill passed.'. . . That was the last time I saw President Kennedy alive."

It fell to Lyndon Johnson, a Texan, to make good on Kennedy's promise, and the interplay between the new president and Martin Luther King, Jr., was a central part of that drama. After Kennedy's assassination, King praised the new president but prodded him, too, voicing confidence that "President Johnson will follow the path charted by President Kennedy in civil rights."

When Johnson phoned to thank him, King suggested that a new civil rights law would be "one of the great tributes" to Kennedy's memory. Johnson chose almost those exact words addressing Congress a few days later, and he persisted until Congress in June 1964 enacted a civil rights law banning segregation in public accommodations. At the bill signing, Johnson gave King one of the pens that he had used.

Then later, in December 1964, King pressed Johnson once again. As King was returning home from receiving the Nobel Peace Prize in Stockholm, Johnson invited him to the White House. America, said King, needs a strong voting rights law. Johnson agreed but said he lacked the votes in Congress. But a month later, on January 18, 1965, Johnson phoned King and urged the civil rights leader to put public pressure on Congress—and on himself as president—to pass a voting rights bill. Without saying so explicitly, Johnson was challenging King to "make me do it!" King understood and responded with a new voting rights campaign, including the bloody march at Selma, Alabama, where the brutal clubbing of John Lewis and others provoked national outrage. Once again, the interaction of people power and presidential leadership achieved concrete results. It produced the Voting Rights Act of 1965—a change in law, in policy, and in expanding American democracy.

Largest One-Day Protest Ever: Earth Day 1970—Twenty Million Strong

Probably the broadest engagement of middle-class political power in modern American politics was the environmental movement. On Earth Day in 1970, in the largest one-day grassroots demonstration this country has ever seen, twenty million Americans staged street marches and held rallies and teach-ins to demonstrate their outrage at pollution. They took to the streets because they were disgusted by such incidents as the Santa Barbara oil spill in 1969, acid rain in the Midwest, the choking smog over Los Angeles, toxic waste in the rivers, and lead paint or asbestos in their own basements.

In the late 1960s, the green movement took off, especially among younger, well-educated suburban voters. Millions joined the Sierra Club, the National Wildlife Federation, Natural Resources Defense Council, the League of Conservation Voters, the Environmental Defense Fund, and the National Audubon Society, among others. Rachel Carson had aroused Americans with her book *Silent Spring* in 1962, but it was the raw, in-your-face ugliness of pollution that fanned the flames of public anger and gave the issue urgency. In the late 1960s, when you stuck an arm into the Potomac River in Washington, it came out covered with green slime. The river wore a filthy floating coat of green algae. That typified the visible, palpable stain of pollution from coast to coast.

"I remember when the Cuyahoga River burned, with flames that were eight stories high," Robert Kennedy, Jr., told me. "I remember the Santa Barbara oil spill in 1969 that closed virtually all the beaches in Southern California. I remember when they declared Lake Erie dead. I remember that I couldn't swim in the Hudson, or the Charles, or the Potomac when I was growing up."

"This Has Got to Stop"

"There was anger at the state of the world, at the state of your own back yard, whether it be a water body or the air or your mountain range," said William Baker of the Chesapeake Bay Foundation. "There was anger that we as a country had let it go so far. And there was a grass roots rebellion saying, 'This has got to stop.'"

So intense was the public interest in the environment and so fierce the political pressure from grassroots America that Nixon, who was far from a tree-hugging environmentalist, felt compelled to declare his fealty to environmental protection on New Year's Day 1970. The coming decade, he declared, "absolutely must be the years when America pays its debt to the past by reclaiming the purity of its air, its waters, and our living environment." Then, echoing a battle cry of the green movement, he trumpeted: "It is literally now or never."

Typically, Washington moves deliberately—which means slowly—on reforms. But on the environment, Congress and the Nixon White House moved with astonishing speed. During his first year, President Nixon set up a White House Council on Environmental Quality, naming environmentalist Russell Train as its chairman. Solid bipartisan majorities in Congress rushed through a flow of environmental legislation under Nixon: the Clean Air Act; the Clean Water Act; a bill establishing the Environmental Protection Agency; the Federal Insecticide, Fungicide, and Rodenticide Act; the Noise Pollution and Abatement Act; the Coastal Zone Management Act; the Marine Mammal Protection Act; the Endangered Species Act; and the Safe Drinking Water Act. More environmental legislation was passed under Gerald Ford after Nixon resigned in 1974.

At the state level, too, there was a rush of action. It seemed as if no politician dared brook the anger of an aroused public. "It was a big issue," observed William Ruckelshaus, Nixon's first EPA chief. "It exploded on the country, and it forced a Republican administration and a president [who] had never thought about this very much, President Nixon. It forced him to deal with it because the public said, 'This is intolerable. We've got to do something about it.' "

In those early years of environmental enthusiasm, quite a lot was achieved. The results were visible. That early wave of government regulation did, in fact, reduce the most egregious pollution, like the green slime on the Potomac. Big industrial polluters and cities were taken to court and fined, until they changed their ways. The public thought the job was done. Voter interest subsided, and as it subsided, so did government action.

Consumer Power: "Nader's Raiders" vs. GM

A similar surge of middle-class power and civic activism, with similar impact on Washington, came from the consumer movement. Although less militant and less well organized than the greens, public interest consumerism took off in the mid-1960s and had strong policy influence into the late 1970s.

Eleven major new consumer organizations were formed in the 1960s, among them the Consumer Federation of America, Public Citizen, and Congress Watch. They attracted a strong following among well-educated yuppies, suburbanites, and upper-middle-class professionals who were wary of big business. With slogans calling for "Truth in Lending" and "Truth in Packaging," consumer advocates demanded more aggressive action by federal watchdog agencies to protect the public from being unfairly exploited by unsafe products and unscrupulous lenders. Quality of life was key. People took U.S. economic growth for granted, and they wanted higher standards, better quality, and greater transparency from industry.

More than any other single person, Ralph Nader put middle-class consumer activism on the political map. A public figure of no small ego, Nader knew how to work the press, the public, and politicians. His 1965 book, *Unsafe at Any Speed,* captured public attention with the charge that America's Big Three carmakers were responsible for many automobile accidents because they were marketing cars that were mechanically and technically unsafe.

Nader's network ranged widely. His Center for the Study of Responsive Law, whose staff proudly called themselves "Nader's Raiders," grew from just five people in 1967 to two hundred in 1971. In one decade, the center generated a score of popular books that exposed the failure of federal agencies to adequately protect the consuming public. Nader pressed for a more sharply adversarial relationship between government agencies and the business sectors they monitored. His Health Research Group kept tabs on the Food and Drug Administration's oversight of the pharmaceutical industry. His Aviation Consumer Action Project critiqued the Federal Aviation Administration and the Civil Aeronautics Board. His Center for Auto Safety kept score on the National Transportation Safety Board and the Highway Safety Administration. His Congress Watch checked on where Capitol Hill was falling down on oversight. By the mid-1970s, the Nader network, funded by public donations and Nader's speaking fees, employed seventy-five full-time lawyers, researchers, and lobbyists, plus a few hundred college interns.

Nader's slashing personal attacks on industry and government agencies made him a celebrity consumer advocate with political impact. By 1974, *U.S. News & World Report* put Nader on its cover with Nixon and Henry Kissinger, ranking him fourth in its national survey headlined "Who Runs America." Nader was seen by the public as more influential than the big-time corporate CEOs he was hounding. His favorite target was General Motors, and ironically, GM's retaliatory harassment of Nader fueled his popular appeal and his political clout. In 1966, Nader filed a lawsuit charging GM with hiring a private detective to shadow him and trying to entrap him with sex lures. GM had to pay a cash settlement of $425,000, which Nader spent on more investigations of GM.

Nader had significant policy impact. His campaign against U.S. automakers led to congressional imposition of auto safety standards in the National Traffic and Motor Vehicle Safety Act of 1966. That law was a political earthquake that broke congressional resistance and paved the way for expanded regulatory laws in other sectors, such as fair packaging and labeling, control of hazardous substances, meat inspection, and gas pipeline and mine safety. Occasionally, the Senate would pass a bill without a single negative vote.

Politicians had gotten the consumer message: If business did not voluntarily clean up its own act, a highly vocal and influential part of the middle class wanted the government to step in. "Consumerism," wrote political historian David Vogel, "was a beneficiary of rising public expectations about the capacity of government to improve the quality of life in American society." The movement was also riding the tide of citizen activism that reached into all corners of American society.

CHAPTER 4

MIDDLE-CLASS PROSPERITY

HOW "THE VIRTUOUS CIRCLE" WORKED
BEFORE THE NEW ECONOMY

The United States comes closest to the ideal of prosperity for all in a classless society.
— VICE PRESIDENT RICHARD NIXON,
1959

The Great Compression succeeded in equalizing incomes for a long period—more than thirty years. And the era of equality was also a time of unprecedented prosperity, which we have never been able to recapture.

— PAUL KRUGMAN,
The Conscience of a Liberal

HENRY FORD, the pioneering automaker, was the godfather of a central economic idea that powered the great era of American growth and middle-class prosperity in the 1950s, '60s, and '70s, before the New Economy began unraveling the American Dream for millions of average people. Ford's idea was what economists call "the virtuous circle of growth."

Henry Ford gave that idea popular currency when he brought out the famous Model T car and announced in 1914 that he would pay his workers the then unheard-of wage of $5 a day. Not only was it a matter of social justice, Ford later wrote, but it was smart business. When wages are low, Ford argued, business and the economy are at risk. But when pay is high and steady, Ford reasoned, business is more secure because workers earn enough to be good customers and eventually to be able to afford to buy Model Ts.

That was Ford's shorthand formula for the analysis of modern economists that high wages paid to tens of millions of middle-class Americans in the postwar era were the engine of economic growth. Good, steady pay, and job security, they say, are the drivers of strong consumer demand, and strong demand stimulates economic growth. Business is moved to expand production and invest in new plants. Each expansion generates a new round of consumer demand. The virtuous circle keeps on generating growth, unless someone breaks the chain reaction.

With that dynamic at work, the postwar era enjoyed "the best economy America has ever had," asserted economist Paul Krugman of Princeton. "It was an economy that seemingly provided jobs for everyone. What's more those abundant jobs came with wages that were higher than ever, and rising every year. At the bottom end, workers were much better off than they would ever be again. . . ."

A Different Business Mind-Set

People often overlook the critical importance of the mind-set of business leaders to the economic fortunes of the middle class. During the long postwar era of shared prosperity, from the mid-1940s to the mid-1970s, the prevailing ethos of business leaders was radically different from the prevailing mind-set of today's CEOs, just as Richard Nixon's "share the wealth" ideas on taxes and on business regulation were radically different from the prevailing philosophy of the Republican Party today.

During the postwar middle-class boom, good corporate leaders saw a competitive advantage in caring for their workforce. If they wanted to succeed, to expand, and to generate steady profits, they needed to keep well-motivated, high-skilled employees on their payroll, and the key, they felt, was assuring good steady jobs with rising pay and benefits.

No less a figure than Frank Abrams, chairman of Standard Oil of New Jersey, voiced the corporate mantra of "stakeholder capitalism"—namely, balancing the needs and interests of all the stakeholders in the corporate family. "The job of management," asserted Abrams, "is to maintain an equitable and working balance among the claims of the various directly affected interest groups . . . stockholders, employees, customers, and the public at large."

General Electric's manager of employee benefits, Earl Willis, explicitly linked corporate success to worker security. "Maximizing employment security is a prime company goal," Willis declared. "The employee who can plan his economic future with reasonable certainty is an employer's most productive asset."

In a bible for corporate managers in the early 1980s, *In Search of Excellence,* Thomas Peters and Robert Waterman, Jr., preached the virtues of keeping employees on the payroll, even during recessions, a far cry from the mass layoffs and hiring freezes of the 2008 recession and recovery. "Only when we look at excellent companies do we see . . . full employment policies in time of recession," they wrote. "Caring runs in the veins of the managers of these institutions."

The Labor Movement: Shared Power/Shared Prosperity

But the anchor of middle-class power during the long postwar period and its most consistent and effective advocate was the American labor movement. Union power played a central role in creating the world's largest middle class by pushing Corporate America to share the economic gains from rising industrial productivity and efficiency with average Americans. Shared labor-management power delivered shared prosperity.

Organized labor's impact extended far beyond bread-and-butter gains for its own members. The trade union movement fought for and won the eight-hour day, the five-day week, child labor laws, and labor safety laws. Not only did unions bargain with America's biggest corporations for a better middle-class standard of living, but the AFL-CIO, the labor federation, vigorously supported consumer activists, environmentalists, and the drive to strengthen regulatory agencies. It backed political candidates—mostly Democrats, but some moderate and liberal Republicans, too—who voted in Congress for a more level economic playing field. What's more, by establishing a social contract and economic benchmarks that many non-union employers felt compelled to match, labor's tough bargaining with big business gained higher pay levels and better benefits for non-union workers as well as union members.

With strong governmental support during the New Deal period, labor had become a force to be reckoned with during the era of middle-class prosperity. Trade union strength had tripled in size, reaching 35 percent of the private sector workforce by the mid-1950s. By the late 1970s, unionization of public as well as private sector employees had tapered off to 27 percent of the total workforce. But that was still an army of twenty-one million, by far the largest organized body of middle-class Americans. Every big industry—autos, steel, construction, food, trucking, textiles, garment making—had big, muscular unions pressing for a better standard of living for average Americans.

GM and the Treaty of Detroit

As the nation's premier corporation, General Motors became the prime target of big labor and the pace setter for the rest of U.S. industry. The famous 1950 "Treaty of Detroit" between GM and the United Auto Workers union established and codified the social contract of the long postwar era—the economic sharing between labor and management, workers and owners.

Five years earlier, coming out of wartime wage and price controls, GM and the autoworkers union had clashed in a titanic showdown, with 175,000 workers walking off the job at fifty GM assembly facilities. Walter Reuther, the smart, fiery leader of the United Auto Workers, was demanding a 30 percent pay raise plus health benefits. "Engine" Charlie Wilson, GM's chief executive, scoffed at those terms and decided to wait out Reuther. The strike lasted 113 days. In the meantime, the United Steelworkers and the United Electrical Workers settled for considerably less in other industries. Reuther had to back down. But labor unrest continued at GM, and Reuther kept pressing General Motors to provide its workers with corporate welfare—steady pay raises plus health benefits and guaranteed retirement pay.

Finally, Wilson tired of industrial warfare and periodic disruptions of GM's output, and he offered Reuther a grand bargain: shared prosperity for workers in return for labor peace. No more wildcat strikes unpredictably shutting down plants. Reuther seized the moment. The two men reached a monumentally important agreement. GM agreed to give its autoworkers annual pay raises that would increase their living standard roughly 20 percent over five years. It agreed to pay half the cost of worker health insurance. And it promised to provide its longest-term employees with an unprecedented pension of $125 a month. The union eagerly accepted the deal and promised a strike-free contract period. GM got peace on the assembly lines. Hence the name "Treaty of Detroit."

That contract had sweeping impact all across the nation's economy. Its escalator provisions set in motion a steadily rising standard of living for the broad American middle class. Because the deal had the imprimatur of General Motors, it had a powerful ripple effect. It was soon matched by other carmakers and then by major companies in other industries. The pattern set in key industries, such as autos and steel, became a model for the rest of big business, even for non-unionized workers. By the early 1960s, as *New York Times* economics writer Steven Greenhouse reported, "more than half the union contracts in the nation had copycat provisions calling for annual improvement factors and cost-of-living adjustments. . . . With labor unions representing one in three workers and threatening to unionize millions more, many nonunion companies adopted a me-too approach, providing cost-of-living adjustments and annual improvement factors, both to keep their workers happy and to keep them from unionizing."

Nixon to Khrushchev:
The United States Is a "Classless Society"

In Washington, a bipartisan political consensus gave its blessing to sharing America's wealth democratically and to linking corporate profits to the American Dream of steady work, rising pay, and generous benefits.

In 1959, at the heart of the Cold War, Richard Nixon, as vice president under Dwight Eisenhower, bragged about America's shared prosperity in his "kitchen debate" with Soviet premier Nikita Khrushchev at the U.S. exhibition in Moscow. Nixon rattled off to his Communist adversary the bounty enjoyed by the American middle class—three-fourths of America's 44 million families owned their own homes, and collectively they owned 56 million cars, 50 million television sets, and 143 million radios. In a classic rejoinder mocking Soviet claims of a classless Communist society, Nixon taunted Khrushchev: "The United States comes closest to the ideal of prosperity for all in a classless society."

Nixon was right. To a far greater degree than most Americans today realize, our economic boom in the three decades after World War II delivered solid middle-class prosperity to a large majority of Americans.

Of course, the economy had plenty of problems. There were ups and downs in the business cycle, periodic surges of unemployment, and too much poverty. People lived in smaller homes than today, with fewer appliances and gadgets. Families had one car, not two.

And despite the model of the Treaty of Detroit, there were strikes, occasional violence, and stormy labor-management confrontations.

But the prevailing pattern was one of rising middle-class living standards. Ordinary Americans felt they were getting their fair share of the country's economic growth, and the numbers confirmed that. The hourly wage of the average worker essentially kept pace with rising productivity. That hourly wage doubled from 1947 to 1973. Those solid earnings and job security gave average workers enough money to spend and, thus, the ability to power another round of economic growth.

"The Great Compression"

Not only did the middle class enjoy solid prosperity, but the economic playing field was far more level than at other times in American history, especially compared with the last three decades. Government policies, especially the tax code, kept incomes more bunched by easing the economic extremes at both ends. Labor laws put a minimum wage floor under the poorest workers at nearly half the average hourly wage, with the result that the poorest 20 percent of American families experienced income growth over three decades that was as rapid as the richest 20 percent, and so did everyone else in between. In other words, Americans at all income levels moved up together.

The tax system reduced the extreme wealth of the rich—taxing the top bracket at 92 percent under Republican president Dwight Eisenhower, then 77 percent under Democratic president John Kennedy (vs. 35 percent today).

Contrary to claims of anti-tax conservatives today that high taxes are a drag on the economy, the long postwar period from the mid-1940s to the mid-1970s was an era of strong, steady economic growth—much better growth than the past decade with its low tax rates. However plausible it sounds that high taxes on corporations and wealthy individuals cause them to invest less and take fewer risks, several decades of solid growth in the postwar period offer incontrovertible evidence to the contrary. "High taxes did not seem to constrain the economy," observed University of California political economist Robert Reich.

What's more, with steep progressive tax policies at work, income inequalities between the rich and the middle class in that postwar era were the narrowest on record. That phenomenon was so striking that economic historians invented a term for the postwar middle-class boom. They call it "the Great Compression"—meaning that differences in incomes and living standards were compressed back then, with Americans from the top to the bottom of the income scale closer together than ever before or since.

In short, middle-class power, exercised through grassroots movements, through trade union collective bargaining, and through government policies, produced the most democratically shared prosperity in our history—an unparalleled achievement.

"The Great Compression succeeded in equalizing incomes for a long period—more than thirty years," reported economist Paul Krugman. "And the era of equality was also a time of unprecedented prosperity, which we have never been able to recapture."

PART 2

DISMANTLING THE DREAM

IN THE LATE 1990S, Al Dunlap was riding the crest of the New Economy, proud of the fortune he'd made at a string of troubled companies such as Scott Paper and Sunbeam. Dunlap exemplified the New Economy breed of CEOs who had emerged in the 1980s and who came to dominate the corporate landscape in the 1990s.

These new business leaders had shed the old philosophy of stakeholder capitalism, where a CEO tried to balance the competing interests of management, employees, and investors and to share the wealth. The new breed chose instead to focus on maximizing returns to shareholders. The interests of employees were subordinated to the goal of delivering gains for wealthy investors.

By the late 1990s, Dunlap was known on Wall Street as a serial downsizer whose mere appearance as CEO of a troubled company would make its stock price shoot up as investors anticipated savings from his drastic cutbacks. And Wall Street had rewarded him richly.

So Dunlap was touring me around his $2 million Florida mansion, showing me his pride and joy—just off his richly furnished living room, with an outdoor pool visible through French doors. His pièce de résistance was a walk-in, temperature-controlled, cedar-paneled wine cellar, fully stocked.

Cases of wine were carefully cradled in floor-to-ceiling racks—all of it world-class vintages, Dunlap assured me. He pulled out a chilled bottle of premier French champagne for me to admire. "If you're gonna splurge," he said, beaming, "Dom Pérignon!"

Dunlap's office at Sunbeam and the company's executive suites, like his home, were decorated with portraits, statues, and hunting lodge mountings of lions, tigers, and sharks, the Darwinian kings of the jungle and the sea.

"I'm a great believer in predators," Dunlap said, "because a predator has to go get its own lunch. It can never call for room service. So I think anybody that has the ability to provide for themselves, it's a good thing. So you'll see predators throughout the office."

CHAPTER 5

THE NEW ECONOMY
OF THE 1990S

THE WEDGE ECONOMICS THAT SPLIT AMERICA

There's class warfare, all right . . . but it's my class,
the rich class, that's making war, and we're winning.

— WARREN BUFFETT,
CEO, Berkshire Hathaway

If I were to describe the new rules of the '90s, it
would really probably start and finish with the power
of the financial markets . . . to really control the destiny, the strategy of the corporation. . . . Shareholders get rewarded beyond their wildest dreams, but
there's a cost—through stagnant wages, through
downsizing and layoffs, through widening inequalities. Capital wins but at a cost.

— STEPHEN ROACH,
former chief economist, Morgan Stanley

AL DUNLAP PRACTICED what some economists call "predatory
capitalism." Like many other American CEOs in the New Economy
of the 1990s and 2000s, Dunlap made a personal fortune worth hun-

dreds of millions of dollars with a corporate formula of cut-cut-cut—cut costs, cut plants, cut jobs.

More traditional CEOs such as Bob Galvin, who ran Motorola from 1959 to 1990 as CEO or chairman, rejected predatory strategies. Galvin believed the best way to achieve efficiency and market dominance was through the relentless pursuit of high quality. That approach, Galvin told me, would produce better products, bring down costs, and generate higher earnings on a much more solid basis.

But Dunlap's more Darwinian formula was a favorite on Wall Street, and it won financial backing from big investors such as Mutual Series Fund owner Michael Price, whose financial syndicate bought Sunbeam, the appliance/consumer products manufacturer, out of bankruptcy. The syndicate paid $60 million in 1990 to buy Sunbeam, and within five years, Price and Mutual Series Fund made a $1 billion profit by selling off half its ownership in Sunbeam on the market. Price made all that profit, he told me, by installing new bosses to shrink Sunbeam by sharply cutting costs and getting the company growing again. But still holding another half ownership in Sunbeam, Price was eager for more profits. He became impatient with Sunbeam's slow growth, so he called in Dunlap as Sunbeam's new CEO to slash costs even further to help Price make another financial killing.

Galvin was a different kind of owner and CEO. At Motorola, which was once largely owned by his family, he saw employees as a cherished asset who should be trained, not fired—trained and retrained and retrained throughout lifetime employment, as Motorola adopted one new technology after another.

Galvin fought to keep jobs in America. Facing aggressive Japanese competition in 1986, he decided to build Motorola's new cellular phone plant in Arlington Heights, Illinois, rather than in Malaysia, as some senior Motorola executives recommended. When Galvin discovered that half of Motorola's existing workers could not read well enough or do the relatively simple math required in the new plant, he established Motorola University and spent $200 million a year on retraining all Motorola employees, from the janitors to himself.

But by the mid-1990s, CEOs like Galvin were a dwindling minority. After he retired, his successors at Motorola began shutting down the company's plants in the United States and in 2010 sold their wireless networks division to Nokia Siemens, a joint Finnish-German firm.

The CEO Sea Change

Through the 1980s, the model of the American CEO was changing. Wall Street banks and big-time investors like Michael Price were putting the heat on corporate CEOs for ever-higher profit margins, which translated into deep cutbacks for average Americans. In some business quarters, anti-union strategies gained legitimacy from the sharply anti-labor stance of Republican presidential nominee Barry Goldwater in 1964 and the union-busting tactics of President Reagan, who broke the air controllers strike in 1981. By the 1990s, ever-higher profits and share prices had replaced sharing the wealth as the touchstones of corporate success.

London Business School economist Sumantra Ghoshal, among others, pointed to business schools and economic thinkers as the main sources of new corporate attitudes. In an influential essay, Ghoshal cited Milton Friedman, the Nobel economist from Chicago, as the intellectual godfather of the New Economy idea that CEOs should focus narrowly on maximizing shareholder returns. In his 1962 book, *Capitalism and Freedom,* Friedman had rejected as "subversive" the notion that corporations had social responsibilities. "Few trends could so thoroughly undermine the very foundations of our free society as the acceptance by corporate officials of a social responsibility other than to make as much money for their stockholders as possible," Friedman asserted.

Ghoshal disagreed. Employees as well as shareholders create value, he argued, and they should share more equally in corporate gains. But Friedman's views turned out to be much more influential than

Ghoshal's. The aggressive management notions of the Chicago school of economists took root at prominent East Coast business schools, causing Ghoshal to complain years later, after the Enron and World-Com scandals, that "many of the worst excesses of recent management practice have their roots in a set of ideas that have emerged from business school academics over the last 30 years."

Al Dunlap: Wall Street Cult Figure

The New Economy model suited Al Dunlap. He became a cult figure on Wall Street. His specialty was parachuting into troubled companies, staying just long enough to shrink them drastically, boost their stock quickly, and turn a huge profit for Wall Street fund managers like Michael Price.

As a good-looking, sixty-year-old graduate of West Point, Dunlap was eager to play up his tough-guy image, riding to the rescue of troubled companies with his slash-and-burn strategies. Other CEOs would conduct similar brutal surgery on such major companies as General Electric, IBM, General Motors, and AT&T, but they soft-pedaled the carnage in public to avoid offending average Americans. What set Dunlap apart was that he thrived in the limelight and he spelled out the brutal New Economy tactics in plain English. *Mean Business* was the title of his how-to management book. To publicize it, he posed in a Rambo headband with bandoliers of bullets crisscrossing his chest and two automatic pistols drawn at the hips. His patented technique—chopping off whole divisions of companies—earned him the nickname "Chainsaw Al."

The Bloodletting at Scott Paper

In 1997, when I met Dunlap, he was fresh from a ferocious turnaround job at Scott Paper Company, the inventor of paper towels and maker of Scotties tissues and toilet paper. Scott was a century-old company with a family-like corporate culture. But it had fallen on hard times, and under pressure from Wall Street financiers, the board brought in Dunlap. Dunlap quickly chainsawed eleven thousand employees and fired a slew of senior managers. He drastically cut research and development, canceled Scott's charitable giving, and focused on short-term profits. Within a year, Scott's stock doubled in price.

Quite a few Scott executives rode the Dunlap escalator to personal wealth—the same way he did, by getting grants of company stock. "I created sixty-two millionaires at Scott in eighteen months," Dunlap boasted.

Among them was Jerry Ballas. "I am much better off financially than I ever thought I would be," Ballas told me.

I asked Ballas what it was like to work for Al Dunlap. "The word that comes to mind is 'terrorizing.' I mean it, literally, it's terrorizing working for the man," Ballas replied. "What you do is you avoid, at all costs, getting near him, avoid contact with him."

According to Ballas, Dunlap had cut so deeply into Scott's core that Ballas feared Scott could not survive. Some of its operations were teetering near breakdown, he said, and employee morale was in tatters. "Clearly Al did not worry or care about people," said Ballas. "He cared about stockholders. He cared about stock price."

Investor activists like Nell Minow, who represented some large Scott investors, contended that Scott could have been nursed back to profitability without massive layoffs. But by then, Dunlap was into his exit strategy. Eighteen months after taking over, he sold Scott Paper to competitor Kimberly-Clark for $9 billion. The deal paid off richly for his Wall Street backers—and for Dunlap, who made $100 million from stock options. So for his eighteen months at Scott, Dunlap had made $166,000 a day.

The Virtuous Circle Demolished

Neither Dunlap's methods nor his payoff was out of line with much corporate and Wall Street performance over the past two decades.

More often than not, Wall Street's gain derived from Main Street's pain. The dynamics of the New Economy disrupted the virtuous circle of growth, the economy of middle-class power, and the Great Compression, where the destinies of management and labor had been linked.

In the New Economy, wedge economics split the fortunes of CEOs from the fate of their employees. It split Wall Street from Main Street. The destinies of the Two Americas parted company. Wedge economics made for corporate profits and big payoffs for CEOs like Al Dunlap, but it began unraveling the American Dream for millions of average Americans.

That dichotomy never came across to me more vividly than in the small town of McMinnville, Tennessee, where I saw the tale of two Dunlaps—CEO Al Dunlap and longtime employee Marsha Dunlap—play out on July 4, 1997.

Why Kill a Cash Cow?

The plant in McMinnville was one of Sunbeam's most profitable, even after the company softened a slowdown in the late 1990s. When Al Dunlap took over, he swiftly executed his draconian formula. In a few short months, he cut Sunbeam's workforce in half, sold off several divisions and warehouses, and shut down eighteen of Sunbeam's twenty-six factories. Only four plants remained in the United States, and three of them were in low-wage Mississippi. So Dunlap focused on the fourth plant—in Tennessee. Its eight hundred workers were making modern electrical hair clippers for home use or barbershops. Dunlap announced that all but 150 of those jobs would be moved to Mexico.

Art Oxley, the young, soft-spoken plant manager, was baffled. Oxley knew that the McMinnville plant had delivered $100 million in sales in 1996 and that their hair clippers were among Sunbeam's most popular and profitable items. "It's like we thought we made money," Oxley said incredulously. "Why are we losing our jobs? Why is it going to Mexico? We're a profitable business."

When I told Oxley that Dunlap had called Sunbeam's operations "a basket case," he stiffened. "I've never heard of McMinnville as referred to as a basket case," he objected. "Maybe a cash cow. But not a basket case."

I told Dunlap what Oxley had said, and he snapped back, "It was a component of a seriously failing company." From his perspective, the profitability of that plant was not the issue. He could get the work done for less in Mexico, for $3 an hour instead of $9 or more, and that would ring bells on Wall Street, which was the sole standard by which Dunlap lived. He kept a stock ticker right outside his office.

Marsha Dunlap

When Marsha Dunlap, no relation to Al, learned she was one of those cut by Al Dunlap, she was speechless. She had invested thirty-four years of her life at the McMinnville plant and was making $9.30 an hour assembling hair clippers. "It was very devastating, you know, to find out that you're going to lose your job," she muttered numbly. "It's a hurt feeling. . . . People don't understand, you know, not unless you've been there."

Marsha Dunlap had no idea what to do next. The McMinnville area had no other employer, or group of employers, that could absorb all the workers laid off by Dunlap. Unbelievably, the ax fell on Independence Day. In a white porch chair, Marsha Dunlap showed me her termination letter. "It says my termination date is July the Fourth, 1997," she told me, barely able to speak. After punching out on the factory time clock for the last time, she warned her daughter, "Your Christmas is going to be light. I'm not going to pay for it with the unemployment check."

Marsha Dunlap was right about the economic impact on the community. "It affects everyone, the whole community," she said, "the car dealership, the real estate firms, grocery stories, discount stores. Everybody."

But back in Delray Beach, Florida, at Sunbeam's next annual meeting, the investors were toasting Al Dunlap. One well-dressed couple told me they had "done fantastic" with their twenty-five thousand shares of Sunbeam (now worth well over $1 million). The stock price had tripled since Dunlap's arrival in May 1996. Dunlap himself had four million shares, then worth about $160 million.

When I asked Dunlap whether all the layoffs had been necessary, he bristled. "It's like a commander in the field," he shot back. "You don't want to lose a single soldier, but when you go into battle, you're going to lose some. . . . But my job at the end of the day is to save the corporation and save as many jobs as I possibly can. And I've saved over six thousand jobs."

"Layoffs Are Wasteful"

But some of his competitors disagreed. The owners of Wahl Clipper Corporation, which was making similar hair clippers in Sterling, Illinois, disputed Dunlap's claim that you couldn't turn a solid profit making hair clippers in America. Wahl had not laid off a single employee in twenty-five years. "Why the layoffs? They're not necessary. They're extremely wasteful," asserted Jack Wahl, the white-haired CEO. "He's laying off quality people. These are key people. I don't think you can . . . get rid of 25 percent, 30 percent, of your employees without changing radically. . . . They're quality people and they shouldn't be terminated."

Unlike Al Dunlap, who was managing plants from his distant headquarters in Florida, Wahl and his heir apparent, son Greg, lived in the same town as their workers. They were a privately owned, family-run business, operating profitably for seventy-five years. "We actually care about our people," Greg Wahl explained. "Our kids go to school with their kids. We go through life for generations with our workers."

As a private company, the Wahls didn't have to cater to Wall

Street. "We don't have a stock price," Jack Wahl emphasized. "No one is interested in the day-to-day value of the stock."

"That's interesting," I said. "You're suggesting that Wall Street's interest in stock prices is inefficient."

"It can motivate people for the short term," Wahl replied. "You need to look at the long-term value of the corporation. And it's not just one year. It's not just two years. It's decades, as far as I'm concerned."

"Puffery" and "Inventory Stuffing"

Wahl's comment was more prophetic than I realized at the time. Al Dunlap was in deep trouble because his strategy was to make dramatic cuts, boost the stock price, and sell the company to another business quickly to make his exit while Wall Street investors cashed in their winnings. Dunlap had done that half a dozen times. But now his exit strategy was stymied because he couldn't find a corporate buyer for Sunbeam. The stumbling block was Sunbeam's stock price. It had gotten too high.

In addition, as Jack Wahl had suggested, Dunlap's severe cutting had crippled Sunbeam. But that was not obvious to investors because Dunlap had exaggerated Sunbeam's profitability by claiming big write-offs for 1996, so that his first year—1997—looked more profitable than it really was. To maintain the image of success, Sunbeam had been exaggerating its sales and income by what investment analysts call "inventory stuffing"—claiming sales for warehouses full of appliances that it had allocated to customers but which had not been actually bought or paid for.

In June 1998, *Barron's* saw the downside at Sunbeam and accused Dunlap of "accounting shenanigans and puffery," falsifying the impression of success. Sunbeam's stock started tumbling, and two weeks later, Dunlap's unhappy Wall Street sponsors fired him. In February 2001, Sunbeam filed for bankruptcy.

Sunbeam shareholders and the Securities & Exchange Commis-

sion filed lawsuits against Dunlap and his lieutenants, accusing
them of inflating the company's stock price through fraudulent accounting. Without admitting or denying the charges, Dunlap and
other top Sunbeam executives paid $15.5 million to shareholders to
settle the suits. The SEC barred him from ever again serving as a
corporate officer. Still, Dunlap walked away with a fortune big
enough to retire to a much larger estate than the one I had seen—a
9,700-square-foot mansion with its own pond and an indoor swimming pool.

Short-Term vs. Long-Term

At every step, Dunlap's defense echoed the mantra of New Economy
CEOs: He was creating shareholder value. "I work for you," he told
Sunbeam shareholders. "You own the company." To Wall Street, that
signaled a CEO focused on boosting the company's stock price in the
short term for investor gains.

That cost-cutting, shareholder-value formula rankled more traditional corporate leaders such as Bob Galvin at Motorola and Henry
Schacht, former CEO of Lucent Technologies, who believed in
long-term growth and value. "Firing people and slashing things and
selling it to somebody else, that's a no-brainer," Schacht said. "That's
not creating value. That's destroying value, in my view."

"I don't think that the chain-saw mentality knows anything about
growth," agreed Stephen Roach, chief economist for Morgan Stanley
investment bank. "It knows a lot about cutting. And to me, that is a
short-term strategy that is ultimately a recipe for disaster."

"They make a lot of money for the shareholders," Schacht added.
"But the debris they leave behind seems to be unthinkable."

That conflict over the social costs of short-term profits versus the
enduring gains from creating long-term value is still playing out
today in the political debate over Mitt Romney's corporate strategies
at Bain Capital, the private equity firm that Romney ran for nearly

fifteen years. The critique that Schacht and Roach directed against short-term gains from downsizing in the 1990s applies as well to the behavior of the big Wall Street banks that fueled the financial collapse of 2008 by engaging in the highly profitable but ultimately disastrous mortgage and derivatives trade of the 2000s. The risks they took for short-term gains made hundreds of billions of dollars in Wall Street bonuses but had devastating consequences for Main Street and for the American economy.

The 1990s Corporate Killers

Some in the business community would like to dismiss Al Dunlap as an aberration—an extreme downsizer. But while it is true that Dunlap overplayed his hand at Sunbeam and that his Rambo posturing offended some CEOs, other corporate chiefs wielded the ax much as Dunlap did—and often more brutally.

"Once upon a time, it was a mark of shame to fire your workers en masse. It meant you had messed up your business," *Newsweek*'s business columnist Allan Sloan commented in early 1996. "Today, the more people a company fires, the more Wall Street loves it, and the higher its stock price goes."

In a cover story titled "The Hit Men," *Newsweek* listed the big guns of corporate cost cutting in 1990. They represented some of America's most profitable blue-chip companies: IBM CEO Lou Gerstner with 60,000 layoffs; Sears, Roebuck CEO Ed Brennan with 50,000 layoffs; AT&T CEO Robert Allen with 40,000 layoffs; Boeing CEO Frank Shrontz with 28,000 layoffs; Digital Equipment CEO Robert Palmer with 20,000 layoffs; and General Motors CEO Robert Stempel with 74,000 layoffs.

By the mid-1990s, structural layoffs—not temporary layoffs, but jobs that would never come back—were a fixture of America's economic landscape. What caught *Newsweek*'s eye in its 1996 cover story was that large-scale firings had moved from the factory floor to the office suites of white-collar professionals and middle managers at firms such as IBM and Chase Manhattan Bank.

The Gold Standard: Jack Welch

Probably more than any other U.S. business leader in the past three decades, Jack Welch, who headed General Electric from 1981 to 2001, personified the Darwinian New Economy CEO. *BusinessWeek* called Welch "the gold standard against which other CEOs are measured," and *Fortune* named him "the Ultimate Manager" of the twentieth century. Welch gained that reputation by drastically streamlining General Electric, imposing change from within, and boosting its stock price.

Welch's hallmark was downsizing—slashing 130,000 jobs, 25 percent of GE's workforce. He claimed that saved GE $6.5 billion. Welch not only cut rank-and-file employees on the shop floor and in the back office, but made a point every year of firing GE managers rated in the bottom 10 percent by their bosses. Welch's demanding, abrasive management style was legendary, *Fortune* reported, and he ran meetings "so aggressively that people tremble. He attacks almost physically with his intellect—criticizing, demeaning, ridiculing, humiliating." As one executive put it, "Working for him is like a war—a lot of people get shot up."

These tactics made Welch a personal fortune. In one year alone, his final year running GE in 2000, Welch collected $123 million in pay, bonuses, stock, and stock options, plus the guarantee of roughly $2 million a year in perks, lifetime use of a Manhattan apartment (including food, wine, and laundry), access to corporate jets, and a range of other in-kind benefits. All this luxury at stockholder expense for a man so ruthless in cutting GE employees that he was nicknamed "Neutron Jack," for the modern weapon that kills people but leaves buildings standing.

Welch was unabashed in rejecting the employee-friendly legacy of the earlier generation of GE executives, including his widely respected predecessor as CEO, Reginald Jones, who talked of loyal employees as the company's most prized asset. Welch scoffed at the 1950s and '60s mantra that loyalty was the vital ingredient for high corporate performance. "Loyalty to a company, it's nonsense," Welch snorted. "If loyalty means that this company will ignore poor performance, then loyalty is off the table."

Payoff for CEOs

The payoffs for the captains of U.S. industry from wedge economics has been enormous. Average CEO pay has soared since the 1980s compared with earlier, more successful periods of American capitalism. In the 1970s, the Federal Reserve reported that chief executives at 102 major companies were paid $1.2 million on average, adjusted for inflation, or roughly 40 times an average full-time worker's pay. But by the early 2000s, CEOs at big companies had enjoyed such a meteoric rise that their average compensation topped $9 million a year, or 367 times the pay of the average worker. At Wal-Mart, which bills itself as the friend of the struggling middle class and the working poor, former CEO Lee Scott was paid $17.5 million in 2005, or roughly 900 times the average pay and benefits of the typical Wal-Mart worker.

With America's changing political climate and the rising influence of pro-business conservatism, CEOs went from being under fire in the 1960s and 1970s, as Lewis Powell observed, to being lionized as superstars in the 1990s and 2000s, supposedly entitling them to pay on a par with Hollywood celebrities and star athletes.

Paul Volcker: The Lake Wobegon Syndrome

CEOs and their corporate boards boldly argued that rising CEO pay was merited because CEOs increased shareholder value; moreover, they said, the rise was dictated by the invisible hand of the market.

Shareholder activists and scholars dispute this. Princeton economist Paul Krugman suggested that the seedbed for CEO fortunes was the cozy fraternity inside corporate boards of directors. "The key reason executives are paid so much now is that they appoint the members of the corporate board that determines their compensation . . . ," Krugman said. "So it's not the invisible hand of the market that leads to those monumental executive incomes; it's the invisible handshake in the boardroom."

As Krugman was suggesting, a large proportion of corporate board members in recent decades have been other CEOs, former CEOs, or business colleagues with ties to the CEO whose pay they were setting. In one poll of 350 corporations over a fifteen-year period, CEOs said they considered one-third of board directors as their "friends," not just acquaintances, and an even higher proportion—50 percent—of the compensation committee members as "friends." In short, corporate boards are a club, and CEOs as a group have been ratcheting up their own collective pay scales.

Somewhat puckishly, former Federal Reserve Board chairman Paul Volcker suggested that this was "the Lake Wobegon syndrome" at work, alluding to humorist Garrison Keillor's fictional town where "all the women are strong, all the men are good looking, and all the children are above average." As Volcker quipped to Congress, "Everybody wants to be in the top quintile."

In short, every company believes its CEO deserves higher pay than his peers. No company wants to give its CEO below average pay, because as Harvard Business School professors Jay Lorsch and Rakesh Khurana put it, "that would imply that the board of the company . . . believe its performance is below average." In fact, corporate boards, forced by the SEC to disclose how they set pay, have admitted that "peer" comparisons drive CEO pay, and they typically assume their CEO is "above average" and deserves to keep ahead of the pack. Moreover, some companies stack peer comparisons by matching themselves against bigger companies with higher CEO pay.

It irks some former CEOs that peer benchmarking has become more important in setting CEO pay than a company's performance, which is supposed to be the yardstick—pay for performance. Du-Pont CEO Edward S. Woolard, Jr., said that corporate boards keep pushing up their CEOs' pay "because they think it makes the company look strong. So when Tom, Dick, and Harry receive compensation increases, . . . I get one, too, even if I had a bad year," with the result that CEO pay spirals ever upward.

The New CEO Mind-Set

In sum, what lies behind the widening gulf between CEOs and middle-class employees in the New Economy is not only changes in the marketplace, but a fundamental shift in the collective attitudes of American CEOs, the corporate ethos that sets the norms for what constitutes fair and reasonable pay for CEOs and for employees.

America's business leaders have a different explanation. They tell us that the meteoric rise in CEO pay and the wage freezes and job cutbacks of the 1990s and 2000s that have cost average Americans so dearly reflect impersonal market forces, emerging new technologies, and the pressures of low-cost global competition. And while it is undeniable that technological change and globalization have forced major changes, that is at best only part of the story. The American business response to those challenges created a more Darwinian form of capitalism than elsewhere.

Those same forces of change have swept through other advanced countries, such as Germany, Japan, France, Australia, and Scandinavian Europe, yet the Organisation for Economic Co-operation and Development (OECD) reported in 2011 that none of those countries shows the huge disparities in income between the executive class and rank-and-file employees that have developed in the United States.

So disproportionate has America's ratio of incomes become that in late 2011, the OECD ranked the United States thirty-first—fourth from the bottom—among its thirty-four member countries. Only Mexico, Chile, and Turkey did worse. All of the advanced countries of Europe and Asia—the ones whose economies were most affected by globalization and new technology—rank better than America in sharing the wealth. So globalization and technology do not explain the U.S. wealth gap.

Something happened in the United States that was different—a new CEO mind-set. Middle-income Americans, from the assembly line workers to bank tellers, have largely been victims of a U-turn in the ethos of U.S. business leaders.

By the mid-1990s, most CEOs had junked the Old Economy notion that the destinies of labor and management should be linked and that they should share roughly equally in economic and productivity gains. They had torn up the old social contract embodied in the Treaty of Detroit between GM and the United Auto Workers. They had turned their backs on the Great Compression concept of shared prosperity, on the idea of the virtuous circle of growth. Instead, New Economy CEOs were guided by the cold calculus of corporate downsizing and offshoring, a calculus that is guided by one yardstick—short-term profits.

No Countervailing Power

Corporate leaders like Al Dunlap and Jack Welch were able largely to dictate the terms of work and pay to their employees because economic power had shifted so dramatically in favor of management against labor by the 1980s and 1990s. Unlike CEOs in other advanced countries, American CEOs have faced no serious countervailing power to their claim for a growing personal share of company profits.

Inside the corporate family, CEOs and corporate boards have fairly consistently denied shareholders a meaningful role in setting executive pay. With rare exceptions, such as shareholder disapproval of the $15 million pay package of Citigroup CEO Vikram Pandit in April 2012, corporate boards have mostly ignored or rebuffed shareholders' views on the issue of CEO pay. For all their proclamations about serving shareholders, business leaders and organizations like the Business Roundtable and the U.S. Chamber of Commerce have lobbied repeatedly against bills in Congress that have sought to give real power to shareholders by making their votes on company proxies legally binding. Even though the financial reform bill passed in 2010 contained a requirement for shareholder votes on executive pay, business lobbyists succeeded in watering down that measure so that the shareholder votes were not binding, but only advisory to corporate boards.

More broadly, the American trade union movement has been in retreat since the 1970s and has increasingly had to bow to terms set by management. Union membership has declined from 27 percent of the private sector labor force in 1979 to roughly 7 percent today. The nation's most powerful unions in the auto, steel, electrical, and rubber industries saw hundreds of thousands of their jobs exported overseas, massively shrinking their rolls. "Right to work" states in the Sun Belt lured industrial plants to move from the pro-union North and Midwest to the anti-union South, with the promise of laws, regulations, and regional attitudes that were often hostile to union organizing.

Some corporate leaders became aggressive union busters, fighting to weaken and decertify unions, sometimes illegally harassing labor organizers. The number of illegally fired workers ordered reinstated by the National Labor Relations Board more than tripled from 1970 to 1980. Unions were hurt, too, by determined anti-union campaigns of big employers like Wal-Mart. Republican administrations, in power twenty of the past thirty-two years, have been unfriendly to unions, and over this same period, Supreme Court decisions have increasingly sided with business.

These trends have left not only union members, but the middle class in general without a voice with sufficient clout to negotiate for moderate, gradual adjustments to technology and globalization rather than instant slashing by Corporate America.

"The Scariest S.O.B. on Wall Street"

The voice heard and heeded most by business leaders since the 1980s has been that of Wall Street. Big-time investors and Wall Street money managers like Michael Price, who put Al Dunlap in charge of Sunbeam, emerged in the 1990s as the "terrors" of the corporate boardroom, as *Fortune* put it. In a cover story reporting on the power of money managers, *Fortune* ran a close-up photo of Price captioned "The Scariest S.O.B. on Wall Street."

In Wall Street's new pressure-cooker atmosphere, corporate leaders have been under the gun to shift their sights away from the solid, steady strategies of building long-term value to hot performance in a hurry, and some at the epicenter of the Wall Street maelstrom have worried about its long-term consequences for the middle class.

Stephen Roach of Morgan Stanley investment bank commented that in the late 1990s, the United States was experiencing an enormous—though unrecognized—shift of wealth from middle-class employees of big U.S. companies to the shareholders, mostly the affluent and the super-rich.

"If I were to describe the new rules of the '90s, it would really probably start and finish with the power of the financial markets . . . to really control the destiny, the strategy of the corporation," Roach told me. "Shareholders get rewarded beyond their wildest dreams, but there's a cost—through stagnant wages, through downsizing and layoffs, through widening inequalities. Capital wins but at a cost. . . . The 1990s is the ultimate triumph of shareholders around the world. The worker is pretty much a pawn in the process."

That was how the New Economy worked—the middle class got squeezed.

CHAPTER 6

THE STOLEN DREAM

FROM MIDDLE-CLASS TO THE NEW POOR

The view that America is the "land of opportunity" doesn't entirely square with the facts.

—ISABEL V. SAWHILL,
economist, Brookings Institution

America has entered the age of the contingent or temporary worker, of the consultant and subcontractor, of the just-in-time work force—fluid, flexible, disposable. This is the future. Its message is this: You are on your own. . . . This is the new metaphysics of work. Companies are portable, workers are throwaway.

—LANCE MORROW,
Time *magazine*

The biggest failure that I've had and that Congress has had . . . is the failure to slow the transfer of income up the income scale, which has left this a two-tiered society. . . . The economic elite of this country has performed the biggest rip-off of the middle class in the history of the universe.

—FORMER REPRESENTATIVE DAVID OBEY,
Wisconsin Democrat

THE WORLD OF OPPORTUNITIES that greeted Pam Scholl coming out of high school in Chillicothe, Ohio, in 1971 was a universe apart from the tough economic world that lies in wait for average high school graduates today.

On the Monday after graduation, Pam went to work full-time for the RCA television tube plant that was opening in nearby Circleville. Pam was a well-organized, gregarious teenager, a five-foot-five bundle of energy with a quick smile. In her senior year, she had worked half-time for RCA as a co-op secretarial student. After her graduation, RCA hired Pam for human relations to help build a workforce that grew to fifteen hundred.

"I got $1.75 an hour," Pam recalled. "I didn't have a car my first year. But about a year later, I bought me a Vega, a new little brown Chevrolet. It was cheap—$2,500. My car payment was $50 a month and I could fill it up for $5, and run two weeks on that. I thought I was hot. I had a new car and I had a job. I was in HR and I met all the guys."

One guy she helped was her classmate Mike Hughes. One Sunday afternoon, Pam tipped Mike off to apply for a job the next day. "Mike came in, he took a test and got hired," she said. "We took just about anybody who was healthy and could lift things."

Living The American Dream: 1970s–2000

"The early seventies were a good time around here," remembered Roy Wunsch, for thirty-five years a chemical engineer at the local DuPont plant and, later, the Republican mayor of Circleville. "Living standards were going up. Everyone was growing or expanding— all the local plants." High school graduates were in demand.

Circleville (pop: 12,000) calls itself "the Pumpkin Capital of the World." It lies at the heart of the Pickaway Plains, the rich farmlands of south-central Ohio honed smooth by prehistoric glaciers. But despite its small-town façade, Circleville was a magnet for brand-name U.S. corporations because it was close to major transportation arteries. RCA, DuPont, General Electric, Pittsburgh Plate Glass, Owens-Illinois, and Container Corporation all had factories there. Purina processed the local crops.

So towns like Circleville rode the escalator of American economic growth from the 1970s into the 2000s, and middle-class people like Pam Scholl and Mike Hughes lived the American Dream. Each bought a home, raised a family, and moved up the ladder at RCA, enjoying steady pay, good benefits, five weeks of paid vacation a year, and a company-financed retirement plan. From secretary, Pam rose to a $47,000-a-year job as stockroom supervisor. Mike got good technical training and promotions. By 2000, he was a senior quality control inspector making $50,000 to $60,000 a year.

"I liked working there," Pam Scholl said, speaking for both of them. "It was great. I knew everybody. It was wonderful."

Wonderful, but it didn't last.

2004: The Bottom Falls Out

The bottom fell out in 2004, even though the U.S. economy was then on the upswing. Facing lower-cost competition from China, RCA sold the plant to the French firm Thomson, which cut back production in 2003 and finally shut down the plant in July 2004. Mike Hughes sensed it coming: The plant was not bringing in as much raw material as it had during boom times.

Even so, the shutdown was a body blow. Suddenly cast adrift in his early fifties, Hughes could not find steady work. He tried changing careers. With federal displaced worker assistance, he was able to take a year's course in industrial maintenance. But even that did not lead to a job. Hughes pumped out scores of job inquiries but kept being told that despite his long technical experience at RCA, he wasn't qualified for entry-level manual labor.

Eventually, he took a night job as part-time custodian at a local high school for $13,000 a year. A second part-time job at a local glass company earned him another $4,000. Only his wife's public sector job at Head Start kept Hughes from sinking below the poverty line.

"What made it difficult for us, we had children coming out of high school wanting to get a college education," Mike explained. "That's where my thirty-one years of severance pay went. All of it went to college tuition. I had to choose between my kids' future and our future.

Talking about his predicament, Mike Hughes put on a brave front, papering over his hurt and anger. "I've got a home. I got a good pension. I somewhat lived the American Dream," he said. "They just cut me off. They cut off the dream."

"The Hardest Thing—Not Being Wanted"

At first, Pam Scholl fared better than Mike. She found a job as office and traffic manager for a small American Wood Fibers plant. The pay was good, $47,000 a year, *until*—until they downsized her out of a job in May 2009. Then life went black. By then, she was a single mom, carrying the costs of a home all by herself. For the next eighteen months, the only work Pam could find was three months as a census taker in 2010. Otherwise, she ran through her savings and had to live on unemployment benefits and rising credit card debt.

"The hardest thing is not being wanted—not feeling worthy," she told me. "I didn't realize how bad I felt about it, until I got the census job. Even though it didn't pay that well, it was uplifting to have something to do. I felt like I was contributing to society. The hardest thing is everybody looking at my résumé and saying, 'What a wonderful résumé you have—all this experience.' But I *have no job*. I know I have completed over five hundred applications and I have had only four job interviews, all for much less money than I was making."

Taking tests for public sector jobs, Pam Scholl ran into other people who had been laid off with her at the RCA plant in 2004. Like Pam, they were still hunting for a steady job. "The same 200 people are there," she noticed. "We are all taking the test for the same job. The very first test I took was for water meter reader for the city of Chillicothe. That was in June 2009. The job paid $14 an hour, and there were 250 people. The bottom line was, there was not even a job. The job was filled internally."

A year later, still without a job, she said it was a nightmare not knowing what to do or where to turn. "Oh, it's horrible," Scholl told me. "I never dreamed that I would be unemployed for a year. Right now, I am about to sink." She gave an uneasy laugh that betrayed her anxiety and too many sleepless nights. "I barely stay afloat between charge cards and unemployment benefits. I have depleted my savings at this point, just surviving. . . . This terrifies me to death."

The New Poor—Middle-Class Dropouts of Opportunity

Pam Scholl and Mike Hughes represent a new phenomenon in America: the New Poor. They have become what might be called "middle-class dropouts"—middle-class Americans sliding down-scale, people slipping backward late in life, which is the exact opposite of the American Dream. In six short years, those two fell from the middle of the American middle class, the middle 20 percent of all income brackets, into the bottom 20 percent or barely above it, and their stories mirror wide trends in American society.

As a nation, we have just been through the worst decade in seventy years, with fewer jobs at the end of 2011 than ten years earlier and with the income of the typical middle-class family winding up lower than in the late 1990s. But the story begins far earlier than this past decade. Millions of middle-class Americans like Pam Scholl and Mike Hughes started their economic decline *before* the Great Recession of 2008.

Their lives reflect "the long arc" of our economic history. They and millions like them are victims of the long-term stagnation of middle-class living standards since the 1970s. The squeeze they feel marks the long, slow erosion of America's claim as the land of opportunity. Blacks have been harder hit than whites—roughly 45 percent of blacks born into solid middle-class families had lower incomes than their parents by 2007.

Their experience has been happening all across America, to real estate agents in Florida, to bank tellers in New York, to computer programmers in Colorado, even to people with Ph.D. degrees. The numbers of New Poor are legion, certainly among the nation's 6 million long-term unemployed. In 2010, the Census Bureau reported, another 2.6 million Americans slipped below the official poverty line, bringing the total to 46.2 million people—the highest number in fifty-two years. "We think of America as a place where every generation is doing better," commented Harvard economist Lawrence Katz, "but we're looking at a period when the median family is in worse shape than it was in the late 1990s."

Baby boomers in their late fifties and early sixties, like Pam Scholl and Mike Hughes, have been especially hard hit. By late 2011, 4.3 million of them, roughly one in six Americans age fifty-five to sixty-four, were unable to find full-time work, and half of them have been looking for more than two years. As a group, joblessness or contingent work has cost them roughly $100 billion a year in lost wages. "This is new. . . . It is worse than we have experienced before and it is very widespread," asserts Carl Van Horn, head of the John J. Heldrich Center for Workforce Development at Rutgers University. "It is going to get worse. You are going to have a higher level of poverty among older Americans."

The United States: Low Mobility in a New "Caste Society"

There is growing, and disturbing, evidence that America has evolved into a caste society, increasingly stratified in terms of wealth and income, with people at the bottom almost frozen there, generation after generation, and people at the top more and more frequently passing on the self-fulfilling advantages of high status to their children and grandchildren. Increasingly, privilege sustains privilege; poverty begets poverty.

"Children born to parents in the top [income] quintile have the highest likelihood of attaining the top," asserts social scientist Julia Isaacs. "And children born to parents in the bottom quintile have the highest likelihood of being in the bottom themselves."

Several countries in Scandinavia and continental Europe, which we used to mock as class-bound hierarchies, have now surpassed us as places where people can move up the social and economic ladder. To gauge such things, experts track how near or far the apple falls from the tree or, in economic terms, how closely the incomes of sons match those of fathers and grandfathers. In those terms, evidence shows that countries like Norway, Finland, Denmark, and Canada offer young people the greatest chances of breaking out of the family mold, and even France, Germany, and Sweden offer young people better chances than America for moving up.

In fact, America is now classified as "a *low-mobility* country in which about half of parental earnings advantages are passed onto sons," reports economist Isabel Sawhill. Isaacs adds that "starting at the bottom of the earnings ladder is more of a handicap in the United States than in other countries."

One major reason that a caste society is emerging in the United States is that education is no longer the great social leveler that it once was. Just the opposite. Recent academic studies have found that the educational attainment gap between affluent and low-income families has grown by 40 percent since the 1960s, even as the educational gap between blacks and whites has narrowed. "We have moved from a society in the 1950s and 1960s in which race was more consequential than family income to one today in which family income appears more determinative of educational success than race," reports Stanford sociologist Sean Reardon. At the college level, one-half of the children from high-income families completed college in 2007 versus only 9 percent of low-income families—again a wider gap than existed in 1989.

An important driver of these radically different educational outcomes, scholars have determined, is the significant additional time and money that affluent families invest in extracurricular learning and tutoring for their children compared with what low-income families can afford—a spending gap that has been increasing. In addition, the quadrupling of average college tuition and room fees from the late 1970s to the early 2000s has put teenage children of average middle-class families at a large financial disadvantage compared with children of wealthy and affluent families in the basic ability to pay for a college education.

America can still point to individual rags-to-riches stories of self-made men and women who leapfrog to success. But for all the glitz of sudden stardom on *American Idol,* for all the hoop stars and gridiron heroes from the inner city, and for every surprise Wall Street billionaire, the unpleasant truth is that a typical child born at the bottom of the heap in America has far less chance of rising into the middle class or above than one born in France, Germany, or Scandinavia. In fact, one study found that it would take five or six generations, 125 to 150 years, for a child from America's poverty caste to rise to the middle of the middle class.

"Being born in the elite in the U.S. gives you a constellation of privileges that very few people in the world have ever experienced," explained David I. Levine, an economist at the University of California at Berkeley. "Being born poor in the U.S. gives you disadvantages unlike anything in Western Europe and Japan and Canada."

Three Decades of Getting Nowhere

Even people who have kept their middle-class status have been stuck in a rut. While the U.S. economy had growth cycles in the 1980s, 1990s, and 2000s, the average middle-class family made almost no headway. The rising tide did *not* lift all boats, or even most boats.

That dichotomy, between the nation's growth and stagnant middle-class incomes, is captured in a few stark statistics:

- From 1948 to 1973, the productivity of all nonfarm U.S. workers grew by 96.8 percent and the hourly compensation of the average worker rose by 93.7 percent. In short, as America enjoyed booming economic growth in the postwar period, middle-class workers got a solid share of the nation's gains in productivity.

- From 1973 to 2011, the productivity of the U.S. workforce rose 80.1 percent, but the wages of the average worker rose only 4.2 percent, and hourly compensation—wages plus benefits—rose only 10 percent. So while productivity was rising close to 3 percent a year, hourly wages of the average worker, adjusted for inflation, were essentially flat, the same in 2011 as in 1978. Three decades of getting nowhere.

- The living standards of middle-class Americans have fallen behind a dozen countries in Europe. Americans worked longer hours, often for lower pay and benefits, and made up the difference with the highest ratio of two-income households of any advanced economy.

- Despite economic ups and downs since 1975, corporate profits have trended upward while workers' wages stagnated. In 2007, before the Great Recession, corporate profits garnered the largest share of national income since 1943, while the share of national income going to wages sank to its lowest level since 1929.

- Gaping inequalities in wealth and income now characterize the U.S. economy. While the middle class stagnated, the ultra-rich (the top 0.01 percent) jumped from an annual average income of $4 million in 1979 to $24.3 million in 2006—*a 600 percent gain per family*. The super-rich (the top 1 percent) gained so much that they captured 23.4 percent of the national economic pie in 2007, more than 2½ times their share in 1979.

Inequalities are inevitable under capitalism, but no other advanced economy has such a hyperconcentration of wealth. In fact, as we've seen, America looks far different from its own past. The contrast between America in the era of the New Economy and America in our earlier era of middle-class prosperity is stark. Business leaders contend the fault lies with technology and globalization, but as we've seen, other countries such as Germany enjoy more widely shared prosperity than the United States. The primary cause of middle-class stagnation lies in the wedge economics practiced by business leaders.

At every turn, average Americans have been forced to swallow cutbacks. Trade unions, trying to hang on to jobs under intense pressure from Corporate America to cut costs, have felt compelled to accept what was once anathema—two wage tiers for the same work, with new workers hired at lower pay and benefits than existing workers. Airline pilots pushed into feeder airlines have had to accept de facto demotions at lower pay for similar work. Ticket clerks, back-office workers, and bank cashiers as well as factory workers have been pushed out of full-time jobs and then hired back by the old company as theoretically "independent contractors" at lower pay as temporary or part-time workers with few or no benefits.

"Permatemps": A New Economy Lower Caste

One hallmark of the New Economy in the 1990s was the rapid expansion of part-time and temporary work. So-called contingent workers became the fastest-growing segment of the U.S. workforce.

In 2005, roughly 30 percent of the labor force—42.6 million people—were classified as contingent workers, paid lower wages and lower benefits than regular workers and highly vulnerable to layoffs. By late 2011, more than 8 million Americans were working part-time against their will. Tens of millions more were hired through temp agencies or classified, questionably, as "independent contractors" to keep them off the company payroll but permanently on the job, doing the same work as regular employees for years on end but at lower pay and benefits.

"Permatemps," they were called, the wage serfs of the New Economy.

As the corporate poster child of "permatemping," Microsoft used thousands of long-term temps for the sophisticated designing, editing, and testing of software, among other jobs. Regular employees wore blue badges, permatemps wore orange. The two groups worked side by side. But Microsoft denied permatemps its employee health benefits, 401(k) plans, and company stock options. Hundreds of other companies copied Microsoft.

Eventually, the IRS charged Microsoft with violating tax laws by failing to deduct taxes from permatemp pay. In 1992, permatemps filed suit against Microsoft to obtain benefits due employees under labor laws. After a long battle, Microsoft agreed to pay $97 million in damages to twelve thousand permatemps. A federal district judge, upheld by the Supreme Court, outlawed hiring temp workers for longer than six months. To get around the ruling, Microsoft and other companies fire temp workers after six months, lay them off for one hundred days, and then rehire them. People are so desperate for work that they bow to those terms.

Men Drop Out, Replaced by Young Mothers

American workers have gone from being the best paid with the best conditions in the 1970s to falling behind other advanced economies by the 1990s. "Their hourly compensation dropped below that of a dozen European labor forces," former Nixon political strategist Kevin Phillips reported in 2002, and median U.S. pay has fallen since then. What's more, Americans typically work 350 more hours per year than the average European worker. By 2010, many men had gotten so discouraged at being unable to find good jobs that they have been dropping out of the workforce entirely. From 1948 to 2011, male participation in the labor market dropped from 87 to 74 percent. That adds up to several million male dropouts.

Economists point out that the only reason average family incomes have risen over the past four decades, even if only slightly, is that so many more women have gone to work. Women have had to work to keep their families financially afloat, often adding enormous strains on families, especially those with small children. "It's probably true that the typical middle-class family earns more now than thirty years ago—the actual income is probably up," observed Larry Mishel, director of the pro-labor Economic Policy Institute in Washington. "But you have to balance that out with the fact that they are also working more hours—two of them are working. But it's an amazing thing that an economy that grows in productivity by 80 to 90 percent still leaves so many people actually worse off."

Working women are now the norm, but the toll on young mothers is stunning. In 1960, only 15 percent of American women with children under six worked, but by 2010 that number had shot up to 64 percent—the highest percentage in the world. In fact, the massive movement of women into the workforce, as Kevin Phillips observed, had by the late 1990s already given the United States "the world's highest ratio of two-income households, with its hidden, de facto tax on time and families."

Paradoxically, the second income stream wound up putting many middle-class families in an even tighter financial bind because of the sharply rising costs of housing from the 1980s through the 2000s. Middle-class parents wanted homes in good neighborhoods with good schools, but, as Elizabeth Warren and Amelia Warren Tyagi reported in their book, *The Two-Income Trap,* they found themselves in an ever-escalating bidding war, having to spend a bigger share of their combined incomes on housing. As the quality of education and safety on the streets deteriorated, people felt the need to pay premium prices for desirable housing. Even two paychecks did not seem enough to keep up with the rising cost of living. As Warren and Tyagi wrote: "The crisis in education is not only a crisis of reading and arithmetic, it is also a crisis in middle-class family economics."

Having a college education helped—but it didn't generate as much of a gain as people imagine. The typical college graduate today makes only about $1,000 a year more than in 1980, adjusting for inflation. In the past decade, entry-level college graduate salaries actually went backward. Their annual pay in 2010 was about $2,000 below their pay in 2000. Young men were averaging $45,000 in 2010 and women were averaging about $38,000. Not bad for starters, but that means typical college graduates, like high school graduates, have been falling further and further behind the executive elite, such as Carol Bartz, CEO of Yahoo!, or Leslie Moonves, CEO of CBS, who were making about $150,000 *a day*.

The enormity of the wealth gap between the top and the middle, Harvard economist Larry Summers said in late 2008, raises "a critical problem of legitimacy" for American capitalism.

It Didn't Have to Be This Way

It didn't have to be this way. Economists have calculated that if the laws and the social contract widely accepted by Corporate America during the middle-class boom of the 1960s and '70s had continued, average Americans would be far better off today. Sharing the gains from America's economic growth from 1979 to 2006 in the same way they were shared from 1945 to 1979 would have given the typical middle-class family $12,000 more per year. Overall, 80 percent of Americans, from the bottom through the entire middle class, would have earned $743 billion more a year; the richest 1 percent would have made $673 billion less; and the next 4 percent down from the top would have made $140 billion less.

So it was the changes in our laws and in the way American business decided to divide its revenues that cost average Americans roughly three-quarters of a trillion dollars since the late 1970s. All that money went to the richest 5 percent of Americans.

Of course, hard times are not new to ordinary Americans. Cycles of boom and bust have periodically wreaked havoc with our economy and disrupted the lives of average families for many decades. Unemployment took its cyclical toll, and people tightened their belts. But after the downturns ended and the recovery came, people got their jobs back, the economy expanded, and the middle class got back on the up escalator.

Today, mass layoffs are no longer a cyclical convulsion during hard times, but a permanent grinding reality even in good times. Firings and job cuts, antiseptically clothed in the corporate euphemisms of "restructuring" and "downsizing," have become a chronic economic malignancy for average Americans in good times as well as bad. In a survey of one thousand companies, the American Management Association found rising numbers of business managements reporting big job cuts during the boom years of the late 1990s. When times got tough, from 2001 to 2003, roughly 5.4 million people were thrown out of work, mostly for reasons unrelated to their work performance. When they were surveyed in 2004, one-third had failed to find new jobs, and more than half of those who had found work were making less than before—a pattern repeated in the latest recession.

Overall, more than fifty-nine thousand factories and production facilities were shut down all across America over the last decade, and employment in the core manufacturing sector fell from 17.1 million to 11.8 million from January 2001 to December 2011, a punishing toll for what historically had been the best sector for steady, good-paying middle-class jobs. By pursuing a deliberate strategy of continual layoffs and by holding down wages, both of which yielded higher profits for investors, business leaders were not only squeezing their employees, they were slowly strangling the middle-class consumer demand that the nation needed for the next economic expansion.

This trend has made it far harder for the private sector to pull the country out of a slump, and it has increased the need for government action to stimulate the economy. The evidence is clear. With each recession since 1990, it has taken longer and longer for the U.S. economy to dig out of the hole and to regain the jobs lost in recession. After the 1990 downturn, economists coined the term "jobless recovery" because it took much longer than usual—twenty-one months—to gain back the lost jobs. It was twice as bad after the 2001 recession. Getting the jobs back took forty-six months.

Stephen Roach, as chief economist for Morgan Stanley, called the painfully slow 2002–03 recovery "the weakest hiring cycle in modern history." Roach was especially alarmed that even when jobs did come back, they paid less, offered fewer benefits, and provided less security. As he said, 97 percent of the new hiring from the economic bottom in 2002 through mid-2004 was for part-time work. Millions of the better-paying, full-time jobs were gone for good—sent offshore to increase corporate profits. Unemployment was increasingly a long-term structural cancer rather than a cyclical headache from which the middle class could more readily recover.

During the most recent recession, that highly profitable but job-crushing trend accelerated so that by early 2011, *The Wall Street Journal* ran a front-page story about Corporate America sitting on idle capital amid high unemployment. "No Rush to Hire Even as Profits Soar," the headline read. Corporations were reporting year-end profits of more than $1 trillion—up 28 percent from a year earlier—and promising dividend increases to affluent shareholders. The Dow Jones Industrial Average ran up above 12,000, while roughly twenty-nine million Americans were either unemployed, involuntarily working part-time, or dropping out of the labor market in despair. The rich had recovered from the recession, the middle was wounded and in pain, and Corporate America was hoarding $1.9 trillion in cash and expanding its overseas operations. That put a crimp on America's recovery.

The numbers confirmed the pattern of the past three decades— the toll on average middle-class employees was heavy, while Corporate America was enjoying high profits. The old social contract had been withered away.

CHAPTER 7

THE GREAT BURDEN SHIFT

———————◆———————

FUNDING YOUR OWN SAFETY NET;
CRIPPLED BY DEBT

The burden shift has turned the traditional definition of the American dream "on its ear."
— "THE METLIFE STUDY OF THE AMERICAN DREAM"

More and more economic risk has been offloaded by
government and corporations onto the increasingly
fragile balance sheets of workers and their families.
This . . . is at the root of Americans' rising anxiety
about their economic standing and future.

— JACOB HACKER,
The Great Risk Shift

WHEN PAUL TAYLOR AND RICH MORIN of the Pew Research
Center did a poll on how people were faring during the Great Recession, they put a face on America—actually, two faces. They described
a revealing dichotomy in the public mood—a schizophrenia in which
55 percent of Americans reported they were in deep trouble, but 45
percent claimed to be holding their own.

Taylor was so struck by these two different portraits that he titled their report "One Recession, Two Americas." That dichotomy in attitudes—and experience—helps explain the nation's sharp political divisions on such contentious issues as President Obama's economic stimulus package and raising taxes on the wealthy.

The "Two Americas" report explained the dissonance in people's experience, such as my own puzzlement at reading newspaper accounts of 15 million Americans being unemployed and 6.7 million families being foreclosed out of their homes, then seeing suburban restaurants jammed with people on a night out, spending as if the economy were strong.

We are literally Two Americas, remarkably out of touch with each other—the fortunate living the American Dream but lacking any practical comprehension of how the other half are suffering, month in and month out, unaware of the enervating toll of economic despair on the unfortunate half, many of whom just two or three years before had counted themselves among the fortunate.

The Pew survey documented a class split in America. Among the losers, the picture was bleak: Two-thirds said their family's overall financial condition had worsened; 60 percent said they had to dig into savings or retirement funds to take care of current costs; 42 percent had to borrow money from family and friends to pay their bills; 48 percent had trouble finding medical care or paying for it. The psychological toll was heavy. By contrast, the other half, the relative winners, admitted to some problems such as stock market losses but described their woes as modest and manageable.

The fault lines dividing losers and winners were income and age. Nearly two-thirds of those earning $75,000 or more said they were holding their own, while nearly 70 percent of those making under $50,000 were losing ground. Most seniors over sixty-five, buttressed by Social Security and traditional lifetime pensions, were doing all right. But 60 percent of the people of working age, between eighteen and sixty-four, gloomily reported that they were falling behind.

The Zero Decade: 2000–09

The one thing the two groups had in common was their verdict that the ten-year period from 2000 through 2009 was the worst decade in more than half a century—the first one in half a century where people had more negative than positive feelings. "The single most common word or phrase used to characterize the past 10 years," the Pew Center reported, "is downhill, and other bleak terms such as poor, decline, chaotic, disaster, scary, and depressing are common."

That language tells how average Americans feel. The numbers describe the damage. In just one three-month period, the final quarter of 2008, American households lost $5.1 trillion of their wealth through plunging home values and steep stock market losses—the most ever in a single quarter in the fifty-seven years that the Federal Reserve has kept records. During the full year of 2008, American households lost $11.1 trillion, close to one-fifth of their total accumulated private wealth.

More and more trillions evaporated in 2009, 2010, and into 2011. With housing prices falling steadily for five straight years, unemployment stuck at stubbornly high levels, and the stock market bouncing up and down, periodically spooked by fear of a second dip into recession, those astronomical losses became permanently etched into the lives of millions of middle-class families. Their personal safety nets had been shredded.

The Misery Index

Translating cold numbers into a graphic picture of the hard economic realities in the lives of ordinary people is a challenge. In the 1990s, economist Edward Hyman of the ISI Group devised the Misery Index to capture the stress on average families by costly, unavoidable items that take a big bite out of family budgets and crimp what families have left to live on. The Misery Index tracked four items—income taxes, Social Security taxes, medical costs, and interest payments. In 1960, these four items took 24 percent of family budgets; but by the 1990s, they were taking more than 42 percent. Income taxes were lower, but Social Security payroll taxes had risen along with medical costs and interest payments on mortgages and debt. In sum, necessities, not lavish spending habits, were eating up family income.

More recently, Yale University political economist Jacob Hacker and his research team developed the Economic Insecurity Index, which logs the harshest economic blows a family can face—an income loss of 25 percent or more in a single year; superheavy medical expenses; or the exhaustion of a family's financial reserves. Using this index, Hacker found that in 1985, roughly 10 percent of all Americans had suffered an acute financial trauma that year. By July 2010, the proportion had jumped to 20 percent—one in five American families suffering from an economic tornado ripping through their lives.

As that Pew Center poll discovered, even middle-class families who avoided the most acute distress have experienced rising economic anxiety in the past two decades.

The "Great Risk Shift"

There is good reason for pervasive middle-class angst. Financial insecurity has been written into the DNA of the New Economy. Not only has the New Economy been more volatile and the economic gains been distributed more unequally than during the era of middle-class prosperity, but Corporate America has rewritten the social contract that once underpinned the security of most average Americans. The company-provided welfare safety net that rank-and-file employees enjoyed from the 1940s into the 1970s has been sharply cut back, and a huge share of the cost burden has been shifted from companies to their employees.

In 1980, for example, 70 percent of Americans who worked at companies with one hundred or more employees got health insurance coverage *fully paid for* by their employers. But from the 1980s onward, employers began requiring their employees to cover an increasing portion of the health costs. Other employers dropped company-financed health plans entirely, saying they could not afford them. Many small businesses made employees pay for all, or most, of the health insurance costs. As union membership declined in various industries, this trend gained momentum.

So pervasive did this burden shift become that by the mid-2000s, only 18 percent of workers—one-quarter of the percentage in 1980—were getting full health benefits paid by their employers. Another 37 percent got partial help but had to pick up a large part of the tab themselves. The rest (45 percent) got no employer support. Some companies may have needed this change to survive, but many simply added the cost savings to their profit line.

Wal-Mart, the nation's largest employer, four of whose owners rank among America's eleven richest individuals, decided in October 2011 to roll back health care coverage for its large part-time workforce and to sharply raise health premiums for many full-time staffers. In the early 2000s, Wal-Mart had touted the news that 90 percent of its employees had health coverage, though it neglected to reveal that at least half got coverage from other employers through their spouses. "The truth is more like 38, 39 percent" were covered by Wal-Mart, said Jon Lehman, a former manager of six different Wal-Mart stores. Very often, Lehman told me, he personally had to counsel and even drive Wal-Mart employees to nonprofit charities and organizations that provided indigent care because they had no Wal-Mart health coverage.

Wal-Mart's policies generated so much public controversy that in 2007, Wal-Mart took a more generous approach—picking up a larger share of the health premiums for its full-time employees and offering coverage for part-timers after a year of employment. In 2008, Wal-Mart reported that for the first time in its forty-six-year history, it was covering 50.2 percent of its employees.

But in 2011, Wal-Mart's management decided to back off the new benefits package. The company's decision to deny health coverage to new part-time employees, according to Wal-Mart spokesman

Gene Rossiter, was driven by rising health care premiums. "Over the last few years, we've all seen our health care rates increase," Rossiter explained. "The decisions made were not easy, but they strike a balance between managing costs and providing quality care and coverage." In reaction, some Wal-Mart employees said they could not afford the higher health premiums, and Dan Schlademan, director of Making Change at Wal-Mart, a union-backed campaign, protested that Wal-Mart's move was "another example of corporations putting profits ahead of what's good for everyday Americans."

In the same tough economic climate, Costco, a big-box retail rival of Wal-Mart, took the opposite tack. Costco has maintained health coverage for roughly 85 percent of its employees, while keeping wages steady and avoiding large layoffs. "We try to provide a very comprehensive health-care plan for our employees. Costs keep escalating, but we think that's an obligation on our part," explained Costco CEO Jim Sinegal. "We're trying to build a company that's going to be here 50 and 60 years from now. We owe that to the communities where we do business. We owe that to our employees, that they can count on us for security. We have 140,000 employees and their families . . . who count on us."

Costco is known for a high retention rate among its employees, while Wal-Mart has a reputation for high employee turnover. At Wal-Mart, CEO pay packages have run as high as $20 million in recent years, whereas Costco's Sinegal consistently took a pay package of about $2.2 million. As *The Wall Street Journal* put it, Sinegal chose being kind to his own workers over making Wall Street happy. In recent years, Morningstar, the investment rating service, reports that Costco has outperformed Wal-Mart and other retailers. Even so, the trend in business has moved away from the Costco model.

The Shift from Pensions to 401(K)'s

In terms of the overall financial burden shift from corporations to employees, by far the largest change has come in retirement benefits.

In 1980, 84 percent of the workers in companies with more than one hundred employees were in lifetime pension plans financed by their employers. By 2006, that number had plummeted—only 33 percent had company-financed pensions. The rest either got nothing or had been switched into funding their own 401(k) plans with a modest employer match.

The switch offered big savings for employers. According to long-time pension expert Brooks Hamilton, the lifetime pension system cost companies from 6 to 7 percent of their total payroll, but they spent only 2 to 3 percent on matching contributions for 401(k) plans. Often those savings went directly into corporate profits and bigger stock options bonuses for the CEO and other top executives.

The explanation from corporate chiefs and financial officers echoed Wal-Mart. Businesses said they could no longer afford lifetime pensions. As Jeffrey Immelt, CEO of General Electric, told his stockholders: "[The] pension has been a drag for a decade."

But digging into the records, *Wall Street Journal* reporter Ellen Schultz found that wasn't really true. In fact, pension plans were moneymakers for many a big company. In the bull market of the 1990s, America's blue ribbon companies did so well investing their employee pension funds that many built up huge surpluses, above their obligations to employees, without contributing a cent of company cash for a decade or more. The stock market gains were so large that by November 1999, GE had a $25 billion surplus in its basic employee pension funds; Verizon had $24 billion; AT&T had $20 billion; IBM had $7 billion.

What's more, some of America's largest corporations were able to shift pension fund gains indirectly to their profit lines and, Schultz reported, a few legally took advantage of loose and poorly enforced accounting rules to siphon off money from their employee pension funds to finance portions of their corporate downsizing, restructuring, and mergers and acquisitions.

"Many, like Verizon, used the assets to finance downsizings, offering departing employees additional pension payouts in lieu of severance," Schultz disclosed. "Others, like GE, sold pension surpluses in

restructuring deals, indirectly converting pension assets into cash."
Some companies made billions by shutting down employee pension
plans and shifting surplus assets to company profits. And if company
pension plans got into financial trouble during the stock market decline in the early 2000s, it was either because the company itself was
in deep financial trouble or because company finance officers had
been too aggressive in gambling with pension assets, putting them
into risky equities in hopes of making big gains, rather than investing carefully in safer, more conservative assets like bonds.

Either way, the shift out of lifetime pensions to 401(k) plans and
so-called account balance plans by highly profitable corporations was
a heavy cost blow to employees from assembly line workers at Ford
and GE to software and Internet specialists at IBM.

In the 1950s, U.S. employees nationwide paid collectively about
11 percent of their retirement costs. By the mid-2000s, they were
paying 51 percent. Hundreds of billions of dollars in safety net costs
were shifted from companies to employees without any offsetting
real increase in the typical worker's pay. For ordinary Americans, the
consequences were acute.

"This fundamental transformation, which I call the 'Great Risk
Shift,'" says Yale political economist Jacob Hacker, ". . . is at the
root of Americans' rising anxiety about their economic standing and
future."

The Ownership Society

Some major political leaders and economic analysts have defended
the burden shift from government or employer safety net programs
to individuals as a positive development. They have argued that both
corporate welfare and government welfare were misguided policies
that fostered economic dependency instead of promoting personal
self-reliance and individual responsibility. In the White House,
George W. Bush called this philosophy "the ownership society," and
he pushed hard to make it policy. What Bush meant by an "owner-

ship society" was that individuals should take ownership, or total financial responsibility, for their own economic destinies and not expect employers or the federal government to provide a safety net.

The "ownership" concept lay behind Bush's abortive effort to privatize the Social Security system in 2005 after his reelection. Bush barnstormed the country pushing the plan. His goal was to get government off the hook for guaranteeing lifetime retirement payments for people on Social Security. Instead he wanted people to invest their Social Security contributions in the stock market and finance their own retirement.

That same general concept lay behind the plan that Republican Paul Ryan, as House Budget Committee chairman, proposed for Medicare in 2011. Ryan's plan was to give individual Americans a stipend from Medicare and have them buy their own health insurance. That would relieve government of responsibility for unlimited health care costs. In both the Bush and Ryan plans, the financial risks over the long run would have been put increasingly on ordinary Americans. Individuals would have been at far higher financial risk than at present. Once enough voters understood what was afoot, they objected vociferously to the changes in their safety net. Both Bush and Ryan had to back off.

Turning the American Dream "On Its Ear"

But Corporate America was so successful in shifting a major portion of the cost for health and pension benefits onto individual employees that even a corporate financial giant like Metropolitan Life Insurance Company was moved to comment in 2007 that this shift had essentially turned the old social contract upside down. As MetLife put it, "The burden shift has turned the traditional definition of the American Dream 'on its ear.' "

In nationwide surveys, MetLife reported, it found that the burden shift from employers to employees was "having an impact, with potentially profound implications" on the living standards and finances of middle-class families. In its 2007 "MetLife Study of the American Dream," the firm found that by more than a 3 to 1 margin (65 to 19 percent), Americans believed things had gotten less secure in the last decade, even though the economy had enjoyed a growth spurt in the mid-2000s. When MetLife asked people whether they were living the American Dream of home ownership and a solid economic life, two-thirds said they had not achieved the dream. Roughly half of those over forty said they never expected to achieve it. That was *before* the economic collapse of 2008.

Two years later, as the recession hit bottom in 2009, MetLife did another poll. Once again, only one-third of Americans thought they were living the dream. But this time, half of that group, especially people in their midfifties and older, were worried that the dream was going to slip through their fingers and that they would be unable to sustain the good life in the years ahead.

Bankruptcy—the Red Flag

Perhaps the starkest indicator of mounting middle-class distress has been the sharp rise in personal bankruptcies, now an integral feature of the New Economy. Bankruptcy is a middle-class phenomenon. The poor go broke, but they don't file for bankruptcy, financial experts say, because they have few, if any, assets to protect. Middle-class people and upper-middle-class professionals go into bankruptcy to try to hang on to basic assets such as their home, their retirement nest egg, or their income stream, all of which are protected by law if they file for bankruptcy.

Personal bankruptcies soared in the 1990s. By 2005, there were more than two million personal bankruptcies—roughly seven times as many as two decades earlier, in 1984. "Bankruptcy has become deeply entrenched in American life," Harvard Law School professor Elizabeth Warren wrote in 2003. "This year, more people will end up bankrupt than will suffer a heart attack. More adults will file for bankruptcy than will be diagnosed with cancer. More people will file for bankruptcy than will graduate from college. . . . Americans will file more petitions for bankruptcy than for divorce."

Bankruptcy can happen to almost anyone, even middle-class people who have been riding along comfortably. Some families teeter on the brink for years, but typically when solid families go bankrupt, the cause is almost always some acute and unexpected economic calamity—the loss of a job; a medical catastrophe; divorce; foreclosure or drastic loss of home value; or the slow, relentless ebb tide of poverty in retirement.

Millions of middle-class families go over the financial cliff, pushed inexorably into bankruptcy by ever-mounting debt. In fact, private debt in America has risen far more rapidly than government debt. The total personal debt of American consumers exploded from several hundred billion dollars in 1959 to $12.4 trillion in 2011, according to Federal Reserve statistics.

Pam Scholl Files for Bankruptcy

Pam Scholl, the unemployed former RCA worker, filed for bankruptcy in September 2010. Scholl had been jobless since May 2009, except for a temporary three-month stint as a census taker in 2010. Her unemployment checks were not enough to cover her mortgage, car payments, health care, taxes, food, clothing, and living expenses, so she borrowed on credit cards. Very quickly, she fell into a downward spiral. By the end, she was making $500 a month in minimum payments to her credit card accounts, on top of her living expenses. Her debt climbed—to $50,000.

"I was pretty much borrowing from one credit card to pay for the others," Scholl told me. "I figured that once I got a job, I could pay them off. But I never could catch up. As soon as I realized that I was over my head, I went to the bankruptcy lawyer. You feel horrible. You know you've ruined your credit. I've had excellent credit since I was seventeen years old. But there was nothing I could do. There was nobody I could borrow from."

Her bankruptcy filing was not contested by any credit card company, and in February 2011, the court approved it. "That ended my credit card debt," Scholl said. "It protected my house so I could live. It protected my retirement fund and my 401(k). To keep my car, I had to take $4,000 from my retirement savings to pay off the car loan."

Just after Thanksgiving 2010, Scholl got a job with the Ross County Auditor's Office at $8.50 an hour, but after tax withholding, that job actually paid her less than unemployment insurance had paid. For a year she limped along, borrowing from her savings to pay her bills. Then, a year later, in December 2011, she got a chance to work as a payroll clerk in the Ross County Sheriff's Office, making $12.25 an hour. The pay was about half as much as her RCA salary. But, said Scholl, "I am thrilled—$12.25 an hour seems like heaven to me. I've been without work for so long, I really appreciate having that. And I feel very fortunate to have health insurance again because I am a diabetic."

The Making of the Debt Quagmire

Pam Scholl's nightmare of sinking into ever-deepening debt is a microcosm of middle-class experience. When you combine credit cards, auto loans, home mortgages, student loans, and other forms of credit, the average debt for every adult man and woman in America has nearly quadrupled since the 1950s. "We have gone from a society where most consumer borrowing was episodic and for special purchases, to a society where many families have to use credit to pay for ordinary household expenses and are permanently indebted," University of Illinois bankruptcy professor Robert Lawless told Congress.

The reason is that debt and bankruptcy follow the rise of easy credit.

"Just a generation ago, the average family simply couldn't get into the kind of financial hole that has become so familiar today," observed Elizabeth Warren. "The reason was straightforward: A middle-class family couldn't borrow very much money. High-limit, all-purpose credit cards did not exist for those with average means. There were no mortgages available for 125 percent of the home's value and no offers in the daily mail for second and third home equity loans. There were no 'payday lenders,' no 'live checks,' no 'instant money,' and certainly no offers to 'consolidate' all that debt by moving it from one credit card to another."

"The single biggest determinant of bankruptcy rate is how fast consumer credit goes up," adds Professor Lawless. After Congress deregulated consumer lending in the 1970s and 1980s, the market was flooded with complicated, high-interest, and potentially dangerous credit products that were sold to unwary consumers untutored in the fine print of credit fees and charges that kept them sinking into the debt quagmire.

The Unnoticed Court Decision That Affects All Our Lives

But the single biggest cause of exploding private debt, Lawless contends, was a U.S. Supreme Court decision in 1978 in the Marquette National Bank case. "That really opened the floodgates," Lawless told me. "It's the court decision that has had the most effect on people's lives, that no one has ever heard of. It effectively deregulated the credit card interest rates. Banks hail that as 'democratization' of credit. Their attitude was, we can now charge 30 percent to people who would not qualify for a loan before, because they were too high a risk. For banks, these vulnerable borrowers are the most lucrative borrowers."

For the finance industry, the steep-interest credit card and, even more, the debit card became the ideal vehicles to sell to people with bad credit records, who would get mired in debt and would forever feed bank profits by making the minimum payments while interest and card fees dragged them deeper into debt.

"If they make the minimum payment, . . . then that loan will take almost 20 years to pay back," said Shailesh Mehta, whose firm, Providian Financial, helped pioneer marketing credit cards to low-income people—"bankrupts . . . no credits," Mehta called them. He admitted to PBS *Frontline* correspondent Lowell Bergman that Providian never wanted these bad-risk borrowers to pay off their cards because the firm made so much money off high-penalty fees. They hooked customers, Mehta said, by offering 0 percent interest for a few months. "We made it look like it's a giveaway and took it back in the form of . . . 'penalty pricing' or 'stealth pricing,' " Mehta said. "In a strange way, the banks were charging [these] borrowers higher interest rates in order to give the wealthy people a break . . . because the people who have money were paying in full, and they were getting the break at the expense of the people who couldn't pay in full."

"More than 75 percent of credit card profits come from people who make those low, minimum monthly payments," Elizabeth Warren and Amelia Warren Tyagi reported in *The Two-Income Trap*, "and who makes minimum monthly payments at 26 percent interest? Who pays late fees, overbalance charges, and cash advance premiums? Families that can barely make ends meet, households precariously balanced between financial survival and complete collapse. These are the families that are singled out by the lending industry, barraged with special offers, personalized advertisements, and home phone calls, all with one objective in mind: *get them to borrow more money*."

Preapproved Credit—$350,000 per Family

Once the lid was off interest rates because of congressional deregulation, the banks had a field day. They sold as much debt as possible. In the early 2000s, banks and credit card companies blanketed the nation with preapproved credit card offers totaling $350,000 per family. This profligate policy represented a complete reversal in lending strategy. A generation earlier, banks were extremely careful, almost stingy, about granting credit. They were quick to shut it off if a borrower got in trouble. But by the 1990s, banks had come to see slow-paying borrowers who were in financial peril as their most lucrative targets.

As Pam Scholl's story illustrates, one way to get off the treadmill of endless credit or debit card debt is to file for bankruptcy and get a second chance financially, much the way bankrupt corporations do. But as personal bankruptcies rose through the 1990s, banks and credit card companies saw the bankruptcy process as depriving them of the most profitable segment of their business.

In the early 2000s, the financial industry began lobbying Congress to close the bankruptcy door, or at least tighten the terms for going bankrupt. They told Congress that "high-income deadbeats" were using bankruptcy to welsh on credit card debt. "The idea," explained Professor Lawless, "was to make it harder for people to get to bankruptcy court. The harder it is, the more expensive it is, the longer people put off filing for bankruptcy, the longer they pay the big penalty fees to the banks." Consumer advocates protested, saying the banks were squeezing helpless debtors who didn't have the funds to pay with. The banks countered that they were targeting the "high-income deadbeat," not the "honest and unfortunate debtor" who had truly run out of money.

Two Million Bankruptcies a Year

In 2005, the financial industry got what it wanted. Congress passed the Bankruptcy Abuse Prevention and Consumer Protection Act, which raised the legal and financial barriers to bankruptcy filings. As expected, the number of personal bankruptcies plunged from just over 2 million in 2005 to about 750,000 in 2006. But after a few years, bankruptcy filings climbed sharply again in the wake of mass layoffs and high unemployment. By 2010, bankruptcies were back over 2 million a year, evidence that even with tougher barriers to bankruptcy, financial distress among the middle class was more acute than five years earlier.

What's more, when experts examined who was filing for bankruptcy, it turned out that the banks and their lobbyists had misled Congress. As the financial industry had urged, the law was designed to block supposed high-income deadbeats from improperly filing for bankruptcy by instituting a financial "means test." With the means test as a filter to weed out high-income filers, the average income of bankruptcy filers should have fallen. But that didn't happen. Researchers saw no significant change.

So instead of filtering out high-income cheats, the new law was actually creating obstacles for honest, financially busted debtors, just as consumer advocates had feared. As Professor Lawless put it, the law "functioned like a barricade, blocking out hundreds of thousands of struggling families indiscriminately." So by the time people got to bankruptcy under the new law, they were in far more desperate straits than before. "The families in bankruptcy are much more deeply laden with debt," one study found. "Their net worth, which has always been negative, sank further. . . . Families filing for bankruptcy are in ever-increasing financial distress."

Once again, the New Economy altered the old rules of the virtuous circle economy, and average Americans got hurt. In the Old Economy, bankers issued credit just to strong, creditworthy customers who typically paid off their debts. The go-go New Economy went for easy credit and higher debt for all, especially people with risky credit records, and many more people wound up in bankruptcy. Over the past five years, as the housing market nosed down and twenty-five million Americans lost solid, full-time jobs, more and more middle-class families turned to easy credit to try to stay afloat. That added to the profits of banks and credit card companies, but the more money they made, the more middle-class and working families sank into financial ruin.

So the new credit system, coming on top of the great burden shift on pensions and health care, has contributed to the unraveling of the American Dream for average Americans and to America's ever-widening wealth gap.

Rescuing average Americans from the New Economy credit trap

will require reversing course—steps such as reimposing ceilings on interest rates and requiring down payments on houses. But the determined efforts of Wall Street banks and congressional Republicans to hamstring the operations of the new U.S. Consumer Financial Protection Bureau shows how hard it will be to do that—unless the middle class demands it.

CHAPTER 8

THE WEALTH GAP

THE ECONOMICS "OF THE 1%,
BY THE 1%, FOR THE 1%"

The fact is that income inequality is real—it's been
rising for more than 25 years.

— PRESIDENT GEORGE W. BUSH

By 2004, the richest 1 percent of Americans were
earning about $1.35 trillion a year—greater than the
total national incomes of France, Italy, or Canada.

— ROBERT FRANK,
Richistan

It is absolutely excessive. . . . But it's amazing what
you can get used to.

— LARRY ELLISON,
Oracle CEO, on his 454-foot yacht

IN THE FALL OF 2005, Citigroup put out a glossy investment
brochure with a boldfaced heading, **WELCOME TO THE PLUTONOMY
MACHINE,** that advised its clients: "There is no 'average consumer' in
a plutonomy. . . . Economic growth is powered by and largely con-
sumed by the wealthy few."

Citigroup was steering savvy investors to exploit America's growing economic divide by investing in businesses that cater to the luxury consumption of the super-rich in the world's greatest plutonomy, the United States. As another Citigroup financial brochure put it, "the rich now dominate income, wealth and spending" in America. In fact, Citigroup's pitch suggested that the world had not seen such an eye-popping concentration of wealth since sixteenth-century Spain or seventeenth-century Holland.

To the magazine *Advertising Age,* a wealthy American plutocracy was a golden opportunity. It urged ad agencies and marketing gurus to abandon mass marketing to the middle class, and even to the affluent upper middle class, and to concentrate on the hyper-rich. "The top 1% alone control nearly 40% of the wealth," advised the *Ad Age* blog. "And while the social and political effects of this inequality may be cause for concern, the accrual of wealth among the very few is of great consequence for marketers, since . . . a small plutocracy of wealthy elites drives a larger and larger share of total consumer spending and has outsize purchasing influence. . . ."

It was true. Even with the economy in a stall in the summer of 2011, luxury goods were selling well in Manhattan. *The New York Times* reported that Nordstrom had a waiting list for a Chanel sequined tweed coat retailing at $9,010. Mercedes said July sales of its high-end S-class sedans, which cost $200,000 or more, had jumped nearly 14 percent—its best July sales in five years. Tiffany's first-quarter sales were up 20 percent to $761 million. Markups in designer clothing and shoes were hot. Higher prices made for hungrier buyers, advised Arnold Aronson, former CEO of Saks. While most of the retail economy was flat, the luxury category recorded its tenth consecutive month of rising sales.

The New Plutocracy

Americans, far more than people in the advanced economies of Europe and Asia, accept and even endorse economic inequality as an integral feature of modern capitalism. Americans believe in material incentives for hard work and talent.

Even so, very few people grasp the dimensions of the economic schism that divides America today. People know that CEOs take home more, but they don't imagine how much more. In a 2007 nationwide survey, most people estimated the pay of an average big-company CEO at $500,000, when in fact CEOs of companies in the Standard & Poor's 500 were then averaging $14 million a year.

Although most people underestimated the wealth gap, most Americans thought income inequality had gone too far. Eleven different polls from 1984 to 2007 found that a 60 to 30 percent majority of Americans, including majorities of Republicans and high-income earners, thought that money and wealth in America should be more evenly distributed.

The explosive Jack-and-the-Beanstalk growth of a new economic oligarchy in America took off in the late 1970s, along with the power shift in Washington and the dawn of downsizing in Corporate America. As I mentioned earlier, it spawned the third wave of great private wealth in U.S. history. First came the robber baron era of railroad, oil, and mining fortunes during the Gilded Age, which left average Americans in what historians call "the long depression" of the 1880s and 1890s. Then came the wildly bullish flapper era of the Roaring Twenties that ended with the disaster of Black Monday, the 1929 stock market crash, and the Depression. The new Gilded Age emerged during the Reagan 1980s, when "Go for the Gold" was the official U.S. slogan for the 1984 Los Angeles Olympics and the unofficial mantra for economic Darwinism on Wall Street and in Corporate America that ended in the financial collapse of 2008.

During the past two decades, while the incomes of 90 percent of Americans barely inched forward, America's super-rich, the top 1 percent, reaped astronomical gains. This small elite garnered half of the nation's overall economic growth from 1993 to 2008, according to "Striking It Richer," a detailed study of U.S. tax records by economist Emmanuel Saez of the University of California at Berkeley. The trend hit new peaks in the 2000s, Saez and French economist Thomas Piketty reported. The farther up the wealth pyramid—which looks more like a steeple—the steeper the income gap.

According to the studies of U.S. income tax returns by Piketty and Saez:

- The top 1 percent super-rich, people with incomes over $352,000 a year, made $1.35 trillion in 2007—more money than entire countries like France, Italy, or Canada. As we've seen, the top 1 percent garnered two-thirds of the gains of U.S. national income growth from 2002 to 2007, twice as much as the other 99 percent of Americans combined. And this tiny group reaped 93 percent of the nation's gains in 2010, the first full year of economic recovery after the financial collapse of 2008.

- The top 0.01 percent, comprising just 15,426 families, enjoyed an *average* income of $9.1 million in 2007. Collectively, they were raking in 6 percent of the nation's overall income, or six hundred times their share in terms of numbers.

- The seventy-four people at the pinnacle each made $50 million or more in 2009, while recession was squeezing millions of American families. In this economic stratosphere, the average income was $518.8 million—*$10 million a week.*

- In 2008, the year of financial collapse, half a dozen hedge fund managers each made more than $1 billion: David Tepper of Appaloosa Management, $4 billion; George Soros, $3.3 billion; James Simons of Renaissance Technologies, $2.5 billion; and John Paulson, $2.3 billion. In

2007, Paulson had already made nearly $4 billion by betting against the housing market; in 2010, he made $5 billion more by betting on rising commodity prices and the recovery of America's big banks, thanks to a taxpayer bailout.

The Geography of Richistan

Translating these astounding numbers into human terms, *Wall Street Journal* reporter Robert Frank wrote a travelogue to the exotic domain of "Richistan." In a book by that title, Frank described the world of the wealthy:

· *Lower Richistan* (7.5 million families), worth $1 million to $10 million, many of them doctors, lawyers, and other professionals.

· *Middle Richistan* (2 million families), worth $10 million to $100 million, mostly entrepreneurs and small-business owners.

· *Upper Richistan* (thousands of families with net worth over $100 million), mainly corporate executives, bankers, financial advisers, and Hollywood and sports superstars.

· *Billionaireville* (the Forbes 400 Richest Americans plus a few more), where net worth of $1 billion is the price of admission.

· *The Walton family* (with an estimated wealth of $90 billion). At the apex of the wealth pinnacle, other writers have pointed out, are the heirs of Wal-Mart founder Sam Walton. Epitomizing the extremes of inequality in America today, this one family enjoys wealth equal to all the assets of the entire bottom 40 percent of the U.S. population—120 million people.

In Upper Richistan and Billionaireville, Frank wrote, the super-rich and ultra-rich often compete with each other in conspicuous consumption. Their primary residence costs an average of $16.9 million. Many of these families set up "family offices," where their personal management staff is dedicated to running their households, paying bills, arranging travel, and handling day-to-day needs. In this group, butlers are back in fashion. According to Frank, super-rich families spend up to $2 million a year on staff, $107,000 for annual spa bills, and up to $182,000 each on watches and $319,000 for cars. For investments, they don't buy mutual funds; they buy timber, land, oil rigs, and office towers.

In the Billionaireville of thirty-thousand-square-foot mansions, private jets, and elite art collections, Frank reports, "luxury fever" is the norm. The hyper-rich compete with ever more expensive toys, such as Oracle CEO Larry Ellison's 454-foot yacht, *Rising Sun,* which is loaded with sports complexes, a cinema, a speedboat, a helicopter pad and a crew of thirty. "It is absolutely excessive. No question about it," Ellison admitted to a writer for *Vanity Fair.* "But it's amazing what you can get used to."

The outlandishly conspicuous consumption of the super-rich might seem merely a shocking gossip tidbit—except that as economist Robert H. Frank pointed out, when the rich build ever more lavish mansions and bid up the cost of high-end estates, "that shifts the frame of reference for the near rich, and so on down the income ladder." So the push at the top helped cause housing prices at almost all levels to shoot up above historic norms until the bubble burst in 2007. For middle-class families, even the median new house built in 2007 was 50 percent larger and much more expensive than the median home in 1970, and that put financial pressure on hard-pressed middle-class families to spend more to get homes near good schools.

Did SBTC Cause the Wealth Gap?

The key question is, how did we get into this bind? How did these vast income and wealth disparities develop?

The conventional answer from business leaders, Republican presidents, and conservative economists is that the wealth divide is the unavoidable price of progress. In the lingo of the New Economy, the Two Americas schism was created by SBTC—skill-based technological change.

Speaking on Wall Street in early 2007, President George W. Bush laid out this rationale. "The fact is that income inequality is real— it's been rising for more than 25 years," Bush acknowledged. "The reason is clear: We have an economy that increasingly rewards education and skills because of that education."

But the supposed causal link between technology/education and the wealth gap does not match the facts. As we have seen in Germany and other European countries, which have also experienced SBTC, none has come out with the hyperconcentration of wealth of America. The middle class in several other countries is faring better than the American middle class.

So in today's global economy, where technology goes worldwide in a nanosecond, technological change cannot explain the disparity between the wealth trends in America and the economics of other leading countries.

Back in the 1970s, America's top 1 percent of income earners were netting a smaller share of the nation's riches than the top 1 percent in France, Germany, Switzerland, and Canada. We were economically more democratic than the Europeans. But by 2000, the picture had reversed: America's ultra-rich had pulled away from the world. In terms of their share of the nation's economic pie, the U.S. super-class easily outdistanced their peers in Germany, Great Britain, Canada, Australia, France, Japan, and Switzerland. America is now the most unequal society among industrialized countries in the West.

Is It Education? CEOs Outearn Ph.D.s

If educational differences were the key to America's economic disparities, as we are told, a different set of people would constitute today's super-rich. Some of the most highly educated people in America, Ph.D. physicists, astroscientists, top heart, brain, and cancer surgeons, and brilliant engineers, earn only a fraction of the astronomical pay of CEOs and Wall Street's top bankers. Bank traders earn far more than "quants"—the mental geniuses who dream up the derivatives that traders use to make money.

"Those at the top are often highly educated, yes, but so, too, are those just below them who have been left increasingly behind," write political economists Jacob Hacker of Yale and Paul Pierson of the University of California at Berkeley.

Blue-collar middle-class workers are constantly chided by business for not getting a college education. But contrary to conventional wisdom, getting a B.A. or B.S. is not a ticket to wealth. Some college graduates have done extremely well—but the degree is not what explains that. "Hard as it may be to believe," Hacker and Pierson report, "a typical entry-level worker (ages 25–34) with a bachelor's degree or higher earned only $1,000 more for full-time, full-year work in 2006 than did such a worker in 1980 ($45,000 versus $44,000, adjusted for inflation)."

In fact, experts find far greater financial differences among people with the *same level* of education than between groups with *different levels* of education. Several economists have reported much larger income disparities among college graduates than between the average income of college graduates and the average income of high school graduates. "To me, the most telling fact is that wages of both college grads and high school grads have gone nowhere for ten years," reports Larry Mishel, director of the pro-labor Economic Policy Institute in Washington, D.C. "College graduates haven't done better than high school graduates. I mean, they earn more, but their incomes are not growing faster. In this decade we have seen the slowest demand for college grads in the whole postwar period, and their wages have gone nowhere."

"The Most Political Law in the World"

Two trends are primarily responsible for today's hyperconcentration of wealth in America—the collective decisions over time by America's corporate power elite to take a far bigger share of business earnings for themselves, and the increasingly pro-rich, pro-business policy tilt in Washington since the late 1970s.

The U.S. tax code is where economics and politics intersect most powerfully. "The U.S. tax code is the most political law in the world," comments Jonathan Blattmachr, a top tax attorney at the blue ribbon Manhattan law firm of Milbank, Tweed, Hadley & McCloy.

The long-term trend of tax cutting since the 1970s has dramatically widened America's wealth divide. As the tax code has been written, rewritten, and rewritten again since 1978, it has been tilted so heavily in favor of the super-rich that many millionaires and billionaires today actually pay lower tax rates than many people in the middle class. The key driver of this lopsided outcome is the sharp cut in the capital gains tax—from 48 percent in 1978 to 15 percent today. Capital gains go primarily to the people at the top of the economic pyramid. The top 0.1 percent—about 315,000 people out of 315 million Americans— garner roughly *half of all capital gains* in the United States. Among the ultra-rich, the Forbes 400, the richest four hundred people in the country, capital gains account for 60 percent of their income.

The 15 percent capital gains tax means that the monumental investment gains of the wealthy are now taxed at lower rates than the W-2 withholding rate for many salaried middle-class professionals and middle managers, whose tax rates run up to 35 percent. Hedge fund managers, who make hundreds of millions of dollars per year, are also taxed at that same low 15 percent rate, well below the rate paid by their secretaries, chauffeurs, or butlers.

"If you make money with money, you get taxed at very low rates," explains billionaire investor Warren Buffett. "If you make money with muscle or hard work or sweat of your brow, you get taxed at rates that move on up. . . . In a very high percentage of cases, the very rich are paying less in the way of taxes than the people that clean their offices."

Personally, Buffett admitted that in 2010 he paid the lowest income tax rate of anyone in his office (twenty people)—a 17.4 percent rate on his taxable income of $39.8 million, most of which was capital gains—a much lower rate than his secretary and other aides paid on their W-2 salaries.

To make matters worse, ordinary employees typically pay a higher payroll tax rate—7.65 percent to finance Social Security and Medicare—than corporate CEOs and super-rich investors. Their investment gains are not subject to the payroll tax, and their pay over $106,800 is also exempt. As a result, the super-rich pay as little as 1 to 2 percent of their earned income in payroll taxes, far below the 7.65 percent rate of middle-class Americans.

Superclass Wealth: Trillions in Tax Cuts

A rainbow of across-the-board tax cuts starting in 1978, and especially the massive tax cuts enacted by President Ronald Reagan in 1981 and President George W. Bush in 2001, have produced a pot of gold for the super-rich. That is no accident. Well-organized business lobbies and anti-government tax cut activists have mounted a relentless campaign since the late 1970s to lower tax rates for the wealthy, and they have won a financial bonanza.

Several trillion dollars were added to the wealth of America's superclass by the Reagan and Bush tax cuts. Starting in 1981, Reagan lowered the top personal income tax rate from 70 to 28 percent, the capital gains rate from 28 to 20 percent, and the corporate tax rate from 46 to 35 percent. Even though Reagan presided over a couple of modest tax increases, the windfall from his tax cuts for America's wealthiest 1 percent was massive—roughly $1 trillion in the 1980s and another $1 trillion each decade after that. The Forbes 400 Richest Americans, enriched by the Reagan tax cuts, tripled their net worth from 1978 to 1990.

The Bush tax cuts of 2001, 2002, and 2003 were also highly skewed in favor of the wealthy by lowering the top income tax rate and the capital gains rate and phasing out the estate tax on America's top 2 percent. In the decade since the Bush tax cuts, the top 1 percent bracket reaped a collective windfall of more than $1 trillion. America's four hundred highest earners, boosted by the Bush tax cuts, saw their average income jump fivefold from the mid-1990s to 2010, while the typical American family's income went down.

At the other end of the income scale, the Bush tax cuts offered virtually nothing to low-income families and only modest breaks to middle-income families. The nonpartisan Congressional Budget Office estimated the middle-income tax cut at $1,180 a year compared with an average tax cut of $58,000 per year for the top 1 percent and a cut of $520,000 a year for the top 0.1 percent (those making over $3 million a year).

While the rich were showered with tax cuts, average Americans were hit by a near doubling of the payroll tax, which funds Social Security and Medicare. The employee's share of the payroll tax, which falls hardest on the working middle class, was increased from 3.45 percent in the 1970s to 7.65 percent today. In December 2010 and December 2011, President Obama persuaded Congress to temporarily lower the Social Security tax by 2 percent, but in exchange, he was forced by congressional Republicans to extend the Bush tax cuts for the wealthy along with cuts for the middle class.

"Creative Minority" to "Dominant Minority"

The other powerful force in creating the lopsided concentration of wealth in America today was the shift in the prevailing mind-set and mores of America's business leaders—a shift from the inclusive style of leadership from the 1940s into the 1970s that shared the nation's gains widely with the middle class, into a more self-centered style of leadership from the 1980s onward that kept most of the economic gains for the business elite itself.

In Arnold Toynbee's terms, such a shift may reflect the time in a civilization when the business and political leadership class changes from acting as "the creative minority" that inspires and leads the rise and flowering of a civilization, into becoming "the dominant minority" of "exploiters" focused primarily on sustaining and expanding their own wealth and power. When this happens, Toynbee reports, it opens up perilous rifts in maturing societies. This shift in the mind-set and motivation of the elite, he contends, is a major cause of the schisms in the body politic that contribute to the disintegration of a civilization.

The Corporate Mind Shift

In America today, a CEO's personal enrichment is taken as a hall-mark of success, whereas in the late 1960s, pay restraint was a core tenet of the corporate ethic. Harvard economist John Kenneth Galbraith wrote in 1967 that a CEO's pay was geared to the size of the company, not to its stock price, as today. Pay was good, but not out-landish. In the 1950s, Charles Wilson, as CEO of General Motors, was at the top of the pay pyramid since he ran America's largest corporation. His annual salary in 1950 was $626,300, roughly equal to $5 million today—a fraction of today's top corporate pay packages. That is mainly because Wilson did not get massive grants of stock options, which were taboo in the era when management shared prosperity with middle-class employees.

"Management does not go out ruthlessly to reward itself—a sound management is expected to exercise restraint," Galbraith reported. Since top company executives were privy to inside company information, they could obviously cash in big-time by trading in company stock. But the unwritten code frowned on that. "Were everyone to seek to do so . . . ," Galbraith wrote, "the corporation would be a chaos of competitive avarice."

By the 1980s, competitive avarice was in. Tom Wolfe captured the winner-take-all creed in his book *Bonfire of the Vanities,* and so did Oliver Stone's 1987 movie, *Wall Street.* "Greed, for lack of a better word, is good," preached Gordon Gekko, the movie's mogul investor. "Greed is right, greed works. . . . Greed, in all of its forms . . . has marked the upward surge of mankind." It certainly marked the upward surge in CEO pay, which rocketed from forty times the pay of an average company worker in 1980 to nearly four hundred times by 2000.

Stakeholder Capitalism

Certainly in the 1980s and '90s, there were CEOs like David Packard of Hewlett-Packard, who practiced stakeholder capitalism, balancing the needs of various corporate stakeholders—employees, customers, and suppliers as well as shareholders and management. James Burke, CEO of Johnson & Johnson, won accolades in 1982 for corporate integrity by recalling and repackaging the company's entire supply of Tylenol, at a cost of $100 million to J&J's bottom line, after someone put cyanide into Tylenol capsules on drugstore shelves and several people died. Burke lived by the Johnson & Johnson corporate "credo" that put the company's commitment to patients, parents, and caregivers and to employees ahead of profits and returns to stockholders.

Ken Melrose, CEO of Toro, brought the lawn mower and snow blower company back from bankruptcy to market success with an employee-centered philosophy during his tenure from 1983 to 2005. "In our culture," Melrose said, "the CEO in effect works for the management, management works for the employee, employees work for customers, and thus the customer is the ultimate boss." As he took charge of his failing company, Melrose took a "substandard salary," giving up a cash salary for stock—but stock that would pay off only over the long term if the company actually prospered. It worked—to everyone's advantage. But as Melrose said later, "I'm not a big fan of large stock-option grants year after year after year to already well-paid executives. I don't buy the argument that each slug of stock options is needed to continue to motivate the CEO to get the stock value up. And it's a hollow argument to say it's good for the small shareholder."

Stock Options—Corporate Alchemy

But CEOs like Ken Melrose, Jim Burke, and David Packard were not the norm in the New Economy. Wall Street was unimpressed with Melrose's logic that CEOs did not need vast stock options to be motivated to run a company well. In fact, just the opposite happened. Wall Street saw company stock as the key to generating managerial success.

In the 1980s, stock options became the golden goose of Corporate America, the avenue to stunning fortunes among the business elite. Year after year, corporate boards would award CEOs and other top executives huge grants of company stock or stock options—either shares for free or shares at a bargain price. Unlike ordinary shareholders, the corporate brass did not face a downside risk. They would exercise their stock options only if the company's stock went up, and as Al Dunlap showed, a fast-talking CEO can often cause a short-term run-up in the market price.

The payoffs were astronomical, enough to vault a previously affluent corporate executive into the stratosphere of the super-rich. In earlier times, inherited wealth accounted for most of America's super-rich, but today the top echelons of business and Wall Street constitute 60 percent of the very richest people in America—the richest 0.1 percent and stock options were the primary vehicle for the corporate super-rich.

Larry Ellison, CEO of software giant Oracle, epitomized the *nouveau super-riche* of Corporate America. Ellison, whose board richly rewarded him every year with a grant of seven million shares of Oracle stock, topped a *Wall Street Journal* compilation of the ten largest CEO payouts in a single year from 1995 to 2005 by garnering $706.1 million in 2001 through the combined value of his stock grants, options, cash, and bonuses. Close behind were Michael Eisner, former CEO of Disney, with $575.6 million in 1998 and another $203 million in 1993; and Sandy Weill, former Citigroup CEO, who pulled down $621.8 million in three big years between 1997 and 2000.

Pay for Performance

The economic rationale for those big stock grants by Corporate America was "pay for performance"—rewarding CEOs and senior executives by supposedly aligning management's interests with stockholder interests. As Milton Friedman put it, that would motivate the captains of industry to "maximize shareholder value" by steadily improving the stock price of their companies. "Shareholder value"—that is, stock price—became the be-all and end-all of corporate CEOs in the New Economy.

The idea sprang from an academic paper by two of Friedman's graduate students who became assistant professors, Michael C. Jensen of Harvard Business School and William H. Meckling of Rochester University. Writing about potential conflicts between CEO and shareholder interests, Jensen and Meckling argued that one way to match the interests of the two sides was to make the CEO an owner of the company, like stockholders—"to give him stock options." At first the idea met with resistance, but Jensen became its apostle, and slowly it gained traction.

By 1980, only about 30 percent of CEOs had been granted company stock options, and by 1994, 70 percent were getting options. By 2000, "mega-option grants" of a million shares or more had become the norm. Perhaps unwittingly, the Clinton administration fueled the option trend by limiting the tax deduction that companies could take for executive salaries to $1 million. Options were not counted under that ceiling. What also made them attractive to corporate boards was that for many years stock options theoretically cost the company nothing. They were not counted as an expense. They were a freebie with an enormous bang, and no buck, and that lasted until international regulatory changes forced reforms in America in 2006.

Huge Payoffs for Failure, Too

But from the 1980s onward, the corporate options game touched off what *New Yorker* writer John Cassidy called "an orgy of self-enrichment." Payoffs were huge, even for failures. CEOs learned how to game option grants. Some, such as Al Dunlap, would talk up their stock price and cash in before the stock dropped. In other cases, boards would time massive option awards to the CEOs just before announcing major expansion plans that shot up the stock price. The whole operation smacked of insider trading, ripe for manipulation.

"There was a sea change in the mid-1990s," observes Stephen Young, executive director of the Caux Round Table, which studies business ethics and promotes moral capitalism. "I think it was a generational shift. It was when baby boomers became increasingly important as CEOs. Baby boomers are the Me generation. If we are running a company, we are running it for ourselves. We have performance standards that always come back to *us*—stock options, golden parachutes. We are not in it for anybody else. CEOs are not doing moral capitalism because that's not what's being rewarded on Wall Street or at business schools."

Sometimes there was a connection between pay and performance, but just as often there was not. Year after year, *The Wall Street Journal, The New York Times,* and a few independent executive compensation experts such as Graef Crystal would run exposés showing that many CEOs had harvested inflated incomes from stock options, even when stockholders lost money. Bob Nardelli, for one, was forced out as

CEO at Home Depot in 2007 because of the company's disastrous performance under his leadership. But Nardelli walked away with $210 million.

Probably the most egregiously distorted pay packages went to the Wall Street bosses at Bear Stearns and Lehman Brothers, who drove their companies to extinction in 2008. A Harvard University study documented how the top five executives at these two banks piled up private fortunes worth $2.4 billion in stock option profits and cash bonuses, even as they left stockholders with next to nothing. From 2000 to 2008, the study reported, Lehman CEO Richard Fuld cashed out $461 million in stock options—more than $160 million in the final months. Bear Stearns CEO James Cayne cashed out $289 million in stock options, much of it as Bear Stearns went into its death spiral.

And as the housing bubble rose and went bust, Angelo Mozilo, CEO of subprime lender Countrywide, pocketed $410 million in salary, bonuses, and stock option grants and then got another $112 million in his severance package when his company went bust.

Options Cheating

The options game had an even more sinister flaw. At several hundred major corporations, including Apple, UnitedHealth Group, and Silicon Valley start-ups such as Symbol Technologies and Mercury Interactive, CEOs cheated their shareholders by manipulating their stock options.

When their company's stock did not go up and deliver them easy profits, these CEOs persuaded their boards of directors to rig the game. The boards would backdate the CEO's stock options to a lower strike price, or buying price, than originally granted, so that even if the company's stock had gone down, the CEO and senior executives would still get a handsome payoff while shareholders lost money. For example, if the original options were issued at a stock price of $50 and the stock went down to $40, the CEO got the board to pick an earlier date for the options grant, when the price was only $30 a share. Suddenly, the CEO could cash in his options for a $10 profit on each share. A million options equaled $10 million. So the CEO made money while the shareholders were losing. This, of course, defeated the entire concept of pay for performance.

In addition, ordinary taxpayers took a hit from options cheating. The SEC found that some CEOs were falsely reporting their option strike date so that the stock price would appear higher than what they actually paid, thus reducing the taxes on their gains.

The highest-profile case of stock option payola involved the late Apple CEO Steve Jobs. After ducking media inquiries about whether Apple's board had improperly changed the dates of its stock option grants, Apple finally admitted to the SEC that between 1997 and 2002, there were 6,428 separate instances where the dates of Apple stock options had been altered.

Steve Jobs had been personally involved in picking "favorable" dates for backdating options, Apple confessed. Nonetheless, Apple's internal report cleared Jobs of wrongdoing. Initially, Apple said Jobs had not profited personally, but it later turned out that Jobs had made a whopping profit, getting $295.7 million from selling half the shares that he'd been allowed to buy for $75 million. Worse, Apple disclosed to the SEC that it had fabricated—that is, totally made up—a fictional meeting of the board of directors in October 2003 that supposedly approved 7.5 million options for Jobs. That meeting never took place, Apple admitted; in fact, the options had been approved on December 18, 2001, when they would have cost Jobs more.

Apple's whitewash of Steve Jobs met with catcalls of corporate hypocrisy. "They pretty much admitted he was directly involved in the fraud," asserted New York University finance professor David Yermack. "You are torturing the English language to say he did not benefit from the options," echoed Patrick McGurn of Institutional Shareholder Services. Even with Apple shareholders grumbling, there was no legal prosecution. Strange as it may sound, while backdating options is obviously fraudulent, it is not against the law.

Nationwide, the scale of stock option cheating was staggering. But the public knew little about it because this corporate fraud took place behind closed doors. Except for a few high-profile cases such as Apple's, most of the bogus option deals got no media attention. In part, this is because the SEC under Bush relied mostly on internal company probes to ferret out wrongdoing rather than launching its own legal actions.

In one revealing case, William McGuire, former CEO of United-Health Group, was forced out by his own board in October 2006 because an internal inquiry found he had been backdating and manipulating stock options for eight years—from 1994 through 2002. To settle claims by both his company and the federal government, McGuire eventually agreed to forfeit $620 million of his $1.1 billion in stock option gains.

The size of McGuire's settlement suggests the huge sums at stake. In a detailed study, professors at Harvard and Cornell documented options cheating on an epidemic scale. At least 850 CEOs, they said, were involved in fraudulently manipulating stock options, dishonestly cheating their own employees as well as mutual fund and 401(k) investors. One reason so many CEOs got away with options cheating was that some corporate board members got payola, too. As the Harvard-Cornell team put it, there were "lucky directors" motivated to manipulate the option dates of their "lucky CEOs" because the board members also "luckily" got backdated options.

Options: A Smokescreen for Wealth Transfer

Some of the sharpest criticism of the stock options game came not from academics or liberal politicians, but from staunch capitalists such as John C. (Jack) Bogle, founder and longtime chairman of the Vanguard mutual fund family. Bogle contended that ordinary shareholders were being cheated by the massive stock grants given to CEOs because the value of everyone else's shares was being diluted by the gift of free or low-cost shares to the executive elite. In his book *The Battle for the Soul of Capitalism,* Bogle derided the whole concept as a smokescreen for a massive "wealth transfer to [corporate] insiders" from ordinary investors.

Bogle also derided the idea that stock options linked the interest of management with the interest of shareholders. "This oft-repeated and widely accepted bromide turns out to be false," Bogle protested. "Managers don't *hold* the shares they acquire [like shareholders]. They *sell* them, and promptly. . . . We rewarded our executives not for the reality of creating long-term economic value but for pumping up the perception of short-term stock market prices."

Even before the Great Recession hit, there was a rising chorus of criticism. At Harvard Business School, one of the original seedbeds of the pay-for-performance concept, dissenting academics charged that this concept of pay was narrowing the focus of CEOs and corporations, at a high cost to society at large. "The dominant ethos today legitimates the notion that human beings are relentless market maximizers who need literally to be *bribed* to focus solely on shareholder value—undermining other commitments managers might have to employees, customers, the community, or larger national and global concerns such as the environment or human rights," asserted Harvard Business School professors Jay Lorsch and Rakesh Khurana. "It relieves the corporate institution of any meaningful responsibility to anyone but the transitory group of stockholders who buy and sell shares constantly."

By 2002, even Michael Jensen was dismayed. Executive stock options, Jensen told *The Economist,* had turned into "managerial heroin" that encouraged CEOs to focus on short-term highs with destructive long-term consequences. "Once a firm's shares became overvalued," *The Economist* explained, paraphrasing Jensen, "it was in managers' interests to keep them that way, or to encourage even more overvaluation, in the hope of cashing out before the bubble burst. Doing this not only meant being less than honest with shareholders, or being creatively optimistic with corporate accounts. It also encouraged behaviour that actually reduced the value of some firms to their shareholders. . . ."

Firestorm over "Gnomes of Norwalk"

But the real political firestorm over stock options was triggered by an obscure quasi-regulatory body, the Financial Accounting Standards Board, or FASB, known in Washington lingo as "Faz-bee," whose officials SEC chairman Arthur Levitt nicknamed "the gnomes of Norwalk," because Norwalk, Connecticut, is FASB's home. In 1993, FASB announced its intention to issue an accounting rule that would end "the freebie" for stock options on grounds that failing to charge options as a business expense was deceptive accounting. To fix that, FASB would require companies to "expense" executive stock options—charge them as a cost against the corporate balance sheet, the same as salaries.

Corporate America went ballistic. Congress was inundated with phone calls, emails, and visiting delegations of CEOs. Business groups issued "Chicken Little" warnings: The stock market would collapse, companies would fold, unable to recruit top talent without the lure of options; the economy would be irreparably damaged. Arthur Levitt and the SEC, which oversees FASB, were besieged. Corporate leaders argued that options were not an expense because no check was issued and also that options could not be precisely valued because of fluctuations in stock prices. This ignored the fact that companies already valued stock options on their tax returns, as required by the IRS.

"During my seven and a half years in Washington . . . ," Arthur Levitt later wrote, "nothing astonished me more than witnessing the powerful special interest groups in full swing when they thought a proposed rule or a piece of legislation might hurt them, giving nary a thought to how the proposal might help the investing public. With laserlike precision, groups representing Wall Street firms, mutual fund companies, accounting firms, or corporate managers would quickly set about to defeat even minor threats. Individual investors, with no organized labor or trade association to represent their views in Washington, never knew what hit them."

Business leaders reacted so explosively because making options a corporate expense would make major companies look bad. Big-name Silicon Valley companies had been issuing such a cornucopia of stock options that if they were charged as an expense, company profits would plummet. Merrill Lynch estimated that expensing options would slash profits among leading high-tech companies by roughly 60 percent. At Cisco, the Internet equipment giant, a yearly $2.6 billion profit would have been cut nearly in half.

Warren Buffett of Berkshire Hathaway, probably America's best-known investor, accused Corporate America of an "Alice in Wonderland" attitude on stock options. Buffett backed the FASB rule. Expensing options, he asserted, would be more honest because it would expose the naked truth to investors. "Options are a huge cost for many corporations and a huge benefit to executives," Buffett declared. Failing to value options fairly, he wrote in a *Washington Post* op-ed piece, "enables chief executives to lie about what they are truly being paid and to overstate the earnings of the companies they run."

But Congress bowed to the political heat from Corporate America. In the spring of 1994, Senator Joe Lieberman of Connecticut, then an ardently pro-business Democrat, introduced a Senate resolution that condemned the FASB rule as reckless and warned of "grave consequences for America's entrepreneurs." Under intense lobbying from powerful CEOs, the Senate voted 88–9 for Lieberman's resolution. Although it was nonbinding, SEC chair Arthur Levitt took the Senate vote as a warning shot at both FASB and the SEC. Fearing that Congress would strip FASB of its powers and cut funding for the SEC, Levitt backed down. He directed FASB to withdraw its rule.

But out of office, Levitt told me how deeply he regretted forcing FASB to retreat. "It was probably the single biggest mistake I made in my years at the SEC," Levitt said. A decade later, after the Enron and WorldCom scandals, in which dishonest accounting played a major role, there were new pressures in Congress from Republicans as well as Democrats for expensing stock options, but the bills died in Senate gridlock.

The hand of U.S. regulators was finally forced in February 2004, when the International Accounting Standards Board adopted universal rules to expense stock options. Ten months later, in December 2004, America followed the world standard, adopting FASB's Rule 123R to expense stock options.

But business opposition succeeded in stalling the new rule from taking effect until 2006. The decade-long political siege over options testified to the power of business to protect its financial interests.

PART 3

UNEQUAL
DEMOCRACY

JUST BEFORE SITTING DOWN in the glittering East Room of the White House to sign the $350 billion tax cut bill of 2003, President George W. Bush thanked his cabinet, congressional leaders, and "my friend Dirk Van Dongen."

To most Americans, Van Dongen was an unknown. He held no elected office or high appointment. He avoided TV appearances. And he enjoyed no celebrity status. But inside the Beltway, Van Dongen was known—and is still known—as a key power player who has been an important influence in tilting Washington policy in favor of business and the super-rich. He is a no-nonsense six-footer in his midsixties, with salt-and-pepper hair and rimless glasses. He's a master organizer who loves the power game but avoids the limelight. And he had a pipeline into the Bush White House.

Right after George W. Bush's inauguration in January 2001, the president's master political strategist, Karl Rove, had lunch with Van Dongen and asked him to organize and run a tax relief coalition. "They knew I was loyal to Bush," Van Dongen said later. "I was a Bush Pioneer, which meant you raised lot of money for the campaign—$100,000. I knew a lot of the senior staff."

Van Dongen was Rove's man to orchestrate the business chorus behind the Bush tax cuts. Some business leaders wanted corporate tax cuts right away, but the Rove–Van Dongen deal was individual cuts first, business tax cuts later.

So in 2001, and again in 2003, Dirk Van Dongen became the field marshal for the business lobbying forces that helped move Congress to pass two massive Bush tax cuts, the first of which delivered more than $1 trillion in lower taxes for the richest 5 percent of Americans and added $2.9 trillion to the federal deficit.

CHAPTER 9

THE NEW 2000S POWER GAME

WHY CONGRESS OFTEN
IGNORES PUBLIC OPINION

Whatever elections may be doing, they are *not* forcing elected officials to cater to the policy preferences
of the "median voter."

— LARRY BARTELS,
Unequal Democracy

Current U.S. tax policies do the opposite of what
most Americans want. . . . The mystery is how politicians can get away with tax policies that are so out
of harmony with the wishes of the American public.
— BENJAMIN I. PAGE AND LAWRENCE R. JACOBS,
Class War?

This is the ultimate Washington insiders-versus-
America issue. . . . Washington derives so much of
its power from the tax code—not just congressmen
on the Ways and Means Committee, but lobbyists
and lawyers.

— STEPHEN MOORE,
Club for Growth

THE ALLIANCE BETWEEN George W. Bush and Dirk Van Dongen—"Dirkus," the president called him—was formalized on February 23, 2001, in the Indian Treaty Room of "the old EOB," the gray Victorian-era Executive Office Building, next door to the White House.

Bush was getting ready to go to Congress to push for his groundbreaking tax cuts that would become not only a hallmark of his administration, but a lightning rod of controversy a decade later in the 2011 congressional battle over whether the rich should pay higher taxes to help bring down the federal deficit.

Many people today forget, but even in 2001, the Bush tax cuts were so massive that they were controversial. And before President Bush went public with them, Karl Rove wanted to cement Bush's political partnership with business on the tax package. So that morning, Bush, Rove, and Treasury Secretary Paul O'Neill walked over to the EOB to sit down with fifty leaders of the Tax Relief Coalition, a new political syndicate of powerful business trade organizations headed by Dirk Van Dongen.

As president of one of the coalition's major business groups, the forty-thousand-member National Association of Wholesaler-Distributors, Van Dongen was a veteran of political wars. He was a shrewd lobbying strategist. "Over the years, I got a reputation for knowing how to organize coalitions, how to run them," Van Dongen explained to me. "My staff serves as the coalition bureaucracy. We call the meetings. We push the paper around. But this is not Van Dongen at the top of a juggernaut without anyone else. This is a team sport. You do not win these things on your own. You gather like-minded stakeholders and create a coalition."

The like-minded stakeholders were in the Indian Treaty Room that morning to meet with the new president. The goal that day was to make sure that everyone walked out of that session singing the same tune. "There's a chorus out there," said one White House official, "and we're trying to make sure it's heard as loudly and clearly as possible."

Tax Wars: Insiders vs. the Public

Most of Corporate America had backed Bush in the tight election of 2000. Now, he was in his honeymoon period, but the fate of his tax proposal was uncertain. Moderates on Capitol Hill, Republicans included, worried that Bush's proposal for $1.78 trillion in individual tax cuts over the next decade risked runaway federal deficits. At Treasury, Secretary O'Neill was warned by his communications director, Michele Davis, that the public was wary. In a memo, she told him: "The public prefers spending on things like health care and education over cutting taxes."

That very morning, February 27, 2001, *The Washington Post* ran a poll reporting that 35 percent of the public thought Bush's top priority should be higher spending on domestic programs such as education and health care. Another 25 percent favored strengthening Social Security; 17 percent wanted to spend budget surpluses inherited from Clinton on reducing the national debt; and only 22 percent—about one in five—wanted to cut taxes. And if there was going to be a tax cut, 53 percent favored a small cut over a large cut; and 47 percent worried that Bush's tax cut would be tilted in favor of the wealthy.

An NBC/*Wall Street Journal* poll found that while most people welcomed a tax cut, a 52 to 41 percent majority said it should be only "for middle- and low-income taxpayers so the government has enough money for debt reduction and specific spending increases in priority areas such as education." An even stronger tilt toward a smaller, middle-class tax cut came in a *Los Angeles Times* poll on March 8. Even in polls that supported a tax cut in principle, the public wasn't buying the scale or the financial tilt of the Bush tax cuts.

The Gang of Six

Enter Dirk Van Dongen and what he calls "the Gang of Six"—the heart of the Tax Relief Coalition—determined to override the public's view.

In the three decades since Lewis Powell's business manifesto of 1971, Van Dongen's six groups had become the core of business political power in Washington: 1) the U.S. Chamber of Commerce; 2) the Business Roundtable; 3) the National Association of Manufacturers; 4) the National Federation of Independent Business; 5) the National Restaurant Association; and, of course, Van Dongen's own 6) National Association of Wholesaler-Distributors. Together, Van Dongen says, they represent 1.8 million businesses, from the Fortune 1,000 to the multitude of small businesses. By 2001, the Gang of Six dominated Washington lobbying.

In Washington, the biggest political wars are invariably about money, especially taxes. "This is the ultimate Washington insiders-versus-America issue," asserts Stephen Moore, president of the Club for Growth, a right-wing group that is passionate about cutting taxes. "Washington derives so much of its power from the tax code— not just congressmen on the Ways and Means Committee, but lobbyists and lawyers."

Dirk Van Dongen cut his political teeth on tax bills—fighting for President Reagan's tax cuts in 1981 and 1986, trying to torpedo President Clinton's tax increases in 1993. As a Republican loyalist and a canny operative with a golden Rolodex, Van Dongen has the inside track; he knows whom to call and how to move things. "Dirk is always well positioned . . . ," said an admiring Chamber of Commerce official. "His political tentacles run deep." Others talk about his talent for organization and his skill at leveraging business influence with Congress.

For the 2001 tax battle, Van Dongen's Tax Relief Coalition ramped up with surprising speed. Even though corporations would not directly benefit from individual income tax cuts, individual business leaders in the Gang of Six coalition stood to reap huge personal windfalls from a drop of 5 percent in the maximum individual tax rate or a cut in capital gains taxes. Those with small businesses, where company profits pass through to their individual tax returns, got an added benefit. So they were all motivated to push a big tax cut.

"That coalition was very important," said Nick Calio, Bush's chief congressional liaison. "There were a lot of recalcitrant Democrats and some Republicans [in Congress]."

Van Dongen's specialty is grassroots politicking. He is a strong believer in district-by-district face-to-face lobbying. His strategy was to mobilize thousands of CEOs of companies in his wholesalers group and in the National Federation of Independent Business to lobby senators and House members back in their home districts. The Chamber of Commerce and Business Roundtable flew in high-powered CEOs to meet with committee chairmen and pivotal lawmakers. Professional business lobbyists buttonholed fence-sitters on Capitol Hill. All pushed the big tax cut.

The Critics: "Reverse Robin Hood"

On the other side was a liberal coalition of organized labor, women's groups, civil rights organizations, Common Cause (the nonprofit public advocacy group), and Ralph Nader's Public Citizen. They favored a smaller, middle-class-friendly tax cut. In a TV ad campaign, the AFL-CIO attacked President Bush for spending the budget surplus inherited from Clinton on a tax cut tilted to favor the wealthy. "The President has it backwards," declared AFL-CIO president John Sweeney. The Service Employees International Union staged protests in several cities, trying to mobilize the opposition. "Let's call it what it is," Georgia State Democratic senator Vincent Fort shouted to a union rally in Atlanta. "This is reverse Robin Hood. [Bush] is stealing from the poor to give to the rich." Although opinion polls showed a majority of Americans against the Bush tax cut formula, there was little evidence that much of the public was writing or calling Congress with their views. In fact, Bush was the one urging voters to press Congress—to back his plan. On a swing through the Midwest promoting his tax cuts, the president told audiences time and again, "You're just an e-mail away from making a difference in somebody's attitude."

In the nitty-gritty of Washington lobbying, the opposition was no match for the Gang of Six. Members knew that in one year, the six big business groups could spend a staggering $2 billion on lobbying and hundreds of millions more on political campaigns, backing President Bush and members of the House and Senate who favored their tax-cutting agenda. Just one group from the Gang of Six, the Business Roundtable, and its 208 corporate members and their executives poured $143 million into the 2010 congressional elections, according to the Center for Responsive Politics, which tracks political money. The business advantage was so great, observed Yale Law School professor Michael Graetz, "you have an 800-pound gorilla battling no one."

With a faltering economy in 2001 and rising unemployment, the Gang of Six made the pitch that large tax cuts would jump-start the economy and create jobs. The Bush White House said it would revive "our sputtering economy." As it turned out, that economic logic was wrong, but it swayed Congress.

In terms of who wins and loses in a tax bill, ordinary voters get confused by the crossfire of claims and counterclaims. Tax policy, as one academic study put it, is "a highly technical realm that is ripe for concealment and mystification," and the Gang of Six and the Bush White House were not above exploiting public confusion or gullibility. Democrats warned that 43 percent of the tax cut would go to the top 1 percent on the income scale. But the White House highlighted the promise of a quick tax rebate for average taxpayers—$300 for single people and $600 for couples. But that pitch masked the larger truth that as the years rolled on, the lion's share of tax cuts would go to the super-rich.

With a full court press by the Gang of Six reinforcing the White House push, the Bush bill, offering $1.35 trillion in tax cuts over a decade, passed the House by 240–154 in May 2001. In the Senate, Republicans sidestepped a Democratic filibuster by invoking the process of budget reconciliation—which required them to guarantee there would be no net loss of revenue, an impossibility with such a huge tax cut. The Republican majority ignored that requirement and the looming deficits and passed the bill 58–33.

McCain in Opposition

No less a conservative than Arizona Republican John McCain voted against the Bush tax cut. McCain had advocated tax relief for "millions of hardworking Americans." But when he saw that the Bush package was stacked against the middle class, he voted no. "I cannot in good conscience support a tax cut in which so many of the benefits go to the most fortunate among us, at the expense of middle-class Americans who most need tax relief," McCain protested.

When economists did the numbers, they found that 52.5 percent of the Bush tax cuts went to the richest 5 percent of U.S. households, while 80 percent of Americans got one-fourth of the tax breaks through 2010. Bush had abandoned the "compassionate conservatism" of his 2000 campaign. Backed by the Gang of Six, he had rammed through a tax bill that ran contrary to public opinion.

"Far from representing popular wishes, the size, structure, and distribution of the tax cuts passed in 2001 were directly at odds with majority views," noted political scientists Jacob Hacker and Paul Pierson. Instead, they observed, the Bush White House was rewarding its political base—"the partisans, activists, and moneyed interests that are their first line of support. . . ."

Business vs. Labor: 16-to-1 Odds

What powered the business community's ability to persuade Congress to buck public opinion on the Bush tax cuts was a political machine with unparalleled clout in political campaigns and influence deep in the tax-writing committees of Congress—a machine that far outstripped that first business coalition after the 1971 Powell memo.

The media still treat business and labor as rough equals in the Washington power game, but that image is forty years out of date. Business vastly outguns organized labor in its ability to marshal money and political muscle. The gap between the two is far, far greater than the public realizes or than most political reporters reflect.

Not only did business respond to the Powell memo by dramatically expanding its lobbying presence in Washington, but it has moved aggressively into campaign politics. Unions were the first to form PACs, or political action committees, to funnel dollars to friendly candidates. But once corporate PACs got the green light, they surged ahead.

The explosive growth of corporate PACs dates from a 1975 ruling by the Federal Election Commission, which approved not only company PACs, but the right of corporate management to solicit funds from employees and to use company funds to manage their PACs. Before that, labor PACs outnumbered corporate PACs by 201 to 89. Today, business PACs have an overwhelming advantage. Companies and business trade associations have set up 2,593 PACs to 272 for labor unions.

Important as they are, PACs are only part of the story in the changing balance of power. PACs are subject to specific legal limits on donations from individuals to candidates. Really big donors look for ways to get around those legal limits. One way is through "bundling"—the kind of fund-raising that business lobbyists like Dirk Van Dongen specialize in. They gather lots of individual donations from their friends and business colleagues and put them together in a "bundle." That gives them credit—and political chits with officeholders who receive those "bundles."

But the biggest campaign donations come in the form of what is known in campaign argot as "soft money"—"soft" because the donations are not subject to fixed, hard, legal limits. Soft money donations cannot go directly to candidates, but they can be contributed to parties or to independent groups, including Super-PACs, which are not legally supposed to have any direct connection with candidates. Until the last couple of years, when Super-PACs took off in size and activity, soft money donations were typically designated for organizational and educational efforts by the political parties—to the Republican National Committee or the Democratic National Committee, or to state and local party committees, or the party committees that back campaigns for the U.S. Senate, Congress, and so on, down the line, for get-out-the-vote efforts or TV issue ad campaigns. Party organizations at all levels are forever on the hunt for soft money, and with no legal limits on the size of donations, the financial floodgates are wide open. The checks can run into the hundreds of thousands and even the millions.

In the pivotal congressional elections of 2010, business interests pumped in $972 million in soft money contributions mostly to the Republican Party vs. $10 million for labor—a staggering 97-to-1 business advantage. In PAC donations, the business tilt was significant, too: Business PACs outdid labor PACs by $333 million to $69 million, according to the Center for Responsive Politics. Add it all together, the center says, and business outspent labor 16 to 1 in the 2010 elections.

The Shadow Government on K Street

Corporate money has also fueled the explosive growth of the Washington lobbying industry. In fact, while most of America was mired in economic stagnation during the zero decade, lobbying enjoyed boom times. The banner years were 2009 and 2010, when Washington was busy doling out taxpayer bailout money to troubled banks and Congress was writing laws on health care and regulating Wall Street. In all, $7 billion was spent on lobbying—$3.5 billion a year—in 2009 and 2010, and $6 billion, or more than 87 percent, was spent by business interests. No other lobbying interest was even a close second. Business outspent labor on lobbying by 65 to 1. Not surprising, since business lobbyists as early as 2006 had outnumbered labor lobbyists by more than 30 to 1 (12,785 business lobbyists to 403 for labor). In fact, business leaders did not even bother to mention labor or public interest lobbyists when they were asked to name their primary targets or opponents. They seemed not to regard labor or public interest lobbyists as serious competition.

Since the early 1990s, a shadow government has taken root along K Street, the Washington corridor that is home to block after stately block of law firms and lobbying offices. Over the years, this army of influence peddlers has gone well beyond the hunt for votes on Capitol Hill. Smart lobbyists know that it is not just the final vote on a bill that counts, but every step along the way. Business enjoys huge political advantages by having its lobbying agents meet day in and day out with key legislators and their staffs, either to kill bills or provisions in them that business considers hostile or to insert arcane subparagraphs that its lobbyists have drafted and tailored to specific corporate interests, often with multibillion-dollar bottom-line consequences.

Most of the time, lobbying is done in private, but sometimes it emerges in public view. In 2007, for example, the Business Roundtable dug in its heels when Barney Frank, then Democratic chair of the House Financial Services Committee, proposed giving shareholders the right to vote on CEO pay, bonuses, and options. For a decade, shareholder groups and investor advocates had complained that CEO pay packages were far too lavish and that Congress should give shareholders a vote on executive pay. But despite the corporate mantra about CEOs working for shareholder interests, CEOs were up in arms at the thought that shareholders might get a deciding voice on their pay.

The Business Roundtable, representing the CEOs of America's 180 largest corporations, sent its president, John Castellani, to inform Congress that the nation's most powerful corporate leaders objected vehemently—even to a nonbinding advisory vote. "Corporations were never designed to be democracies . . . ," Castellani told a House Finance Committee hearing. "While shareholders own a corporation, they don't run it."

Barney Frank and his fellow Democrats were unmoved. The Democratic majority in the House passed a pro-shareholder bill. But typical of the power of stealth lobbying in Washington on a relatively low-profile issue, the Business Roundtable and its allies in the Gang of Six found ways to stifle the shareholder bill in the Senate Banking Committee. Without a vote being taken, the bill died in its legislative crib. The investing public was largely unaware that its interests had been suppressed. It took the financial collapse of 2008 finally to get Congress and the Securities & Exchange Commission to authorize shareholder votes on executive pay—but even those were nonbinding.

The Mystery of High-End Tax Cuts

As we saw on the Bush tax cuts, public opinion often gets ignored and special financial interests prevail when Congress and the White House make policy, even though that runs counter to our notions of how American democracy is supposed to work.

Political scientists, tracking votes in Congress since the 1980s, have developed broad evidence that this is fairly typical—that senators and House members simply tune out the opinions of average Americans when voting on legislation, especially when powerful financial interests get engaged.

On issues as varied as civil rights, the minimum wage, abortion, and government spending, Princeton professor Larry Bartels found that in the 1980s senators were "vastly more responsive to affluent constituents than to constituents of modest means." Two decades later, in 2005, another Princeton professor, Martin Gilens, found an even stronger upper-class impact on policy makers on a wide range of policy questions. "Influence over actual policy outcomes appears to be reserved almost exclusively for those at the top of the income distribution," Gilens concluded.

After citing a series of public opinion polls from 1998 through 2007, in which significant majorities said they favored higher taxes on the wealthy, two other scholars asserted, "The mystery is how politicians can get away with tax policies that are so out of harmony with the wishes of the American public."

Do High-End Tax Cuts Generate Growth?

The political and economic rationale for tax cuts for the rich made by President George W. Bush and other Republican leaders is that the wealthy are the prime source of job-creating investments that stimulate the nation's economic growth. That argument is based on classical economic theory, dating from the British economists Adam Smith and David Ricardo in the late eighteenth and early nineteenth centuries.

Classical economists advocate lowering taxes on the wealthy on grounds that only the wealthy can provide large sums of capital for business investment to drive the economy because the rich can afford to save a larger portion of their income than hard-pressed middle-class families. Accordingly, classical economists and business leaders have seen high concentrations of wealth as justified and have argued that wide income inequalities are actually desirable because they promote growth.

But a host of modern economic studies contradict the old classical theories. Several studies have analyzed American economic history in twenty-five-year segments, and as Boston College Law School professor James R. Repetti reported, they "are remarkably unanimous in suggesting that high concentrations of wealth correlate with poor economic performance in the long run." Other studies have examined the modern economic performance of eighty different countries and have come to a similar conclusion that "a more unequal size distribution of income is bad for growth in democracies."

Other analysts point to the hesitancy of American businesses to invest in growth during America's painfully slow economic recovery from 2009 to 2012 as evidence that offering low tax rates to promote investment did not work. Even former Fed chairman Alan Greenspan was moved to comment in 2011 that Corporate America was sitting on nearly $2 trillion in idle capital. Greenspan asserted that the reluctance of business leaders to spend on new plants and equipment and on hiring more workers "accounted for almost all of the rise in unemployment" from 2007 to 2011.

Economic historians such as Professor James Livingston of Rutgers University contend that it is not business investment but consumer demand that actually drives economic growth. According to Livingston, America's twentieth-century history shows that businesses don't invest heavily in growth without strong and growing consumer demand. As if in confirmation, many American businesses, from major banks to big pharmaceuticals, were laying off workers in 2011 while collectively allocating $445 billion of their cash flow to buy back their own stock, thus delivering a payoff for investors while adding to unemployment.

Exhibit number one showing that there is no direct link between low taxes and high growth was America's dismal economic record following the massive tax cuts enacted under George W. Bush in 2001, 2002, and 2003. The ten years following the Bush tax cuts, David Leonhardt wrote in *The New York Times,* were "the decade with the slowest average annual growth since World War II. Amazingly, that statement is true even if you forget about the Great Recession and simply look at 2001–7."

What's more, Bush was also wrong in promising that start-up businesses would create jobs and bring people back into the workforce. Just the opposite happened: The rate of start-up job creation fell, and so did workforce participation. As Princeton economist Alan Krueger reported, "The 2000s saw the worst record of job creation in 50 years, even before the recession that started in 2007." By contrast, during Bill Clinton's presidency, U.S. economic growth was strong even though Clinton had pushed through a significant tax increase. Going back further in time, growth was strong under Presidents Eisenhower and Kennedy when the personal income tax rate was more than double today's rates.

In short, the economic rationale for low tax rates on the wealthy was wrong.

The Tax Cut Fight of 2010

But the historical record had little influence on political Washington in December 2010 when President Obama, trying to help push economic recovery, proposed extending the modest Bush tax cuts for middle- and upper-middle-class Americans, 98 percent of all taxpayers, but letting the tax cuts for the top 2 percent expire. Obama argued that it made no sense to extend tax cuts for the rich because that would add heavily to the budget deficit and just "provide tax relief to primarily millionaires and billionaires. It would cost us $700 billion to do it. On average, millionaires would get a check of $100,000."

In opinion polls, a majority of Americans endorsed the Obama approach. As the president noted in a press conference on December 7, "The American people, for the most part, think it's a bad idea to provide tax cuts to the wealthy." That same day, a Bloomberg poll reported that 59 percent wanted to "eliminate tax cuts" given to the wealthiest Americans in recent years. Earlier, a CNN poll had reported that 64 percent opposed extending tax cuts for the wealthy.

Even some Reaganite conservatives and billionaires called it folly to continue tax cuts for the rich. Bruce Bartlett, a senior Treasury Department official under President George H. W. Bush, said Republicans had fallen under the spell of an idea that he called "frankly, nuts—the idea that there is no economic problem that cannot be cured with more and bigger tax cuts. . . ." Multibillionaires like Warren Buffett, head of Berkshire Hathaway, a multinational holding company and investment fund, Bill and Melinda Gates of Microsoft fame, and CNN founder Ted Turner came out in favor of letting taxes go back up for America's superclass.

"The rich are always going to say that, you know, just give us the money and we'll go out and spend more and then it will all trickle down to the rest of you," Buffett observed. "But that has not worked the last 10 years, and I hope the American public is catching on."

Reenter the Gang of Six

But Buffett did not reckon on the power of Dirk Van Dongen and the Gang of Six to keep the low Bush tax rates. "We kept the coalition in business to protect those rates," Van Dongen told me. "We activated again to extend the Bush tax cuts." In July 2010, Van Dongen's Tax Relief Coalition called for Obama and Congress "to immediately support at least a temporary extension of *all* [emphasis added] the tax relief passed in the prior decade." *All* meant not only the huge 2001 personal income tax cuts, but lower capital gains taxes, a sharp cut in taxes on corporate dividends, a phase-out of the estate tax, and hundreds of business tax breaks, which Senator John McCain had derided as "the worst example of the influence of special-interest groups I have ever seen."

The Gang of Six got the jump on the Obama White House. In September 2010, when members of Congress were desperate for campaign dollars, the Gang of Six launched a lobbying blitz on Capitol Hill. The Chamber of Commerce generated seventy-five thousand letters to senators and House members pushing for the tax cuts. The Business Roundtable sent eighty-seven CEOs knocking on doors on Capitol Hill. "Our position is that this is not the time to raise any taxes," asserted Johanna Schneider, the Roundtable's executive director for external affairs.

In the lame duck session, after the Republican sweep in the midterm elections, President Obama urged congressional leaders to extend middle-class tax cuts, end high-end cuts for the rich, and use $700 billion in revenues from the rich to reduce the federal deficit. But Senate Republicans slammed the door. They refused "to proceed to any legislative item" on any issue, from arms control to food safety, until Obama and the Democrats agreed to extend tax cuts for the wealthy along with everyone else. Obama protested that middle-class tax cuts were being "held hostage to the high-end tax cuts," and he was opposed to negotiating with hostage takers.

But in the end, Obama felt compelled to agree to a two-year extension of all the Bush tax cuts in return for Republican acceptance of some added benefits for the middle class—an extension of jobless benefits for the long-term unemployed and a one-year payroll tax cut for most workers. But Republicans extracted a final concession for the super-rich—cutting the estate tax rate from 55 to 35 percent and exempting estates of married couples up to $10 million. Congress passed this package swiftly, and the Gang of Six, which had barely said a kind word about President Obama in months, applauded him for surrendering.

And Dirk Van Dongen vowed that business forces would be ready to fight Obama again, when the tax cuts are scheduled to expire at the end of 2012.

CHAPTER 10

THE WASHINGTON—
WALL STREET SYMBIOSIS

———

THE INSIDE TRACK OF "THE MONEY MONOPOLY"

> I sincerely believe, with you, that banking establish-
> ments are more dangerous than standing armies. . . .
>
> — THOMAS JEFFERSON,
> *letter to a friend, 1816*

> In a political system where nearly every adult may
> vote but where knowledge, wealth, social position,
> access to officials, and other resources are unequally
> distributed, who actually governs?
>
> — ROBERT A. DAHL,
> *Who Governs?*

> The finance industry has effectively captured our
> government. . . .
>
> — SIMON JOHNSON,
> Atlantic *headline, "The Quiet Coup"*

NO SLICE OF AMERICAN BUSINESS has amassed more political
power or more astronomical profits—and contributed more to the
acute economic divide and the hyperconcentration of wealth in

America today—than what Woodrow Wilson once called "the money monopoly," meaning Wall Street.

Wall Street has enjoyed meteoric growth before—in the Gilded Age and the Roaring Twenties—but the scale of its financial boom in the past two decades is unprecedented in American history.

Since the late 1980s, Finance has become the heart of the New Economy. It has far outpaced other sectors, exploding from $1.2 trillion of assets in 1978 to $11.8 trillion in 2007. It overtook manufacturing to become the largest sector of the U.S. economy. Its profits soared—from 17 to 18 percent of total U.S. corporate profits in 1980 to 46 percent in 2005. As former Nixon political strategist Kevin Phillips put it, Wall Street "hijacked" the U.S. economy for its own profit, causing a "perilous overconcentration" of economic power.

In terms of political power, Wall Street has no peer. Over the past two decades, the bankers portrayed by Tom Wolfe in *Bonfire of the Vanities* as arrogant "Masters of the Universe" have been even more successful than the leaders of other sectors of business, such as oil or the military-industrial complex or the pharmaceutical industry, in influencing Washington to adopt their agenda. They have lobbied successfully to overturn New Deal–era laws and time-tested government regulations. They have won several government bailouts in one financial crisis after another, culminating in the collapse of 2008. They have gained repeated concessions from Washington's Wall Street–friendly regulators. Most important for them, and costly for the nation, the powers-that-be on Wall Street managed in the 1990s and 2000s to break down the walls separating different types of banking and to fence off their gold-plated derivatives business from regulation.

What has made "the money monopoly" explosively dangerous is that its power and wealth have been built on debt—debt that dwarfed the debt of the U.S. government. The debt of the financial sector metastasized from $2.9 trillion in 1978 to $36 trillion in 2007, plus another $33 trillion of exposure in derivatives. What Wall Street likes to call its leveraging, its debt, had become well over four times the size of the $15 trillion federal government debt—far more debt than the superbanks could sustain. When Wall Street's bubble burst, it pushed the nation to the precipice, and only government action saved the rest of us from going over the edge.

Wall Street Corners the Policy Market

But in spite of the wide peril it posed, Wall Street has escaped serious oversight. It has gotten its way in Washington to an extraordinary degree. It wields influence not only through lobbying power and lavish campaign donations, but even more through the tight symbiotic relationship it has built with official Washington.

The chieftains of the financial world have acted on the evident conviction that money spent on lobbying and political campaigns pays big policy dividends. In those terms, too, finance has no rival. In the 2009–10 election cycle, the financial sector poured roughly $318 million into congressional campaigns and spent another $946 million on lobbying—$1.25 billion in all. Most other high-profile sectors—oils, defense, pharmaceuticals—did less.

Even more striking than the flow of money is the steady flow of Wall Street luminaries and master financiers into the most important policy posts of government. At times, the line between government and banking has become blurred: Alan Greenspan, head of an elite New York financial consulting firm and board member at J. P. Morgan & Co., served as chairman of the Federal Reserve for twenty years; Robert Rubin and Henry Paulson, former top executives of Goldman Sachs, have run the Treasury for both Democrat Bill Clinton and Republican George W. Bush, respectively; so many Goldman alumni were recruited by Paulson to manage the taxpayer bailout for Wall Street banks that they were called "the Guys from Government Sachs"; former New York Fed president Tim Geithner, who for five years worked under a Fed board dominated by Wall Street bank CEOs, was chosen to head Treasury by President Barack Obama; and former Harvard president and economist Larry Summers, who was paid nearly $8 million in fees in 2008 by Wall Street firms and hedge funds, became the head of Obama's National Economic Council. Under Democrats as well as Republicans, Wall Street cornered the policy market.

Fourteen Hundred
Ex-Government Officials Lobby for Wall Street

What's more, the Washington–Wall Street axis works as a two-way street. Wall Street recruits its lobbying army from the ranks of government. During the battle over the 2010 law to regulate Wall Street, the financial services sector hired 1,447 former government officials as lobbyists—former members of Congress, Capitol Hill staffers, or White House and Treasury Department policy makers as well as former high officials from other key agencies.

Finance had a lobbying team that included 73 former members of Congress, headed by two former House majority leaders, Democrat Dick Gephardt and Republican Dick Armey, and two former Republican Senate majority leaders, Bob Dole and Trent Lott. Less visible but no less influential were 115 former staff aides for the key House and Senate banking committees that were actually writing the financial reform bill. These staffers were inside experts who possessed not only intimate knowledge of the intricacies of the law, but also access to key members of Congress. Their job was to turn every conceivable subparagraph and semicolon to Wall Street's advantage.

Under *The Atlantic*'s headline, "The finance industry has effectively captured our government," economist Simon Johnson observed. "A whole generation of policy makers has been mesmerized by Wall Street. . . . The American financial industry gained political power by amassing a kind of cultural capital—a belief system. Once, perhaps, what was good for General Motors was good for the country. Over the past decade, the attitude took hold that what was good for Wall Street was good for the country."

What Johnson called "the Quiet Coup" was a matter not just of people, but of ideology. In the 1990s, with Greenspan chairing the

Federal Reserve and Robert Rubin leading Treasury, Wall Street's laissez-faire market philosophy became Washington's conventional wisdom. Its "capture" of Washington was evident in practically every major financial policy battle under Clinton in the late 1990s and under Bush in the zero decade, and even into the battles over financial regulation under Obama.

Brooksley Born's Warning on Derivatives

In 1998, Brooksley Born, a tough-minded, iconoclastic lawyer who headed the Commodity Futures Trading Commission, saw danger ahead and began pushing for government regulation of over-the-counter derivatives—the esoteric investments that renowned investor Warren Buffett called "financial weapons of mass destruction." Over-the-counter derivatives were not standard products. Each was different from the next one, making them almost impossible for regulators to monitor. When Born dared to challenge the Wall Street power axis by suggesting that these derivatives be standardized and made more transparent, Rubin, Greenspan, and then Treasury deputy secretary Larry Summers tried to muzzle her. They contended that the mere release of her concept paper on derivatives regulation would trigger a market collapse. Born, seeing unregulated derivatives as a greater danger, released her paper anyway. Wall Street bankers were apoplectic, but nothing dire happened.

In September 1998, Born was vindicated when Long Term Capital Management, a huge hedge fund deeply invested in derivatives, collapsed. Born told Congress that the hedge fund's disaster "should serve as a wakeup call about the unknown risks that the over-the-counter derivatives market may pose to the U.S. economy. . . ." But instead of hailing Born's prescience, Greenspan, Rubin, and Summers cut off her regulatory arms. They asserted that the big banks could protect themselves and that regulators should not interfere with the market. They pushed Congress to pass a bill blocking the commission that Born headed from taking any action on derivatives.

Born accused them of "muzzling" her agency and abruptly announced her intention to quit the government when her term expired in April 1999. But eight years later, just as she had warned, the derivatives market started to blow up and spread financial mayhem worldwide.

Repealing Glass-Steagall

An even more pivotal victory for the Wall Street–Washington axis was repeal of the Glass-Steagall Act (the Banking Act of 1933) by Congress in 1999, at the urging of Rubin and Greenspan. Glass-Steagall had been passed as one of the first reforms of the New Deal to try to prevent a repeat of the 1929 market crash. Its purpose was to separate commercial banking from investment banking. The law walled off the dull but vital business of safe, reliable banks, where consumers could put their savings and their checking accounts, from the risky business of investment banks engaged in mergers and acquisitions, "financial engineering," marketing derivatives, and playing the market with company assets for their own profit.

But by the 1980s, Wall Street banks chafed at any limitation on their operations. They wanted total deregulation. Investment bankers like Rubin began a drumbeat for tearing down the Glass-Steagall wall. It was constricting their operations and limiting their profits.

In Washington, they had powerful allies. As John Reed, former CEO of Citicorp, told me, "Greenspan was sympathetic. Greenspan was always against Glass-Steagall. He had been on the J. P. Morgan board of directors, and Morgan was always against Glass-Steagall. Greenspan and the Fed had been watering down Glass-Steagall for years. The key phrase [in that law] was that commercial banks were not permitted to be 'principally engaged in' investment banking. The question was, what constituted 'principally engaged in'?" Starting in 1987 and then reaching a climax in 1996, Greenspan chose to reinterpret the wording of the law to create a loophole that weakened the Glass-Steagall separation of commercial and investment banking, and then he greatly enlarged it. He and the Federal Reserve Board, lobbied by Wall Street bankers, permitted an escalating expansion by commercial banks into underwriting securities and other investment banking operations by allowing them to do first 5 percent, then 10 percent, and finally 25 percent of their business in those higher-risk areas by the late 1990s.

The Rise of "Too Big to Fail"

But that was not enough for Sandy Weill, Wall Street's most ambitious banker. Weill wanted to create the world's largest superbank. To do that, he needed to demolish Glass-Steagall. By the late 1990s, Weill had formed a financial giant that combined Travelers Insurance and Salomon Brothers investment house. His next step was to arrange a megamerger with a big commercial bank. He tried first with J. P. Morgan and then, when that failed, with Citicorp.

Weill knew that his dream merger would violate Glass-Steagall, but after some private soundings with Greenspan, Rubin, and President Clinton, he decided to force the government's hand. On April 6, 1998, Weill and Citicorp CEO John Reed announced the breathtaking merger of Travelers and Citicorp.

Greenspan quickly gave his blessing and allowed Weill and Reed some breathing time for the merger to solidify. Rubin, who had been pushing Congress to repeal Glass-Steagall since 1995, lobbied Congress to ratify the merger and open the field to more megabanks. Consumer groups and community bankers protested that this would create uncontrollable financial empires. Former commerce undersecretary Jeffrey Garten, then dean of the Yale School of Management, warned prophetically that bank megamergers would come back to haunt the government. If the superbanks got in trouble, Garten predicted, the taxpayers would have to bail them out because they would be "too big to fail" without causing a wider financial disaster.

But with Wall Street lobbyists in full cry and with "wise men" from Wall Street like Greenspan and Rubin arguing that superbanks would generate "synergies" that would "enhance the competitiveness" of U.S. banking in the global economy, Congress repealed Glass-Steagall, a law that had worked well for six decades.

Just as Jeff Garten had forecast, Citigroup and other megabanks created massive havoc when the financial earthquake hit Wall Street in 2008. The damage was all the more colossal because the multitrillion-dollar market in derivatives was unregulated, which meant there was nothing to stop banks from overplaying their risks even when they had inadequate reserves to cover their losses. And there was no Glass-Steagall wall shielding commercial banking and the deposits of ordinary customers from the disastrous collapse of high-rolling investment banks like Bear Stearns and Lehman Brothers. All the big banks were linked to one another, as vulnerable as dominoes. Wall Street maimed itself with self-inflicted wounds, and when Bear Stearns and Lehman Brothers went under and other firms like Merrill Lynch had to be rescued by rivals, the taxpayers were stuck with the bill—not only for the reckless greed on Wall Street, but also for the myopia of the Wall Street gurus who were making policy in Washington.

The Banks: "Obstruct and Delay"

The moment had come for reversing two decades of policy. But given the high stakes for the nation's economy, the federal government had little choice but to step in to rescue Wall Street once again. With former Goldman Sachs CEO Henry Paulson running Treasury, even a limited-government Republican like President George W. Bush scrapped his free market ideology to push Congress into appropriating $700 billion for the country's largest corporate welfare program—a bailout for the superbanks—while the Federal Reserve handed out $7.8 trillion more in low-interest loans. All that cheap money enabled the surviving banks to grow even larger and to get back to making the same kinds of profits they had made before the collapse.

The surprise was not that the Washington–Wall Street symbiosis was still at work. The surprise was that once the hemorrhaging slowed and Congress sat down to write a new law to prevent a future collapse, Wall Street was back at lobbying full throttle, resisting almost every regulatory idea. Equally surprising was the fact that at the very moment when Wall Street's credibility should have been in tatters, it still had enormous political clout—proof that the power shift begun in the 1970s still dominated political Washington despite the dangers to the U.S. economy.

In 2009, the political climate demanded action. The public, mired in unemployment and home foreclosures, was in an anti-bank uproar, clamoring for change. But the bank and business lobbies defied the public mood. Their brazen strategy paid off, and President Obama, guided by former Wall Street bank regulator Tim Geithner, moved timidly. The banking sector, with its fourteen hundred lobbyists, fought off a potential historical reversal of policy with the tactics of "obstruct and delay." The banks shrewdly calculated that mass amnesia would save them: The longer it took to craft regulatory reforms, the greater the likelihood that the drive for reform would lose momentum. The public lost track—and lost interest.

In May 2010, a group of Democratic senators tried to pass a provision shrinking the biggest banks and limiting their size to deal with the "too big to fail" problem, but the banks and their allies in Congress killed that measure. President Obama wanted a freestanding consumer protection agency. The bankers hated the idea. They lobbied successfully to have the new agency tucked inside the Federal Reserve and then, in 2011, got Senate Republicans to block any consideration of Elizabeth Warren, the vigorous consumer advocate who was Obama's choice to head it, forcing her to quit the administration and abandon her chance to head the new agency that she had proposed and helped to organize.

When reformers wanted to revive Glass-Steagall protections, bank advocates argued that it was too late, and they won. When it was proposed that the banks pony up a bank tax to help pay for future bank failures, the banks got the bank tax killed. When Senator

Blanche Lincoln of Arkansas proposed barring banks from marketing derivatives, she came under withering fire from business interests as well as the banks. The Obama administration, in retreat,
pushed to make the derivatives trade more open and regulated, but
the banks fought successfully to exempt certain derivatives, such as
the credit default swaps that played a big role in the mortgage
blowup. Former Fed chairman Paul Volcker advocated barring all
regulated banks from proprietary trading on their own account (what
came to be called "the Volcker Rule"), to keep superbanks from
speculating recklessly and putting the whole system at risk again.
Volcker won backing from former Citicorp CEO John Reed, who
apologized for what he now called the mistaken Citi-Travelers megamerger. Congress passed a vague version of the Volcker Rule but left
its definition to regulators who were besieged by bank lobbyists.

In mid-2011, a full year after the financial regulatory law was
passed, Treasury Secretary Tim Geithner accused Wall Street banks
of stalling the whole process in order to water down the new rules.
"There's an attempt to kill this through delay," asserted Michael
Greenberger, a former member of the Commodity Futures Trading
Commission staff, and the delay "could be cataclysmic." That did
not trouble Wall Street. The big banks wanted to stave off regulation, even regulation to improve the safety of the financial system.

Volcker: The Reforms Fall Short
The Danger: Another Future Collapse

It is true that passing any major regulatory legislation over the near
unanimous opposition of Republicans was a major achievement for
the Obama administration. Creating the Consumer Financial Protection Bureau was a milestone. Passing the Volcker Rule against
proprietary trading was a gain, though it was watered down with
one loophole that allowed banks to speculate with up to 3 percent of
their assets and another loophole that delayed implementing the
Volcker Rule for seven years, long enough for banks to fight to ex-

pand the loophole and perhaps to elect a bank-friendly president in 2012 or 2016 who would wipe the Volcker Rule entirely off the books. Ultimately, the concessions made to win the final crucial Senate votes largely emasculated the reform.

Volcker later voiced his dismay: Reform was inadequate, and the biggest banks were larger than before the 2008 collapse. In late 2011, he suggested that the government was still stuck with the structural problem of megabanks too large and too interconnected to be allowed to fail. His solution was bold: Reduce the risks either "by reducing their size, curtailing their interconnections, or limiting their activities." Similarly, Paul Krugman, a Nobel laureate in economics, found the law's penalties and incentives not tough enough to force bankers to stop the risky trading practices that had caused the financial collapse. Jeffrey Lacker, president of the Federal Reserve Bank of Richmond, said the reform was so weak that it was destined to perpetuate the cycle of boom and bust and taxpayer rescue.

Politics—the enormous political power of the banks—was the core problem, as the conservative, pro-business London *Telegraph* pointed out. "Such is the lobbying power of the big Wall Street institutions," the British paper said, "that they not only caused a global economic crisis and then forced the US government to pay for a massive bail-out but then used a slice of that bail-out cash to bribe politicians with campaign donations in order to block rule changes that might prevent a repeat performance."

A "Starkly Unequal Democracy"

For our democracy, the danger is that the balance of power has moved so far away from the middle class and into the hands of the financial and business elite that average Americans today feel they have little impact on policy, and they have largely given up on real democracy.

In the 1960s, just 28 percent of Americans said that "the government is pretty much run by a few big interests looking out for themselves." Today, that figure is 78 percent. Poll after poll has recorded that most Americans feel cut out of government and that roughly four out of five distrust lobbyists, resent their power, and want the government to curtail it.

Ordinary people dislike this unfair state of affairs, but they feel powerless to change it. Without knowing the details, they sense that all the advantages accrue to powerful insiders with the money and resources to fight the daily trench warfare over policy. The gulf between the Washington Power Game and the electorate has widened steadily as ordinary people feel cut out of the political process. They have, we all have, become increasingly passive and disengaged and, in the apt comment of Ernie Cortes, one of America's most energetic grassroots organizers of minority voters, immobilized by our sense of our own powerlessness. The danger, Cortes said, is that Americans over the past three decades have "been institutionally trained to be passive."

The peril for our society and for our democracy is that we have been sliding into an economic and political oligarchy where a self-reinforcing process is at work: The wealthy and the corporate elite use their vast financial resources to buy political influence and then leverage that added political power to obtain further policies that exponentially multiply the economic returns to the financial elite at the expense of average Americans.

We instinctively shy away from this conclusion since it violates our concept of America as a land of equal opportunity and it desecrates our vision of an American Dream accessible to all. But, sadly, the record since the late 1970s shows that the concentration of wealth and the concentration of power in America are mutually reinforcing.

"The available evidence is striking and sobering," wrote political scientist Larry Bartels. "In Aristotle's terms, our political system seems to be functioning not as a 'democracy,' but as an 'oligarchy.' If we insist on flattering ourselves by referring to it as a democracy, we should be clear that it is a starkly *unequal* democracy."

PART 4

MIDDLE-CLASS
SQUEEZE

PAT O'NEILL had it all figured out. Like many average Americans who started out in the 1970s during the era of middle-class prosperity, he had worked a lifetime for the same employer. He had earned a company pension, added a 401(k) plan, and even bought employee stock options. With that nest egg, he felt he could retire secure.

As a lead mechanic for United Airlines, he put in thirty-five hard years, working at night, often in freezing winds, on the flight line at Chicago's O'Hare International Airport and Seattle's SeaTac Airport. His job was to keep DC-8s, DC-10s, and Boeing 737, 757, and 777 airliners flying and to keep his fellow Americans on the move. O'Neill is a plucky, friendly, go-getter Irish American. He poured himself into his job heart and soul.

"Of course, workin' there at O'Hare, it's not a normal nine-to-five job," he recalled. "Planes are fixed at night, when everybody's home asleep. You work graveyard. I worked graveyard for twenty-two years. It was a seven-day operation. You didn't call up an' say, 'Aw, I can't make it in tonight. I'm gonna stay home.'. . . I had a work ethic. I was very loyal to the company. An', you know, we were loyal to our customers. That airplane had to leave every mornin' six o'clock or eight o'clock or whatever."

To O'Neill, United Airlines was like family. He knew his bosses; they knew him. They all trusted one another. He knew that United counted on him when they needed him. He counted on United when he needed them.

But just as he was getting ready to retire, in May 2003, financial havoc at United tore up his well-laid plans for retirement, and it cost thousands of average employees like O'Neill dearly. So nearly a decade later, O'Neill is still at work, his eventual retirement day receding like a desert mirage—and his predicament a symptom of the financial squeeze that middle-class Americans feel across the board.

CHAPTER II

BROKEN PROMISES

BANKRUPTING MIDDLE-CLASS PENSIONS

The essence of {a company} bankruptcy is that whatever promises the company has made, they can't live up to all of them and they need to find a way to deal with the fact that they've promised more than they have.

—JAMES H. M. SPRAYREGEN,
corporate bankruptcy lawyer

Bankruptcy's terrible for the employee. It's an absolutely horrific experience for the people who worked hard to build a company. . . . It means being forced to negotiate changes to your working conditions, to your terms of employment, with a gun to your head.

—GREG DAVIDOWITCH,
flight attendants union leader

LIKE SO MANY OTHERS in the airline industry—pilots, flight attendants, mechanics—Pat O'Neill had a romance with the airplane. As a boy growing up on a dairy farm in Wisconsin, he had looked up at planes flying overhead and had fallen in love. He finished high school in 1966 and took a year's course in aircraft mechanics, and on November 6, 1967, he went to work for United. He was nineteen.

"It was an exciting time for me—working on airplanes," O'Neill recalled proudly. "The one factor that really threw a curveball at us was Old Man Weather. You couldn't bring these airplanes into a hangar, nice'n warm, and work on 'em. You had to work on 'em outside, in the elements. . . .

"The responsibility you have as an aircraft mechanic is . . . really, people don't realize it," he said. "A mechanic could ground an airplane. Here you got an airplane that holds lots of people, and you work on it. You gotta fix 'em right the first time."

O'Neill did his job well, got promoted, and eventually became chief of a team of flight-line mechanics. He went from a starting pay of $10,000 a year in 1967 to making $50,000 or $60,000 a year in the 1990s, depending on how much overtime he got. With longevity and a good pay scale, O'Neill was counting on the lifetime pension plan that his union, the International Association of Machinists and Aerospace Workers, had negotiated with United for anyone who wanted to retire at fifty-five after thirty years of steady work. That was O'Neill's plan—put in thirty-five years and retire.

The Deal: Less Pay in Exchange for a Lifetime Pension

Pat O'Neill was pretty typical of his generation. Millions of people born in the 1940s, 1950s, and early 1960s were promised lifetime pensions by their employers after a career of work at one company. These plans got started after World War II, when strong labor unions were demanding—and getting—steady wage increases year after year.

Corporate America made a counteroffer: Take some money now, but take part of it later and we'll put the second part into a pension. Companies liked that idea; it was cheaper for them. In the 1980s, employers were operating 114,000 of these so-called defined benefit plans that, at their peak, covered 35 percent of America's private sector workforce and reached a maximum of about 34.5 million participant workers and retirees. Today, 26 million older employees still have these lifetime pension plans.

Labor unions and their workers bought the pension idea from management. The "defined benefit" is what the unions liked most because it meant employees would get a predictable monthly pension payment for as long as they lived, paid for and guaranteed by the company. Strong unions like the United Auto Workers and the United Steelworkers negotiated contracts with a fixed pension formula.

Typically, a big company promised workers the equivalent of 1.5 percent or 2 percent of their salary or wages in their last five years, multiplied by the number of years they'd worked. It came out to something between 45 and 60 percent of their final pay. Pat O'Neill, who ended up making $50,000 plus, could count on an annual retirement of roughly $36,000, or about $3,000 a month—*for the rest of his life*. United Airlines was committed to that under its union contracts and the 1974 Employee Retirement Income Security Act (ERISA).

Bankrupt Promises

The crunch began in the 1990s. Low-cost carriers like Southwest Airlines began eating into United's market share, and its profit margins slipped. In 1994, United's finances were so shaky that management struck a grand bargain with its unions—management would trade 55 percent majority ownership in the company to its unions in exchange for their agreeing to $4.9 billion in pay cuts and reduced benefits. Union members could buy company stock.

Pat O'Neill, who had rock-solid faith in United, invested $80,000 of his hard-earned savings in United stock. With the union givebacks on wages and benefits and an infusion of new capital, United had a strong spurt in the second half of the 1990s. Stock, bought by union members for $22 a share, shot up to $90.

But it turned out that those were phantom gains, way beyond the value of United's profits. Even in good times, United had been struggling. It piled up a multibillion-dollar debt buying or leasing a fleet of new wide-bodied Boeing 747s and 777s and Airbus A320 airliners. It got into periodic fights with the powerful pilots union. In 2001, United ran a $3.8 billion operating loss. After the 9/11 terrorist attack in 2001, fear of flying panicked the American public. United lost more traffic and revenue than most carriers. By early 2002, it was deep in debt. It desperately needed big new bank loans to survive, and to get that money, United sought a government guarantee.

The Bush administration's Air Transportation Stabilization Board gave loan guarantees to other airlines but turned down United. Union leaders said they had heard that anti-union hard-liners around President Bush wanted to push United into bankruptcy to force major concessions from its unions and to erode union power. Whether that was the plan or not, that's what happened. United filed for bankruptcy on December 9, 2002, the largest American airline ever to take such a desperate step.

Bankruptcy's "Triple Whammo"

United's eighty-one thousand employees got slammed hard by the company's bankruptcy. Pat O'Neill, then on the verge of realizing his dream of retiring at fifty-five, suffered what he calls "a triple whammo"—on his employee stock plan, on his 401(k) plan, and on his United pension.

"The stock went zippo," O'Neill recalled. Stockholders were virtually wiped out. United's stock plunged from roughly $100 a share in the late 1990s, when O'Neill bought it, down to $1. United's unions were left with near worthless stock in return for the $4.9 billion in wage and benefit cuts that they had surrendered in 1994. O'Neill's $80,000 investment in the employee share ownership program shrank to $1,800. O'Neill got hurt again on his 401(k) plan, which also had a bundle of United stock. Finally, his pension was cut by one-third. When United Airlines dumped its vastly underfunded pension plans on the quasi-governmental Pension Benefit Guaranty Corporation, O'Neill's pension was automatically reduced from $3,012 to $1,994 a month because the government formula was less generous than United's contract.

As Pat O'Neill retired from United in 2003, he knew that for the rest of his life he would lose $1,000 a month, money that he had earned over thirty-five years. Like his co-workers, O'Neill was angry at United's management. He blamed them for mishandling the airline's finances and for forcing harsh bankruptcy concessions on union employees while executives got "retention bonuses" and came out of bankruptcy with the prospect of large personal gains from the new United.

"I never thought it would come to this. Hell, no," O'Neill said. "There's a lot of other people who felt the same way. People worked. People cared. They went the extra mile, and now look at it."

Companies Exit Lifetime Pensions

Pat O'Neill's predicament is a microcosm of the devastating impact of bankruptcy, not just on United's eighty-one thousand employees, but on workers all across the country. Probably one million workers and retirees, and perhaps as many as 1.6 million, have been casualties of corporate restructuring under Chapter 11 of the bankruptcy code or of companies on the brink of bankruptcy shutting down pension plans. They have seen their pensions, wages, and benefits drastically cut over the past couple of decades by some of the best-known names in Corporate America. In addition, millions of other average Americans without union contracts to protect them have lost their lifetime pensions or had them frozen, even at profitable companies such as IBM, Verizon, and Hewlett-Packard.

When the economy was growing in the 1980s and '90s, big corporations liked the pension programs because the billions that accumulated in their pension plans showed up as assets on the corporate balance sheet. When markets went up, so did the stock portfolios in their pension plans. Those gains made the profit line look even rosier on the company books. But when the markets hit rough going in the early 2000s, those pension plans took losses and became a balance sheet eyesore. Suddenly, chief financial officers were being blamed by CEOs for generating losses that made the company look bad.

So some highly profitable firms headed for the exits. Companies such as IBM, Verizon, and Hewlett-Packard froze the benefits in their existing lifetime pension plans and shifted their workforce into employee-run and largely employee-financed plans, either 401(k)'s or similar options. In one year alone, 2.6 million employees had their lifetime pensions frozen and were switched into 401(k)-style plans. New Economy companies in computers, the Internet, or telecommunications, such as Intel, Microsoft, and Cisco, adopted 401(k) plans from the beginning.

Overall, the percentage of large and medium-sized American firms that offered traditional lifetime pensions fell from 83 percent in 1980 to 28 percent in 2011.

Bankruptcy: Efficient Capitalism or a Legal Way to Burn Promises?

Bankruptcy became the typical route for troubled companies to bail out of lifetime pension obligations in a hurry. The financial meltdown in 2008 triggered a flood of high-profile bankruptcies such as those of Lehman Brothers, CIT Financial, General Motors, Chrysler, Washington Mutual, and many more. The early 2000s saw a previous wave of bankruptcies by major corporations such as Enron, WorldCom, Global Crossing, Texaco, Pacific Gas and Electric; steel companies such as LTV, Bethlehem, National, and Weirton; airlines such as Pan Am, Eastern, United, Delta, and US Airways (twice); plus many others.

Some companies were being liquidated and their meager assets divvied up. But far more frequently, bankruptcy was used by corporate management as a strategy to restructure the company—a vehicle for management to shed old labor contracts and write new ones, to dump old debts to creditors and trade suppliers, and to revive a debt-ridden firm as a leaner, slimmer company ready to compete without the weight of old obligations. The logic of the strategy: Better an amputated company with fewer jobs, lesser benefits, and lower wages than a dead carcass.

Bankruptcy, Jamie Sprayregen asserted, represents "the efficient working of American capitalism."

Sprayregen was United's chief bankruptcy attorney and one of the nation's most successful bankruptcy lawyers. By the mid-2000s, bankruptcy had become such a popular corporate strategy that big law firms all over the country set up special bankruptcy practices and made hundreds of millions of dollars from that business.

Companies needed bankruptcy, Sprayregen explained, as a legal way to bail management out of a financial jam. In his words, "The essence of bankruptcy is that whatever promises the company has made, they can't live up to all of them and they need to find a way to deal with the fact that they've promised more than they have."

"Bankruptcy," retorted Elizabeth Warren, then a Harvard Law School professor specializing in bankruptcy, "is a way to take legal promises and burn them."

"Bankruptcy's terrible for the employee," added Greg Davidowitch, head of the United Airlines section of the flight attendants union. "It's an absolutely horrific experience for the people who worked hard to build a company. . . . It means being forced to negotiate changes to your working conditions, to your terms of employment, with a gun to your head."

That's no accident. That's the way the 1978 bankruptcy law was written and the way bankruptcy courts have applied it. Technically, a bankrupt company such as United Airlines tells a bankruptcy judge that it cannot pay its bills and asks the judge to defer claims on its assets and to impose losses on its creditors—but not on the banks.

The law and the courts give top priority to the banks that loan money to the besieged corporation—in this case United and United's management—to make sure that banks don't lose money on their loans. The 1978 bankruptcy law also leaves corporate management in control of the bankruptcy process and gives employees very low priority—unlike some countries in Europe and Latin America where employee interests are better protected.

"The Dip Club"

In reality, as I learned from Hugh Ray, a Texas attorney with thirty years of experience in bankruptcy law, the process is run by and for what insiders call "the DIP club"—the small group of big banks that loan funds to the bankrupt company, which is legally known as "the DIP," meaning "the debtor in possession." The 1978 bankruptcy law gave the DIP, the corporate management, the primary initiative and control of the company's restructuring during bankruptcy.

In a so-called Chapter 11 bankruptcy such as United's, the company's attorneys go into court on the first day with drafts of court orders, worked out in advance and in private with the banks, which they give to the judge as a road map for the bankruptcy process. Generally, Ray reported, bankruptcy judges sign off on the company drafts, which then become the judge's "first day orders." They govern the bankruptcy process—especially the financial winners and losers.

"It says right here in the United first day order that the lenders are given superpriority claims—superpriority, not just priority, but superpriority," Hugh Ray pointed out to me. "Employee rights are inferior here [in the United States]. They are superior in other countries, but here, that's the way it works."

"It sounds [to me] as though through the first day orders, the whole deal, the whole outcome, is pre-cooked," I said, astonished at the thought that a judge would render the most critical verdict in advance of testimony and most of the arguments.

"Absolutely." Ray nodded. "The die is cast. Certain players have been made irrelevant at the end of the first day."

"What's the typical outcome in terms of who gets hit?" I asked.

"The typical outcome is the employees get new contracts that are much less generous than what they had before," Ray said. "The trade people [suppliers] get very little, very few cents on the dollar [of what they are owed]. Typically, the people who own stock in the company get wiped out."

"So the banks win?" I asked.

"That's correct," said Ray.

"It sounds like money is flowing from little people, middle-class, maybe poor people, to rich people, the rich institutions," I suggested.

"That's the norm in these situations," Ray agreed.

The Bankruptcy Script

The United Airlines bankruptcy followed Hugh Ray's script. CEO Glenn Tilton, who came to United from a previous bankruptcy, talked initially about how all of United's stakeholders would need to "share the pain" financially to save United. "This is going to take sacrifice by every single member of United's family," Tilton urged.

But before long, Tilton was focused mainly on major sacrifices from rank-and-file employees. Within a few months, United's four major unions agreed to $3.3 billion in "givebacks," mostly in lower wages and smaller health benefits. Not enough, insisted United's management; more cuts were needed. "No way to exit this bankruptcy case," United attorney Jamie Sprayregen asserted, "without taking on what I had called the silent elephant in the room. That is, addressing the pension issue."

United's lifetime pensions had become an elephant-sized problem because for several years, United Airlines, like many other companies, had been largely ignoring its obligations to fund them. Management had put little or no cash into the pension funds for pilots, mechanics, flight attendants, and office employees. Management's assumption was that its pension obligations would be covered by stock market growth from past contributions.

$450 Billion in Underfunded Pensions

In the 1990s, that stratagem worked as long as the stock market was booming, but by 2001–02, those rosy assumptions were wildly off the mark. When the market plunged in 2002, United's pension funds were more than $10 billion in the red.

By declaring bankruptcy, United Airlines was able legally to shift its $10 billion pension debt onto a little-known federal agency, the Pension Benefit Guaranty Corporation (PBGC), which is the safety net and payer of last resort that insures failed pension plans. United was a granddaddy of failures, but it was also, unfortunately, a proxy for much of Corporate America.

According to Bradley Belt, then executive director of PBGC, more than eighteen thousand U.S. companies had been welshing on their promises to their employees, skimping on legally required contributions to their pension plans. By 2006, Belt said, corporate pensions were underfunded by $450 billion. Even though ERISA, the nation's pension law, required companies to put up the money, the law was so full of loopholes that corporate accountants and attorneys had found ways to dodge their obligations, and PBGC was left to pick up the pieces. But often, as in Pat O'Neill's case, PBGC's payout formula offered much less money than what the company had promised. So average employees lost out.

United's Bankruptcy: Winners and Losers

During the course of United's three-year bankruptcy, CEO Glenn Tilton used the leverage of the bankruptcy process to squeeze United's employees into accepting larger and larger financial concessions.

In the end, United cut twenty-six thousand jobs for good. It furloughed thousands more employees temporarily. And it reaped $5 billion in givebacks and cuts from employees and retirees, changed work rules, revised pay scales, and instituted a new type of pension system. In all, fifty thousand employees and retirees, like Pat O'Neill, either had their pensions cut or were shifted over to 401(k)-style plans where they, not United, would foot most of the bill.

But the banks got back all of their loans, plus tens of millions of dollars in interest, plus millions more in loan and administrative fees. Jamie Sprayregen told me that his law firm had pocketed $100 million in fees on the United bankruptcy and that collectively, the law firms, accounting consultants, and restructuring experts that handled United's bankruptcy had made at least $400 million—close to 10 percent of the money surrendered by the unions.

"That's a tremendous amount of money," I said. "Workers giving up, you know, $3 billion worth of pensions, and it's costing $400 million to get the job done."

"I wouldn't call it cheap," Sprayregen conceded. "But . . . that's in the range of what happens in restructurings, even in healthy companies, in Corporate America."

In addition, CEO Glenn Tilton preserved his own $4.5 million retirement benefit from a previous employer that United's board had promised to pay when it hired him, and his management team got paid healthy "retention bonuses" during bankruptcy, offsetting the losses they took on their pensions. But the big payoff for executives was a grant of $400 million worth of stock for management in the new post-bankruptcy United Airlines, after union members lost their worthless stock in the old United.

The New United: More Hours, Less Pay

Pat O'Neill had retired from United, but others such as Robin Gilinger, a picture-postcard image of a smart, slim, attractive flight attendant in her midforties, had to live with the altered regime at United after the harsh cutbacks forced by bankruptcy.

After two decades of flying with United, Gilinger found that she had to increase her flight hours by 30 percent to make up for a 30 percent cut in her pay. Even with more hours, she said, she was making less than she had in the 1990s. She resented having to be away from home all that extra time.

"You are juggling all the time," she said. "You are very tired. You are in a different bed every night. You don't really get to connect with your family. I have a fifteen-year-old daughter. In four years, she'll be gone. I feel like I have to reconnect with her every time I come home. And then, before you know it, you are repacking and going back out again."

What angered her the most, however, was United's refusal to continue funding her lifetime pension and its decision to thrust its fifteen thousand flight attendants into the uncertain do-it-yourself world of retirement saving. By Gilinger's calculations, confirmed by the union, United's bankruptcy had cost her about 40 percent of her anticipated pension benefits. For years, she had counted on being able to retire at fifty-five, after thirty-plus years of flying. Now she expects to work until sixty-five or beyond.

"The pension was like a final straw that we lost," she said bitterly.

After the United bankruptcy, what troubled her most was the uncertainty of having to manage her own finances for retirement—"not knowing if I'll be able to make the right decisions." Her sense of security was shattered not only by the United bankruptcy, but by her husband's loss of his job in early 2009, after thirty years of work with one employer. He eventually got rehired, but that layoff left sickening doubts, not just about how to pay for her daughter's college tuition, but about surviving financially over the long term.

"I feel very uneasy about where I'm going to be in 20 years," Gilinger told me. "And I'm afraid that I'm going to end up having to work my golden years. . . ."

Pat O'Neill: Retirement Detours

That prospect was already reality for Pat O'Neill. Financially crippled by the United bankruptcy, O'Neill had to scramble to find a new job instead of being able to stop work and kick back after thirty-five years. O'Neill was supporting himself and his wife, paying college tuition for his daughter, and handling mortgage payments on a $141,000 farm north of Seattle. He needed another job.

For three years, O'Neill drove a sixteen-wheeler rig, hauling cargoes out of Port Seattle to Oregon, Utah, Idaho, and Montana. He was on the road six or seven days a week, for a slim weekly paycheck of $400. That plugged part of the hole left by his reduced pension, but it didn't rebuild his lost retirement nest egg. Plus, being away from home for weeks at a time took a toll. "You'd do six hundred miles a day in a heartbeat—that's eleven hours of driving," O'Neill said. "I couldn't take being away from my wife all the time."

After three years, O'Neill quit trucking and moved with his wife to rural eastern Washington State, where the cost of living was lower but where work was tough to find. "I put in forty applications," he said. "Couldn't find a job to save my soul." Finally, he went into business for himself, mowing lawns for a new subdivision. The pay was poor, but it kept him afloat until a relative of the subdivision owner bumped him out of the job.

Still needing income, O'Neill took a wild plunge. Even though he was unknown locally and was a Democrat in solidly Republican Whitman County, he decided to run for county commissioner. To everyone's surprise, he upset the incumbent Republican. He did it the old-fashioned way, by knocking on hundreds of doors and winning people over with his gregarious Irish charm. The job pays him $4,847 a month for a four-year term, and even though he puts in sixty-hour weeks, he's thinking about running for reelection and serving into his seventies.

"That is the only thing that saves my bacon," O'Neill chirped. But it's still not enough to rebuild his retirement nest savings. For extra cash, he works part-time on weekends for a local company, setting up events and conferences.

"I'm still struggling, just trying to keep my head above water," he confessed. "That's all I know—is work. But I'm gettin' tired, gettin' older. My body doesn't jump back the way it used to. Twenty-two years on [the] graveyard shift is taking its toll."

CHAPTER 12

401(k)'S: DO-IT-YOURSELF

———◆———

CAN YOU REALLY AFFORD TO RETIRE?

A million people are turning sixty-five every year,
a million people retiring, year after year, and they're
not prepared for it.

— TERESA GHILARDUCCI,
pension economist

Left to their own devices, most employees don't put
enough into their 401(k)s to make a dent in their
retirement needs. . . . It's time to stop pretending
that the 401(k) can get us where we need to go.

— ERIC SCHURENBERG,
CBS MoneyWatch

I would blow up the system and restart with something totally different. . . . Now this monster is out
of control.

— TED BENNA,
an architect of the 401(k) system

WHEN THE 401(K) WAS BORN, no one dreamed—or
intended—that it would become the mainstay of the retirement

system for the American middle class. It was enacted as an executive perk.

In the pivotal Congress of 1978, as we have seen, the 401(k) was inserted into the tax code, like many arcane technical provisions, as a favor to two major corporations by Representative Barber Conable, a Republican from upstate New York. Conable's district included the corporate headquarters of Kodak and Xerox, and the two companies had lobbied Conable to get them a legal tax shelter for deferred compensation for their top executives. The executives already had regular company pensions. The new wrinkle was to help executives who set aside a portion of their annual profit-sharing bonuses by giving them a long-term tax shelter. The goal was to cut the tax bite on executive pay.

As the ranking Republican on the tax-writing House Ways and Means Committee, Conable was perfectly positioned to tuck the 401(k) provision into a major tax bill as a tiny subparagraph. It was a classic Washington move. Almost no one else in Congress or the Carter White House even noticed.

Three years later, the Reagan administration's Treasury Department opened the floodgates by transforming the 401(k) into something radically different. Lobbied by corporate tax and pay consultants, the Reagan Treasury in 1981 adopted an aggressive interpretation of the tax code. It ruled that the ordinary income of rank-and-file employees could qualify for the 401(k) tax shelter along with the executive elite.

Things did not change overnight. Most companies moved gingerly in the early 1980s. Many were not sure they wanted to give this savings option to their rank-and-file employees. Their banks, which were making good money by managing traditional corporate pension plans, did not want to lose that lucrative pension business. What turned the pension game upside down, starting in the mid-1980s, was the discovery by the mutual fund industry that 401(k) plans represented an opportunity to capture an enormous windfall of new business if they could get 401(k) plans under their management.

"Be Your Own Money Manager"

"The technology and methodology of mutual funds were a big advantage," recalled Bob Reynolds, an early apostle of 401(k)'s as vice president of the Fidelity Investments mutual fund group. "The structure was perfect for the mutual fund industry—participant-directed, daily valuations, educating people on investing."

With aggressive marketing, the mutual fund industry drove a boom in 401(k)'s in the 1980s. Mutual funds weaned Corporate America away from lifetime pensions by pointing out the savings to business of switching to mostly employee-financed retirement. For employees the siren lure was, "Be your own money manager." Millions of Americans, imagining that they could all beat the market averages, took the bait. "It had a lot of sex appeal. And it was power to the people . . . ," recalled Brooks Hamilton, a veteran pension consultant. "That's the way it was sold."

Riding the tide of financial populism, 401(k) plans grew from 7 million people with $92 billion in assets in 1984, to 25 million participants with $675 billion in 1994, to more than 44 million people with nearly $2.2 trillion in assets in 2004. No longer was the 401(k) the executive elite's supplemental savings plan. It had become one of the two principal pillars of American retirement, along with Social Security.

This was a monumental transformation for the American middle class. "When the 401(k)'s came in, there was a sea change, a huge shift in who was paying for retirement," observed Brooks Hamilton. "In the old system, employers put up most of the money—89 percent. The employees contributed 11 percent. Those figures are from the Department of Labor. Fast-forward to the 401(k) system and today, employees are paying more than half—51 percent—and the companies, 49 percent. So there was a huge shift in costs from employers to employees—hundreds of billions of dollars."

The Track Record

With up to 65 million average Americans now heavily dependent on 401(k) plans, the key question is, How well has the 401(k) done for middle-class families?

For an on-the-ground look, I visited National Semiconductor, one of America's leading-edge computer chip companies and one of the first to adopt the 401(k) as its retirement plan. National Semiconductor prided itself on being an industry leader in employee benefits. It aggressively promoted its 401(k) plan to employees.

At the company's chip fabrication plant in Arlington, Texas, managers boasted of their unusually high participation rate—90 percent. Their secret was a higher-than-normal match—$1.50 from the company for each employee dollar—6 percent of pay for every 4 percent put in by individual employees. "What we found is that if we could provide an additional 50 cents on every dollar to the employees . . . we could raise our participation rates," reported Brian Conner, National's benefits manager. "We could actually get them to be responsible for their retirement." And once employees were enrolled, the company's responsibility ended. It was the employees' job "to manage their dollars."

Gil Thibeau

That last point was crucial. Some people are good at it. Some are terrible.

The 401(k) was made for Gil Thibeau, who, like high-level executives, made enough money to save easily and who had a knack for investing. A tall, quiet-spoken New Englander who had moved to Texas, Thibeau was trained as an industrial engineer, plus he had an M.B.A. in business administration. For National Semiconductor, he was a technical troubleshooter for big corporate clients.

Thibeau's job paid well—$90,000 to $100,000 a year. Not only did he religiously pump 6 percent of his salary into the 401(k) plan, but he put another 5 to 10 percent into National's employee stock option program. Thibeau loved researching stocks on the Internet. His picks were good and his timing was lucky. He bought National stock when it slumped to a low of $8 a share and saw it climb to $30 plus. In fourteen years with National, Thibeau built up a solid retirement nest egg. By the time National laid him off in 2001, his retirement funds were a bit under "half a million," he said half apologetically. "If I had started earlier, I would have set my target at a million. But I waited too long. . . ."

When he was laid off, Thibeau was not yet eligible for Social Security. Rather than use his retirement savings, he swallowed his pride and took a new job—at a huge pay cut, working at Aetna Insurance for $30,000 a year, plus health insurance. When he retired from Aetna in 2008 at sixty-seven, Thibeau decided to tap his Social Security, but he earned extra money as a part-time high school teacher. The financial crash of 2008 took his 401(k) assets on a roller coaster, but, he told me later, "I am still ahead of what I put in." By taking other jobs, Thibeau had protected his main nest egg for the future.

Winson Crabb

Winson Crabb could have used Thibeau's luck and head for money. Crabb worked for sixteen years at National Semiconductor as a skilled maintenance technician, making $50,000 a year. Like Thibeau, Crabb said, he made his 401(k) contributions every month, assuming the 401(k) would pretty well run itself.

Crabb is a solid, salt-of-the-earth guy, good with his hands, smart about machinery and guns, but not quick at math and finance. "My assumption was that when I got to be 65, well, there would be a large amount of money in there for me to take cash out to put in our bank to utilize for whatever," Crabb said. "Well, that didn't work out."

The biggest problem, said his wife, Bess, was the sudden sharp market plunge during the two years before her husband retired in 2003. Before that, she said, Crabb had about $120,000 in his 401(k) plan. "That was our goal, and that's what was there," she said. But when the market fell, the Crabbs lost more than half of their 401(k) balance. "It went down to forty-five [$45,000], and we built it back up to sixty-four [$64,000]," Bess recalled. "And then . . . the day that he drew out the 401(k), it was fifty-two [$52,000]."

In fact, the Crabbs had less than the $52,000 that showed on his 401(k) statement, because Crabb had twice borrowed money from his 401(k)—$20,000 for his daughter's medical training, which he paid back, and another $10,000 to buy a motor home, which he had not paid back. So that reduced his total. Worse, Crabb got socked with a hefty tax bill when he cashed out his 401(k) in one lump sum instead of rolling it over into a tax-sheltered IRA. "I just went with the information that I had and thought I was doing the right thing, which I wasn't," Crabb said sheepishly. In the end, his 401(k) was down to just $26,000.

"It was a jolt when we got to counting funds," Crabb admitted, rubbing a weathered hand through his white hair.

"Well, I thought when he retired, it was going to be a lot different, you know, money-wise," Bess Crabb added.

"So, how do you manage financially?" I asked.

"Well, you do what you have to do . . . ," Crabb said. "I had a couple jobs in between there, and my wife works."

In bits and pieces, the Crabbs were cobbling together barely enough to keep afloat and hang on to their brick rambler home in Cleburne, Texas. Bess Crabb's job in a local real estate office was bringing in some money. Crabb was drawing Social Security and getting $400 a month from a lifetime pension at an earlier job covered by a steamfitters union contract. Now and then, he would get temporary jobs doing repair work or driving a truck. To help make ends meet, Crabb sold off his prized gun collection for $12,000. "Broke my heart," Crabb said in a whisper.

The big news during my visit was a job offer as a safety officer in a computer chip plant in New Mexico. So at sixty-eight, Winson Crabb was heading out to Albuquerque alone, without his wife, for a temporary job. For how long? He didn't know. The Crabbs had no long-term plan.

Financial Cancer in the System

The stark contrast between Gil Thibeau and Winson Crabb left me wondering whether these were just two random cases or whether they told a larger story. Both had worked for the same company, enrolled in the 401(k) plan, faithfully made contributions, and benefited from a good company match. Of course, the two men had made different salaries, and that would explain why one would have twice as much saved as the other. But the gap was far larger: Thibeau had twenty times more than Crabb. Why such wildly different results?

Brooks Hamilton, the Dallas pension consultant who had been advising major companies on their benefits programs for fifty years, gave me the answer. Hamilton is a high-energy brainstormer with a law degree and a mathematician's mind for figures. He loves statistical puzzles. When 401(k)'s first appeared, Hamilton believed in their magic. He was an early apostle, persuading companies to buy into the 401(k) concept and then helping them set up and run their programs. But by the late 1990s, Hamilton was troubled by the different results he noticed among employees in the fifteen corporate 401(k) plans he was then running, each with thousands of participants and each with total balances of $100 million to $200 million or more. Hamilton dug into the records of every single employee to find out what was going wrong.

The huge gap between Thibeau and Crabb was no aberration, Hamilton told me. It mirrored a wide and disturbing pattern. Their track records were dots on a chart, and when Hamilton connected those dots with thousands of other dots, he was shocked. Year after year, in one 401(k) plan after another, he saw a similar pattern that totally changed his views of the 401(k).

"In every case, the 20 percent at the top not only had the highest investment income, like 30 percent or whatever, they also had the highest pay," Hamilton told me, "whereas the bottom 20 percent not only had the lowest investment income, 4 percent, they had the lowest average annual pay."

To Hamilton, this was a systemic flaw. The best-educated, best-paid employees and executives were getting investment returns that were six or seven times greater than the returns for average workers. That gap was compounded year after year. The top brackets were not only able to put away much more money each year, but they got far better returns than rank-and-file workers like Winson Crabb. They didn't borrow from their 401(k)'s or make Crabb's mistake of pulling out their retirement fund in one lump sum, triggering a tax penalty. They left the money in and let it grow. They knew how to get the best results and how to avoid costly pitfalls.

"I label this [the] 'yield disparity,' " Hamilton said. "I thought, 'We have a yield disparity that is a financial cancer in this, in our great beautiful 401(k) movement.' And I had never seen it before, but it was everywhere I looked."

"What do you mean, a financial cancer?" I queried.

"It would destroy the opportunity for ordinary workers to retire in dignity," Hamilton declared. Then he said very slowly, underlining each word: *"They can't get there from here."*

Rough Ride Ahead for Baby Boomers

Hamilton's conclusion is reinforced by other retirement experts, and that points to a critical problem for middle-class baby boomers nearing retirement and for the next generation.

Half of America's workers get no retirement plan from their employers. About 40 percent are enrolled in a 401(k) plan, an account balance plan, or a similar system where the employee makes a regular contribution, partially matched by the employer, and the employee picks investments from a basket of mutual funds offered by the employer. Ten percent have a mix of lifetime pensions, 401(k)'s, or variations on the 401(k).

The 401(k) track record is not good. After twenty-five years, the typical account balance was just $17,686 on January 1, 2011, according to the Employee Benefits Research Institute (EBRI), which tracks 401(k) records for twenty-two million people. The typical 401(k) nest egg of people in their sixties, who have been in a 401(k) plan for twenty years and are nearing retirement, is $84,469. The Center for Retirement Research at Boston College puts the figure at $79,000 for those between fifty-five and sixty-five.

Either way, that's far, far short of what people will need. Those balances represent less than two years of pay for a typical American family, when average life expectancy for people retiring at sixty-five is seventeen years. Even adding Social Security, which replaces about 35 percent of the pre-retirement income for a typical individual, many middle-class Americans are far below what's needed.

By the estimate of EBRI's Jack VanDerhei, 45 percent of the next generation of retirees are seriously "at risk" in retirement, which means that they will *fall short of meeting their basic financial needs*—not a comfortable retirement, but basic needs. "They will not have enough money to afford the basic necessities of life and necessary medical care," said VanDerhei. "They will still have Social Security and maybe something from a defined benefit program [a lifetime pension]. But it won't be enough to cover their basic expenses. . . . I would say unless you're fortunate to be in the upper-income quartiles that you're probably going to be in for a very rough ride."

Alicia Munnell's Center for Retirement Research at Boston College estimates that more than half of American families (51 percent) are "at risk" of being squeezed into a lower standard of living in retirement. That's without adding in medical costs.

The number jumps to 65 percent of American families at financial risk when analysts add in typical medical costs during retirement.

Even for people on Medicare, average health costs are a huge item. Financial analysts project that most retired couples will spend $200,000 on supplemental insurance, Medicare premiums, co-pays for chronic illnesses or serious accidents, and drugs, glasses, and other items only partially covered by Medicare.

"They are not going to be penniless because they have Social Security," Munnell told me. "But it's a very serious situation. Middle-class people are going to be very hard-pressed. People will feel destitute, absolutely forced to cut expenditures, maybe forced to sell their houses, forced to dramatically change their lifestyle. Making ends meet is going to be a consuming task. It will be the focus of their lives. And that is not what it was supposed to be. After a lifetime of work, that is a terrible state for older Americans to end up in."

The Pitfalls

The puzzle is how did we, as a nation, wind up with such an enormous shortfall from a system that seemed so attractive to millions of average Americans who were eager to manage their own retirement savings?

After a quarter of a century, the reasons are now clear. Success requires discipline over a lifetime of work, but most people lack sufficient discipline, especially in the New Economy, where periodic layoffs force many average Americans to change jobs, employers, and 401(k) plans.

Retirement specialists like Brooks Hamilton and Alicia Munnell question whether, in this turbulent economy, the task of financing retirement is too fraught with risk and too complicated for most average Americans, especially the millions who are gun-shy about financial markets.

"The individual has to make a choice every step along the way," Munnell observed. "The individual has to decide whether or not to join the plan, how much to contribute, how to allocate those contributions, how to change those allocations over time, decide what to do when they move from one job to another, think what to do about company stock. And then the hardest thing is, what are they going to do when they get to retirement and somebody hands them a check? How do you figure out how to use that money over the span of your retirement?"

These are the most common pitfalls that Munnell identified:

- **No plan:** Half of U.S. workers get no retirement plan from their employers.

- **Failure to sign up:** Historically, roughly 25 percent of those who are eligible have not signed up. Prodded by a new retirement law in 2006, about 40 percent of employers instituted automatic enrollment for new employees. That reduced nonparticipation to about 15 percent.

- **Low contributions:** Among eligible employees, 23 percent made no contribution in 2010. With automatic enrollment, typical contributions have declined and only 10 percent typically contribute the maximum.

- **Leakage:** People start out with good intentions but later drop out. The biggest leakage comes when people change jobs. Munnell reported that half of the millions of Americans who changed jobs in recent years also fully cashed out their 401(k)'s. Typically, that money never shows up again in retirement savings.

- **Borrowing:** Many other people use their 401(k) as a rainy day fund. They borrow from it to buy a pickup truck, remodel their home, get new furniture or appliances, send kids to college, or pay medical bills. "Now, they may even use [the money] for something *good* . . . ," Munnell observed, "but it means it's not there when they come to retirement." Even if they repay later, they have already lost the interest the money would have earned if it had been kept continuously in the 401(k). That defeats the vital compounding effect of long-term savings.

Even experts have trouble juggling all those problems, including Munnell, who has imposing academic credentials as a tenured professor of management sciences. "I have made virtually every mistake that I look out there and see other people doing," Munnell admitted candidly. "We live busy, complicated lives. Saving for retirement is a really hard thing to do."

When I asked her what went wrong, she laughed. "Everything! Everything has gone wrong . . . ," Munnell confessed. "I wish I could say that I've stopped making mistakes. . . . I've stopped taking money out because my children are grown. But I still buy high and sell low, because I get panicked when the stock market collapses and think, 'God! I can't lose all my money,' and get out."

In Bad Times, Companies Back Off from 401(k)'s

That panicky reflex during market collapses can hurt long-term retirement saving. Even for steady savers, recessions are a jolt. During the market collapse of 2008–09, 401(k) plan holders lost an estimated $2.8 trillion in savings—roughly 30 percent of their assets. By January 2011, they had recovered considerably, but they were still $800 billion below their 2007 savings levels.

People's panicky reflex in bad times can compound losses. If, understandably, they decide to cut down or stop their 401(k) contributions, they lose an opportunity to make investments when stock prices are at bargain levels.

Many employers cut back, too. During the Great Recession, several hundred companies cut their 401(k) match contributions, including General Motors, Eastman Kodak, Saks, Sears, Motorola, UPS, FedEx, Hewlett-Packard, Resorts International, and National Public Radio. Overall, one in five employers reduced or eliminated their match; 30 percent reported a drop in employee contributions, according to the Profit Sharing/401(k) Council of America. A few reported that 30 percent of their employees had increased their contributions, and 10 percent of the companies increased theirs.

In June 2011, more than two years into the recovery, Corporate America was still pinching retirement pennies. More than half of the companies that had slashed their 401(k) matches still had not restored them. Their cutbacks and those of employees during the market lows of 2009 permanently hurt the long-term performance of hundreds of company 401(k) plans.

False Expectations

One basic problem that has come back to haunt many in the middle class, according to Jack Bogle, founder and longtime CEO of the Vanguard Group, an investment management company specializing in mutual funds, is that people had totally unrealistic expectations of stock market returns because of what Bogle called "the phantom gains" of the abnormally hot stock market of the 1990s. "The phantom wealth of the stock market gains fueled the notion that 401(k) investing was easy," Bogle said. "Then the market went bust."

By "phantom wealth," Bogle means that stock prices were inflated by speculative fever that exaggerated the actual growth of the economy and individual companies. Bogle explained it this way: If a company generates 4 percent income a year and grows 6 percent, that's a real gain of 10 percent; but if the stock price goes up 17 percent, speculative fever added 7 percent of phantom wealth. "The market in the 1980s and 1990s was going up 17 percent a year for two decades, year after year," said Bogle. "We've never had that before and we'll never have it again." When the phantom wealth bubble burst, Bogle said, the 2008 market crash cost investors $8 trillion and sixty million 401(k) holders took an icy bath.

A reasonable growth rate, based on long-term market performance, Bogle averred, is 5 percent a year from an equal mix of stocks and bonds. With steady, patient investing over long periods, said Bogle, 5 percent a year delivers astounding results: $1 over forty years becomes $7.04, or $100,000 becomes $704,000. For retirement savings, the length of time is crucial. Over twenty-five years, Bogle calculated, that same $1 in savings goes up to only $3.39, not $7.04. The growth is slow at first, but it shoots up steeply in later years, said Bogle, "like the shape of a hockey stick."

The Mutual Fund Bite

But ordinary 401(k) and mutual fund investors don't reap the full benefit of those long-term results, Bogle said, because of the large bite taken out of 401(k) plans by the financial industry—the mutual funds and banks that manage 401(k) accounts. According to Bogle, their fees and transaction costs average 2 percent a year. Subtracting that from the average 5 percent gain leaves individual investors with a net gain of 3 percent. Over the long term, the mutual fund bite has a compounding effect. That means, Bogle said, that over forty years, the projected gain from $1 to $7.04 gets cut way down—to $3.26.

"Where did the nearly $4 difference go?" Bogle asked. "It went to Wall Street [in fees]. So you the investor put up 100 percent of the capital. You take 100 percent of the risk. And you capture about 46 percent of the return. Wall Street puts up none of the capital, takes none of the risk, and takes out 54 percent of the return."

That is why Bogle is a staunch advocate of stock index funds, a basket of diverse stocks combined in an index to represent the whole market. Index funds cost the customer much less, Bogle pointed out, because the index has a fixed portfolio and does not require a fund manager to trade in and out of stocks. "You can buy an index fund for one-tenth of 1 percent," he said. "No turnover expense. No sales load or commission. You get 4.9 percent investment gain out of the 5 percent growth. You get $6.78 out of that $7.04 instead of seeing most of it go to the financial industry."

How Much to Save?

On a personal level, the main reason average Americans do poorly with 401(k) plans is that they don't invest enough, largely because they have no practical idea of how much they will need for their retirement years. Typically, people underestimate their longevity and how many more people are living into their eighties and nineties. Long life is the upside. The downside is the money it takes to pay for all those extra years.

Most people are shocked to hear the estimates of financial experts of what they will need. Based on the actual spending of current retirees, EBRI has developed the following sliding scale: To best secure the likelihood of having enough money to last over a lifetime, people who earn $50,000 to $100,000 a year should build a retirement fund seven to thirteen times their highest earnings, in order to have enough money to last their lifetimes. Using a midrange, that translates into a $500,000 retirement fund for a $50,000-a-year employee and a $750,000 fund for a $75,000-a-year worker.

The Boston College Center for Retirement Research sets slightly lower targets—a savings of $300,000 for a $50,000-a-year earner; $550,000 for people making $75,000; and nearly $800,000 for people making $100,000. But their numbers, unlike EBRI's, leave out medical costs, which can run another $200,000 for a couple over sixty-five. Either way, those professionally developed targets are five to ten times greater than the 401(k) balance of middle-income Americans on the lip of retirement.

Most Plans Are "Half What They Need To Be"

Take Rich Kidner, a wry, friendly computer geek who handles customer help calls for Perot Systems, the software company founded by Texas billionaire Ross Perot.

Since he joined Perot in 1992, Kidner has regularly contributed to his 401(k) plan, recently about $5,000 a year, out of his yearly salary of $75,000. By late 2007, Kidner's balance had hit $149,000, but then, he said, "I got hit like everyone else, and it fell to $111,000."

Still, that sounds pretty good, and Kidner was feeling very fortunate because he kept his job when Perot sold out to Dell and the company health plan paid out $175,000 for his major heart valve operation and recuperation. Now sixty and back at work, Kidner, who is an avid golfer, dreams of retiring at sixty-five and traveling to major golf tournaments worldwide.

But he was stopped dead in his tracks when I asked how he could afford to quit five years from now when the financial experts say he'll need a nest egg of $550,000 to $750,000 to retire on—five or six times what he then had.

"Where am I going to get that kind of money in five years?" Kidner gulped. "I've saved my whole life for retirement, and I can't get near that kind of money."

The hard truth, according to several experts, is that building the nest egg you need takes much more ambitious savings than virtually any 401(k) plan envisions for employees below executive levels. The best plans typically let employees sock away 6 percent of their pay each year and match it with 3 percent from the company, for a total of 9 percent.

But the experts at EBRI told me 15 percent a year should be the combined target. Vanguard founder Jack Bogle also said 15 percent. Brooks Hamilton, the corporate pension consultant, put the figure higher—15 to 18 percent. Most plans, said Hamilton, "are half what they need to be."

The Nation's Retirement Fund Deficit—$6.6 Trillion

Add it all up—what people really need when they turn sixty-five compared with what they have in their 401(k) plans, IRAs, and the other savings—and you get a price tag on the nation's retirement shortfall. Anthony Webb, research economist at Alicia Munnell's

Boston College Center for Retirement Research, did just that. He calculated what he called "the national retirement income deficit" in 2010. It came to $6.6 trillion.

"That $6.6 trillion is a call to action for us as a country," said Webb. "It's telling us that the whole system isn't working."

What's more, Webb's figure did not include the enormous short-falls in corporate and public pension funds, both of which are vastly underfunded. In 2009, the PBGC, the federal agency that oversees business pensions, estimated the corporate pension shortfall at roughly $500 billion. City and state pension funds are estimated to be even deeper in the red—$1.5 trillion or more.

Anyone faced with paying those bills is in shock. In 2011, pension fund deficits fueled controversy over public employee pensions in Wisconsin, Ohio, New Jersey, and Indiana. Unions had won pensions for public employees to retire at fifty-five, even though life expectancy was rising. The burden became impossible for taxpayers. Government officials, like corporate CEOs and CFOs, had been overly optimistic about pension plan investment returns, and that produced massive red ink in state and city budgets. Even union leaders conceded the need to raise retirement ages and to scale back benefits.

"Our nation's system of retirement security is imperiled, headed for a serious train wreck," Jack Bogle warned Congress.

The 401(k): Steady Savings or Roulette Wheel?

The 401(k) system has come under increasing fire from some of its original architects, such as pension consultant Ted Benna, widely called the "father" of the 401(k) system for his role in persuading the Reagan administration to extend the original executive 401(k) deferred compensation plan to the rank-and-file.

"Now this monster is out of control," Benna told *SmartMoney,* the *Wall Street Journal* blog, in November 2011. "I would blow up the system and restart with something totally different. . . . We're throwing tons of money away trying to teach participants how to become skilled investors—we said, we are going to make people smart and savvy enough to make the right investment decisions, but it just hasn't worked."

In Benna's eyes, the beauty of the original 401(k) concept was that it offered only two options—a guaranteed income fund and a stock equity fund. The problem with the modern 401(k), Benna said, is that it offers too many options and it has baffled average Americans who are not savvy at making sound investment decisions.

Financial professionals such as Thomas C. Scott, CEO of Scott Wealth Management and author of *Fasten Your Financial Seatbelt,* report that the public yearns for the predictable security of the old lifetime pensions. Scott cited a Fidelity Investments mutual fund survey, which found that "85 percent of investors 55 to 70 years old placed greater importance on a guaranteed monthly retirement income than on above-average investment gains."

Advocates of 401(k)-style plans such as David Wray, president of the Profit Sharing/401(k) Council of America, assert that the 401(k) system can be made to work if average employees can be pushed to stick to their plans over the long run. Given recent innovations such as automatic enrollment and "target date funds," Wray contends that the 401(k) system has been improved. Target date funds do the long-term financial planning through an investment formula targeted to an employee's projected retirement date, periodically reallocating investment objectives to match the investor's age.

But skeptics such as Eric Schurenberg, editor in chief of CBS MoneyWatch, consider the 401(k) plan inherently risky. Instead of being a steady, reliable savings plan, Schurenberg said, the 401(k) has become like a roulette wheel that "randomly creates winners and losers." The accident of market timing, Schurenberg wrote, can demolish the best-laid plans. "It all depends on when in your working life the inevitable market downturn falls," he said. "If early, you'll build your nest egg by buying cheap assets and retire rich. If late, you'll find your life savings decimated when it's too late to re-build."

The End of Retirement?

The poor 401(k) track record to date, said Alicia Munnell of Boston College, has left individuals with three options: Save more, work longer, or live on less. "They're all unattractive," Munnell admitted, "but the least unattractive is working longer."

It's already happening. The official retirement age under Social Security is creeping upward, from sixty-five to sixty-seven, and it will go higher, as it should, to mirror increases in lifetime longevity. Surveys confirm that more people are coming to the tough realization that they will need to keep working during their "golden years." In late 2010, nearly three out of four Americans said that they expect to work well into their retirement years, because they know their financial nest egg won't be nearly enough.

Older workers (fifty-five and up) are already growing as a share of the total workforce, from 12 percent in 1999 to 19 percent in 2009 and likely to be 25 percent a decade from now. Even among people seventy-five and up, the number with jobs is rising. In 2011, about 7.5 percent of that group were working, with predictions of 10 percent or more by 2018.

"Baby boomers will be facing a very different kind of retirement life than their parents . . . ," observed Teresa Ghilarducci, a senior pension economist at the New School for Social Research in New York City. "The only way they can do it is if they work. The only source of income to retirees—and I understand the irony in what I'm just going to say—the only increasing source of income to retirees is from work. . . .

"So what is the meaning of the word *retirement*, if the only way you can live in retirement is to work—or look for work?" she asked. "The answer is, there is no meaning to retirement anymore. We're now shifting from lifetime pensions to lifetime work. It's the end of retirement."

Is There a Better Way? Ask Nebraska

In the face of that bleak assessment, retirement experts like Alicia Munnell and Brooks Hamilton suggest there is a better way for people to do their retirement saving. Most average Americans, they argue, would be much better off giving up do-it-yourself investing and putting their savings, with company match, into a company-wide investment fund run by professional financial managers. People would have individual accounts—their share of the company fund based on their contributions and longevity. But their funds would be locked in until retirement, and pros would manage the investing.

The state of Nebraska actually ran a test of this concept, using two different retirement plans. Starting in 1964, one group of Nebraska's state employees went into a traditional, professionally managed lifetime pension plan, and another group went into a 401(k)-style plan funded and run by employees. Both plans set mandatory participation and contribution levels. Both got the benefit of a generous, steady 6 percent state employer match.

About a decade ago, retirees in the do-it-yourself plan complained that their retirement funds were insufficient. The state legislature demanded an outside study, which examined results from 1980 to 2004, one of the best periods for stock investing in U.S. history. The study delivered the unambiguous finding that the pooled funds in the professionally managed defined benefit pension had done far better than the 401(k)-style funds. With pooled assets and professional management, "the average rate of return for the last twenty-plus years has been over 10½ percent," reported Anna Sullivan, executive director of Nebraska's state retirement funds agency. In the employee-run plan, she said, "the average rate of return was somewhere between 6 and 7 percent."

That may not sound like much of a difference, but it is huge. Compounded over twenty years, that 4 percent earnings gap meant that the retirement accounts in the professionally managed program were double the size of the do-it-yourself accounts. The study also confirmed the retirees' complaint—that the 401(k)-style plan left them short of retirement funds. "It's just not adequate," Sullivan reported. So Nebraska killed its 401(k)-style plan and put everyone into a state-run lifetime pension.

A New Nationwide Plan?

"This is a national problem and we have to come up with a national solution," asserted Karen Friedman, executive vice president of the Pension Rights Center, a public advocacy group.

"We need a new tier of retirement savings," echoed Alicia Munnell. "The 401(k) system has proven to be totally inadequate. It can't do the job. I don't think the answer is to throw it away. But we need a new program with pooled assets, mandatory contributions, funds professionally managed, and assets locked up so that people can't get at them until they retire."

Jack Bogle advocates something like the Nebraska model on a national scale: converting people's savings from their 401(k)'s, IRAs, and other plans into personal retirement accounts with one big new U.S. retirement fund run by America's best professional money managers. These experts would be picked and overseen by a new Federal Retirement Board. Bogle urges that the plan include the 50 percent of Americans whose employers currently offer no retirement plan.

Teresa Ghilarducci, the pension economist from New York, has proposed a similar idea but with one important wrinkle: Participation by all employees and all employers should be mandatory, with an annual contribution of 5 percent of pay, shared equally by employers and employees.

Any reform of this nature faces an uphill battle as long as Corporate America, the mutual funds, and the banks are reaping huge financial benefits from the current 401(k) system and while politicians at the state and federal levels are pushing public employees away from the old lifetime pensions into 401(k)-style programs.

For a people-first program, it will take a populist revolt among baby boomers—the people who face possible poverty in retirement, unless the current system is changed.

CHAPTER 13

HOUSING HEIST

———◆———

PRIME TARGETS: THE SOLID MIDDLE CLASS

Right here in America, if you own your own home, you're realizing the American Dream. . . . That's why I've challenged the industry leaders all across the country to get after it . . . by achieving the goal of 5.5 million new minority home owners.

— PRESIDENT GEORGE W. BUSH,
June 2002

I didn't think I was in an economic position to buy a house. I didn't think I made enough money. . . . It was a nightmare. . . . I was angry—angry at myself because I shouldn't have believed the promises they made to me. . . . They knew I could not afford that loan.

— ELISEO GUARDADO,
subprime borrower

The banks are playing to brokers who specialize in driving people into loans that people don't understand. . . . They take a product that was exotic and move it to the category of a weapon—seriously.

> These loans go from being an exotic product to a
> hand grenade. . . .
>
> — KATHRYN KELLER,
> *mortgage broker*

WHEN YOU THINK OF THE HOUSING CRISIS and millions of Americans being foreclosed out of their homes, you don't imagine a bright, successful thirty-year-old like Bre Heller. When I met her, Heller was still reeling from the forced sale of her home in Orlando, Florida, stuck with a mountain of debt and furious at her bank. She didn't seem like a typical victim. She's street smart, quick as a whip with numbers, and a picture of cool composure. From the knowing way that she marched me through her loan documents, it was clear that she understood home finance.

Even so, she got stung. She got locked into a mortgage loan that she did not qualify for. By the time it was approved, she couldn't afford it and did not want it. So on October 22, 2008, with the ominous shadow of foreclosure looming over her $513,000, four-bedroom home, she emailed the Florida attorney general's "fraud hotline."

"I am a victim of predatory lending practices executed by Washington Mutual Bank in November 2006," Heller told the attorney general's office, "and would like to know the necessary steps to filing a formal complaint. I do have a full breakdown of fair lending practices that were violated, inclusive of:

"1. Being steered into a higher interest rate than necessary.
"2. Structuring loans with payments borrowers cannot afford.
"3. Falsifying loan applications in regards to income to qualify for a loan."

What made Bre Heller's case so striking was that her mortgage lender, Washington Mutual Bank (WaMu), was also her employer.

For almost four years, Heller had been a very successful loan account executive in the white-hot Florida home loan market for the Long Beach Mortgage Company, a subsidiary of Washington Mutual.

So in her email to the Florida attorney general, Heller was accusing her own bank of locking her into two loans totaling $513,525 by falsifying her loan application, downgrading her to a below prime loan, and charging her a higher rate of interest—all without telling her. It was a story familiar to legions of middle-class Americans.

The Switch on Bre Heller

In 2003, fresh out of Seattle Pacific University with a major in business and sociology, Bre Heller had joined Long Beach Mortgage and had ridden its rocket growth until suddenly, in 2006, Heller found herself a casualty of her own business.

Heller had applied for a half-million-dollar loan in September 2006 when she was easily making enough to cover that loan. But just two months later, in November 2006, her salary had fallen off a cliff. Washington Mutual, spotting big trouble at Long Beach, had suddenly put restrictions on the riskiest—and most profitable—loans in the Long Beach portfolio. The Long Beach mortgage business hit a wall. Suddenly, loan officers in Florida were doing only one-fifth the volume they had done a month or two earlier. Incredibly, Heller's pay fell from $13,374 in September to $2,288 in November.

Bre Heller figured her loan and her dream house were history. She knew that Washington Mutual required an updated review of all loan applications prior to closing to make sure that the borrower's income and bank balances had not changed and the borrower could still afford the loans. She also knew that as a Washington Mutual employee, her pay information was instantly accessible to the bank's loan officers; they would see that under the bank's loan standards, she no longer qualified for her loan, and it would be rejected. "If this had been done the way it is supposed to be done," Heller told me, "my loan should have been declined."

Instead, without telling her, WaMu rewrote her loan application, stated her income as $1 a year, shifted her into a totally different kind of loan—a no-document, no-questions-asked loan—and charged her a higher interest rate. When Heller talked to the WaMu loan officer, she was told that using a so-called $1 stated income loan was a courtesy to employees. That kind of high-interest, high-fee loan was also widely used with other customers who had irregular income.

This was not unusual. I have talked to several other people who also had their loan terms altered by the bank, without being informed, and to lawyers who represented dozens of other borrowers caught by similar bank switches on their loans. During the go-go years of the housing boom, altering loan applications to qualify people improperly was a fairly routine maneuver by banks and mortgage loan companies to generate high loan volume and higher profits.

When Bre Heller was told about her new loan, she felt trapped by her bank and her building contractor, both of whom had a financial interest in pushing the deal through. Personally, she was in a jam. She had sold the home she was living in and had to move out. She had a signed contract with the builder and had put down a $24,000 deposit as a guarantee of her serious intent to buy. If the bank had blocked her loan and denied her financing, that would have annulled her builder's contract and she would have recovered her $24,000. "But if I were to walk away on my own," she explained, "I was going to lose that $24,000." Plus, she might have faced a lawsuit for breach of contract.

So she took a risk. She went ahead with the deal, gambling at the age of twenty-six on the hope that the real estate market—and her salary—would recover. "We knew things were changing rapidly, but we didn't know if this was temporary or whether it would turn around," Heller told me. "We didn't know at that time, at the end of November 2006, that our industry would die."

Her personal plot unfolded inexorably like a Greek tragedy. Heller spent much of the money she made from selling her first home to help pay for the big mortgage on her second home. She struggled gamely for a couple of years to make her payments, with the help of a boyfriend who moved in with her. But she couldn't keep it up for years to come. Finally, she had to bow to the inevitable—the forced sale of her house in the spring of 2010 at a crushingly low price. Her home, by then in a neighborhood of foreclosed homes, was deep "under water"—its market value well below her loan balance, like eleven million other homes across America at that time.

"Considering that I lost $250,000 on that house," Heller admitted in hindsight, "I would have been better off to have walked away and left that $24,000."

From Family-Friendly to "The Power of Yes!"

The irony in that episode is that Washington Mutual had carefully cultivated the reputation since 1889 as a bank that was a "friend of the family"—a bank that earned the trust of its customers by knowing them personally, treating them like neighbors, and taking their interests to heart. But in the New Mortgage Game, Washington Mutual's character and mantra morphed into "The Power of Yes!"—a tagline in its TV ads that meant you got a loan no matter what.

WaMu CEO Kerry Killinger was not satisfied with the plodding, modestly profitable business of plain vanilla thirty-year fixed-rate mortgages to carefully screened borrowers (the old "Power of No"). That strategy wasn't getting WaMu or its CEO rich enough, fast enough. Killinger heard the siren call of Wall Street's new mortgage money machine and its voracious appetite for high-interest, high-risk, high-profit mortgage bonds—in reality, "junk mortgages," like the high-interest junk bonds of the 1980s.

Moving into junk mortgages required a radical shift in thinking at WaMu, but the financial calculus was seductive. Instead of the old business of selling mortgages, hanging on to them, and collecting interest, a home loan bank such as WaMu could make much more money by originating high-interest loans and then selling them off to Wall Street.

Killinger's fastest way of getting into the new junk mortgage game was to buy an existing subprime lender. So in 1999, WaMu bought Long Beach Mortgage Company, a high-flying, aggressive pioneer in junk mortgages.

Killinger was warned in advance that buying Long Beach was a dangerous, perhaps fatal, mistake. That warning came from WaMu executive vice president Lee Lannoye, whose job as WaMu's chief credit officer was to protect the bank against bad credit risks. Within WaMu's inner circle, Lannoye told me, he had vigorously opposed buying Long Beach. He said he had warned Killinger—prophetically—that the go-for-broke subprime culture at Long Beach would corrupt the "Friend of the Family" culture at Washington Mutual and would ultimately destroy WaMu.

As an old-line credit officer, Lannoye contended that the subprime business had to be predatory to succeed. Lending to borrowers with bad credit histories, as subprime did, was bound to lead many of those borrowers to default on their mortgages. Those defaults would cause losses to the bank in the long run, even though selling subprime loans netted some short-term gains. That system would not work, Lannoye warned, because it violated the rules of sound lending, under which banks require a creditworthy record for someone to obtain a loan.

But if credit standards are relaxed and poor credit risks are accepted, Lannoye asserted, the only way to cover the losses from bad credit risks would be to unfairly sucker solid middle-class prime borrowers into taking subprime loans at higher interest rates. "Predatory lending means finding uneducated, uninformed borrowers to take subprime loans—people who qualify for a prime loan," Lannoye explained. "You have to charge them a higher rate and a higher fee in order to subsidize the losses that will occur [on loans] to people with bad credit. This kind of lending did not fit the character and culture of our bank. It would have violated our family-friendly motto."

Twice, Lannoye fought against buying Long Beach, and it got him fired. Not literally—he got pushed into premature retirement by Killinger, who not only bought Long Beach in 1999, but also changed WaMu's operations. "He put underwriting and quality assurance under sales management," Lannoye said. "When you put credit under someone whose responsibility is sales, credit quality goes out the window, you eliminated the checks and balances. There was nobody to say 'No. . . . Hey, wait a minute. We're out of control.'"

Long Beach: Volume over Reliability

Long Beach Mortgage Company may not have been out of control in 1999, but it was pushing the limits. Congress had opened the door for high-cost subprime loans in 1980 by effectively eliminating the ceiling on mortgage interest rates set by state usury laws. In the 1990s, subprime had been an iffy business. It often lacked the capital to make large volumes of loans. But in 2001, Federal Reserve Board chairman Alan Greenspan gave subprime banking a shot in the arm. By dramatically cutting interest rates, Greenspan opened wide the profit margins on lending, especially subprime lending, and ignited the real estate and financial boom that powered the U.S. economy up to the financial bust of 2008.

Subprime lending was heavily promoted by Presidents Bill Clinton and George W. Bush. Clinton's White House had urged Fannie Mae (the Federal National Mortgage Association), Freddie Mac (the Federal Home Loan Mortgage Corporation), and other lenders to ease credit requirements and offer subprime loans to lower-income Americans, especially to ethnic minorities whose credit records were too weak to qualify for prime. In the late 1990s, Fannie Mae and Freddie Mac, the quasi-governmental companies that guarantee about half of the nation's home mortgages, pressed banks to lend to minorities and to be more flexible on loan standards. In the next administration, President Bush championed the "ownership society" for lower-income Americans, later boasting that home ownership reached record levels in his tenure—temporarily.

Long Beach Mortgage thrived in this New Mortgage Game. It was an edgy lender, always testing the limits, cutting corners, riding the fast track. So fast that in a confidential report to Washington Mutual, the Federal Deposit Insurance Corporation (FDIC) said that in reviewing four thousand Long Beach loans made in 2003, they found that only one in four qualified for sale to investors; half were deficient and needed to be corrected; the final quarter were totally disqualified for resale. As Lee Lannoye had warned Killinger, Long Beach's record was so bad that WaMu's legal department stopped all Long Beach securitizations, or sales of its bundled mortgages, to Wall Street. But the suspension was temporary. Long Beach was soon tripling its loan volume from $11.5 billion in 2003 to nearly $30 billion in 2006.

Just Out of College: $200,000 a Year

As a mortgage loan officer at Long Beach, Bre Heller worked frenetic, fourteen-hour days. She was constantly on the road, dealing with one hundred different mortgage broker firms, all pushing loans as fast as possible. The incentives at Long Beach and Washington Mutual were all based on volume—volume, not reliability or prospects for the loans' being repaid.

"We were paid by the total volume of loans that we handled, and the [commission] percentage was tiered," Heller explained. "The larger the volume, the higher the percentage. If you handled $5 million a month, that would pay you $20,000 a month. In a normal month, we would each handle from $3 million to $10 million worth. . . .

"At twenty-three and twenty-four, I was making $200,000 a year," she said proudly. "I bought my first house in 2004. I had it only two years, sold it, and made over $100,000 on it."

Strange as it may sound, Heller almost never met a live borrower. Banks such as Long Beach and Washington Mutual were by then doing the bulk of their sales through legions of independent mortgage brokers, most of whom were hustling newcomers in their twenties and thirties with little experience in finance.

Brokers: The Engine of Subprime

Brokers were the powerhouses of the subprime market. Like Long Beach account executives, they were paid on loan volume, and they got fat bonuses for talking borrowers into high-interest junk mortgages. The bonus could go as high as 3 percent: On a single $300,000 loan, a broker could make $9,000. Turn fifty or sixty of those loans in one year, and a hustling young broker could make $500,000 a year.

Brokers learned how to game the system to get loans approved; often, instead of filtering out bad loans, Long Beach loan officers would coach brokers on how to jimmy loan applications for easy approval. Then both broker and loan officer would get bonuses. "A lot of coaching takes place," Bre Heller reported. "As a sales rep I could tell the broker, 'This is how to get a loan passed. If you bring us this, this, and this, your loan will go through.' You're pointing out the loopholes. Every bank has loopholes."

The loopholes, the exotic loans, and the aggressive marketing by New Economy mortgage firms such as Long Beach were planting a time bomb in the nation's financial system that blew up on Wall Street in 2007. How? By creating volumes of explosive loans headed toward default and foreclosure and then selling them to distant investors who couldn't see the flaws in the loans. The brokers and the banks didn't care whether the mortgages would ever be paid back. They made their money by pushing volume and ignoring bad quality. Brokers got paid up front for floating the loan. Its ultimate fate was of no consequence to them.

"It was a fast-buck business," former Salomon Brothers mortgage bond trader Sy Jacobs told Michael Lewis in *The Big Short*. "Any business where you can sell a product and make money without having to worry how the product performs is going to attract sleazy people."

To make matters worse, mortgage brokers pressured banks to ease their credit standards, thus generating more defaulted loans and foreclosures. In the New Mortgage Game, brokers had the whip hand. As the frontline salespeople promoting junk mortgages, they were the point of contact with buyers, scouring phone books and ethnic groups, finding borrowers, hawking loans. They could take their customers to any lender they chose—to Long Beach, to WaMu, to competitors such as Countrywide and Ameriquest, or to affiliates of big Wall Street banks. Competition was fierce. To keep brokers at their door, Long Beach and WaMu kept loosening their loan standards.

The Exotic Loans Arsenal: From No Doc to Ninja

The mortgage banks had an arsenal of exotic loans that were far from the traditional thirty-year fixed-interest loan, where borrowers had to put 20 percent down and file pay stubs or W-2 forms to prove their income. In the New Mortgage Game, the banks' loans of choice were Option ARMs, subprime loans, 100 percent financing, teaser rates, serial refinancing, negative amortization, yield spread premiums, or home equity loans, almost all of which carried a sting that few borrowers understood.

To qualify risky borrowers, a favorite tactic of high-volume brokers was to sell a "stated income loan"—the kind of loan Bre Heller was given. Originally, such loans made sense. Banks had invented them for self-employed business consultants, contractors, writers, actors, and others with good earnings but not a steady income recorded on W-2 forms. The borrowers stated their income and then submitted tax returns or bank statements to show enough assets to pay off the loan, and they provided a business license or some official document to prove that they were actually working as stated.

But in the fever of the housing boom, the stated income loan was corrupted. WaMu and Long Beach dropped their safeguards. They let practically anyone apply for a stated income loan. Instead of requiring a state license, Heller said, they would accept letters of recommendation from anyone—easy to forge or fictionalize. Even when people had real documents, such as W-2 forms, checking on them slowed down the loan process, and that interfered with volume. So the trade gravitated in 2004, 2005, and 2006 to "no doc" loans, where no documents were required. One variation was the NINA loan—no income, no assets given. And finally came the NINJA loan—no income, no job, and no assets required.

"Loan officers dropped their duty to truly qualify home buyers for homes," Heller reported. "Instead, the loan officer did whatever was necessary to get them qualified. The system was very wishy-washy. We were pushing the boundaries."

The obvious potential for fraud troubled Heller, but as she told me, lowering the bank's standards "brought us a lot more customers." Risk was piled on risk, increasing the odds that the borrowers would default and the house of cards would crash.

The 2/28 Arm and the Piggyback Loan

At Long Beach Mortgage, the vintage subprime loan was the 2/28 ARM—an adjustable-rate mortgage that lured borrowers with a low initial "teaser rate" that after two years abruptly shot up to the normal "fully indexed rate." Some senior officials later admitted that these loans were designed to fail and to force borrowers into refinancing.

Often, to get poor credit risks approved, mortgage officers would grant loans on the borrower's ability to pay the teaser rate, rather than making sure they could afford the normal monthly payment. So pervasive was this practice that one senior WaMu executive admitted that one-third of the bank's refinancing loans would have been rejected if loan officers had properly qualified borrowers. In other words, savvy WaMu loan officers understood that borrowers who were qualified by the lender only on their ability to pay the teaser rate were headed for inevitable default, but the loan officers often ignored that reality to keep loan volume and profits rising.

Most buyers suffered severe "payment shock" when the interest rate reset after two years, potentially doubling their mortgage payments or worse. Unable to meet that steep bill, they got talked into refinancing their mortgage with a larger loan principal and a new low teaser rate. As Bre Heller explained, this started a refinancing cycle, with borrowers going deeper into debt each time, while the brokers and bankers kept pocketing handsome fees on each new loan.

With low-income borrowers, the 2/28 ARM was often combined with "the piggyback loan"—a second 20 percent mortgage piled on top of an 80 percent first mortgage. That dramatically increased the risks of default, but the sales pitch was almost irresistible—no money down. The downside was that this dangerously eliminated the time-tested credit requirement that the buyer have some financial stake in the home as protection for the bank. But by 2000, that requirement had largely gone by the boards at Long Beach, WaMu, and elsewhere.

WaMu's longtime credit expert Lee Lannoye found 100 percent financing inconceivable, especially for subprime borrowers with poor credit. Such loans were doomed at the outset, Lannoye told me, because the borrowers could simply default and walk away. "The only way to repay this loan is to refinance and refinance again, and at some point, the merry-go-round stops," Lannoye said. "Home prices don't always go up. We know that from experience."

But on the front lines, what Bre Heller recalls is the frenzy to buy, buy, buy, get your offer in before the house price goes up again, and the bottomless appetite for 100 percent financing and low teaser rates. "The big thing was the sign up there in front of the new development: '100% Financing and No Money Down,' " she said. "People think, 'I can buy this house, this brand-new house'—and everyone wants a brand-new house—'and no one can tell me I don't qualify.' "

"They [the banks] were playing to brokers who specialize in driving people into loans that people don't understand," observed

Kathryn Keller, an experienced, play-it-safe-and-fair broker with Guarantee Home Mortgage in Seattle. "They take a product that was exotic and move it to the category of a weapon—seriously. These loans go from being an exotic product to a hand grenade, and WaMu clearly did it only for marketing reasons."

Subprime Whirlpool

Eliseo Guardado was one of millions enticed by a gossamer story of the American Dream of home ownership with 100 percent financing. Guardado had come to America in 2003 as a legal immigrant from El Salvador. An earthquake had laid waste to parts of his country, and the U.S. State Department agreed to permit thousands of Salvadorans to come work in the United States under "temporary protected status," a designation that has enabled them to obtain annual extensions until the present. Guardado, who was in his late thirties and spoke no English, got a steady job as a subcontractor for HMS Drywall in Laurel, Maryland, installing walls in new homes. By his account, he made about $2,000 a month, and, living alone in a one-room basement apartment, he saved about $15,000.

But by late 2010, when I first met Guardado, he'd been through "a nightmare." Now in his midforties, he said he'd been lured into a subprime loan based on false income figures that he blamed on his broker; had been slapped with repeated foreclosure threats; had lost one job and found another; and had spent all his savings trying to hang on to a tiny two-bedroom cracker box house in Hyattsville, Maryland.

Buying a home in America was never his idea, Guardado said. "I didn't think I made enough money." Then in January 2006, he got a cold call. "There were realtors calling people all the time," he told me. "One guy called me, a real estate man who spoke really good Spanish. His name was William, but we called him El Gringo. He said to me, 'With the money you are making, you should buy a house. You are throwing your money away by renting. You'll be approved for a loan, fast and easy.' He told me I could refinance in six months and be making money on the house."

Guardado was wary but admitted that William's call had started him thinking. William took him out to see a white shingled home in Hyattsville—price tag $310,000. Then William took him to a loan office, Congressional Funding in Vienna, Virginia. There, Guardado met a Peruvian-born mortgage man named Carlos. Guardado told them he couldn't afford that house on $2,000 a month, but he says Carlos reassured him: "Don't worry. We'll fix it. You'll get your loan"—100 percent financing.

Despite his misgivings, Guardado persuaded his brother, Armando, to go in fifty-fifty with him to buy the house and live together. They were never shown the documents that federal law requires loan applicants be shown prior to closing. When they got to the closing, Eliseo and Armando were told to sign documents prepared by Carlos. It was rush, rush rush, Guardado said. Sign here. Sign there. Because they could not read English, the brothers relied on William and Carlos to fill out the forms honestly. Only years later, when he turned to a nonprofit for help, did Guardado find out that his loan application falsely showed his monthly income as $8,750, not the $2,000 he had told Carlos. It also listed him, wrongly, as a U.S. citizen. By 2010, when I tried to check Guardado's information, the Congressional Funding office was closed. Two former employees, Freddy Cova and Brian Rios, confirmed that Carlos had worked in the Tysons Corner office, but that office had closed in 2007 and the firm went out of business. Both had lost track of Carlos.

Guardado showed me his loan documents, which he kept in neat, well-organized folders. There were two 2/28 subprime ARMs—adjustable-rate mortgages with 8.65 percent interest on the first and 10.85 percent on the second. After two years, the interest floated as high as 14 percent. The monthly payments were $2,600—difficult even when shared by the brothers—plus another $4,400 a year in taxes and insurance, which Eliseo said the broker had never mentioned to him. He said he spent his precious $15,000 in savings to cover his payments, but when the mortgage charges bumped up, his brother left and things got beyond him.

With the economy turning sour, Guardado lost contracting work. He managed to land a steady job working for a landscaper, but with his savings depleted, he quit paying the mortgage in April 2008. Four months later, the foreclosure notices started.

"It was a nightmare. It was chaos," he said in a crushed voice. "I was depressed. I did not know if I was going to get kicked out of the house. Where was I going to go? To the street? Begging? . . . I was angry—angry at myself because I shouldn't have believed the promises they made to me. And I was angry at the loan officer and the realtor. They knew better. They knew I could not afford that loan. They should have told me very seriously, 'You can't make the payments. You can't afford a house.' "

Liars' Loans

Lili Sotello, an attorney for the Los Angeles Legal Aid Foundation, heard that same story thousands of times. Her team of five public service attorneys was flooded with complaints from home buyers who claimed to have been defrauded by mortgage brokers. The office handled about two thousand cases a year and turned away many times more. "We know that in 2006 there was a high demand for subprime loans on Wall Street," Sotello said. "There were not enough subprime loans to satisfy demand from the mortgage-backed trusts. That created very loose underwriting by the lenders, which allowed for predatory loans. It became a very aggressive business."

"Affinity marketing" was how loans were mass-produced, she explained. That is, Latinos, blacks, Asian Americans, and church members were being marketed by others in their own community, even relatives. By Sotello's account, thousands of seniors living on Social Security checks or lower-middle-class workers making the minimum wage were sweet-talked into home ownership on totally unrealistic terms.

"Waves of defaults were inevitable," Sotello said. "It was so easy to originate loans. All a broker had to do was fill out the application for the borrower, upload it to the loan office. They were not refusing anybody. They were overriding their own risk assessments. I filed hundreds of lawsuits on behalf of African American families, the elderly, Spanish-speaking people. Many didn't understand English very well. These were people who should not have been given loans."

Their mortgages became known as "liars' loans." But contrary to public opinion, Sotello asserted, most of the lying was done by the brokers and bank loan officers rather than by the customers. Perhaps collusion, but always with broker involvement, she said. Why? Because it took an insider's knowledge to plug in the right numbers to qualify the loan, Sotello said, and non-English-speaking borrowers could not even read the forms.

Quality Control: Black Sheep of the Family

A Long Beach insider confirmed Sotello's story—a quality control officer named Diane Kosch, who confessed to me her constant angst about fraud at Long Beach. Kosch, who is in her early sixties, had spent a lifetime in the mortgage business, eight years as a senior loan closer for Washington Mutual in Seattle. She knew how loans should be processed, and she was horrified when she moved to the Long Beach office in California's central valley region in 2004. Loan officers didn't seem to care whether they were making good loans or bad loans. "They were in business to make money for themselves, not to do good for the company," she said.

In theory, Kosch's team at quality assurance was there to stop bad loans—to protect the company and investors in Long Beach Mortgage bonds. But quality control was constantly overruled by upper management, she said, and was regarded as pariahs by everyone else because their reviews slowed the loan process, threatening to reduce loan volume and profits. Management treated the quality control staff like second-class citizens, cramming them in a conference room

instead of giving them offices and then ousting them during meetings. "I don't think there was ever a time when people in the firm
paid attention to us," Kosch said. "We were the black sheep of the
family. Everyone hated us. . . .

"The fraud was there—you could see it," she went on. "I am not
saying everyone was fraudulent. But the loan officers who were making the most money and the most loans were the most fraudulent.
And they were rewarded with trips to Hawaii and to Florida. Two or
three years down the road, a lot of those loans turned out to be foreclosures because the borrowers couldn't make the payments."

The most obvious fraud, she said, was on stated income loans, especially for relatively low earners like self-employed gardeners and
housekeepers. To Kosch, one telltale sign was that brokers would use
the same inflated income figures loan after loan—about $4,000 a
month—without any documentation, and they would cite impossible bank balances. When I asked if she saw fraudulent pay stubs, she
shot back: "We saw that all the time—pay stubs, or statements saying people made so much money. You can forge a letterhead or a
credit statement or a 1099 form."

When Kosch or other quality control officers challenged dubious
loan applications, they were overridden by management. "The loan
officers went over our heads and submitted the loan anyway," she
said. Output was all that counted. "Loan officers were fired because
they couldn't meet their goal of so many dollars per month," Kosch
reported. "In quality control, we got incentive pay for the number of
loans we reviewed. Some of our people would review a file in five
minutes."

Financial kickbacks and fancy gifts from brokers to mortgage loan
officers were a constant office topic. "I never actually saw it happen,"
Kosch told me, "but you overheard a lot of people saying, 'I closed
this loan, so I get this much money.' Brokers talking to loan officers
or loan processors, they would say: 'Do not alter the amount that I
am putting on the loan application. I will give you so much money
not to change the application, and to pass it.' "

This was more than office gossip. In December 2007, the Justice

Department indicted John Ngo, a senior loan officer at the Long Beach office in Dublin, California, where Kosch worked, for taking $100,000 in kickbacks from a mortgage broker. Ngo pleaded guilty. He admitted that he also received payments from certain Long Beach sales representatives to push loan applications through, knowing that many were fraudulent. Ngo said that he had "fixed" loan applications by creating false documents or adding false information.

Subprime for the Middle Class

One major popular misconception was that subprime loans were sold mainly to low-income people with bad records. But in fact, most of the people who were sold subprime mortgages at the height of the housing boom were solid middle-class borrowers who would have qualified financially for prime loans and probably did not understand how they were being stung. In 2005, *The Wall Street Journal* found that 55 percent of subprime borrowers should have been given prime-rate loans. In 2006, 61 percent of subprime borrowers qualified for prime, according to First American Loan Performance.

In other words, millions of middle-class home buyers were manipulated into loans that profited the brokers, the banks, and Wall Street but cost middle-class borrowers with good credit records billions of dollars in excess fees and interest. Many are probably still paying excess rates today.

The Option Arm

Washington Mutual had a potent variation on subprime that lured millions of solid middle-class and upper-middle-class borrowers. It was a below-prime loan known as "the Option ARM." This was WaMu's signature product. It was a floating-rate mortgage that fooled lots of well-educated people and was especially lucrative for the bank and for brokers. WaMu's prime targets for its Option ARMs were professionals, small-business owners, college-educated office workers, or high-tech employees, borrowers who qualified for a prime loan at favorable rates but got steered into Option ARMs often by a misleading teaser rate. Interest on the Option ARM could balloon suddenly. The loan usually carried a stiff prepayment penalty in case the borrower suddenly wanted out. Since it cost big money to bail out, borrowers typically hung on, and WaMu moved them onto a treadmill of refinancing with ever-rising loan balances.

The floating-rate mortgage, Bre Heller told me, is "the biggest dupe of all" for home buyers "because you just can't predict them," meaning the cusomer cannot know how high the interest rates will go. For the banks, she explained, the easiest target "was a customer wanting a beautiful home at the lowest rate possible. That is the perfect scenario. The broker would give the customer a choice—the cheapest rate with an adjustable-rate mortgage, or a higher rate on a straight, fixed-rate mortgage. Nine times out of ten, the customer would take the adjustable rate. And the pitch to the client was, 'Look how quickly house values are appreciating. You'll be able to refinance after it appreciates.' That was a gamble, and everybody took it."

Stingers in the Option Arm

WaMu's Option ARM had a bait-and-switch lure. It was an extremely low teaser rate, often as low as 1 or 2 percent, way below the loan's normal rate of 7 percent or higher. So if the bank or the broker didn't spell out the terms very clearly, borrowers could get hoodwinked into thinking they were getting an unbelievable bargain.

The second stinger was the "option" feature. Like a credit card, the Option ARM let the borrower choose the monthly payment level. The four options typically included (a) a bare-bones minimum payment; (b) an interest-only payment; (c) principal plus interest on a thirty-year loan; and (d) principal and interest for a speeded-up fifteen-year payoff.

For people who picked option (a), the catch-22, the most perilous aspect of the Option ARM, was that it generated what bankers call "negative amortization." That is, instead of your loan balance going down, it went up. If a borrower made the minimum payment, that was not enough even to pay the monthly interest on the loan, let alone any of the principal. So making the minimum payment left a big chunk of interest unpaid, and the bank simply tacked on that unpaid interest to the loan balance. So the balance went up month after month.

But there was another catch—a ceiling. When the rising loan balance hit a prescribed ceiling, usually 110 percent of the original loan balance, the borrower immediately had to start paying the full interest and principal on the new, larger loan balance. In most households, that caused acute payment shock—an instant doubling or tripling of the monthly payment—that pushed the borrower into either hasty refinancing or foreclosure.

John Terboss: "YSP" and Serial Refinancing

John Terboss, a small-business owner in North Miami Beach, got a triple sting. He was trapped into serial refinancing by WaMu's Option ARM—plus he was victimized by yet another hidden wrinkle in WaMu's sales arsenal known as "the yield spread premium."

This was WaMu's most enticing kickback payment to brokers, to spur them to sell loans with the highest possible interest rates, costing the homeowner dearly. The yield spread premium was based on "the interest spread"—the difference between the interest rate at which the bank borrowed money and the rate that it charged on the loan. The higher the yield spread, the higher the bonus for the broker. If an aggressive broker could maneuver an unknowing buyer into a high-interest $500,000 or $600,000 loan, he could net a bonus of $11,000 to $20,000.

The borrower paid that fee but didn't know it—because the yield spread premium was disguised. It was not shown in the column that most buyers check on the HUD-1, the main document at closing, in the column labeled "Paid from Borrower's Funds." Bre Heller showed me how the yield spread premium is typically disguised on page 2, off on the left, on line 806, in small print—"ysp" with a number. If a borrower happened to be sharp-eyed enough to spot the "ysp" and ask about it, she said, the broker would typically say that it was a fee paid to the broker by the bank. Technically that was true, but what the broker didn't explain was that the bank simply added the "ysp" amount to the interest on the loan. The borrower wound up paying for it.

WaMu's "ysp" bonus was so attractive that brokers scoured the country hunting for borrowers who could be talked into an Option ARM. John Terboss in Miami was pitched by a broker with Homegate Mortgage in Ohio in late 2007.

Four years earlier, Terboss had moved to Florida after a successful thirty-year career as an executive at radio stations in Syracuse and Philadelphia, pulling down six-figure salaries and stock options. In his late fifties, Terboss decided to go into business for himself. He bought a small advertising business, Creative Connection. Terboss and his wife, Sonia, bought a $725,000 three-bedroom ranch house in a secluded, upscale neighborhood of North Miami Beach on an inland waterway canal. The house came with a seventy-foot dock, where Terboss berthed a Silverton Cabin Cruiser that sleeps six.

Terboss spent $200,000 of his own money remodeling the house, on top of a $100,000 down payment, and he took out a loan for $627,000. In 2006, with the Florida market still rising, Terboss refinanced with a Washington Mutual Option ARM, on which the interest-only payment was about $3,900 a month. But as the Florida economy started to crater and Terboss's ad business faltered, that $3,900 payment became a strain. So he was looking for a way to cut his costs.

Enter a second WaMu Option ARM offered in a mailer from Homegate Mortgage in Ohio. When Terboss phoned Homegate, he said they told him that they could cut his payments by about $1,000. Terboss shared with me the loan proposal that Bob Norris at Homegate had sent him. It showed an interest-only payment of $3,027.56 a month, a minimum payment of $500 below that, and a big black arrow pointing to a "fully indexed rate" (interest) of 5.025 percent. That was well below Terboss's existing WaMu loan interest rate. Eager to save nearly $1,000 a month, Terboss bought the proposal, and Homegate did his loan application over the phone.

Before settlement, Terboss said, he never saw any documents from Homegate. They did the closing in Terboss's office—in a rush. "It was a very strange closing," Terboss said. "Homegate hired a local guy to handle the closing. He was very unorganized, didn't have half the papers with him. That should have been a signal. I guess I was more trusting of banking interests than I should have been. He was a total sham."

The next surprise was his first payment notice—for $1,600. Terboss, thinking it was a mistake, called Washington Mutual. They told him it was a teaser rate for the first month; the normal rate would kick in next month. And kick in it did! The interest-only payment was $4,900—$1,000 more than his old payment, not $1,000 less, as promised.

Terboss, who is normally soft-spoken, was livid. "I immediately called the bank and said, 'There's been some confusion here.' The bank would not even talk to me. They said to me: 'This came through a broker. We are not responsible. We have sold off your mortgage already.' They would take no ownership at all." Terboss fought back. On December 11, 2007, less than a month after signing the loan agreement, Terboss faxed WaMu requesting that the bank revise the mortgage: "This is not how it was represented. . . . I am not in a position to make payments of $4,928.95 a month. . . . We need to figure out a better arrangement or we'll have to void this mortgage." WaMu gave him the cold shoulder.

As a lifelong businessman, Terboss was shocked. At first, he had assumed that it was all a mistake and that Washington Mutual would correct things. But on second thought, he concluded that he had been deliberately cheated and that WaMu was part of the scam. When he checked his loan documents more carefully, he found he'd bought a high-cost, non-prime loan, even though he qualified for prime. The basic interest rate was 8.263 percent—significantly higher than the rates on his two previous loans. And then he saw the payoff to the broker—the "ysp" in tiny print, tucked in a corner of one form—$18,875.

"The guy made $18,875 for getting me into that terrible loan!" Terboss fumed.

The Final Sting

But that wasn't the end of his troubles. When Terboss tried to get out of his loan by paying it off, he discovered the final sting—a prepayment penalty of $21,000 that would sock him if he paid off the loan ahead of time. It was a provision stuck into the loan, according to Seattle housing attorney David Leen, precisely to stop people like Terboss from exiting their loans once they discovered they'd been snookered. Leen had seen scores of such cases, and they infuriated him: "It's as if the broker sold you a house, set it on fire, and locked the back door so you couldn't escape!"

Infuriated, Terboss paid his way out of the WaMu loan, but it cost him dearly—$50,000 in prepayment penalties, closing costs, and fees for a new loan from CitiMortgage. What's more, his new loan was for $777,500—almost exactly $150,000 more than his first mortgage when he bought the house. Each time he had refinanced, he got hooked into a bigger loan, meaning that he had effectively lost $150,000 of the equity he had put into his home. He thought about selling, but he couldn't recover his money.

As a businessman, Terboss had long trusted bankers, but no longer. When I asked Terboss about lessons learned, he replied coldly: "I learned that the banking industry is not what you think it is. It is not your local bank trying to help you. It is big banks trying to make money off the consumer in ways that are not appropriate. . . . Dealing with these guys was a nightmare. It was a totally fraudulent deal.

They lied all around. They were unethical. It pains me even to think about it now."

John Terboss, Bre Heller, and Eliseo Guardardo—and many others like them who talked to me—were all casualties of the New Mortgage Game, victims of hidden financial stings in their mortgages that wound up taking value out of their homes, leaving them poorer at the end or permanently in hock to their banks. People saw their equity shrink and their savings evaporate. That was actually the strategy of the New Mortgage Game, and that is how it played out all across America.

CHAPTER 14

THE GREAT WEALTH SHIFT

HOW THE BANKS ERODED MIDDLE-CLASS SAVINGS

> The American people realize they've been robbed.
> They're just not sure by whom.
>
> —GRETCHEN MORGENSON AND JOSHUA ROSNER,
> *Reckless Endangerment*

> Our present economic crisis was, by and large, foist-
> ed on Main Street by Wall Street—the mostly inno-
> cent public taken to the cleaners, as it were, by the
> mostly greedy financiers.
>
> —JOHN C. BOGLE,
> *founder, the Vanguard Group*

HOUSING EPITOMIZES DIVIDED AMERICA. It lies astride
the fault line of the economic earthquake that split the country. The
housing bubble and bust did more to devastate middle-class wealth
in a relatively short span than any other single development.

In the 1990s and 2000s, the secondary market in housing mortgages gave birth to probably the most massive operation for creating, packaging, and selling debt in American history. It powered the
growth of debt on a logarithmic scale, *making the home mortgage market even larger than the market for U.S. Treasury obligations.*

When that massive debt bubble burst, people quickly pointed to the subprime mortgage market as the villain. It is true that the implosion of the subprime market set off the housing collapse, but subprime was not the cause of our economic debacle. It was a symptom.

The underlying causes of the massive depletion of middle-class wealth lay both in the mind-set of the New Mortgage Game and in a sequence of new laws and policies that changed the rules on banking. These changes fundamentally—and dangerously—altered the relationships between bankers and homeowners. Mortgages got passed on from mortgage brokers to banks, from regional banks to Wall Street banks, and then got bundled into huge anonymous investment pools and sliced into segments so that the vital link between lender and borrower got lost—and along with it the financial safety of the system.

The Flaw in Greenspan's Model

The crash and its waves of foreclosures and high unemployment were no accident of the unfettered workings of a free market. They sprang from the deregulatory fever that burst forth in the pivotal Congress of 1978 and gained momentum in waves of deregulation passed from the Reagan era to the Bush era, as well as from former Federal Reserve chairman Alan Greenspan's belief that Wall Street banks and the subprime market could regulate themselves and his unyielding faith that the free market could be trusted.

When Cassandras warned as early as 2003 that the housing market was overheated and headed for disaster, Greenspan dismissed the risk of "a sharp decline, the consequences of a bursting bubble" as "most unlikely."

Greenspan was wrong, as we saw, tragically. But only in hindsight, well after what he termed "the greatest global financial crisis ever," did Greenspan admit to Congress that "I found a flaw in the model"—the economic model he had been using for forty years—and "I was shocked." For a man given to painstakingly qualified circumlocutions, that was an astonishing admission from Greenspan. He was referring to his long-held laissez-faire premise that government oversight and regulation were unnecessary impediments to the market because the banks could manage their own risk. In 2011, Greenspan went on to admit that the crash of 2008 "has cast doubt on this premise."

The Upside-Down Mortgage

At its core, the New Mortgage Game turned the basic concept of a home mortgage upside down.

Since the 1930s, banks had helped average Americans purchase and eventually own their homes by enabling them over thirty years to build up home equity. The banks made long-term loans and patiently enabled borrowers to pay off their debt and, ultimately, take full title to their homes, free and clear. That gave average people a foundation for financial security in retirement.

The cruel New Economy twist was that bankers developed strategies that did exactly the opposite. Instead of enabling ordinary Americans to achieve The Dream, they fashioned stratagems that stole the dream. The sales pitch from Washington Mutual, Long Beach Mortgage, and hundreds of other profit-hungry banks and brokers was that homeowners should think of their houses not as nests or nest eggs for their retirement years, but as ATM machines where they could withdraw money. Subprime junk loans were structured and marketed in ways that put new homeowners in perpetual hock to the bank. The Option ARMs, home equity lines of credit, and other arcane loans sold to millions of solid middle-class borrowers sucked rivers of money out of their homes into the banking system. "Equity stripping," bankers called it. People saw their equity shrink and their savings evaporate.

Washington Mutual senior vice president Harry Tomlinson extolled the New Mortgage Game in an interview with James Grant, editor of *Grant's Interest Rate Observer*. "What I see," said Tomlinson, "is a shift in the mortgage product, going from a product used to buy one's home . . . to a product where people can leverage their home as a financial asset. And that's a big shift."

Greenspan and "Home Equity Extraction"

Think of it this way: All those exotic mortgage loans and Wall Street's vehicles of "structured finance" were debt machines. They were instruments of a financial system that destroyed value for middle-class Americans. The housing boom of the 1990s and 2000s enriched the banks and steadily impoverished millions of middle-class Americans—and not just at the end, when housing prices fell, but all along. Trillions were lost even before the crash because homeowners were pulling so much equity out of their homes.

Greenspan hailed this trend, which he called "home equity extraction." He saw it as good for the nation's economy after the dot.com collapse. In 2002, Greenspan estimated home equity withdrawals at $700 billion a year. Other economists worried. They saw average American families going $700 billion deeper into debt, year after year, but Greenspan welcomed that mountain of borrowing.

Greenspan wanted homeowners to draw savings out of their homes to finance their consumption and thus power the economy. As he told Congress on November 13, 2002, that process was rescuing a sick economy. "It is important to recognize that the extraction of equity from homes has been a significant support to consumption during a period when other asset prices [that is, stock markets] were declining sharply," Greenspan testified. "Were it not for this phenomenon, economic activity would have been notably weaker. . . ."

Many borrowers happily collaborated in that process, figuring the housing boom would replenish their savings. Some stripped their homes of value to live a more luxurious life—to buy second and third cars or plush yachts, build home entertainment centers, or take fancy vacation trips.

But far more people took out high-interest home equity loans for practical necessities because their salaries or wages were not keeping pace with inflation. They pulled money out of their houses to pay medical bills, to fund college educations for their kids, to finance home improvements, or simply to keep up with the rising cost of living. A hefty chunk of the new borrowing put no money into the homeowners' pockets. It went to pay high loan fees and yield spread premiums to aggressive and sometimes deceptive brokers, and to fatten the bonuses of bankers and the financial elite on Wall Street.

A Seismic Shift of Wealth

At its peak, the New Mortgage Game worked for several years, but when the housing boom that Greenspan promoted went bust, the losses were titanic. American homeowners lost trillions in plummeting home prices from mid-2006 to the start of 2012. But that's only half of the story.

Less visible was the massive loss of equity in their homes that average Americans suffered before the housing bubble burst in 2006. Back in 1985, Americans actually owned 69.2 percent of the value of their homes (the banks owned the rest), according to Federal Reserve data. By 2011, the homeowners' share of housing wealth had plunged to just 38.4 percent of the total value. Homeowners lost nearly a 30 percent stake in what had been the nation's $20 trillion housing stock—a collective loss of about $6 trillion primarily through equity stripping.

In short, the fantasy promise that housing prices would go up forever and you could borrow on your home time after time, combined with deceptive sales pitches on junk mortgages, seduced millions of middle-class families into draining the precious equity that they had painstakingly built up in their homes.

That steep national drop in homeowner equity, from nearly 70 percent down to below 40 percent of total housing value, represented a monumental transfer of the absolute core of middle-class wealth from homeowners to banks. Trillions of dollars in accumulated middle-class wealth were shifted from average Americans to the big banks, their CEOs, and their main stockholders. For the first time in decades, banks owned more of the cumulative value of American homes than the so-called owners.

That seismic shift of wealth represented the theft from millions of middle-class families of a vital component of the American Dream. A large portion of the baby boomer generation, heading for retirement, were left in dire straits. Instead of having paid off their thirty-year mortgages, they were stuck with homes "under water" and they may literally have to pay money to get out of them.

Before the New Mortgage Game took over, people would plan on cashing out of the homes where they had raised their families and on using the proceeds to move to smaller, hopefully cheaper quarters in sunny Florida or Arizona. The housing bust changed all that. Even for those who hung on to their homes, it meant in many cases that *sellers* had to *bring cash to settlement* to cover the costs at closing. By economist Dean Baker's estimate, nearly one-fifth of older boomers in their sixties face this new financial challenge right now, and unless the housing market changes dramatically, roughly one-third of the younger boomers, in their fifties, are on track for a similar shock when they retire.

The Secondary Market—Separating Profit from Risk

In going back to see how things got so badly off track, what emerges is a fatally flawed concept at the heart of the New Mortgage Game. It is the dangerous disconnect—the separation of Profit from Risk. The primary place where that happened was in what bankers call "the secondary market," where regional banks sold their home mortgages and where Wall Street banks could buy those mortgages by the millions.

The secondary market was the engine of the housing bubble of the 2000 decade. It financed the "originate and sell" strategy that became the hallmark of the New Mortgage Game. One predictable consequence of regional banks' quickly selling off mortgages to Wall Street was that the brokers and bankers who originated the loans no longer cared whether those loans were paid back or defaulted, because they no longer owned the risk. They could pass the risk downstream to distant investors on Wall Street and beyond. Reliability was sacrificed on the altar of volume and profits.

This was a watershed change for the banking industry. Traditionally, banks closely scrutinized the three Cs of borrowers—credit, collateral, and cash flow (income)—to make sure that 99 percent of their loans paid off. But as we saw with Bre Heller and the Florida brokers using the no doc, stated income, and NINJA loans, checking the borrowers carefully no longer mattered to the loan originators in the New Mortgage Game. They made fast, big profits from handsome closing fees.

Then, Wall Street firms sliced, diced, and repackaged these mortgage loans into what became known as "synthetic" derivatives, or security pools with various levels of risk, and sold multibillion-dollar bundles of mortgages—or mortgage parts—known as "collateralized debt obligations," to hedge funds, college endowments, pension funds, insurance companies, or investors in Germany, Japan, Abu Dhabi, or wherever. The investors loved them because mortgages used to be very safe investments and Wall Street bond-rating agencies still gave them AAA ratings.

When Risk Is Everywhere, It's Nowhere

The growth of these pyramiding bank loans and derivatives followed the policy prescriptions of Fed chairman Alan Greenspan, who credited this process with diversifying risk and having "contributed to the stability of the banking system. . . ."

What Greenspan evidently discounted was the colossal danger in separating profit from risk—the problem that when risk resides everywhere, risk resides nowhere in particular. No one was minding the store the way the old-fashioned bank did when it lent money from its own depositors to their neighbors.

When the roof fell in, the banks blamed borrowers who defaulted for behaving irresponsibly. But the banks themselves—and the Fed—had created a system of irresponsibility, by lending to millions of people who could not reasonably be expected to repay and then not carefully regulating the process for safety.

"Ordinarily, the instinct for financial self-preservation should prevent lenders from making too many risky loans," observed Simon Johnson, former chief economist for the International Monetary Fund (IMF). "The magic of securitization [reselling mortgages in bundles] relieved lenders of this risk . . . leaving them free to originate as many new mortgages as they could. Because mortgages were divided up among a large array of investors, neither the mortgage lender nor the investment bank managing the securitization retained the risk of default. That risk was transferred to investors, many of whom lacked the information and the analytical skills necessary to understand what they were buying. And the investors assumed that they didn't need to worry about what they were buying, because it was blessed by the credit rating agencies' AAA ratings."

The secondary market turned the New Mortgage Game into a game of musical chairs that was destined for disaster. Because of the financial disconnect, it worked like a multitrillion-dollar Ponzi scheme. The secondary market grew so enormous that it constantly needed new money to cover losses and to keep the game going. But when the music stopped, the game brought down Bear Stearns, Lehman Brothers, Washington Mutual, Countrywide, and hundreds of regional banks, and it left millions of average Americans foreclosed out of their homes and millions more vastly poorer—$9 trillion poorer—from both equity stripping and plunging home values.

The Legislative Seeds of Crisis

The New Mortgage Game and the enormous loss of wealth by middle-class Americans were the direct consequences of new policies in Washington—New Economy policies that wiped out laws and regulations that had worked well for decades.

The first major step was taken under President Jimmy Carter—the Depository Institutions Deregulation and Monetary Control Act of 1980. That law effectively abolished limits on interest rates for first mortgages that had long been imposed by state usury laws. It thus removed a basic protection for financially vulnerable borrowers and opened the door to unscrupulous subprime lenders. "More than anything else," asserted former Federal Reserve Board governor Edward Gramlich, "this elimination of usury law ceilings [on interest rates] paved the way for the development of the subprime market."

In 1982, Congress took an even bigger step. It adopted legislation proposed by President Reagan that authorized the exotic loans that became the pathological hallmarks of the housing craze of the 2000s. This law enabled state banks to sell adjustable-rate mortgages (national banks had gotten that authority in 1981). It also permitted something never allowed before—equity stripping loans, known in banking lingo as "negative amortization." This meant authorizing banks to sell loans where the principal balance would go up over time, digging homeowners into ever-deepening debt. Finally, the law empowered the Office of the Comptroller of the Currency to issue rules in 1983 that permitted up to 100 percent financing, by canceling restrictions that required down payments from buyers.

These three items—ARMs, negative amortization, and 100 percent financing—in a law that President Reagan hailed as "the most important legislation for financial institutions in the last 50 years," were the grist, as *New York Times* financial columnist Gretchen Morgenson observed, for home mortgages loaded "with poisonous features that made them virtually impossible to repay."

Two years later, in 1984, the Reagan administration delivered the coup de grâce for the New Mortgage Game—the separation of Profit from Risk. In partnership with Wall Street bankers, the Reagan White House wrote the Secondary Mortgage Market Enhancement Act of 1984. This law sanctioned the "securitization" of mortgages on the secondary market, which powered the explosive growth of

America's mortgage market to the point that it outstripped even the market for U.S. Treasury bonds and bills.

For banks that originated loans, such as Washington Mutual and Long Beach Mortgage, securitization provided the avenue for selling their mortgages and the source for raising more capital to finance another round of lending. For investment banks such as Goldman Sachs, it created a new venue and new vehicles to reap lucrative fees and a casino for betting against the subprime market that they were getting their clients to finance.

The 1984 law was written to Wall Street's specification. By several accounts, Lewis Ranieri, a legendary Salomon Brothers trader, whom some have called the father of the modern mortgage bond market, worked hand in glove with the Reagan White House to craft the legislation. From experience in the 1970s, Ranieri knew exactly what legal barriers the investment bankers needed to eliminate in order to create a grand new mortgage marketplace. Then in 1986, Ranieri and the investment banks won another round of lucrative concessions in the tax reform law that established the real estate mortgage investment conduit, or REMIC, which granted complex special tax advantages for the mortgage bond market.

Greenspan: Engineering a Turnaround

If the White House and Congress provided the legal blueprint for the New Mortgage Game, Alan Greenspan became its point man— its prime policy architect and its most influential advocate. Three elements were central to the New Mortgage Game—cheap money, subprime loans, and a portfolio of flexible interest rate mortgages— and all of them were either created by Greenspan or vigorously championed by him.

Greenspan instituted the Federal Reserve's cheap money policy after the dot.com bubble burst and the stock market collapsed in early 2000. Greenspan turned to real estate and home construction as the new driving force for the U.S. economy. He led the Fed to cut interest rates eleven times from 2001 to mid-2003. The Federal Open Market Committee cut the federal funds rate from 6.5 percent in January 2001 to 1 percent by mid-2003, providing mountains of cheap money for banks to lend and for Wall Street to invest.

Greenspan's strategy worked. It rescued the economy from a free fall. It gave housing a kick start, and the housing sector soared, generating more than 40 percent of new private sector jobs starting in November 2001. Operating at full steam in 2005, housing, construction, and real estate were pumping an enormous stimulus into the nation's economy—more than $1 trillion a year, by one economist's estimate.

But danger lay in what became the meteoric rise of housing prices. Cheap money and rising home prices made people feel richer than they really were, so everyone took big risks. People borrowed more than they should have.

Yale University's Robert J. Shiller, one of America's premier housing economists, compared the price binge to a "rocket taking off," a spurt without precedent, except after World War II. In the 114 years from the 1890s to 2004, Shiller reported, housing prices had risen only 66 percent, adjusted for inflation, or less than ½ percent a year on average. But from 1997 to 2004, in just eight years, prices had shot up 52 percent. Such a white-hot housing market, Shiller said, should be a warning to the Fed. Other dire prophecies came from financial experts warning that Greenspan's cheap money was fueling a dangerous speculative fever, but Greenspan brushed aside those warnings as overblown.

Greenspan Blesses Subprime and Exotic Loans

Greenspan did more than provide cheap money. He vigorously promoted the subprime market, flexible-rate mortgages, and other exotic loans. Both Presidents Clinton and Bush had called for extending the American Dream of home ownership to those who had been left behind, especially to minorities. Greenspan became a cheerleader for that policy. "Where once more-marginal applicants would simply have been denied credit, lenders are now able to quite efficiently judge the risk posed by individual applicants and to price that risk appropriately," Greenspan declared in April 2005.

Unfortunately, by then, lenders such as Countrywide, Washington Mutual, and the main New York banks were doing just the opposite. Instead of weeding out the bad risks, they were dropping their standards and giving loans to poor risks. But Greenspan took heart from the rapid growth in subprime mortgage lending, boasting that it had risen from just 1 or 2 percent of the U.S. mortgage market in the 1990s to 10 percent in 2005.

Greenspan also told solid middle-class homeowners that they would have been better off if they had stayed away from safe, traditional thirty-year fixed-rate loans. The Fed's research, Greenspan said in early 2004, "suggests that many homeowners might have saved tens of thousands of dollars had they held adjustable-rate mortgages rather than fixed-rate mortgages during the past decade." He urged bankers to be more daring: "American consumers might benefit if lenders provided greater mortgage product alternatives to the traditional fixed-rate mortgage."

But then, rather inconsistently, Greenspan imposed a penalty on the borrowers who followed his advice and bought flexible-rate loans. He led the Fed through fourteen interest rates hikes from mid-2004 to January 2006, quadrupling the federal funds rate from 1 to 4.5 percent. That spelled rough weather for people with 2/28 subprime loans or Option ARMs.

"No One Wanted to Stop That Bubble"

The push on subprime by the Clinton and Bush administrations sounded great—egalitarian, inclusive, progressive. But the strategy had a fundamental flaw that one might have expected the Federal

Reserve as the repository of financial expertise to spot: The low-income homeowner strategy did not match economic reality.

Housing prices from the late 1990s onward were rising far faster than people's incomes, economist Robert Shiller pointed out. Millions of subprime borrowers were being thrust into a race that they were bound eventually to lose. Subprime mortgages pushed them into a cycle of refinancing, and each time they refinanced, the size and cost of their mortgage went up. But their income stayed flat or fell. Keeping up with the housing bubble was a stretch even for many prime borrowers. Starting in 1997, former IMF economist Simon Johnson observed, "the growth of *housing prices outstripped income growth* [emphasis added]; after 1999, real median household income *fell* for five consecutive years as housing prices soared." With a growing gap between housing prices and personal incomes, massive defaults were inevitable. Too many people couldn't afford their loans.

Inside the Federal Reserve, Ed Gramlich cautioned Greenspan that the subprime market, swollen to $625 billion in 2005, 20 percent of the total U.S. mortgage market that year, was operating like "the Wild West," with almost no regulatory protection. The Fed, Gramlich charged, had abdicated its role as sheriff, allowing "carnage" among low-income borrowers. Gramlich underscored that 51 percent of subprime loans in 2005 were originated not by banks, but by consumer finance companies or mortgage brokers, not subject to regulatory supervision. He urged the Fed to step in. Otherwise, Gramlich asserted, subprime "is like a city with a murder law, but no cops on the beat." Greenspan shot down Gramlich's proposal for Fed oversight to bring the subprime market under better control.

Bush's Treasury secretary, John Snow, later admitted, "What we forgot in the process was that it has to be done in the context of people being able to afford their house. We now realize there was a high cost." But Lawrence Lindsey, Bush's first chief economics adviser, said no Bush official wanted to raise the alarm. "No one wanted to stop that bubble," said Lindsey. "It would have conflicted with the president's own policies."

The Warnings

Those were comments made in hindsight. But there were warnings ahead of time from outside economists. In 2003, Dean Baker and Mark Weisbrot of the Center for Economic and Policy Research in Washington cautioned that rising mortgage debt had reached dangerous levels and this was "especially scary" because housing prices "may be inflated by as much as 20 to 30 percent." Other warnings that the housing market was dangerously overheated came from economists Stephen Roach of Morgan Stanley and Paul Krugman of Princeton.

In 2004, Robert Shiller, whose book *Irrational Exuberance* had foretold a stock market bust in 2000, reported ominous housing bubbles in key regional markets, warning that speculative fever could bring widespread mortgage defaults. Shiller recalled that waves of mortgage defaults in 1929 had contributed to the biggest banking crisis in U.S. history in the 1930s. A few months later, in early 2005, Shiller's warning was more stark. The housing frenzy, he said, "may be the biggest bubble in U.S. history"—destined to end with a crash. Renowned global investor Sir John Templeton forecast an inevitable downturn. "When home prices do start down," he said, "they will fall remarkably far" and cause widespread bankruptcies.

But Alan Greenspan dismissed talk of a housing "bubble." In June 2005, he conceded "signs of froth in some local markets," but he rejected calls from economists like Shiller for the Fed to raise interest rates more sharply to cool speculative fevers, asserting that "the U.S. economy seems to be on a reasonably firm footing."

A year later, the housing market began its tumble. In hindsight, *The Wall Street Journal* editorial page, normally among Greenspan's admirers, judged that "Alan Greenspan's policies at the Fed contributed to the credit and housing manias that led to the financial meltdown. . . ."

WaMu—Shifting Clients: From Main Street to Wall Street

But out across the country, in the boom years, Greenspan was the oracle, the north star for bank presidents like Washington Mutual CEO Kerry Killinger. They followed his course, and their operations in the 2000 decade graphically illustrate how Greenspan's strategies played out across the country.

Bank CEOs such as Killinger took Greenspan's cheap money policies, his advocacy of subprime, and his promotion of variable-rate mortgages as the green light for more aggressive lending through exotic loans such as Option ARMs intended for resale on the secondary market. So WaMu shifted priority from serving Main Street to serving Wall Street. Home buyers were no longer its primary customers. They were a means to an end—feeding Wall Street.

This was a pivotal shift for old-line banks such as Washington Mutual—and for American banking in general. At WaMu, it seemed a cynical shift. Killinger, in an internal email in March 2005, worried about the high level of risk in the housing market that "typically signifies a bubble." But rather than retreat to safety, Killinger raced ahead.

Wall Street stock analysts asked Killinger in mid-2005 how he protected WaMu from losses in its large inventory of risky Option ARMs and subprime mortgages. Killinger first said WaMu had internal risk control measures, but bank documents contradict him. His real defense, Killinger admitted, was to sell off potentially toxic loans to Wall Street investors: "You've seen us sell in the secondary markets more than what we historically have done."

Accolades for Fraud, Not Penalties

What Killinger didn't reveal was how rapidly the tide of rotten—even fraudulent—liars' loans was rising, based on bogus information on loan applications. This was happening not just at Long

Beach, which had the highest loan delinquency rate of any bank in the country in February 2005 and had to be shut down entirely and absorbed into WaMu in June 2007 after being forced to buy back $837 million worth of mortgages it had sold to Wall Street. But by then the infection of predatory marketing had spread to WaMu itself.

What is surprising in retrospect is that Wall Street was so slow to detect the poison in the New Mortgage Game that it had fostered and financed. Wall Street banks were so hungry for WaMu's Option ARMs that WaMu sold a staggering $130 billion worth in 2004 and 2005. But by mid-2006, more and more borrowers were defaulting, and much later, Ronald Cathcart, WaMu's chief risk management officer, admitted in hindsight that too many Option ARMs had been recklessly approved and, ultimately, they "were a significant factor in the failure of WaMu and the financial crisis generally."

Worse, WaMu's internal investigators in 2005 confirmed what Lili Sotello and her staff of lawyers at the Los Angeles Legal Aid Foundation had reported. They found massive broker fraud and abuse inside Washington Mutual at two of the bank's highest-volume loan offices, near Los Angeles. Like Sotello, WaMu's internal memos blamed the fraud not on borrowers, but on the bank's loan officers. "Virtually all of it [is] . . . attributable to some sort of employee malfeasance," WaMu investigators reported.

The prime offenders, investigators said, were two of the bank's all-time high-volume champion loan officers—Thomas Ramirez, the top mortgage loan salesman in Downey, California, and Luis Fragoso, the kingpin loan performer in Montebello, California. Both were experts in affinity marketing within the Hispanic community.

In a year-long probe, WaMu investigators found documentary evidence of "an extremely high incidence of confirmed fraud"—58 percent of the loans handled by Ramirez and 83 percent of those managed by Fragoso. The fraud, investigators said, covered a gamut of bogus information on loan applications—false credit records, phony employment information, inflated income figures, false statements about owner occupancy of homes, and illegal Social Security numbers. In one file, investigators reported: "The credit package was found to be completely fabricated."

But no firings or shake-ups at WaMu followed the probe. In fact, eighteen months later, in June 2007, the insurance giant AIG, which had insured WaMu's loans, protested about the new fraudulent loans from Luis Fragoso in WaMu's Montebello office. AIG demanded that WaMu buy back these "Fragoso loans," and it filed formal complaints with federal and California bank regulators. When WaMu investigators went back to Montebello, they verified "the elements of fraud found by AIG." Still, WaMu's top brass did nothing to root out the fraud or penalize its perpetrators, according to an investigation by the Senate Permanent Subcommittee on Investigations.

In fact, just the opposite happened. WaMu's leaders showered Fragoso and Ramirez with accolades, despite the fraudulent loans linked to them by WaMu's investigators. Fragoso and Ramirez were not only paid handsomely, they were given WaMu's highest corporate honor, year after year, from 2004 to 2007—selection to the bank's highly touted President's Club. This gave them all-expenses-paid first-class trips to Hawaii, private suites at a swanky hotel, and a cornucopia of valuable gifts as well as personal praise from CEO Kerry Killinger and home loans president David Schneider.

"Arts and Crafts Weekends"

By many accounts, this kind of insider fraud was pervasive. Fannie Mae, the quasi-governmental guarantor of many mortgage loans, was getting fraud warnings about the mortgage industry as early as 2003. The FBI first publicly warned of mounting fraud in 2004— and that was only reported fraud; most fraud went unreported. Once the bubble burst, insiders such as Richard Bitner, a wholesale mortgage lender in Texas, disclosed that fraud was epidemic because the financial temptations were so immense.

"The level of fraud we experienced as a lender . . . was unprecedented," Bitner told the Financial Crisis Inquiry Commission. "In my firm's experience, between the years of 2003 to 2005, *more than 70 percent* of all brokered loan files that were submitted for initial review were somehow *deceptive, fraudulent or misleading* [emphasis added]."

The problem was not individual bad apples, but a system run amok, according to University of Missouri's William Black, executive director of the Institute for Fraud Prevention. Most liars' loans, Black reported, were generated by bank insiders using false information to get loan applications approved. "They had these sessions where they would rework the applications—what in the trade were called 'arts and crafts weekends,' where they would cut out the bad numbers and paste in the good numbers to hit the needed ratios [to qualify borrowers for loans]. They actually kept the original numbers, so that we know that the lies came from loan officers and brokers."

Come 2006, even the Mortgage Bankers Association admitted that "stated income and reduced documentation loans . . . are open invitations to fraudsters." In November 2007, the Fitch bond-rating agency bucked the silence in the bond-rating industry that consistently gave mortgage bond pools AAA ratings and notified its clients that when it checked loan records in detail, "there was the appearance of *fraud or misrepresentation in almost every file* [emphasis added]."

Hedge Funds Spot the Flaws, Cash In

Most of Wall Street, as well as two Fed chairmen, Alan Greenspan and Ben Bernanke, failed to anticipate the pathological danger in the stream of toxic loans flowing into America's financial system. But a handful of hedge fund mavericks saw disaster coming. They realized that if millions of poor-credit-risk borrowers were sold 2/28 subprime loans in 2004, 2005, and 2006, then two years later, when their low teaser rates ran out and their monthly payments ballooned, they would default en masse. This would bust the secondary mortgage market. So they bought insurance on mortgage bonds, in the form of credit default swaps, and cashed in big-time when the market collapsed.

Hedge fund managers such as John Paulson, Mike Burry of Scion Fund, and Steve Eisman of FrontPoint Partners made a mint betting against the flimsy promise of home ownership for virtually everyone. Eventually, traders at Goldman Sachs smelled blood in the water and made a killing, too.

For the most devious minds on Wall Street, Long Beach Mortgage loans were attractive precisely because they were so unreliable. They figured prominently in Goldman's high-profile mortgage loan pool, the $2 billion Abacus 2007–AC1, for which Goldman was fined $550 million by the SEC. Goldman was accused of duplicity by regulators for failing to disclose to investors that Abacus 2007–AC1 had been put together by John Paulson, who had designed the loan package to fail. Paulson had included six Long Beach Mortgage loan trusts. By betting against such loan pools, Paulson & Company made $15 billion in 2007, and Paulson himself made $4 billion.

Goldman Sachs, too, bet against Abacus 2007–AC1 after selling it to investors such as the Royal Bank of Scotland, IKB Deutsche Industriebank, and the Dutch bank ABN Amro, which lost huge sums. Goldman's double-dealing caused an uproar among investment experts. "The simultaneous selling of securities to customers and shorting them because they believed they were going to default," said Sylvain R. Raynes of R&R Consulting, "is the most cynical use of credit information that I have ever seen."

In a highly publicized resignation from Goldman Sachs in March 2012, Greg Smith, a veteran of twelve years in Goldman's derivatives business, claimed that disregard for client interests had become the norm at Goldman. "It makes me ill how callously people still talk about ripping off clients," Smith wrote in an op-ed in *The New York Times*. "To put the problem in the simplest terms, the interests of the client continue to be sidelined in the way the firm operates and thinks about making money." Smith charged Goldman CEO Lloyd C. Blankfein with overseeing "the decline in the firm's moral fiber" and urged the firm's leaders to restore Goldman's integrity by "weed[ing] out the morally bankrupt people, no matter how much money they make for the firm." Goldman executives took issue with Smith, saying that his version did not accurately reflect how Goldman treats its clients.

The Role of Bond-Rating Agencies

In hindsight, it seems hard to understand why sophisticated investors like the Royal Bank of Scotland would get sucked into buying $840 million worth of highly dubious mortgages from Goldman. One reason is that mortgage loans had long been very safe investments. But that changed with the emergence of junk mortgages, except that the bond-rating agencies, Moody's, Standard & Poor's, and Fitch Ratings, kept on rating most mortgage bonds as AAA in terms of safety.

Financial experts point out that "without those AAA ratings, the flow of money" into the secondary mortgage market would have stopped. "I view the ratings agencies as one of the key culprits," said Joseph Stiglitz, a Nobel Prize–winning Columbia University economist. "The banks could not have done what they did without the complicity of the ratings agencies."

The ratings agencies had, and still have, a conflict of interest to this day. They were supposedly rating the quality of mortgage loans and other bonds for potential buyers. But they were being paid huge fees by the sellers, the investment banks, which need the raters' vital seal of approval for their mortgage pools. Bank traders were constantly threatening rating agencies to take their lucrative business elsewhere if they didn't get AAA ratings. The agencies were making huge earnings. Moody's earnings from exotic financial vehicles tripled from 2001 to 2007, and it enjoyed operating margins of 50 percent, more than three times higher than ExxonMobil's—and they didn't want to rain on the parade of profits.

Even if bank insiders belatedly realized that lots of loans were rotten, they engaged in a game of hot potato. They just kept passing on risky mortgages and derivatives to someone else, piling up profits. In May 2007, the Fed's Ben Bernanke said he saw no threat to U.S. prosperity and "no serious broad spillover" from the troubled subprime market to the big Wall Street banks, because, he said, they were not involved in subprime. Bernanke was wrong. They were deeply involved. Two months later, with the housing market already in steep decline, Citigroup CEO Charles Prince pooh-poohed the dangers. "When the music stops, in terms of liquidity, things will be complicated," Prince told the *Financial Times*. "But as long as the music is playing, you've got to get up and dance. We're still dancing."

Prince had a tin ear. Within a week, Wall Street's bond-rating agencies turned thumbs down on hundreds of subprime mortgage bundles on Wall Street, and the liquidity on the mortgage secondary market froze. As Eric Kolchinsky, a dissident bond rater at Moody's later admitted, Moody's inflated ratings had "caused hundreds of billions of losses for the world's financial institutions."

Liars' Loans Are Suicidal

Even the sellers got burned. "Making liars' loans is not risky—it is suicidal," said fraud expert William Black. "That is why every significant lender specializing in liars' loans has failed."

Black was right. By October 2006, the housing market was into its sharpest fall in thirty-five years and the junk mortgage dominoes began to fall: New Century, Ameriquest, Bear Stearns, Countrywide, IndyMac Bank, and, finally, Wall Street titan Lehman Brothers, filing for bankruptcy on September 15, 2008, setting off global shock waves.

Ten days later came the biggest bank failure in American history—Washington Mutual—eight times larger than any previous bank failure. At the eleventh hour, the bank had desperately sent emissaries abroad to Asia, to find buyers who didn't yet know the score. Its number crunchers had figured out which of WaMu's loans were the most default-prone, and WaMu's high command cynically gave the go-ahead to sell them. WaMu managed to sell $1.5 billion worth without warning investors of their poor quality. But that did not save WaMu from going broke.

The bank swooned into bankruptcy and a federal takeover on September 25, 2008. Its books listed $307 billion in assets, but it was sold for a pittance—$1.9 billion—to JPMorgan Chase.

Hundreds of bank failures like WaMu's hit middle-class Americans in multiple ways. Borrowers were not the only ones burned by predatory loans; employees and investors were also affected. At WaMu, CEO Kerry Killinger walked off with more than $100 million in salary and bonuses, but bank employees saw their retirement fund collapse from $300 million to virtually nothing. They filed suit, but with WaMu gone, there was no one to pay. The terms of JPMorgan Chase's buyout barred lawsuits against either WaMu or JPMorgan Chase. The same happened to several pension funds for police and teachers in Detroit, Ontario, and Pompano Beach, Florida, which had invested in WaMu and were stuck with millions of shares of worthless WaMu common stock and bonds.

Fraud but Almost No Prosecution

What is striking about the housing crisis is that unlike the savings and loan scandal of the 1980s, where hundreds of bank officials and board members went to jail on felony charges, only relatively low-level officers have been criminally prosecuted in the housing bust. Only belatedly have a few high-level government officials even acknowledged massive deception. Late in 2010, Alan Greenspan conceded that fraud had played a central role in the crisis, though he did not say whether the Fed's lax oversight had contributed. "Things were being done which were certainly illegal and clearly criminal in certain cases," Greenspan told a Federal Reserve conference in November 2010.

Even that did not trigger criminal action by the Justice Department. Government agencies pushed for fines and won modest settlements with big banks like Citigroup and Wells Fargo. Countrywide, an aggressive subprime lender, paid the largest residential fair-lending settlement in U.S. history—$335 million on civil charges that it had levied higher fees and loan rates to more than two hundred thousand minority borrowers than to whites with similar credit ratings. The firm's CEO, Angelo Mozilo, agreed separately with the SEC to pay a $67.5 million fine, $20 million of which was paid by Bank of America, which bought Countrywide. Mozilo's personal fine amounted to less than 10 percent of the $500 million fortune he amassed at Countrywide, and by settling, Mozilo avoided criminal prosecution and the risk of jail.

Washington Mutual was targeted by the FDIC in a $900 million lawsuit against its top executives—CEO Kerry Killinger, COO Steve Rotella, and home loans president David Schneider. The FDIC accused them of taking "extreme and historically unprecedented risks" and pursuing policies ". . . to increase their own compensation, with reckless disregard for WaMu's long-term safety and soundness." The bank executives scoffed at the government action as "political theater." Ultimately, the FDIC collected $190 million in damages, mostly from WaMu assets or executive insurance policies. Killinger and his two lieutenants paid only $425,000 in cash penalties, though they also forfeited nearly $25 million in funds they claimed WaMu owed them.

Senator Carl Levin, a Michigan Democrat who led a Senate investigation of Washington Mutual, was deeply disappointed. "Today's settlement," Levin asserted, "shows again how bank executives can beat the system. Former WaMu executives Killinger, Rotella, and Schneider are truly the 1 percent: they got bonus upon bonus when the bank did well, but when they led the bank to collapse, insurance and indemnity clauses shielded them from paying any penalty for their wrongdoing."

In case after case, the pattern was familiar: legal charges of fraud, deception, or violation of securities laws, followed by a financial settlement but no admission of guilt by the banks, except as implied by the bank's promise of better behavior in the future—never to violate the anti-fraud provisions of securities laws in the future. But when *The New York Times* checked the record after Citigroup agreed in November 2011 to a $285 million settlement, it found that Citigroup had made the same vows of good conduct in July 2010, May 2006, April 2005, and April 2000. In fact, nineteen of the biggest financial firms, the major Wall Street banks, were repeat offenders.

An Opportunity Missed

The Wall Street bust and bailout offered an opportunity to correct some of the misguided policies that led to the financial collapse, through regulatory reform and rescue measures for millions of homeowners in trouble. But despite getting a taxpayer bailout and going back to multibillion-dollar profits, the big banks blocked Washington from taking strong action to rescue average Americans. Instead of using some of the $700 billion taxpayer bailout to help 22 million homeowners stuck with high-interest loans and houses "under water," the banks mounted a foreclosure assembly line against 6.7 million families. One result was that by mid-2011, banks found themselves stuck with a glut of 820,000 unsold and largely unsalable properties.

Some foreclosures were so slipshod that bankruptcy judges objected to what they feared were bogus evictions. In the frenzied finale of the housing boom, so many mortgages had been bought, sold, repackaged, and resold that banks lost track of the documents that proved who actually owned the homes and the right to evict. At Bank of America, GMAC, and JPMorgan Chase, employees confessed to being "robo-signers"—signing thousands of affidavits to oust people from their homes without even reading the documents. Under threat of prosecution from state attorneys general, the banks agreed in February 2012 to set up a $26 billion fund to compensate some homeowners who were unjustly foreclosed and to adjust the principal on some loans of people whose homes were "underwater." But rather than offer immediate relief, the process would take three years and would cover only a fraction of the millions of homeowners who were forced out or put under financial pressure by banks.

"Frankly, They Own the Place!"

Earlier, the banks had fought off the Obama administration's appeal to Congress in early 2009 for legislation to pressure banks into rewriting bubble-era mortgage loans at lower interest rates. Part of the bill passed, the part that left bank participation voluntary. But the mandatory part was eviscerated, with the result that the administration's hopes to provide relief for up to 4 million families was defeated, and only 894,000 were ultimately helped to refinance their homes. Among them was Eliseo Guardardo. The Treasury Department under Timothy Geithner compounded the problem by moving slowly to help beleaguered homeowners, spending only $217 million of the $7.6 billion fund set up to help "the hardest hit."

A stronger measure for middle-class relief that would have given bankruptcy judges the power to modify the terms of home mortgages for creditworthy borrowers was stymied by bank lobbyists. The banks objected that the bankruptcy provision would undermine the sanctity of contracts, even though the 1978 bankruptcy law already gave bankruptcy judges the power to rewrite business contracts with unions and to modify mortgages on vacation homes, farms, and even luxury yachts, but *not primary residences*. Extending those provisions to average homeowners, bank lobbyists told Congress, would be unfair.

The House Democratic majority overrode the bank lobbyists and passed the bankruptcy provision. But in the Senate, the banking lobby succeeded in getting the bankruptcy provision stripped from the bill. Senator Richard Durbin, the measure's main sponsor, was almost speechless with frustration and incredulous at the political clout that banks still had in Congress. "Hard to believe in a time when we're facing a banking crisis that many of the banks created, they are still the most powerful lobby on Capitol Hill," Durbin told a radio interviewer, "and they frankly own the place!"

If middle-class Americans find the political domination of the banks unacceptable, they will have to make housing fairness a more salient political issue through direct citizen action. The experts have come up with ideas for reform and recovery. Both Republican and Democratic economists have offered specific measures to help hard-pressed homeowners refinance their bubble-era mortgages at lower interest rates, arguing that would help generate more consumer demand and accelerate economic recovery. But the banks, joined by Freddie Mac and Fannie Mae, have resisted pressures or regulations that would force them to write down large numbers of old loans—even though most economists say this would give a shot in the arm to the economy.

The nation has paid a steep price. Five years after the housing bubble burst, the backlog of foreclosed homes and the depressed housing market are a huge drag on economic recovery, crippling construction and consumer spending. As investment guru Warren Buffett noted: "We won't come back big time until we've worked off the excess inventory that was created during our binge on housing . . ."

CHAPTER 15

OFFSHORING THE DREAM

THE WAL-MART TRAIL TO CHINA

Wal-Mart and China have a joint venture. Both of them are geared to selling products in the United States at the lowest possible price, . . . and both are determined to dominate the U.S. economy as much as they can in a wide range of industries.

— PROFESSOR GARY GEREFFI,
Duke University

Over the past 8 years, China has cored out our manufacturing base and we have closed over 43,400 factories in the United States and lost almost 8 million manufacturing jobs. Not only did our government ignore all of this, but they intentionally refused to enforce the trade laws. When the Chinese figured that out, they had a field day.

— DAN SLANE,
U.S.-China Economic and Security Review Commission

THE AUCTION WAS IN FULL SWING by the time my camera crew and I arrived to film the shutdown of Rubbermaid's home plant in Wooster, Ohio. It was a cavernous white edifice, nearly half a mile long, massive as an airline hangar. Inside, people looked tiny. For decades, this had been the heart of Rubbermaid, the plant where it fabricated garbage cans, rubbish containers, large totes, and a world of plastic products. Rubbermaid made them so well that in 1994 it was named America's Most Admired Company by *Fortune* magazine.

At its peak, nearly one thousand people worked here. But now the plant was an empty carcass. On this day, June 16, 2004, they were auctioning off all its equipment. A few small knots of men were inspecting the machinery, mentally calculating its age and utility— businessmen, engineers, and contractors, hunting for bargains among the tools and the top-of-the-line plastic injection machines, big as dinosaurs, made by Cincinnati Omicron.

"A lot of this stuff is going cheap," gushed Larry Ptak, an equipment buyer for Beaver Excavating. "We picked up some real good deals."

But if Ptak saw an upside, Harry Frank was crestfallen, watching the plant's dying gasp. He had worked here for thirty-one years. Then one day, Frank and eight hundred others had been summoned by management to the plant floor and told: " 'We're shutting it down.' . . . You could see people crying. . . . What are you supposed to do? You have to make a living. You have to eat, and pay rent, buy a house, a car."

The auctioneer was a sturdy young guy in his thirties from Cleveland named Scott Mihalic, embarrassed to admit that lately his business had been very good, with so many plants in Ohio closing down. I asked him where the equipment buyers were from.

"They're from all over," Mihalic replied. "We've got guys that flew in from all over the fifty states. We've got two guys in from South America, two guys from Italy, a guy from Spain, two guys from over in Japan or China. . . . They bought the one big machine today."

"The Chinese guys bought the big machine?" I asked, to make sure.

"Right. You know, it's an injection machine," he said. "They bought it, I believe, for $850,000."

The Rubbermaid shutdown was a body blow to the town of Wooster. "When you think of Wooster, you think of Rubbermaid," Scott Mihalic explained. "I mean, this is what this town is all about. . . . There's about a thousand jobs that were lost here."

"It was the backbone of this community," Larry Ptak agreed. "You've got a lot of home folks around here, their grandfathers, their fathers, their daughters, and their sons are working here, *were* working here. And you see a lot of houses for sale. You see a lot of people trying to figure out where they're going to make a living. A lot of debt. It's pretty devastating."

The ripple effects were felt for half a dozen years. Town fathers worried about the loss of tax revenues. School bond issues had rough sledding. Stores like Hawkins Supermarket and Restaurant, long a favorite of Rubbermaid workers, went under. The real estate market froze. "You could have bought a home for nothing," Ptak said. "Those houses just sat there for a long time. The bank took a lot of them over."

Doing Business with Wal-Mart: A Double-Edged Sword

A couple of months later, filming in southern China for the PBS *Frontline* documentary "Is Wal-Mart Good for America?," I came across a Rubbermaid plant in a huge industrial sprawl that the Chinese named Plastics City. The Chinese guard wouldn't let me in, but one young woman emerging from the plant told me that it was churning out consumer goods for America—actually, more likely, for Wal-Mart to sell in America.

Wal-Mart had been Rubbermaid's most important customer. Stanley Gault, Rubbermaid's longtime CEO, had been prescient enough to sense in the 1980s that big-box retailers like Wal-Mart were the wave of the future. Gault shifted Rubbermaid from marketing to thousands of retail outlets to focusing mainly on five or six large chains. Wal-Mart was the big prize. It took 25 percent of Rubbermaid's output and gave Rubbermaid products prime shelf space and prominent display. "They can take a new product and make it a success overnight," Gault told me proudly.

They can also cut a supplier to ribbons. Forging a tight relationship with Wal-Mart was a double-edged sword because the heat was always on from Wal-Mart to cut costs—every year, cut product cost by 5 or 10 percent, or else bring out a new and better product for less. Rubbermaid had been skillful at that game until 1996, when it was hit by a skyrocketing 50 percent price hike for resin, a key component for plastic products. Wolfgang Schmitt, Rubbermaid's new CEO, informed the big-box retailers that Rubbermaid would have to raise its prices. Target and Kmart agreed, but Wal-Mart said no.

A Clash of Cultures

It was a clash of corporate cultures and a microcosm of the power shift and changing strategies in U.S. business that would have a devastating impact on some of the best middle-class jobs in U.S. industry.

Rubbermaid was intent on maintaining product quality, afraid that if it tried to save money by skimping on its plastics formula, its products would crack or crinkle. Wal-Mart's focus was single-minded—price. Frictions had already developed over Wal-Mart's pressures on Rubbermaid to shift some Rubbermaid operations to China.

In a last desperate effort, Wolfgang Schmitt flew to Wal-Mart headquarters in Bentonville, Arkansas, to meet with Bill Fields, then head of Wal-Mart stores. Schmitt made Rubbermaid's case for price increases to offset higher raw material costs. But according to Carol Troyer, president of Rubbermaid's Office Products Division, the session was ugly. Fields, she said, had told Schmitt: "We're big enough that we can tell you that we're not gonna take your price increase. We *don't care* what it's gonna do to Rubbermaid. We don't care what kind of price increases you've had in your raw materials. We're just not gonna take it."

"They were very public in those days . . . about saying, 'One of the advantages we as big-box retailers have is we can put the hammer to the manufacturers and we can give American consumers lower prices,' " Schmitt recalled.

Fields, who had retired, never returned my calls. But an insider told me that Schmitt and Fields actually stood nose to nose, jabbing fingers into each other's chests. Even though Fields, at six feet six, towered over Schmitt, who was five feet ten, Schmitt could not contain his frustration. "You don't *understand*," he blurted out. But before he could finish, Fields thundered: "No, *you* don't understand!"

That confrontation caused irreparable damage to Rubbermaid. Wal-Mart punished Rubbermaid by cutting back its purchases and giving a competitor, Sterilite, choice shelf space. "They dropped a number of our products for a couple of years," Carol Troyer reported. "That impacts the company tremendously. To me, it was one of the first signs of the decline of Rubbermaid."

Rubbermaid's management scrambled for three more years, and then in 1999 it sold out to Newell, a major competitor. The plant closing in Wooster reflected cutbacks by Newell Rubbermaid, which, bowing to Wal-Mart, shut down U.S. plants and opened some in China.

The Power Shift Inside Our Economy

Wal-Mart's ability to outgun Rubbermaid illustrates the pivotal shift of power in American business in the 1980s and '90s. That shift now shapes supply lines that reach worldwide, especially from China to America. It reflects the globalized economy that has disrupted old ways and cost America the loss of an estimated 3.5 million jobs.

Before the rise of big-box retailers—specifically Wal-Mart— manufacturers were the kings of the hill. They decided what to produce and what retailers would offer consumers. Wal-Mart changed all that. Not right away. It took time for Wal-Mart to build muscle. But Sam Walton and Wal-Mart were aggressive and their ascent was steep. Wal-Mart grew from 38 stores in 1970, to 276 in 1980, to 1,400 by 1990. In 1991, less than three decades after Walton opened his first discount store, Wal-Mart overtook Sears and Kmart to become the nation's biggest retailer. By 2011, it was a $260 billion-a-year behemoth, with 140 million customers shopping weekly in its 3,800 American stores.

With 1.2 million employees, Wal-Mart has become America's largest employer, with power and influence over the whole economy. Consumers reap cost savings every time they push a shopping cart out of the checkout line. During the 1990s and early 2000s, economists credited Wal-Mart's tightfisted low-price strategy with not only helping millions of American families on low budgets, but also helping to hold down the nation's overall rate of inflation. By one Wal-Mart-friendly estimate, the retail giant cut America's overall inflation from 1995 to 2006 by about 3 percent, or roughly 0.15 percent a year, impressive for a single company.

The Impact of the Wal-Mart Model

Wal-Mart's business model became the template for companies all across the corporate landscape. "In the nineteenth century, it was the Pennsylvania Railroad which called itself 'the standard of the world,'" recalled economic historian Nelson Lichtenstein. "Early twentieth century, it might have been U.S. Steel. General Motors, of course, in the mid–twentieth century. But clearly, Wal-Mart . . . today is setting a new standard that other firms have to follow. . . . It's setting standards for the nation as a whole."

The Wal-Mart model was built on the simple formula that "Mr. Sam," as Sam Walton was widely known, trademarked in his early days: Buy cheap, sell for less, and make your profit on high volume and fast turnover. Sounds simple, but it required a revolution in marketing and distribution. Wal-Mart had to find out what products to stock in its stores. It had to anticipate the demands of tens of millions of shoppers daily, in different parts of the country where tastes differ—straight-leg jeans in the North, flared jeans in the Sun Belt; loose-fitting clothes for old folks in Florida and Arizona, tight-fitting for young folks near college towns; polka-dotted blouses here, striped over there.

Knowledge Is Power

The magic key to predicting the market was—the bar code. As Linda Dillman, Wal-Mart's chief information officer, showed me, flashing a handheld "Telxon" gadget at the bar codes of several items: "It tells me the sales price of the item, how many I currently have. It knows what the history looks like and what we think it will do, going forward." With supercomputers, Wal-Mart was able at the end of each shopping day to tote up sales and inventory, store by store, region by region, and nationwide, so that it could project future sales and order exactly the right resupplies. By now, the system is everywhere, but in the 1980s, Wal-Mart pioneered it and gained a competitive advantage.

In marketing, as in war or science, knowledge is power. The information that Wal-Mart teased out of bar codes enabled its buyers in Arkansas to tell its suppliers—companies like Rubbermaid, Procter & Gamble, Black & Decker, Huffy bicycles—what products it needed, how many, and what models, colors, and sizes, long before these companies heard from their own salespeople.

Jon Lehman, who managed six different Wal-Mart stores during seventeen years at Wal-Mart, described the blizzard of detail Wal-Mart got from the bar code, even on a simple item like pet food. "A can of 9Lives cat food has a bar code, and every flavor—chicken, liver, beef—they all have different bar codes," Lehman explained. "And as the item is scanned through the front checkout, the item is tracked, and you're able to determine what flavor's sellin', how much you're makin' on that item . . . and an order is automatically generated that evening at midnight and it's sittin' back on the shelf the next night or the following night. . . . It's just really incredible."

"Wal-Mart, as an efficiency machine, has just done better than any other U.S. retailer—or, perhaps, any other U.S. company in history," observed Duke University professor Gary Gereffi, who studies global supply chains. "They were more single-minded in terms of global cost cutting and internal efficiency than any other U.S. retailer. And that helps us understand how and why they were able to pass companies like Kmart and Sears that were the early leaders in U.S. retailing and offshore sourcing."

The Shift from "Push" to "Pull"

With its blinding informational efficiency, Wal-Mart became a world leader in logistics, number one in the science of just-in-time supply from a global network of suppliers. And it used its unprecedented informational power to turn the system of production upside down. With other mass retail chains such as Target and Kmart, Wal-Mart generated a revolution—a shift from "push production" to "pull production."

"The push system involved manufacturers deciding what they're going to produce and then trying to get retailers to buy it and sell it for them," explained Edna Bonacich, a marketing sociologist with the University of California at Riverside. "The pull system involves retailers deciding what is being sold, collecting information on what is being sold, and then telling manufacturers what to produce and when to produce it, based on what is actually being sold. . . . There has been a power shift from manufacturers to retailers."

In the new commercial solar system, Wal-Mart is the sun, holding suppliers in its orbit. Size and scale have given Wal-Mart gravitational magnetism. Its headquarters is located in rural northeast Arkansas, in Bentonville, but its pull is so powerful that hundreds of its suppliers have set up a village of satellite sales offices in several storefront malls, just to cater to Wal-Mart. They call it "Vendorville." Mighty Fortune 500 companies such as Procter & Gamble and Disney gather like vassals to pay tribute to the inner kingdom of Wal-Mart, the retail Brahmins of Bentonville.

When their moment comes, vendors are led one by one into tight little cubicles for tough bargaining with Wal-Mart buyers. Wal-Mart officials describe these sessions as normal business give-and-take, ignoring the vast power disparity between a $260 billion-a-year colossus like Wal-Mart and small producers who are dependent on Wal-Mart for survival. Wal-Mart's incentive bonuses richly reward buyers for arm-twisting every last cent out of suppliers, according to former Rubbermaid CEO Wolfgang Schmitt. "In a large organization," Schmitt said, "you're going to have buyers who overdrive that part and will step over the line."

Former Wal-Mart managers concede that it played hardball. "It's very one-sided," former Wal-Mart store manager Jon Lehman told me. "I've been in these little cubicles. . . . The manufacturer walks in . . . and the buyer says, '. . . We want you to sell it to us for 5 percent . . . lower this year than you did last year.' . . . They know every fact and figure that these manufacturers have. They know their costs. They know their business practices—everything. So, what's a manufacturer left to do? They sit naked in front of Wal-Mart. Wal-Mart calls the shots: 'If you want to do business with us, if you want to *stay* in business, then you're going to do it our way.' It's all about driving down the cost of goods."

The "Opening Price Point"

The key to Wal-Mart's marketing strategy—and one big reason that its supply lines from China have become so all-important—is what Wal-Mart calls its "opening price point." That is the rock-bottom price that Wal-Mart showcases on each aisle, like the $29.97 microwave oven, the $19.14 saucepan, or the trick-or-treat jack-o'-lanterns for 78 cents. Every line of goods has an opening price point—the bait to lure customers to that line of goods.

"It's the heart of Wal-Mart's pricing strategy. Wal-Mart puts [a] tremendous amount of planning, organization, and thinking into what their opening price points are going to be, based on last year's sales, based on customer requests . . . ," Jon Lehman explained. "[It's] to get you in. You look at that, and you think, 'Wow! What a great price!'. . . Then they've got you, because you walk about ten more feet, and you see the item you really want in that same category. Then you buy that item. But it's not going to be, probably, the lowest price in town. . . . Once you walk past that opening price point, they've got you, because you've already formed the perception that everything in that department is the lowest price in town."

"And maybe it's not?" I queried.

"No, it's not— No." Lehman flashed a knowing smile. "I can tell you from experience, *it's not.*"

"If You Want to Play, Go to China"

To hit those all-important opening price points, Wal-Mart reached increasingly for suppliers in Asia and especially China, where costs were practically subterranean. Soon, Wal-Mart was pressuring American suppliers to move production to China. In one meeting in Bentonville, I was told, a Wal-Mart vice president bluntly advised a group of two hundred suppliers that if they wanted a good chunk of Wal-Mart business, especially at the opening price point, they had to shift at least 25 percent of their productive capacity to China.

"Their message to us is, 'There's a broad market out there. If you want to focus on the lowest-cost part of the market, it's obvious that you can't do that in the United States,' " Bill Nichol, CEO of Kentucky Derby Hosiery, reported to me.

"So, if you want to play in that 25 percent of the Wal-Mart market, you've got to be in a very low-cost place—China or someplace like China?" I asked.

"That's correct," Nichol replied. "But China, practically speaking, is *it.*"

To Kentucky Derby Hosiery, Wal-Mart was so vital a customer that Bill Nichol felt he had no choice. "We will open those facilities and buy product or make product, or both, in China as soon as possible," he told me.

Wal-Mart's "Move offshore or die" message cropped up in my conversations with other suppliers, but they shied away from being quoted out of fear of angering Wal-Mart. But back in Circleville, Ohio, people said point-blank that Wal-Mart's guillotine had killed the RCA-Thomson television tube plant where Pam Scholl and Mike Hughes had worked. The plant had been highly profitable through the 1990s, former plant manager Ray Strutz said. They were supplying not only RCA-Thomson television plants in Arkansas and Mexico, but also Sanyo, the big Japanese electronic firm, which was selling low-end television sets to Wal-Mart.

In 2003, the Thomson-RCA plant began to feel price competition on TV sets with low-cost Chinese components. "They were selling at prices that most people couldn't even manufacture out[side] of the U.S.," Strutz told me. That put a crunch on the Thomson plant, according to Roy Wunsch, the former mayor of Circleville. Wunsch said he was told that Sanyo, under pressure from Wal-Mart, demanded drastic cost cuts from Thomson.

"Wal-Mart's going to say, 'If you want our space, you're going to have to match our price or figure something else to do,' " Strutz confirmed. "And so it forces a supplier like Sanyo to go back upstream . . . in our case, to the glass manufacturer—to look for price concessions." But if Sanyo can't get a price cut from Thomson-RCA, what happens? I asked. Ruefully, Strutz replied: "Then they go to China."

That's exactly what happened. The Thomson plant, like Rubbermaid in its showdown with Wal-Mart, could not swallow the cost cutting that Wal-Mart was demanding through Sanyo. So Thomson lost its big Sanyo contract in 2003, and eighteen months later, the Thomson plant shut down. Eight hundred workers lost their jobs, and the work all wound up in China.

Wal-Mart Sets Up Shop
in Shenzhen, South China's "Miracle City"

China was a gold mine for Wal-Mart. Like other U.S. multinationals, it set up shop in China big-time, with headquarters in Shenzhen, the miracle city that embodies China's breathtaking explosion of economic growth since 1978. For centuries, Shenzhen had been a sleepy little fishing village just across Kowloon Bay from Hong Kong. Then in 1978, Chinese leader Deng Xiaoping proclaimed a new strategy of economic reform. He blessed private farming, free markets, and an "open door" to world trade. He named Shenzhen a customs-free zone for trade—a springboard for China's export strategy to the West. Overnight, Shenzhen shot up. Its economy grew at the rate of 50 percent a year.

When I first saw Shenzhen in 1996, it was already a raw city of half a million or more, a magnet for bright, adventurous young people from all over China. It exuded the coarse, cocky self-confidence of gold rush territory. It looked like a naked construction site—cranes dominating the skyline, the skeletons of buildings rising from the mud, concrete pylons and idled machinery littered everywhere, tiny figures of construction workers climbing like flies on the honeycombs of future skyscrapers. The mood was electric and the atmosphere permissive, epitomized by Deng's famous dictum "Black cat, white cat—it's a good cat if it catches mice." Translation: It doesn't matter whether the Chinese economy is Communist or capitalist, as long as it works.

Eight years later, in 2004, when I got back to Shenzhen, it had been transformed into a modern-looking city of *seven million people.* Along boulevards now neatly lined with low trees and hedges were ten- and twelve-story glass office buildings and towering twenty-five-story apartment houses. It was still a city of young people, now nicely dressed; not a single Mao suit or old padded peasant outfit in sight. Cellphones were ubiquitous. Unhappily, I didn't see the Chinese shopping for American products. Electronic goods were being hawked everywhere—laptops, boom boxes, and TV sets, almost all Chinese made. Even in the local Wal-Mart, the goods were overwhelmingly Chinese.

In Shenzhen, down a side street behind one of the thirty-five supercenter stores that Wal-Mart had opened in China, I found the epicenter of Wal-Mart's China operations. What Wal-Mart calls its "global procurement center" opened in 2002. Two years later, more than five hundred people were working there. Their mission was to keep the import pipeline to America full. But Wal-Mart kept a low profile with the U.S. media; its deep dependence on China was at odds with its "Buy America" ad campaigns. Wal-Mart/Shenzhen didn't talk to American correspondents. So I found a scholar, Gary Gereffi, a marketing sociologist from Duke University, who had talked to Wal-Mart's Shenzhen managers.

What Wal-Mart told Gereffi was that China accounted for 80 percent of Wal-Mart's six thousand suppliers worldwide. "China is the largest exporter to the U.S. economy in virtually all consumer goods categories," Gereffi explained. "Wal-Mart is the largest retailer in the U.S. economy in virtually all consumer goods categories."

"It sounds like a commercial marriage made in heaven," I observed.

"Wal-Mart and China have a joint venture. Both of them are geared to selling products in the United States at the lowest possible price, . . . and both are determined to dominate the U.S. economy as much as they can in a wide range of industries," Gereffi replied.

He explained how Wal-Mart coaches Chinese producers how to capture the American consumer market. "Wal-Mart gives Chinese suppliers the specifications for Wal-Mart products and they teach those suppliers how to meet those specifications. They have to do with price. They have to do with quality. They have to do with delivery schedule," Gereffi said. "So Chinese suppliers learn how to export to the U.S. market through large retailers like Wal-Mart."

The Wal-Mart Cost Squeeze

With Chinese suppliers, Wal-Mart can be even more brutal than with American companies. So said Kenneth Chan, an experienced Hong Kong entrepreneur in his early forties who had sold many low-cost items to Wal-Mart and other big-box U.S. retailers. "Wal-Mart is—they are very shrewd people. They know that they have the volume orders behind them and they can go into a factory and almost demand, 'These are my list of demands. This is what I need,' " Chan reported. "There's always going to be somebody that will say, 'Okay, I will take this order at whatever cost and I'll find a way to do it,' whether it's using inferior materials or just finding a way to cut corners."

Chan described the Wal-Mart squeeze. Its buyers would call three or four vendors into a bargaining booth and pit them against one another. "They just put the product in front of you and ask everybody to bid a cost on the product—it's very high pressure," Chan said. "The things that I was involved in were inexpensive, less than a dollar."

"So they're pounding you for a few pennies?" I asked.

"Yeah, they're pounding, in a lot of cases, for *just one penny*," he replied.

Wal-Mart: Huge Profits on Chinese Imports

At the other end of the pipeline, in America, former store manager Jon Lehman saw the payoff for Wal-Mart in 1993, when the high command in Bentonville turned on the spigot of Chinese imports. Sam Walton had died a year earlier and the U.S. economy was slowing. Wal-Mart's sales were sluggish and the company's stock price fell sharply. In a panic, Wal-Mart's new management cranked up the flow of cheap imports to recover.

"I saw this as a store manager, a *giant* influx of imported merchandise . . . ," Lehman recalled. "The stores were *inundated* with inventory—*inundated*. I mean, we had so much of this cheap crap floatin' around the store, we didn't know what to do with it." Overwhelmed, Lehman called a vice president at headquarters to ask what was going on. "He said, 'Jon, we've got to bring our profit in for the quarter, for the month, for the year. You know our stock has been declining. You do understand, Jon, that these imports have a high margin and they're going to help your profit and loss statement. They're going to help the company's profit-and-loss statement.' "

In fact, the flood of Chinese imports delivered exactly the kick start that the top brass wanted. The impact was dramatic. "The margins on the merchandise that were coming in from—the Wal-Mart import items—were *incredible* . . . ," Lehman told me. "Like 60 percent, 70 percent, 80 percent, you know—*incredible*!"

"Compared with what from American-made items?" I asked.

"Well, compare that to an electric razor that you might be makin' 20 percent on, 18 percent on," he said.

"We understand that Wal-Mart is delivering us lower prices," I said. "But you're saying not just lower prices, but much bigger profits for Wal-Mart?"

"Well, absolutely, yeah, . . ." Lehman asserted. "Wal-Mart pays billions—not millions, but billions of dollars to make you believe that as a consumer. That's all you see on television: 'Low prices every day.' That is what Wal-Mart wants you to believe. . . . But what's really goin' on is Wal-Mart's finding a cheaper way to get it, and Wal-Mart's getting' rich. They're makin' tons of profit."

Shenzhen Port: From Zero to Number Four in the World

The sheer volume of goods streaming out of China to America through Shenzhen Port is staggering. A steady torrent of flatbed trucks converges seven days a week on Shenzhen Port, hauling containerized shipments from a beehive of factories all over the Pearl

River Valley of South China. The port is the funnel for a colossal profusion of plastics, footwear, appliances, jeans, bicycles, lawn mowers, lamps, cellphones, TV sets, laptops—roughly 80 percent of the 120,000 items carried in a typical Wal-Mart superstore.

At Shenzhen Port, I saw a veritable city of containers stacked ten and twelve stories high, sprawling over several square miles of territory, waiting to be loaded onto fleets of container ships bound for America's West Coast ports. Shenzhen Port hummed with activity. As flatbed trucks raced up to dockside, tall, computerized cranes leaned down like giant mechanical giraffes to pluck up ten-ton containers and then set them down neatly on board the ship. The tempo was swift and steady—up, down, up, down, up, down.

Shenzhen was a natural deep-water port, but the rush of its development was astounding. In 1994, the modern port did not exist; it was nothing but a barren rocky outcrop. Ten years later, in 2004, the modern Port of Shenzhen was already the world's fourth busiest, busier than Shanghai, Rotterdam, Hamburg, and Singapore and challenging Hong Kong as number three. It was handling nearly eleven million containers a year, more cargo than America's two big West Coast ports—Los Angeles and Long Beach, California—combined. Two-thirds of its traffic was headed for America. No one spends on Chinese goods like American consumers. Western Europeans are less profligate.

Shenzhen Port officials boasted that Wal-Mart is one of their top customers. "Wal-Mart sources a huge amount of products from China," Kenneth Tse, general manager of the export terminal, told me. "We have our contacts in Bentonville. We show them how market-oriented we are. They have to satisfy themselves that China has the infrastructure that they need and that their shipments will flow smoothly. They do their comparative shopping, and I can see now that South China has become the preferred manufacturing base for them."

"Wal-Mart is providing a gateway into the American economy for overseas suppliers in China and elsewhere—and it's doing it on a scale that is unprecedented," Professor Gereffi confirmed.

Aware of growing anger among Americans about job loss to China, Wal-Mart has played down the scale of its China trade. As early as 2004, I was told, Wal-Mart's direct imports were more than $30 billion, plus tens of billions more imported for Wal-Mart by its U.S. suppliers, and those imports were rising sharply. "Next year [the figure] will be higher, and the year after that, it's likely to be higher as well," Wal-Mart vice president Ray Bracy told me.

At Long Beach: The Lopsided Trade

In California, at the Port of Long Beach, I got a firsthand look at our lopsided trade with China—the opposite of what our business and political leaders had promised. On a water tour, Yvonne Smith, the port's communications director, pointed out ships from China, Japan, and other nations. "But they're all carrying Chinese cargo," she advised. "China is where it's being manufactured."

"So what are they shipping in and what are we shipping back?" I asked.

"Well, we're bringing in consumer products. We're bringing in about $36 billion worth of machinery, toys, clothing, footwear—$36 billion from China comes through Long Beach alone," Smith said.

"And what are we shipping back?" I asked.

"We're shipping out about $3 billion worth of raw materials," she said. "We export cotton, we bring in clothing. We export hides, we bring in shoes. We export scrap metal, we bring back machinery."

"So, they're doing all the . . . ," I stammered. "We're like a third world country."

Her litany went on: "We're exporting waste paper, we bring back cardboard boxes with products inside them."

Even more important were cargoes that Yvonne Smith didn't mention—high-tech equipment, industrial machinery, advanced telecom devices, Internet backbone components, high-quality lasers used in fiber-optic cable systems.

I stumbled into a discovery when I asked Smith about the computerized cranes that were unloading the cargoes for the Port of Long Beach. Proudly, Smith told me that these were leading-edge technology. Long Beach had sixty of them, costing $6.5 million apiece. They used to be made in Germany; now, mostly in Shanghai.

The U.S.-China Trade Deficit: $2 Trillion

Wal-Mart may have been the prime mover in pushing the China trade and driving American jobs to China, but almost everyone was in the game: Target, Costco, Best Buy, an army of mass retail chains, plus big manufacturers such as Boeing, which has contracted with the Chinese and Japanese to make parts for the new 787 Dreamliner jet, as well as other U.S. multinationals such as Apple with its iPhones and iPads made in China or Hewlett-Packard and Cisco importing components for laptops, printers, cellphones, and Internet switching gear.

Apple's longtime CEO, Steve Jobs, won praise for creating jobs in America from Republican leaders like Indiana governor Mitch Daniels, but in fact, Apple under Steve Jobs had only forty-three thousand employees in the United States, while it indirectly employed seven hundred thousand at its overseas suppliers, mainly in China. As *The New York Times* reported, Apple overlooked sweatshop conditions and fatal explosions at supplier plants in China, not just because Chinese labor was cheap, but because state-subsidized Chinese suppliers jumped to meet Apple's tight deadlines by rousting workers out of bed at midnight and reportedly working them fifteen hours a day. With a competitive advantage from these illegal labor practices, confirmed by an outside audit inspection, Foxcomm, Apple's biggest supplier in China of iPads and iPhones could undercut and beat out American rivals. "The speed and flexibility is breathtaking," said one Apple executive. "There's no American plant that can match that."

Many other American firms found the pull of China's low-cost, moderately skilled workforce and its state-supported industrial clusters irresistible. With overseas production based in China shipping goods home to American consumers, U.S. multinationals were contributing to America's record $273 billion trade deficit with China, triple the level a decade earlier. From 2001 to 2010, right after Washington approved free trade with China, the red ink was overwhelming. We Americans *bought $1.928 trillion more* in goods from China than we sold to China.

As a result, China has become not only America's main supplier, but America's main banker, the largest holder of U.S. debt, with financial reserves topping $3.2 trillion, giving it enough financial leverage to wreak havoc with the American economy if it ever chose to sell off a large slice of its U.S. Treasury holdings.

This is the opposite of what America's business and political leaders promised.

The Hyped Sell on China Trade

When the House passed the new free trade agreement with China in May 2000, President Clinton proclaimed that it would "open China's markets to American products made on American soil—everything from corn to chemicals to computers." In September, as the Senate was voting, George W. Bush, then the Republican presidential nominee, supported the trade deal and, through his spokesman, declared that it would "open markets to American products and help export American values, especially freedom and entrepreneurship." Charlene Barshefsky, the U.S. Trade Representative, rhapsodized about the export potential for the United States "across all sectors and all fields of a magnitude unprecedented in the modern era."

Business eagerly pushed for the new permanent trade agreement with China, replacing the annual agreements that were subject to bargaining and delays. The Business Roundtable, drumming up congressional votes, ran an ad envisioning massive export gains. "With 1.3 billion people, China is the world's largest marketplace," the Roundtable ad asserted. "A new trade agreement opens China's market to our goods and services."

General Motors predicted it would sell $2 billion in exports to

China within five years. Telecom companies saw a potential bonanza. Caterpillar and Deere forecast strong exports of farm tractors and combines. Drug companies were optimistic. "The potential is explosive," declared Mark Grayson, speaking for the pharmaceutical industry trade group. Dave McCurdy, president of the Electronics Industries Alliance, gushed over new sales on the horizon: "From semiconductors to circuit boards, from PC's to cellphones, China is simply the most dynamic international market for U.S. high-tech exports."

In hindsight, the bravado of American industrial and political leaders sounds like a pipe dream that failed to note that in 2000, the U.S. trade deficit with China was already $83 billion. Not everyone was so hopeful. Organized labor opposed the trade pact, warning of massive job losses at home as U.S. firms moved plants to China in the chase for cheap labor. Smaller and midsized U.S. manufacturing firms feared that big multinationals were angling for ways to cut costs and squash smaller domestic competitors by producing cheap goods in China for export back to America.

"We were sold a bill of goods," asserts Alan Tonelson of the U.S. Business and Industry Council, a trade group of two thousand smaller manufacturers. "We thought that expanding trade with countries like China, using multinational companies as the main traders, would tremendously increase U.S. exports to this huge, rapidly growing market. But that assumed that the multinationals largely saw China as an end-use customer. In fact, if you check their websites, it's clear that they saw China as a production and export platform. I think the multinationals did this quite knowingly. They understood exactly what China offered. They looked at China like a super-Mexico."

In fact, Tonelson contended, instead of generating net American exports, America's biggest corporations have been adding to the U.S. trade deficits by importing more than they export. "Despite their export mantra," Tonelson observed, "U.S. multinationals are now running big and steadily growing trade deficits with the world overall and with their favorite offshoring sites in particular." In 2008, for example, Tonelson calculated the trade deficit of U.S. multinationals at $172 billion.

"The big argument is that trade deficits don't matter," Tonelson said, parroting the rationale of free trade economists. "Who cares? The economy is going strong. That was the main argument through mid-2007. Then when the economy got into deep trouble, it became clear to many politicians and economists that trade deficits hurt growth. So they really matter. In fact, they mattered all along, but throughout the 1990s and into the first decade of this century, their growth-destroying effects were masked by a series of bubbles—the tech and stock bubble of the late 1990s and the real estate and credit bubble of late in this last decade. But now, we can no longer rely on real estate or financial gimmickry for growth. So the losses from trade are really holding us back."

The Cost of U.S.-China Trade: 3.5 Million Jobs

Job loss is where ordinary Americans have felt the crunch. According to Robert Scott, an economist with the Economic Policy Institute, a progressive Washington think tank, America lost 2.6 million jobs to China from 2001 to 2010, the decade following the free trade agreement with China, and close to another 1 million in the 1990s. Scott compiles his estimates the same way the government and business calculate the job gains from U.S. exports. In toto, he says, in the last twenty years, 3.5 million American jobs have been wiped out by offshoring work and by Chinese imports.

Economists differ over those figures. Some trade specialists, including Mike Wessel, a member of the bipartisan U.S.-China Economic and Security Review Commission, think Scott has understated the job losses, because Scott counts only those jobs that were actually destroyed and not jobs forgone by U.S. corporations, which might have expanded their U.S. operations but for China.

Orthodox market fundamentalists, such as Alan Greenspan and free trade thinkers such as Columbia University economics professor Jagdish Bhagwati, dispute the notion that trade with China—or trade anywhere—has caused job losses in the United States. Their view is that trade is a win-win for every country. Citing the theory of competitive advantage put forth by early-nineteenth-century British economist David Ricardo, orthodox free trade economists argue that each country shifts out of production where it is inefficient and gravitates to sectors where it is more efficient; old, outworn jobs are replaced by new and better jobs.

Bhagwati, author of *In Defense of Globalization,* contends that "putting these jobs overseas is, in economic terms, no different than importing labor-intensive textiles and other goods. . . . The fact is, when jobs disappear in America it is usually because technical change has destroyed them, not because they have gone anywhere." Gregory Mankiw, who headed President George W. Bush's Council of Economic Advisers, adds that whatever "dislocations" are caused by "outsourcing" of U.S. production in the short run, trade delivers long-run gains in new high-tech jobs. Trade deficits don't matter, according to Brink Lindsey, vice president and senior economist at the Cato Institute, a libertarian research institute in Washington, because the gains of the new winners in America more than offset the losses of those thrown out of work by trade.

"I think that trade policy or trade flows, one way or another, don't have an effect on overall employment numbers," Lindsey asserted. "They affect the kinds of jobs we have. And so some number of jobs have definitely been eliminated because of Chinese competition. Elsewhere in the economy, other jobs have been created because of Chinese competition. . . . The net effect, most economists think, is a wash. . . ."

Others disagree. Economic revisionists like Clyde Prestowitz, the Reagan administration's chief trade negotiator for Asia, dispute the old orthodox argument, contending that it denies reality and defies common sense. "For some time now our 'best and brightest' have been invoking false doctrines that are systematically undermining American prosperity," Prestowitz wrote. "Leading among these is the economic orthodoxy of market fundamentalism, simplistic pure free trade. . . ."

Former IBM vice president Ralph Gomory contended, in testimony to Congress, that Ricardo's nearly two-hundred-year-old theory does not match modern conditions. What America has lost to China, Gomory asserted, is not just a shift in production, but a shift in productivity, which puts the United States on the defensive. "When the U.S. trades semiconductors for Asian T-shirts, for example, that is trade in the narrow sense. And the conclusion of the most basic economic theories is that this exchange clearly benefits both countries," Gomory testified. "But when U.S. companies build semiconductor plants and R&D facilities in Asia rather than in the U.S., then that is a shift in productive capability, and neither economic theory nor common sense asserts that shift is automatically good for the U.S. even in the long run."

The longtime dean of American economists, Paul Samuelson, a Nobel laureate from MIT, was so irked by orthodox economists that at eighty-nine he waded into the debate and accused the free market economists of purveying a "polemical untruth" about America reaping net benefits from trade.

"There are no such neat *net* benefits, but rather there are now new, net harmful U.S. terms of trade," Samuelson asserted. Sometimes, he said, trade does benefit both sides. But at other times, he said, America can suffer *"permanent* hurt" when a country like China improves its productivity. He challenged the contention that the balance works in America's favor. "It is dead wrong about *necessary* surplus of winnings over losings—as I proved in my 'Little Nobel Lecture of 1972,' " Samuelson declared. " And although he agreed with Bhagwati that technology accounts for some of America's wage losses, he contended that trade exacts a toll in driving down real wages. Mainstream trade economists, he declared, were ignoring the "drastic change" in incomes between the rich, who are further enriched by free trade, and average Americans, whose "real wage has been lowered" by trade.

That issue—the different winners and losers from trade—is central to Larry Mishel, president of the Economic Policy Institute. "Theoretically, the gains from trade offset the losses from trade," Mishel said. "But nothing says there were more winners than losers, and . . . that for the bottom three-fourths of America that they are net gainers. In fact, I believe that most people have been losers from trade."

How People Fared at the Grass Roots

Since free trade economists contend that people thrown out of work by trade eventually bounce back and get even better jobs, I decided to check that out. Six years after Rubbermaid shut down its plant in Wooster, Ohio, I went back to find people I had first met in 2004. Most were significantly worse off than before.

Two of the lucky ones were Ron Wright and Mike Kendall. Each had piled up more than thirty years of seniority at Rubbermaid by 2004, and their seniority qualified them for the small workforce that Rubbermaid retained to operate a small distribution center in Wooster. Initially, their pay was cut sharply, but gradually they have inched it back up. Now in their sixties, they are on track for a reasonable retirement.

But others in their age group with less seniority were forced into premature retirement in their midfifties. They have wound up with far less than if Rubbermaid had kept operating.

Jump down half a generation to people in their midforties, and the pain is palpable. The people in the worst shape are almost impossible to find. They're long gone, seeking work somewhere else. I heard their stories second- or thirdhand. Those whom I found were struggling.

Sylvian Greene, who had put in eighteen years at Rubbermaid, said he and his wife, Lois, could not have survived without charity and public assistance. Together they had made about $80,000 a year at Rubbermaid; since then, even with federal assistance, their income has been cut roughly in half. At first, Greene found work in a fertilizer plant and his wife as a home nurse. But in her first week, Lois severely injured her back lifting a patient and has not been able to work since. Two years later, Sylvian lost his fertilizer job. For three years he had little work, and the couple chewed through their Rubbermaid severance pay and savings until they were broke.

"It is hard—really hard," Greene admitted stoically. "Faith Harvest Church, they brought us groceries, paid our electric. The People to People ministry, they would pay our bills, give us money. It was nothing to go to the mailbox and there would be a $50 bill in there. My mom helped with house payments." But eventually they fell behind and the bank foreclosed. Only the intervention of an understanding local judge gave them time to sell the house and get cash to pay off the mortgage and buy a cheap mobile home. By then Greene had been diagnosed with congestive heart failure, eventually qualifying for federal disability insurance. Otherwise, the Greenes survived on charity, welfare, and food stamps.

Don and Ginny Lingle were in their midthirties when the plant closed. Full of optimism and energy, they decided to go into business for themselves. Ginny, who had worked in accounting, set up shop doing budgets and tax returns for small businesses. Don, who had done carpentry and maintenance at Rubbermaid, launched a contracting business. Ginny's clients have been pretty steady. Don's contracting has faced rougher sledding. People are slow to decide on projects—slower still in a tight economy. Fortunately, while at Rubbermaid, the couple had paid off the mortgage on a contemporary home. But with their income now uncertain, their big worries are the rising cost of health insurance and their lack of retirement savings. "It's the unpredictability that gets to you," Don admitted. "When you own your own business, you can't tell what your work is going to be like. It fluctuates with the economy. There's no security now."

Pam Constantino, a lively bundle of energy in her late forties, was a product processor at Rubbermaid. For her, as a single parent, the plant's closing hit like a tornado. "After I lost my Rubbermaid job, I couldn't make my house payments and my utilities," she said. "So I had two people move in with me, my sister and a good friend—for three years." Then Constantino got a temporary job at a nursing home and more recently at the Wayne County Kidney Center, making $10 an hour, 40 percent below her Rubbermaid pay, with slim benefits. "I am frugal," she said. "I know how to go without, but I couldn't live from paycheck to paycheck. I had to have roommates. Thank God I didn't have a car payment. I had to borrow money for gas sometimes. "

The common thread in these and other stories that I heard from computer programmers in Silicon Valley or information technology workers in New Jersey is that even people who find new work come out behind, with lower pay and fewer benefits. That pattern is confirmed by a nationwide study done by the U.S. Bureau of Labor Statistics. In January 2010, only half (49 percent) of those thrown out of work in the three previous years had found a new job. The other 51 percent were still looking or had given up. Among the fortunate half, most were making less than before; more than one-third were down more than 20 percent. In short, job loss from global trade means a chronic drop in income and economic security.

How Offshoring Widens the Economic Divide

While technology and automation are certainly destroying some out-of-date jobs, economists increasingly see globalization as the heart of the problem. The figures show a stark shift from the 1990s to the 2000s. In the 1990s, American companies were hiring both at home and abroad. In the zero decade (2000s), the U.S. Commerce Department reports that major American multinational corporations added 2.4 million employees to their overseas workforces while cutting 2.9 million workers in America.

Whether U.S. multinationals are chasing cheap labor or chasing customers, as business leaders contend, offshoring has sharpened America's economic divide, according to Nobel Prize–winning economist Michael Spence of New York University. By his analysis, the United States has had two economies with very different track records since 1990. One is what Spence terms "the nontradable sector," fields that do not face global trade competition, such as health care, retail, and public service. The other is "the tradable sector," such as autos, electronics, and other manufacturing, all of which face foreign trade competition.

From 1990 to 2008, Spence and a colleague found, virtually all (97.7 percent) of U.S. job growth came in the nontradable sector, mainly health care and government jobs, where the growth outlook now is poor. In the tradable sector, they found big job losses, lower pay and insecurity, and a widening income gap between the vulnerable U.S. middle class and a small fraction of high-income jobs in management, consulting, and finance.

"You could say, as many do, that shipping jobs overseas is no big deal because the high-value work—and much of the profits—remain in the U.S.," writes former Intel CEO Andy Grove. "That may well be so. But what kind of a society are we going to have if it consists of highly paid people doing high-value-added work—and masses of unemployed?"

Grove's answer, revealing for an American CEO, is that offshoring U.S. jobs is far too important an issue for our nation to be left to our multinational companies and their CEOs. Grove argues that it will take a new national strategy and a broad commitment in U.S. industry to regenerate America's muscle in manufacturing. A few glimmers have begun to appear—a handful of plants coming back from China, a modest uptick in manufacturing employment, and business leaders such as Grove speaking out. But much more needs to be done, as you will see in the final section of this book.

CHAPTER 16

HOLLOWING OUT
HIGH-END JOBS

————◆————

IBM: SHIFTING THE KNOWLEDGE
ECONOMY TO INDIA

Merchants have no country. The mere spot they stand
on does not constitute so strong an attachment as
that from which they draw their gain.

— THOMAS JEFFERSON,
letter, 1814

What we are trying to do is outline an entire strategy
of becoming a Chinese company.

— JOHN CHAMBERS,
CEO of Cisco

In this new era of globalization, the interests of
companies and countries have diverged. In contrast
with the past, what is good for America's global corporations is no longer necessarily good for the American people.

— RALPH GOMORY,
former IBM vice president

AMERICA'S RESPONSE to the challenge from China in the 1990s was to shift toward high tech. That became the new rallying cry for business and political leaders. Some economists reckoned that traditional U.S. manufacturing was doomed because China and the rest of Asia were becoming the workshops of the global economy with their three hundred million or more low-cost, moderately skilled workers. America's new high ground would be the knowledge economy—the Internet, IT, scientific research, product development, corporate services, finance—areas where American universities would generate high-end skills and where start-ups would smartly innovate the United States to a long-term competitive advantage.

Bill Clinton, seeking support from Silicon Valley's high-tech leaders, made the promise of masses of high-skill, high-wage, high-tech jobs a centerpiece of his 1992 presidential campaign and one of his first White House initiatives. The normally Republican CEOs of Apple, Oracle, Compaq, and Xerox backed Clinton. "Going digital" became the mantra for free traders on both left and right. That was the title chosen for an economic strategy book by William Niskanen, head of the libertarian Cato Institute, and economist Robert Litan of the liberal Brookings Institution. Free trade economist Jagdish Bhagwati forecast that "in the end, Americans' increasing dependence on an ever-widening array of technology will create a flood of high-paying jobs. . . ."

The older generation coached Generation X to stake its future on becoming engineers, computer programmers, and systems architects—an irreplaceable army of "knowledge workers"—because knowledge economy expertise would protect them from low-cost Asian competitors. The dawning of the digital era, its enthusiasts asserted, was altering the global balance of economic power back in our favor. "You could think of it as brain power vs. muscle power," said Harvard economist Richard B. Freeman.

Free traders in Washington think tanks and in Congress, wanting to put the best face on America's global trade policies and seeing high-technology industries as America's strong suit, had pressed the government in 1989 to establish a new category of foreign trade—"Advanced Technology Products." This category was set up to embrace high-tech products that require significant research and development to create and produce—the sectors of the economy where Americans had long outperformed the world. So trade in high-technology products was going to be the new yardstick for measuring America's global performance.

America's Deficit in High-Tech Trade

Through the 1990s, the United States did maintain its historic edge in high-tech trade, as expected. But all too quickly, blue skies turned gray. In 2002, America suffered a high-tech trade deficit—importing more high-tech goods than it exported. Initially, it was dismissed as an anomaly. But very quickly America became stuck in the red in high-tech trade. By 2006, America's deficit in advanced technology trade had risen to $38 billion, and by 2011, only five years later, it had nearly tripled—to $99.3 billion.

And what was the main source of America's huge shortfall? Not the highly developed economies of Germany and Japan. With most of the world, the United States ran a slight high-tech trade surplus. China was the big exception. In 2010, only a decade after President Clinton and U.S. business groups were trumpeting American advantages in trade with China, the United States ran a $94.2 billion high-tech trade deficit with China, and it kept climbing—to $109 billion in 2011. To the consternation of U.S. free trade advocates, the Chinese were shipping more high-tech products to the United States than we were shipping to them.

China's steep upward leap in high tech caught many Americans by surprise, even though in 1985 China's leaders had announced their goal of reaching technological parity with the West. With a big boost from the China-based production of leading U.S. multinationals, the mix of U.S. imports from China changed dramatically in just one decade. America went from importing mostly low-end garments, home appliances, and consumer electronics from China to importing sophisticated high-end technology, according to Alan Tonelson, trade analyst for the U.S. Business and Industry Council. "Semiconductors . . . advanced telecommunications equipment . . . the lasers that send light through fiber optic communication systems . . . aerospace parts are all coming from China," said Tonelson.

To former Reagan trade negotiator Clyde Prestowitz, the Chinese success in high tech was foreseeable. "It is a fallacy to believe that America will somehow dominate high-tech industries while the rest of the world concentrates on low- and medium-tech," Prestowitz said. "The dynamics that have moved production of steel, autos, wind turbines, and the reading of brain scans abroad will also move biotech and nanotech and any other tech. . . ."

Knowledge Economy Offshoring

Suddenly, no career was immune to the Asian challenge, no job safe from offshoring: Computer programmers, systems analysts, white-collar bank and insurance employees, and millions more were as vulnerable as assembly line workers. As Tonelson noted, the Chinese had shown their mastery not only of routine production jobs, but of skill-intensive jobs, so that among big U.S. multinationals, "not only the production jobs but the research jobs, the development jobs, the engineering [jobs] within those industries are rapidly moving to China as well."

When Robert Scott at the Economic Policy Institute broke down America's job loss through trade with China in 2010, by far the hardest-hit sector was computers and their components, communications, and audio and video equipment. That sector lost 627,000 jobs, one-fourth the total loss nationwide, and this was between 2001 and 2008, *before* the recession. After Scott pinpointed Silicon Valley as ground zero for the worst job losses nationwide, one engineer concurred and emailed Scott: "We're now calling it *Skeletal Valley.*"

Even the service sector, another supposedly safe zone for Americans, was not immune. By 2008, Scott calculated, nearly 140,000 jobs in the high-end services area were wiped out by trade with China and another 153,000 in back-office administration and support. This was China alone. Add offshoring to India and the rest of Asia, and the Hackett Group, which tracks global personnel trends, estimated that from 2000 to 2010, roughly 2.8 million jobs in finance, IT, HR, and procurement were lost in North America and Europe to "electronic offshoring."

Contrary to earlier predictions, knowledge economy jobs seemed especially vulnerable because digital work can be flashed across the globe by the click of a mouse. Work in information and finance follows repetitive processes and transactions that can, like assembly line production, be "commoditized," in the argot of globalization. Since "commoditized" translates as "can be done anywhere cheaply," it is the kiss of death for American businesses and employees.

With China and India educating more engineers and computer scientists than the United States, no level of education provides protection, according to Princeton economist Alan Blinder. "Millions of skilled workers in developing countries are educated about as well as Americans are. And those numbers are bound to increase as poor countries, notably China and India, continue to participate more vigorously and effectively in the world economy," Blinder told Congress in 2007. "There is little doubt that the range and number of jobs that can be delivered electronically is destined to increase greatly as technology improves and as India, China, and other nations educate more and more skilled workers—in the case of India, *English-speaking* workers."

Eroding the U.S. High-Tech Base

America's high-tech problems were partly of our own making. High-level advisers to the Bush administration had warned that U.S. multinationals were themselves eroding the U.S. high-tech base and helping China jump up the high-tech ladder, according to Reagan trade negotiator Clyde Prestowitz in his book *The Betrayal of American Prosperity*.

In 2003, the Defense Department's Advisory Group on Electron Devices warned that the offshore migration of U.S. semiconductor chip fabrication plants "must be addressed" or it "will potentially slow the engine for economic growth." The group's chairman, Thomas Hartwick, told Congress that America's global lead in innovation was being put at risk. "The structure of the U.S. high-tech industry is *coming unglued,*" Hartwick said, "with innovation and design losing their tie to prototype fabrication and manufacturing [emphasis added]." President Bush's Council of Advisors on Science and Technology warned that the steady offshoring of U.S. production facilities would lead to the loss of research, development, engineering, and design capability, too. "The continuing shift of manufacturing to lower-cost regions, and especially to China," the council cautioned, "is beginning to pull high-end design and R&D capabilities out of the United States."

Not "beginning" to happen, it was already happening. Prestowitz reported that foreign corporations, led by U.S. multinationals, have set up at least 1,160 high-end research installations in China since 1999, plus more in India. The challenge from China, he noted, was sharply different from the Japanese trade challenge in the 1980s. Japan had resisted attempts by American multinationals to set up factories in Japan. By contrast, China welcomed foreign investors as a way to capture their technology and know-how. "China was much more clever than Japan with its investment policies," observed C. Fred Bergsten, director of the Peterson Institute for International Economics. "It invited foreign direct investment and then took the American corporations hostage," requiring them to transfer valuable technologies to China as a price of doing business there.

The roster of those who went along reads like a corporate *Who's Who*—GM, IBM, Microsoft, Intel, Cisco, Motorola, Hewlett-Packard, Dell, Applied Materials, and more. By 2005, GE had twenty-seven labs in China working on projects from composite-materials design to molecular modeling. In November 2010, GE announced plans to invest an additional $2 billion in R&D, technology, and financial services partnerships in China. Just two months later, GE disclosed a joint venture agreement to share its most sophisticated avionic systems on the Boeing 787 Dreamliner with the Chinese state-owned firm AVIC.

General Motors broke ground in mid-2010 on its highly touted GM China Advanced Technical Center—science lab, vehicle engineering lab, work on alternative energy vehicles. Microsoft, already spending $300 million on a research facility in Beijing, committed another $1 billion in late 2008 to more R&D centers around China. Another "milestone" investment was announced by Microsoft in 2010 for a new Shanghai Technology Park to "expand innovations in 'Cloud Computing' and green technology" as well as software development.

Symbolically, the most stunning decision came from Applied Materials of Silicon Valley, the world's biggest supplier of equipment to make semiconductors, solar panels, and flat-panel displays. In 2010, the company disclosed that it would base its chief technology officer, Mark R. Pinto, in China to head up a new 360-person lab complex in the ancient city of Xi'an.

Technology Theft at Unprecedented Levels

Some American corporate leaders concede that they are walking a delicate line by sharing know-how with China, but they say that is an unavoidable cost of doing business there. "China has a carrot and stick strategy—to sell to the Chinese government and state-owned enterprises, you have to make it in China," Clyde Prestowitz explained. "The Chinese even have a policy of *indigenous innovation*. The idea is that in order to sell to the Chinese government, you have to have R&D and new technology done in China incorporated into your products. It's a technology transfer requirement."

The heads of some U.S. multinationals dislike this policy and note that it goes against global trading rules, but they shy away from strong public comments. Privately, they have told the U.S. Chamber of Commerce that China's policy is simply "a blueprint for technology theft on a scale the world has never seen before." But, said the Chamber of Commerce, many U.S. multinationals are so "increasingly dependent on their China profits" that they "can't afford to antagonize China."

They have asked Washington for help. In January 2011, the Chamber of Commerce and corporate CEOs asked President Obama to raise American objections to "indigenous innovation" when he spoke with President Hu Jintao in Washington. Hu reportedly agreed to end that policy, but U.S. officials were skeptical, noting that in the past, powerful groups in the Chinese military and industry had blocked some of Hu's pledges and that before Hu came to power, the Communist Party leadership had made "indigenous innovation" a cornerstone of its drive to make China "a technology powerhouse by 2020."

Willingly or not, some big U.S. companies have become integrated into China's export drive to the United States, as smaller U.S. businesses predicted. Typically, U.S. multinationals try to hide homebound exports, but occasionally word leaks out. Cooper Tire & Rubber Company of Findlay, Ohio, America's second largest tire company, invested $70 million in 2004 in a Chinese joint venture plant. Only three years later did Cooper Tire admit to the U.S. International Trade Commission that for the first five years, it had agreed that not a single tire would be sold in China; everything would be for export "to North America and Europe."

China's Billion-Dollar Lures

"That kind of thing is the stick part of China's strategy," Prestowitz explained. "The carrot is that they offer foreign corporations all kinds of benefits. The Chinese say, 'Hey, come on over here. To make it here, you have to transfer technology, but if you do, we will make it worthwhile. We will subsidize your factories.' Intel, Applied Materials, and these companies are getting tax abatements for fifteen to twenty years. They are getting free land or land at very reduced prices. They are getting free infrastructure, getting a break on utility costs, and some are even getting capital grants from the Chinese. This is the carrot side of Chinese policy. I know it very well. I was on Intel's advisory board. I can't discuss the details, but there were lots of 'bennies.' We don't have anything like that in America to match it."

Paul Otellini, CEO of Intel, which opened a $2.5 billion chip-fabricating plant in Dalian, China, in October 2010, confirmed the power of China's financial lures. "It costs $1 billion more per factory for me to build, equip, and operate a semiconductor manufacturing facility in the United States," Otellini said, because in China, Intel could save that $1 billion. It "wasn't because the labor costs are lower," Otellini reported, "it was because the construction costs were a little bit lower, but the cost of operating, when you look at it after tax, was substantially lower." In short, the Chinese government was offering subsidies and tax breaks that made it cheaper for Intel to operate there. Prestowitz, among others, believes the United States should change tax laws and other incentives to U.S. firms to match and counter the Chinese lures.

Beijing's strategy has succeeded, economists point out, not only in luring major U.S. multinationals to locate sophisticated plants in China, but also in drawing top American companies into helping China's high-tech offensive in global trade. In a 2005 *BusinessWeek* op-ed tellingly titled "The High-Tech Threat from China-America Inc.," former undersecretary of commerce Jeffrey Garten warned of the perilous partnerships being formed. "U.S. companies are understandably seeking the best talent and lowest cost of operations anywhere. But in the process they are sharing America's intellectual treasures with a foreign rival in unprecedented ways," Garten asserted. "They are training foreign scientists and engineers and giving them and the omnipresent Chinese government access to their proprietary research programs."

The Corporate Mind Shift

What's at work is not only China's inducements, but also a radical shift in the mind-set of some leading American corporate chiefs. Most of us equate the success of the American economy with the success of American corporations. But many corporate CEOs don't see it that way. To them, America is no longer ground zero. It is just one of many global markets, and selling here does not necessarily mean producing here.

Alex Trotman, the CEO of Henry Ford's old company, was among the first to openly sound that theme in the late 1990s. "Ford isn't even an American company, strictly speaking," he said. "We're global." Ron Rittenmeyer, CEO of EDS, the largest American-based IT services company, described his firm as "agnostic about specifically where we operate." In 2005, former Intel CEO Craig Barrett was so bullish about Intel's global presence and operations in an interview with *New York Times* columnist Thomas Friedman that Friedman paraphrased Barrett as contending that "Intel can be a totally successful company without ever hiring another American." In 2006, Cisco CEO John Chambers went further. "What we are trying to do," he said, "is outline an entire strategy of becoming a Chinese company."

Today's corporate thinking is the opposite of what Charlie Wilson, chairman of General Motors, famously said in the 1950s: "What's good for our country is always good for GM and vice versa." Those days are long gone, says former IBM vice president Ralph Gomory. "In this new era of globalization, the interests of companies and countries have diverged," Gomory told Congress in 2007. "In contrast with the past, what is good for America's global corporations is no longer necessarily good for the American people. . . . Globalization has now made it possible for global corporations to pursue their profits by building capabilities abroad. . . . But in creating their profits this way, they are building up the GDP of other countries while breaking their once tight links with America's own GDP."

Summarizing the impact of this new corporate mind-set on the American economy, the National Science Board reported that 85 percent of the growth in R&D workers by U.S. multinationals between 2003 and 2009 had been abroad, while American-based employment in high-tech manufacturing had dropped 28 percent since 2000.

IBM: Flagship for Outsourcing Knowledge Economy Jobs

No high-tech company epitomizes this mind shift and job shift more than Ralph Gomory's alma mater—IBM—which now bills itself as the *world's* largest technology employer and computer services provider. Once the iconic American company, IBM has become the flagship for outsourcing technology services, helping a fleet of U.S. firms to relocate as many as a couple of million high-end IT jobs to Asia, especially to India.

If Wal-Mart pushed consumer manufacturing to China, IBM has been the driving force for pushing IT work offshore. Its own transformation has been stunning, implemented largely out of public view. In seven short years, from 2003 to 2010, IBM fired so many American IT professionals and hired so many engineers and computer programmers in India that IBM India's workforce is now larger than that of IBM USA.

The *Times of India* had to break that news. Since 2006, IBM has been secretive about revealing just where its 400,000-person global workforce is stationed. But the *Times of India* dug out the news that IBM's Indian workforce—a mere 6,000 in 2003—had catapulted to 100,000, maybe even 130,000, by August 2010. In those same seven years, IBM cut its American workforce by 30 percent or more, from 135,000 in 2003 to under 100,000 in early 2011, according to piecemeal corporate announcements plus inside information provided by the Alliance@IBM/CWA Local 1701, an IBM employee group trying to unionize the workforce and track IBM's hiring and firing.

Close behind IBM came a rush of other U.S. firms in IT, finance, insurance, accounting, and corporate services. Accenture, a technology and consulting firm, jumped from a tiny workforce in India to 50,000 by 2010. Computer giant Hewlett-Packard also now has roughly 50,000 employees in India. Dell Computer doubled its Indian head count in one year alone. In 2009, the major accounting firm Deloitte disclosed plans to triple its Indian staff to nearly 35,000 by the end of 2012. India also became a favored home for American IT outsourcing firms—EDS, ACS, CSC—Electronic Data Systems, Affiliated Computer Services, and Computer Sciences Corporation.

Even Perot Systems got on the India bandwagon—the company founded by Ross Perot, whose trademark comment in the 1992 presidential race was the blistering quip that the North American Free Trade Agreement would lead to a "giant sucking sound" of American jobs lost to Mexico. But India, it seems, was somehow different. James Champy, Perot's chairman of consulting, told the Indian media that Perot Systems would offshore about half of its work within five years. Said Champy: "Many of our clients who have resisted offshoring before will be more receptive now."

India's Disruptive Business Model

Like China, India has burst upon the global economy with warp speed. Two decades ago, as *The Economist* reported, India had no global companies worth mentioning. But now Arcelor-Mittal and Tata Steel in steelmaking, Hindalco in aluminum rolling, and Sundram Fasteners in auto parts can hold their own globally. But with what Indians call their "software miracle," India has largely leapfrogged over manufacturing to make its global business presence felt most powerfully in the digital world, with such information services firms as Infosys, Wipro, Cognizant, HCL Technologies, and Tata Consulting Services. By one United Nations estimate, India accounts for at least 35 percent of the nearly $100 billion global business in cross-border information outsourcing, but India claims closer to 50 percent of that market.

Three upstart Indian companies, Wipro, Infosys, and Tata Consulting, provoked the exodus of American IT jobs. Initially, in the early 2000s, when they began trying to lure U.S. corporations to outsource their IT work to low-cost, college-educated, English-speaking Indian professionals, IBM and other big American IT companies laughed at them, according to Ron Hira of Rochester Technology Institute.

Hira, who tracks global trends in IT services, said that American firms had a lock on that lucrative business back then, but Indian firms could underbid them because they were paying roughly one-tenth of U.S. salaries (engineers at $7,000 to $10,000 a year, accountants $5,000, project managers $15,000). "The Indian firms had a disruptive business model," Hira explained—low costs and very high profits. "Wall Street spotted how profitable the Indian companies were and put the heat on American firms to match the Indians. Infosys was a $5 billion revenue company and it turned a $1.5 billion profit. So Wall Street said to the U.S. firms, 'Why should you get 6 percent profit and Infosys gets 27 percent?' "

That asymmetry sparked a corporate revolution, and the Indian IT gold rush was on. IBM adopted the Indian model, and other major U.S. players followed. In a twinkle, the Americans were rushing to hire those same Indian IT professionals at low pay, to fire much of their American workforce, and to boost their own profits.

IBM Adopts the Indian Model

In March 2003, IBM signaled its shift to an offshoring strategy with a company-wide global teleconference among its personnel chiefs focused on what IBM liked to call "cross border job shifting." Tom Lynch, IBM's global employee relations director, outlined a big personnel push out of North America and Europe. The 1990s had seen manufacturing move offshore, but from now on, Lynch said, "we're looking at an emerging trend now to move services offshore." Lynch conceded that the road might be bumpy given the "anemic" American recovery from the dot.com bust. Moving jobs offshore in that environment, Lynch said, "is going to create more challenges." Besides, he added, "U.S. workers . . . will, in many cases, be asked to train their replacements."

In short, the old paternalistic IBM of CEO Tom Watson, Jr., which had carefully nurtured the security and loyalty of its employees, was about to morph into what former IBM'ers now call a New Economy "slash and burn" employer under CEOs Lou Gerstner and Sam Palmisano.

In the 1990s, but even more in the 2000s, news headlines began to catch the shift at IBM. "Cutting Here but Hiring over There," *The New York Times* reported in June 2005. Three months later, CNNMoney.com reported that IBM had hired fourteen thousand Indian workers while laying off up to thirteen thousand in the United States and Europe. TechWeb quoted IBM's CFO, Mark Loughridge, as saying that job reductions would save IBM $1.8 billion in 2005 and 2006.

But to reduce the unflattering headlines, IBM went sub rosa with its firings. Although federal and state laws require companies to report "material events" such as large layoffs, IBM stopped announcing large job cuts in 2006. It said that it did not have to make reports because there was not one big cutback. The cuts were being rolled out in modest batches and spread out geographically. In January 2009, without an IBM announcement, CBS reported that four thousand IBM jobs had been cut in one week at IBM sites in Tucson, Arizona; San Jose, California; Austin, Texas; Burlington, Vermont; Rochester, Minnesota; and Research Triangle Park, North Carolina. Two months later, *The Wall Street Journal* and *The New York Times* reported that IBM had fired another five thousand employees across America.

"Sometimes People Don't Realize They Are Training Their Own Replacement"

Inside IBM, longtime employees watched for clues. Tom Midgley, a $75,000-a-year IT systems administrator at the large IBM operation in Fishkill, New York, tracked trends by watching the parking lot and the cafeteria. Over time, the parking lot developed hundreds of empty spaces. In the cafeteria, Midgley noticed a growing population of Indian IT workers, Chinese engineers, and other foreigners. In twenty-seven years at IBM, Midgley said, he had witnessed the Fishkill facility shrink from more than ten thousand workers to about five thousand, though he said that IBM keeps the numbers secret. Also, Midgley added, IBM managers became surreptitious in arranging training for foreign employees.

"They used to bring the people over here and train them," Midgley recalled, "but now they don't even want to spend the money. You do the training over the phone. People are told, 'You are leaving. You are fired. You have thirty days. You have to train somebody in India to take your place or you won't get your severance pay.' IBM is firing proven workers. These are good performers. And they are training rookies, people with no track record. Sometimes people are training someone overseas and they don't even realize that they are training their own replacement."

That happened to Kristine Serrano in Colorado, who had put in sixteen years working either directly for IBM or indirectly for an IBM client, the IT department of Qwest Communications. At IBM, Serrano managed Oracle software and databases for Qwest and other corporate clients. She survived several rounds of IBM job cuts, but toward the end of 2009, she noticed something troubling.

"I was responsible for Oracle software installation. Every request for help on Oracle came through me," she explained. "What I saw were a lot of requests from India—twenty installations or more at once. I had to provide the software because they were going to go through training for how to do an Oracle software installation. That's when I kind of knew something was coming. But nobody ever says anything."

About three months later, in March 2010, Serrano's boss called her in and said she was being laid off. No cause, she said, "just GR"—"Global Resourcing," IBM's euphemism for firing Americans and moving their jobs overseas. Serrano was given sixty days' notice and told to train a young Chinese woman in Atlanta, hired on contract. But that woman was just a fill-in; four months later, she was fired and phoned Serrano to say that the job had been permanently offshored to India.

Serrano was offended at IBM's explanations and its stealth firings. "When you read that the company is parroting that there is a skills mismatch, that they can't find Americans with the right skills, that's dishonest," she complained. "These people who are being fired, people like me, are experienced IT workers. They know their job, and now that very same job is over in India. That's what happened to me. My job is in India—except at a different pay level."

IBM's Indian Empire

In India, IBM was anything but covert. It was eager to showcase its burgeoning empire, which by 2006 numbered forty-three thousand strong, a sevenfold growth in just three years. In June 2006, IBM invited Wall Street financial analysts to a gala celebration of its new India-based strategy at the Bangalore Palace Hotel in India's version of Silicon Valley. With the president of India at his side, a live audience of ten thousand IBM employees in Bangalore, and thousands more in Delhi, Mumbai, Kolkata, and Pune linked by satellite, IBM CEO Sam Palmisano spelled out India's central role in his vision of the "globally integrated enterprise."

In India, Palmisano emphasized, IBM would do cutting-edge R&D, write breakthrough software, and take on back-office projects on a huge scale. "India and other emerging economies are an increasingly important part of IBM's global success," Palmisano declared. "In the next three years, we will triple our investment in India—from $2 billion over the last three years to nearly $6 billion in the next three years."

Already IBM was gearing up a campaign to market its new offshore IT capabilities to major business clients in America and Europe. Out went glossy brochures and blast emails promoting IBM's "global centers of excellence." Its early promotional materials did not reveal that IBM intended to take outsourced work from U.S. clients and shift it to India and other low-cost foreign sites such as Brazil or Russia. But its big pitch was low costs, going after market share from Indian firms. "We aggressively drive to new levels of cost competitiveness," IBM told its would-be clients.

Big Blue did so well marketing its low-cost IT services in America that it had to keep expanding in India, adding up to seventy thousand more employees there by 2010. It became so India-based that it often had to call in its Indian staff for clients in America. Occasionally, IBM overstepped and stubbed its toe.

In late 2009, IBM flew in seventeen Indian engineers and computer consultants from Mumbai to analyze and update old databases at New York City's Department of Finance and Taxation. When the *New York Post* heard about it, the paper ran a story headlined "NYC Hit by Nerd Job Rob; City $$ for India Hires." One of the Indians, Sunny Amin, a twenty-five-year-old engineer from Aurangabad on his first trip to the Big Apple, was ecstatic. He told a reporter that his job was "a dream come true." He had rented an apartment in Parsippany, New Jersey, for nine months. He was coy about discussing his pay but bragged that "I make about ten times more than I would in India"—yet still well below American salary levels.

Local 2627, a union of city-employed computer consultants, exploded in outrage at IBM's hiring of foreigners with taxpayer money. "It's like a slap in the face," said union president Robert Ajaye. "We have people in-house who could do this job."

IBM: Patents for Offshoring U.S. Jobs

But IBM, unembarrassed and eager to capitalize on its own experience moving to India, moved ahead aggressively. It created a major new profit center to teach other U.S. companies how to go offshore: how to decide which jobs could be moved most profitably; what was the most efficient work flow to manage the offshore move; how to qualify for subsidies and tax breaks in the offshore country; how to hang on to tax breaks in America while walking out the door. IBM marketed its offshoring systems to such diverse clients as Disney, Hertz, Hartford Insurance, A&P grocery chain, and Accelerated Auto Parts, as well as to financial, consumer goods, and pharmaceutical giants.

So lucrative did this business become that IBM decided to patent its offshoring blueprint. On January 3, 2006, IBM systems experts filed an application to patent a computerized "Method for Identifying Human-Resource Work Content to Outsource Offshore" in finance, human resources, logistics, infrastructure, and training. IBM claimed its unique vehicle would enable clients to develop a "migration project plan" to achieve an "end-to-end knowledge transfer." Cost saving was central.

In September 2007, IBM applied for another patent on what it evidently thought was an even smarter blueprint, promising clients a computerized "Workforce Sourcing Optimizer" to assess the pros and cons of moving out of one country (unnamed) to other countries such as India, China, and Hungary (named). IBM's application boasted that its program could help clients achieve "50% of resources in China by 2010."

When the U.S. Patent and Trademark Office made IBM's patent application public in March 2009, it was a bombshell. Congressman John Hall of Dover Plains, New York, a Democrat to whom IBM had made campaign contributions, denounced IBM as "downright unpatriotic and un-American." IBM workers were in an uproar. "This is obviously outrageous—a patent on how to offshore U.S.

jobs," objected Lee Conrad of the Alliance@IBM/CWA Local 1701. "IBM is obviously doing all it can to decimate the U.S. work force, and it is all the more reason why IBM should not get any tax breaks or stimulus money. They clearly are abandoning the U.S. work force."

Within twenty-four hours, IBM pulled its patent application.

Cloning the American Office in Madras, India

Even so, losses of solid middle-class jobs now ripple throughout the knowledge economy. Banks, airlines, hotels, retailers, investment banks, law firms, and even hospitals and American states have been shipping work offshore. In Madras, India, a *Los Angeles Times* reporter came across an offshore operation where "task by task, function by function, the American office is being hollowed out and reconstituted in places like this. . . ." He described a local shopping arcade where researchers, librarians, claims processors, investment analysts, typists, proofreaders, accountants, and graphic designers were churning out work for U.S. tax accountants, insurance companies, and law firms.

Offshoring today involves brainpower jobs. Wall Street investment bankers use Indian analysts to gather information on potential merger or acquisition targets. Massachusetts General Hospital in Boston hires radiologists in India to process X-ray images of American patients. In 2002, the state of California outsourced the processing and delivery of some state welfare benefits to Citicorp Electronic Financial Services Inc., and Citicorp turned the work over to English speakers in Bangalore and Pune, India. The volume of such offshore work, not only in India but in China, Brazil, the Philippines, Russia, and Eastern Europe, has shot up exponentially since 1990, from next to nothing to roughly $100 billion a year.

"They told all the workers when manufacturing jobs were leaving the country, 'Train in computers. Jump to computers,' " protested Lee Conrad of Alliance@IBM/CWA. "Well, now computer jobs are going out of the country. These are high-skilled jobs—IT specialists, HR specialists, IT architects—college-educated. Desk jobs. Good pay. They're just decimating white-collar people. It's devastating."

Recession: Offshoring Rises; Job Cuts at Home

Offshoring may not have been a hot issue during the booming 1990s, but in the recent recession, public opinion swung against it. In October 2010, most people blamed offshoring as the main reason for the slow U.S. economic recovery, according to a *Wall Street Journal/ NBC News* poll. Among blue-collar workers, 83 percent cited outsourcing as the reason U.S. companies were not hiring. Even more professionals and managers—95 percent—said the same.

And no relief is in sight. At the depths of recession in January 2009, the Hackett Group, a strategic consulting firm, reported that in the United States, "companies are clearly . . . accelerating the pace of their globalization efforts, particularly in finance and IT, while at the same time implementing hiring freezes and/or staff cuts for their other back-office staff positions." In sum, job cuts at home, big hiring overseas. In the decade from 2000 to 2010, Hackett said, offshoring had been "a major culprit" in the estimated loss of 3.9 million jobs in finance, IT, human resources and business support functions in North America and Europe.

During recession, the big Wall Street banks bailed out by taxpayers rebuffed President Obama's pleas to "hire American." Instead, they pushed ahead with overseas hiring, but like IBM, they kept it quiet. The Indian press broke the news that in 2011, JPMorgan Chase, Bank of America, and Citigroup had signed contracts to offshore $5 billion worth of new IT and back-office work to Indian firms. At home, the big banks were firing tens of thousands of employees.

In November 2010, Hackett put out a report entitled "How Offshoring Could Prolong the Jobless Recovery," predicting that offshoring of white-collar and professional jobs would be a persistent source of "net job destruction." Hackett forecast that offshoring in the knowledge economy would keep rising, wiping out another 1.3 million jobs in North America and Europe by 2014.

Looking over the long term, Princeton economist Alan Blinder spelled out the implications for the upper echelons of the American middle class. Roughly one-quarter of all the jobs in the U.S. economy are vulnerable to be offshored, Blinder said: That "corresponds to about 30–40 million jobs" vulnerable to loss—unless, as some business groups are now advocating, the federal government changes tax policies and investment incentives and business leaders find ways to keep more jobs at home, to prevent that massive job loss from happening.

CHAPTER 17

THE SKILLS GAP MYTH

IMPORTING IT WORKERS COSTS MASSES OF U.S. JOBS

> We have seen numerous instances in which Ameri-
> can businesses have brought in foreign skilled work-
> ers after having laid off skilled American workers,
> simply because they can get the foreign workers
> more cheaply.
>
> — ROBERT REICH,
> *secretary of labor, 1995*

> These are not Einsteins or superstars. That has always
> been a lot of hype. H-1B never required that they be
> the best and brightest in the world. It only required
> a bachelor's degree.
>
> — BRUCE MORRISON,
> *former congressman, 2011*

> We find neither an inadequate supply of STEM
> [scientific, technical, engineering, mathematical]
> workers to supply the nation's current needs, nor
> indications of shortages in the foreseeable future.
>
> — RAND CORPORATION STUDY,
> *2004*

IN AMERICA, one of the most controversial causes of job loss in the high-tech industry involves not offshoring but "onshoring"— importing college-educated foreigners to come work in the United States and replace Americans—a strategy favored by such major U.S. companies as AIG, Disney, IBM, Microsoft, and Pfizer.

The high-tech world has long looked to recruit hot new talent through immigration, and in fact, immigrant scientists and entrepreneurs have played key roles in sparking America's preeminence in high tech. Among them, Andy Grove from Hungary, the ex-CEO of Intel; Jerry Yang from Taiwan, a co-founder of Yahoo!; Andreas von Bechtolscheim from Germany and Vinod Khosla from India, co-founders of Sun Microsystems; Pierre Omidyar, founder of eBay, from France; and Sergey Brin, a co-founder of Google, from Russia.

For America to stay on top, Bill Gates of Microsoft and other high-tech industry leaders have told Congress and the White House, the United States needs to recruit the world's "best and brightest." By the late 1980s, high-tech industry leaders were sounding the alarm that U.S. global leadership was endangered by a "skills gap" in the critical STEM fields—science, technology, engineering, and mathematics. They said there was a shortage of qualified Americans and a slowdown in the flow of foreign talent to industry from America's premier graduate schools in the sciences, where roughly half of the students were foreign born. There was a logjam, they said, in the government's approval of green cards to foreigners to let them work in the United States while they applied for citizenship.

Gates and others pressed Congress, from the late 1980s into the 2000s, to take action to help them recruit foreign talent. "It makes no sense to educate people in our universities, often subsidized by U.S. taxpayers, and then insist they return home," Gates testified. "These top people are going to be hired. It's just a question of where."

The H-1B Visa Program

In response to intense industry lobbying, Congress enacted a special visa program in 1990 as a stopgap measure. The new H-1B visa program would permit an annual quota of sixty-five thousand temporary three-year visas to be issued to college graduates to work in the United States in "specialty occupations."

Former Democratic congressman Bruce Morrison of Connecticut, who helped write the law, saw it as a temporary fix—a bridge for channeling talented foreign students into high-tech America while the government broke the immigration logjam. The visas were made renewable for a second three years to help keep precious talent in America long enough to recruit them as U.S. citizens. The visa quota was kept fairly low, Morrison said, to encourage bright foreigners to become Americans.

Inevitably, there was hot debate over how to protect Americans from being shoved out of solid, high-paying high-tech jobs and replaced by younger, cheaper foreigners. In speech after speech, members of Congress vowed that American jobs would be protected. But in the end, Morrison said, no ironclad protections for Americans were written into the 1990 law. The law did require U.S. employers to pay H-1B visa holders at prevailing wages and not to undercut existing U.S. salary scales. But there was no legal mandate requiring employers to keep qualified Americans in their jobs or to scour the labor market and hire Americans before foreigners for any high-tech opening. "H-1B does not require that and never has," Morrison said.

The law had so many loopholes that it was easy for companies to evade it, Morrison told me. American companies figured out a legal dodge: They could legally get rid of American employees and replace them with foreigners by working the switch through subcontractors. Under the law, Morrison explained, "you can't fire your own worker and hire an H-1B worker, but you can fire a contractor that has supplied you with American workers and hire another contractor who will supply you with H-1B foreign workers."

Fired and Replaced by Cheaper Foreigners

With such loopholes, the H-1B program soon altered the economic landscape in the high-tech world, eliminating hundreds of thousands of prime American jobs. IT giants such as Microsoft, Intel, Oracle, Cisco, and IBM, which had pushed the H-1B legislation, were among the first to exploit it. But other companies quickly saw its benefits. One was AIG, the insurance giant, which wanted to cut costs by replacing much of its main information staff in Manhattan, New Jersey, and New Hampshire.

Linda Kilcrease, a former AIG computer systems manager, described how in September 1994 senior AIG executives summoned 250 of the company's most experienced IT staffers to a sudden meeting at a local hotel. "After we were seated, an executive stood in front of the room and coldly told us that the computer systems were outsourced," she said. "We were each handed a folder of papers that detailed our 60-day notice and severance." Summarily fired, the Americans were being replaced by H-1B visa workers from India—workers they were ordered to train, or else lose all severance benefits. The firings came as a shock to Kilcrease and her colleagues because they had been instrumental in developing AIG's IT capabilities and the company was then enjoying strong profits. They knew that theoretically H-1B visas are designated for foreigners with special, otherwise unavailable job skills. But Kilcrease, a ten-year veteran at AIG who led a team of twenty computer programmers and systems analysts, commented after working with the Indians that "it was clear that Syntel [the firm supplying the Indian workers] did not bring in any special skills that we did not have."

Cost-cutting was AIG's evident motive, Kilcrease asserted. "This profitable company boasted they were saving $11 million as they made us train our H-1B replacements," she said. "The company that provided the foreigners to AIG, Syntel, was punished for paying foreigners less than the prevailing wage. I sought to sue AIG via four government agencies. This failed as they did nothing illegal, no matter the harm to their employees. I secured [another] job, but retirement benefits were destroyed. In my fifties, I cannot start over, [and] there remain no protections to prevent abuse."

Such mass firings were terrifying to employees, but a boon to companies. H-1B fever spread rapidly during the dot.com boom of the late 1990s and the Y2K angst over a potential computer apocalypse at the stroke of midnight on December 31, 1999. Silicon Valley and its political allies in the Clinton administration, claiming they needed more foreign "techies" to head off trouble, got Congress to triple the annual H-1B visa quota from 65,000 to 195,000. Companies such as IBM and Microsoft, which have overseas subsidiaries, added to that total by using another visa, the L-1, to bring in their own foreign employees without any quota.

So the numbers of "onshored" foreign workers in America shot up. Microsoft acknowledged in 2007 that one-third of its 46,000-member workforce in the United States was foreigners on work visas or green cards. Even in hard times, when Americans were being laid off in large numbers, the foreign worker tide kept rising. In 2009, the industry lobbying group TechAmerica reported that while the industry cut 245,600 U.S. jobs, it added more than 100,000 H-1B visa workers.

Syntel: Grad Student to Billionaire

Once again, the driving force behind the wave of imported IT workers on H-1B visas was the aggressive coterie of Indian offshoring firms, Infosys, Wipro, Satyam, and Tata. They have recruited tens of thousands of Indian knowledge workers at home and sent them into America. Other so-called body shops or multinational temp agencies, some owned by Americans, have copied the Indian strategy. But the four Indian firms have dominated the field. During the recession, from 2007 to 2009, four of the five largest users of H-1B visas were Indian firms—Tata, Infosys, Wipro, and Satyam—each receiving several times more visas than American giants such as Microsoft and

Cisco, according to Ron Hira of Rochester Institute of Technology, who has frequently testified to Congress on offshoring issues.

"Tata has about 18,000 people in the United States, 17,000 of them are on H-1B or L-1 visas," Hira said. "Infosys has 8,000 H-1Bs visas and L-1 visas in the U.S. Wipro is similar. The visas cost them about $11 million a year." A small investment, given how profitable the H-1B trade has been for these Indian companies. From 2000 to 2010, Infosys exploded from a $203 million company with 5,400 employees to a $4.8 billion company with 113,800. Syntel Inc. was founded in 1980 by Bharat Desai, a graduate of the Indian Institute of Technology and the University of Michigan, and its H-1B trade made Desai into one of America's four hundred richest people, with a net worth of $1.35 billion.

Milton Friedman: H-1Bs Unneeded Subsidy

With the American economy going through rocky years, the explosive growth of the H-1B visa program has fueled charges that it is undercutting American wage scales and job security. Labor Department reports have repeatedly charged that H-1B visa firms are breaking the law by paying wages well below prevailing American rates and often submitting fraudulent visa applications. In 1994, former labor secretary Robert Reich singled out Syntel for enabling AIG to fire 250 American workers and hire Indians. An investigation, Reich said, had found that "Syntel had willfully underpaid its Indian computer programmers by nearly 20 percent below the wage they were required under law to be paid." Reich also cited eighteen other cases of underpaid H-1B workers. A year later, the Labor Department's inspector general reported evidence of pervasive cheating by U.S. companies that were paying substandard wages.

In 1995, Reich was back on Capitol Hill urging Congress to fix what he called the "seriously flawed" H-1B program. Not only were U.S. employers cheating by paying submarket salaries, he said, but they were improperly firing American workers. "We have seen nu-

merous instances in which American businesses have brought in foreign skilled workers after having laid off skilled American workers,
simply because they can get the foreign workers more cheaply,"
Reich said. The H-1B visa program, he went on, "has become a
major means of circumventing the costs of paying skilled American
workers or the costs of training them."

Even Milton Friedman, the normally pro-business free market
economist from the University of Chicago, criticized the H-1B program as an improper subsidy to Corporate America. He mocked the
idea that big corporations such as Microsoft, IBM, or Intel needed
help from Washington to build a foreign talent farm system. "There
is no doubt," said Friedman, "that the program is a benefit to their
employers, enabling them to get workers at a lower wage, and to
that extent, it is a subsidy."

One Million Foreign Visa Workers

With the expansion of the annual H-1B quota and with renewable
visas, the accumulation of "onshored" foreign workers expanded far
beyond the original, limited stopgap program.

The Labor Department does not keep track of the totals. But in
2011, Paul Almeida, president of the AFL-CIO's Department of
Professional Employees, estimated that one million or more foreigners were working in the United States on H-1B visas. His estimate
was based on the expanded annual quota of 195,000 visas, renewable
for up to six years, meaning 195,000 more workers could be added
each year for six years. High-tech industry spokesmen discounted his
estimate as a wild exaggeration. But a 2010 report from the Department of Homeland Security lent credence to the AFL-CIO figures. In
just one three-year period, from 2006 to 2008, the DHS reported
that the government had approved 828,677 H-1B visas. Add another three years of visas and the total could be well over 1 million.

What's more, early backers of the H-1B program, like former con
gressman Bruce Morrison, contend that the program has strayed far

from its original intent of recruiting the world's "best and brightest," as Bill Gates had put it. "These are not Einsteins or superstars," Morrison objected. "That has always been a lot of hype. H-1B never required that they be the best and brightest in the world. It only required a bachelor's degree."

But what most disturbs Morrison and reformers in Congress is how H-1B visas have been misused to knock hundreds of thousands of Americans out of good high-tech jobs in hard economic times. "If I had known in 1990 what I know today about offshore companies using the H-1B program to import foreign workers, I wouldn't have drafted the law so that they could use it that way," Morrison told me. "You know, some jobs are going to wind up going abroad because of globalization, but the government shouldn't have its thumb on the scale, making it easier."

Indian information industry leaders bristle at American criticism. India has "been viewed as taking away American jobs," wrote Som Mittal, president of NASSCOM, India's National Association of Software and Services Companies, which includes the H-1B staffing companies. In an op-ed for the San Jose *Mercury News* in December 2010, Mittal argued that India should be seen as "a country that is creating jobs in the United States."

NASSCOM contends that Indian firms are saving U.S. corporations $20 billion to $25 billion a year in costs. Trade union and academic critics contend that money should have been spent on jobs for Americans.

Pfizer's Switch

What makes the operations of the Indian companies so controversial is that typically they help American companies get around the H-1B law. The Indian firms act as buffers that shield U.S. business from the reach of the law. Pfizer's huge offshoring shift starting in late 2008 offers a window on how the H-1B game works.

In late 2008, Pfizer forced drastic cutbacks among one thousand information specialists at its global research center in Groton and New London, Connecticut. These workers, almost all Americans, had been hired years earlier through outside contractors, but they had worked at Pfizer for so long and had become so integrated into Pfizer's operations that they were widely regarded as tantamount to permanent Pfizer employees.

For many years, Pfizer liked this system. But when similar contract workers and long-term temp employees at Microsoft—its so-called permatemps—sued for health and retirement benefits and won their lawsuit in 2005, Pfizer became gun-shy and decided on a massive personnel switch. In November 2007, Pfizer adopted Corporate Procedure 117, a new personnel policy that laid the groundwork for it to shed hundreds of long-term American contract or contingent workers by discontinuing their contracts.

What made Pfizer's massive personnel switch possible was the availability of a large complement of less expensive Indians. In 2005, Pfizer signed up two Indian staffing agencies, Infosys and Satyam, now known as Mahindra Satyam, as "strategic partners" to provide IT specialists as part of its drive to cut $4 billion in costs. Months before the big layoffs, people at the Groton research center noticed a trickle of Indians arriving for three-month assignments to be trained by Americans.

In late 2008, the big layoffs came. They swept through Pfizer's Informatics Division, which did the intricate computerized work for Pfizer's complex clinical drug trials. Informatics IT teams developed databases and software for Pfizer's pharmaceutical R&D and assembled the data for Pfizer's applications to the Food and Drug Administration for approval of new drugs. That work required especially skilled people, not only masters of complex information software, but people who could work well with Pfizer scientists, earn their trust, and keep the whole process moving on schedule.

When the first Indian IT specialists arrived to replace the fired Americans, Pfizer's scientific administrators at Groton worried that the Indians were not up to the job and that relying on them was seriously hurting Pfizer's performance on new drugs, according to Lee

Howard, a reporter for *The Day,* New London's daily newspaper. They appealed to CEO Jeffrey Kindler to stop the Indian "onshoring." But Kindler and his aides rejected their appeal and the job cuts rolled on.

"Everybody was scared to death," I was told by one former systems analyst with ten years' experience at Pfizer. "You wouldn't know if one day you would show up and find out that you didn't have a job. Some people's contracts had two or three years to go, but Pfizer could let you go before renewal. And if your contract expired, forget it. You were done. In my time, I saw three hundred people laid off, well over three hundred. That's Americans. People who were there at Pfizer for fourteen to fifteen years. Pfizer people who had been transferred to Connecticut from Ann Arbor, Michigan. People who bought a house in this worst economy of all times. They couldn't sell their house and leave. No job and they were stuck in their houses. And these were people who had devoted their lives to Pfizer!"

How Pfizer Avoided the Reach of the Law

A stream of Indian IT workers took up posts in Pfizer's three-story computer center at 194 Howard Street in New London, where some three hundred IT specialists worked. "Five years ago, the Howard Street building was probably all American contractors," Lee Howard told me. "Then there was a gradual shift, maybe not all H-1Bs, but a handful of Indians. And then it switched to a completely Indian workforce." Pfizer people talked about them as H-1B visas employees, but some could also have come to the U.S. on B-1 or L-1 visas, which are similar but have even more flexible rules, allowing for pay abroad and no payment of American taxes.

"These contracting companies have apartments rented across the street from Pfizer," said the former Pfizer systems analyst, who as a $125,000-a-year project coordinator dealt directly with the Indian staffing companies before being fired in mid-2009. "They'd stick five or six people in one apartment. You'd see these people walking over to Pfizer in winter—in sandals, because no one had prepared them. . . . We never looked at the visas. They were Indians working for an Indian company. . . . Pfizer did not want to deal with visas. That makes them complicit in the process."

That last point was crucial. Like scores if not hundreds of other U.S. companies, Pfizer maintained that its hands-off policy on H-1B visas protected it against any charge of violating the visa law by firing Americans to hire Indians. Pfizer contended that these were not its employees, that it was merely switching from one outside contractor to another, and the contractors were doing the layoffs and replacements. That was the gist of Pfizer's response to Senator Chris Dodd and Representative Joe Courtney, two Connecticut Democrats who wrote Pfizer CEO Jeff Kindler in November 2008, to "urge you in the strongest terms to reconsider" Pfizer's replacing American workers with foreign workers. In reply, Pfizer said it was using a dozen outside contractors, some foreign, some American, and they, not Pfizer, had hired the replacements and obtained their H-1B visas. "Pfizer would have had no involvement," Pfizer asserted, except for a small number of high-level scientists with "specialized knowledge and expertise."

Calls for Reform

Cases like Pfizer's and charges that what critics call the "Indian body shops" are broadly abusing the H-1B visa system have triggered a push for reform in Congress to focus the H-1B program on a small window of truly unusual foreign talent and to stop the influx of routine IT workers taking good high-tech American jobs.

In April 2009, a bipartisan bill was introduced by Republican Senator Chuck Grassley of Iowa and Democratic Senator Richard Durbin of Illinois. They proposed requiring U.S. firms to "attest" that neither they nor their subcontractors have fired Americans and "that they have tried to hire an American before they hire a foreign worker." Others suggested limiting H-1B visas to foreigners with graduate degrees.

"The H-1B visa program is riddled with loopholes and is in need of serious reform," Senator Grassley declared. "Senator Durbin and I have been highlighting fraud and abuse within the H-1B program for years. . . . It's time we get the program back to its original intent where employers use H-1B visas only to shore up employment in areas where there is a lack of qualified American workers."

Rand: No High-Tech Skills Gap

Grassley threw the spotlight on the central question: Is there, in fact, a genuine shortage of qualified American professionals, as industry spokesmen claim?

During the feverish dot.com boom in the late 1990s, as the H-1B program was gaining momentum, Norman Matloff, a professor of computer science with the University of California at Davis, debunked "the myth of a desperate software labor shortage." Matloff provided figures to Congress showing ample pools of well-educated American job applicants at Microsoft, Intel, and other high-tech companies.

High-tech industry claims were even more sharply challenged during the long, slow "jobless recovery" after the dot.bom bust and the 2000–2002 recession. In 2004, Rand, the California research giant, did a detailed study and rejected high-tech industry claims of a "skills gap." Rand asserted that there was no gap—no evidence of a shortage of highly qualified people in science, technology, engineering, and mathematics (STEM). "We find neither an inadequate supply of STEM workers to supply the nation's current needs, nor indications of shortages in the foreseeable future," Rand stated.

Another study in 2009 by Rutgers University, the Urban Institute, and Georgetown University found that the STEM pipeline from American universities to high-tech industry was working well.

In fact, this study charged that the high-tech industry's off-shoring strategies were causing some of the personnel problems that industry was complaining about. By giving good jobs to foreigners, the study asserted, U.S. high-tech companies made themselves look less attractive to the most promising American students.

American universities, the Rutgers study asserted, "graduate many more STEM students than are hired each year. . . . The problem may not be that there are too few STEM qualified college graduates, but rather that STEM firms are unable to attract them." Some of the best math and science students were choosing other careers, Rutgers reported, because they offered higher pay, better prospects for advancement, and more job security, and the other careers were "less susceptible to offshoring."

Faced with strong evidence that the skills shortage had been exaggerated by industry, Congress dropped the quota on H-1B visas to sixty-five thousand a year in 2004 but created a special category of twenty thousand more visas for foreign students studying in American universities and transitioning to the U.S. high-tech sector. Despite the change in law, the numbers of foreign workers on either H-1B, B-1, or L-1 visas remained high.

To try to curb the importing of foreign workers, Senator Charles Schumer proposed in August 2010 to more than double the H-1B visa fees to $3,750 a head. The New York Democrat lauded companies such as Oracle, Cisco, and Apple for using the H-1B visa program as intended and then sharply attacked firms that violate the spirit of the law by operating "a glorified international temp agency for tech workers." Schumer claimed that he was not trying "to target Indian companies," but to penalize firms whose business model was built around importing H-1B workers—a description that mostly fit Indian companies and a few American firms that copied the Indian business model.

As Congress passed Schumer's legislation, the Indian IT industry, treating Schumer's bill as a salvo at them, protested that the United States was violating international trade practices. Jeya Kumar, CEO of a top Indian IT company, said that raising the visa fee would "erode cost arbitrage" and force changes in the operations of "Indian offshore providers."

"Exactly," Schumer shot back. "That is what we want."

But the higher visa fees have had only modest impact, and the fundamental reform pushed by Senators Chuck Grassley and Dick Durbin to overhaul the H-1B program, clamp down on low pay and other abuses, and improve protections for American workers has been tied up in congressional deadlock. Their bill, strongly opposed by the high-tech industry, has been bottled up for more than three years.

One potentially helpful step, taken by Congress in late 2011, was to eliminate the annual limits on green cards for foreigners who want to work and live permanently in the United States and become tax-paying U.S. citizens, not foreign nationals taking both American wages and taxes abroad. Over time, this step could ease some of high-tech America's demand for H-1B visas. But much broader reforms are needed to stop foreign "body shops" from undercutting the jobs of American middle-class professionals and to recoup one million jobs already lost to foreigners.

PART 5

OBSTACLES
TO A FIX

EIGHTEEN MONTHS BEFORE PUBLIC ANGER boiled over at congressional gridlock on the deficit in August 2011, Senator Evan Bayh of Indiana gave public voice to what angers so many Americans today about Congress—it operates like a dysfunctional family.

"The people's business is not being done," Bayh declared in February 2010. Congress suffers from multiple pathologies, he said, and he ticked them off: "strident partisanship, unyielding ideology, a corrosive system of campaign financing, gerrymandering of House districts, endless filibusters, holds on executive appointees in the Senate, dwindling social interaction between senators of opposing parties and a caucus system that promotes party unity at the expense of bipartisan consensus."

It is a list worth rereading. It spells out, item by item, what ails the machinery of our democracy and stands in the way of fixing the nation's most pressing problems.

The surprise was not in what Bayh said, but who said it and what he was doing about it. Evan Bayh was no stranger to the Washington power game. He grew up in politics. His father, Birch Bayh, held the same Senate seat from Indiana from 1968 to 1980. Evan Bayh entered politics young and rose fast: governor at thirty-four for two terms, then senator for two terms. In 2008, at fifty-four, he was prominent enough to make the short list of potential running mates for Barack Obama.

By 2010, he was a moderate, centrist Democrat with a shot at the presidency if he stayed in the political game. But Evan Bayh was so sickened by the partisan gridlock and inertia on Capitol Hill that he announced he was quitting the Senate—giving up his political career in Washington.

CHAPTER 18

THE MISSING MIDDLE

⎯⎯⎯⎯⎯⎯⎯

HOW GRIDLOCK ADDS TO THE WEALTH GAP

Over the past thirty years, the parties have deserted the center . . . in favor of the wings. . . . First, at the level of individual members of Congress, moderates are vanishing. Second, the two parties have pulled apart.

—NOLAN MCCARTY, KEITH T. POOLE, AND HOWARD ROSENTHAL, *Polarized America*

It's the incredible shrinking middle.

—FORMER SENATOR JOHN BREAUX, *Louisiana Democrat*

There are still times when you get Democrats and Republicans talking to one another. But in public settings, no. They are teams and they are at war. You don't fraternize with the enemy.

—TOM MANN, *Brookings Institution*

WHAT MADE EVAN BAYH'S INDICTMENT of political Washington so striking was his description of personally witnessing the Senate decline.

At one time, he recalled, the Senate had functioned well as a legislative body because a bipartisan atmosphere made compromises possible. People found ways around roadblocks. But in recent years, Bayh said, the Senate was so marked by partisan acrimony that it was frequently paralyzed by the refusal to compromise or by a small group of senators who threatened to filibuster and talk a bill to death. "Just one or two determined senators can stop the Senate from functioning," Bayh said.

As a boy whose father was a senator—Birch Bayh, a progressive Democrat from Indiana—young Evan Bayh remembered a different political climate in the 1960s and 1970s. He saw his father enjoying friendships with senators of sharply different views—Republicans and conservative southern Democrats. Their social mingling and personal ties, Bayh said, had lubricated the process of government. Personal chemistry often created a way out of political deadlocks.

"Members of Congress from both parties, along with their families, would routinely visit our home for dinner or the holidays," Bayh recalled. "This type of social interaction hardly ever happens today and we are the poorer for it. It is much harder to demonize someone when you know his family or have visited his home. Today, members routinely campaign against each other, raise donations against each other and force votes on trivial amendments written solely to provide fodder for the next negative attack ad. It's difficult to work with members actively plotting your demise."

By contrast, he recalled an episode in 1968, when his father was seeking reelection. "Everett Dirksen, the Republican leader, approached him on the Senate floor, put his arm around my dad's shoulder, and asked what he could do to help," Bayh recalled. "This is unimaginable today."

Today, ideological purists dictate "all or nothing" tactics, Bayh said. They see "compromise [as] a sign of betrayal." Gridlock reigns. Little gets done.

The Last Straw

For Bayh, the last straw—the action that finally provoked him to quit—was the Senate's rejection in January 2010 of a proposal for a bipartisan task force to bring the Congress a blueprint for an up or down vote on how to get the deficit under control. A Senate majority actually voted in favor of the commission, 53–46, but the vote failed because, under Senate rules, passage required sixty votes—a filibuster-proof supermajority.

The margin of victory, the seven missing votes, had evaporated at the eleventh hour, Bayh noted, "for short-term political reasons." The commission had been born as a bipartisan idea, with fourteen Republican and eleven Democratic co-sponsors, Bayh among them. President Obama had initially reacted coolly, but when he belatedly endorsed the bill, seven previously enthusiastic Republicans switched sides—six of the GOP co-sponsors plus Senate minority leader Mitch McConnell. Previously, McConnell had ardently endorsed the plan. It was, McConnell said, "the best way to address" the budget crisis. "It deserves support from both sides of the aisle," McConnell had declared, chiding President Obama for hesitating to back it.

But when the president endorsed the bill three days before the vote, McConnell switched sides. Outsiders were astonished. "It's impossible to avoid the conclusion that the only thing that changed . . . is the political usefulness of the proposal to McConnell's partisan goals," wrote Fred Hiatt, editorial page editor of *The Washington Post.* "He was happy to claim fiscal responsibility while beating up Obama for fiscal recklessness. But when Obama endorsed the idea . . . and when the commission actually, against all odds, had the wisp of a chance of winning the needed 60 Senate votes—McConnell bailed."

Health Care Bills, Then and Now:
The Vanishing Middle

The past few years have seen a siege of partisan conflict. But it would be hard to find a more vivid contrast between the politics of then and now, between the mid-1960s and today, between the bipartisan politics of middle-class power and the partisan ferocity of the New Power Game, than the votes on major health care legislation in 2010 under President Obama and in 1965 on President Johnson's proposal for Medicare.

The debate in each case was furious. While liberals and moderates urged a broad new government insurance program as a safety net for the needy, conservative opponents ran angry newspaper ads with dire warnings that the new health program would lead to rationed care and a dangerous tide of "socialized medicine." Business groups charged that patients would lose "the freedom to choose their own doctor" and that Washington bureaucrats would intrude on "the privacy of the examination room." The hyper-rhetoric was the same in 1965 as in 2010.

In 1965, with Congress considering the first significant expansion of the government's social safety net since Franklin Roosevelt's New Deal of the 1930s, it was the strong centrist vote, the pivotal middle ground in Congress, that carried the day.

When the votes were tallied, 65 Republicans joined 248 Democrats to give Medicare a huge 313–115 majority in the House. In the Senate, 13 Republicans joined 57 Democrats for a 70–24 majority. Yes votes were cast by some of the most prestigious Republican moderates in Congress—Senators Jacob Javits of New York, Clifford Case of New Jersey, Hugh Scott of Pennsylvania, Leverett Saltonstall of Massachusetts, Margaret Chase Smith of Maine, George Aiken of Vermont, Everett Dirksen of Illinois, John Sherman Cooper of Kentucky, and Thomas Kuchel of California.

In 2010, the vote on Obama's health care plan—to extend health insurance to thirty-two million financially strapped Americans and to prevent insurance companies from barring coverage for average Americans with preexisting medical conditions or charging them steep fees—was sharply partisan. There was no middle ground. No moderates offered a compromise bill, as Republicans had done in 1965. GOP opposition was monolithic in 2010. Even the few Republican moderates toed the party line, though the Obama bill was a less ambitious expansion of government-backed health care than the health reform proposed by Republican Richard Nixon in 1974.

Facing a wall of Republican opposition, the Obama White House had to make concessions to pro-business conservative Democrats and independents to piece together enough votes for passage. Senator Joe Lieberman of Connecticut extracted a White House promise to kill "the public option," a government insurance program that was anathema to the private insurance industry. In the end, a watered-down health care bill barely scraped through.

Signficantly, the final vote did not bring closure. With today's sharp ideological schisms, no issue is ever settled. Every issue is forever in dispute. When the new Congress convened in January 2011, House Republicans set out to repeal, defund, and cripple not only the new health program, but other new Obama initiatives, such as the bill establishing the Consumer Financial Protection Bureau. That did not happen in the era of powerful centrist politics. Laws were enacted and Congress moved on.

Bipartisanship Has Helped Both Parties

Government worked better when bipartisan collaboration was the norm. Republican presidents benefited as well as Democrats— Dwight Eisenhower in the 1950s and Richard Nixon in the 1970s.

As a Republican from Kansas dealing with a Democrat-controlled Congress, Eisenhower regularly shared drinks of bourbon and branch water at the White House with Lyndon Johnson, then the Senate Democratic majority leader, and with House Speaker Sam Rayburn. Ike's openness was reciprocated. Once, when the archconservative Senate Republican leader William Knowland of California left his front-row seat and refused to floor-manage the passage of an Eisenhower foreign policy bill, Johnson took over and passed Eisenhower's legislation—cross-party collaboration that is unimaginable today.

Although Nixon won the presidency in 1968 by running as a conservative and forging a new Republican electoral base in the South, he governed more from the political center. His historic anticommunism, pursuit of the Vietnam War, and strong law-and-order stance at home won favor with conservatives. But his governmental activism won favor with liberals. He took strong government action in the economy, imposing wage and price controls, taking America off the gold standard, and shocking balance-the-budget conservatives with the surprising admission "I am now a Keynesian," meaning that he supported deficit spending to stimulate the economy. On Capitol Hill, Nixon's environmental, consumer, and regulatory legislation won strong bipartisan support, as did his modest expansion of Social Security, his tax increases on the wealthy, and his novel idea of guaranteed income for the poor.

When Johnson was in the worst jams of his political life, he often turned to Republicans for help—and got it. Right after John F. Kennedy was assassinated in Dallas on November 22, 1963, Johnson made one of his first phone calls, as the newly sworn-in president, to Eisenhower, asking for help and advice. Ike promised to meet him in Washington the next day and delivered an eight-page memo that Johnson used as a blueprint in his early months.

On the most contentious legislation, such as the Civil Rights Act of 1964, Johnson reached across the aisle to the Senate Republican leader, Everett Dirksen of Illinois, for help in breaking a determined filibuster by southern Democrats. With that kind of bipartisan cooperation, Johnson and Kennedy compiled the most productive legislative records during the half century from the end of World War II to the year 2000, according to an in-depth study of the work of each session of Congress.

"The Pull to the Center"

Perhaps the most compelling demonstration of bipartisanship came during the battles over the civil rights legislation in the mid-1960s. Without major Republican support, President Johnson could not have enacted those historic laws.

The pivotal figure was Senate Republican leader Everett Dirksen. From his long years in the Senate, Johnson understood the political risk of his taking on the entrenched southern Democratic barons of the Senate, especially his old mentor Senator Richard Russell of Georgia, on civil rights. Johnson saw Dirksen and the Republicans as the key. He needed to harness them to a bipartisan coalition.

As a business-friendly midwest conservative, Dirksen initially opposed a new law and regulations requiring desegregation of hotels, restaurants, and public accommodations. But patiently, methodically, Johnson worked on Dirksen. Bill Moyers, then LBJ's press secretary, recalled seeing Johnson grab a *New York Times* article reporting that in 1964 racial segregation was still increasing in the South. He scribbled, "Shame, Shame, Shame," on it and sent it to Dirksen. As longtime friends, they would sit together at the White House for a quiet drink in Johnson's small private room just off the Oval Office, where the president would josh and cajole Dirksen. He worked on Dirksen's pride in America, arguing that the time had come to grant Negroes their rights and that Dirksen, as a patriot, should support that goal.

But LBJ also played to Dirksen's vanity with an arsenal of flattery, according to Harry McPherson, Johnson's longtime Senate aide and White House speechwriter. Imitating LBJ's Texas drawl, McPherson acted out the famous Johnson treatment on Dirksen: "There is no way on earth that I'm going to be able to pass this without you, Everett, and I want to tell you that you're going to hear yourself referred to in the warmest terms you've ever heard. I've told Hubert [Senator Humphrey of Minnesota] I don't want any bad word about

Everett Dirksen ever to issue from his mouth. . . . You know, Everett, I've been to Pekin, Illinois [Dirksen's hometown]. I've seen that statue of Lincoln in the town square, and I want to tell you, Everett, if you help with this [civil rights bill], and make it possible for Nigras to live like decent human beings under the law like the rest of us, one day there's going to be another statue in that town square, and it's going to be a statue of you—you and Abraham Lincoln in your hometown."

McPherson paused, then added with an impish grin: "Now, you know, that's pretty broad paint, but, Judas Priest, hard to resist."

Slowly, Dirksen morphed from adversary to ally, but not before mildly recrafting the civil rights bill to insert some limits on the powers of federal enforcement. Yet when the crucial moment came—the vote on a motion of cloture that is the parliamentary procedure for killing a filibuster—Dirksen produced twenty-seven Republican votes, joining forty-four Democrats. That easily quashed the southern filibuster and paved the way for final passage. True to Johnson's word, Democrats fell all over themselves praising Dirksen as the savior of the civil rights bill.

To Johnson, Dirksen's decision was natural and wise. Not only was it morally right, in Johnson's view, it was smart politics: Dirksen had moved toward the middle, where Eisenhower had been. As Johnson saw it, the genius of American politics was that the two parties "pull to the center, where the vast majority of the votes traditionally are in this country."

A National Political Realignment

But even as Johnson uttered those words, the precious political center was under assault. Right-wing Republicans, with a power base in the Sun Belt, had taken control of the party, and in the 1964 presidential election, Johnson would face a challenge from the champion of the Republican Right, Senator Barry Goldwater of Arizona. Johnson felt Goldwater was too extreme to win in the general election, and he thought Goldwater's loss would fatally wound right-wing extremism. He was right about his beating Goldwater but wrong about its impact. Goldwater's loss in 1964 did not quiet the right wing, which fought back against the political center over the next four decades.

Johnson was prophetic about something else—the way America's political map was about to be redrawn. He foresaw a political transformation of monumental proportions taking shape. He understood that the foundations of the two major parties were about to be shaken to their core, with the southern reaction to the new civil rights laws fracturing the old New Deal coalition of the Democratic Party and with militant new forces altering the traditional conservatism of the Republican Party.

Johnson had been euphoric as he signed the historic Civil Rights Act of 1964 within hours of its passage in Congress. But that very evening his press secretary, Bill Moyers, found the president in bed, brooding. When Moyers asked what was the trouble, Johnson replied: "I think we just delivered the South to the Republican Party for a long time to come."

Johnson was right. As a Texan, he knew his region and its politics. He understood that by pushing a Democrat-controlled Congress to pass the Civil Rights Act of 1964 and then the Voting Rights Act of 1965, he had triggered what would be a prolonged backlash against the Democratic Party among southern whites. The once "Solid South," the historic bastion of the Democrats, would go Republican.

The realignment began even faster than Johnson expected. In November 1964, Barry Goldwater carried only six states against Johnson: his home state of Arizona and five states in the Deep South—South Carolina, Georgia, Alabama, Mississippi, and Louisiana. In 1968, Richard Nixon broadened the GOP's southern beachhead, piling up enough electoral votes in the Old Confederacy to narrowly defeat Vice President Hubert Humphrey for the White House. From 1972 onward, the South and the Sun Belt Southwest became the most reliable voting base of the Republican Party.

The Center: An Endangered Species

Moderates in both parties came under pressure, but especially moderate Republicans. As the South went Republican, states in the Northeast and Mid-Atlantic swung more Democratic. Moderate northern Republicans became an endangered political species—either defeated, purged, or gerrymandered out of their seats by party leaders eager to craft safe seats for more militant party loyalists. Or else moderates were defeated in party primaries engineered to favor extremist candidates. Democrats did much the same, crafting House districts to favor reelection of liberals, especially in big cities. And the conservative wing of the Democratic Party shrank as Republicans took away seats in the Sun Belt from conservative Democrats.

In the latest Congress, Republican Senate moderates have dwindled from the twenty-two recruited by Dirksen on civil rights to just three—Scott Brown of Massachusetts and Olympia Snowe and Susan Collins of Maine. But now Snowe has decided to resign, like Evan Bayh, out of frustration with the brutal partisanship on Capitol Hill. The seats of northern Republican moderate senators such as Javits in New York, Case in New Jersey, Scott in Pennsylvania, Aiken in Vermont, and Saltonstall in Massachusetts are now held by Democrats. Where Kentucky once elected Republican moderate John Sherman Cooper, it now has Tea Party libertarian Rand Paul. In the House, the sixty-five moderates who voted for Medicare with Johnson have shrunk to fewer than a dozen.

The swing to the Republican Right has been especially strong in the South. From 1964 to 2010, Republican strength in Congress from the eleven states of the Old Confederacy plus Kentucky and Oklahoma shot up from just 4 Senate seats to 20, and from 14 House seats to 102. Those gains helped power Republicans to control of the Senate in 1980, the House in 1994, and periodically since then. The impact of the Republican surge shows up not only in the numbers, but in the tenor of politics. Sun Belt Republicans have typically been opposed to the government's social programs and economic intervention that old-line Republican moderates used to support.

A Tribal Divide

The parties used to overlap, with conservative Democrats joining forces with Republicans on some issues and moderate Republicans voting with Democrats. But over time, the political center has been chewed away from both sides, mainly from the right. "Over the past thirty years, the parties have deserted the center of the floor in favor of the wings," concluded the authors of *Polarized America,* an academic study of Congress.

Political scientists Keith Poole and Howard Rosenthal have literally diagrammed the demise of the center. They have constructed inkblot charts that graph the growing gulf between the two political parties by plotting the votes of individual members of Congress on many issues. You can see the widening gulf between the parties. Over time, the R dots marking Republican vote patterns can be seen migrating away from D dots marking Democratic vote patterns. At one time the two clusters overlapped, but today the inkblot charts show clear white space between the parties. No overlapping vote patterns. The parties eye each other warily, like two armies, across a no-man's-land.

The few remaining moderates who might be inclined toward bipartisan cooperation are under intense pressure to prove their loyalty to their political tribe, said Tom Mann, an expert on Congress at the Brookings Institution, a liberal Washington think tank. In earlier times, Mann recalled, "there wasn't this sense of the tribe, this sense that no one can venture out of the tribe. Today, there are still some people in both parties who would like to do [bipartisan] deals, but the camps are too far apart. They don't play that game. They are two teams and they are at war. You don't fraternize with the enemy."

The partisan vitriol during the fight over Obama's health care reform in 2009–2010 epitomized the ideological schism that now divorces the parties from each other. "In the forty years that I have been here, this is the sharpest, most rancorous polarization that I have seen," said Norman Ornstein, a well-known congressional scholar at the conservative American Enterprise Institute. "We have had sharp divisions over Vietnam, around the impeachment of Nixon, real issues when Reagan first came in trying to implement a different agenda. But those differences did not play out strictly along party lines. This is more partisan, more ideological."

Max Baucus, the Montana Democrat who chairs the Senate Finance Committee, pointed to the senators' private dining room as a graphic example of the partisan divide, the political chill that keeps senators even from breaking bread together. "Nobody goes there anymore," said Baucus. "When I was here 10, 15, 30 years ago, that was the place you would go to talk to senators, let your hair down, just kind of compare notes, no spouses allowed, no staff, nobody. It is now empty."

Polarized Politics Plus
Filibusters Equals Senate Gridlock

Polarized parties and the missing middle spell policy stalemates. Gridlock has risen almost exponentially since the early 1990s, according to Professor Sarah Binder of George Washington University. "Partisan polarization and ideological diversity both contribute to policy stalemate," she found. When voters split control of Congress and the White House between the two parties, it's worse: The odds of gridlock escalate.

The Senate has become particularly paralyzed by the explosive use of the filibuster. Even the mere threat of filibuster by one or two senators, as Evan Bayh reported, can stop the action. The stepchild of the filibuster, "the personal hold"—a filibuster threat by a single senator—has become the parliamentary weapon of choice for the Senate minority party. There is no easier way for a minority, or even a few senators, to kill a bill than to threaten to shut down the Senate with a filibuster—or even the threat of a filibuster.

In the 1950s and 1960s, filibusters were used rarely, and then mostly on social issues such as civil rights legislation, but not on economic issues. Today, filibuster tactics are used frequently on economic issues. "Republicans began using filibusters on almost every issue, because it would bollix up the majority," observed Norman Ornstein. "It was like throwing molasses on the tracks."

"The Phantom Filibuster"

Average Americans frustrated by the eternal gridlock in Congress have no idea of the machine-gun frequency with which the filibuster—or the threat of a filibuster—is exploited. This is mainly because voters do not see live filibusters. The Senate long ago found a way to sidestep the televised drama of marathon filibusters like the one Jimmy Stewart staged in Hollywood's *Mr. Smith Goes to Washington* or the twenty-four-hour, eighteen-minute talkathon by Senator Strom Thurmond, the die-hard segregationist from South Carolina who defied biology and a Senate majority to block a civil rights bill in 1957.

To avoid tying up the Senate full-time in prolonged filibusters with senators sleeping in their offices, former Senate majority leader Mike Mansfield devised a two-track procedure in the 1960s. On one track, the Senate proceeded with normal business, while on a second track it took a quick test vote to see if it had a sixty-vote majority to invoke cloture. If the majority leader lacked the sixty votes, that bill was deemed dead on arrival. No fuss, no muss, no vote—not even a debate. Voters rarely realized that a bill had been killed by a phantom filibuster.

What this meant was that a minority of forty-one senators—and often fewer than that—could prevent a majority of fifty-nine from even bringing up a bill for debate. In practical terms, said Senator Tom Udall, a New Mexico Democrat, "every vote in the Senate now is sixty votes, which is what you need to cut off the debate. The will of the majority can be blocked by a minority. You have *tyranny of the minority*—and the public doesn't even realize it."

What's more, because the Senate operates under the rule of *unanimous* consent to bring up any bill, a single senator can block action by invoking a "personal hold"—long known as "the silent filibuster" because the senator did not have to identify himself or utter a word in public. The senator could set up a legislative blockade by sending a private written notice to the leadership of intention to filibuster a bill or a presidential appointment. A hold stopped the action because it forced the majority leader either to drop the proposal, make a backroom deal, or go through the Sisyphean task of scouring up sixty votes and using many hours of precious floor time to apply cloture. A silent filibuster was, in effect, a one-senator veto.

Originally, personal holds were granted as a courtesy to a senator who was ill, was out of town, or needed more time to consider a measure. But in the modern era of partisan combat, holds are used routinely to tie the majority in knots or to extract some concession from the White House or Senate leaders on an unrelated measure. As Norman Ornstein explained, "A hold is a hostage-taking weapon for individual senators."

The Senate: 70 Percent of All Bills—Death by Filibuster Tactics

Today, filibuster tactics are used across the board, and particularly on economic issues such as health care and taxes. "The statistics just blow you away," commented Tom Mann of Brookings. "The use of delaying tactics has just skyrocketed. In the 1960s, about 8 percent of significant legislation was subject to delaying tactics like filibusters and holds. It is now about 70 percent. Obstructionism is now the hallmark of the Senate."

With the escalation of filibuster tactics in the early 1990s as Republicans waged partisan warfare against President Clinton, Mann pointed out, the Senate has become the graveyard for legislation passed by solid House majorities. Hundreds of House-passed bills have been "condemned to death-by-filibuster."

As reform-minded senators have pointed out, the Senate has become such a bottleneck that the 2009–10 Congress was unable even to pass a normal budget bill or just one of the thirteen appropriations bills needed to fund the normal operations of the government. For years, those bills had routinely passed the Senate. Now, it takes emergency, cliff-hanging, eleventh-hour deals to get minimal routine work done.

So crippled has the Senate become—and Congress as a whole— that Thomas Mann and Norman Ornstein titled their major study on Congress, in 2008, *The Broken Branch,* and its sequel, out this year, *It's Even Worse Than It Looks.*

An Opportunity for Reform

Many people assume that the Senate filibuster is a constitutional prerogative, but neither the filibuster nor the personal hold is mentioned in the Constitution. These procedures have evolved over time through changes in Senate rules.

Historians tell us that the filibuster came into being by mistake. In 1805, as the Senate was codifying its rules on the advice of Vice President Aaron Burr, it accidentally omitted a rule for proceeding to its agenda, as the House does, and unknowingly, by default, that omission allowed extended debate. Only in 1917 did the Senate pass a cloture rule to have a formal way for cutting off debate. That backfired. Because of the very high threshold for cloture (then, a two-thirds vote of the Senate), the cloture rule worked perversely. It seemed to sanction filibusters. Senator Mansfield's two-track strategy backfired in the same way. It no longer took an actual filibuster to stop Senate action. A phantom filibuster did the trick.

To curb the use of phantom filibusters, reform-minded senators argue that the actual filibuster should be brought out of the closet and exposed to public scrutiny. They reason that the voters, already angry at congressional gridlock, would be even more fed up if forced to watch live filibusters tying up the Senate for weeks on end, and that might be a deterrent. In January 2011, twenty-six senators led by Democrats Jeff Merkley of Oregon, Tom Harkin of Iowa, and Tom Udall of New Mexico pushed for rule changes to bar some of the procedural delaying tactics. They persuaded the Senate to vote for a ban on the silent filibuster—the anonymous hold. But they failed to win a majority for a more important change—to bar filibusters on the procedural motion to bring a bill to the floor for debate and to eliminate Mansfield's old two-track procedure.

"We want to force a talking filibuster," explained Udall. "We want to get to the substance and not get stuck on procedure. A talking filibuster means that you would have to come to the floor and actually talk—talk as long as you wanted *on the issue,* which is the way it always had been, and then we would move to cut off debate and have a majority vote." That rule change failed to pass in January 2011, but reformers say they will try again.

The Economic Impact of Gridlock

Gridlock is not merely Washington's worry. It has real-life impact on the nation's economy and on the wealth gap. When Congress is polarized by partisan warfare and crippled by phantom Senate filibusters, budgets fail to pass and programs that are intended to help average Americans and strengthen the social safety net get stranded. Gridlock protects the status quo at a time when most tax laws and other economic legislation favor corporations and the wealthy—as people saw in 2010 and again in 2011 when President Obama tried to raise taxes on the top income bracket.

Political scientists have documented a link between polarized politics and rising economic inequality. The ever-increasing wealth gap and ever-sharpening partisan divisions go hand in hand. Over the past century, the two trends have moved up and down together, according to the authors of *Polarized America,* political scientists Nolan McCarty, Keith T. Poole, and Howard Rosenthal.

Graphs of the two trends overlap almost perfectly. In the early twentieth century, before the Depression of the 1930s, the income share of the top 1 percent in the country was at its peak, more than 24 percent of the total, and the division between the political parties was sharp, according to McCarty, Poole, and Rosenthal. From the 1940s through the 1970s, during the era of middle-class power and broad bipartisanship, we had less income inequality in the period of the Great Compression. Since the 1980s, the schism between the parties has widened and so has the wealth gap.

Litmus Tests:
The Minimum Wage and the Estate Tax

There is ample evidence that the collapse of the political middle and America's modern polarized politics have helped bring about policies that accentuate the nation's wealth divide. These political trends have powerfully affected key pocketbook issues at both ends of the economic spectrum, altering the way the pie is shared among winners and losers in the American economy.

Two litmus tests are the minimum wage and the estate tax, each intended to narrow the wealth gap.

Not only does the minimum wage put a floor on the lowest American pay scales, but that floor exerts an upward push on average wages. Since the late 1960s, as the political middle shrank and business lobbies gained power, the real value of the minimum wage has fallen by more than 40 percent, despite consistent public support for a higher minimum wage.

That change is no accident. It reflects the new partisan politics.

Traditionally, liberals seek to raise the minimum wage and to cover as many workers as possible. Conservatives, arguing that the minimum wage artificially raises the cost of labor, have fought to keep the minimum wage low and to limit its scope. From the 1930s through the 1960s, many moderate Republicans joined Democrats in supporting periodic increases in the minimum wage to help workers keep up with inflation. But in the Carter Congress of 1977, Republicans refused to index the minimum wage to inflation. After that, as inflation rose and eroded the purchasing power of minimum wage workers, their pay fell behind inflation. Finally, in 2007, Congress raised the federal minimum to $7.25 an hour, or full-time yearly pay of $15,080—but that is still 15 percent below the real value of the federal minimum back in 1968. In 2005, twelve states passed state minimum wages above the federal level, and eight of them, from Ohio to Arizona and Florida to Washington, have boosted their minimum wage again in 2012 by indexing it to inflation.

At the other extreme, the estate tax on inherited wealth, which affects only the richest 2 percent of Americans, has shifted increasingly in favor of the super-rich. The tax was established under President Woodrow Wilson in 1916, and until the mid-1970s, it imposed a levy of 77 percent on estates over $250,000. Anti-tax conservatives have fought to lower or abolish the estate tax, while political moderates and liberals supported the tax. In 1976, the exemption from the estate tax was raised to $1 million, adjusting for inflation, and under President Reagan, the estate tax rate was cut to 55 percent.

But President George W. Bush made the big changes in 2002. He passed a bill to phase it out entirely, reducing it in stages from a 55 percent rate in 2001 to zero in 2010, saving the super-rich $186 billion in taxes.

With the Bush cuts due to expire in 2011, President Obama proposed in December 2010 to restore the old pre-Bush tax rates (55 percent on estates over $1 million), but congressional Republicans blocked him.

Gridlock was the ally of the wealthy. With the Senate filibuster rule working for Republicans, they refused to extend Bush's tax cuts for the middle class unless Obama agreed to extend Bush's tax cuts for the rich, including a 35 percent cap on the estate tax rate and a tax exemption for estates worth $10 million for couples instead of the old pre-Bush rate of 55 percent on estates larger than $3 million. To break the gridlock, Obama had to accept estate tax cuts for the rich.

Those two policies—the failure of an increasingly polarized Congress to help the working poor and lower middle class by indexing the minimum wage to inflation and congressional approval of ever more generous estate tax cuts for the super-rich—have contributed to the great economic divide in America today. They illustrate the economic costs of polarized politics.

"The fight over estate tax repeal seems uniquely symbolic of the skewed class politics of the New Gilded Age . . . ," commented Princeton University political economist Larry Bartels. "To protect the inherited wealth of multimillionaires seems perversely contrary to the interests of the 98% of American families whose estates will never reach the threshold for taxation. How could a democratic political system arrive at such a policy?"

Good question.

CHAPTER 19

THE RISE OF THE RADICAL RIGHT, 1964–2010

ASSAULT ON THE MIDDLE-CLASS SAFETY NET

Let me now . . . warn you in the most solemn manner against the baneful effects of the spirit of party. . . . It serves always to distract the public councils and enfeeble the public administration. It agitates the community with ill founded jealousies and false alarms, kindles the animosity of one part against another. . . .

— PRESIDENT GEORGE WASHINGTON,
Farewell Address, 1796

The GOP's evolution in Congress since the 1970s has been one long move to the right. Like a retreating glacier, the GOP's moderate edges continually vanish . . . leaving a hardened core of increasingly unflinching conservatives.

— JACOB S. HACKER AND PAUL PIERSON,
Winner-Take-All Politics

Zero-sum politics and ideological siege warfare are the new order of the day.

ROBERT GATES,
former secretary of defense

THE MOST STRIKING and profound change in American politics during the last half century—a change that has sharpened America's political divide—is the transformation of the Republican Party and its takeover by the radical Right.

From its beginning in the 1960s, the militant New Right has been bent on political revolution. "We are different from previous generations of conservatives," asserted Paul Weyrich, the 1970s political genius nicknamed the Robespierre of the New Right for his revolutionary zeal and ideology. "We are no longer working to preserve the status quo. We are radicals working to overturn the present power structure in this country."

They have largely succeeded, reshaping the Grand Old Party with a series of political mutinies beginning with Senator Barry Goldwater in the 1960s and running up to the Tea Party today. Their persistent ideological insurgency has largely overthrown the Old Right, the mainstream Republican Establishment. In its place, the New Right has preached and practiced a new brand of conservatism, rejecting traditional bipartisanship, pushing the country into confrontation politics, and moving the nation's political center of gravity in its own direction.

"Bathtub" Conservatism

In terms of policy, the New Right has turned its back on the old mainstream consensus. Its hallmarks have been periodic assaults on the once sacrosanct bulwarks of the middle-class safety net, Social Security and Medicare, its relentless push for lower taxes, especially for the super-rich, and its desire to shrink government by shutting down entire cabinet departments and agencies.

Its goals were vividly voiced in a radio interview in 2011 by Grover Norquist, a leader of the College Republicans in the 1980s and now Washington's most influential anti-tax activist. "I don't want to abolish government," Norquist began, tongue-in-cheek, "I simply want to reduce it to the size where I can drag it into the bathroom and drown it in the bathtub."

In terms of tactics, the New Right has mirrored the confrontational politics of the firebrand Old Left. Its leaders normally reject compromise. They put ideological purity ahead of winning short-run victories. Their technique has been to sharpen partisan divisions by exploiting wedge issues that play upon concerns of white middle-class religious voters, such as abortion, school prayer, and ERA (women's rights), and by taking extreme positions and then waging uncompromising battle on "anti" issues—anti-tax, anti-union, anti-gay, anti-Washington, anti-government.

As Yale historian David Critchlow put it, "The Right's ideology [is] vehemently antistatist . . . the belief that centralized government should be feared as an enemy to individual liberty."

With this strategy, the radical Right has engineered the Republican Party's steady (if interrupted) march to the right, decade after decade. As scholars have noted, the Republican Party of Ronald Reagan in the 1980s was to the right of Richard Nixon's Republican Party in the 1970s; the party of former House Speaker Newt Gingrich in the 1990s was to the right of Reagan's party; the party of George W. Bush in the 2000s was to the right of Gingrich's party; and the party of Tea Party activists is the furthest right of all.

The Democratic Party has changed, too, but far less than the Republicans. Democratic officeholders have become philosophically more alike, more cohesive. Liberals from safe congressional districts dominate their caucuses more now than in the past, especially after many conservative Democrats lost in the 2010 elections. But paradoxically, as a group, congressional Democrats have been dragged toward the right by the gravitational pull of the Republican Right.

Goldwater: A New Brand of Conservatism

The Republican Right call themselves conservatives. So do 34 percent of all Americans. But there are many brands of conservatism. The Eastern Establishment conservatism of Wall Street and Corporate America promoting the global trade and tax agenda of big business differs from the heartland conservatism of small towns and rural counties that dislikes big government in principle but wants farm subsidies, federal loan guarantees for small business, and subsidized rural hospitals and electrification. Both of those differ from the social conservatism of Catholics and Evangelicals moved by issues like school prayer, abortion, and gay rights.

The trademark conservatism of the militant New Right was coined by Senator Barry Goldwater of Arizona, a handsome, straight-talking, ardently anti-government, anti-union conservative who lit the fire of ideological rebellion within the Republican Party in the 1960s. By breaking with traditional GOP conservatism and spurning the bipartisan consensus that governed America, Goldwater opened a polarizing cleavage between the two parties and provided an ideology for New Right crusaders for the next fifty years.

As a vehemently anti-union head of two family-owned department stores in Phoenix, Goldwater was an apostle of pure laissez-faire capitalism. He rejected the mainstream conservatism of Dwight Eisenhower and Richard Nixon, who talked about limited government but embraced the status quo, including New Deal programs, and who pushed government regulation of business to protect consumers and workers.

By contrast, Goldwater advocated repealing or revamping Social Security and warned that the welfare state and a permissive society were undermining America's morals. He accused Eisenhower, a small-town, middle-of-the-road Kansas conservative, of succumbing to the "siren song of socialism." Goldwater lashed out at Ike's budget. "It subverts the American economy," he declared, "because it is based on high taxes, the largest deficit in history, and the consequent dissipation of the freedom and initiative and genius of our productive people."

On many issues, Goldwater struck themes that are echoed by today's Tea Party. He tapped into the suspicions of the newly Republican Sun Belt toward Eastern Establishment Republicans and corporate leaders who had accommodated the welfare state. His vows to stop government from poking its nose into business won favor with ranchers, oilmen, and nouveau riche entrepreneurs in the Southwest. His attacks on Washington resonated with southerners who remembered that Goldwater had opposed Johnson's civil rights laws. His fervent anticommunism appealed to isolationist patriots furious at Eisenhower's internationalism, his support of the United Nations. And Goldwater's strident denunciations of labor unions gave him a beachhead in Corporate America. In one major speech, he lashed out at Walter Reuther and the United Auto Workers as "more dangerous to our country than *Sputnik* or anything Soviet Russia might do."

Above all, Goldwater infused a zeal for ideological purity into New Right movement conservatism. At the 1964 Republican convention in San Francisco, where Goldwater accepted the party's presidential nomination, the militancy of the Goldwater delegates alarmed mainstream Republicans. "What has been really frightening here is not the tactics, but the tacticians. They are a new breed," wrote *New Yorker* political analyst Richard Rovere. "The spirit of compromise and accommodation was wholly alien to them. . . . They came for a total ideological victory and the total destruction of their critics." To those who accused Goldwater of ideological extremism, Goldwater retorted, "Extremism in the defense of liberty is no vice. . . . Moderation in the pursuit of justice is no virtue." That memorable battle cry became a mantra of the New Right.

In the general election campaign, Goldwater's New Right rhetoric did not go over well with voters. He tried to downplay his pet issues like privatizing Social Security, expanding the Vietnam War, and opposing federal enforcement of civil rights, but an image of rampant extremism had been fixed in voters' minds by the GOP convention. Johnson won in a landslide—61 percent of the popular vote to Goldwater's 38.5 percent. But to Goldwater crusaders, being right was more important than winning. Staying true to principle trumped victory. The Goldwater legions vowed to fight another day, and with good reason. The finale of the Goldwater campaign was an electrifying half-hour anti-Communist, anti-government speech on national television by Ronald Reagan that immediately established the then fading fifty-three-year-old actor as America's most compelling new right-wing politician.

Paul Weyrich:
Building the Right-Wing Network

By the time Reagan ran for the presidency in 1980, a New Right apparatus was in place—a core leadership group, a bevy of think tanks, and a formidable network of organizations with their own political action committee and direct-mail fund-raising machine.

Paul Weyrich, a former Goldwater campaign volunteer, was the mastermind of the right-wing network. Weyrich, who spearheaded several right-wing organizations, was a one-man brain trust, constantly dreaming up ideas. He coined the terms *New Right* and *Moral Majority*. As the New Right trailblazer, he organized others for the mutiny against the Republican Establishment.

Weyrich was an unlikely looking revolutionary—a baby-faced Roman Catholic from Wisconsin in his midforties. But looks were deceiving. I remember watching him in action, suddenly seeing Weyrich as an American in a gray flannel suit and gold-rimmed spectacles who could match the ideological fervor and political skill of any Lenin in the world. He was a born crusader, a leader with a fertile mind, political passion, steely discipline, and contempt for compromise.

Weyrich strategized on a grand canvas. He understood that a revolution needed a department of propaganda, and he founded National Empowerment Television, a New Right channel. He saw Congress as the key to power and established the Committee for the Survival of a Free Congress, and he raised seed money from conservative business leaders like Joseph Coors of Coors Brewing Company to help elect true believers. He helped gear up the New Right for ideological battle by persuading Joe Coors and Richard Mellon Scaife, heir to the Mellon fortune, to put up millions to found the Heritage Foundation, a right-wing think tank, in 1973. Soon, other right-wing think tanks such the Cato Institute and American Enterprise Institute blossomed, funded by conservative foundations, corporations, and wealthy individuals such as David and Charles Koch of Wichita, Kansas, who poured more than $14 million into conservative think tanks.

Weyrich was also instrumental in drawing Jerry Falwell's Moral Majority, Pat Robertson's Christian Coalition, and other fundamentalist groups into the New Right political movement. Weyrich not only shared the religious faith and family values of social conservatives, but he understood the power of televangelists to mobilize the anger of born-again Protestants and traditional Roman Catholics against legalized abortion, women's rights, and the banning of prayer in schools. Their agenda was far different from Corporate America's, but Weyrich found ways to bridge the gap and, in Reagan's comforting phrase, bring them all under "one big tent."

Reagan Disappoints the Hard-Core Right

With Reagan's election in 1980, the New Right activists thought they had reached the Promised Land. In his campaign, Reagan had spoken contemptuously about government and limned his memorable refrain: "Government is not the solution; government is the problem." He had ridiculed the Environmental Protection Agency and the Occupational Safety and Health Administration with stories about their bedeviling business with excessive regulation. He had vowed to abolish entire cabinet departments.

But in office, Reagan disappointed the hard-core Right. He never came close to fulfilling his promise to kill several agencies. Instead of cutting cabinet departments, Reagan actually added one—the Department of Veterans Affairs. Paul Weyrich and the New Right were alarmed when Reagan chose mainstream Republicans for his cabinet and staff—especially White House chief of staff James A. Baker III, who had run Gerald Ford's presidential campaign against Reagan in 1976. Later, Weyrich went to see Baker to try to stop Reagan's nomination of Sandra Day O'Connor to the Supreme Court, on grounds that she was not a conservative true believer. But he failed.

Reagan did please the New Right, however, by turning Republican economic orthodoxy on its head. He delivered tax cuts—individual tax cuts, corporate tax cuts, and capital gains tax cuts—even as he was sharply boosting military spending. That combination generated a meteoric rise in the federal budget deficit. And it marked a philosophical turning point for the Republican Party.

Before, balanced budgets were a foundation stone of mainstream Republican economics. But Reagan and the New Right changed that. Their new mantra became "Starve the Beast"—meaning cut taxes first, create big deficits, and then use runaway deficits to pressure Congress and future presidents to cut programs—often important middle-class programs such as Medicare and Social Security.

Even so, the New Right activists were disgruntled with Reagan. His own budget director, David Stockman, faulted Reagan for perpetuating almost all government programs and accused him of waging a "phony war on spending." Paul Weyrich's verdict: "No Reagan Revolution." According to Weyrich, Republicans were too focused on the presidency—"conservatives are monarchists at heart"—whereas the real opportunity for change lay in taking over Congress.

The Gingrich Revolution

Enter Newt Gingrich, who as Speaker of the House in 1995 made the most concerted effort so far to enact the New Right political agenda and to roll back the middle-class safety net.

Gingrich personified the confrontational politics of the New Right. He arrived in Congress in 1978 as a brash, boyish-looking thirty-six-year-old history professor with the energy of a tornado, a machine-gun tongue, and a mop of bushy gray hair on a lion-sized head with an ego to match. He had not come to Congress to work with Democrats or the Republican leadership to pass laws. He had come to fight them both and take power.

Gingrich believed in polarizing politics. Boy Scout manners don't work in politics, he told a gathering of Young Republicans in Georgia. "Be nasty," he advised. "Fight, scrap, issue a press release, go make a speech." In Washington, he practiced guerrilla warfare. As a tireless media hound, Gingrich angled for coverage by getting into high-profile scraps with Democratic House Speaker Tip O'Neill and his successor, Jim Wright, and even with his own party leaders. He quickly became a star on Paul Weyrich's National Empowerment Television, and he exploited C-SPAN's coverage of the post-session hours in Congress to deliver diatribes to New Right followers across the country.

"Even before being sworn in as a member, Newt had this vision of how Republicans could take the majority," recalled Norman Ornstein of the American Enterprise Institute, who befriended Gingrich in 1978. "Newt saw that the country hates Congress in general, but people love their own congressman. He said, We can't win the way we're going. We have to nationalize the elections, mobilize the hatred for Congress nationally, and intensify it, and make Congress look so bad to people that they will think, 'Anyone is better than what we've got now.' That strategy encouraged polarizing the parties."

Over the years, too, Gingrich built a formidable political machine, using GOPAC, which he ran, to recruit, train, fund, and elect a whole new army of radical Republicans to do battle with liberal Democrats. In Gingrich's mind, the conflict was literally to be a civil war. "This war has to be fought with a scale and a duration and a savagery that is only true of civil wars," Gingrich caustically declared in 1988.

A Political Watershed—Clinton's Budget

When Bill Clinton entered the White House in 1993, Gingrich was battle ready. He had ousted the old Republican bosses and gotten elected as House Republican leader. He had a disciplined minority of

175 Republicans, and he was out to block every Clinton initiative, to make Clinton and the Democratic majority look bad by tying them in knots, and then to capitalize on voter frustration to win a House majority in the 1994 elections. He was out to destroy the Congress as a working institution, in order to capture control of it.

The first big test in 1993 came on Clinton's budget. It was a bold initiative, because it included a tax increase to help close the budget deficit left behind by Reagan and George H. W. Bush. It was smart economics because it eventually yielded the first budget surplus in years as well as helping to generate the solid economic growth of the 1990s. But Gingrich and his Republicans were dead set against any tax increase on ideological grounds. So all 175 House Republicans voted against Clinton's five-year economic plan.

It took a titanic effort by Clinton to hold together enough Democrats to pass the budget in the House, 218–216. The Senate deadlocked, 50–50, and Vice President Al Gore had to cast the deciding vote. Those budget votes marked a political watershed. It was the first time since World War II that a major piece of legislation had passed without a single yes vote from the opposition party.

Close as it was, that fragile victory was a high point for Clinton in that session of Congress. Clinton's health care plan never got out of committee. A whole list of other legislation was defeated or bottled up: aid to housing, aid to education, funding for the EPA's Superfund, and much more. More than half the bills (56 percent) died in gridlock.

In fact, the 1993–1994 Congress was one of the two *least productive sessions in half a century,* according to a study by political scientist Sarah Binder of George Washington University. *The Washington Post* commented that it would "go into the record books as perhaps the worst congress—least effective, most destructive, nastiest—in 50 years."

That was the verdict Gingrich had wanted. His strategy was to generate public disgust with Congress so that voters would reject the incumbent Democratic majority. The strategy worked brilliantly. In the 1994 congressional elections, Gingrich and the New Right hit the jackpot—seventy-three new Republicans to give the GOP the House majority for the first time in forty years.

Gingrich could not have done it without talk radio, especially right-wing commentator Rush Limbaugh. Sharply partisan talk radio had shot up since the Federal Communications Commission in 1987 repealed "the Fairness Doctrine," which previously required broadcasters to balance opposing political views. According to Republican pollster Frank Luntz, people who listened to ten or more hours of talk radio a week voted 3 to 1 for Republicans in 1994. Gingrich's freshmen understood Limbaugh's importance. They lionized him when he spoke at their freshmen orientation.

Gingrich—Bent on Reversing History

As the first Republican Speaker of the House in half a century, Gingrich set out in January 1995 to reverse the tide of history. His blueprint was "the Contract with America," the GOP's 1994 campaign platform that had promised a constitutionally balanced budget, a slew of tax reductions, cuts in safety net spending, and reforms to curb Washington's power. Backed by a passionate army of Class of '94 freshmen, Gingrich launched a legislative blitzkrieg.

By mid-November, Gingrich and Bob Dole, the Senate Republican leader, had set up a confrontation with President Clinton over the budget. Federal funds were about to run out, raising the specter of a government shutdown. Gingrich thought he had Clinton cornered. But Clinton outfoxed Gingrich by immediately furloughing eight hundred thousand federal workers, including those who processed Social Security checks. He put the political onus for the shutdown on the Republicans, accusing them of "unacceptable" cuts in education, public health, and the environment and creating a "winner-take-all society" that left out average Americans.

Gingrich fought back, pushing through a mammoth seven-year balanced budget package with even heavier program cuts. It contained a stinger, a proposal to privatize Medicare. The Gingrich plan would push seniors into private health care plans by putting future Medicare dollars into "medical savings accounts" and forcing seniors to shop for their own health insurance. The plan passed the House easily and barely squeaked through the Senate, but its impact got lost in press coverage on the government shutdown.

For several weeks, from mid-November 1995 to early January 1996, the partisan war between the Republican-led Congress and the Clinton White House raged on. Voters were appalled. In a CBS poll, a 51 percent majority blamed the Republicans for the government shutdown; only 28 percent blamed Clinton.

What Gingrich failed to reckon on was the ideological gulf between House and Senate Republicans. Gingrich had a New Right army in the House, but Dole led a more traditional Republican majority in the Senate. Dole himself was a mainstream conservative whom Gingrich had once mocked as "the tax collector for the welfare state."

By early January, Dole and the Senate Republicans had tired of the shutdown and of Gingrich and his abrasiveness. The GOP had been taking a political beating. With Dole ready for a deal, Gingrich had to back down and swallow Clinton's budget. His political revolution never regained momentum.

Purging Rinos

But New Right legions kept tightening their grip on the Republican Party and intensifying their drive to purify the party and rid it of what they derisively called RINOs—"Republicans in name only." Target No. 1 was Pennsylvania's Arlen Specter, the lone Republican moderate elected to the Senate in the GOP sweep of 1980 that elected a surge of new right-wingers and gave Republicans control of the upper chamber for the first time since 1954.

Specter had entered politics as a Kennedy Democrat in Philadelphia, but, feeling more in tune with moderate Pennsylvania Republicans like Senators Hugh Scott and John Heinz, he switched parties.

Once elected to the Senate, Specter was a straddler. He voted mostly with the Reagan White House in the early 1980s but crossed party lines on 40 percent of his votes—enough for Democrats to hail him as a sometime ally and Republican purists to mock him as "Specter the defector." Specter opposed Reagan's spending cuts on Social Security, unemployment benefits, child health care, food stamps, and programs for the poor, and he fought against a ban on abortions and a constitutional amendment legalizing school prayer. *National Review* put Specter on its cover in 1983 as the "Worst GOP Senator."

But what most infuriated the hard-core Right was his vote in 1987 in the Senate Judiciary Committee against Reagan's nomination of Robert Bork to the Supreme Court. Specter's no vote helped defeat Bork. The New Right smoldered.

In 2004, the hard-core Right decided to purge Specter by challenging him in Pennsylvania's Republican primary and intimidating other Senate RINO moderates. "If we beat Specter, we won't have any trouble with wayward Republicans . . . ," asserted Stephen Moore, president of the Club for Growth, a militantly anti-tax, anti-government right-wing group. "It serves notice to Chafee, Snowe, Voinovich and others who have been problem children that they will be next," meaning moderate Republican senators Lincoln Chafee of Rhode Island, Olympia Snowe of Maine, and George Voinovich of Ohio.

Moore's group spent $1 million, and its wealthy members individually added another $800,000, to fund Specter's challenger, right-wing Republican congressman Pat Toomey. Toomey tore into Specter as a "Ted Kennedy" liberal. Specter shot back that the Club for Growth was a gang of "Wall Street tycoons" and Toomey was "not far right, he's far out." In 2004, Specter beat the challenge.

But the hard-core Right was undaunted. They prepared Toomey for another run against Specter in 2010. Long beforehand, Specter could see that the political landscape had shifted against him. Pennsylvania's once moderate GOP electorate was now dominated by its extreme wing. "Since my election in 1980 . . . the Republican Party has moved far to the right," Specter commented. "Last year, more than 20,000 Republicans in Pennsylvania changed their registration to become Democrats." In April 2009, Specter announced that he, too, was switching parties.

But his switch came too late. Democratic voters saw it as too opportunistic, with the result that Specter lost in the Democratic primary. Then, in the general election, Toomey won Specter's old Senate seat and aligned himself with the Tea Party caucus.

The purge of Specter, wrote *Washington Post* columnist Dana Milbank, exemplified right-wing Republican "ideological cleansing." To Specter, it was political cannibalism—"eating or defeating your own."

The New Right vs. Obama

Riding the populist enthusiasm of his 2008 election victory, Barack Obama came into the presidency believing he could transform the fierce partisan divide in Washington. He talked hopefully about moving America into a new era of "postpartisan politics."

Obama never got a chance. He did not even get a traditional presidential honeymoon. A partisan red line split the 111th Congress from day one. The first two years of the Obama presidency echoed the instant war that former House Republican leader Newt Gingrich had declared on Bill Clinton in the 1993–1994 Congress. Confronting Obama in January 2009 was John Boehner, the new House Republican leader, who had been a top lieutenant to Gingrich in the 1990s. Boehner reused Gingrich's obstructionist game plan. He sought to defeat or discredit every Obama initiative and to make the president and the Democratic majority look bad in the eyes of voters.

The first test was Obama's emergency bill to rescue the U.S. economy from a free fall. In the winter of 2008–2009, private employers were firing six hundred thousand people a month and the economy had a gaping $2 trillion hole. To turn things around and to create jobs, economists of all stripes were calling for a shot in the arm from the government—a major stimulus package of tax cuts for average

Americans; funds for state governments to stave off mass layoffs of teachers, firemen, and others; and money for construction projects. Christina Romer, chairman of Obama's Council of Economic Advisers, recommended a $1.2 trillion stimulus. Keynesian economists such as Nobel laureates Paul Krugman and Joseph Stiglitz urged a supersized stimulus of $1.5 trillion to $2.4 trillion. But Obama's economic policy chief, Harvard economist Larry Summers, cautiously warned that anything larger than $600 billion to $800 billion could "spook markets . . . and be counterproductive." Summers feared Wall Street banks would raise interest rates, triggering inflation, and he told Obama that if more money was needed, Obama could get it later. Summers was wrong on both counts—there would be no inflation danger and no second chance with Congress.

Obama was in a hurry. He immediately sent a Summers-sized $787 billion stimulus plan to Congress. It had the backing of Republican governors from Connecticut's M. Jodi Rell to California's Arnold Schwarzenegger. But just nine days into Obama's presidency, all 177 House Republicans voted no on his plan to boost the economy. In the end, Democratic majorities pushed through the stimulus. Just three Republican senators voted yes. Obama's "postpartisan" politics had died on arrival.

On health care reform, the next big issue, the Republican Right was not only rock solid in opposition, but scathing in its rhetoric. Despite numerous concessions as the bill worked its torturous way through both houses, it got not a single Republican vote.

On financial regulation, the battle lines were sharp. Despite widespread public anger against Wall Street for the financial collapse, Republicans stalled, fought, and voted against legislation to impose new regulations on Wall Street to head off another catastrophe and to protect consumers. In the end, only six Republicans—three in the Senate and three in the House—saw merit in policing Wall Street and voted for the bill.

Just as in 1994, Republican obstructionism paid off politically in the 2010 congressional elections. With high unemployment, massive home foreclosures, and wide economic discontent, voters vented their anger at incumbent Democrats and handed sweeping victories and control of the House of Representatives to Republicans and their new Tea Party faction.

The Tea Party—Viral Rage

The Tea Party was born in anger in February 2009, when Chicago hedge fund trader Rick Santelli went into a nationally televised tirade against taxpayer-funded bailouts to foreclosed homeowners. In an angry rant on CNBC's *Squawk Box,* Santelli shouted that taxpayers had no desire to "subsidize the losers." His message was: Stop the government from helping other Americans. "We're thinking of having a Chicago Tea Party in July," Santelli boomed. "All you capitalists that want to show up to Lake Michigan, I'm going to start organizing."

Thanks to YouTube, Santelli's burst of rage went viral on the Internet. It struck a nerve. Two months later, more than half a million people turned tax day, April 15, into a mass protest at eight hundred Tea Party rallies coast to coast. By midsummer, the new "anti" movement—anti-tax, anti-government, anti–safety net—was targeting members of Congress for purging in the 2010 elections. Big-time right-wing political donors such as the energy magnates David and Charles Koch of Kansas, with a long record for underwriting right-wing causes, poured millions into the Tea Party's "educational" organizing.

The Tea Party looked like a populist movement, but when its profile emerged, it was not a movement of average Americans. The 18 percent who identified themselves in polls as Tea Party followers were predominantly white, male, older, more college-educated, and better off economically than typical Americans, and 63 percent chose Fox News as their primary news source. They were far to the right of average Americans, identifying themselves as "very conservative" and always or usually voting Republican. Some 92 percent wanted smaller government (vs. 50 percent of Americans overall); 73 percent said they would favor cutting domestic programs, including Social Security, Medicare, education, and defense; and while most Americans (by 50 to 42 percent) favored government spending to create jobs, Tea Party supporters were 5 to 1 against that policy. They cared far less about jobs than cutting government and the deficit.

Contrary to most Americans, Tea Party followers were not angry about the Wall Street bailout (only 1 percent were). But they were furious at Obama's health care program and at what they saw as his policy tilt in favor of the poor and blacks over whites. In all, 92 percent said Obama was leading America into socialism; 30 percent said, incorrectly, that Obama was not born in the United States; and, again wrongly, 64 percent said Obama had increased taxes, whereas Americans got a tax cut from Obama's stimulus package in 2009.

In the Republican primaries, Tea Party candidates defeated Republican Senate incumbents or mainstream politicians in Delaware, Florida, Kentucky, and Utah, and they won a slew of upsets in House races. In the general elections, the Tea Party planted its flag firmly on Capitol Hill, helping to lift Republicans to control of the House and to important gains in the Senate. Tea Party–backed candidates won Senate seats in Florida, Kansas, Kentucky, Pennsylvania, Utah, and Wisconsin, plus forty-two of the eighty-seven new Republican seats in the House. After the election, the House Tea Party Caucus picked up more members.

The Tea Party in Power

In power, the Tea Party Right pursued an agenda out of Goldwater and Gingrich, with a sharper, more cutting edge than Reagan. Very quickly, Tea Party caucuses on Capitol Hill signaled their intention to challenge their own leaders, if need be, in order to slash the size of government and the national debt—without touching tax breaks for corporations and the wealthy. Like Gingrich's Class of 1994 Republicans, the Class of 2010 was out to shut down government programs by the bushel, even those designed to help average voters.

With three thousand Americans dying and forty-eight million getting sick every year from tainted food, House Republicans cut millions of dollars from the budget of the Food and Drug Administration for overseeing the safety of the nation's food supply. They balked at renewing funds to retrain Americans thrown out of work by foreign competition. They opposed disaster relief after Hurricane Irene.

"They are more rigid than the Class of '94," said Norman Ornstein. "These are people who say we can cut most of government and nobody would notice, and they believe it. They seem to view Washington and the whole process as a leper colony. The more time you spend with the lepers, the greater the likelihood that you are going to get infected yourself."

The Tea Party's uncompromising absolutism on taxes and on across-the-board cuts of government programs left older conservatives like Bill Kristol, once a young Republican firebrand in the 1980s and now editor of the conservative *Weekly Standard,* worrying that many American voters would shy away from the Republican Party if it appeared to be "in the grip of an infantile form of conservatism."

GOP Right vs. Boehner and Obama

Taxes were the touchstone issue.

By rights, it fell to John Boehner as House Speaker to negotiate with President Obama on how to get the national debt under control. In early July 2011, Boehner shared his ambition with other House Republican leaders: He had not spent twenty years working his way up to the top job just for the title. He wanted to achieve something big, like a huge debt reduction package.

Boehner and the Republicans had staked out their position, calling for big cuts in government spending. Obama argued that taxes had to be part of the package, and taxes on the wealthy had to go up. "You can't reduce the deficit to the levels that it needs to be reduced without having some revenue in the mix," Obama asserted.

During a round of golf at Andrews Air Force Base in mid-June 2011, Boehner turned to Obama in the golf cart and urged the president to join him in striking a grand bargain: "Come on, you and I," Boehner said, "let's lock arms and we'll jump out of the boat together." For the next three weeks, the two leaders tried in private to craft a package to reduce the national debt by $4 trillion over ten years through a combination of large spending cuts and $800 billion in tax increases.

It was a political gamble. If they could strike the bargain and get Congress to pass it, both men would rise in stature. The president would be stronger running for reelection in 2012, and Boehner would raise his stature by winning huge spending cuts from Obama yet showing voters that Republicans were not out to gut Social Security and Medicare. The risk was that the hard-core Republican Right and/or militant liberal Democrats would revolt and block the deal.

As Obama and Boehner edged close to a deal, word about Boehner got out to House Republicans touching off rebellion. On Saturday night, July 9, Boehner phoned the president at Camp David and told him that it wouldn't work. House majority leader Eric Cantor, who had maneuvered into becoming the point man for the Republican Right and/or who was irked at being cut out of the secret Obama-Boehner talks, had torpedoed the deal. He told Boehner that House Republicans would not accept any tax increases and that Boehner had to back out of talks with Obama. Boehner bowed to that dictum and rejoined the Republican chorus against any tax increase.

Republican-friendly columnist David Brooks exploded in exasperation at the adamant refusal of the Tea Party–dominated Republicans to accept what he saw as Obama's lopsided concessions. In a *New York Times* column headlined "The Mother of All No-Brainers," Brooks wrote: "A normal Republican Party would seize the opportunity to put a long-term limit on the growth of government," but not a Republican Party in the grip of the Tea Party Right. "The members of this movement do not accept the logic of compromise, no matter how sweet the terms. If you ask them to raise taxes by an inch in order to cut government by a foot, they will say no. If you ask them to raise taxes by an inch to cut government by a yard, they will still say no."

That unflattering image evidently gnawed at Boehner because he decided to reopen his secret talks with President Obama in mid-July. In this final push, their grand bargain became even more ambitious. Boehner wanted an additional $450 billion in cuts from Medicare and Medicaid on top of $2.6 trillion in spending cuts previously agreed upon. Obama responded by demanding $360 billion more in tax revenue increases on top of $800 billion that Boehner had previously accepted. But on July 17, as Boehner talked with Cantor about making a counteroffer, Cantor flatly vetoed any tax increases. Boehner was stymied. He could not even go back and pick up the more modest deal that he and Obama had largely agreed upon a few days earlier. He had to call Obama once again and back out.

The Republican refusal to budge an inch on tax increases on the wealthy ignored the fact that the size of the deficit from 2009 through 2012 was heavily determined by the weak state of the U.S. economy and the fact that U.S. tax revenues, as a percent of the nation's economy, were already at their *lowest level in sixty years*—since 1950. It ignored the fact that the United States has the *third lowest overall tax rates* of the twenty-eight most advanced economies in the world. Not only do Germany, France, Canada, the United Kingdom, Japan, and New Zealand all have higher tax rates than the United States, but so do Turkey, Korea, Israel, and Iceland. Among developed countries, only Mexico and Chile tax less than the United States.

The Tea Party Millionaires Club

A hidden factor was at work on the tax issue—the Tea Party millionaires club.

Among the eighty-seven new House Republicans elected in 2010, low taxes suited not only their politics but their pocketbooks. Thirty-three of the sixty members of the House Tea Party caucus were millionaires when elected. Six were worth more than $20 million, according to the Center for Responsive Politics, which tracks money in politics. "What unites these freshmen," said the center's Dan Auble, "is that, on balance, they're rich." On average, Tea Party members were twice as rich ($1.8 million net worth) as other House members ($755,000).

Congress as a whole has a large crop of millionaires, which puts them among the richest 1 percent in America. In net worth, 261 out of the 535 senators and House members are millionaires—49 percent of the total, compared with 1 percent of the U.S. public. The wealthy have long been well represented in Congress, from prosperous landowners in the early 1800s, railroad barons and industrialists in the 1900s, to the new Wall Street and dot.com millionaires of today. What is striking is that the average wealth in Congress has shot up by 250 percent from 1984 to 2009, while average Americans were going backward.

Politically, the most powerful millionaire in Congress is House majority leader Eric Cantor, a handsome workaholic who recruited many of the new Tea Party House Republicans as candidates and who epitomizes their views and their financial profile.

First elected in 2000, Cantor is a multimillionaire real estate businessman from Richmond whose wife is an attorney serving bank clients. According to his financial disclosure statement, Cantor's personal portfolio in 2010 was worth about $5 million.

Not only do his investments and family real estate and banking connections give Cantor a vested interest in low tax rates for millionaires and in deregulating the financial industry, but the financial industry showered Cantor in 2010 with more than $2 million in campaign donations, double what they gave to Speaker Boehner. As *The Washington Post* commented, Cantor is their voice at the bargaining table.

Grover Norquist: Anti-Tax Lobbyist

Republican intransigence on tax increases also owes much to what Massachusetts governor Deval Patrick called the "hypnotizing" influence of an unlikely-looking Pied Piper—a stocky, bearded, owl-eyed anti-tax lobbyist named Grover Norquist.

In the 1980s, Norquist worked with Karl Rove at the national headquarters of the College Republicans. At President Reagan's urging, he formed Americans for Tax Reform to carry out Reagan's "Starve the Beast" strategy. He built a nationwide anti-tax movement and became what columnist Arianna Huffington called "the dark wizard of the Right's anti-tax cult"—an epithet that pleases Norquist. He posted it on his webpage.

Norquist, whom Senate majority leader Harry Reid called the de facto leader of congressional Republicans on tax issues, presses relentlessly for ever lower taxes, using that strategy to push constantly for across-the-board reductions in all discretionary programs and an across-the-board freeze in pay levels at such diverse agencies as the Pentagon, Medicare, FBI, Centers for Disease Control, and the National Park Service. Norquist, who seems to oppose virtually all government, led other budget deficit hawks after the Republican sweep in the 2010 elections in calling for a Congressional "crusade" against government spending that accepts "no sacred cows." More broadly, Norquist has laid out a strategy of cutting government in half by privatizing Social Security, eliminating welfare, cutting defense, education, and farm subsidies, as well as aid to the disabled, at-risk youth, and early child development, and selling off government facilities like airports; and then cutting government in half again.

As an anti-tax missionary, Norquist has no peer. He has set up anti-tax coalitions in every state. In Congress, as his website advertises, he has cajoled, persuaded, and threatened 238 House members and 41 senators—mostly Republicans—into signing a pledge never to raise taxes (as well as 13 governors and 1,249 state legislators). Since 1990, Norquist boasts, no congressional Republican has voted for any tax increase, and if anyone breaks his pledge, he will mount a mass effort to purge the offender.

Obama: Unable to Govern as a Democrat

Norquist is so confident of disciplining his anti-tax army that he once boasted: "We will make it so that a Democrat [in the White House] cannot govern as a Democrat."

That's exactly the political bind in which Barack Obama found himself in 2011—cornered by a radicalized Republican House majority and blocking-sized Senate minority, both dug in against raising taxes.

Just as Grover Norquist had predicted, Obama was unable to govern as a Democrat. In the battle over the federal debt ceiling, the Republican hard Right forced both GOP leaders in Congress and President Obama to accept their no-tax agenda along with nearly $1 trillion in immediate spending cuts, plus another $1.2 trillion to $1.5 trillion to come later. Even as American politics moved toward the 2012 election, the Republican Right in Congress adamantly refused to accept any tax increase on the rich to pay for extending middle-class payroll tax cuts, even though opinion polls indicated that's what the public favored. And as Yale professor David Bromwich observed, "It is an unhappy fact of politics that victory goes to the pressure that will not let up."

Tea Party Republicans were triumphant, but some mainstream Republicans were alarmed by what one called the "dangerous folly" of the Tea Party's game of chicken against the president. Former two-term Republican senator Chuck Com of Nebraska, who left the Senate in 2009, said he was appalled at the "irresponsible actions of my party, the Republican Party. . . . I had never seen anything like it in my, in my lifetime. I think about some of the presidents that we've had on my side of the aisle—Ronald Reagan and George Bush senior, and go right through them, Eisenhower. They would be stunned. . . . I was very disgusted in how this played out in Washington, this debt ceiling debate. It was an astounding lack of responsible leadership by many in the Republican Party."

The GOP Mainstream Bends

Six months later, Maine's Olympia Snowe, a moderate Republican, voiced similar anger when she announced last February that she was quitting the Senate after thirty-four years in Congress and would not seek reelection despite being a strong favorite. "I find it frustrating that an atmosphere of polarization and 'my way or the highway' ideologies [have] become pervasive in campaigns and in our governing institutions," Snowe declared. Seeing no realistic prospect for change, Snowe said bluntly: "I am not prepared to commit myself to an additional six years in the Senate."

Some mainstream Republican senators such as Orrin Hatch of Utah and Richard Lugar of Indiana, like GOP presidential candidates playing to the hard-core Right in the primaries, swerved to adopt hard right positions in their reelection campaigns to ward off Tea Party purging. Hatch survived the initial Tea Party purge, but Lugar was knocked off.

Conservative columnist David Brooks likened Republican primaries to "heresy trials" imposing ideological purity, and he sharply chided Hatch and Lugar for bowing to these pressures. "It's not honorable to kowtow to the extremes so you can preserve your political career," Brooks commented. "Of course, this is exactly what has been happening in the Republican Party for the past half century. Over the decades, one pattern has been constant: [Right] Wingers fight to take over the party, mainstream Republicans bob and weave to keep their seats. Republicans on the extremes ferociously attack their fellow party members. Those in the middle backpedal to avoid conflict." The danger, Brooks warned, is that the new right-wing extremists "don't believe in governance. They have zero tolerance for the compromises needed to get legislation passed. . . . It's grievance politics."

In the past, mainstream Republicans and Democrats have tackled politically explosive issues such as the national debt or the future of Social Security and Medicare through bipartisan commissions that work out of the political limelight to forge compromises based on shared sacrifice. But in the New Power Game, the time-tested approach of mutual give-and-take has been discarded in favor of what politicians themselves deride as "the permanent political campaign," pushed especially by the Republican hard Right.

"Today's Republican Party," observed Congressional scholars Thomas Mann and Norman Ornstein, "is an insurgent outlier. It has become ideologically extreme; contemptuous of the inherited social and economic policy regime; scornful of compromises; unpersuaded by conventional understanding of facts, evidence and science; and dismissive of the legitimacy of its political opposition, all but declaring war on the government."

The Democratic Party is "no paragon of virtue," Mann and Ornstein contend, but they find Congressional Democrats more ideologically diverse, more open to incremental changes of policies, and more prepared to seek compromise and bargaining with Republicans.

For Washington to get functioning properly again, Mann and Ornstein argue, the Republican Party has to return to its more traditional footing. "Bringing the Republican Party back into the mainstream of American politics and policy," they assert, "and [a] return to a more regular, problem-solving orientation for both parties, would go a long way toward reducing the dysfunctionality of American politics."

It would also help revitalize the U.S. economy and recover the American Dream, as would a reduction of America's ambitious global military footprint and operations.

CHAPTER 20

THE HIGH COST
OF IMPERIAL OVERSTRETCH

HOW THE U.S. GLOBAL
FOOTPRINT HURTS THE MIDDLE CLASS

To amass military power without regard to our economic capacity would be to defend ourselves against one kind of disaster by inviting another.

— PRESIDENT DWIGHT EISENHOWER,
State of the Union Address, February 2, 1953

The total amount that we spend on our military every year in the United States is roughly the same as the sum total of all defense expenditures by every other country on the planet.

— CHRISTOPHER PREBLE,
The Power Problem

MATTHEW HOH KNOWS the Afghan war from the inside. He volunteered to go, and he was a perfect fit for Afghanistan. At thirty-five, he had the right mix of experience, energy, courage, and commitment. After college, Hoh had enlisted in the U.S. Marines. By 2006, with the Iraq war at its worst, he was a marine captain commanding a combat engineer company in what Hoh called "the hell that was Anbar Province"—a hotbed of Sunni resistance where Americans suffered extremely heavy casualties.

Hoh knew how to get Iraqis to cooperate with Americans. In 2004–2005, he had supervised a major reconstruction effort by five thousand Iraqis in Saddam Hussein's hometown of Tikrit, spending tens of millions of dollars to rebuild roads and mosques. His program had been singled out for praise. Then came Hoh's sixteen-month combat tour in Anbar Province, where he was cited for "uncommon bravery" and recommended for promotion. But, suffering from post-traumatic stress disorder, Hoh mustered out of the U.S. Marines. However, when President Obama ramped up the Afghan war and sent in twenty-one thousand more U.S. troops in March 2009, Hoh volunteered to serve again.

The State Department grabbed him and sent him to heavy combat zones, first in the east and then into the southern heartland of the Taliban. Hoh studied the local culture and dug into Afghan history. In Zabul Province, he worked to help local officials increase their effectiveness and win support among the tribes. In the east, he had seen that the tribes had little affinity for the Taliban but had been driven into a working alliance with the Taliban out of resentment against American military intrusions. In the south, Hoh found people motivated not by Taliban ideology, but by family ties and loyalty to tribe and village. There was not one insurgency, he discovered, but hundreds, and what united them was their hostility toward the corrupt central government in Kabul, especially after the fraud-ridden reelection of President Hamid Karzai in August 2009.

A War Gone Off Track

Over time, Hoh came to the conclusion that the war had gone off track. He was troubled both by the American rationale for fighting in Afghanistan and by the way the war was being fought. As he saw it, the United States was no longer fighting al-Qaeda and global terrorism, but we had gotten sucked into an Afghan quagmire—a civil war between feuding Afghan tribes and warlords. Al-Qaeda's terrorists had fled to Pakistan or to Yemen, Somalia, and beyond. What was left now, he thought, was a domestic Afghan conflict that pitted urban, secular, educated Afghans in Kabul against the rural, religious, illiterate Pashtun tribes in the south and east. Initially, America had arrived as an ally that ousted a hated Taliban regime. Now, Hoh believed, America was widely perceived as the occupier.

"I believe that the people we are fighting there are fighting us because we are occupying them—not for any ideological reasons, not because of any links to al-Qaeda, not because of any fundamental hatred toward the West," Hoh would later say. "The only reason they're fighting us is because we are occupying them."

Within a year, Hoh resigned. "I have lost understanding of and confidence in the strategic purposes of the United States' presence in Afghanistan . . . ," Hoh wrote to the State Department. "My resignation is based not upon how we are pursuing this war, but why and to what end. . . . We are mortgaging our Nation's economy on a war, which, even with increased commitment, will remain a draw for years to come. Success and victory, whatever they may be, will be realized not in years, after billions more spent, but in decades and generations. The United States does not enjoy a national treasury for such success and victory."

"Rebuild Afghanistan or Rebuild America? . . . We Cannot Do Both"

Matthew Hoh had put his finger on what the Bush administration ignored and the Obama administration played down—the impact of the Afghan and Iraqi wars on the U.S. economy and the toll they were taking on domestic programs for average Americans.

President Bush sidestepped a guns-vs.-butter debate by never raising taxes to pay for the wars in Iraq and Afghanistan or for America's global war against al-Qaeda. The wars have added more than $2 trillion to the U.S. national debt. In Matthew Hoh's terms, Bush mortgaged the nation's economy for years to come. Not until the tenth year of the Afghan war, when domestic programs faced severe cutbacks as Congress grappled with the national debt, was there a public clamor for cutting military spending.

Paradoxically, it was President Obama's first draw-down of U.S. troops in Afghanistan that triggered protests. There was wide public disappointment in June 2011 over Obama's long-awaited announcement that the initial withdrawal would be just ten thousand U.S. troops by the end of 2011 and twenty-three thousand more by mid-2012.

Both Republican conservatives and Democratic liberals rebelled. In the House of Representatives, they pushed for a faster pullout. To loud applause, Republican Walter Jones of North Carolina declared: "If we're going to cut programs for children who need milk in the morning, if we're going to cut programs for seniors who need a sandwich at lunch, if we're going to cut veterans benefits, then, for God's sake, let's bring back our troops from Afghanistan." The resolution for a faster pullout was beaten—but only very narrowly, by 215–204—a vote that posed a warning for the future.

Out in the country, there were echoes of discontent. The U.S. Conference of Mayors passed a resolution urging an early end to the wars and rechanneling funds from military to domestic programs. Minneapolis mayor R. T. Rybak protested that American cities were being forced to make "deeply painful cuts to the most core services while the defense budget continued to escape scrutiny." Los Angeles mayor Antonio Villaraigosa angrily objected: "That we would build bridges in Baghdad and Kandahar and not Baltimore and Kansas City absolutely boggles the mind." During the Senate's partisan wrangling over the debt ceiling, West Virginia Democrat Joe Manchin III remonstrated: "We can no longer, in good conscience, cut services and programs at home, raise taxes or—and this is very important—lift the debt ceiling in order to fund nation-building in Afghanistan. The question the president faces—we all face—is quite simple: Will we choose to rebuild America or Afghanistan? In light of our nation's fiscal peril, we cannot do both."

War Costs Will Total $4 Trillion

What had pushed the guns-vs.-butter debate to the front burner was uneasiness at the staggering costs of the wars in Iraq and Afghanistan and a growing awareness that they were fueling the national debt because they had not been paid for.

Congress has directly appropriated $1.4 trillion in funds earmarked for the wars in Iraq and Afghanistan from September 11, 2001, through 2012, but those figures vastly understate the total costs. They leave out $2.5 trillion to $3 trillion of increases in other war-related spending and national security costs supporting the two wars and the war on terrorism.

From government budget documents, the Eisenhower Study Group, a team of scholars at Brown and Boston Universities, totaled the costs of the war through fiscal year 2015 this way:

$1.430 trillion—Direct war appropriations through fiscal year 2012

326 billion—Additions to Pentagon base budget, indirectly supporting wars

185 billion—Interest on Pentagon borrowing for war appropriations

864 billion—War-related foreign aid assistance through fiscal year 2012

33 billion—Veterans' medical and disability payments and expenses

401 billion—Department of Homeland Security

$2.461 trillion—Total war costs through FY 2012

168 billion—Projected war appropriations through fiscal year 2015

589 billion—Guaranteed lifetime health and disability care for 2.2 million veterans of the two wars through fiscal year 2051

295 billion—Projected social costs to veterans and their families

$3.513 trillion—Total projected costs and obligations

The Eisenhower Study Group called the $3.5 trillion figure a conservative estimate. A more realistic "moderate" estimate, they said, would be $4.4 trillion.

All those costs represent deficit spending, added to the national debt and far, far above the forecasts of the Bush administration, which suggested the two wars would be short and cheap. Bush's budget director, Mitch Daniels, estimated the Iraqi war costs at $50–$60 billion. Bush fired his top economic adviser, Lawrence Lindsey, for telling a reporter that the Iraq war might cost from $100 billion to $200 billion. The Pentagon estimated the Afghan war would cost $1 billion a month, or $120 billion over ten years.

The Perils of "Mission Creep"

The costs skyrocketed because both wars lasted much longer than the Bush administration expected—and as policy experts remind us, they lasted longer for two reasons.

One was Bush's decision not to raise taxes to finance the wars—a decision attacked by conservatives as well as liberals. Wars that are unpaid for last longer, according to Bruce Bartlett, a former high Republican official in the Reagan and first Bush presidencies. "History shows that wars financed heavily by higher taxes, such as the Korean War and the first Gulf War [1991], end quickly, while those financed largely by deficits, such as the Vietnam War and current Middle East conflicts [Iraq and Afghanistan], tend to drag on indefinitely," Bartlett wrote. Cato Institute researchers William Niskanen and Benjamin Friedman said unfunded wars drag on because "deficit financing sends war bills to future taxpayers. . . . The effect is to make war feel cheaper. . . ."

The other main reason that wars drag on is what generals call "mission creep"—U.S. forces are sent in with a narrow mission and that evolves over time into a much more ambitious and costly mission. In Iraq, the mission was to overthrow Saddam Hussein and to find and destroy his weapons of mass destruction. When there were no such weapons, the mission shifted to building Iraqi democracy.

In Afghanistan, America's initial goal was to avenge the terrorist attack of 9/11 and to disrupt, dismantle, and decapitate al-Qaeda by destroying its Afghan bases and killing Osama bin Laden and other al-Qaeda leaders. "The mission is to bring al-Qaeda to justice and to make sure Afghanistan no longer serves as a haven for terrorists," President Bush asserted on November 26, 2001.

Bush emphasized that he did not want to get drawn into a protracted guerrilla war. Soon after the first U.S. attacks against al-Qaeda bases in Afghanistan, a reporter asked him how the United States was going to avoid being drawn into a Vietnam-like quagmire.

"We learned some very important lessons in Vietnam," Bush replied. "Perhaps the most important lesson that I learned is that you cannot fight a guerrilla war with conventional forces." In his 2000 campaign, Bush declared his aversion to nation building and chided President Clinton for peacekeeping and democracy-building missions abroad. As president, in July 2001, Bush underscored the point that he "thought that our military should be used to fight and win wars. . . . And that I was concerned . . . about how we use our troops for nation-building exercises, which I have rebuffed as a, basically rebuffed as a kind of a strategy for the military."

But once al-Qaeda had been routed, the Taliban regime in Kabul had been overthrown, and bin Laden had fled into Pakistan, Bush widened his objectives. In April 2002, the president proclaimed a "Marshall Plan" for Afghanistan. "We know that true peace will only be achieved when we give the Afghan people the means to achieve their own aspirations," Bush declared. He ticked off an ambitious agenda for nation building. "Peace will be achieved," he said, "by helping Afghanistan develop its own stable government . . . train and develop its own national army . . . [build] an education system for boys and girls which works. We're working hard in Afghanistan. We're clearing minefields. We're rebuilding roads. We're improving medical care. And we will work to help Afghanistan to develop an economy that can feed its people without feeding the world's demand for drugs."

Then in 2003, as Bush plunged America into war in Iraq, he shifted resources away from Afghanistan, but he still spoke glowingly about "Afghanistan's journey to democracy and peace." At a White House meeting with Afghan president Hamid Karzai in June 2004, Bush emphasized America's "ironclad commitment to help Afghanistan succeed and prosper."

From "Counterterrorism" to "Counterinsurgency"

The mission creep was not merely rhetorical. As the president changed his stance, America's military objectives morphed into new ones. Al-Qaeda, once in the Pentagon's bull's-eye in Afghanistan, faded. By 2006 if not earlier, al-Qaeda and its Arab recruits had for all practical purposes disappeared from Afghanistan, according to General David McKiernan, the U.S. commander there. Al-Qaeda had found better, safer havens in Pakistan and was able to mount attacks against the West from other bases around the world. So the original rationale for U.S. military operations in Afghanistan, which had made sense and had strong popular support, had become defunct.

The Pentagon simply shifted gears. Following the president's lead, the nation's military leaders took on the immense mission of nation building in Afghanistan. To Robert Blackwill, Bush's deputy national security adviser during 2003–2004, that shift was a strategic blunder. "The mistaken mission creep in Afghanistan during the Bush years was moving from counterterrorism after 9/11—to destroy al-Qaeda—to nation building . . . ," said Blackwill. "Given the history and culture of Afghanistan, that was always many bridges too far."

In the lexicon of national security, as Blackwill observed, the White House and the generals slipped from a "counterterrorism strategy" to a "counterinsurgency strategy." They are very different. Counterterrorism targets the terrorist network, using small operations by highly trained forces such as the Navy SEAL team that killed Osama bin Laden. In the past five years, its main field of operations has been outside of Afghanistan. Its primary weapons have been drones operating over the tribal areas of Pakistan or Yemen.

Counterinsurgency is far broader and much more expensive. It involves taking on the full range of tribal forces allied with the Taliban. It means pacifying an entire vast mountainous country and simultaneously trying to create an effective national army and police and to establish a stable Afghan government. It takes much longer than counterterrorism and requires much larger forces and much more foreign development aid.

Counterinsurgency is precisely the kind of complicated, long-term nation building that Bush had once so staunchly opposed. But by the end of his term, President Bush had switched. He enshrined an open-ended U.S. commitment to Afghanistan. "We have a strategic interest and I believe a moral interest in a prosperous and peaceful democratic Afghanistan. And no matter how long it takes," Bush vowed, "we will help the people of Afghanistan succeed."

Obama Expands the Afghan War

The Pentagon's push to keep expanding the U.S. mission in Afghanistan found new momentum under President Obama. True to his campaign promises in 2008, Obama moved to reduce and withdraw all U.S. combat forces from Iraq. But denying Afghanistan as a potential future base for terrorists had long been his priority, and two months into his term, Obama committed twenty-one thousand more troops to Afghanistan. Even before they arrived, Obama was under intense pressure from General Stanley A. McChrystal, the new U.S. commander in Afghanistan, and the top Pentagon brass to send yet another forty thousand troops. Failure to send in more troops and stop a "deteriorating" war situation, McChrystal warned Obama in August 2009, "risks an outcome where defeating the insurgency is no longer possible."

McChrystal had put the squeeze on the new president by framing a dilemma: Go in deeper or risk losing. His stated goal of *defeating* the Taliban represented mission leap—not creep, but leap. Until then, the more modest U.S. goal had been to "disrupt and dismantle" the Taliban. *Defeat* was setting the bar higher, sharpening the imperative for more troops and more years in Afghanistan. Secretary of Defense Robert Gates and the Joint Chiefs of Staff wanted *defeat* written into Obama's official orders to McChrystal.

That quickly became a bone of contention in heated internal policy debates. In the end, Obama and his national security advisers rejected the "defeat" language. Obama's final orders were for the military to "degrade" the Taliban insurgency and to "deny [the Taliban] the ability to overthrow the Afghan government." In short, block the enemy, but you don't have to crush them. Nonetheless, Obama did agree to send thirty thousand more troops, meaning that in his first year he had more than doubled the U.S. fighting force in Afghanistan.

Just over a year later, in January 2011, General David Petraeus, the new U.S. Afghan commander, reported that the American troop surge had given U.S. and NATO forces the military initiative and had thrown the Taliban on the defensive. NATO coalition and Afghan forces had "inflicted enormous losses" on the Taliban in the past year, Petraeus said, and "took away some of their most important safe havens." In mid-2011, Petraeus reported a modest decline in Taliban attacks from the peak levels of 2010. The ultimate goal of leaving the Afghans able to provide for their own security, Petraeus said optimistically, was "very hard, but it is doable."

Afghanistan and Vietnam: Déjà Vu All Over Again

As the Afghan war dragged on, longtime counterinsurgency experts saw pregnant parallels between the war in Afghanistan and the fateful U.S. war in Vietnam in the 1960s. Rufus Phillips, who had headed the U.S. civilian counterinsurgency effort in Vietnam in the early 1960s, went to Afghanistan on an official mission in mid-2009 and came home to write an essay titled "Déjà Vu All Over Again." The war estimates of Generals Petraeus and McChrystal bore echoes of the rosy military assessments in Vietnam. U.S. commanders seemed in both wars to focus more on enemy casualties and body counts, on territory won or lost, than on the political dimensions of the conflict, which in Vietnam ultimately undid the American cause.

Of course, history does not literally repeat itself, but as Mark Twain reportedly quipped, "It rhymes." As Rufus Phillips saw it, the U.S. military campaign in Afghanistan, as in Vietnam, might appear to be going well, but the Afghan government, like the Vietnamese, was weak, corrupt, and disliked; its national police force was inept and unreliable; and out in the rural homeland of the insurgency, Afghans, like the Vietnamese, felt little connection with the government in Kabul. Ambassador Richard Holbrooke, whom I had met in Vietnam in 1963 and who was running the U.S. civilian counterinsurgency campaign in Afghanistan for the Obama administration, told me in late 2010 that he, too, saw worrisome parallels between the two wars.

There is good reason to look at the Vietnam and Afghan wars in tandem because of their economic impact on America at home. Over the past seven decades, the United States has girded for security threats in Europe and now in the Pacific, but it is actually in the Arc of Danger, stretching from Afghanistan, Pakistan, Iraq, and Somalia to Indochina, that the United States has spent heavily in blood and treasure. This volatile region, as Defense Secretary Robert Gates would warn as he ended his tour, is where the projection of our military power has mired us in long, expensive wars whose economic and political costs have outweighed whatever they might have added to our long-term national security.

In each war, American leaders cast the struggle in grand terms, as a critical battle in a global Armageddon. The White House and Congress in the 1960s insisted that Vietnam was the linchpin of security in Asia. If Vietnam fell, policy makers insisted, other dominoes would fall—Cambodia, Laos, Thailand, Southeast Asia. America itself would be threatened. Eventually Vietnam fell, but the disaster never happened. More recently, Saddam Hussein in Iraq was portrayed as a mortal nuclear threat, but that turned out to be false. Now, in Afghanistan, we are said to be fighting the decisive battle against Islamic terrorism, but in fact, al-Qaeda was largely routed six years ago and Islamic jihadists have shifted their operating bases to Pakistan, Yemen, Somalia, or the Internet.

In Afghanistan, as in Vietnam, as former U.S. ambassador Karl Eikenberry repeatedly warned the White House and State Department, the war is more political than military, more about winning "the hearts and minds" of the Afghan people than about military firepower and kill ratios. Both were guerrilla wars in which the awesome technology of the U.S. military has provided only modest advantages. In Vietnam, and now again in Afghanistan, most American policy makers have focused on the enemy's ideology, but as Matthew Hoh observed, they have underestimated nationalism as the unifying motivator for the other side—the simple but unquenchable drive for national independence and for expelling the outsiders.

In both wars, the American cause has been crippled by corrupt governments that failed to rally the loyalty of their people. In each case, the United States has invested heavily to build an effective indigenous army and police, but the local forces have been riddled with defections and often unwilling to fight. Their weakness has forced the American military to take the lead, but that has only deepened the gulf between the local government and its people, by making it look like a puppet. Moreover, the high U.S. military profile has left a burning popular resentment when America's high-tech weaponry has caused civilian casualties, as President Hamid Karzai has often complained.

The "Good War" Gone Bad

To a majority of Americans, including those such as President Obama who disagreed with the war in Iraq, the military campaign to dislodge al-Qaeda from Afghanistan was justified. But as mission creep moved American forces into nation building, the downside emerged: Afghanistan's weak and mercurial leadership; rising tensions and violence between Afghan and American forces; and President Karzai's frequent and often blistering denunciations of the American war effort.

Over time, some American officials have become disillusioned with Karzai, especially after the massive ballot stuffing and election fraud cast a shadow of illegitimacy over Karzai's reelection in August 2009. Ambassador Eikenberry was so mistrustful of Karzai's reliability that he warned President Obama that reinforcing U.S. troops would probably be futile unless the Karzai government could curb rampant corruption, show stronger leadership, and muster public support.

Although the United States has spent $6 billion since 2002 in building the Afghan army and the national police to take over security in 2014, as U.S. and NATO combat troops are scheduled to depart, the reliability of those forces is questionable. Crooked Afghan cops have been reported selling arms and ammunition to the Taliban. Desertions and resignations from the police have been estimated at 47 percent or more.

While the Afghan army has grown more rapidly, only a tiny fraction of its recruits—just 1.5 percent—have come from southeastern Afghanistan, the heartland of the Taliban, home to roughly five million of the country's thirty million people. Afghan loyalties are a looming question mark. While some U.S. officers praise certain Afghan military units, others are alarmed that Afghan soldiers have been turning their weapons against U.S. and other NATO forces. Initially, these killings were dismissed as isolated incidents. But in early 2012, one classified U.S. military report said killings of allied soldiers "reflect a rapidly growing systemic homicide threat" among Afghan recruits. A *New York Times* reporter who obtained that report pointed to the killings of U.S. GIs by Afghan soldiers as "the most visible symptom of a far deeper ailment plaguing the war effort: the contempt each side holds for the other, never mind the Taliban. The ill will and mistrust run deep among civilians and militaries on both sides. . . ."

That mistrust sharpened acutely in the spring of 2012 after a video circulated showing U.S. Marines urinating on the dead bodies of Taliban fighters and after NATO forces mistakenly burned Korans near Bagram Air Base. Two dozen Afghans were killed in clashes with NATO military forces during bloody protests in several Afghan cities over the Koran burnings, and two U.S. advisory officers were killed inside the heavily guarded Afghan Interior ministry. But the most inflammatory incident was an apparently unprovoked killing rampage by an American Army sergeant, who allegedly murdered sixteen villagers in their homes in southern Afghanistan. In Washington, the string of explosive episodes heightened talk of accelerating the U.S. military withdrawal. In Kabul, President Karzai responded to widespread public anger by pressing the U.S. to pull back from rural operations and to confine its troops to military bases by 2013. Officials in both countries feared that the new tensions played into the hands of the Taliban insurgency.

"People are still kind of under the spell of the Taliban," asserted Dr. Mahmood Khan, a member of parliament from Kandahar. "They believe it is not only stronger than the government, but that their intelligence is stronger. They can find out very soon if your son or brother is serving in the army." The Taliban are reported to have beheaded army recruits and recruited others.

Friendly Afghans warn Americans not to be deceived by appearances of cooperation. "I can tell you this very clearly," Munshi Abdul Majid, governor of Baghlan Province, told a *Washington Post* reporter: "50 percent of the people working with the Afghan government, their hearts are with the Taliban." Muhammad Mohaqeq, a former tribal warlord and current member of parliament, said ominously in late 2011: "The Taliban are coming back. They have deeply infiltrated the Afghan forces, the police and the army. Security is getting worse as the Taliban are getting stronger."

The Warning from Bob Gates

Although Defense Secretary Robert Gates steadfastly promoted the broad counterinsurgency strategy in Afghanistan and spoke confidently about the American war effort there, on the verge of his retirement from the Pentagon in 2011, Gates vented his frustration at waging war in the Arc of Danger.

"I must tell you, when it comes to predicting the nature and location of our next military engagements, since Vietnam, our record has been perfect," Gates quipped puckishly in a speech to West Point cadets. "We have *never once gotten it right,* from the Mayaguez to Grenada, Panama, Somalia, the Balkans, Haiti, Kuwait, Iraq, and more—we had no idea a year before any of these missions that we would be so engaged."

Then, Gates soberly underscored the grave risks of committing large U.S. forces to guerrilla wars and nation building. "In my opinion," Gates said, "any future defense secretary who advises the president to again send a big American land army into Asia or into the Middle East or Africa should 'have his head examined,' as General MacArthur so delicately put it."

America's Global Footprint: An "Empire of Bases"

The wars in Afghanistan and Iraq epitomize America's global military footprint. We Americans don't like to think of our country as an empire, but, as the Pentagon's own figures confirm, our military forces have an imperial reach that girdles the globe. Unlike Great Britain, France, or Spain in the eighteenth and nineteenth centuries, we have not built an empire of overseas colonies, with some notable exceptions such as the Philippines and Puerto Rico.

But the United States has been driven by a sense of manifest destiny to carry our concept of freedom and democracy across the world and to fight when we see liberty—or our lanes of commerce—threatened. We did not covet territory per se. Instead, as Professor Chalmers Johnson of the University of California at Berkeley observed, America chose a politically more expedient and cost-efficient strategy for projecting its power. The United States developed what Johnson called an "Empire of Bases" that circled the globe.

America's military imperium has become so natural to us and so embedded in the structure of global power that by the end of 2011, nearing seven decades after the end of World War II and more than two decades after the close of the Cold War, the United States still had more than 580,000 personnel—in uniform or defense contractors—stationed in fifty-seven countries.

The magnitude of America's worldwide network of bases is stunning. The Pentagon's "Base Structure Report" in 2011 listed 611 U.S. overseas military sites, not counting those in hot war zones—then 411 in Afghanistan, 88 in Iraq, and half a dozen in Kuwait. Nor did it count another half dozen bases in Saudi Arabia or U.S. covert facilities in Pakistan used for drone missions against al-Qaeda. Even subtracting family housing complexes, schools, resort hotels, and golf courses (the Pentagon owns 172 golf courses), there are more than 1,000 overseas U.S. military installations.

"No other military in world history has been deployed as widely as that of the United States," the conservative Heritage Foundation reported. Simply maintaining those bases in 2010 cost $41.6 billion, not counting the costs of troops stationed overseas or new construction, according to Deputy Undersecretary of Defense Dorothy Robyn.

America's omnipresent global footprint today is a legacy of the Cold War. The global menace of Soviet-led communism was its rationale. The United States built a system of deterrence through alliances with NATO in Europe, SEATO in Southeast Asia, CENTO in the Middle East, and special defense links to Japan and South Korea in the Far East. Every region, every country, every civil war, every coup d'état, every nascent threat, became a potential trip wire for U.S. involvement.

From Harry Truman to George W. Bush, America's leaders gauged U.S. national interests as broadly as the rulers of ancient Rome. Economist Joseph Schumpeter's description of the Roman Empire resonates vividly today: "There was no corner of the known world where some interest was not alleged to be in danger or under actual attack. If the interests were not Roman, they were those of Rome's allies; and if Rome had no allies, then allies would be invented. When it was utterly impossible to contrive such an interest—why, then it was the national honor that had been insulted. The fight was always invested with an aura of legality. Rome was always being attacked by evil-minded neighbors, always fighting for a breathing space. The whole world was pervaded by a host of enemies, and it was manifestly Rome's duty to guard against their indubitably aggressive designs."

The Mismatch: Projecting Military Power on Waning Economic Power

The Cold War rationale for America's universal military presence largely disappeared with the collapse of the USSR and its Warsaw Pact alliance in the early 1990s, as many foreign policy experts have noted. Nonetheless, the United States maintains eighty thousand troops in Europe. When former defense secretary Donald Rumsfeld made plans to bring seventy thousand troops home from Europe and elsewhere, regional military commanders blocked him.

Whatever the new threats from terrorism, our "Empire of Bases" remains in place largely because both political and military leaders today echo the Cold War mind-set, the notion that the United States is *the* global policeman, whether protecting Bosnian Muslims, invading Iraq, or helping to overthrow Libyan dictator Muammar Gaddafi. "America stands alone as the world's indispensable nation," President Clinton proclaimed in 1997. In 2005, President Bush tied America's security not to military threats, but to spreading democracy around the world. "The survival of liberty in our land increasingly depends on the success of liberty in other lands . . . ," Bush declared. "America's vital interests and our deepest beliefs are now one."

In its defense doctrine, the Bush administration held that U.S. power alone was crucial to global order. It stipulated that the United States would act—preemptively, if necessary—to halt the rise of potential challengers in any corner of the world. More modestly, but still with sweeping implications, President Obama observed that "more than any other nation, the United States of America has underwritten global security over six decades. . . ." But later, in his Nobel Peace Prize address, he injected a note of caution. "America's commitment to global security will never waver," Obama vowed. Then he added that "in a world in which threats are more diffuse and missions more complex, America cannot act alone. America alone cannot secure the peace."

Obama's subtext was the economic limits to American power: The United States could no longer afford a universal military role.

In its prime, coming out of World War II, the United States dominated the global economy. With a monopoly of atomic weapons, ninety-five military divisions, a blue-water navy of twelve hundred major warships, and more than two thousand heavy bombers, it had the means to enforce Pax Americana worldwide. But by the early 1970s, America's economic ebb tide had begun. With the nation's first trade deficit in 1971, President Nixon tacitly acknowledged a more limited U.S. role by devaluing the dollar and suspending its convertibility into gold. In the 1970s, with U.S. domestic oil production in irreversible decline and foreign oil suppliers jacking up prices, Americans personally experienced the U.S. economic vulnerability—a punishing 40 percent spike in gasoline prices and long lines at filling stations.

President Jimmy Carter tried to preach austerity, but Ronald Reagan told Americans to "go for the gold" and keep consuming. He mounted a massive defense buildup while sharply cutting taxes. "Reagan severed the connection between military spending and all other fiscal or political considerations—a proposition revived by George W. Bush after September 2001," historian Andrew Bacevich observed.

Bush's Defense Spending:
$200 Billion Higher Than in the Cold War

Spending beyond our means became America's modus operandi, as illustrated by the nation's pre-recession global trade deficits of more than $800 billion in 2006 and again in 2007. The years of the Bush presidency brought not only the trillions spent on two new wars, but a doubling of the overall defense budget, which actually ran *$200 billion a year higher than at the height of the Cold War,* even adjusting for inflation.

With the exploding costs of new weapons and intelligence systems on top of the costs of war, U.S. spending on national security leapt to nearly $1 trillion a year ($993 billion), according to Winslow Wheeler, a veteran analyst of Pentagon spending for Congress and the nonprofit Center for Defense Information. Christopher Preble, another analyst, at the libertarian Cato Institute, as well as some former defense officials calculated that U.S. defense spending was roughly equal to the total of defense expenditures for all the other nations in the world.

"Imperial Overstretch"—the Problem of Empires

The heart of the problem, thoughtful analysts assert, is that America's defense empire today is the largest and most costly the world has ever known—at a time when the U.S. economy is in deep trouble. This has happened to other nations in other eras—with dire consequences. As historian Paul Kennedy pointed out in *The Rise and Fall of the Great Powers,* nations have a pattern of becoming the world's number one economy and the number one military power and then overreaching with their military ambitions while their economies sputter past their prime.

"It has been a common dilemma facing previous 'number-one' countries," Kennedy wrote, "that even as their relative economic strength is ebbing, the growing foreign challenges to their position have compelled them to allocate more and more of their resources into the military sector, which in turn squeezes out productive investment and, over time, leads to the downward spiral of slower growth, heavier taxes, deepening domestic splits over spending priorities and a weakening capacity to bear the burdens of defense."

Kennedy drew parallels between the United States today and the historical arcs of imperial Spain in 1600 and the British Empire in 1900, in the twilight of their power. Like the two earlier imperial powers, Kennedy observed, the United States "now runs the risk . . . of what might roughly be called 'imperial overstretch': that is to say, decision-makers in Washington must face the awkward and enduring fact that the sum total of the United States' global interests and obligations is nowadays far larger than the country's power to defend them all simultaneously."

America's challenge, Kennedy concluded, is to find a more reasonable balance between its military commitments and trying to "preserve the technological and economic bases of its power from relative erosion in the face of the ever-shifting patterns of global production."

Kennedy wrote that in 1987, when America's global economic position was stronger than today—making his comments an even more trenchant augury of the current dangers of America's excessive global commitments and military spending.

Eisenhower's Warning

Six decades ago, at the height of the Cold War with the Soviet Union, President Dwight Eisenhower warned of precisely that danger—the danger that the United States, by overspending on defense, would damage its domestic economy, its engine of growth.

Eisenhower, who is remembered for his parting admonition about the excessive political power of the military-industrial complex, had worried earlier in his presidency that the United States was becoming so obsessed with the Soviet threat and its urge to build a network of overseas bases that it risked undermining the nation's long-term economic security. As Eisenhower put it: "To amass military power without regard to our economic capacity would be to defend our- selves against one kind of disaster by inviting another."

Eisenhower was explicit about the trade-offs between guns and butter. Making one heavy bomber, he said, meant sacrificing thirty modern schools or two fully equipped hospitals or two electric power plants. "We pay for a single destroyer with new homes that could have housed more than 8,000 people . . . ," he said. "This is not a way of life at all, in any true sense. Under the cloud of threatening war, it is humanity hanging from a cross of iron."

In 2008, presidential candidates Hillary Clinton and Barack Obama applied Eisenhower's trade-offs to the war in Iraq. "Instead of fighting this war . . . ," Obama told primary voters in Charleston, West Virginia, "we could be fighting to put the American Dream within reach for every American. . . . For what folks in this state have been spending on the Iraq war, we could be giving health care to nearly 450,000 of your neighbors, hiring nearly 30,000 new ele- mentary school teachers, and making college more affordable for over 300,000 students."

Clinton spelled out the benefits nationwide for average Americans if $1 trillion spent on Iraq went instead to domestic programs. "That is enough," Clinton declared, "to provide health care for all 47 mil- lion uninsured Americans and quality pre-kindergarten for every American child, solve the housing crisis once and for all, make col- lege affordable for every American student, and provide tax relief to tens of millions of middle-class families."

Increasingly, members of Congress have been pressing Obama to apply this economic logic to Afghanistan. Tea Party Republicans in the House have joined liberal Democrats in calling for defense cuts and faster withdrawal from Afghanistan. Several national security experts have offered a foreign policy rationale: Reverse mission creep and go back to the original anti-terrorism mission in Afghanistan and forget about building Afghan democracy. With Osama bin

Laden dead and buried at sea and with al-Qaeda operating from Pakistan and beyond, these experts say the United States can legitimately declare, "mission accomplished."

"Afghanistan is no longer a war about vital American security interests," asserted Leslie Gelb, a former State Department policy maker. "With Osama bin Laden now swimming with the fishes, the U.S. has but one sensible path: to draw down U.S. forces to 15,000–25,000 by the end of 2013, try cutting a deal with the Taliban, and refocus American power in the region on containment, deterrence and diplomacy."

What Gelb and others are urging is not just a faster pullout from Afghanistan, but a more restrained strategy throughout the Arc of Danger. That approach would reduce the need for our "Empire of Bases," including what the Obama Administration initially planned as a $6 billion-a-year, later cut to the $3.7 billion-a-year, U.S. embassy in Iraq with its sixteen thousand personnel, including five thousand U.S. military trainers and a force of civilian security contractors.

Political Washington's recent focus on the national debt has accelerated the push for a less aggressive foreign policy and a smaller U.S. global footprint. As Congress and the White House clashed in 2011 over the national debt, the key question about the Afghan war changed from "Is the strategy working?" to "Can we afford it?"

"We should be working toward the smallest footprint necessary . . . ," asserted John Kerry, the Democratic chair of the Senate Foreign Relations Committee, and he had the backing of the committee's ranking Republican, Dick Lugar of Indiana. "Make no mistake, it is fundamentally unsustainable to continue spending $10 billion a month on a massive military operation with no end in sight."

While Kerry was talking about Afghanistan, his comments conveyed a broader, deeper impulse for the United States to reduce its global military overstretch and to trim its overseas commitments to fit its more modest economic means—a cutback that would provide resources for many programs badly needed by average Americans.

PART 6

CHALLENGE
AND RESPONSE

IN ARNOLD TOYNBEE'S ANALYSIS of the rise and fall of human civilizations, we Americans fall among those, like ancient Greece and Rome, whose most dangerous challenge comes from within—from the rifts and schisms that we have allowed to develop within our economy and our body politic in the decades since the peak of our power and prosperity from the 1940s to the 1970s.

The new global economy makes it tempting for Americans to blame China or India or the irresistible sweep of technology and globalization for causing the dangerous divide that imperils America today. But in fact, we Americans have done it to ourselves. We could have protected our country better and provided for our people better by pursuing different strategies and policies that minimized our economic erosion, our glaring financial inequalities, and the weakening of our industrial strength. But we decided to pursue a market strategy and to go our separate ways, and in doing so, we have stretched our social fabric close to the breaking point.

The challenge now is to find our way back to common ground, to rise above the economics of selfishness and the politics of partisan advantage and revenge, and to reknit the bonds of a people committed to building a strong common destiny.

A powerful response must come from all of us. At the commanding heights of business and government, we need to restore the economics of shared prosperity. At the pinnacle of wealth, we need a revived ethic of social responsibility. At the grass roots, we need a renaissance in the politics of citizen action to restore and reclaim the American Dream.

CHAPTER 21

RECLAIMING THE DREAM

A DOMESTIC MARSHALL PLAN:
A TEN-STEP STRATEGY

A free people ought not only to be armed but disciplined . . . and their safety and interest require that
they should promote such manufactories as tend to
render them independent of others for essential, particularly military, supplies.

— PRESIDENT GEORGE WASHINGTON,
First Annual Message to Congress, January 8, 1790

Today, our most important task is to restart this virtuous cycle of invention and manufacturing. . . . We need
to create at least 20 million jobs in the next decade to
offset the effects of the recession and to address our
$500 billion trade deficit in manufactured goods.

— SUSAN HOCKFIELD,
president, Massachusetts Institute of Technology

One key to Germany's success: "The social contract,
the willingness of business, labor, and political leaders to put aside some of their differences and make
agreements in the national interest."

— KLAUS KLEINFELD,
Alcoa CEO

FOR THREE DECADES, we have pursued the laissez-faire economics of lower taxes, less regulation, and trust in the market to lift all boats, and we have seen the dangerous schisms this has created. Just in the past two years, there has been a dramatic increase in people's sense of a class division and a sharp class conflict in America.

To reverse that trend, to heal our schisms, to restore our sense of community, and to rejuvenate our competitive economic strength, we need a new direction and a new agenda—a new political and economic response, in Toynbee's terms. Changing America's direction will not be easy. It will happen only if there is a populist surge demanding it, a peaceful political revolution at the grass roots, like the mass movements of the 1960s and 1970s.

In the economy, we need to get the virtuous circle working once again to rebuild middle-class prosperity. That challenge requires a positive response from business—a change in the business mind-set: smart CEOs committed to rebuilding productive capacity at home in America and then sharing more of the fruits of higher productivity with average Americans through higher pay. Even if that means lower dividends for Wall Street and for wealthy shareholders in the short run, everyone will profit in the longer run from a vigorous economy where the spoils are shared more evenly.

And in the world at large, we need to step back from Imperial Overstretch that has exceeded our means and refocus our resources and our energies on regenerating America's economic might and shared prosperity.

A Domestic Marshall Plan

Many good people from different walks of life sense the need for a new direction. Some top corporate executives have joined economists and political moderates and liberals in calling for a national economic strategy that will generate an American industrial renaissance and revive America's global competitiveness. Advocating a comeback for manufacturing in America is one issue that Mitt Romney, Rick Santorum, Newt Gingrich, and other contenders for the Republican presidential nomination shared with President Obama.

One group of top corporate executives, the Horizon Project, advocates a domestic Marshall Plan, evoking the generous American aid that put Western Europe back on its feet after World War II by financing reconstruction of its infrastructure and its war-ravaged industry. In other words, a massive collective effort—a public-private partnership sparked at the outset by government initiatives and investments.

"Job creation must be the number one objective of state economic policy," declares former Intel CEO Andy Grove. "The government plays a strategic role in setting the priorities and arraying the forces and organization necessary to achieve this goal."

It's a mistake, says Grove, for America to count on individual companies, even big ones like Intel, to meet the job and growth needs of the nation without government policies that stimulate them to do so. "Each company, ruggedly individualistic, does its best to expand efficiently and improve its own profitability," says Grove, who ran Intel from 1987 to 1998. "However, our pursuit of our individual businesses, which often involves transferring manufacturing and a great deal of engineering out of the country, has hindered our ability to bring innovations to scale at home. Without scaling [mass production], we don't just lose jobs—we lose our hold on new technologies. . . . [We] damage our capacity to innovate."

Business organizations, such as the Alliance for American Manufacturing and the U.S. Business and Industry Council, as well as organized labor, endorse Grove's thinking. So do many economists.

New York University's Michael Spence, a Nobel laureate in economics, explains their logic. Spence has documented how global competition has stunted the growth of the "tradable" sectors of the U.S. economy—the industries that make cars or cellphones or energy equipment and that are directly exposed to foreign competition. Their poor performance, Spence explains, has left nearly 98 percent of America's job growth since 1980 to the lower-paid health care, service, and public sectors, the so-called nontradable sectors where work has to be done locally. These domestic-oriented sectors have generated 26.7 million of the 27.3 million new jobs in the United States from 1980 to 2008. But those sectors face dim prospects for future growth, Spence asserts, and so America needs "to devote public funding to developing infrastructure and the technological base of the U.S. economy with the specific goal of restoring competitiveness and expanding employment in the tradable sector."

To the free market thinking that has dominated our politics and our economics for three decades, the Grove-Spence approach is anathema. Market advocates reject the very idea of a national economic strategy as heresy. Government involvement in the economy, they argue, amounts to Washington's picking winners and losers. That, they contend, is un-American. It goes against the grain of American history.

But that's not really true.

From George Washington to George W. Bush: A Government Industrial Policy to Spur America's Growth

The Founding Fathers, and many other American presidents from both major political parties, have favored what other nations call an "industrial policy."

Not only did George Washington make a point of wearing an American-made suit for his inauguration, when British tailors were reputedly the world's best, but he advocated a government plan to promote domestic manufacturing against British imports.

In his first annual address to Congress on January 8, 1790, Washington emphasized in words that resonate today: "A free people ought not only to be armed but disciplined . . . and their safety and interest require that they should promote such manufactories as tend to render them independent of others for essential, particularly military, supplies."

Washington's Treasury secretary, Alexander Hamilton, promoted high tariffs and "buy American" policies, endorsed by Washington. Thomas Jefferson, the Virginia plantation owner who was originally an agrarian foe of merchants, switched to Hamilton's view after the British sacking of the nation's capital during the War of 1812. That war, Jefferson wrote to a friend, had showed "that manufactures are now as necessary to our independence as to our comfort." He argued that American industry needed support, contending that "He, therefore, who is now against domestic manufacture, must be for reducing us either to dependence on that foreign nation, or to be clothed in skins, and to live like wild beasts in dens and caverns." Presidents James Madison, James Monroe, John Adams, and John Quincy Adams, holding similar views, supported subsidies and tariffs to promote domestic industry.

In fact, American history is replete with examples, from the Erie Canal to the transcontinental railroad to the *Apollo* moon project to the Internet and the GPS, where the government has backed economic and industrial projects to build the nation's transportation backbone or to create new technologies to enhance America's competitiveness and then has handed them off to the private sector.

In 1842, Congress awarded Samuel F. B. Morse a $30,000 appropriation to test the feasibility of an experimental telegraph line, and another $10,000 in 1843 to lay a telegraph line from Washington to New York via Baltimore and Trenton, New Jersey. In 1862, Abraham Lincoln got Congress to pass the Pacific Railroad Act, which made huge land grants to railroads that became the springboard for America's astonishing economic surge in the late nineteenth century. Nearly a century later, in response to the Soviet *Sputnik* space shot, Dwight Eisenhower got Congress to vote funds for a nationwide highway network that still serves us today. The nation's space program, which Eisenhower launched and nine other presidents kept going, generated many of the technologies that led to America's supremacy in aerospace and computers.

Reagan's Economic Interventions

Even Ronald Reagan, despite his mocking remark that "government is not the solution; government is the problem," used governmental power to bolster U.S. industry. When Japanese computer firms threatened American computer chip makers in the early 1980s, the Reagan administration put political pressure on the Japanese government to guarantee U.S. firms a 20 percent share of the Japanese market by initiating an unprecedented trade case against Japan. Reagan persuaded Congress to approve the government's investment of $1 billion in Sematech, a new public-private partnership with a dozen computer companies, to create "precompetitive" technologies to keep America's high-tech industry in the vanguard and to prevent the Pentagon from becoming dangerously dependent on foreign suppliers for components of military weapons systems.

Reagan also moved forcefully to protect America's automakers. When Toyota and Honda made deep inroads into the U.S. car market, Reagan forced a 40 percent devaluation of the dollar, making Japanese imports much more expensive. Then Reagan pressed Tokyo to accept quotas on Japanese auto exports to America and pushed Japanese automakers to set up assembly plants in the United States to generate jobs for American workers.

So there was ample precedent for Barack Obama to extend an $80 billion rescue fund to General Motors and Chrysler during the economic collapse of 2008 with funds that George W. Bush had gotten from Congress to rescue Wall Street banks.

In short, contrary to modern right-wing political rhetoric, presidents of both parties have used government funds and authority to protect American industry and have poured hundreds of billions of dollars into the nation's transportation, communications, and financial systems. They have fostered the development of new technologies since the dawning of our Republic, though Americans have often remained unaware of the government's role in what are marketed as private sector innovations.

As CEO of Apple, Steve Jobs won a deserved reputation as the creative and entrepreneurial genius behind many groundbreaking products. But as former Reagan administration trade negotiator Clyde Prestowitz observed, "Virtually everything Jobs has developed—the mouse, Mac/Windows displays, operating systems, touch screens—began in or received support from a government office."

That is hardly surprising since federal agencies such as NASA, the Departments of Defense, Energy, and Agriculture, the National Institutes of Health, and the National Science Foundation are so large and spend so many hundreds of billions of dollars a year in the economy that there is no such thing as a free market without government influence. Without announcing it, the United States already has a de facto industrial policy—in effect, picking winners—by pouring life-blood into such huge contractors as Boeing, Lockheed Martin, United Technologies, IBM, Microsoft, Intel, Apple, and hundreds more.

Reconnecting America's Genius at Innovation with Production and Job Growth

So the question now is not whether, but how—how should the existing influence of government be used most effectively to help the private sector revitalize our economy, to share the economic gains more widely, to create millions of jobs for average Americans, and to make our nation more globally competitive again?

Corporate CEOs such as Jeffrey Immelt of General Electric, Andrew Liveris of Dow Chemical, and former Intel CEO Andy Grove, as well Nobel Prize–winning economists such as Michael Spence, Joseph Stiglitz of Columbia, and Paul Krugman of Princeton declare that we must urgently restore the nation's industrial strength.

"The United States became the world's largest economy because we invented products and then made them with new processes . . . ," asserted MIT president Susan Hockfield. "Today, our most important task is to restart this virtuous cycle of invention and manufacturing. . . . We need to create at least 20 million jobs in the next decade to offset the effects of the recession and to address our $500 billion trade deficit in manufactured goods."

The key, these corporate leaders and economists contend, is to re-establish vital connections in our economy in order to reinforce the crucial ways in which America's genius at innovation translates into economic growth for the nation and job growth for the middle class through large-scale production, which then powers the next generation of innovation, production, and job growth.

The dynamic interaction between innovation, production, and job growth in America was disrupted, they say, when major U.S. multinationals moved overseas the mass production of commodities—from computer and aircraft components to auto parts, appliances, and cellphones—to places like China. "Not only did we lose an untold number of jobs, we broke the chain of experience that is so important in technological evolution," cautions Andy Grove. "Abandoning today's 'commodity' manufacturing can lock you out of tomorrow's emerging industry."

Behind Germany's Success:
A Social Contract for Jobs and Exports

As the United States looks ahead, many economic analysts see valuable lessons in Germany, the linchpin of the euro zone, over the last two decades. Germany's response to the challenge of globalization and low-cost competition from China and Asia has been different from ours, as we saw earlier, and its outcome has been better.

Since the mid-1990s, the German economy has grown faster than the U.S. economy, and its middle class has shared more of the gains. Since 1985, Germany's average wage went up nearly 30 percent versus only 6 percent in the United States. In foreign trade, Germany generated $2 trillion in trade surpluses from 2000 to 2010, while the United States racked up $6 trillion in trade deficits. So today,

Germany still has twice as many people working in manufacturing as the United States—21 percent of its workforce to 9 percent of ours.

"The German model shows that a developed country can remain competitive even in a world where new economic giants, such as China, India, and others, are emerging," observes Wall Street investment manager Steve Rattner. One reason is that German consumers import less than half as much, per capita, from China as Americans do, and German industry, with its marquee brands and precision machine tools, exports more successfully. BMW, for example, makes 25 percent of its profits selling luxury cars in China.

But what explains Germany's so-called economic miracle is a social contract that brings together business, labor, and government working for the nation's benefit. "It isn't a miracle," former German economy minister Michael Glos explained. "It's because we stuck to manufacturing whereas other countries de-industrialized"—moved into services and shifted their production offshore.

Klaus Kleinfeld, former CEO of the German electrical giant Siemens and now CEO of Alcoa, asserts that the key ingredient of Germany's success is "the social contract, the willingness of business, labor, and political leaders to put aside some of their differences and make agreements in the national interest."

Trade union leaders sit on the supervisory boards of major firms such as Volkswagen, Daimler, and Siemens, positioned to persuade management to keep the highest value-added work in Germany. As a trade-off, unions have eased demands for pay increases.

"To keep work at home, German unions also agreed to continual productivity and efficiency increases," noted commentator Harold Meyerson. "They can afford to do this because, as is not the case in the United States, such increases don't necessarily mean their members will be sacked."

In fact, during the 2008 economic collapse, big German companies adopted a "short work" policy to spread the pain of recession. Instead of laying off masses of workers, German companies shortened everyone's workweek, saving five hundred thousand jobs, so Germany's unemployment rate went down during the recession while America's rose sharply and stayed high.

Ten Steps to Reclaim the Dream

Reclaiming the American Dream will not be quick or simple. We have a long-term structural jobs problem that demands new thinking and an ambitious new economic agenda. Hence the call from the Horizon Project CEOs for a domestic Marshall Plan. What they advocate is a government-led industrial policy focused on generating millions of new jobs, exporting more products, modernizing our infrastructure, making our tax laws smarter and fairer, restoring America's manufacturing at home, and legally challenging or retaliating against China's unfair trade practices.

From their thinking and that of others, here are ten steps for reclaiming the American Dream.

Step #1: Infrastructure Jobs to Compete Better

Step #1 is to form a new public-private partnership to modernize America's outdated transportation networks and create five million jobs—and maybe many more—with major investments over the next decade. Follow the model of President Lincoln, who used government aid to promote and subsidize the transcontinental railway, or President Theodore Roosevelt, who built the inland waterways, or President Dwight Eisenhower, who fathered America's modern interstate highway network.

Wall Street is reported to be eager to invest in infrastructure projects if the government puts up seed money. That plan wins backing from such traditional political adversaries as the U.S. Chamber of Commerce and the AFL-CIO. It wins bipartisan endorsement from politicians like New York mayor Michael Bloomberg, Texas senator Kay Bailey Hutchison, and former California governor Arnold Schwarzenegger, all Republicans, and Democrats such as Senators John Kerry of Massachusetts and Mark Warner of Virginia and former Pennsylvania governor Ed Rendell.

The U.S. Chamber of Commerce estimates that America's faltering infrastructure costs the United States $1 trillion in economic growth and hampers U.S. exports. In world rankings of infrastructure, the United States has fallen from No. 1 to No. 15 . Not only do we have sixty-nine thousand structurally deficient bridges, but our national rail network has such serious bottlenecks that it takes a freight train longer to get through the city of Chicago than it does to go from Chicago to Los Angeles. In high-speed rail development, China is outspending the United States $300 billion to $10 billion. Our aviation control system is so outdated and overloaded that the Federal Aviation Administration predicts it "will reach total gridlock by 2015" unless it is urgently modernized. Our ports are overloaded. Our highways are clogged. In 2009, Americans wasted 4.8 billion hours and 3.9 billion gallons of fuel sitting in traffic at an estimated cost of $115 billion.

Leaders from both parties as well as business-oriented task forces advocate responding to this challenge with a national infrastructure bank to spark the financing of a ten-year plan to improve our ports, airports, and commercial and commuter rail systems, as well as our bridges and highways. Because of current low interest rates and high unemployment, one economic study pointed out that it will "never be cheaper" for the nation to undertake a major infrastructure push because "capital costs are now at historic lows . . . and labor is in abundant supply. . . ."

The U.S. Chamber of Commerce estimates that $10 billion to $30 billion in government start-up funds could attract up to $600 billion in private investments. Another $1 trillion in private investments could be generated, some economists suggest, from the overseas profits of U.S. multinational corporations, if they were given attractive terms to bring those funds home and invest them in financing U.S. infrastructure development. They could profit from that investment, while paying U.S. taxes—a win-win for all sides.

As a parallel move, former CEO Leo Hindery, Jr., and United Steelworkers president Leo Gerard have proposed that the government provide funds to put five million young people to work on modest infrastructure projects, especially in urban areas. A youth jobs program, similar to the New Deal Civilian Conservation Corps, they assert, would not only reduce the much higher than average unemployment rates among young people, but reduce the risk of idled youth turning to crime. Hiring young people would have a multiplier effect on the economy, economists explain, because young people are known for spending their earnings fast.

Step #2: Push Innovation, Science, and High-Tech Research

Step #2 is a major new national commitment to rebuild America's capacity to out-invent and out-innovate the world. Despite breakthroughs by companies such as Apple and Google, the United States has slipped in innovation, which has long been America's bedrock advantage in the world. In 2007, the National Academy of Sciences, joined by leaders in industry and education, reported that a "gathering storm" from foreign competitors was threatening America's traditional edge in science, high tech, and innovation. In a second major report three years later, the academy issued an even sharper warning of a "rapidly approaching category 5" disaster.

Scientists date the American slide in research from the Reagan administration's sharp cuts in government funding for basic research in the early 1980s—from nearly $9 billion in 1979 to $1.4 billion in 2006, figures adjusted for inflation. The impact has been disastrous on America's once invincible lead in research and innovation. From a No. 1 innovation ranking in 2000, the United States fell to No. 4 in 2011, behind Finland, Singapore, and Sweden. Georgia Tech University's global study of high-tech indicators found that China in 2008 surpassed the United States in overall "technological standing." The World Economic Forum ranked the United States fifth in global competitiveness in 2011.

The trends in patents, a key indicator of innovation, are worrisome. After decades of domination by U.S. firms, universities, and individuals, 51 percent of the U.S. patents awarded in 2009 went to non-American companies. In clean energy development and production, the United States was once the undisputed leader but has been surpassed in production by China, Japan, and South Korea. Without large new U.S. investment, the Information Technology and Innovation Foundation predicts that the United States will soon be importing "the overwhelming majority" of its clean energy technologies, jeopardizing the U.S. economic recovery and our balance of trade.

Business and Science Leaders Look to Government to Take the Lead

Not only scientists and educators, but corporate leaders such as former CEOs Norman Augustine of Lockheed Martin, Craig Barrett of Intel, and Roy Vagelos of Merck support the National Academy of Sciences finding that it will take dramatically expanded government funding for the United States to bounce back in the R&D race. The private sector and universities will do the work, they say, but they need a big financial shot in the arm from Washington. In 2007, industry leaders urged Congress to appropriate $130 billion over the next decade for government funding of research, innovation, and targeted aid to education, plus tax credits to industry for research and development.

In April 2009, President Obama provided a kick start. He announced plans to add $42.6 billion to science and technology research over the next decade and he set up a new Advanced Research Projects Agency at the Department of Energy (ARPA-E). It was modeled on the Pentagon's DARPA (Defense Advanced Research Projects Agency), which has spawned thousands of important new technologies with commercial as well as defense applications. Obama put $400 million in his 2009 stimulus package to launch ARPA-E and to fund more than thirty of the most daring new energy projects. But as we saw from the bankruptcy of the solar energy firm Solyndra after it got more than $500 million in government loan guarantees, the government has to be much smarter in picking the companies it funds and much tougher in overseeing their performance.

Step #3: Generate a Manufacturing Renaissance

Step #3 is to generate a manufacturing renaissance in America—perhaps the boldest step of all, and one that will require not only a series of public-private partnerships, but a reset in New Economy thinking.

To those on Wall Street, in Washington, or within academia who say that the United States does not need an industrial base, General Electric's CEO Jeffrey Immelt and Intel's Andy Grove retort that this is dangerous nonsense. "Many bought into the idea that America could go from a technology-based, export-oriented powerhouse to a services-led, consumption-based economy—and somehow still expect to prosper," Immelt told the Detroit Economic Club in 2009. "That idea was flat wrong."

Richard McCormack, editor of *Manufacturing & Technology News,* points to the slow, jobless U.S. recovery as evidence of the fallacy in that thinking. "Without an industrial base, an increase in consumer spending, which pulled the country out of past recessions, will not put Americans back to work," McCormack argues. "Without an industrial base, the nation's trade deficit will continue to grow. . . . Without an industrial base, the United States will be increasingly dependent on foreign manufacturers even for its key military technology."

Immelt, too, insists that technology-based manufacturing must be central to reviving the U.S. economy. His goal is to see manufacturing employment double, from 9 to 20 percent of the nation's workforce—a target endorsed by the Horizon Project, a task force of former CEOs led by Leo Hindery, Jr., who used to run AT&T Broadband. "You cannot survive as a nation of such size and complexity with such a small manufacturing workforce as we have," Hindery asserts. "If you have only 9 percent making things, the only way you can grow is to have credit bubbles."

In the decade from 2001 to 2011, U.S. employment in manufacturing fell from 17.2 million to 11.7 million, and more than fifty-nine thousand factories were shut down. The damage was even wider because of the ripple effect. Each job lost in manufacturing cut 2.5 other jobs in the rest of the economy.

"Close a manufacturing plant, and a supply chain of producers disappears with it," says Richard McCormack. "Dozens of companies get hurt: those supplying computer-aided design and business software; automation and robotics equipment, packaging, office equipment and supplies; telecommunications services; energy and water utilities; research and development, marketing and sales support. . . . The burden spreads to local restaurants, cultural establishments, shopping outlets, and then to the tax base that supports police, firemen, schoolteachers, and libraries."

Reversing the multiplier effect—to make it work for economic expansion—is essential to America's economic growth, but it is a tough challenge. Rebuilding our industrial base, Andy Grove points out, means being sharp enough to convert American innovations into American-based production for U.S. jobs, and that requires new government initiatives and public-private partnerships.

Take clean energy. Before the recession, the green energy sector was growing faster than the economy in general, and many forecast great job potential. The consulting firm Booz Allen Hamilton predicted a jump from 2.4 million jobs in 2008 to 7.9 million jobs in 2013 in construction of green energy projects. More modest job growth in producing clean energy devices was expected—from a few hundred thousand to 1.7 million jobs. But the test is whether the United States can move fast enough to ensure that technologies invented in the United States are produced here and not in Asia.

To do that, the Alliance for American Manufacturing wants help from Washington—federal loan guarantees to help finance new energy infrastructure projects, tax credits for clean energy manufacturing, and tax changes that permit up-front expensing on capital investment in plant and equipment. More broadly, the alliance wants the government to fund a new investment facility to initiate and promote financing for new U.S. energy plants and other domestic manufacturing, and to do it before fragile American start-up firms are driven out of business by government-subsidized competitors in China, Korea, Singapore, and Hong Kong.

Buy American

One other major change in government policy—and in the actions of American consumers—could bolster U.S. manufacturing, and that is to Buy American. Many in business urge that state and federal governments tighten the "Buy American" requirements for government contracts, consistent with U.S. trade agreements.

In two recent high-profile cases, the state of California hired U.S. contractors to help rebuild the San Francisco–Oakland Bay Bridge, but the steel was imported from China. And in Washington, the monument to Martin Luther King, Jr., was designed by a Chinese architect, built by workmen from China, and constructed from marble that came thousands of miles from China.

To prevent such episodes in the future, job-first advocates say that both the federal and state contracts should establish tighter "Buy American" standards that require at least 75 percent domestic content in products and services.

Step #4: Make the U.S. Tax Code Fairer

Step #4 is to rebalance the U.S. income tax code to reduce its heavy tilt in favor of the super-rich. As nonpartisan economists have reported, the large Reagan tax cuts of the 1980s and the even larger George W. Bush tax cuts in 2001 to 2003 contributed greatly to the vast economic inequality in America today by generating more than $1 trillion in tax savings for America's superclass every decade, with only modest benefits to the middle class.

Large majorities of the public favor taxing the super-rich more by letting the 2001 Bush tax cuts for the wealthy expire. An alternative idea is to let the Bush tax cuts expire for all Americans and then pass a new tax reform to lower tax rates, especially for 90 percent of American families earning less than $138,925 a year—and to simplify the tax code by eliminating loopholes and tax breaks that benefit mainly the wealthy.

Simplifying the tax code will make it easier to enforce. So many exotic tax shelters have been invented by ingenious tax lawyers and accountants to reduce the taxes of the super-rich that former IRS commissioner Charles Rossotti, a Republican businessman, estimated the tax loss to illegitimate tax evasions at $250 billion to $350 billion a year. As a result, Rossotti told me, honest taxpayers have to pay 15 percent more in their taxes.

"Stop Coddling the Super-Rich," declares Warren Buffett, the famous billionaire investor from Omaha. "I know well many of the mega-rich and, by and large, they are very decent people. They love America and appreciate the opportunity this country has given them. . . . Most wouldn't mind being told to pay more in taxes as well, particularly when so many of their fellow citizens are truly suffering."

As Buffett has frequently pointed out, the super-rich make most of their money from the stock market and other investments, which are taxed at the 15 percent capital gains rate, much lower than the tax rate on most middle-class salaries. As we saw earlier, Buffett paid a rate of 17.4 percent on his multimillion-dollar income in 2010, and that was the lowest tax rate in his office. Buffett advocates not only repealing the Bush tax cuts for the super-rich, but imposing a supertax on income over $1 million a year and a super-super rate on income over $10 million a year. Others propose a special tax on corporate stock options to CEOs and other top executives.

Another important move would be to close the exemption in the payroll tax now enjoyed by the rich. Ordinary employees pay a 7.65 percent payroll tax to fund Social Security and Medicare, but the income from investment gains of CEOs and super-rich investors is exempted from the payroll tax. In fact, multimillionaires pay a much lower payroll tax rate on their salaries and bonuses—as low as 1 percent—because all their income over $106,800, even their salaries and bonuses, is also exempt from the payroll tax. Removing that $106,800 tax cap would not only make everyone pay the same rate, it would go a long way toward solving the funding shortfall for Social Security and Medicare.

But the simplest, broadest tax reform to achieve a more level economic playing field would be to end the special low 15 percent capital gains tax rate and to tax investment gains at the same rate as wages and salaries (35 percent). Exceptions could be made for assets such as a house, a farm, a small business, or even a stock investment owned for a truly long term, say, for twenty years or more—to compensate for long-term inflation.

A majority of Americans favor raising capital gains taxes to 35 percent or higher, according to a *New York Times* poll taken in January 2012, when the political controversy broke out over Republican presidential candidate Mitt Romney's 13.9 percent tax rate in 2010 on his $27 million income. Romney is fairly typical of the super-rich since virtually all of his income came as capital gains, which are by far the main source of income for the richest Americans. Those gains are heavily concentrated at the top. The tiny sliver at the peak of our economy—the top 0.1 percent of all income earners—captures almost half of all the capital gains in America.

All these tax reforms taken together—on capital gains, on payroll taxes, on closing loopholes, and on a special tax on executive stock options—would make the U.S. tax code much fairer, plus it could cut the national debt by $1 trillion over a decade.

Step #5: Fix the Corporate Tax Code to Promote Job Creation at Home

Step #5 is to fix the corporate tax code by lowering the rate and closing loopholes, because that would make the United States more globally competitive by enacting reforms that would discourage U.S. firms from offshoring jobs and reward those that hire at home.

American business leaders complain that they are hurt competitively by the U.S. corporate tax rate, and it is true that the U.S. corporate tax rate is one of the highest in the world. But in practice, most U.S. multinationals pay far less than the official 35 percent rate. When Citizens for Tax Justice examined the records of 280 major firms, it found that from 2008 to 2010, their true federal tax rate averaged 18.5 percent. What's more, the rate varied widely. Some companies paid the full 35 percent rate or close to it. Others cashed in heavily on loopholes and tax breaks that corporate lobbyists and pro-business members of Congress have written into the tax code—loopholes that were worth $1.2 trillion in reduced business taxes over a decade, according to the Treasury Department.

The multinationals that have been most successful in avoiding U.S. federal taxes include Boeing, DuPont, ExxonMobil, General Electric, IBM, Merck, United Technologies, and Wells Fargo, according to Citizens for Tax Justice, because the way they do business qualifies them for large tax credits. General Electric, for example, made nearly $10.5 billion in profits from 2008 through 2010, and instead of paying taxes, GE got a federal tax rebate of $4.7 billion by using loopholes and claiming tax credits. Companies that pay roughly 35 percent in taxes include retailers such as CVS Caremark, Home Depot, Target, and Wal-Mart; domestic-oriented insurance companies such as Aetna and Humana; trucking companies; and electric utilities, food processors, restaurants, and hotels—mostly firms that do the bulk of their business inside the United States.

In terms of the tax code's impact on jobs in America, what counts most is that U.S. multinationals that have large overseas operations often pay very low U.S. taxes or none at all. Many of them are high-tech firms that qualify for tax credits for spending on research and development or on new plants and equipment, but often their biggest loophole is paying no taxes at all on their overseas profits—unless and until they transfer their foreign earnings back to the United States.

Apple: Shifting Profits to Avoid Taxes

High-tech companies such as Apple have big moneymaking products like iPads and iPhones made overseas, often in China. They can allocate their profits on lucrative patents on iPads and iPhones to their overseas operations or they can sell software applications from low-tax countries overseas, shifting around tens of billions in income from country to country with legal but cleverly devised bookkeeping to avoid taxes in the United States and in other countries, too. Earlier this year, *The New York Times* reported that Apple had pioneered an accounting technique known as the "Double Irish with a Dutch Sandwich," which cut Apple's taxes drastically by routing profits through Irish subsidiaries to the Netherlands and then to the Caribbean. Today, hundreds of other U.S. corporations have copied tactics invented by Apple, which, in 2011, paid only $3.3 billion in taxes on $34.2 billion in profits.

Under current tax law, U.S. multinationals are allowed to write off all their overseas costs immediately, even though they don't pay tax on those overseas profits until the money is repatriated. One big loophole, created inadvertently by the U.S. Treasury and worth billions in tax reductions for multinationals, allows them to "Check the Box" on IRS form 8832 to identify their subsidiaries as doing business overseas, not subject to U.S. taxes. This is an automatic process, rarely given close IRS scrutiny. On paper, U.S. companies can work accounting rules to their advantage by shifting profits realized in America (for products sold in the United States) to the financial books of overseas subsidiaries (where the products were made).

In this way, U.S. multinationals periodically accumulate $1 trillion or more in foreign earnings over several years, and then, as a group, they lobby Congress for "a tax holiday"—a very low tax rate on foreign profits repatriated to the United States. In 2005, the Bush administration pushed through a low 5.25 percent tax rate on repatriated profits and gave 843 of America's largest corporations a $265 billion windfall gain.

All sides agree on the need to rewrite the corporate tax code. Pro-business conservatives want to lower the maximum corporate tax rate from 35 to 25 percent. In terms of job creation in the United States, that would leave more capital in the hands of companies that operate inside America, enabling them to expand and hire. To balance such a tax reduction, pro-jobs progressives want to close the $1.2 trillion in corporate tax loopholes—above all, the tax exemption on overseas profits. Economists estimate that if overseas corporate profits were fully taxed, it would generate $100 billion a year in new corporate tax revenues—$1 trillion over a decade. What's more, they argue, taxing corporate profits at the full rate would curb questionable corporate accounting stratagems used to avoid U.S. taxes. It might even persuade U.S. multinationals to keep more production at home and bring jobs back from China and India.

Policy makers within both parties agree in principle on giving businesses tax credits for research, innovation, and new facilities, to stimulate more job creation at home. But jobs advocates such as Leo Hindery Jr., want tax reform to require proof from employers that their tax credits are actually being used to expand their U.S.-based workforce. They also want to tie tax breaks to job creation at home to apply to companies repatriating profits from overseas. When U.S. multinationals were given a special 5.25 percent tax rate on repatriated profits in 2005, they said the money would create jobs, but economists tracked those funds and found out that 92 percent of that money went to investors and corporate executives through dividends and stock buybacks and only 8 percent went for job creation. This time, jobs advocates want ironclad provisions to make sure the multinationals actually create more jobs in the United States.

Step #6: Push China to Live up to Fair Trade to Generate Four Million Jobs in the United States

Step #6 is strong action by the United States and other countries to combat China's unfair trade practices and to rebalance global trade. Economists estimate it would generate four million jobs in America and significantly cut the U.S. trade and budget deficits if world currencies were revalued and if China was required to live up to the fair trade rules of the World Trade Organization.

The American economy and American workers are being hurt in three major ways by Chinese trade practices, experts say. First, they contend, China manipulates the value of its currency by fixing a low rate of exchange between the Chinese yuan and the U.S. dollar. A low exchange rate boosts Chinese exports by making them very cheap, and it cuts down U.S. exports to China by making them very expensive. Economists say the yuan would be priced 25 to 50 percent higher if it were allowed to float freely, letting trade flows and the global market determine the value of the yuan relative to the U.S. dollar. It is not just the Chinese yuan that poses a problem for the United States and Western European countries. Other Asian currencies in Hong Kong, Singapore, Taiwan, and Malaysia are pegged to the Chinese yuan, and their low currency values also hurt the U.S. trade balance with Asia.

Second, American businesses accuse the Chinese of widespread intellectual piracy—stealing copyrighted intellectual property, patents, and inventions and illegally copying foreign-made products, from Microsoft software to General Motors cars. A major national intelligence report to Congress on economic theft and espionage stated bluntly in late 2011 that "Chinese actors are the world's most active and persistent perpetrators of economic espionage" and went on to cite several cases where American companies had lost patented material through cyberespionage.

Finally, Americans accuse the Chinese government of regularly violating rules of the World Trade Organization by dumping products on the world market at below the cost of production and giving illegal subsidies, land grants, and other cost-saving advantages to both Chinese and foreign firms. In fact, American CEOs say they save more on their investments in China through Chinese subsidies and tax breaks than from cheap labor.

Correcting those problems would have a major impact on the U.S. job market. The United States would gain 2.25 million jobs if China let its currency (and others linked to it) rise 25 percent, according to Robert Scott, a China trade specialist at the Economic Policy Institute. If this happened, Scott says, the U.S. unemployment rate would fall by 1 percent and the government's budget deficit would be cut by at least $621 billion and perhaps by as much as $857 billion over a decade.

The United States would gain another 2.1 million full-time jobs if the Chinese stopped violating international copyright laws and intellectual property protection, according to the U.S. International Trade Commission.

Congress is ready to take a tougher line toward China. "China's currency manipulation is like a boot on the throat of our economic recovery," asserted New York Democratic senator Charles Schumer. "There is no bigger step we can take to promote U.S. job creation, particularly in the manufacturing sector, than to confront China's currency manipulation." Republicans such as Senator Lindsey Graham of South Carolina have shown a willingness to co-sponsor legislation with Democrats to impose stiff tariffs on Chinese goods unless China raises its currency value. The last time Congress threatened action, China allowed its currency value to rise a fraction but pressures have been building again for action by Congress.

Confronting China is not easy. Foreign policy experts urge collective action rather than unilateral U.S. moves. Western European and Latin American countries such as Brazil and Mexico are also hurt by China's cheap currency and restrictive trade policies. International economists suggest that the best way to move China and other Asian countries on the currency issue is through global negotiations on rebalancing world trade. On China's unfair trade policies, economists point to the success of the case brought by several Western nations that accused China of violating free trade rules through export controls on certain industrial minerals that are essential components for producing sophisticated electronics. The World Trade Organization ruled against China in early 2012 and ordered Beijing to end those policies, a ruling that offers precedent for future cases.

In the meantime, it is essential for Congress to fund the retraining of Americans thrown out of work when trade with China and other low-cost countries wipes out their jobs. Under the Trade Adjustment Assistance program, which started in the 1960s, the government spent close to $1 billion in 2008 to give aid to plants shut down by import competition and to provide career retraining for displaced American workers. But in 2011, Tea Party budget deficit hawks blocked all funding for this retraining program. House Republican leaders finally relented after the Obama administration refused to send Congress Washington's new trade agreements with South Korea, Panama, and Colombia until the worker benefits were guaranteed. Corporate America wanted the trade agreements, so Republican leaders agreed to restore modest funds for worker retraining. Now this vital worker safety net needs to be expanded.

Step #7: Save on War and Weapons

Step #7 is to cut spending on wars overseas and to reduce the Pentagon budget by $1 trillion over the next decade—savings that would generate funds for a domestic Marshall Plan and underwrite a middle-class agenda.

The Obama administration began in 2012 by announcing $450

billion in projected defense cuts, plans for a leaner army and marines, and moves to bring home troops from Europe and reorient U.S. defense strategy. Another $500 billion in cuts would be imposed in January 2013 under the 2011 congressional debt reduction agreement— unless Congress comes up with an alternative.

Military advocates from the Joint Chiefs of Staff and Defense Secretary Leon Panetta to defense hawks in Congress oppose a $1 trillion overall cutback, protesting that it would endanger the nation. But former Pentagon officials such as Assistant Defense Secretary Lawrence Korb and other experienced defense experts disagree. They assert that $1 trillion can be cut from projected defense spending over ten years without jeopardizing national security. Former Pentagon officials point out that defense spending now runs $200 billion a year higher than at the peak of the Cold War, adjusted for inflation, and the United States faces no comparable strategic nuclear threat today. Moreover, cutting $1 trillion in military spending over ten years, says longtime congressional defense analyst Winslow Wheeler, would still leave defense spending at the very high 2007 level of $470 billion a year. That level would still enable the Pentagon to spend more than the defense budgets of the next largest-spending seventeen nations *combined*.

Defense spending cuts are long overdue. This is not just because the United States is pulling back from the wars in Iraq and Afghanistan, wars that will ultimately cost the nation more than $3.5 trillion in deficit spending. It is also because the basic Pentagon budget has been given unprecedented increases for thirteen years in a row.

A cutback of $1 trillion over the next decade would fit past precedents. After the Korean War, President Dwight Eisenhower reduced defense spending by 27 percent. After the Vietnam War, President Richard Nixon reduced Pentagon spending by 29 percent. As the Cold War ended, President Reagan scaled back military spending, too, and so did his successors George Herbert Walker Bush and Bill Clinton. But then it shot back up again after 2001, under President George W. Bush.

What is more, Pentagon critics contend that the U.S. military establishment has become grossly inefficient and wasteful in buying new weapons and needs to be more strictly controlled. Even such defense advocates as Senator John McCain and Vice Admiral Norb Ryan, Jr., president of the Military Officers Association, have chastised the Pentagon for weapons programs that keep escalating in cost far beyond original estimates and that are so out of control that the Defense Department cannot pass an outside audit.

In November 2011, Admiral Ryan decried the "gross mismanagement and cost overruns in expensive weapons programs, few of which have any relevance to the wars our troops are fighting today." In a Senate floor speech, McCain issued a savage critique of one weapons system after another, pointing at "spectacular, shameful failure" and accusing the Pentagon of "a shocking lack of any accountability" for cost overruns or matching new weapons to actual combat needs.

It was Dwight Eisenhower, the Republican president who had commanded Allied forces in Europe against Nazi Germany during World War II, who warned against the danger of overspending on the military and, in the process, sapping the nation's economic strength—America's primary source of national security.

Better than anyone, this West Point–trained five-star general understood the trade-offs. "Every gun that is made, every warship launched, every rocket fired signifies, in the final sense, a theft from those who hunger and are not fed, those who are cold and are not clothed," Ike declared. "This world in arms is not spending money alone. It is spending the sweat of its laborers, the genius of its scientists, the hopes of its children."

In 2008, candidate Barack Obama opposed the war in Iraq and promised a peace dividend: "Instead of fighting this war, we could be fighting to rebuild our roads and bridges. I've proposed a fund that . . . would generate nearly two million new jobs. . . ."

Now, four years later, the time has come to cash in that peace dividend. With the Afghan war costing more than $100 billion a year, a faster draw-down of U.S. forces could free tens of billions for programs to revive our domestic economy. Untold billions more could be saved by bringing home some of our eighty thousand troops still stationed in Western Europe nearly twenty-five years after the end of the Cold War. Billions more could be saved by eliminating wasteful and irrelevant weapons—and still leave America with the largest, most modern military force in the world.

There is bipartisan support for reducing military spending. In 2010, the bipartisan deficit commission headed by former Republican senator Alan Simpson and former Clinton White House chief of staff Erskine Bowles proposed $750 billion in defense cuts over the next decade. Sentiment for deeper cuts has grown since that report. In today's sharply divided Congress, cutting defense is one issue on which Tea Party Republicans and liberal Democrats agree.

Step #8: Fix Housing and Protect the Safety Net

Step #8 is to fix the housing market by arranging massive refinancing of millions of homes now "under water" to help get the economy moving and to strengthen the nation's safety net programs, especially Social Security and Medicare.

The housing market today is both symptom and symbol of the nation's economic quagmire and its gross inequalities. Wall Street's megabanks, which fueled the housing bubble and bust, have been bailed out with more than $700 billion of taxpayer money and are back to multibillion-dollar profits, while six million average families have been foreclosed out of their homes and twenty-two million more families are trapped in homes that are "under water"—worth less than their mortgages. Not only have those families been hurt, but the dead housing market has put a damper on a strong economic recovery.

For those twenty-two million homeowners—mostly creditworthy borrowers who are paying their mortgages regularly—it's a catch-22. Most can't afford to sell their homes and take a loss. Many would like to benefit from today's low interest rates (around 4 percent) and shed their old 7 to 10 percent bubble-era rates. That would give them more cash to spend and to fuel the economics of the virtuous circle and lift the economy. But they are trapped. Banks won't approve loans for more than the value of the house, and government-backed enterprises such as Fannie Mae and Freddie Mac have balked at writing down loans they have guaranteed in the past, because on their books they would lose some money.

One modest improvement was the agreement in February 2012 by the main Wall Street banks, under pressure from state attorneys general and the Obama administration, to commit $26 billion to reduce the principal or interest on the mortgages of a million homeowners with loans that exceed the market value of their homes. The banks agreed to spend $1.5 billion on small ($1,500 to $2,000) payments to about 75,000 people who lost their homes in wrongful foreclosures. But the deal was only a partial step forward. It did not cover mortgages insured by Fannie Mae and Freddie Mac (roughly half of all mortgages), it gave the banks three years to take these actions, and it fell far short of fully compensating people who were foreclosed improperly. While hailing the agreement as a step forward, President Obama commented: "No compensation, no amount of money, no measure of justice is enough to make it right for a family who's had their piece of the American dream wrongly taken from them."

Waiting for the market to correct itself is no solution. Establishment bankers such as William C. Dudley, president of the Federal Reserve Bank of New York, assert that "the infrastructure of the residential mortgage market is wholly inadequate to deal" with the massive debt overhang and with getting real upward movement in home sales. Unless the government takes action, Dudley said, the housing market will "destroy much more value in housing than is necessary."

Smart economists have suggested multiple ways to break the housing logjam. Glenn Hubbard, former chief economic adviser to President George W. Bush, has urged Fannie Mae and Freddie Mac to reduce loan balances on some of the homes now "under water" and to rewrite their rules so that up to ten million homeowners can qualify for refinancing their mortgages at lower rates. Economists Nouriel Roubini of New York University, Robert Hockett of Cornell University, and Daniel Alpert of Westwood Capital have proposed that the federal government buy up near worthless second mortgages and home equity loans whose holders are blocking first-mortgage lenders from refinancing their loans. William Dudley has proposed easing red tape and long delays both at banks and at government agencies to grant new credit to homeowners and temporary bridge loans for homeowners thrown out of work. To reduce the massive backlog of foreclosed homes that are still empty, Dudley has suggested that the banks be pushed by regulators to convert many of these homes into rentals. Other economists advocate having the Federal Housing Administration offer loan guarantees to banks to induce them to refinance millions of home loans at lower interest rates, a move adopted in early 2012 by the Obama administration. Finally, bankruptcy judges should be given the legal power to alter the terms of mortgages, just as judges now help troubled companies rewrite their contracts with labor unions, creditors, and suppliers.

Social Security and Medicare

Equally important are steps to protect and strengthen Social Security and Medicare, something overwhelmingly supported by Republican, Democratic, and independent voters. Privatizing them or altering their basic structures, as some in Congress propose, would spell financial disaster for millions of average Americans, and people know that. Whenever politicians have moved to privatize or radically alter these safety net programs, as Speaker Newt Gingrich did in 1995, as President Bush did in 2005, and as the Republican-led House did in 2011, voters have objected vehemently.

Conservatives are right that some adjustments and cost controls are needed to prevent health care inflation and our longer life span from undermining the financial viability of Social Security and Medicare. One suggestion is to readjust the formula for the annual cost-of-living increases in Social Security payments so as not to exaggerate inflation. The 2010 health care law included measures to slow Medicare cost growth, partly by curbing overpayments to private health insurance plans that cost more than Medicare and by rewarding health providers for quality of care rather than volume.

But the easiest way to put Social Security and Medicare on more solid financial footing is to remove the income cap on the payroll tax. Economists have estimated that taxing now exempt incomes over $106,800 would entirely eliminate the anticipated Social Security shortfall over the next seventy-five years. Added revenue could be raised by increasing Medicare premiums for the top 10 percent of income earners (income over $138,925) or by applying a means test for Medicare's low-cost health coverage.

Without these safety net programs, retirement security for average Americans is in serious peril. As we have already seen, roughly 50 percent of U.S. workers already face long-term poverty in their senior years. To prevent that, we may need to expand retirement protection with new laws requiring all companies with one hundred or more employees to provide some retirement program and to contribute a minimum of 4 percent of each employee's salary. Where 401(k) plans are offered, people need help—both a guaranteed employer contribution and the option of joining a pool of professionally managed funds with low fees.

Finally, as long as we claim to be a "land of opportunity," the United States must keep open the economic ladder upward for the sixty million in America's "aspiring middle class"—the hardworking poor. They depend on such safety net programs as college student loans, Medicaid, food stamps, child care support, housing assistance, and the earned income tax credit. Without those programs, the chances for rising into the middle class would almost disappear. Certainly poverty would be far more severe. Opinion polls show that majorities of Americans favor such programs, and the country can afford them. Over the next thirty years, our economy is projected to grow by 60 percent. That's another $8 trillion to $9 trillion. Steps #4, #5, and #7 suggest ways to generate funds for these programs through tax reform, defense cutbacks, and long-term savings on entitlements.

The Role of Politics

Thirty or forty years ago, in the era of middle-class power, a broad political consensus supported the kind of middle-class agenda outlined in this chapter. But in today's harsh partisan climate with the Senate often immobilized by filibuster tactics, the opposition will be formidable and Washington gridlock will be hard to overcome.

An authentic populist agenda won't be achieved without altering the power equation in Washington, so the political challenge (steps #9 and #10) is to revive middle-class power and to reduce polarized gridlock in our government by returning more power to the political center, the terrain inhabited by moderates and independents.

CHAPTER 22

POLITICS:
A GRASSROOTS RESPONSE

REVIVING THE MODERATE CENTER
AND MIDDLE-CLASS POWER

There is a disconnection between the people and their
leaders. Citizens do not trust their government. And a
variety of polls indicate that the distrust extends to
corporations and the media. People do not feel that
they have much control over their lives, and the sense
of impotence grows like a great life-endangering
tumor.

— JOHN W. GARDNER,
cabinet secretary to President Lyndon Johnson

Either democracy must be renewed, with politics
brought back to life, or wealth is likely to cement a
new and less democratic regime—plutocracy by some
other name.

— KEVIN PHILLIPS,
Wealth and Democracy

CHANGING THE POWER EQUATION in Washington will take a
mass movement at the grass roots to force the White House and Con-

gress to listen to average Americans and to put a middle-class agenda into law. It will also require reforms in our political system to increase the influence of political moderates and independent voters by reducing the built-in advantages now enjoyed by partisan extremists.

Voting is critical, of course, but experience teaches that voting is not enough. Even when voters elect a middle-class-friendly president and Congress, the hard grit of policy is chiseled out between elections, when voters have turned their backs on politics. That is when the influence game in Washington goes to work and undoes much of what voters thought they had voted for. The public may vent its frustration to pollsters, but as we have seen, Congress doesn't listen to polls.

Congress—and presidents, too—listen to money. The business of members is getting reelected. As the costs of political campaigns have soared, the power of political money has grown to the point where we have a government responsive largely to the superclass, what economist Joseph Stiglitz called government "of the 1%, by the 1%, for the 1%." Or as Senator John McCain, the conservative Republican presidential nominee in 2008, put it, the flow of money into lobbying and into election campaigns is "nothing less than an elaborate influence-peddling scheme in which both parties conspire to stay in office by selling the country to the highest bidder."

Action to Counter the Influence of Money

To counteract the influence of money in the New Power Game, average Americans need to exercise their unique political leverage—direct personal engagement in politics. As John Gardner, longtime head of Common Cause, the nonpartisan public advocacy group, observed, "The sad, hard truth is that at this juncture the American people themselves are part of the problem." Average Americans have become disenchanted and politically disengaged and, as a consequence, disenfranchised.

If we genuinely want government of the people, by the people, and for the people to fix the deep problems that plague our country, then millions of average Americans will have to become directly involved once again in citizen action—making their presence felt, taking to the streets, just as millions did in the 1960 and 1970s—to restore the vital link between Washington and the people.

There is ample tinder to fire a new populist rebellion. Public discontent over the gaping economic inequalities in America today is at a new high. Two-thirds of Americans now say there are "strong" conflicts between rich and poor—up roughly 20 percent from just two years ago. And this is not the view just of liberals. The perception of class conflict has risen sharply among white people, middle-income earners, political independents—even among a majority of Republicans (55 percent).

Confidence in government, especially in Congress, has plunged to historic lows. The popular sense of alienation is acute. Americans are fed up with the mean-spirited partisan warfare in a Congress that fails to do the people's business. In the summer of 2011, 70 percent told a CBS News poll that special interests have too much influence in Washington, and 85 percent said that ordinary people have too little influence. Voters in focus groups told Democratic pollster Stanley Greenberg: "There's just such a control of government by the wealthy. . . . We don't have a representative government anymore."

Hard facts support this conclusion. Political scientists have documented in detail that without active grassroots pressure, Washington ignores large majorities of Americans. When Larry Bartels of Princeton University analyzed a host of congressional votes in the 1980s and 1990s, he found that senators were "vastly more responsive to affluent constituents" than to middle-class and poorer voters.

In 2005, Martin Gilens, another Princeton political scientist, made a detailed comparison of the policies that voters preferred with the policies Washington adopted and concluded that politicians had disregarded the views of middle-class voters. "Influence over actual policy outcomes," wrote Gilens, "appears to be reserved almost exclusively for those at the top of the income distribution."

Correcting the obvious inequalities in our democracy, as well as in our economy, will require political reforms—pushed from the bottom up.

Step #9: Rebuild the Political Center

Step #9 is to regenerate the centrist core of American politics both by rejecting extremist candidates in both parties and by opening up our political process in every state to give more influence to moderate and independent voters.

Historically, when there has been mass disenchantment with both major political parties, public anger has spawned third party movements. In the 1992 presidential election, Texas billionaire Ross Perot ran for president and won nearly 20 percent of the popular vote running as an independent.

At that time, 39 percent of the voters voiced dissatisfaction with how government was being run. Today, dissatisfaction with both parties in Washington is far higher—81 percent—and it has once again spurred an urge to reach beyond party lines and revive the political center. The 2012 political year has seen a wave of new political movements such as Americans Elect, Votocracy, Third Way, and No Labels. "There is just so much unrest out there that something is going to explode," commented Democratic pollster Peter Hart.

Americans Elect is the most ambitious effort to promote a bipartisan middle ground in the presidential election. Capitalizing on the Internet, Republican strategist Kahlil Byrd and wealthy philanthropist Peter Ackerman have been promoting what Byrd calls a "widespread draft movement for presidential candidates," with strong appeal to moderate and independent voters. Their idea is to bypass the Republican and Democratic nominating conventions with more direct democracy: Offer registered voters a forum to nominate their own presidential candidate via the Internet, with the proviso that whoever is chosen as presidential nominee must select a running mate from the opposite party. By early 2012, Americans Elect accomplished a major goal—getting the organization listed on the ballot in all fifty states.

The key, of course, is fielding a high-profile, vote-getting candidate and sustaining the movement. After the 2010 midterm elections, New York's Republican mayor, Michael Bloomberg, seemed to cast himself as a centrist contender with his broadside blast at both major parties. "Despite what ideologues on the left believe, government cannot tax and spend its way back to prosperity, especially when that spending is driven by pork barrel politics," Bloomberg declared. ". . . Despite what ideologues on the right believe, government should not stand aside and wait for the business cycle to run its natural course. That would be intolerable. . . ." But having staked out the political middle, Bloomberg did not throw his hat in the ring. Even when third-party movements have run a potent vote-getter, such as Theodore Roosevelt and the Bull Moose Party in 1912 or Ross Perot in 1992, third parties have never offered a long-term solution to a sharp divide between the two major parties. Perhaps the most important role of Americans Elect in the future may be in state and Congressional races because it has gotten its own ballot line all across the country.

Another sign of rising protest against political extremism—at the state and congressional level—is the birth of No Labels, a group formed by longtime Democratic fund-raiser Nancy Jacobson and Republican Mark McKinnon, a media strategist for the Bush presidential campaigns in 2000 and 2004. No Labels won early blessings from Mayor Bloomberg, Florida's former Republican governor Charlie Christ, and former Clinton administration official Jonathan Cowan. As Cowan puts it, the goal is to counteract "this kind of hyper-partisanship, my party, right or wrong, damn the consequences" and to pressure politicians in all 435 congressional districts into "setting aside their [party] labels" and moving toward compromises on the nation's most pressing issues.

But Third Way, a think tank linked to No Labels, has a more focused and practical agenda. Its leaders see parties as the main cause of today's "pathological polarization" of politics, and they want to break party control over primary elections, the gerrymandering of congressional districts, and party line election of congressional leadership. "Political parties have turned out to be a disaster," argues former conservative Oklahoma Republican congressman Mickey Edwards. "The problem is the party system itself. And No Labels has on its mission statement to move toward open primaries and to take away party control over districting."

Reforming the Primary System

To revive the political center, Third Way asserts, it's essential to break the iron grip of parties by opening primaries to all voters and turning over the once-a-decade redrawing of congressional district lines to nonpartisan commissions. Such moves, reformers assert, will change the mix of voters and the dynamics of political campaigns. The idea is that open primaries would expand the electorate and therefore push candidates to cater more to moderates, who at 44 percent of the electorate in the presidential election of 2008 outnumbered both conservatives (34 percent) and liberals (22 percent). Third Way argues that open primaries should lead to the election of more moderates, making Congress less polarized and more prone to compromise.

Actual experience is limited, but it supports Third Way's logic. Twice since the 1970s, California's legislative redistricting was forced into the courts and carried out by a panel of retired federal judges instead of the legislature. Each time, the parties wound up with less of a lock on legislative districts. Elections swung from Republican to Democrat and vice versa. Voters had more sway.

So far, eleven states have so-called open primaries in the presidential nominating contest for both parties—that is, primaries where each party, running its own candidates, opens the balloting to all voters, whether they are registered in that party or are independents or in the opposite party. Eighteen states follow the same pattern in congressional elections—all voters can take part and vote for that party's candidates.

So far, only Washington State has taken the next step—running one nonpartisan primary in congressional races, where candidates for both parties run together in a single primary race and voting is open to everyone. The top two vote getters then oppose each other in the general election. Washington State did that in 2010 and the impact was dramatic. The average vote in Washington State's nine congressional districts tripled the turnout in 2008. That seemed to favor more moderate candidates because higher turnout typically reduces the pull of extremist candidates. California has now decided to follow Washington State in its congressional elections in 2012, and if it works well there, the idea may spread.

Ways to Boost Voter Turnout

Since American elections with low turnout usually go to the party that can fire up the political emotions of its most ardent partisan supporters, the most obvious way to increase the influence of moderate and independent voters would be to increase American voter turnout. In 2010, just 37 percent of eligible voters cast ballots. When so many Americans move their residences from year to year, local variations in voter registration pose obstacles to higher turnouts. In the 2008 president election, an estimated 2.2 million Americans were unable to cast ballots because of voter registration problems, according to the Pew Center on the States.

The Pew Center and other groups have urged states to adopt automated online voter registration and computerized voting, to make voting more accessible to people whose jobs are distant from their homes and voting sites. A few states such as Maine, Minnesota, and Wisconsin have instituted election-day voter registration and seen voter turnouts rise. Other countries have gotten better turnouts by putting election days on weekends or holidays to reduce conflicts with work schedules. In America, 25 percent of eligible voters have told pollsters that work and schedule conflicts impede their ability to vote.

To boost turnout, about thirty countries have compulsory voting and some actually penalize voters for failing to exercise their franchise. Australia achieves roughly 95 percent voter turnout by holding elections on Saturdays and fining citizens A$20 for not voting, with the fine escalating each time a voter misses an election. This system changes the dynamics of the campaign and elevates the caliber of debate in Australian elections, according to Norman Ornstein of the American Enterprise Institute.

"The way to gain votes does not come from working your base to fever pitch, it comes from persuading the persuadables, the centrists who are increasingly left out of the American political process," Ornstein has written. "Appealing to the extremes is a formula for failure. If there were mandatory voting in America, there's a good chance that the ensuing reduction in extremist discourse would lead to genuine legislative progress."

The Corruptive Influence of Money

The toughest nut in U.S. politics today is how to reduce the influence of money in elections and on legislative policy making. As Arizona's Republican senator John McCain once admitted, "All of us [politicians] have been corrupted by the process where big money and big influence—and you can include me in that list—where big money has bought access, which has bought influence."

So far, legislative efforts at reform have repeatedly been undermined. Each time Congress has tried to impose limits on donations to political candidates, either the Supreme Court has voided those measures as unconstitutional limits on free speech or ingenious political operatives have found ways around the laws. In its January 2010 decision on the *Citizens United* case, the Supreme Court rejected two precedent decisions and ruled that government may not ban campaign spending by corporations on behalf of political candidates. The high court gave the green light to unlimited donations to independent groups, meaning technically independent of candidates and parties. That decision, reinforced by the loose rules for independent groups adopted by the Federal Election Commission, has effectively nullified the existing $2,500 limit on personal contributions to political candidates and opened the floodgates to hundreds of millions of campaign dollars flowing from super-rich donors and corporations to theoretically independent Super-PACs.

The Sudden Surge of Super-Pacs

Very quickly in the 2012 elections, Super-PACs emerged to play a commanding role, acting as surrogates for the candidates they favored. In Iowa's Republican caucuses, Restore Our Future, the Super-PAC backing Mitt Romney, demolished Newt Gingrich with a multimillion-dollar television ad blitz. In South Carolina, the pro-Gingrich Super-PAC, Winning Our Future, crippled and defeated Romney. Other candidates, such as former Pennsylvania senator Rick Santorum and Governor Rick Perry of Texas followed suit. "The Super-PACs are plainly an avenue for candidates to evade the law that limits contributions," Mann and Ornstein commented ruefully.

By late spring, Super-PACs had raised $160 million, bankrolled mainly by a small group of billionaire would-be kingmakers such as Las Vegas casino owner Sheldon Adelson and his wife, Miriam; Harold C. Simmons of Dallas and his chemical and metals conglomerate, Contran Corporation; Houston home builder Robert J. Perry; PayPal co-founder Peter Thiel; Hollywood producer Jeffrey Katzenberg, CEO of Dreamworks; and hedge fund managers John A. Paulson and Paul Singer of New York. Just three super-donors—the Adelsons, Simmons/Contran, and Perry—contributed close to one fourth of all the Super-PAC cash.

In the 2012 general election campaign, Super-PACs have cast themselves as weapons of political mass destruction. Long before the party conventions actually nominated presidential candidates, runaway campaign fund-raising by Republicans, Democrats, and independent groups was on track to outspend the record-breaking $1.8 billion presidential election of 2008. Charles and David Koch, billionaire owners of Koch Industries, an energy conglomerate head-quartered in Wichita, Kansas, pledged $60 million to defeat President Obama and recruited other wealthy conservative super-donors to help raise $100 million. American Crossroads and Crossroads GPS, the Super-PACs masterminded by Karl Rove, longtime political strategist for George W. Bush, set a goal of raising $300 million to blitz Obama. Initially, President Obama had rejected Super-PACs. But facing a Republican Super-PAC offensive, Obama relented and gave the go-ahead for Democratic funders to try to match Republicans, presaging a fierce crossfire of negative attack ads in the fall campaign.

More broadly, the explosive rise of Super-PACs and their super-donors has overwhelmed the campaign finance reform legislation enacted since 1974 and has thrown America once again into an era of essentially unregulated campaign funding.

Reformers like Senator McCain have warned that unregulated funding corrodes American democracy and corrupts the legitimacy of American elections, and so they have fought to impose limits on donations. Other reformers have advocated large-scale public financing to put political unknowns and challengers on a more equal footing with incumbents and to reduce the lopsided political influence of big corporations and wealthy donors. But decisions by the Supreme Court and the Federal Election Commission have punched large loopholes in those reforms. Fred Wertheimer of Democracy 21 and others have attacked the fictional independence of some Super-PACs from their favored candidates and now call for new laws to ban Super-PACs with any links to candidates, however indirect.

But politicians and their campaign strategists have been so ingenious and adept at getting around laws and regulations that it will almost surely require a constitutional amendment to ban campaign contributions from corporations, labor unions, and other institutions and specifically to empower Congress to impose limits on campaign donations from individuals. But that is a formidable process, sure to be fiercely opposed by entrenched interests. Only a groundswell of grassroots political activism, fueled by public revulsion at the power of Super-PACs and inflated campaign spending by America's super-rich, will be able to overcome resistance from politicians, and especially from congressional incumbents who have thrived on the present system.

Step #10: Mobilize the Middle Class

The only sure way to alter today's patently unequal democracy is for average Americans to mobilize politically—to break out of their political inertia and to move forcefully back into the political arena.

Important as it is to open up party primaries, arrange for nonpartisan legislative redistricting, and provide a floor of public financing for elections, the fundamental need of American democracy is the practical exercise of democracy—a rebirth of citizen activism. That requires not only a populist rebellion against the political and economic inequalities of our divided nation, but a hopeful rebirth of American idealism, a revival of the belief that ordinary people can, in fact, make a difference and turn the tide.

At election time, American voters seem flattered and even seduced by the ritualistic declarations of presidential contenders that America's best years lie ahead and America's democracy is the greatest in the world. But it is clear from a multitude of opinion polls and reporting that once the inflated rhetoric of campaigns subsides, people don't really believe that anymore. They doubt their own power.

"The loss of civic faith is an obstacle," John Gardner remarked in the late 1990s. "One might imagine that the solution would be for government to make itself worthy of our faith. But the plain truth is that the government . . . will not become worthy of trust until citizens take positive action to hold them to account. Citizen involvement comes first."

Politicians are afraid of mobilized voters. They open their doors when home-state residents flood the corridors of Capitol Hill—evidence that continuing political pressure from the middle class can push Washington to generate what nineteenth-century British philosopher Jeremy Bentham called "the greatest good for the greatest number."

So the time has come for direct political action by millions of ordinary Americans to use their physical involvement as a countervailing power to Washington influence peddlers.

*You Think Government
Doesn't Work? Take Another Look*

But what's the point? people say. Government doesn't work.

Well, take a closer look. Government may not work well for average Americans, but it has been working very well for Wall Street, for multinational corporations, and for the financial superclass. They get the government they want, and they pay handsomely to get it.

During 2009 and 2010, when Congress was writing laws on financial regulation, health care, and taxes, business interests spent $6 billion on lobbying. In "soft money" campaign donations, business outspent labor 97 to 1 in the 2010 elections, and it got a Congress eager to roll back regulations on banks, health insurers, and other businesses and refusing to close corporate tax loopholes or raise taxes on the rich. Over the years, the multinationals have won new trade deals, tax holidays on overseas earnings, and laws that let them import cheaper foreign labor to displace American workers. Some of America's richest families bankroll anti-tax conservatives like the Tea Party, which has wielded huge influence in two short years, even though it represents only a small fraction of Middle America.

So government can work. You just have to make it work for you.

People are understandably skeptical. Many say they want smaller government, but that may be because they don't realize how much they already depend on government, like the South Carolina man who in an anti-government tirade told his congressman to "keep your government hands off my Medicare"—not realizing that Medicare was a government program.

In a 2008 survey by Cornell University, people were asked if they had ever benefited from federal policies and government programs. In response, 57 percent said, "No, never." But when they were questioned more closely, it turned out that 94 percent had actually benefited from at least one government social program and the average person had used four programs.

So government has an impact on our lives, and we in the middle class need to learn from Wall Street, Corporate America, and the Tea Party how to make it work better for us. That may sound impossible. Ever since the late 1970s, the power game has been dominated by money. Of course, people in the middle-income brackets cannot hope to outspend the rich and the big corporations.

The most powerful action that average Americans can take is *to organize at the grass roots,* as the Tea Party did, and then *put ourselves on the line.* Ordinary people need to personally join the battle: Show up at town meetings with members of Congress; get out on Main Street and demonstrate for jobs and homes; head for the state capital; take the bus or train to a march on Washington. Like the civil rights protesters, or the military veteran bonus marchers during the Great Depression—or the Tea Party people today—average Americans can stage rallies and demonstrations and put up tent cities on the Washington Mall that make it impossible for Congress and the White House to ignore the needs and demands of ordinary people.

The Touchstone Issues—Jobs and Fairness

It would help rekindle public faith in government if political leaders would demonstrate that Washington actually works for average Americans, that the White House and Congress are ready to help out Main Street the same way they bailed out Wall Street.

The test should focus on two touchstone issues—jobs and fairness. Both issues can mobilize the middle class. People have an existential understanding of jobs and fairness, either from their own lives or from the lives of their family, friends, and neighbors.

If enough average Americans mobilize around jobs and fairness and demand action from Congress and the White House, politicians will get the message and respond. As the Tea Party has demonstrated, a highly vocal activist minority with a clear agenda and focused demands can change the debate and direction of policy in Washington.

Jobs come first. They are the essential economic lever to lift the middle class back to shared prosperity and to jump-start the consumer engine to drive the American economy. The test of whether business leaders are committed to America's growth or just to their own company's profits is whether they invest their $1 trillion or $2 trillion in cash reserves and their overseas profits in *creating jobs in America* and not primarily in stock options, higher dividends, and buying back their own company's stock.

Practical programs to promote and create jobs are the political litmus test of whether Congress and the White House are committed to a middle-class revival or just to a futile repetition of the failed litany of the lower taxes, less regulation, free market mantra that in the 2000s generated the worst economic performance for most Americans of any decade since World War II.

Catch-22 for Twenty-Two Million Homeowners

Fairness is the touchstone for money issues—a test of whether America can return to a more equitable sharing of the nation's economic gains.

As we have seen, the middle class won't have enough spending power to regenerate "the virtuous circle" in the economy unless a much larger share of America's national income goes to average Americans. Fairness requires rebalancing how business profits are divided between shareholders and employees, and it calls for rebalancing government policies more in favor of average Americans.

Some quick symbolic steps such as closing corporate tax loopholes, raising taxes on the rich, and imposing new fees on Wall Street's stock transactions and executive stock options could help restore government's credibility with ordinary people.

But a more central long-term yardstick of fairness to the middle class is how the Congress and the White House handle housing, since homes are the heart of the American Dream and the cornerstone of middle-class wealth. As Harvard economist Kenneth Rogoff noted, "There is widespread agreement among economists that housing debt is at the heart of the slow recovery, and that finding a way to bring it down faster would accelerate the recovery."

The biggest debt now overhangs twenty-two million families stuck in homes that are "under water." Like the big Wall Street banks, which were bailed out not only with $700 billion in taxpayer funds, but with $7.7 trillion in loans from the Federal Reserve, these creditworthy homeowners desperately need help with rewriting and refinancing their mortgages, and smart economists have spelled out steps to speed massive refinancing—steps that would be a shot in the arm to the whole nation.

A dead housing market hurts everyone. It not only depresses home values, it cuts consumer demand. Even people whose homes are above water cut back their spending when housing prices fall. Economists tell us that the housing collapse from 2006 to 2009 has cost the U.S. economy an estimated $240 billion a year in lost consumer spending.

"Consumer spending is not only the key to economic recovery in the short term," economic historian James Livingston of Rutgers University has written. "It's also necessary for balanced growth in the long term. If our goal is to repair our damaged economy . . . that entails a redistribution of income away from profits toward wages, enabled by tax policy and enforced by government spending."

What's Needed: Armies of Volunteers

Getting help for homeowners and jobs for the roughly twenty-five million unemployed and underemployed Americans will require changing the political dynamics in Washington. The reflexive instinct of most Americans is to ask for a new Lincoln to pull the nation together again and restore a national sense of purpose. But great as he was, Lincoln could not have done it without armies of volunteers—without regiments from New York, Illinois, Ohio, and Pennsylvania, without average Americans prepared to put themselves and their lives on the line to reunite America and reforge a common destiny for our nation.

So, too, today it will take armies of volunteers to get the country back on track. People regularly sign up for causes. They join demonstrations—to oppose the new Keystone XL Pipeline from Canada to Oklahoma, to raise money for the Susan G. Komen Race for the Cure, to fight obesity in America, or to take part in comedian Jon Stewart's Rally to Restore Sanity and/or Fear at the Lincoln Memorial in October 2010. In 1979, several hundred farmers drove their tractors to Washington and camped on the Mall for a few weeks to protest high interest rates. But these are disparate causes.

What's needed now is an army of volunteers prepared to battle for the common cause of reclaiming the American Dream. Occupy Wall Street and its spin-offs in more than fifteen cities around the country began that process, focusing more of the national dialogue on the hyperconcentration of wealth and power in America—the costly divide of gross inequality between the top 1 percent and the other 99 percent. But for significant long-term impact, either Occupy will need to mature or some new movement will need to emerge with broader participation, better organization, more clearly articulated goals, and specific policy targets.

If Americans are daunted by that challenge, consider what happened in Arab countries that had been under the boot of dictators for decades. The people who took over Middle East capitals in the winter and spring of 2011 had never known our freedoms or our democracy. Yet, amazingly, long passive Egyptians, Tunisians, Libyans, Yemenis, and Syrians dared to challenge entrenched power with their "Arab Spring." Change has been swift in some countries, slow in others. But it has happened.

In Israel, less noticed but more relevant to Americas issues, hundreds of thousands of people marched through the summer of 2011, demanding that the Israeli government narrow the gap between rich and poor and ease the hardships caused by a housing shortage and a sharply rising cost of living. Israelis threw up tent cities in parks from Haifa to Beersheba and along fashionable avenues in Tel Aviv to protest against the concentrated wealth of the "tycoons," as Israel's richest families are known. They called on the Israeli government to take action to "minimize social inequalities."

Under pressure from the street, Prime Minister Benjamin Netanyahu and the Israeli cabinet set up an economic commission to study the popular demands, and then, when the commission delivered its findings, the government approved its call for increased taxes on companies and on capital gains and a surtax on the wealthy, as well as its proposals for easing financial burdens on the middle class. "The consumer will feel the government's decision today in his pocket," said Netanyahu.

If there can be protests and government action against a lopsided division of the economic spoils in Israel, why not in America?

If there can be an "Arab Spring" among peoples who have never known democracy, why not in the homeland of democracy?

Why not a springtime for American democracy? A jobs-first crusade? A movement to reclaim the American Dream?

We are at a defining moment for America. We cannot allow the slow, poisonous polarization and disintegration of our great democracy to continue. We must come together and take action to rejuvenate our nation and to restore fairness and hope in our way of life. We see the challenge. It is now time: We the People must take action.

ACKNOWLEDGMENTS

SCORES OF PEOPLE CONTRIBUTED to this book, whether by giving me interviews, by sharing their expertise with me, or, as colleagues, by their reporting for the PBS documentaries that we created together. I am grateful to all of you. But several people made special and continuing contributions to my work and deserve to be singled out for particular acknowledgment and appreciation.

My first reader and editor and the most important believer in this project has been Susan Zox, my wife and longtime collaborator in journalistic enterprises. Susan has deftly managed to find that indefinable but vital place that combines enthusiasm and support with a helpful critical eye and that enables an independent-minded friend to offer sometimes difficult advice to keep a writer from getting off track. Susan also provided a wonderful environment for me during two years of writing—relief, amusement, and incredible patience with my long hours and selfish concentration on the work at hand. Her belief in this book and her backing have been invaluable.

I have been most fortunate to have Kate Medina, one of the finest and most dedicated editors in modern American publishing, as my editor for this book and three previous books. In a publishing world much focused on coping with new technologies and new marketing challenges, Kate personifies the time-tested virtues of classical editing—working closely with an author on the substance, voice, and architecture of the book. The final version of *Who Stole the American Dream?* has benefited greatly from the skill, passion, and care that Kate invested in this book, and I am most grateful.

I owe a debt of gratitude as well to my researcher, Owen Smith, who for two years dug into a mountain of books, often impenetrable government reports and documents, and online sites to seek out the information that I tasked him to find. Owen has been tireless, tenacious, and ingenious as a researcher and reporter and in mastering the technical challenges in our project. Through it all, he has been a cheerful, unflappable colleague and companion whose support has been essential to me.

David Black, my literary agent, has been a resourceful and knowledgeable friend and ally from start to finish. For a writer who last published a book in the mid-1990s, David has been a steadying influence, wise in his comments and advice, patiently tutoring me on how the world of American publishing and the audience of readers have changed in the past seventeen years.

Olga Seham, a former Random House editor, brought a fresh and extremely helpful perspective to the late stages of editing. She combined an immediate enthusiasm for my book and its range of topics with thoughtful and provocative questions that prodded me to fill holes and answer questions that needed sharper, smarter explanations. Quite a few chapters bear the imprint of her tough-minded critiques and my responses to her friendly challenges.

Anna Pitoniak, as Kate Medina's assistant, has been resourceful, ubiquitous, and ever invaluable in shepherding me and variations of my manuscript through the byways of a large publishing house. I found her personal reactions and editing suggestions insightful and her quick and lively interest in this book project helpful and heartwarming.

I owe special thanks and appreciation to WGBH, the PBS station in Boston, to *Frontline,* and to my friend David Fanning, the founder and senior executive producer of *Frontline,* for granting me permission to use material from my reporting on several *Frontline* documentaries.

My appreciation goes as well to my colleagues at Hedrick Smith Productions, especially Rick Young, Catherine Rentz, and Cory Ford, for sharing their reporting and insights with me. I am grateful, too, for the generous assistance of David Heath, formerly of *The Seattle Times* and more recently of the Center for Public Integrity, on the topics of Washington Mutual, Long Beach Mortgage, and the intricacies of exotic home mortgages.

Many scholars and academicians have provided me with assistance, but several deserve special recognition because they responded so generously to my repeated inquiries and requests: Larry Mishel, director of the Economic Policy Institute, and his EPI colleague Robert Scott; Jack VanDerhei and Dallas Salisbury of the Employee Benefits Research Institute; Alicia Munnell and Andy Eschtruth of the Boston College Center for Retirement Research; pension consultant Brooks Hamilton; Karen Friedman of the Pension Rights Center; Tom Mann of the Brookings Institution; Norman Ornstein of the American Enterprise Institute; Robert Lawless of the University of Illinois; Alan Tonelson of the U.S. Business and Industry Council; Ron Hira of the Rochester Institute of Technology; Winslow Wheeler of the Center for Defense Information; and the researchers who track money in politics for the Center for Responsive Politics.

APPENDIX

Stolen Dream Timeline:
Key Events, Trends, and Turning Points, 1948–2012

JANUARY 1914—Henry Ford announces the $5 day—reckoning that if workers are well paid, they can afford to buy Ford's Model T cars, and Ford could move into mass production. Ford's strategy sparks a trend.

1948 "TREATY OF DETROIT"—Labor agreement between General Motors and the United Auto Workers union gives GM labor peace and autoworkers annual pay increases, health benefits, and monthly pensions, setting a pattern for other industries, ensuring that gains from U.S. economic growth are shared between labor and management.

1950—Top CEO salary in America: GM chairman Charlie Wilson is paid $663,000, roughly $5 million in today's dollars, and about 40 times the annual wage of his average assembly line worker. Corporate ethic frowned on CEOs taking stock grants as unfair "competitive avarice." Economists call this period "The Great Compression" because the income gap between the rich and the middle class is at its narrowest in the twentieth century.

MID-1940S TO MID-1970S—Heyday of the middle class, when the U.S. economy is driven by the dynamics of "the virtuous circle." Companies paid high wages and tens of millions of families had steady income to spend, generating high consumer demand. Robust consumer demand propels businesses to invest in new plants and technology and to hire more employees, fueling the "virtuous circle of growth" to another round of expansion and higher living standards.

AUGUST 1963—March on Washington led by Martin Luther King, Jr. Student sit-ins, Freedom Rides, other civil rights demonstrations, and citizen grassroots movements force change, demonstrating the political power of average Americans.

JUNE 1964—Congress passes the 1964 Civil Rights Act with strong bipartisan support, outlawing segregation of public accommodations, following mass protests.

NOVEMBER 1964—Barry Goldwater, a strongly anti-union, anti-government senator from Arizona, beats the mainstream Republican Establishment to win the GOP presidential nomination, but loses to Democrat Lyndon Johnson. Goldwater's defense of political extremism and rejection of compromise as a matter of principle spark the birth and growth of the Republican New Right, culminating in today's Tea Party.

MARCH 1965—Bloody Sunday in Selma, Alabama: Civil rights protesters led by John Lewis are brutally clubbed by Alabama State troopers and sheriff's deputies during a march for voting rights for African Americans.

JULY 1965—Congress enacts Medicare with strong bipartisan support: 65 House Republicans and 13 Senate Republicans join majorities of Democrats in both chambers to pass President Johnson's historic legislation.

AUGUST 1965—Voting Rights Act is pushed through Congress by President Johnson, on the momentum of massive grassroots civil rights demonstrations. The act removes legal obstacles to the right to vote for African Americans, especially in southern states.

1965 — Consumer advocate Ralph Nader publishes his searing attack on U.S. auto industry, *Unsafe at Any Speed*, charging automakers with marketing defective cars, and giving consumer activism new political leverage. The burgeoning consumer movement presses Congress and the White House to create new watchdog agencies and standards for truth in packaging and truth in lending.

NOVEMBER 1967 — Pat O'Neill, at nineteen, starts a thirty-five-year career with United Airlines as a jet airline mechanic, working the overnight "graveyard shift" at Chicago's O'Hare field. He works his way up to chief mechanic, making $60,000 a year, leading a crew that does repairs and safety checks so that planes are ready to be airborne by dawn.

APRIL 22, 1970 — EARTH DAY — The largest single mass public protest in U.S. history. Twenty million Americans participate in marches, teach-ins, and other demonstrations to protest against pollution of the environment.

1970 — President Nixon, responding to public pressures, establishes the Environmental Protection Agency. Congress passes the Clean Air act in 1970, the Clean Water Act of 1972, and other strong laws to protect the environment. Nixon also sets up a Consumer Product Safety Commission and the Occupational Safety and Health Administration, and expands the powers of the Federal Trade Commission to protect consumers and curb the excesses of capitalism.

AUGUST 1971 — Corporate attorney Lewis Powell sparks a political rebellion with his call to arms for Corporate America. Circulated by the U.S. Chamber of Commerce, Powell's memo warns that anti-business attitudes and government regulation are threatening to "fatally weaken or destroy" the American free enterprise system. Powell declares that business must arm itself politically, battle organized labor and consumer activists, and mount a long-term campaign to change the balance of power and policy trends in Washington.

1971–1972—The CEOs of America's biggest corporations, responding to Powell's memo, organize the Business Roundtable, which becomes the most potent political lobbying arm of Corporate America. The National Association of Manufacturers moves its headquarters to Washington. In one decade the U.S. Chamber of Commerce doubles its membership and the National Federation of Independent Business (small business) grows from 300 to 600,000 members.

SUMMER 1971—After graduating from high school, Pam Scholl and Mike Hughes land solid middle-class jobs at the brand new RCA television tube plant in Circleville, Ohio. For the next three decades, Scholl and Hughes and their classmates enjoy their version of the American Dream of secure jobs, rising pay, health benefits, and lifetime pensions—a solid middle-class standard of living.

1973—The productivity of U.S. workers rises 96 percent since 1945, and average hourly compensation rises in tandem—94 percent from 1945 to 1973. Average Americans share in the nation's prosperity. In the next three decades, from 1973 to 2011, worker productivity rises another 80 percent but hourly compensation rises only 10 percent. Ordinary Americans are cut out of their share of the nation's economic gains.

OCTOBER 1976—Inspired by their mentor, free market economist Milton Friedman, business school professors Michael Jensen and William Meckling propose in an academic study that CEOs be given stock options to align their interests with those of stockholders. Corporate boards, seeing an advantage because options are not charged as a company expense, adopt this "pay for performance" idea, and by 1980, 30 percent of CEOs are receiving stock option grants.

LATE 1970S—Business mobilizes politically. The number of companies with Washington lobbying offices grows from 175 in 1971 to 2,445 a decade later. Along with 2,000 different trade associations, businesses have a combined Washington staff of 50,000, plus 9,000 lobbyists and 8,000 public relations specialists. Business lobbyists and advocates now outnumber members of Congress by 130 to 1.

1977–1978—In the pivotal 95th Congress under President Jimmy Carter and the Democrats, business shows its new political muscle. Its lobbyists block organized labor's legislation and Ralph Nader's push for a consumer protection agency. They win deregulation of airlines, railroads, and trucking. They get Congress to reject Carter's plan to close tax loopholes for the rich and, instead, they push to cut the corporate tax rate and the capital gains tax on investment income from 49 percent to 28 percent.

1978—Two major bills alter the economic landscape for decades to come. One is an obscure insert in the tax code, paragraph 401(k), initially intended to authorize supplemental executive retirement plans and later extended by the Reagan administration to rank-and-file workers. The other change updates U.S. bankruptcy laws, giving management control during corporate bankruptcy, paving the way for bankruptcies in the 1990s and 2000s that canceled provisions of union contracts.

1980—Congress passes a deregulatory bill that overrules state usury laws and effectively abolishes limits on interest rates for first mortgages, paving the way for the future subprime mortgage boom.

1981—President Reagan pushes through tax cuts that heavily favor the wealthy, dropping the top personal income tax rate from 70 percent to 28 percent, the capital gains rate from 28 percent to 20 percent, and the corporate rate from 46 percent to 35 percent. The Reagan tax cuts add $1 trillion in income for the super-rich 1 percent during the 1980s, and another $1 trillion in each successive decade. The Forbes 400 Richest Americans triple their net worth between 1978 and 1990, thanks to the Reagan tax cuts.

1982—President Reagan persuades Congress to pass a law authorizing the exotic loans that will become the hallmarks of the 2000s housing boom. The law permits loans never previously allowed: adjustable-rate mortgages, or ARMs, with ballooning interest rates, 100 percent financing, and "negative amortization," which permits banks to charge high fees and interest rates and allows minimal payments, causing many people to go deeper into debt, and stripping equity out of many homes.

LATE 1980S TO 1990S—Mutual funds popularize 401(k) plans with the slogan "Be Your Own Money Manager." Millions of rank-and-file employees eagerly adopt do-it-yourself retirement. Companies unload hundreds of billions in retirement costs onto their workers. The employee share of retirement costs goes from 11 percent in 1980 to 51 percent by 2006.

1990—Congress passes the H-1B visa program, permitting U.S. businesses to import college-educated foreign workers for high-tech and knowledge economy jobs. By the early 2000s, close to a million Americans have been replaced by foreigners, even though studies by Rand and others assert that there is no shortage of Americans to fill such jobs.

1993—For the first time since World War II, a major piece of legislation—President Clinton's budget—passes Congress without a single yes vote from the opposition party. In a virtually unprecedented party-line vote, not a single Republican supports Clinton's tax increases.

1993–1994—Hampered by partisan gridlock, the 1993–1994 Congress becomes one of the two least productive legislative sessions in half a century, with the second lowest percentage of major legislation passed.

1994—The CEO stock option boom takes off. Seventy percent of CEOs now receive stock option grants and by 2000, grants of millions of stock options become the norm, hugely increasing CEO pay. Corporate executives overtake the inherited rich as the biggest portion of the nation's richest 1 percent.

1995 — Partisan gridlock shuts down the government after Republicans take control of the House for the first time in forty years and Republican Speaker Newt Gingrich sets up a confrontation with President Clinton over the budget. Eventually, with polls showing the public blames Republicans more than Democrats, Gingrich backs down.

1999—General Electric CEO Jack Welch is named "the ultimate manager" of the twentieth century by *Fortune*. Nicknamed "Neutron Jack" for the weapon that kills human beings but leaves buildings standing, Welch reverses the employee-friendly policies of his predecessor and wins favor on Wall Street for cutting 25 percent of GE's workforce—130,000 jobs. As one executive put it, "Working for him is like a war—a lot of people get shot up."

1995–2000 — By balancing the federal budget and generating budget surpluses, the Clinton tax increases of 1993 help to lower inflation and interest rates and to generate the nation's strongest steady economic growth period since the 1960s, boosting the real wages of average middle-class workers.

2001–2003 — President George W. Bush pushes massive tax cuts through Congress each year, starting in 2001, despite opinion polls showing the public favors using budget surpluses inherited from Clinton to increase spending on education, health, and Social Security, or to reduce the national debt.

2001–2003 — The Federal Reserve, led by Chairman Alan Greenspan, cuts interest rates 11 times from 6.5 percent to 1 percent, providing cheap money to fuel a housing boom and revive the U.S. economy. Home prices rise so fast that Americans borrow $700 billion a year from their home equity. Despite warnings about the dangers of rising personal debt, Greenspan hails homeowners' "equity extraction" as the engine for consumer demand and economic growth.

MAY 2003—At a White House ceremony, President Bush thanks "my friend Dirk Van Dongen" for helping to move the Bush tax cuts through Congress. Unknown to most Americans, Van Dongen is a Washington insider, field marshal of "the Gang of Six"—the six major business organizations that anchor the Tax Relief Coalition that lobbied for tax cuts.

2003—Airline mechanic Pat O'Neill retires from United Airlines after 35 years on the job, but when United Airlines declares bankruptcy, his lifetime pension is drastically cut, and his employee stock option plan collapses. His 401(k) suffers from a sharp stock market decline, and he is forced to take another job. To rebuild financially, O'Neill is still working today, and he expects never to retire.

2004—Pam Scholl and Mike Hughes lose their jobs when the old RCA television tube plant in Circleville, Ohio, shuts down—one of 54,000 American plants to close in the 2000s. Pam gets another job fairly quickly, but Mike can't find steady work.

2004—Bill Nichol, CEO of Kentucky Derby Hosiery, bowing to Wal-Mart executives telling their suppliers to set up low-cost production in China, says he is moving a big chunk of his company there. Wal-Mart gets 80 percent of its products from China-based production, much of it from U.S. companies operating in China.

2004–2005—Alan Greenspan praises the rapid growth of the subprime mortgage market and encourages mainstream borrowers to shift from standard level–rate loans to adjustable-rate mortgages. Then, from 2004 to 2006, Greenspan raises interest rates, making adjustable-rate mortgages riskier.

2003–2007—Small-business owner John Terboss of North Miami Beach is talked into a series of adjustable-rate home mortgage refinancings, each with a higher loan balance. When he discovers that his broker got an $18,875 bonus for putting Terboss into a high-interest loan, Terboss tries to cancel the loan and gets socked with a $21,000 prepayment penalty. In all, he loses $150,000 in equity he had put into his home.

2005–2006—More than half of the people to whom banks sell subprime mortgage loans, at high interest rates with heavy fees, are actually solid mainstream middle-class borrowers who qualified for—and should have been sold—prime loans.

2006—American business has shed much of the cost of the corporate safety net. By the mid-2000s, only 18 percent of employees at companies with more than 100 workers get health insurance fully paid by employers, down from 70 percent in 1980. Only 35 percent still get lifetime monthly pensions, paid by the company, down from 84 percent in 1980.

2006—Oracle CEO Larry Ellison, with $706.1 million in pay and stock in 2001, tops a *Wall Street Journal* compilation of the biggest CEO pay packages from 1995 to 2005. Close behind are Michael Eisner of Disney, with payouts of $575.6 million in 1999 and $203 million in 1993; and Sandy Weill of Citigroup, with pay of $621.8 million in three big years between 1997 and 2000.

JULY 4, 2007—Hundreds of workers at Sunbeam's profitable plant in McMinnville, Tennessee, are laid off and ordered to train their replacements at a factory in Mexico, in a firing ordered by Sunbeam CEO Al Dunlap. Dunlap has made a personal fortune as a serial downsizer of businesses. Jack Wahl, owner of Sunbeam competitor Wahl Clipper Corporation, criticizes the Sunbeam layoffs as shortsighted and "extremely wasteful," and says his company runs profitably with U.S. workers.

2007—The richest 1 percent take a near record 23 percent of the personal incomes paid to all Americans, earning a combined $1.35 trillion a year, which is more than the entire economies of Canada, Italy, or France.

2007—Among economic sectors, corporate profits see their share of national income rise during the Bush years to the highest level since 1943, while the share of national income going to employee salaries and wages sinks to its lowest level since 1929.

2008—In a Cornell University survey, 57 percent of people say they have never benefited from any government program or policy. But after more detailed questioning, it turns out that 94 percent have actually benefited from at least one program. The average person has used four government programs.

2008–2009—In the recession, hundreds of major U.S. companies such as General Motors, Eastman Kodak, Sears, Motorola, UPS, FedEx, Hewlett-Packard, and National Public Radio either cancel or cut back their employer match for 401(k) programs.

2009—After a taxpayer bailout, big Wall Street banks rebuff President Obama's appeal to "hire American" and continue offshore hiring and domestic layoffs. In the 2000s, the Hackett Group reports, 3.9 million jobs in finance, IT, human resources, and back-office functions have been lost in North America and Europe. In 2011, JP Morgan Chase, Bank of America, and Citigroup sign new contracts to offshore $5 billion worth of IT and back-office work to Indian firms.

2009—Millions of average Americans, including Pam Scholl and Mike Hughes, become middle-class dropouts—the New Poor. Pam is laid off for a second time and, despite an intense search for work, remains unemployed for 18 months. The only work Mike can find is as a night custodian at a local high school at about one-fourth of his old pay at RCA. Scholl eventually gets a public sector job, at about half her old RCA salary.

DECEMBER 2009—The United States ends a decade with the slowest economic growth of any decade since World War II. Economic growth was slow prior to 2007, even before the Great Recession, despite President Bush's promise that his tax cuts would spur growth.

DECEMBER 2009—Germany ends the decade having earned $2 trillion in trade surpluses, with 21 percent of the German workforce still in manufacturing, versus America's $6 trillion in trade deficits and 9 percent in manufacturing. Since 1985, average German hourly wages have risen 30 percent versus 5 percent in the United States.

2000–2009—In this decade, the Commerce Department reports, U.S. multinational companies hire 2.4 million people overseas while firing 2.9 million workers at home. IBM now has more employees in India than in the United States. Intel CEO Craig Barrett says his company can be successful without ever hiring another American. Cisco CEO John Chambers says his company is developing a strategy to "become a Chinese company."

2009–2010—With the U.S. economy in a painfully slow recovery, political lobbying in Washington enjoys a boom. As Congress tackles such big-ticket items as a stimulus bill, health reform, and financial regulation, a record $7 billion is spent in lobbying in these two years—87 percent by business interests. Business outspends labor on lobbying by 61 to 1. Wall Street banks hire 1,477 former members of Congress, congressional staff, or Executive Branch officials to lobby against new financial regulation.

2010—The National Retirement Fund deficit is calculated at $6.6 trillion by economists at the Boston College Center for Retirement Research. At year's end, the average 401(k) balance is $17,686. For people in their sixties, on the verge of retirement after 20 years in a 401(k) plan, the average balance is only $84,469. Economists warn that half of baby boomers will not have enough funds to cover their basic financial needs in retirement.

JUNE 2010—Democratic majorities in Congress pass President Obama's health care law. Not a single Republican in either house votes for the final bill—a sharp contrast to the strong bipartisan support for Medicare in 1965.

2010—Escalating use of Senate filibusters or the threat of filibusters has become a major reason for Congressional gridlock, because a minority—sometimes just one or two senators—can prevent even the start of debate. Scholars who now call Congress "the broken branch" of government report that in the 1960s, only 6 percent of all legislation faced a filibuster, but now it is up to 70 percent. Most bills passed by the House die in the Senate.

2010—Wall Street financial firms hire over 1,400 former government officials as lobbyists to fight new banking regulation legislation, attempting to eliminate or water down provisions for strict regulations. After the bill passes, Wall Street bankers and lobbyists continue the battle to delay or weaken new regulations.

2010—In the congressional elections of 2010, business interests outspend labor $1.3 billion to $79 million, a 16-to-1 advantage for business. In soft-money contributions to political parties, rather than donations made directly to candidates through political action committees, the business advantage is 97 to 1 ($972 million for business to $10 million for labor).

2010—Thirty-three of sixty new Tea Party members elected to the House are millionaires. Tea Party members have an average net worth of $1.8 million. Overall, 261 of the 535 senators and House representatives are millionaires—49 percent compared with 1 percent among the public at large.

2010–2012 — Washington's vanishing political center—so vital to bipartisanship in past decades—continues to shrink. Two moderate senators—Democrat Evan Bayh of Indiana and Republican Olympia Snowe of Maine—announce they are so frustrated and disgusted by the harsh partisan divide that hobbles Congress that they are quitting and will not seek reelection—Bayh in 2010, Snowe in 2012.

2011 — The housing boom and bust causes a massive transfer of wealth from ordinary American families to the banks—economists say roughly $6 trillion—mainly because so many Americans have drained equity out of their homes. In 1985, Americans owned nearly 70 percent of the total value of the nation's housing stock, the main anchor of middle-class wealth. By 2011, the homeowners' share had plummeted to just under 40 percent, and the banks now owned a major share.

2012 — The United States struggles with what economists call "a jobless recovery," where the numbers show the economy growing but where unemployment remains stubbornly high. This is the third instance of a jobless recovery in recent decades, after declines in the early 1990s and again in 2000–2002. Corporations sit on $1.9 trillion in cash, spending more money on buying back stock than hiring workers, undermining the dynamics of "the virtuous circle."

2011–2012—Some corporate leaders call for a "domestic Marshall Plan" and revisions in U.S. tax laws to generate more job growth, revitalize America's global competitiveness, and to enable more of the middle class to reclaim the American Dream. Former Intel CEO Andy Grove and GE CEO Jeffrey Immelt, among others, advocate a renaissance in U.S. manufacturing. Other business leaders and economists call for our current leaders to do what past presidents from Washington to Lincoln and Eisenhower have done—take government action to rebuild America's aging roads, ports, and airports; to recoup America's lost lead in technology and innovation; and to educate America's next generation and retrain America's current generation to compete better against global rivals.

NOTES

EPIGRAPH

ix **"We must make our choice"** Raymond Lonergan, "A Steadfast Friend of Labor," in Irving Dilliard, ed., *Mr. Justice Brandeis, Great American* (St. Louis: Modern View Press, 1941), 42.

PROLOGUE: THE CHALLENGE FROM WITHIN

xi **"We are treading"** John W. Gardner, remarks, "The American Experiment," Council for Excellence in Government, April 1, 1998, http://www.pbs.org.

xi **"Thus, it is manifest"** Aristotle, *Politics,* in *The Basic Works of Aristotle* (New York: Random House, 1941), 1221.

xi **Its response to the challenges** Arnold J. Toynbee, chap. 5, "Challenge and Response," in *A Study of History,* abridged vols. 1–6, ed. D. C. Somervell (London: Oxford University Press, 1947), 60–79.

xii **"Schism in the body social"** Toynbee, *Study of History,* chap. 18, "Schism in the Body Social," 371–428; chap. 19, "Schism in the Soul," 429–532; also see part 2, The Geneses of Civilizations, and part 4, The Breakdowns of Civilizations; "A Study of History," *Life,* February 23, 1948.

xiii **"A house divided"** Abraham Lincoln, "A House Divided," speech delivered in Springfield, Illinois, June 16, 1858, in vol. 2 of *The Collected Works of Abraham Lincoln,* ed. Roy P. Basler (New Brunswick, NJ: Rutgers University Press, 1953), 461–69, http://quod.lib.umich.edu/l/lincoln/lincoln2/1:508?rgn=div1;view=fulltext.

xiii **We have gone off track** Naftali Bendavid, "Country Is Headed in Wrong Direction, 74% Say," *The Wall Street Journal,* October 13, 2011; "Just 1 in 5 Americans Happy with Direction of Country," CBS News poll, October 3, 2011, http://www.cbsnews.com.

xiii **One such hidden beginning** Lewis F. Powell, Jr., memorandum, "Attack on American Free Enterprise System," August 23, 1971, http://law.wlu.edu/deptimages/Powell%20Archives/PowellMemorandumTypescript.pdf.

xiv **"America is coming apart at the seams"** Charles Murray, *Coming Apart: The State of White America, 1960–2010* (New York: Crown Forum, 2012), 11, 12.

xv **"Mind-boggling" in its magnitude** Alan Krueger, "The Rise and Consequences of Inequality in the United States," remarks, Center for American Progress, January 12, 2012, http://www.americanprogress.org/events/2012/01/pdf/krueger.pdf. For a "chasm" reference, see Ron Haskins and Isabel V. Sawhill, *Creating an Opportunity Society* (Washington, DC: Brookings Institution Press, 2009), 33.

xv **The top 1 percent . . . reaped two-thirds** Emmanuel Saez, "Striking It Richer: The Evolution of Top Incomes in the United States (Updated with 2008 Estimates)." working paper (Berkeley: Institute for Research on Labor and Employment, University of California at Berkeley, July 17, 2010).

xv **The top 1 percent captured 93 percent** Emmanuel Saez, "Striking It Richer: The Evolution of Top Incomes in the United States (Updated with 2009 and 2010 Estimates)," March 2, 2012, elsa.berkeley.edu/~saez/saez-UStopincomes-2010.pdf.

xvi **A solid majority** "Most in Poll See Growing Wealth Gap," *The Washington Post,* November 9, 2011; "Polls Find Voters Are Deeply Divided," *The Wall Street Journal,* November 8, 2011; also see Andrew Kohut, "Don't Mind the Gap," *The New York Times,* January 26, 2012.

xvi **Drag on today's economy** William H. Gates, Sr., and Chuck Collins, *Wealth and Our Commonwealth: Why America Should Tax Accumulated Fortunes* (Boston: Beacon Press, 2002), 21; Philippe Aghion, Eve Caroli, and Cecilia García-Peñalosa, "Inequality and Economic Growth: The Perspective of the New Growth Theories," *Journal of Economic Literature* 37, no. 4 (December 1999): 1615–60.

xvi **"Impressively unambiguous"** Aghion, Caroli, and García-Peñalosa, "Inequality and Economic Growth," 1616–17.

xvi **Income inequality can be "destructive"** Andrew G. Berg and Jonathan D. Ostry, "Inequality and Unsustainable Growth: Two Sides of the Same Coin?" IMF Staff Discussion Note, International Monetary Fund, April 8, 2011, http://www.imf.org.

xvi **Losing our title as "the land of opportunity"** Isabel V. Sawhill, "Trends in Intergenerational Mobility," in Julia B. Isaacs, Isabel V. Sawhill, and Ron Haskins, *Getting Ahead or Losing Ground: Economic Mobility in America* (Washington, DC: Brookings Institution, 2008), 8–9; see also Isaacs, "International Comparisons of Economic Mobility," in Isaacs, Sawhill, and Haskins, *Getting Ahead,* 37–44, http://www.economicmobility.org.

xvii **"Middle class is the key"** Rush Limbaugh, "Democrats and the Middle Class," *The Rush Limbaugh Show,* October 25, 2011, http://www.rushlimbaugh.com.

xvii **"Middle class that made America great"** Richard Trumka, "Your Money," CNN, September 4, 2011, http://transcripts.cnn.com; and Trumka, remarks, Brookings Institution, September 30, 2011, http://www.brookings.edu.

xvii **Unequal Democracy** The title of Princeton University professor Larry M. Bartels's excellent book on modern U.S. politics and economics: Bartels, *Unequal Democracy: The Political Economy of the New Gilded Age* (New York: Russell Sage Foundation; Princeton, NJ: Princeton University Press, 2008).

xviii **"Powerlessness also corrupts"** William Greider, *Who Will Tell the People? The Betrayal of American Democracy* (New York: Simon & Schuster, 1992), 20.

xviii **"An elaborate influence-peddling scheme"** John McCain, CNN AllPolitics, June 30, 1999.

xix **Business has employed thirty times as many** "Lobbying Database," Center for Responsive Politics, based on data from the Senate Office of Public Records, January 31, 2011, http://www.opensecrets.org/.lobby/index.php; Lee Jared Drutman, *The Business of America Is Lobbying,* online doctoral thesis (Berkeley: University of California at Berkeley, Fall 2010), 5, 140–141, http://www.leedrutman.com.

xix **From 1998 through 2010** "Lobbying Database": With this database, the Center for Responsive Politics covers lobbying expenditures from 1998 through 2011 for thirteen sectors— Labor; "Ideology," or single-issue lobbying; "Other"; and ten business-related categories (listed in descending order of their lobbying expenditures): Health; Miscellaneous Business; Finance/Insurance/Real Estate; Communications/Electronics; Energy/Natural Resources; Transportation; Agribusiness; Defense; Construction; and Lawyers& Lobbyists. That database shows business lobbying expenditures from 1998 through 2010 of $28,562,488,910, compared with $492,244,499 for labor. In all, business groups accounted for 85.71 percent of the total lobbying expenditures and labor for 1.48 percent for those twelve years.

xix **No countervailing power matches** Drutman, thesis, 117.

xx **Share of world trade shrank** William H. Branson, Herbert Giersch, and Peter G. Peterson, "Trends in United States International Trade and Investment Since World War II," in *The American Economy in Transition,* ed. Martin Feldstein (Chicago: University of Chicago Press, 1980), 183–84.

xx **"Empire of consumption"** Charles S. Maier, *Among Empires: American Ascendancy and Its Predecessors* (Cambridge, MA: Harvard University Press, 2006), 255.

xxi **Germany took a different fork** David Leonhardt, "The German Example," *The New York Times,* June 8, 2011; Steven Rattner, "The Secrets of Germany's Economic Success: What Europe's Manufacturing Powerhouse Can Teach America," *Foreign Affairs* 90, no. 4 (July–August 2011); Leslie H. Gelb, "What Germany's Economy Can Teach Us," *Daily Beast,* June 5, 2011, http://www.thedailybeast.com; Kevin Phillips, *Wealth and Democracy: A Political History of the American Rich* (New York: Broadway Books, 2003), 163.

xxi **Multitrillion-dollar trade deficits** The U.S. trade deficits totaled $6 trillion from 2000 through 2010. Germany's trade surplus totaled $2 trillion. "U.S. Trade in Goods and Services, Balance of Payment Basis, 1960–2011," U.S. Census Bureau, Foreign Trade Division, March 9, 2012, http://www.census.gov/foreign-trade/statistics/historical/gands.pdf; German Office of Federal Statistics, "Foreign Trade Data: Overall Development in Foreign

Trade Since 1950," *Statistisches Bundesamt, Deutschland,* February 21, 2012, http://www.destatis.deDocument2.

xxi **Pay of middle-class workers in Germany** Leonhardt, "German Example"; Robert B. Reich, "The Limping Middle Class," *The New York Times,* Sunday Review, September 4, 2011.

xxii **Today, 21 percent of Germans work** In U.S. nonfarm payroll of 131.6 million, the Bureau of Labor Statistics listed 11.8 million in manufacturing in September 2011: "The Employment Situation, September 2011," October 7, 2011, http://www.bls.gov. For German figures, see U.S. Bureau of Labor Statistics, *International Comparisons of Annual Labor Force Statistics: Adjusted to U.S. Concepts, 10 Countries 1970–2010,* table 2–8, "Percentage of Employment in Manufacturing," March 30, 2011, 23, http://www.bls.gov/fls/flscomparelf/lfcompendium.pdf.

xxii **The difference is not in technology** Marcus Walker, "Is Germany Turning into the Strong Silent Type?" *The Wall Street Journal,* July 27, 2011; Gelb, "What Germany's Economy Can Teach Obama."

xxii **Middle class was left behind** Neither ordinary Americans nor experts agree on what constitutes the U.S. middle class. In opinion polls, close to half of Americans, from people who make $45,000 a year to those who make $200,000, call themselves middle class. The U.S. Census Bureau reports the median household income—right in the middle—was $49,445 in 2010 and that 80 percent of all U.S. families had household incomes below $100,065. Typically, economists divide the current U.S. population of 312 million into income quintiles, or fifths. In its income analysis, the Congressional Budget Office uses four groupings: the bottom fifth; the three middle fifths; the top fifth, and the top 1 percent—corresponding to lower-income, middle-income, and upper-income groupings, plus the super-rich. At the high end, income analysts such as Emmanuel Saez of the University of California at Berkeley separate the top 10 percent from the lower 90 percent and then differentiate among the top 1 percent (the super-rich, with annual incomes above $352,000) and the next 9 percent (upper middle class and wealthy). I have followed the CBO groupings with the exception that I have moved the middle class up by ten percentiles. Since the U.S. Census Bureau tops out household income for the lowest quintile at $20,000 (below the official poverty level of $22,811 for a family of four), it seems mistaken to include that level in the middle class. Accordingly, like some other analysts, I group as poor and low income the bottom 30 percent (90 million people with incomes below $28,636). The middle class comprises the thirtieth through the eightieth percentiles, 150 million people with household incomes from just below $30,000 to $100,065; the upper middle class from the eightieth to the ninety-fifth percentiles (45 million making $100,065 to $150,000, using Census Bureau and Saez figures); the wealthy as the top 5 percent (15 million people earning above $150,000), topped by the super-rich 1 percent (3 million people with household incomes topping $352,000). For income and poverty level figures, see U.S. Census Bureau, "Income, Poverty, and Health

Insurance Coverage in the United States: 2010," issued September 2011, 14–16, table A-3, which shows quintile levels and the mean level for the second quintile at $28,636; for total U.S. population, see Census Bureau, "Monthly Population Estimates for the United States, April 1, 2010 to March 1, 2012," http://www.census.gov/popest/data/state/totals/2011/tables/NA-EST2011–01.xls; CBO "Trends in the Distribution of Household Income Between 1979 and 2007," October 2011, http://cbo.gov/sites/default/files/cbofiles/attachments/10-25-HouseholdIncome.pdf; Emmanuel Saez, "Striking It Richer," updated to 2010, March 7, 2012, elsa.berkeley.edu/~saez/saez-UStopincomes-2010.pdf; Lawrence Mishel, director, Economic Policy Institute, email, March 29, 2012; Haskins and Sawhill, *Creating an Opportunity Society*, 48–50.

xxiii **Getting nowhere** Ibid.; Conor Dougherty, "Income Slides to 1996 Levels," *The Wall Street Journal*, September 14, 2011.

xxiii **"More productive, more profitable, flush with cash"** Scott Thurm, "U.S. Firms Emerge Stronger," *The Wall Street Journal*, April 9, 2012.

xxiii **Two-thirds of Americans** "Rising Share of Americans See Conflict Between Rich and Poor," Pew Research Center, January 11, 2012, http://www.pewresearch.org.

xxiii **"Virtuous circle of growth"** Thomas I. Palley, "America's Exhausted Paradigm: Macroeconomic Causes of the Financial Crisis and Great Recession," *New American Contract* (Washington, DC: New America Foundation, June 2009), http://www.newamerica.net.

xxiv **Dynamic thrust of "the virtuous circle"** Ibid.

xxvi **What we need now** Jeffrey R. Immelt, "An American Renewal," Detroit Economic Club, June 26, 2009, http://www.econclub.org.

xxvi **A domestic Marshall Plan** Horizon Project, "Report and Recommendations," February 2007, http://www.horizonproject.us.

xxvi **Management and labor doing give-and-take** Nick Bunkley, "G.M. Contract Approved, with Bonus for Workers," *The New York Times*, September 29, 2011; "GM, UAW Pioneer a Competitive Path," *Detroit News*, September 28, 2011; Bill Vlasic and Nick Bunkley, "In Deal with Ford, Union Wins Wage Increases and Additional Jobs," *The New York Times*, October 4, 2011.

xxvi **Big Three carmakers planned to invest** Joseph B. White, Jeff Bennett, and Lauren Weber, "Car Makers' U-Turn Steers Job Gains," *The Wall Street Journal*, January 23, 2012.

xxvi **Manufacturing employment** Floyd Norris, "Making More Things in the U.S.A.," *The New York Times*, January 6, 2012; David Wessel, "Factory Floor Has a Ceiling on Job Creation," *The Wall Street Journal*, January 12, 2012.

xxvi **Cost advantages of China** "Moving Back to America: The Dwindling Allure of Building Factories Offshore," *The Economist*, May 12, 2011; John Bussey, "Buck Up, America: China Is Getting Too Expensive," *The Wall Street Journal*, October 7, 2011.

xxvi **A few companies such as General Electric** John Schmid, "Master Lock

Reassessing China," *JSOnline, Milwaukee Journal-Sentinel*, January 1, 2011; Eduardo Porter, "The Promise of Today's Factory Jobs," *The New York Times*, April 4, 2012; Annie Lowrey, "White House Offers Plan to Lure Jobs to America," *The New York Times*, February 4, 2012.

xxvi **In all, some 25,000 manufacturing jobs** James R. Hagerty, "Once Made in China: Jobs Trickle Back to U.S. Plants," *The Wall Street Journal*, May 22, 2012.

xxvii **"The American people themselves"** Gardner, "American Experiment."

xxviii **More than half** "Tea Party House Members Even Wealthier than Other GOP Lawmakers," Center for Responsive Politics, January 4, 2012, http://www.opensecrets.org/news/2012/01/tea-party-house-members-wealthy-gop.html.

xxviii **"We are the 99 percent"** Brian Stelter, "Camps Are Cleared but '99 Percent' Still Occupies the Lexicon," *The New York Times*, November 30, 2011.

xxviii **"Powerful thrust of energy"** Gardner, "American Experiment."

PART I: POWER SHIFT

3 **Powell's personal manner** Linda Greenhouse, "Lewis Powell, Crucial Centrist Justice, Dies at 90," *The New York Times*, August 26, 1998.

CHAPTER 1: THE BUSINESS REBELLION

5 **"The danger had suddenly escalated"** Thomas Byrne Edsall, *The New Politics of Inequality* (New York: W. W. Norton & Co., 1984), 113–14.

5 **"There has been a significant erosion"** Ibid., 13.

6 **"Revolt of the Bosses"** Ted Nace, *Gangs of America: The Rise of Corporate Power and the Disabling of Democracy* (San Francisco: Berrett-Koehler, 2003), 137–51.

6 **Powell warned the corporate community** Powell, memorandum, "Attack on American Free Enterprise System," August 23, 1971, http://www.aspenlawschool.com.

6 **Business was being victimized** Ibid.

7 **"Business must learn the lesson"** Ibid.

7 **In a private session** Nixon meeting with Henry Ford II and Lee Iacocca, White House tapes, cited in Tom Wicker, *One of Us: Richard Nixon and the American Dream* (New York: Random House, 1991), 515.

8 **Nixon administration was swept along** Jacob S. Hacker and Paul Pierson, *Winner-Take-All Politics: How Washington Made the Rich Richer—and Turned Its Back on the Middle Class* (New York: Simon & Schuster, 2010), 97.

9 **"He didn't know much"** Excerpt of interview of William Ruckelshaus for the *Frontline* program "Poisoned Waters," September 3, 2008.

10 **"Most of the people"** Ibid., July 28, 2008.

10 **His package also included**   David Vogel, *Fluctuating Fortunes: The Political Power of Business in America* (New York: Basic Books, 1989), 62–63.

10 **"The most 'anti-rich' tax reform"**   Edwin L. Dale, Jr., "It's Not Perfect, but It's the Best Yet," *The New Republic,* May 3, 1969.

11 **Business sprang to life**   Vogel, *Fluctuating Fortunes,* chap. 8, "The Political Resurgence of Business."

11 **The chief executives**   Hedrick Smith, *The Power Game: How Washington Works* (New York: Random House, 1989), 31.

11 **"If you don't know your senators"**   Leonard Silk and David Vogel, *Ethics and Profits: The Crisis of Confidence in American Business* (New York: Simon & Schuster, 1976), 65.

11 **Quickly expanded their agenda**   Edsall, *Politics of Inequality,* 121–26.

12 **The National Association of Manufacturers**   Vogel, *Fluctuating Fortunes,* 193–200; Nace, *Gangs of America,* 137–42.

CHAPTER 2: THE PIVOTAL CONGRESS

13 **"Fifteen years ago, the businessman"**   "The Swarming Lobbyists: Washington's New Billion-Dollar Game of Who Can Influence Whom," *Time,* August 7, 1978, 14.

13 **"Business's new lobbying weapon"**   "A Potent New Business Lobby," *BusinessWeek,* May 22, 1978.

14 **The decisive force**   "The Swarming Lobbyists."

15 **"Never seen such extensive lobbying"**   "Carter Dealt Major Defeat on Consumer Bill," *CQ Almanac 1978* (Washington, DC: Congressional Quarterly, 1979).

15 **A disastrous defeat**   Hacker and Pierson, *Winner-Take-All Politics,* 126–27.

16 **Council on Union-Free Environment**   "Council Is Formed by NAM for Union-Free Environment," *The Washington Post,* December 2, 1977.

16 **It passed the House**   "House Passes Bill Aiding Union Drives," *The New York Times,* October 7, 1977.

16 **"What the filibuster does"**   Ray Marshall, interview, June 14, 2011.

17 **Douglas Fraser . . . resigned**   Jefferson Cowie, " 'A One-Sided Class War': Rethinking Doug Fraser's 1978 Resignation from the Labor-Management Group," *Labor History* 44, no. 3 (2003): 307–14.

17 **Some wins for labor**   "Carter Signs Minimum Wage Bill, Giving Raises of 45 Percent by '81," *The New York Times,* November 2, 1977.

17 **Federal minimum wage fell**   U.S. Department of Labor, "Federal Minimum Wage Rates Under the Fair Labor Standards Act," http://www.dol.gov/whd/minwage/chart/pdf; and U.S. Bureau of Labor Statistics, "B-2: Average Hours and Earnings of Production and Nonsupervisory Workers on Private Nonfarm Payrolls by Major Industry Sector, 1964 to Date," http://www.bls.gov/ces/#tables.

18 **The first priority**   "Congress Clears Trucking Deregulation Bill," *CQ Al-*

manac 1980 (Washington, DC: Congressional Quarterly, 1981); "Congress Clears Airline Deregulation Bill," *CQ Almanac 1978* (Washington, DC: Congressional Quarterly, 1979); "House, Senate Advance Bills to Curb FTC," *CQ Almanac 1979* (Washington, DC: Congressional Quarterly, 1980).

19 **The first major bankruptcy reform**   Lynn M. LoPucki and William C. Whitford, "Corporate Governance in the Bankruptcy Reorganization of Large, Publicly Held Companies," *University of Pennsylvania Law Review* 141, no. 3 (January 1993): 674–75, 688–92, 719; Robert Lawless, email, January 6, 2012.

19 **Labor union contracts**   Lawless, email, December 21, 2011.

19 **Banks got top priority**   "Congress Approves New Bankruptcy System," *CQ Almanac 1978* (Washington, DC: Congressional Quarterly, 1979), 179–82.

19 **"A big part of the selling"**   Elizabeth Warren, interview, February 6, 2006.

21 **Instead of tax increases**   "Congress Preparing Tax Lop-offs: Capital Gains, Retired Get Biggest Relief," Associated Press, October 15, 1978; *How Capital Gains Tax Rates Affect Revenues: The Historical Evidence* (Washington, DC: Congressional Budget Office, March 1988), 34, http://www.cbo.gov.

21 **"Business began to see"**   Arthur Levitt, interview, April 20, 1986.

CHAPTER 3: MIDDLE-CLASS POWER

23 **"This hallowed spot"**   Martin Luther King, Jr., speech, "I Have a Dream," Washington, D.C., August 28, 1963, http://www.pbs.org/newshour/extra/teachers/lessonplans/english/mlk_transcript.pdf.

23 **"Deep public concern"**   Excerpt of interview of William Ruckelshaus for the *Frontline* program "Poisoned Waters," September 3, 2008.

25 **"No one could remember"**   Russell Baker, "Capital Is Occupied by a Gentle Army," *The New York Times,* August 29, 1963.

26 **"Probably the most thoroughly segregated city"**   Martin Luther King, Jr., letter from the Birmingham Jail, in *Reporting Civil Rights,* part 1 (New York: Library of America, 2003), 778.

27 **"A community of fear"**   Harrison Salisbury, "Fear and Hatred Grip Birmingham," *The New York Times,* April 12, 1960.

27 **By his personal involvement**   King, letter, 784–85.

27 **"Money is color-blind"**   Andrew Young, interview, February 8, 2011.

28 **A deal slowly emerged**   Hedrick Smith, "A Dozen Men Hammered Out Birmingham Agreement in Home of Negro Executive," *The New York Times,* May 11, 1963.

28 **"Promissory note"**   King, "I Have a Dream."

29 **"He shook hands"**   John Lewis, interview, April 6, 2011.

29 **It fell to Lyndon Johnson**   Nick Kotz, *Judgment Days: Lyndon Baines Johnson, Martin Luther King Jr., and the Laws That Changed America* (Boston: Houghton Mifflin, 2005), 18–19; Taylor Branch, *Pillar of Fire: America in the King Years, 1963–65* (New York: Simon & Schuster, 2005), 177.

30 Johnson was challenging King   Kotz, *Judgment Days,* 18–19.
30 Bloody march at Selma   Lewis, interview, April 6, 2011.
30 Twenty million Americans   Philip Shabecoff, *A Fierce Green Fire: The American Environmental Movement* (Washington, DC: Island Press, 2003), 103–10.
30 "I remember"   Excerpt of interview of Robert F. Kennedy, Jr., for the *Frontline* program "Poisoned Waters," June 4, 2009.
31 "There was anger"   Excerpt of interview of Will Baker for the *Frontline* program "Poisoned Waters," November 20, 2008.
31 "Now or never"   Richard Nixon, "Statement About the National Environmental Policy Act of 1969," American Presidency Project, January 1, 1970, http://www.presidency.ucsb.edu.
31 The Nixon White House moved   Shabecoff, *Fierce Green Fire,* 103–10, 121–27.
32 "It exploded on the country"   William Ruckelshaus interview excerpt, *Frontline,* "Poisoned Waters," September 3, 2008.
32 Major new consumer organizations   "56 Groups Set Up a Consumer Union," *The New York Times,* April 29, 1968.
33 Nader's network   Vogel, *Fluctuating Fortunes,* 101–03.
33 Put Nader on its cover   "Who Runs America: A National Survey," *U.S. News & World Report* 76, no. 16 (April 1974).
33 Nader filed a lawsuit   "G.M. Settles Nader Suit on Privacy for $425,000," *The New York Times,* August 14, 1970.
34 Politicians had gotten   Vogel, *Fluctuating Fortunes,* 40–46.

CHAPTER 4: MIDDLE-CLASS PROSPERITY

35 "Prosperity for all"   Richard Nixon, quoted in Lizabeth Cohen, *A Consumer's Republic: The Politics of Mass Consumption in Postwar America* (New York: Vintage Books, 2003), 125.
35 "The Great Compression"   Paul Krugman, *The Conscience of a Liberal* (New York: W. W. Norton & Co., 2007), 54.
36 Wage of $5 a day   Henry Ford, *My Life and Work* (New York: Garden City Publishing, 1922), 126–27.
36 Virtuous circle keeps on generating   Palley, "America's Exhausted Paradigm."
36 "It was an economy"   Krugman, *Conscience of a Liberal,* 79.
37 "The job of management"   Frank Abrams, quoted in *Fortune,* October 1951.
37 "Maximizing employment security"   Steven Greenhouse, *The Big Squeeze: Tough Times for the American Worker* (New York: Anchor Books, 2008), 74–76; Krugman, *Conscience of a Liberal,* 73.
37 "Caring runs in the veins"   Thomas J. Peters and Robert H. Waterman, Jr., *In Search of Excellence* (New York: Warner Books, 1982), 238–39.
38 Trade union strength   "Union Membership Trends in the United States,"

Congressional Research Service, August 31, 2004, http://digitalcommons
.ilr.cornell.edu/cgi/viewcontent.cgi?article=1176&context=key_workplace.

38 **"Treaty of Detroit"**   Greenhouse, *Big Squeeze,* 74–76; Krugman, *Conscience of a Liberal,* 49–51.

39 **"More than half the union contracts"**   Greenhouse, *Big Squeeze,* 75.

40 **"Classless society"**   Richard Nixon, quoted in Lizabeth Cohen, *Consumer's Republic,* 125.

41 **But the prevailing pattern**   Economic Policy Institute, *The State of Working America,* February 1, 2011, http://www.stateofworkingamerica.org/charts/view/201.

41 **The poorest 20 percent**   Economic Policy Institute, "Income Inequality," *The State of Working America,* April 1, 2011, http://www.stateofworking america.org.

41 **The tax system reduced**   Internal Revenue Service, U.S. Individual Income Tax: Personal Exemptions and Lowest and Highest Bracket Tax Rates, and Tax Base for Regular Tax: Tax Years 1913–2008, http://www.irs.gov/taxstats/article/0,,id=175910,00.html.

42 **"High taxes"**   Robert B. Reich, *Supercapitalism: The Transformation of Business, Democracy, and Everyday Life* (New York: Alfred A. Knopf, 2007), 37.

42 **That phenomenon was so striking**   Claudia Goldin and Robert A. Margo, "The Great Compression: The Wage Structure in the United States at Mid-Century," *Quarterly Journal of Economics* 107, no. 1 (1992): 1–34.

42 **"Time of unprecedented prosperity"**   Krugman, *Conscience of a Liberal,* 54.

PART 2: DISMANTLING THE DREAM

45 **"If you're gonna splurge"**   Al Dunlap, interviews, July and August 1997, transcript, PBS, *Surviving the Bottom Line,* http://www.hedricksmith.com.

CHAPTER 5: THE NEW ECONOMY OF THE 1990S

47 **"There's class warfare"**   Ben Stein, "In Class Warfare, Guess Which Class Is Winning?" *The New York Times,* November 26, 2006.

47 **"If I were to describe"**   Stephen Roach, interview, July 1997, "Running with the Bulls," transcript, PBS, *Surviving the Bottom Line,* January 18, 1998, http://www.hedricksmith.com.

48 **Traditional CEOs such as Bob Galvin**   Hedrick Smith, *Rethinking America* (New York: Random House, 1995), 319–25.

48 **Price made all that profit**   Michael Price, interviews, May–June 1997, transcript, PBS, *Surviving the Bottom Line,* http://www.hedricksmith.com.

49 **Reagan, who broke the air controllers**   Greenhouse, *Big Squeeze,* 82.

49 **Ghoshal cited Milton Friedman**   Sumantra Ghoshal, "Bad Management

Theories Are Destroying Good Management Practices," *Academy of Management Learning & Education* vol. 4, no. 1 (2005): 75–91.

49 **"Undermine the very foundations"** Milton Friedman, *Capitalism and Freedom* (Chicago: University of Chicago Press, 1962 and 2002), 133.

50 **"Worst excesses"** Ghoshal, "Bad Management Theories."

50 **Turn a huge profit** Price, interview, *Surviving the Bottom Line.*

51 **"The word that comes to mind"** Jerry Ballas, interview, June 1997, transcript, PBS, *Surviving the Bottom Line,* http://www.hedricksmith.com.

51 **Made $166,000 a day** "Running with the Bulls," transcript, PBS, *Surviving the Bottom Line,* http://www.hedricksmith.com.

52 **"It's like we thought we made money"** Art Oxley, interview, July 3, 1977, transcript, PBS, *Surviving the Bottom Line,* http://www.hedricksmith .com.

53 **"A hurt feeling"** Marsha Dunlap, interview, July 2, 1977, transcript, PBS, *Surviving the Bottom Line,* http://www.hedricksmith.com.

54 **"Why the layoffs"** Jack Wahl, interview, August 1997, transcript, PBS, *Surviving the Bottom Line,* http://www.hedricksmith.com.

54 **"We actually care"** Greg Wahl, interview, August 1997, transcript, PBS, *Surviving the Bottom Line,* http://www.hedricksmith.com.

55 **Sunbeam had been exaggerating** Jonathan R. Laing, "High Noon at Sunbeam," *Barron's,* June 16, 1997.

55 ***Barron's* saw the downside** Jonathan R. Laing, "Dangerous Games," *Barron's,* June 8, 1998.

55 **Sunbeam's stock started tumbling** Jonathan R. Laing, ". . . And Take the Chainsaw with You!" *Barron's,* June 22, 1998.

55 **Sunbeam filed for bankruptcy** "Despite Recovery Efforts, Sunbeam Files for Chapter 11," *The New York Times,* February 7, 2001.

56 **Dunlap . . . paid $15.5 million** "Ex-Sunbeam Executives to Pay $15 Million to Settle a Lawsuit," *The New York Times,* January 15, 2002; "Former Sunbeam Chief Agrees to Ban and a Fine of $500,000," *The New York Times,* September 5, 2002.

56 **Retire to a much larger estate** Tax assessor records, Ocala, FL, http:// 216.255.243/135/DEFAULT.aspx?Key=2062061&YR=2011.

56 **"Firing people and slashing"** Henry Schacht, interview, July 1997, transcript, PBS, *Surviving the Bottom Line,* http://www.hedricksmith.com.

56 **"The chain-saw mentality"** Stephen Roach, interview, July 1997, transcript, PBS, *Surviving the Bottom Line,* http://www.hedricksmith.com.

56 **Mitt Romney's corporate strategies** Nicholas Confessore, Christopher Drew, and Julie Creswell, "Buyout Profits Keep Flowing to Romney," *The New York Times,* December 18, 2011.

57 ***Newsweek* listed the big guns** Allan Sloan, "The Hit Men," *Newsweek,* February 26, 1996, http://www.newsweek.com.

58 **"The gold standard"** Geoffrey Colvin, "The Ultimate Manager," *Fortune,* November 22, 1999; Tim Smart, "Jack Welch's Encore," *BusinessWeek,* October 28, 1996, http://www.businessweek.com.

58 **Hallmark was downsizing**   Greenhouse, *Big Squeeze,* 85–86.

58 **Firing GE managers**   Clyde Prestowitz, *The Betrayal of American Prosperity: Free Market Delusions, America's Decline, and How We Must Compete in the Post-Dollar Era* (New York: Free Press, 2010), 193.

58 **Abrasive management style**   Steven Flax, "The Toughest Bosses in America," *Fortune,* August 6, 1984.

58 **These tactics made Welch**   Paul Krugman, "For Richer," *The New York Times,* October 20, 2002.

59 **"Loyalty to a company, it's nonsense"**   Janet Guyon, "Combative Chief, GE Chairman Welch, Though Much Prized, Starts to Draw Critics," *The Wall Street Journal,* August 4, 1988.

59 **367 times the pay**   Krugman, *Conscience of a Liberal,* 142–45.

59 **Former CEO Lee Scott**   Reich, *Supercapitalism,* 108.

60 **"Invisible handshake in the boardroom"**   Krugman, "For Richer."

60 **Board directors as their "friends"**   James D. Westphal, "Collaboration in the Boardroom: Behavioral and Performance Consequences of CEO-Board Social Ties," *Academy of Management Journal* 42, no. 1 (1999): 7–24; update interview, October 13, 2011.

60 **"The Lake Wobegon syndrome"**   Paul Volcker, testimony to Joint Economic Committee, May 14, 2008, http://www.gpo.gov/fdsys/pkg/CHRG-110shrg44539/pdf/CHRG-110shrg44539.pdf.

60 **"That would imply"**   Jay Lorsch and Rakesh Khurana, "The Pay Problem," *Harvard Magazine,* May–June 2010.

61 **CEO pay spirals ever upward**   Edward S. Woolard, Jr., quoted in Charles Elson, moderator, "What's Wrong with Executive Compensation?" *Harvard Business Review* 81, no. 1 (2003): 69–77.

61 **Ranked the United States thirty-first**   Organisation for Economic Co-operation and Development, "An Overview of Growing Income Inequalities in OECD Countries: Main Findings," in "Divided We Stand: Why Inequality Keeps Rising," *An Overview of Growing Income Inequalities in OECD Countries: Main Findings,* accessed December 6, 2011, http://www.oecd.org/dataoecd/40/12/49170449.pdf.

62 **With rare exceptions, such as**   Jessica Silver Greenberg and Nelson D. Schwartz, "Citigroup's Chief Rebuffed on Pay by Shareholders," *The New York Times,* April 18, 2012.

63 **The number of illegally fired workers**   Edsall, *New Politics of Inequality,* 151–54.

63 **Increasingly sided with business**   Jeffrey Rosen, "Supreme Court, Inc.," *The New York Times Magazine,* March 16, 2008; Adam Liptak, "Justices Offer Receptive Ear to Business Interests," *The New York Times,* December 19, 2010.

64 **"Terrors" of the corporate boardroom**   "The Scariest S.O.B. on Wall Street," *Fortune* 4, no. 11 (December 9, 1996).

64 **Close-up photo of Price**   Ibid.

64 **"The power of the financial markets"**   Roach, interview, transcript, *Surviving the Bottom Line.*

CHAPTER 6: THE STOLEN DREAM

65 **"The 'land of opportunity' "** Sawhill, "Overview," in Isaacs, Sawhill, and Haskins, *Getting Ahead,* 4, 7.

65 **"America has entered"** Lance Morrow, "The Temping of America," *Time,* June 24, 2001.

65 **"The biggest failure"** "Retiring Rep. Obey Not Going Out with a Whimper," *The Washington Post,* November 30, 2010.

66 **"I got $1.75 an hour"** Pam Scholl, interview, November 7, 2010.

66 **"The early seventies"** Roy Wunsch, interviews, October 27 and November 7, 2010.

67 **Mike got good technical training** Mike Hughes, interview, June 23, 2010.

68 **"What made it difficult"** Ibid., June 28, 2010.

69 **"I barely stay afloat"** Pam Scholl, interview, June 23, 2010.

69 **Fewer jobs** U.S. Bureau of Labor Statistics, "The Employment Situation, December 2001," January 7, 2002, http://www.bls.gov; U.S. Bureau of Labor Statistics, "The Employment Situation, September 2011," October 7, 2011, http://www.bls.gov. BLS figures show 132.2 million nonfarm jobs in 2001 vs. 131.3 million in September 2011.

69 **Winding up lower** Census Bureau, "Income, Poverty, and Health Insurance Coverage in the United States: 2010"; "Income Slides to 1996 Levels," *The Wall Street Journal,* September 4, 2011.

70 **Roughly 45 percent of blacks** Isaacs, "Economic Mobility of Black and White Families," in Isaacs, Sawhill, and Haskins, *Getting Ahead,* 71–80.

70 **The numbers of New Poor** Census Bureau, "Income, Poverty, and Health Insurance Coverage in the United States: 2010."

70 **"Median family is in worse shape"** "Soaring Poverty Casts Spotlight on 'Lost Decade,' " *The New York Times,* September 14, 2011.

70 **"This is new. . . . It is worse"** E. S. Browning, "Oldest Baby Boomers Face Jobs Bust," *The Wall Street Journal,* December 19, 2011.

71 **Children born to parents** Isaacs, "Economic Mobility of Families Across Generations," in Isaacs, Sawhill, and Haskins, *Getting Ahead,* 19.

71 **Have now surpassed us** Isaacs, "International Comparisons of Economic Mobility," in Isaacs, Sawhill, and Haskins, *Getting Ahead,* 37–44.

71 **America is now classified as "a *low-mobility* country"** Sawhill, "Trends in Intergenerational Mobility," in Isaacs, Sawhill, and Haskins, *Getting Ahead,* 9, italics added; Thomas DeLeire and Leonard M. Lopoo, "Family Structure and the Economic Mobility of Children," Pew Charitable Trusts, April 2010, http://www.economicmobility.org; Jason DeParle, "Harder for Americans to Rise from Economy's Lower Rungs," *The New York Times,* January 5, 2012.

71 **Starting at the bottom** Isaacs, "Economic Mobility of Families Across Generations," in Isaacs, Sawhill, and Haskins, *Getting Ahead,* 19.

71 **"We have moved"** Sean F. Reardon, "The Widening Academic Achievement Gap Between the Rich and the Poor: New Evidence and Possible Explanations," in *Whither Opportunity? Rising Inequality, Schools, and Children's*

Life Chances (New York: Russell Sage Foundation, 2011); "Poor Dropping Further Behind Rich in School," *The New York Times,* February 10, 2012.

71 **At the college level** Martha J. Bailey and Susan M. Dynarski, "Gains and Gaps: Changing Inequality in U.S. College Entry and Completion," Working Paper 17633, National Bureau of Economic Research, December 2011, http://www.nber.org.

72 **An important driver** Study by Sabino Kornrich, Center for Advanced Studies, Juan March Institute, Madrid, and Frank F. Furstenberg, University of Pennsylvania, cited in "Poor Dropping Further Behind Rich in School," *The New York Times,* February 10, 2012.

72 **The quadrupling of average college tuition** Will Hutton, "Log Cabin to White House? Not Any More," *The Observer,* April 28, 2002, http://www.observer.co.uk/comment/story/0,6903,706484,00.html.

72 **Far less chance of rising** Bhashkar Mazumder, "Fortunate Sons: New Estimates of Intergenerational Mobility in the United States Using Social Security Earnings Data," for Federal Reserve Bank of Chicago, July 6, 2004, published in *The Review of Economics and Statistics* 87, no. 2 (2005): 235–55.

72 **Being born in the elite** Janny Scott and David Leonhardt, "Class in America: Shadowy Lines That Still Divide," *The New York Times,* May 15, 2005.

73 **From 1948 to 1973** Lawrence Mishel, Joshua Bivens, and Heidi Shierholz, *The State of Working America, 2012/2013* (Ithaca, NY: Cornell University Press, 2012), figure 4U, "Hourly Compensation for Production/Non-Supervisory Workers and Total Economy Productivity, 1948–2011"; Mishel, emails, March 29 and April 9, 2012.

73 **From 1973 to 2011** Ibid. The contrast is sharper when comparing productivity growth and hourly wages only in the private sector. Over this period, private sector productivity grew by 92.6 percent while the average hourly wage rose by only 4.2 percent. This difference is dampened when figures cover the overall economy, because that data includes government workers, whose productivity is assumed not to grow while their salaries rise.

73 **Hourly wages of the average** Census Bureau, "Income, Poverty, and Health Insurance Coverage in the United States: 2010," September 2011.

73 **The living standards** Phillips, *Wealth and Democracy,* 112, 163.

73 **Corporate profits have trended upward** Aviva Aron-Dine and Isaac Shapiro, "Share of National Income Going to Wages and Salaries at Record Low in 2006," Center on Budget and Policy Priorities, March 29, 2007, http://www.cbpp.org.

73 **Gaping inequalities in wealth and income** Study by Emmanuel Saez, University of California at Berkeley, cited in "It's the Inequality, Stupid," *Mother Jones,* March–April 2011, http://www.motherjones.com.

74 **The super-rich (the top 1 percent)** During recession, the share of the top 1 percent fell, but with recovery that share has been moving back up toward previous highs. Emmanuel Saez, "Striking It Richer: The Evolution of Top Incomes in the United States," *Pathways Magazine,* Stanford Center for the Study of Poverty and Inequality (Winter 2008), and updated version of same

paper to include estimates for 2009 and 2010, March 7, 2012, http://elsa
.berkeley.edu/~saez/saez-UStopincomes-2010.pdf. Also see Thomas Piketty
and Emmanuel Saez, "Income Inequality in the United States, 1913–1998,
updated," table A-3, "Top Fractiles Income Shares (Including Capital Gains)
in the United States," http://elsa.berkeley.edu/~saez/TabFig2010.

74 **Forced to swallow cutbacks**   Catherine Rampell, "In Job Market Shift,
Some Workers Are Left Behind," *The New York Times,* May 12, 2010; Louis
Uchitelle, "Unions Yield on Wage Scales to Preserve Jobs," *The New York
Times,* November 19, 2010; "Still On the Job, but at Half the Pay," *The New
York Times,* October 13, 2009.

75 **Roughly 30 percent of the labor force**   "Employment Arrangements:
Improved Outreach Could Help Ensure Proper Worker Classification," General Accounting Office report, July 2006, http://www.gao.gov.

75 **Working part-time**   U.S. Bureau of Labor Statistics, "The Employment
Situation, September 2011," table A-1, October 7, 2011, http://www.bls
.gov.

75 **Microsoft agreed to pay $97 million**   Steven Greenhouse, "Technology:
Temp Workers at Microsoft Win Lawsuit," *The New York Times,* December 13, 2000; Mike Blain, "Supreme Court Refuses to Hear Appeal of Microsoft 'Permatemp' Settlement," *WashTech News,* November 13, 2002, http://
archive.washtech.org.

75 **To get around the ruling**   Ibid.

76 **Several million male dropouts**   U.S. Bureau of Labor Statistics, "Employment Situation, September 2011."

76 **Only reason average family incomes**   Haskins and Sawhill, *Creating an
Opportunity Society,* 10.

76 **"They are also working more hours"**   Larry Mishel, interview, June 30,
2010.

76 **The toll on young mothers**   Phillips, *Wealth and Democracy,* 113; U.S.
Bureau of Labor Statistics, "Employment Characteristics of Families Summary," March 24, 2011, http://www.bls.gov.

76 **"World's highest ratio of two-income households"**   Phillips, *Wealth
and Democracy,* 113, 164.

76 **An even tighter financial bind**   Elizabeth Warren and Amelia Warren
Tyagi, *The Two-Income Trap: Why Middle-Class Parents Are Going Broke* (New
York: Basic Books 2003), 20–24.

77 **"A crisis in middle-class family economics"**   Ibid., 34.

77 **The typical college graduate**   Hacker and Pierson, *Winner-Take-All Politics,* 35–38.

77 **Entry-level college graduate salaries**   Heidi Shierholz, "New College
Grads Losing Ground on Wages," *Economic Snapshot,* Economic Policy Institute, August 31, 2011, http://www.epi.org. Men's salaries fell from $22.75
per hour in 2000 to $21.77; women's fell from $19.38 to $18.43.

77 **Falling further and further behind the executive elite**   Larry Mishel,
interview, June 30, 2010; Catherine Rampell, "Many with New College Degree Find the Job Market Humbling," *The New York Times,* May 18, 2011;

Joann S. Lublin, "A Closer Look at Three Big Paydays," *The Wall Street Journal,* November 15, 2010.

77 **"A critical problem of legitimacy"** Lawrence H. Summers, "The Future of Market Capitalism," Harvard Business School Forum, October 14, 2008, http://www.hbs.edu.

77 **Average Americans would be far better off today** Hacker and Pierson, *Winner-Take-All Politics,* 25.

77 **Would have earned $743 billion more** Jacob S. Hacker and Paul Pierson, cited in Kevin Drum, "Why Screwing Unions Screws the Entire Middle Class," with statistical table, "Your Loss, Their Gain," *Mother Jones,* March–April 2011.

78 **Rising numbers of business managements** Jacob S. Hacker, *The Great Risk Shift: The New Economic Insecurity and the Decline of the American Dream* (New York, Oxford University Press, 2008), 69.

78 **One-third had failed to find** U.S. Bureau of Labor Statistics, "Worker Displacement, 2001–03," July 30, 2004, http://www.bls.gov/news.release/archives/disp_07302004.pdf. See also U.S. Bureau of Labor Statistics, "Worker Displacement, 2007–09," August 26, 2010.

78 **Fifty-nine thousand factories and production facilities** U.S. Bureau of Labor Statistics, "Quarterly Census of Employment & Wages Database," accessed January 20, 2012, http://www.bls.gov.

78 **17.1 million to 11.8 million** U.S. Bureau of Labor Statistics, "Employment, Hours, and Earnings from the Current Employment Statistics survey (National)," data extracted on January 23, 2012, http://www.bls.gov.

79 **After the 1990 downturn** Peter S. Goodman, "Despite Signs of Recovery, Chronic Joblessness Rises," *The New York Times,* February 21, 2010.

79 **"The weakest hiring cycle"** Stephen Roach, "More Jobs, Worse Work," *The New York Times,* July 22, 2004.

79 **Sitting on idle capital** "No Rush to Hire Even as Profits Soar," *The Wall Street Journal,* February 6, 2011.

79 **Roughly twenty-nine million Americans** U.S. Bureau of Labor Statistics, "The Employment Situation, December 2010," January 7, 2011, http://www.bls.gov. Unemployed, 14.5 million; part-time wanting full-time work, 8.9 million; 2.6 million marginally attached (day laborers); discouraged dropouts from labor market, 3.6 million.

79 **Hoarding $1.9 trillion in cash** Alan Greenspan, citing Federal Reserve data, in "Activism," *International Finance* 14, no. 1 (Spring 2011), www.cfr.org/content/publications/attachments/infi_1277_Rev6.pdf.

CHAPTER 7: THE GREAT BURDEN SHIFT

81 **"The burden shift"** Metropolitan Life, "The MetLife Study of the American Dream," January 25, 2007.

81 **"More and more economic risk"** Hacker, *Great Risk Shift,* xv–xvi.

82 **"One Recession, Two Americas"** Paul Taylor and Rich Morin, Pew Re-

search Center, "One Recession, Two Americas," September 24, 2010, http://www.pewsocialtrends.org.

82 **Survey documented a class split** Ibid. Among other findings: 43 percent had been unemployed at some point; 35 percent had serious difficulty paying their rent or their mortgage.

82 **The fault lines** Ibid.

83 **"The single most common word"** Pew Research Center, "Public Looks Back at Worst Decade in 50 Years," December 21, 2009, http://www.pewresearch.org.

83 **The numbers describe the damage** "Household Wealth Falls by Trillions," *The New York Times,* March 13, 2009.

84 **The Misery Index tracked** Edward Hyman's Misery Index, cited in Phillips, *Wealth and Democracy,* 133.

85 **So pervasive** U.S. Bureau of Labor Statistics, "National Compensation Survey: Employee Benefits in Private Industry," March 2006, http://www.bls.gov/ncs/ebs/sp/ebsm0004.pd.

85 **Four of whose owners** "The Forbes 400: The Richest People in America," net worth calculated September 2011, accessed January 26, 2012, http://www.forbes.com.

85 **To roll back health care** Steven Greenhouse and Reed Abelson, "Wal-Mart Cuts Some Health Care Benefits," *The New York Times,* October 20, 2011.

85 **"The truth is"** Excerpt of interview of Jon Lehman for the *Frontline* program "Is Wal-Mart Good for America?," July 16, 2004. http://www.pbs.org/frontline./frontline.

85 **Wal-Mart reported** Michael Barbaro, "Wal-Mart Says More than Half Its Workers Have Its Health Insurance," *The New York Times,* January 23, 2008.

86 **"Another example of corporations"** Greenhouse and Abelson, "Wal-Mart Cuts."

86 **Costco, a big-box retail rival** John Matthews, Costco senior vice president for human resources and risk management, interview with Owen Smith, January 26, 2012; James Flanigan, "Costco Sees Value in Higher Pay," *Los Angeles Times,* February 15, 2004; Ann Zimmerman, "Costco's Dilemma: Be Kind to Its Workers, or Wall Street?" *The Wall Street Journal,* March 26, 2004.

86 **"We try to provide"** "CEO Interview: Costco's Jim Sinegal," *FastCompany,* November 1, 2008, www.fastcompany.com/magazine/130/thinking-outside-the-big-box.html.

86 **Sinegal consistently took** R. J. Hottovy, "Morningstar's 2011 CEO of the Year Redefined Retail," *Morningstar,* January 4, 2012.

86 **Costco has outperformed Wal-Mart** Ibid.

87 **The switch offered big savings** Brooks Hamilton, interview, December 8, 2010. Hamilton, a corporate pension consultant, based his calculations on Labor Department figures.

87 **"[The] pension has been a drag"** Jeffrey Immelt, GE Annual Outlook Investors Meeting, transcript, December 14, 2010, http://www.ge.com.

87 **Pension plans were moneymakers**   Ellen E. Schultz, *Retirement Heist: How Companies Plunder and Profit from the Nest Eggs of American Workers* (New York: Portfolio/Penguin, 2011), 9.

87 **"Many, like Verizon"**   Ibid., 3–25.

88 **"This fundamental transformation"**   Hacker, *Great Risk Shift,* ix–x.

89 **"The burden shift has turned"**   Metropolitan Life, "The MetLife Study of the American Dream," January 25, 2007.

89 **"Having an impact"**   Ibid.

90 **Two-thirds said they had not**   Ibid.

90 **Two years later**   Ibid. MetLife's nationwide survey found 68 percent said they had not achieved the American Dream; 48 percent of baby boomers and older (over forty-two) said they did not expect to achieve the American Dream. See also "The 2009 MetLife Study of the American Dream."

90 **Personal bankruptcies soared**   American Bankruptcy Institute, Annual Business and Non-Business Filings by Year (1980–2009), http://www .abiworld.org.

90 **"Bankruptcy has become deeply entrenched"**   Warren and Tyagi, *Two-Income Trap,* 6.

91 **Families go over the financial cliff**   Board of Governors of the Federal Reserve System, Federal Reserve Statistical Release Z.1, *Flow of Funds Accounts of the United States,* table L,100, September 16, 2011, http://www .federalreserve.gov; Federal Reserve Statistical Release G.19, *Consumer Credit,* October 7, 2011, http://www.federalreserve.gov.

91 **"I was pretty much borrowing"**   Pam Scholl, interview, December 29, 2011.

92 **"We have gone from"**   Robert Lawless, testimony before U.S. Senate Committee on Judiciary, December 4, 2008, http://www.judiciary.senate .gov/pdf/08-12-04LawlessTestimony.pdf. Also see Federal Reserve Statistical Release G.19, *Consumer Credit;* and Federal Reserve Statistical Release Z.1.

92 **"Just a generation ago"**   Warren and Tyagi, *Two-Income Trap,* 127.

93 **"The single biggest determinant"**   Lawless, interview, November 3, 2010.

93 **"That really opened the floodgates"**   Ibid.

93 **"If they make the minimum"**   Excerpt of interview of Shailesh Mehta for the *Frontline* program "The Card Game," November 24, 2009. http://www .pbs.org/frontline./frontline.

94 **"More than 75 percent"**   Warren and Tyagi, *Two-Income Trap,* 131, 139–140.

94 **Credit card companies blanketed the nation**   Ibid., 130.

95 **"High-income deadbeats"**   Lawless, interview, November 3, 2010.

95 **Bankruptcies were back over 2 million**   Bankruptcy Data Project, Harvard University, accessed February 24, 2011, http://bdp.law.harvard.edu. For 2009, the figure was 1,950,492; and for 2010, it was 2,094,623.

96 **"Functioned like a barricade"**   Robert M. Lawless, Angela K. Littwin, Katherine M. Porter, et al., "Did Bankruptcy Reform Fail? An Empirical

Study of Consumer Debtors," *American Bankruptcy Law Journal* 82 (October 15, 2008).

96 **"The families in bankruptcy"** Ibid.

CHAPTER 8: THE WEALTH GAP

98 **The economics "of the 1%"** Joseph E. Stiglitz, "Inequality: Of the 1%, by the 1%, for the 1%," *Vanity Fair,* May 2011.

98 **"The fact is"** Michael Abramowitz and Lori Montgomery, "Bush Addresses Income Inequality," *The Washington Post,* February 1, 2007.

98 **"By 2004, the richest 1 percent"** Robert Frank, *Richistan: A Journey Through the American Wealth Boom and the Lives of the New Rich* (New York: Crown Publishing Group, 2007), 3.

98 **"It is absolutely excessive"** Matthew Symonds, "Absolutely Excessive," *Vanity Fair,* October 2005.

98 **WELCOME TO THE PLUTONOMY MACHINE** Citigroup, "Plutonomy: Buying Luxury, Explaining Global Imbalances," October 16, 2005.

99 **"The rich now dominate"** Citigroup, "Revisiting Plutonomy: The Rich Getting Richer," March 6, 2006, http://www.ifg.org.

99 **A wealthy American plutocracy** Paul Krugman, "Graduates Versus Oligarchs," *The New York Times,* February 27, 2006; Stiglitz, "Inequality."

99 **"The top 1% alone control"** David Hirschman, "The New Wave of Affluence," *Advertising Age,* May 23, 2011; David Hirschman, "On the Road to Riches," May 22, 2011, *Ad Age* blogs, http://adage.com.

99 **Luxury goods were selling** Stephanie Clifford, "Even Marked Up, Luxury Goods Fly off Shelves," *The New York Times,* August 4, 2011.

100 **Most people estimated** Benjamin I. Page and Lawrence R. Jacobs, *Class War? What Americans Really Think About Economic Inequality* (Chicago: University of Chicago Press, 2009); Inequality Survey, 37–38, pay data cited from simplyhired.com, November 8, 2007, and Corporate Library Survey reported at aflcio.org/corporatewatch/paywatch.

100 **Eleven different polls** Page and Jacobs, *Class War?,* 41.

100 **Jack-and-the-Beanstalk growth** Benjamin M. Friedman, *The Moral Consequences of Economic Growth* (New York: Alfred A. Knopf, 2005), 116–120; Paul Krugman, "The Third Depression," *The New York Times,* June 27, 2010.

100 **This small elite** Emmanuel Saez, "Striking It Richer: The Evolution of Top Incomes in the United States," July 17, 2010.

101 **Incomes over $352,000** Emmanuel Saez, "Striking It Richer: The Evolution of Top Incomes in the United States" (updated with 2009 and 2010 estimates), March 2, 2012. The calculations of Emmanuel Saez and Thomas Piketty cited throughout this book are based on salary, bonuses, and capital gains income—all inclusive. See also Shaila Dewan and Robert Gebeloff, "One Percent, Many Variations," *The New York Times,* January 15, 2012. The *Times* noted there were various ways of calculating income and reported that

the Federal Reserve's Survey of Consumer Finances set the cutoff for the top
1 percent at $690,000 in 2007, the latest year for which Federal Reserve data
is available. Economists at the Tax Policy Center and other institutions have
developed figures close to $600,000.

101 **Made $1.35 trillion in 2007** Frank, *Richistan,* 3.

101 **The top 1 percent garnered two-thirds** Saez, "Striking It Richer," *Pathways Magazine.*

101 **And this tiny group reaped 93 percent** Saez, "Striking It Richer," update, March 2, 2012.

101 **The top 0.01 percent** Ibid., figure 3.

101 **$10 *million a week*** David Cay Johnston, "Scary New Wage Data," October 24, 2010, http://www.tax.com.

101 **Half a dozen hedge fund managers** "Pay of Hedge Fund Managers Roared Back Last Year," *The New York Times,* April 1, 2010.

102 **Paulson had already made nearly $4 billion** Gregory Zuckerman, "Trader Racks Up a Second Epic Gain," *The Wall Street Journal,* January 28, 2011.

102 **Translating these astounding numbers** Frank, *Richistan,* 3–12; see chart, 6.

102 ***Billionaireville*** Frank, *Richistan,* 11–12.

102 ***The Walton family*** Tony Judt, *Ill Fares the Land* (New York: Penguin Group, 2010), 14.

103 **The super-rich and ultra-rich often compete** Frank, *Richistan,* 8–12.

103 **Ever more expensive toys** Symonds, "Absolutely Excessive."

103 **When the rich build** Robert H. Frank, "Why 2 Paychecks Are Barely Enough," *The New York Times,* Sunday Business, January 1, 2012.

104 **"Income inequality is real"** Abramowitz and Montgomery, "Bush Addresses Income Inequality."

104 **America is now the most unequal** Will Hutton, "Log Cabin to White House? Not Any More," *The Observer,* April 28, 2002, http://www.observer.co.uk/comment/story/0,6903,706484,00.html; Organisation for Economic Co-operation and Development, "Divided We Stand: Why Inequality Keeps Rising," *An Overview of Growing Income Inequalities in OECD Countries: Main Findings,* accessed December 6, 2011, http://www.oecd.org/dataoecd/40/12/49170449.pdf.

105 **"Those at the top"** Hacker and Pierson, *Winner-Take-All Politics,* 34–40.

105 **The degree is not what explains that** Ibid., 35–38.

105 **"The most telling fact"** Larry Mishel, interview, July 10, 2010.

106 **"The U.S. tax code"** David Cay Johnston, *Perfectly Legal: The Covert Campaign to Rig Our Tax System to Benefit the Super Rich—and Cheat Everybody Else* (New York: Penguin Group, 2003), 11.

106 **As the tax code has been written** Thomas L. Hungerford, "An Analysis of the 'Buffett Rule,' " Congressional Research Service, October 7, 2011, fpc.state.gov.

106 **The key driver** U.S. Treasury Department, "Capital Gains and Taxes Paid

on Capital Gains for Returns with Positive Net Capital Gains, 1954–2008," http://www.ustreas.gov/offices/tax-policy/library/capgain1–2010.pdf.

106 **Garner roughly *half of all capital gains***   Robert Lenzner, "The Top 0.1% of the Nation Earn Half of All Capital Gains," *Forbes,* November 20, 2011.

107 **"If you make money with money"**   "Warren Buffett Tells Charlie Rose Why Congress Should Stop 'Coddling' the Super-Rich," transcript, PBS, *Charlie Rose,* August 17, 2011, http://www.cnbc.com.

107 **Personally, Buffett admitted**   Ibid.; and Warren Buffett, "Stop Coddling the Rich," *The New York Times,* August 14, 2011.

108 **The Forbes 400 Richest Americans**   Howard Zinn, *A People's History of the United States, 1492–Present* (New York: HarperCollins, 1999), 580; see also Conor Dougherty, "Income Slides to 1996 Levels," *The Wall Street Journal,* September 13, 2011; Census Bureau, "Income, Poverty, and Health Insurance Coverage in the United States: 2010."

108 **The Bush tax cuts**   Internal Revenue Service, U.S. Individual Income Tax: Personal Exemptions and Lowest and Highest Bracket Tax Rates, and Tax Base for Regular Tax: Tax Years 1913–2008, http://www.irs.gov/taxstats/article/0,,id=175910,00.html.

108 **The top 1 percent bracket reaped**   Edmund L. Andrews, "Tax Cuts Offer Most for Very Rich, Study Says," *The New York Times,* January 8, 2007; Fieldhouse and Pollack, "Bush-Era Tax Cuts," Economic Policy Institute, June 1, 2011; Thomas L. Hungerford, "Changes in the Distribution of Income Among Tax Filers Between 1996 and 2006: The Role of Labor Income, Capital Income, and Tax Policy," Congressional Research Service, December 29, 2011, fpc.state.gov.

108 **Average income jump fivefold**   Fieldhouse and Pollack, "Bush-Era Tax Cuts."

108 **At the other end**   Dougherty, "Income Slides to 1996 Levels"; Census Bureau, "Income, Poverty, and Health Insurance Coverage in the United States: 2010."

108 **The middle-income tax cut**   Andrews, "Tax Cuts Offer Most for Very Rich"; Fieldhouse and Pollack, "Bush-Era Tax Cuts."

108 **President Obama persuaded Congress**   "Tax Deal Suggests New Path for Obama," *The New York Times,* December 7, 2010; "Congress Sends $801 Billion Tax Cut Bill to Obama," *The New York Times,* December 17, 2010.

109 **In Arnold Toynbee's terms**   Toynbee, *Study of History,* vols. 7–10, 365–68.

109 **When this happens**   Toynbee, *Study of History,* vols. 1–6, 245–46.

109 **His annual salary**   Nace, *Gangs of America,* 180–81.

109 **"Management does not go out ruthlessly"**   John Kenneth Galbraith, *The New Industrial State* (New York: New American Library, 1968), 120–21.

110 **"Greed, for lack of a better word"**   Nace, *Gangs of America,* 180; Krugman, *Conscience of a Liberal,* 142; Reich, *Supercapitalism,* 108.

110 **James Burke, CEO of Johnson & Johnson**   Jim Collins, "The 10 Great-

est CEOs of All Time," *Fortune,* July 21, 2003; James E. Burke, Harvard Business School Alumni Achievement Awards, accessed October 20, 2011, http://www.alumni.hbs.edu.

110 **Burke lived** Johnson & Johnson, "Our Credo," accessed October 20, 2011, http://www.jnj.com.

110 **"In our culture"** "Kendrick B. Melrose: Caring About People: Employees and Customers," *Ethix,* October 1, 2007, http://ethix.org; and Ken Melrose, "2005 Minnesota Business Hall of Fame," *Twin Cities Business,* July 2005, http://www.tcbmag.com.

111 **The top echelons of business** Jon Bakija, Adam Cole, and Bradley T. Heim, "Jobs and Income Growth of Top Earners and the Causes of Changing Income Inequality: Evidence from U.S. Tax Return Data," research paper (Bloomington: School of Public and Environmental Affairs, Indiana University, November 2010), http://www.indiana.edu.

111 **Larry Ellison** Graef Crystal, "Larry Ellison Rides Again!" *Crystal Report on Executive Compensation,* July 13, 2009, http://www.graefcrystal.com.

112 **A *Wall Street Journal* compilation** John S. Lublin and Scot Thurm, "Behind Soaring Executive Pay, Decades of Failed Restraints," *The Wall Street Journal,* October 12, 2006. In his three big years, Weill was paid $230.5 million in 1997, $166.9 million in 1998, and $224.4 million in 2000.

112 **The idea sprang** Michael C. Jensen and William H. Meckling, "Theory of the Firm: Managerial Behavior, Agency Costs and Ownership Structure," *Journal of Financial Economics* 3, no. 4 (October 1976): 305–60.

112 **Jensen became its apostle** Michael C. Jensen and Kevin J. Murphy, "Performance Pay and Top-Management Incentives," *Journal of Political Economy* 98, no. 2 (April 1990): 225–64.

112 **Perhaps unwittingly** John Cassidy, "The Greed Cycle," *The New Yorker,* September 23, 2002.

113 **"An orgy of self-enrichment"** Ibid.

113 **"There was a sea change"** Stephen Young, interview, October 19, 2011.

113 **Bob Nardelli, for one** "Home Depot's Nardelli Ousted After Six-Year Tenure," Bloomberg, January 3, 2007, http://www.bloomberg.com.

114 **Probably the most egregiously distorted** Lucian A. Bebchuk, Alma Cohen, and Holger Spamann, "The Wages of Failure: Executive Compensation at Bear Stearns and Lehman 2000–2008," Discussion Paper No. 657 (Cambridge, MA: John M. Olin Center for Law, Economics, and Business, Harvard University, February 2010).

114 **Angelo Mozilo, CEO** Frank Ahrens, "Big Payday Awaits Chairman After Countrywide Sale," *The Washington Post,* January 12, 2008.

115 **The SEC found** Eric Dash, "Dodging Taxes Is a New Stock Options Scheme," *The New York Times,* October 30, 2006; "Stock-Options Scandal Fugitive Puts Roots Down in Namibia," *The Wall Street Journal,* November 17, 2006; "How Backdating Helped Executives Cut Their Taxes," *The Wall Street Journal,* December 12, 2006.

115 **Steve Jobs had been personally involved** "Jobs Helped Pick 'Favorable' Dates for Options Grants," *The Wall Street Journal,* December 30, 2006; and

Alan Sipress, "Apple Chief Benefited from Options, Records Indicate," *The Washington Post,* January 11, 2007.

116 **One revealing case, William McGuire**   "Embattled CEO to Step Down at United Health," *The Wall Street Journal,* October 16, 2006; "How a Giant Insurer Decided to Oust Hugely Successful CEO," *The Wall Street Journal,* December 7, 2007.

116 **One reason so many CEOs got away**   Lucian Bebchuk, Yaniv Grinstein, and Urs Peyer, "Lucky CEOs and Lucky Directors," Discussion Paper No. 573 (Cambridge, MA: John M. Olin Center for Law, Economics, and Business, Harvard University, December 2006), published in *Journal of Finance* 65, no. 6 (December 2010); John Hechinger, "Backdated Options Pad CEO Pay by Average of 10%," *The Wall Street Journal,* November 17, 2006.

117 **Bogle also derided the idea**   John C. Bogle, *The Battle for the Soul of Capitalism* (New Haven, CT: Yale University Press, 2005), 10–26.

117 **Dissenting academics**   Jay Lorsch and Rakesh Khurana, "The Pay Problem," *Harvard Magazine,* May–June 2010.

117 **Executive stock options**   Despite his dismay, Jensen was against abandoning the pay-for-performance stock options. To solve the problem, he suggested better-designed stock options. "How to Pay Bosses: Michael Jensen Still Thinks He Has the Answer," *The Economist,* November 14, 2002, http://www.economist.com/node/1441839.

118 **"During my seven and a half years"**   Arthur Levitt, *Take On the Street: What Wall Street and Corporate America Don't Want You to Know* (New York: Pantheon Books, 2002), 236.

119 **Merrill Lynch estimated**   Merrill Lynch & Co., study by Gary Schieneman, C.P.A., 5, June 19, 2001, 5.

119 **Buffett backed the FASB rule**   Warren Buffett, "Who Really Cooks the Books?" *The New York Times,* July 24, 2002; and Buffett, "Fuzzy Math and Stock Options," *The Washington Post,* July 6, 2004.

119 **Levitt backed down**   Levitt, *Take on the Street,* 106–11.

119 **"Probably the single biggest mistake"**   Arthur Levitt, interview, March 12, 2002.

120 **The hand of U.S. regulators**   "Foreign Firms to Expense Options: New International Rule Pressures U.S. to Handle Stock Grants the Same Way," *The Wall Street Journal,* February 20, 2004.

120 **Ten months later**   Gary Rivlin, "Regulators Adopt Tighter Rules on Accounting for Stock Options," *The New York Times,* December 18, 2004.

120 **But business opposition succeeded**   John Nester, SEC communications director, and SEC, email and interview, October 18, 2011.

PART 3: UNEQUAL DEMOCRACY

121 **Unequal Democracy**   Bartels, *Unequal Democracy.*

123 **"My friend Dirk Van Dongen"**   President George W. Bush, remarks, White House, May 28, 2003, PR Newswire, http://www.prnewswire.com;

Bush, remarks, U.S. Chamber of Commerce, May 6, 2003, PR Newswire, http://www.prnewswire.com.

123 **"They knew I was loyal"** Dirk Van Dongen, interview, April 25, 2011.

123 **Van Dongen was Rove's man** Kristin Jensen, Jonathan D. Salant, and Michael Forsythe, "Bush Relies on Corporate Lobbyists to Help Him Push U.S. Agenda," Bloomberg, September 23, 2005, http://www.bloomberg.com.

123 **Added $2.9 trillion** A Congressional Budget Office study estimated that Bush tax cuts reduced tax revenues by $2.9 billion from 2001 to 2011, while less than expected growth reduced revenues another $3.5 billion, cited in Bruce Bartlett, "Are the Bush Tax Cuts the Root of Our Fiscal Problem?" *New York Times Economix,* July 26, 2011, http://economic.blos.nytimes/2011/07/26.are-the-bush-tax-cuts-the-root-of-our-fiscal-problem; James Horney and Kathy Ruffing, "Economic Downturn and Bush Policies Continue to Drive Large Projected Deficits," Center on Budget and Policy Priorities, May 10, 2011, http://www.cbpp.org/ms/index.fm?fa=view&id=3490; "The Bush Tax Cuts Costs Two and a Half Times as Much as the House Democrats' Health Care Proposal," Citizens for Tax Justice, September 8, 2009, http://www.ctj.org.

CHAPTER 9: THE NEW 2000S POWER GAME

125 **"Whatever elections may be doing"** Bartels, *Unequal Democracy,* 287.

125 **"Current U.S. tax policies"** Page and Jacobs, *Class War?,* 88, 93.

125 **"This is the ultimate"** Richard W. Stevenson, "Itching to Rebuild the Tax Law," *The New York Times,* November 24, 2002.

126 **"Over the years"** Dirk Van Dongen, interview, April 25, 2011.

126 **"There's a chorus"** Alison Mitchell, "Interest Groups Are Gearing Up for High-Stakes Tax Cut Fight," *The New York Times,* February 24, 2001.

127 **Bush's proposal for $1.78 trillion** Estimate, Joint Committee on Taxation, "Congress Cuts Deal on Taxes," *CQ Almanac 2001* (Washington, DC: Congressional Quarterly, 2002), http://www.cqpress.com.

127 **At Treasury** Michele Davis, memo, February 27, 2001, in Ron Suskind, *The Price of Loyalty: George W. Bush, the White House, and the Education of Paul O'Neill* (New York: Simon & Schuster, 2004), 150.

127 **That very morning** "Key Goals Face Early Obstacles," *The Washington Post,* February 27, 2001.

127 **An NBC/*Wall Street Journal* poll** "Public Buys Bush's Tax-Cut Plan, but Details Magnify Differences," *The Wall Street Journal,* March 8, 2001.

127 **An even stronger tilt** "Poll Analysis: Bush in Honeymoon Period," *Los Angeles Times,* March 8, 2001.

128 **"Washington derives so much of its power"** Stevenson, "Itching to Rebuild the Tax Law."

128 **"Dirk is always well positioned"** Jeffrey Birnbaum, "The Man in the Middle," CNNMoney.com, April 1, 2002, http://money.cnn.com.

128 **"That coalition was very important"** Jensen, Salant, and Forsythe, "Bush Relies on Corporate Lobbyists."

129 **"The President has it backwards"** "Bush Pushes Huge Tax Cut in U.S. Congress Debut," *Dallas Morning News,* February 28, 2001.

129 **Protests in several cities** "Union Campaigns to Thwart Tax Cut Plan," *Atlanta Daily World,* April 8, 2001.

129 **Bush was the one urging voters** Marc Lacey, "Bush Deploys Charm on Daschle in Pushing Tax Cut," *The New York Times,* March 10, 2001.

130 **A staggering $2 billion** Jensen, Salant, and Forsythe, "Bush Relies on Corporate Lobbyists."

130 **The Business Roundtable** The Center for Responsive Politics reported business interests pouring $333 million into the 2009–10 election campaign cycle. By the center's calculations, just one of Dirk Van Dongen's six groups, the Business Roundtable, and its 208 corporate members and their executives and families contributed $142,955,958 to that campaign cycle. Email April 16, 2012. See also "Business-Labor-Ideology Split in PAC & Individual Donations to Candidates and Parties," Center for Responsive Politics, based on Federal Election Commission data, March 27, 2011.

130 **"You have an 800-pound gorilla"** Jensen, Salant, and Forsythe, "Bush Relies on Corporate Lobbyists."

130 **Tax policy** Benjamin I. Page and Robert Y. Shapiro, *The Rational Public: Fifty Years of Trends in Americans' Policy Preferences* (Chicago: University of Chicago Press, 1992), 166, 287.

130 **Exploiting public confusion** "Bush Pushes Huge Tax Cut."

130 **White House highlighted the promise** Richard W. Stevenson, "Congress Passes Tax Cut, with Rebates This Summer," *The New York Times,* May 27, 2001.

131 **John McCain voted against** John McCain statement on final tax reconciliation bill, press release, May 26, 2001, http://mccain.senate.gov.

131 **52.5 percent of the Bush tax cuts** "The Bush Tax Cuts Costs Two and a Half Times as Much as the House Democrats' Health Care Proposal," Citizens for Tax Justice, September 8, 2009, http://www.ctj.org.

131 **"Far from representing popular wishes"** Jacob S. Hacker and Paul Pierson, "Abandoning the Middle: The Bush Tax Cuts and the Limits of Democratic Control," *Perspectives on Politics* 3, no. 1 (March 2005): 33–53.

132 **The explosive growth of corporate PACs** Nace, *Gangs of America,* 148–49.

133 **Business interests pumped in $972 million** Based on Federal Election Commission data, the Center for Responsive Politics reported total business donations to the 2009–10 campaign cycle as $1,362,777,162 compared with $96,824,239 for labor, with soft-money contributions from individuals representing business interests of $971,645,729 versus $9,906,072 for labor, and $332,951,693 in contributions from business PACs compared with $69,073,927 from labor PACs. "Business-Labor-Ideology Split in PAC & Individual Donations to Candidates and Parties," Center for Responsive Pol-

itics, based on Federal Election Commission data, March 27, 2011, http://www.opensecrets.org/overview/blio.php.

133 **In all, $7 billion was spent** "Lobbying Database," Center for Responsive Politics, opensecrets.org, based on data from Senate Office of Public Records, January 31, 2011. Business groups spent $5.998 billion in those two years compared with $91.7 million by labor groups. That pattern is fairly typical in recent years. Even though the media generally treat business and labor as roughly equal "special interests," business interests heavily outspent labor interests on lobbying from 1998 through 2010 by roughly a 60-to-1 ratio ($28.6 billion to $492 million). See http://www.opensecrets.org/lobby/index.php.

133 **No other lobbying interest** Ibid.; see also Drutman, *The Business of America Is Lobbying,* online doctoral thesis, 3–6.

133 **Business leaders did not even bother** Drutman, *Business of America,* 117.

134 **The Business Roundtable** Jonathan Peterson, "Lawmakers Debate Bill on Executive Pay," *Los Angeles Times,* March 9, 2007.

135 **Gang of Six found ways** Thomas, "Shareholder Vote on Executive Compensation Act," HR1257, Bill Summary and Status, 110th Congress, Library of Congress, accessed October 24, 2011, http://Thomas.loc.gov.

135 **It took the financial collapse** "New Rule Tries to Rein In the Pay of Corporate Executives," *Los Angeles Times,* January 25, 2011.

135 **On issues as varied** Bartels, *Unequal Democracy,* 253–54.

135 **An even stronger upper-class impact** Martin Gilens, "Inequality and Democratic Responsiveness," special issue, *Public Opinion Quarterly* 69, no. 5 (2005): 778–96.

135 **"The mystery is how politicians"** Page and Jacobs, *Class War?,* 93.

136 **A host of modern economic studies** James R. Repetti, "Democracy, Taxes, and Wealth," Research Paper No. 2001–03 (Newton, MA: Boston College Law School, June 14, 2011), 831.

136 **Come to a similar conclusion** Torsten Persson and Guido Tabellini, "Growth, Distribution, and Politics," in *Political Economy, Growth, and Business Cycles,* ed. Alex Cukierman, Zvi Hercowirtz, and Leonardo Leiderman (Cambridge, MA: Massachusetts Institute of Technology Press, 1992).

136 **Alan Greenspan was moved to comment** Alan Greenspan, remarks, Council on Foreign Relations, March 15, 2011, http://www.cfr.org; Greenspan, citing Federal Reserve data, in "Activism," *International Finance* 14, no. 1 (October 2011): 165–82, http://onlinelibrary.wiley.com.

137 **Not business investment but consumer demand** James Livingston, "It's Consumer Spending, Stupid," *The New York Times,* October 25, 2011.

137 **Major banks to big pharmaceuticals** Nelson D. Schwartz, "As Layoffs Rise, Stock Buybacks Consume Cash," *The New York Times,* November 21, 2011.

137 **"The 2000s saw the worst"** Alan Krueger, "The Rise and Consequences of Inequality in the United States," remarks, Center for American Progress, January 12, 2012, http://www.americanprogress.org.

137 **By contrast, during Bill Clinton's presidency** David Leonhardt, "Were

the Bush Tax Cuts Good for Growth?" *The New York Times,* November 18, 2010.

138 **Historical record had little influence**   President Barack Obama, "Investing in America: A CNBC Town Hall Event with President Obama," September 20, 2010, http://www.cnbc.com.

138 **A majority of Americans endorsed**   President Barack Obama, press conference, December 7, 2010, White House transcript.

138 **A CNN poll**   CNN Opinion Research Poll, November 17, 2010, http://i2.cdn.turner.com/cnn/2010/images/11/17/rel16e.pdf. CNN found 49 percent opposed tax cuts for people making over $250,000 a year; 15 percent opposed any tax cut; 64 percent in all opposed tax cuts for upper income brackets. See also Bloomberg News Poll, December 4–7, 2010, http://media.bloomberg.com.

138 **Republicans had fallen under the spell**   Bruce Bartlett, "Supply-Side Economics, R.I.P.," Capital Gains and Games blog, October 10, 2009, http://www.capitalgainsandgames.com.

138 **"The rich are always going to say"**   "The Giving Pledge," *ABC This Week,* November 28, 2010.

139 **"We kept the coalition in business"**   Van Dongen, interview, April 25, 2011.

139 **Van Dongen's Tax Relief Coalition**   U.S. Chamber of Commerce, "Jobs for America: An Open Letter to the President of the United States, the United States Congress, and the American People," July 14, 2010, http://www.uschamber.com.

139 *All* **meant**   "Bush Scores Win on Tax Cuts," *CQ Almanac 2003* (Washington, DC: Congressional Quarterly, 2004), http://www.cqpress.com; Edmund L. Andrews, "Greenspan Throws Cold Water on Bush Arguments for Tax Cut," *The New York Times,* February 12, 2003; "Nobel Laureates, 450 Other Economists Fault Bush Tax Plan," Economic Policy Institute, February 10, 2003, http://www.epi.org; "A Tax Bill, Full of Breaks, Passes Senate," *The New York Times,* October 12, 2004; "Buffett Slams Dividend Tax Cut," CNNMoney.com, May 20, 2003, http://money.cnn.com.

139 **The Gang of Six got the jump**   Jeanne Cummings, "Business Pushes to Extend Tax Cuts," *Politico,* September 14, 2010, http://www.politico.com.

139 **Senate Republicans slammed the door**   Republican letter to Majority Leader Harry Reid, *Congressional Record,* S8327, December, 1, 2010, http://www.gpo.gov.

139 **Obama protested**   President Barack Obama, press conference, December 7, 2010; "Obama Defends Tax Deal, but His Party Stays Hostile," *The New York Times,* December 8, 2010.

140 **Republicans extracted a final concession**   David M. Herszenhorn, "Congress Sends $801 Billion Tax Cut Bill to Obama," *The New York Times,* December 16, 2010.

140 **Congress passed this package**   "Obama Tax Deal Wins Praise from Business-Lobby Critics," Bloomberg, December 7, 2010, http://www.bloomberg.com.

140 **Business forces would be ready to fight** Van Dongen, interview, April 25, 2011.

CHAPTER 10: THE WASHINGTON–WALL STREET SYMBIOSIS

141 **"I sincerely believe"** Thomas Jefferson to John Taylor, May 28, 1816, in *The Writings of Thomas Jefferson,* vol. 6 (Washington, DC: Taylor & Maury, 1854), 604–8.

141 **"In a political system"** Robert A. Dahl, *Who Governs? Democracy and Power in an American City* (New Haven: Yale University Press, 1961), 1.

141 **"The finance industry"** Simon Johnson, "The Quiet Coup," *The Atlantic,* May 2009, http://www.theatlantic.com/magazine/archive/2009/05/the-quiet -coup/7364.

142 **What Woodrow Wilson once called** Woodrow Wilson, "Money Monopoly Is the Most Menacing," speech, Harrisburg, Pennsylvania, reprinted in Philadelphia *North American,* June 6, 1911, cited in John Milton Cooper, Jr., *Reconsidering Woodrow Wilson: Progressivism, Internationalism, War, and Peace* (Baltimore: Johns Hopkins University Press, 2008), 68.

142 **The scale of its financial boom** U.S. Bureau of Economic Analysis, National Income and Product Accounts, figure 3–1, "Real Corporate Profits, Financial vs. Nonfinancial Sectors," shows financial sector profits growing 800 percent from 1980 to 2005, while nonfinancial sector profits grew by 250 percent. See Simon Johnson and James Kwak, *13 Bankers: The Wall Street Takeover and the Financial Meltdown* (New York: Pantheon Books, 2010), 59–61; and John Bellamy Foster and Hannah Holleman, "The Financial Power Elite," *Monthly Review* 62, no. 1 (May 2010).

142 **It overtook manufacturing** Johnson and Kwak, *13 Bankers,* 59; Kevin Phillips, *Bad Money: Reckless Finance, Failed Politics, and the Global Crisis of American Capitalism* (New York: Penguin Group, 2009), xiii, xv, 31. The financial sector jumped from 11–12 percent of U.S. GDP in the 1980s to 20–21 percent by the mid-2000s. See U.S. Bureau of Economic Analysis, "Gross Domestic Product by Industry," table B-12, November 11, 2004.

142 **Its profits soared** Johnson and Kwak, *13 Bankers,* 60–61.

142 **They have lobbied successfully** Multiple financial analysts have developed these themes. See, for example, Phillips, *Bad Money,* xii–xvii; xxxii–xxxix; Johnson and Kwak, *13 Bankers,* 1–10, 75–88, 148–50.

142 **Debt that dwarfed** Johnson and Kwak, *13 Bankers,* 59–60.

143 **Financial sector poured roughly $318 million** Center for Responsive Politics, "Long-Term Contribution Trends," based on Federal Election Commission data, March 27, 2011, http://www.opensecrets.org; "Lobbying: Finance, Insurance & Real Estate, Sector Profiles 2009 & 2010," accessed March 8, 2012, http://www.opensecrets.org/lobby/indus.php?id=F&year= 2010.

143 **The line between government and banking** Julie Creswell and Ben

White, "The Guys from 'Government Sachs,'" *The New York Times,* October 19, 2008.

143 **Former New York Fed president** Jo Becker and Gretchen Morgenson, "Geithner, Member and Overseer of Finance Club," *The New York Times,* April 27, 2009.

144 **1,447 former government officials as lobbyists** Center for Responsible Politics and Public Citizen, report, *The Washington Post,* June 3, 2010.

144 **Finance had a lobbying team** Kevin O'Connor, "Big Bank Takeover: How Too-Big-To-Fail's Army of Lobbyists Has Captured Washington," Institute for America's Future, May 10, 2010. http://www.ourfuture.org/files/documents/big-bank-takeover-final.pdf. "For Lobbyists, Banks Tap Washington Pipeline, Report Finds," *The Washington Post,* May 11, 2010. Center for Responsive Politics, "Lobbying: Finance, Insurance & Real Estate, Sector Profiles 2009 & 2010" http://www.opensecrets.org/lobby/indus.php?id=F&year=2010. DealBook," Minting Bank Lobbyists on Capitol Hill,"*The New York Times,* April 13, 2010; Erika Lovley, "Washington Draws Ex-Lawmakers," Politico, June 3, 2010.

144 **"Effectively captured our government"** Johnson, "Quiet Coup."

144 **A matter not just of people, but of ideology** Ibid.

145 **"Financial weapons of mass destruction"** Warren Buffett, "Chairman's Letter," Berkshire Hathaway annual report, 2002, http://www.berkshirehathaway.com.

145 **"Should serve as a wakeup call"** Brooksley Born, testimony, House Committee on Banking and Financial Services, October 1, 1998, http://www.cftc.gov.

145 **Greenspan, Rubin, and Summers** Brady Dennis and Robert O'Harrow, Jr., "A Crack in the System," *The Washington Post,* December 30, 2008; Manuel Roig-Franzia, "Credit Crisis Cassandra," *The Washington Post,* May 26, 2009.

146 **"Greenspan was always against Glass-Steagall"** John Reed, interview, December 18, 2002.

147 **Federal Reserve Board . . . permitted an escalating expansion** Nathaniel C. Nash, "Banks Ask Fed for Power to Underwrite Securities," *The New York Times,* October 26, 1988; and Federal Reserve press release announcing proposed revision of regulation, raising to 25 percent from 10 percent the percentage of total revenues that commercial banks may derive from underwriting and securities dealings, December 20, 1996, effective March 6, 1997.

147 **Weill knew that his dream merger** Reed, interview, December 18, 2002; Carol Loomis and James Aley, " 'One Helluva Candy Store!' That's What Sandy Weill Called the Megameld of his Travelers Group and John Reed's Citicorp," *Fortune,* May 11, 1998.

147 **Come back to haunt the government** Jeffrey E. Garten, "Mega-Mergers, Mega-Influence," *The New York Times,* October 26, 1999.

148 **The country's largest corporate welfare** "Secret Fed Loans Gave Banks $13 Billion Undisclosed to Congress," Bloomberg, November 28, 2011, http://www.bloomberg.com.

148 **All that cheap money**   "In Obama's Tenure, a Resurgent Wall Street," *The Washington Post,* November 7, 2011.

149 **A group of Democratic senators**   "Senate Rejects Bid to Shrink Biggest U.S. Banks," *The New York Times,* May 7, 2010.

149 **When reformers wanted to revive**   Michael Hirsh, "Bonfire of the Loopholes," *Newsweek,* May 21, 2010.

150 **John Reed, who apologized**   Bob Ivry, "Reed Says 'I'm Sorry' for Role in Creating Citigroup," Bloomberg, November 6, 2009.

150 **"There's an attempt to kill this"**   "Resistance Bogs Down Financial Overhaul," *The New York Times,* June 7, 2011.

151 **Volcker later voiced his dismay**   Paul Volcker, lecture, "Three Years Later: Unfinished Business in Financial Reform," September 23, 2011, graphics8.nytimes.com/packages/pdf/business/23gret.pdf; see also Gretchen Morgenson, "How Mr. Volcker Would Fix It," *The New York Times,* Sunday Business, October 23, 2011; and Zachary A. Goldfarb, "In Obama's Tenure, a Resurgent Wall Street," *The Washington Post,* November 7, 2011.

151 **The law's penalties and incentives**   Paul Krugman, "Making Financial Reform Fool-Resistant," *The New York Times,* April 15, 2010; Krugman, "Bubbles and the Banks," *The New York Times,* January 10, 2010.

151 **The reform was so weak**   Jeffrey Lacker, "The Regulatory Response to the Financial Crisis: An Early Assessment," May 26, 2010, http://www.richmondfed.org/press_room/speeches/president_jeff_lacker/2010/lacker_speech_2000526.cfm.

151 **"Such is the lobbying power"**   Liam Halligan, "Obama Signs a Bill That Lets Banks Have US over Barrel Once More," *The Telegraph* (London), July 26, 2010, http://www.telegraph.co.uk.

151 **"The government is pretty much run"**   Center for Political Studies, University of Michigan, cited in William Greider, *Who Will Tell the People: The Betrayal of American Democracy* (New York: Simon & Schuster, 1992), 23; "Poll Finds Edge for Obama over GOP among the Public," *The New York Times*/CBS News Poll, February 12, 2010. See poll data, 15, question 30, http://s3.amazonaws.com/nytdocs/docs/192/192.pdf.

151 **Poll after poll has recorded**   The September 21, 2008, Zogby poll found 82 percent thought that political parties, presidential candidates, and candidates for the U.S. Congress should be banned from receiving financial contributions from lobbyists or other representatives from those industries that are vital to the financial and national security of the country (Zogby, "Voters Not Sold on Government Bailout," http://www.zogby.com/news/ReadNews.cfm?ID=1555). The January 2, 2007, poll from Roper recorded 81 percent saying Congress should move to enact "new regulations to reduce the power and influence of lobbyists in Washington" (*The Wall Street Journal,* January 3, 2007). The January 11, 2006, Pew poll found that 81 percent thought it was common for lobbyists to bribe members of Congress (PewCenter for the Press, "Americans Taking Abramoff, Alito and Domestic Spying in Stride," http://people-press.org/reports/display.php3?ReportID=267).

152 **"Institutionally trained to be passive"** Greider, *Who Will Tell the People,* 20.

152 **"The available evidence"** Bartels, *Unequal Democracy,* 287.

PART 4: MIDDLE-CLASS SQUEEZE

155 **As a lead mechanic** Pat O'Neill, interview, December 21, 2010.

155 **"Of course, workin' there"** Excerpt of interview of Pat O'Neill for the *Frontline* program "Can You Afford to Retire?," March 13, 2006, http://www .pbs.org/frontline.

CHAPTER 11: BROKEN PROMISES

157 **"The essence"** Excerpt of interview of Jamie Sprayregen for the *Frontline* program "Can You Afford to Retire?," February 17, 2006, http://www.pbs .org/frontline.

157 **"Bankruptcy's terrible"** Excerpt of interview of Greg Davidowitch for the *Frontline* program "Can You Afford to Retire?," http://www.pbs.org/ frontline.

158 **"It was an exciting time"** Pat O'Neill, interview, December 21, 2010.

158 **Employers were operating 114,000** Pension Benefit Guaranty Corporation databook, accessed April 4, 2012. Table S-31 shows 112,000 single employer–defined benefit (lifetime pension) plans in 1985, plus 2,000 multi-employer plans. Peak coverage at 35 percent of active workforce was achieved in 1980 (table S-33), but peak participation of 34.5 million employees was in 2004 (table S-31) because this included retirees receiving benefits as well as active workers. See http://www.pbgc.gov/res/data-books.html.

159 **Pat O'Neill, who ended up making** Pat O'Neill, interview, July 13, 2010.

159 **Management struck a grand bargain** Adam Bryant, "July 10–16: Lean, Hungry Skies; United's Employees, After 7-Year Fight, Buy Their Own Airline," *The New York Times,* July 14, 1994.

159 **United had a strong spurt** Roger Lowenstein, "Into Thin Air," *The New York Times Magazine,* February 17, 2002.

160 **Those were phantom gains** Ibid.

160 **Union leaders said they had heard** Davidowitch, interview, "Can You Afford to Retire?"

160 **United filed for bankruptcy** Edward Wong, "Airline Shock Waves: The Overview; Bankruptcy Case Is Filed by United," *The New York Times,* December 10, 2002.

160 **"The stock went zippo"** Pat O'Neill, interview excerpt from *Frontline,* "Can You Afford to Retire?"

161 **Finally, his pension was cut** O'Neill, interview, July 13, 2010.

161 **Probably one million workers and retirees**   Pension Benefit Guaranty Corporation databook, table S-5, reports that 1,897,253 employees and retirees were affected by companies' terminating their pension plans between 1975 and 2010. The ten largest pension plans with 543,825 participants were closed down through bankruptcy, and PBGC officials reported that was also true of 85 percent of 102 of the largest plans, with more than 1 million participants. PBGC officials say that is a typical pattern. If so, roughly 1.6 million participants would have had their benefits diminished by corporate bankruptcies or by companies on the verge of bankruptcy. Marc Hopkins and Jeff Speicher, PBGC press officers, emails and briefings, April 10 and 13, 2012; PBGC databook, 2010, http://www.pbgc.gov/res/data-books.html.

162 **In one year alone**   PBGC background briefing, December 8, 2010.

162 **Overall, the percentage**   U.S. Bureau of Labor Statistics. "National Compensation Survey: Employee Benefits in the United States, March 2011," accessed January 31, 2012, http://bls.gov/ncs/ebs/benefits/2011/ownership/private/table01a.htm; Hacker, *Great Risk Shift,* 14.

162 **Bankruptcy became the typical route**   Since 2000, there have been waves of corporate bankruptcies in the airline, steel, automotive, energy, and financial industries. PBGC background briefing, press spokesman, December 8, 2010; PBGC databook, table S-5, reported 4,140 corporate pension plans terminated and more than 90 percent of the time, PBGC officials said, bankruptcy was the vehicle for companies' dumping their pension plans. Speicher, email, April 14, 2010.

163 **"The efficient working of American capitalism"**   Jamie Sprayregen, interview excerpt, from *Frontline,* "Can You Afford to Retire?"

163 **"Bankruptcy," retorted Elizabeth Warren**   Excerpt of interview of Elizabeth Warren for the *Frontline* program "Can You Afford to Retire?," February 6, 2006, http://www.pbs.org/frontline.

163 **"It's an absolutely horrific experience"**   Greg Davidowitch, interview excerpt from *Frontline,* "Can You Afford to Retire?"

164 **"It says right here"**   Excerpt of interview of Hugh Ray for the *Frontline* program "Can You Afford to Retire?," February 28, 2006, http://www.pbs.org/frontline.

164 **"Certain players have been made irrelevant"**   Ibid.

165 **"That's the norm"**   Ibid.

165 **CEO Glenn Tilton**   Wong, "Airline Shock Waves."

165 **"No way to exit"**   Sprayregen, interview, "Can You Afford to Retire?"

166 **United's pension funds were . . . in the red**   Pension Benefit Guaranty Corporation background briefing, December 8, 2010.

166 **Corporate pensions were underfunded**   Excerpt of interview of Bradley Belt for the *Frontline* program "Can You Afford to Retire?," February 10, 2006.

167 **"I wouldn't call it cheap"**   Jamie Sprayregen, interview excerpt from *Frontline* program "Can You Afford to Retire?"

167 **Tilton preserved his own $4.5 million retirement benefit**   Glenn Tilton, testimony responding to Sen. Ron Wyden, Senate Finance Com-

mittee hearing, June 7, 2005. http://finance.senate.gov/hearings/hearing/download/?id=d028276c-611f-447e-a266-f3b1cd6a62c6.

168 **"You are juggling all the time"** Robin Gilinger, interview, August 5, 2010.

168 **By Gilinger's calculations . . . United's bankruptcy** Gilinger, interview, August 5, 2010.

168 **The uncertainty** Excerpt of interview of Robin Gilinger for the *Frontline* program "Can You Afford to Retire?," March 15, 2006, http://www.pbs.org/frontline.

168 **"I feel very uneasy"** Gilinger, interview, August 5, 2010.

169 **"You'd do six hundred miles a day"** O'Neill, interview, July 20, 2010.

169 **"Twenty-two years on [the] graveyard shift"** Ibid.

CHAPTER 12: 401(k)'S: DO-IT-YOURSELF

170 **Can you really afford to retire?** "Can You Afford to Retire?" PBS *Frontline,* May 16, 2006, http://www.pbs.org.

170 **"A million people"** Teresa Ghilarducci, interview, December 22, 2010.

170 **"Left to their own devices"** Eric Schurenberg, "The 401(k) Has Failed. Admit It," *Huffington Post,* July 14, 2009.

170 **"I would blow up"** Ted Benna, quoted in Jeremy Olshan, " 'Father' of the 401(k)'s Tough Love," *WSJ SmartMoney,* November 22, 2011, http://blogs.smartmoney.com.

171 **Like many arcane technical provisions** Excerpt of interview of David Wray, president, Profit Sharing/401(k) Council of America for the *Frontline* program "Can You Afford to Retire?," February 17, 2006, http://www.pbs.org/frontline.

171 **It was a classic Washington move** Excerpt of interview of Dallas Salisbury, EBRI president for the *Frontline* program "Can You Afford to Retire?," December 1, 2005, http://www.pbs.org/frontline.

172 **"The technology and methodology"** Excerpt of interview of Bob Reynolds, vice president of Fidelity Funds, for the *Frontline* program "Can You Afford to Retire?," http://www.pbs.org/frontline.

172 **"It had a lot of sex appeal"** Excerpt of interview of Brooks Hamilton for the *Frontline* program "Can You Afford to Retire?," February 23, 2006, http://www.pbs.org/frontline.

172 **401(k) plans grew from 7 million people** U.S. Department of Labor, "Private Pension Plan Bulletin Historical Tables and Graphs," December 2011, table E20, "Number of 401(k) Plans, Total Participants, Active Participants, Assets, Contributions, and Benefits Payments, 1984–2009," http://www.dol.gov/ebsa/pdf/historicaltables.pdf.

172 **"There was a sea change"** Brooks Hamilton, interview, December 8, 2010.

173 **Their secret was** Excerpt of interview of Brian Conner for the *Frontline* program "Can You Afford to Retire?," February 26, 2006, http://www.pbs.org/frontline.

174 **"If I had started earlier"** Excerpt of interview of Gil Thibeau for the *Frontline* program "Can You Afford to Retire?," February 22, 2006, http://www.pbs.org/frontline.

174 **When he retired** Gil Thibeau, interview, August 5, 2010.

174 **"My assumption was"** Excerpt of interview of Winson and Bess Crabb for the *Frontline* program "Can You Afford to Retire?," February 22, 2006, http://www.pbs.org/frontline.

177 **"In every case, the 20 percent"** Brooks Hamilton, interview excerpt, from *Frontline* program "Can You Afford to Retire?"

177 **"I label this [the] 'yield disparity' "** Ibid.

178 **The 401(k) track record** Jack VanDerhei, email, January 5, 2012.

178 **The typical 401(k) nest egg** Ibid., January 12, 2012.

178 **The Center for Retirement Research** Andrew Eschtruth, Center for Retirement Research at Boston College, email, October 31, 2011.

178 **Seriously "at risk"** VanDerhei, interview, December 10, 2010. See also Jack VanDerhei, "Measuring Retirement Income Adequacy: Calculating Realistic Income Replacement Rates," EBRI Issue Brief No. 297, September 2006, http://www.ebri.org; and VanDerhei, "Evaluation of the Adequacy and Structure of U.S. Voluntary Retirement Plans, with Special Emphasis on 401(k) Plans," Employee Benefits Research Institute, *Benefits Quarterly* (Third Quarter 2010).

178 **More than half of American families** Alicia Munnell, interview, July 9, 2010; and Andrew Eschtruth, emails, January 23 and October 30, 2011. Economists and other experts at Boston College created the National Retirement Risk Index (NRRI) to measure the adequacy of retirement savings by individual households in their 401(k)'s, IRAs, Social Security, and other savings. The index compares the ability, at retirement age, of individuals and households to generate 70 percent of the final pre-retirement income, a target chosen because the financial industry estimates that is what is needed to maintain one's standard of living after retirement. Munnell describes the NRRI as a conservative index, not intended to exaggerate the problem. It uses average life span expectations and average market returns on a balanced bond-stock retirement account. See Alicia Munnell, Anthony Webb, Francesca Golub-Sass, et al., "Long Term Care Costs and the National Retirement Risk Index," Brief No. 9–7 (Chestnut Hill, MA: Center for Retirement Research at Boston College, March 2009); and Alicia Munnell, Anthony Webb, and Francesca Golub-Sass, "The National Retirement Risk Index: After the Crash," Brief No. 9–22 (Chestnut Hill, MA: Center for Retirement Research at Boston College, October 2009).

179 **"Not going to be penniless"** Munnell, interview, December 8, 2010.

180 **Failure to sign up** Press release, "54th Annual Survey of Profit Sharing and 401(k) Plans," Profit Sharing/401(k) Council of America, October 11, 2011, http://www.psca.org.

180 **Low contributions** Anne Tergesen, "401(k) Law Suppresses Saving for Retirement," *The Wall Street Journal,* July 7, 2011.

180 **Only 10 percent** Ibid.; Eschtruth, email, January 23, 2011; see also Popula-

tion Reference Bureau, "U.S. Labor Force Trends," *Population Bulletin* 63, no. 2 (June 2008); Alicia Munnell, interview, February 6, 2006, transcript, "Can You Afford to Retire?," PBS *Frontline*, May 16, 2006, http://www.pbs.org.

180 **Many other people** Excerpt of interview of Alicia Munnell, interview for the *Frontline* program "Can You Afford to Retire?," February 6, 2006, http://www.pbs.org/frontline.

181 **"Everything! Everything has gone wrong . . ."** Ibid.

181 **Plan holders lost an estimated $2.8 trillion** Eschtruth, email, November 7, 2011.

181 **Many employers cut back, too** "In Need of Cash, More Companies Cut 401(k) Match," *The New York Times*, December 21, 2008; David Kansas, "Has the 401(k) Failed?" CNNMoney.com/*Fortune*, June 16, 2009.

181 **Overall, one in five** "Good News for 401(k) Plans, Just in Time for the Holidays," Profit Sharing/401(k) Council of America, December 17, 2010, http://www.psca.org.

182 **Corporate America was still pinching** "Retirement Plans Make Comeback, with Limits," *The Wall Street Journal*, June 14, 2011.

182 **People had totally unrealistic expectations** John Bogle, interview, December 12, 2010.

182 **Cost investors $8 trillion** John Bogle, testimony, House Committee on Education and Labor, February 24, 2009, http://johncbogle.com/wordpress/wp-content/uploads/2009/03/statement2009.pdf ; Hamilton, interview, December 8, 2010.

183 **Don't reap the full benefit** Ibid.

183 **That is why Bogle** Ibid.

184 **Most people are shocked** VanDerhei, email, July 20, 2010.

184 **Sets slightly lower targets** Eschtruth, email, December 15, 2010.

185 **"I got hit like everyone else"** Rich Kidner, interview, July 12, 2010.

185 **"Where am I going to get"** Ibid.

185 **But the experts at EBRI** Dallas Salisbury, interview excerpt from *Frontline*, "Can You Afford to Retire?," November 9, 2005.

185 **Put the figure higher** Brooks Hamilton, interview excerpt from *Frontline*, "Can You Afford to Retire?"

185 **Add it all up** Andrea Coombes, "U.S. Retirement Income Deficit: $6.6 Trillion," *WSJ MarketWatch*, September 15, 2010, http://www.marketwatch.com.

186 **"That $6.6 trillion"** Anthony Webb, interview, January 20, 2011.

186 **The corporate pension shortfall** The Pension Benefit Guaranty Corporation gave an estimate of $504 billion. *Pension Insurance Data Book* 2009 14 (Summer 2010): table S-49, http://www.pbgc.gov.

186 **City and state pension funds** Peter Whoriskey, "Economists: State, Local Pension Funds Understate Shortfall by $1.5 Trillion or More," *The Washington Post*, March 3, 2011.

186 **"Our nation's system"** Bogle, interview, December 12, 2010.

186 **"Now this monster"** Benna, in Olshan, "Father of the 401(k)'s Tough Love."

187 **Financial professionals** Thomas C. Scott, "The Risk-Averse Future," in "Room for Debate," *The New York Times,* online running commentary on the news, March 25, 2009, http://www.nytimes.com/roomfordebate.

187 **401(k) system can be made to work** Press release, "54th Annual Survey of Profit Sharing and 401(k) Plans."

187 **Has become like a roulette wheel** Schurenberg, "The 401(k) Has Failed."

188 **Nearly three out of four** "Working in Retirement Is the New Normal for Middle Class Americans, Wells Fargo Retirement Survey Finds," Business Wire, December 8, 2010, http://www.businesswire.com.

188 **Older workers (fifty-five and up)** Maria Heidkamp, Nicole Corre, and Carl E. Van Horn, "The 'New Unemployables,' " Issue Brief No. 25 (Chestnut Hill, MA: Sloan Center on Aging & Work at Boston College, November 2010).

188 **Even among people seventy-five and up** Kelly Greene and Anne Tergesen, "More Elderly Find They Can't Afford Not to Work," *The Wall Street Journal,* January 21, 2012.

188 **"Baby boomers will be facing"** Excerpt of interview of Teresa Ghilarducci, for the *Frontline* program "Can You Afford to Retire?," February 17, 2006, http://www.pbs.org/frontline.

190 **"It's just not adequate"** Excerpt of interview of Anna Sullivan for the *Frontline* program "Can You Afford to Retire?," February 13, 2006, http:// www.pbs.org/frontline.

190 **"This is a national problem"** Karen Friedman, interview, December 6, 2010.

190 **"We need a new tier"** Munnell, interview, December 8, 2010.

190 **Jack Bogle advocates** Bogle, testimony, February 24, 2009.

190 **Participation by all employees** Teresa Ghilarducci, testimony, House Education and Labor Committee, October 7, 2008; Jacob F. Kirkegaard, "Stop Rewarding the Wealthy," Peterson Institute for International Economics, in "Room for Debate," *The New York Times,* online commentary, March 25, 2009, http://www.nytimes.com/roomfordebate.

CHAPTER 13: HOUSING HEIST

192 **"Right here in America"** President George W. Bush, remarks on home ownership, Atlanta, GA, June 17, 2002, http://georgewbush-whitehouse .archives.gov.

192 **"I didn't think I made enough money"** Eliseo Guardado, interview, October 3, 2010.

192 **"The banks are playing to brokers"** Kathryn Keller, interview, August 9, 2010.

193 **Even so, she got stung** Bre Heller, interview, August 4, 2010.

193 **"I am a victim"** Bre Heller, email to Florida Attorney General's Office, October 22, 2008.

194 **Bre Heller figured her loan**   Heller, interview, August 4, 2010.

196 **Was deep "under water"**   CoreLogic reported that 11.2 million homes, 24 percent of residential properties with mortgages, were in negative equity on March 31, 2010; CoreLogic, "Real Estate News and Trends: New Core-Logic Data Shows Decline in Negative Equity," media alert, May 10, 2010, www.corelogic.com/about-us/researchtrends/asset_upload_file155_1435 .pdf.

196 **"Considering that I lost $250,000"**   Heller, interview, August 4, 2010.

196 **The irony in that episode**   Robin Updike, " 'Friend of the Family'— Washington Mutual New TV Ads Focus on 'The Little Guy,' " *Seattle Times,* September 3, 1991.

197 **Killinger was warned in advance**   Lee Lannoye, interviews, August 27, 2010, and September 27, 2010. Sen. Carl Levin, summarizing the investigation of Washington Mutual by the Senate Permanent Investigations Subcommittee, identified WaMu's purchase of Long Beach Mortgage as the pivotal change in Washington Mutual's loan strategy from prudent conventional lending to borrowers with solid credit records to high-risk subprime lending with the goal of profiting by selling those loans to Wall Street, leading to development of WaMu's own high-risk, high-profit Option-ARM loans. As Levin put it, "WaMu built its conveyor belt of toxic mortgages to feed Wall Street's appetite for mortgage-backed securities." James Vanasek, former chief risk officer at Washington Mutual, testified that bank insiders had warned of the dangers of WaMu's new high-risk loan strategy. According to Vanasek, "There is ample evidence in the record to substantiate the fact that it was clear that the high-risk profile of the entire industry, to include Washington Mutual, was recognized by some but ignored by many. Suffice it to say, meeting growth objectives to satisfy the quarterly expectations of Wall Street and investors led to mistakes in judgment by the banks and the mortgage lending company executives." The subcommittee's ranking Republican, Sen. Tom Coburn of Oklahoma, echoed Levin's assessment. Coburn said that under Killinger, "WaMu's corporate culture had no place for individuals concerned about high-risk lending, but instead brushed them aside and ignored them." Levin and Coburn, opening statements, and Vanasek, testimony, Senate Permanent Subcommittee on Investigations, hearing on Washington Mutual, April 13, 2010, http://www.hsgac.senate .gov/subcommittees/investigations.

197 **Subprime business had to be predatory to succeed**   Lannoye interview, August 27, 2010.

197 **Predatory lending means finding uneducated**   Ibid.

197 **Twice, Lannoye fought**   Lannoye, interview, September 27, 2010.

198 **Congress had opened the door**   The Depository Institutions Deregulation and Monetary Control Act of 1980 effectively abolished state usury laws limiting rates of interest on first-lien mortgages.

198 **Fannie Mae . . . Freddie Mac**   Gretchen Morgenson and Joshua Rosner, *Reckless Endangerment: How Outsized Ambition, Greed, and Corruption Led to Economic Armageddon* (New York: Times Books, 2011), 34–40.

199 **Long Beach loans made in 2003**   Federal Deposit Insurance Corporation, report to Washington Mutual Bank's board of directors, January 13, 2004, and visitation report by FDIC and Washington State director of banks to Washington Mutual, October 14, 2003, Exhibit 8B, Senate Permanent Subcommittee on Investigations, hearing chaired by Senator Carl Levin, April 13, 2010, http://www.hsgac.senate.gov/subcommittees/investigations. Hereafter "Levin subcommittee."

199 **Long Beach's record was so bad**   Ibid. Also, Washington Mutual internal email memo detailing Fitch rating agency review of Long Beach loan performance, April 14, 2005, Exhibit 8a, Levin subcommittee, April 13, 2010.

199 **"We were paid by the total volume"**   Heller, interview, August 9, 2010.

200 **"A lot of coaching takes place"**   Ibid.

200 **"It was a fast-buck business"**   Michael Lewis, *The Big Short: Inside the Doomsday Machine* (New York: W. W. Norton & Co., 2010), 9.

202 **"Loan officers dropped their duty"**   Heller, interview, August 9, 2010.

202 **The obvious potential for fraud**   Bre Heller, email, November 2, 2010.

202 **One-third of the bank's refinancing loans**   Cheryl Feltgen, internal Washington Mutual memo, March 17, 2007, Exhibit 40B, Levin subcommittee.

203 **"The only way to repay"**   Lannoye, interview, August 27, 2010.

203 **"The big thing was the sign"**   Heller, interview, August 9, 2010.

204 **"A product that was exotic"**   Kathryn Keller, interview, August 9, 2010.

204 **"One guy called me"**   Eliseo Guardado, interview, October 3, 2010.

205 **The Congressional Funding office was closed**   Freddy Cova, interview, November 11, 2011; Brian Rios, interview with Owen Smith, January 9, 2012.

206 **"It was a nightmare"**   Guardado, interview, October 3, 2010.

206 **"There was a high demand for subprime"**   Lili Sotello, interview, August 30, 2010.

207 **"Waves of defaults"**   Ibid.

208 **"The fraud was there"**   Diane Kosch, interview, August 22, 2010.

208 **"Loan officers were fired"**   Ibid.

209 **John Ngo, a senior loan officer**   U.S. Department of Justice, news release, December 17, 2007, Exhibit 82, Levin subcommittee, hearing April 13, 2010, www.hsgac.senate.gov/public/_files/Financial_Crisis/041310Exhibits.pdf.

209 **55 percent of subprime borrowers**   "Subprime Debacle Traps Even Very Credit-Worthy," *The Wall Street Journal,* December 3, 2007; "Policing Main Street," *Newsweek,* July 25, 2010.

210 **The floating-rate mortgage**   Heller, interview, August 4, 2010.

212 **Terboss spent $200,000**   John Terboss, interview, September 2, 2010.

212 **Terboss shared with me**   Homegate Mortgage Company, fax letter, "Proposal for John Terboss, Prepared by Bob Norrris, 10/03/07," provided by Terboss.

213 **"It was a very strange closing"**   Terboss, interview, September 2, 2010.

213 "I immediately called the bank" Ibid.
213 "This is not how it was represented" John Terboss, fax letter to Washington Mutual, December 11, 2007.
214 "It's as if the broker" David Leen, interview, August 30, 2010.
214 "I learned that the banking industry" Terboss, interview, September 17, 2010.

CHAPTER 14: THE GREAT WEALTH SHIFT

216 "The American people" Morgenson and Rosner, *Reckless Endangerment,* xiv.
216 "Our present economic crisis" John C. Bogle, testimony, House Committee on Education and Labor, February 24, 2009.
216 It powered the growth of debt Frank J. Fabozzi, Anand K. Bhattacharya, and William S. Berliner, *Mortgage-Backed Securities* (Hoboken, NJ: John Wiley & Sons, 2007), preface.
217 Greenspan dismissed the risk Alan Greenspan, remarks, annual convention of Independent Community Bankers of America, Orlando, FL, March 4, 2003.
217 "Greatest global financial crisis ever" Alan Greenspan, citing Federal Reserve data, in "Activism," *International Finance* 14, no. 1 (Spring 2011), http://www.cfr.org.
217 "I found a flaw in the model" Alan Greenspan, testimony, House Committee on Oversight and Government Reform, October 23, 2008.
218 Greenspan went on to admit that the crash Greenspan, citing Federal Reserve data, in "Activism."
219 "A shift in the mortgage product" James Grant, *Mr. Market Miscalculates: The Bubble Years and Beyond* (Mt. Jackson, VA: Axios Press, 2008), 138.
219 Greenspan hailed this trend Alan Greenspan and James Kennedy, "Sources and Uses of Equity Extracted from Homes," Finance and Economics Discussion Series, working paper, March 2007, http://www.federalreserve .gov.
219 Greenspan welcomed that mountain of borrowing Greenspan, remarks at annual convention of the Independent Community Bankers of America, Orlando, Florida (via satellite), March 4, 2003, http://www.federalreserve.gov.
219 "Were it not for this phenomenon" Alan Greenspan, testimony before the Joint Economic Committee, November 13, 2002, www.federalreserve .gov/boarddocs/testimony/2002/20021113/default.htm.
220 American homeowners lost trillions Dean Baker, *False Profits: Recovering from the Bubble Economy* (San Francisco: Berrett-Koehler, 2010), 2; also Dean Baker, co-director of the Center for Economic and Policy Research, interview, October 15, 2010.
220 The homeowners' share of housing wealth Board of Governors of the Federal Reserve System, "Flow of Funds Accounts of the United States, Annual Flows and Outstandings," chart B.100, 1985–1994, 1995–2004, 2005–2010, and Current (fourth quarter 2011), March 8, 2012, http://www

.federalreserve.gov/releases/z1/Current/annuals/a2005–2010.pdf; and 2011
figures from http://www.federalreserve.gov/releases/z1/Current/z1/pdf.

220 **Homeowners lost nearly a 30 percent stake** Dean Baker, interview, October 25, 2010.

221 **Nearly one-fifth of older boomers** Baker, *False Profits,* 46–56.

222 **Greenspan, who credited this process** Alan Greenspan, "Risk Transfer and Financial Stability," remarks, Federal Reserve Board of Chicago, May 5, 2005.

223 **"Ordinarily, the instinct"** Johnson and Kwak, *13 Bankers,* 130–31.

223 **Vastly poorer—$9 trillion poorer** Federal Reserve System, "Flow of Funds Accounts," chart B.100, 1985–1994, 1995–2004, 2005–2010, and Current (fourth quarter 2011), March 8, 2012, reports a homeowner loss of equity from $15.3 trillion in 2005 to $6.2 trillion at the end of 2011, figures adjusted for inflation to 2012 values, http://www.federalreserve.gov/releases/z1/Current/z1.pdf.

224 **"This elimination of usury law ceilings"** Edward Gramlich, *Subprime Mortgages: America's Latest Boom and Bust* (Washington, DC: Urban Institute Press, 2007), 16.

224 **It also permitted something never allowed** Johnson and Kwak, *13 Bankers,* 72; Lewis, *Big Short,* 51.

224 **"The most important legislation for financial institutions"** President Ronald Reagan, signing remarks, Public Law 97–320, October 15, 1982, http://www.Reagan.utexas.edu.

224 **Mortgages loaded "with poisonous features"** Gretchen Morgenson, "Some Bankers Never Learn," *The New York Times,* July 31, 2011.

224 **This law sanctioned the "securitization" of mortgages** Fabozzi, Bhattacharya, and Berliner, *Mortgage-Backed Securities,* preface.

225 **Lewis Ranieri, a legendary Salomon Brothers trader** Johnson and Kwak, *13 Bankers,* 72–76; Lewis, *Big Short,* 8.

225 **Greenspan instituted** William A. Fleckenstein with Frederick Sheehan, *Greenspan's Bubbles: The Age of Ignorance at the Federal Reserve* (New York: McGraw-Hill, 2008), 120, 128; Board of Governors of the Federal Reserve System, "Open Market Operations Archive: Intended Federal Funds Rate, Change and Level," accessed March 19, 2012, https://www.federalreserve.gov/monetarypolicy/openmarket_archive.htm; and https://www.federalreserve.gov/monetarypolicy/openmarket.htm#calendars.

226 **It gave housing a kick start** Asha Bangalore, Northern Trust Company, "Housing Market—Another Information Tidbit," May 23, 2005, www.northerntrust.com/library/econ_research/daily/us/dd052305.pdf.

226 **More than $1 trillion a year** Baker, *False Profits,* 34.

226 **A "rocket taking off"** Robert J. Shiller, *Irrational Exuberance,* 2nd ed. (New York: Broadway Books, 2005), 12.

226 **In the 114 years** Ibid., 12, 20.

227 **But Greenspan took heart** Alan Greenspan, remarks, Federal Reserve Community Affairs Research Conference, April 8, 2005.

227 **"Many homeowners might have saved"** Alan Greenspan, "Understanding Household Debt Obligations," speech to Credit Union National Association, Governmental Affairs Conference, February 23, 2004.

227 **He led the Fed through fourteen interest rate hikes** Board of Governors of the Federal Reserve System, http://www.federalreserve.gov/monetary policy/default.htm. The first raise on June 30, 2004, increased the rate to 1.25 percent, and the final one, on Greenspan's last day as Fed chairman, on January 31, 2006, raised the rate to 4.5 percent.

228 **Housing prices from the late 1990s** Shiller, *Irrational Exuberance,* 13.

228 **"The growth of *housing prices*"** Johnson and Kwak, *13 Bankers,* 112.

228 **Massive defaults were inevitable** Shiller, *Irrational Exuberance,* 13.

228 **Gramlich cautioned Greenspan** Gramlich, *Subprime Mortgages,* 6; Gramlich, "Booms and Busts: The Case of Subprime Mortgages," lecture, Federal Reserve Bank of Kansas City symposium, August 30–September 1, 2007, 106, published in *Economic Review* (Fourth Quarter 2007), Federal Reserve Bank of Kansas City, http://www.kansascityfed.org/publicat/econrev/PDF/4q07Gramlich.pdf.

228 **51 percent of subprime loans** Gramlich, *Subprime Mortgages,* 21; Greg Ip, "Did Greenspan Add to Subprime Woes?" *The Wall Street Journal,* June 9, 2007.

228 **"Like a city with a murder law"** Gramlich, "Booms and Busts."

228 **"What we forgot"** Johnson and Kwak, *13 Bankers,* 142–44.

228 **No Bush official wanted** Jo Becker, Sheryl Gay Stolberg, and Stephen Labaton, "White House Philosophy Stoked Mortgage Bonfire," *The New York Times,* December 21, 2008.

229 **Mortgage debt had reached dangerous levels** David Cay Johnston, "Business; In Debate Over Housing Bubble, a Winner Also Loses," *The New York Times,* April 11, 2004.

229 **Shiller's warning was more stark** Robert J. Shiller, "Household Reactions to Changes in Housing Wealth," Discussion Paper 1459 (New Haven, CT: Cowles Foundation, Yale University, April 2004), http://cowles.econ.yale.edu.

229 **"May be the biggest bubble in U.S. history"** Robert J. Shiller, cited in Paul Krugman, "Running Out of Bubbles," *The New York Times,* May 27, 2005.

229 **"When home prices do start down"** Fleckenstein, *Greenspan's Bubbles,* 145.

229 **Greenspan dismissed talk of a housing "bubble"** Alan Greenspan, "The Economic Outlook," opening statement, Joint Economic Committee, U.S. Congress, June 9, 2005; Johnson and Kwak, *13 Bankers,* 147.

229 **"Greenspan's policies at the Fed"** "Perry's Public Service," *The Wall Street Journal,* August 18, 2011.

230 **Bank CEOs such as Killinger** "Home Loans Discussion," confidential memo from home loans president David Schneider to Washington Mutual board of directors, April 18, 2006; Exhibit 3, Levin subcommittee, hearing April 13, 2010.

230 **Worried about the high level of risk**   Kerry Killinger, email to James Vanasek, March 10, 2005, Exhibit 78, Levin subcommittee.

230 **Wall Street stock analysts asked Killinger**   Washington Mutual, pricing guides, November 2, 2006, belie Killinger's contention about risk control. In November 2006, the bank was still offering huge bonuses to brokers for steering borrowers into high-risk Option ARMs.

230 **"You've seen us sell"**   Kerry Killinger, Strategic Decisions Conference, Sanford C. Bernstein & Co., June 1, 2005.

231 **The highest loan delinquency rate of any bank**   Office of Thrift Supervision, internal memo, April 14, 2005, Exhibit 8a, Levin subcommittee, April 13, 2010; James A. Vanasek, chief risk management officer, Washington Mutual, 1999–2005, statement to Levin subcommittee hearing, April 13, 2010. By comparison, Vanasek reported losses on fixed-rated thirty-year mortgages as less than one-tenth of 1 percent.

231 **Had to be shut down entirely**   Senator Levin, opening statement, hearing, April 13, 2010; see also memorandum to Washington Mutual Board of Directors from General Auditor Randy Melby, April 17, 2006, Exhibit 10, Levin subcommittee, April 13, 2010.

231 **Wall Street was so slow to detect**   Senator Levin, transcript, hearing, April 13, 2010, Senate Permanent Subcommittee on Investigations, 66, citing SEC filings by Washington Mutual, Levin noted that the bank's Option ARM sales had been $67 billion in 2004 and $63 billion in 2005.

231 **Option ARMs had been recklessly approved**   Ronald Cathcart, chief risk management officer, Washington Mutual, December 2005–April 2008, prepared statement, April 13, 2010, Levin subcommittee hearing.

231 **"Employee malfeasance"**   Memo to James Vanasek, Washington Mutual, November 17, 2005, Exhibit 22a, Levin subcommittee; Retail Risk Overview, Washington Mutual Credit Risk Management, November 16, 2005, with attached chain of email messages, Exhibit 22b, Levin subcommittee, April 13, 2010.

231 **The prime offenders**   Final report, "Wall Street and the Financial Crisis: Anatomy of a Financial Collapse," April 13, 2011, Levin subcommittee, 95–101.

231 **"Extremely high incidence of confirmed fraud"**   Tim Bates, email to James Vanasek, August 30, 2004, Exhibit 23b, Levin subcommittee; "Memorandum of Results: AIG/UG and OTS Allegation of Loan Frauds Originated by [name deleted]," Washington Mutual, April 4, 2008, Exhibit 24, Levin Subcommittee, April 13, 2010; Ann Hedger, Office of Thrift Supervision examiner, "Loan Fraud Investigation," to David Schneider, president of home loans, Washington Mutual, June 19, 2008, Exhibit 12a, Levin subcommittee, hearing, April 6, 2010, www.hsgac.senate.gov/public/_files/Financial_Crisis/041610Exhibits.pdf.

232 **"Found to be completely fabricated"**   Washington Mutual, string of emails, August 29, 2005, to November 19, 2005, and December 14, 2007, Exhibits 23a and 23b, Levin subcommittee, April 13, 2010.

232 **But no firings or shake-ups**   Loan Fraud Investigation Report, Washing-

ton Mutual, January 7, 2007, Exhibit 25, Levin subcommittee; Risk Mitigation and Mortgage Fraud Review, September 8, 2008, Exhibit 34, Levin subcommittee, April 13, 2010.

232 **Insurance giant AIG** "Wall Street and the Financial Crisis: Anatomy of a Financial Collapse," *Majority and Minority Staff Report,* Senate Permanent Subcommittee on Investigations, April 13, 2011, 96–101.

232 **"Elements of fraud found by AIG"** Loan Fraud Investigation Report, Washington Mutual, Jan. 7, 2007, Exhibit 25; Risk Mitigation and Mortgage Fraud Review, Sept. 8, 2008, Exhibit 34, Levin subcommittee, April 13, 2010.

232 **Still, WaMu's top brass** *Majority and Minority Staff Report,* "Wall Street and the Financial Crisis," April 13, 2011, 63.

232 **WaMu's leaders showered Fragoso** "Awards Night Show Script," Washington Mutual Home Loans President's Club 2005—Maui, Exhibits 63a and 63b, Levin subcommittee, April 13, 2010.

232 **Insider fraud was pervasive** Federal Housing Finance Agency Inspector General Report, 2003, cited in "Fannie Mae Knew Early of Abuses, Report Says," *The New York Times,* October 4, 2011.

232 **The FBI first publicly warned** "FBI Warns of Mortgage Fraud 'Epidemic,' " CNN, September 17, 2004, http://articles.cnn.com.

232 **Fraud was epidemic** Richard Bitner, *Confessions of a Subprime Lender: An Insider's Tale of Greed, Fraud, and Ignorance* (Hoboken, NJ: John Wiley & Sons, 2008), 39–72.

233 *"More than 70 percent"* Richard Bitner, prepared statement, Financial Crisis Inquiry Commission, April 7, 2010, http://fcic-static.law.stanford .edu/cdn_media/fcic-testimony/2010–0407-Transcript.pdf.

233 **" 'Arts and crafts weekends' "** William Black, interview, September 26, 2010.

233 **"Open invitations to fraudsters"** "Eighth Period Mortgage Fraud Case Report to Mortgage Bankers Association," Mortgage Assets Research Institute, April 2006.

233 *"Fraud or misrepresentation in almost every file"* Fitch Ratings, "The Impact of Poor Underwriting Practices and Fraud in Subprime RMBS Performance," November 28, 2007.

234 **Hedge fund managers** In *The Big Short,* Michael Lewis tells the compelling tale of how each of them doped out the ugly reality beneath the mythic conventional wisdom on Wall Street and in Washington and then took the risk of betting against the crowd, and won.

234 **Long Beach Mortgage loans were attractive** Goldman Sachs Flipbook, "Abacus 2007–AC1, $2 Billion Synthetic CDO," February 26, 2007.

234 **Goldman was accused of duplicity** "SEC Accuses Goldman of Fraud in Housing Deal," *The New York Times,* April 17, 2010; "Goldman Pays $550 Million to Settle Fraud Case," *The New York Times,* July 16, 2010.

234 **Paulson had included** "Profiting from the Crash," *The Wall Street Journal,* October 31, 2009.

234 **Goldman's double-dealing** Gretchen Morgenson and Louise Story,

"Banks Bundled Bad Debt, Bet Against It, and Won," *The New York Times,* December 24, 2009.

234 **"It makes me ill"** Greg Smith, "Why I Am Leaving Goldman Sachs," *The New York Times,* March 14, 2012.

235 **Goldman executives took issue** "Public Rebuke of Culture at Goldman Opens Debate," *The New York Times,* March 15, 2012.

235 **"Without those AAA ratings"** "Bringing Down Wall Street as Ratings Let Loose Subprime Scourge," Bloomberg, September 24, 2008, http://www .bloomberg.com; and " 'Race to Bottom' at Moody's, S&P Secured Subprime's Boom, Bust," Bloomberg, September 25, 2008, http://www.bloomberg.com.

235 **A conflict of interest** Eric Kolchinsky, internal Moody's memo, August 28, 2009.

235 **Moody's earnings from exotic financial vehicles** Elliot Blair Smith, "Bringing Down Wall Street as Rating Let Loose Subprime Scourge," Bloomberg, September 24, 2008.

236 **Bernanke said he saw no threat** Binyamin Appelbaum and David Cho, "Fed's Approach to Regulation Left Banks Exposed to Crisis," *The Washington Post,* December 21, 2009; Ben Bernanke, "The Subprime Mortgage Market," speech, Federal Reserve Bank of Chicago, May 17, 2007, http://www.federal reserve.gov.

236 **"When the music stops"** "Citigroup Chief Stays Bullish on Buy-Outs," *Financial Times,* July 9, 2007.

236 **Bond-rating agencies turned thumbs down** "Rate Agencies Move Toward Downgrading Some Mortgage Bonds," *The New York Times,* July 11, 2007; "Ratings Cut Near for Debt Products," *The New York Times,* July 12, 2007; "Market Shock: AAA Rating May be Junk," *The New York Times,* July 20, 2007.

236 **"Caused hundreds of billions of losses"** Eric Kolchinsky, statement to Financial Crisis Inquiry Commission, June 2, 2010.

236 **"Making liars' loans"** Black, interview, September 26, 2010.

236 **Find buyers who didn't yet know the score** Drew DeSilver, "Reckless Strategies Doomed WaMu," *Seattle Times,* December 23, 2009; string of Washington Mutual emails, February 14–20, 2007, Exhibit 40b, Levin subcommittee; Dave Beck, testimony given April 13, 2010, Levin subcommittee.

237 **The bank swooned** "FDIC Crashes WaMu's Birthday Bash," Reuters, September 25, 2008, http://blogs.reuters.com.

237 **Killinger walked off with more than $100 million** Washington Mutual Securities Litigation, amended class action complaint, U.S. Western District Court, Seattle, WA, June 15, 2009, http://www.blbglaw.com.

237 **"Clearly criminal in certain cases"** Alan Greenspan, remarks, Federal Reserve Bank of Atlanta, November 6, 2010, http://www.federalreserve.gov; http://dailybail.com/home/bombshell-video-greenspan-admits-to-rampant -fraud-illegal-ac.html.

238 **Did not trigger criminal action** Joe Nocera, "Biggest Fish Face Little Risk of Being Caught," *The New York Times,* February 26, 2011.

238 **Countrywide, an aggressive subprime lender**   "Countrywide Will Settle a Bias Suit," *The New York Times,* December 21, 2011.

238 **Angelo Mozilo, agreed**   "Lending Magnate Settles Fraud Case," *The New York Times,* October 15, 2010. In an email in April 2006, Mozilo had told a business colleague that "in all my years in the business, I have never seen a more toxic product" than the subprime loans that Countrywide was then selling.

238 **Mozilo's personal fine**   "Big Payday Awaits Chairman After Countrywide Sale," *The Washington Post,* January 12, 2008.

238 **Washington Mutual was targeted**   "Feds Sue WaMu Ex-CEO Killinger and Two Others," *Seattle Times,* March 17, 2011; "F.D.I.C. Sues Ex-Chief of Big Bank That Failed," *The New York Times,* March 17, 2011.

238 **The bank executives scoffed**   "WaMu Ex-CEO: Lawsuit 'Unworthy of the Government,' " *The Wall Street Journal,* March 17, 2011.

238 **FDIC collected $190 million in damages**   Gretchen Morgenson, "Slapped Wrists at WaMu," *The New York Times,* Sunday financial section, December 18, 2011.

238 **"Bank executives can beat the system"**   Senator Carl Levin, office press release, "Statement on Settlement of Claims Against Washington Mutual Bank," December 13, 2011, http://levin.senate.gov.

238 **The pattern was familiar**   Edward Wyatt, "Promises Made, and Remade, in S.E.C. Fraud Cases," *The New York Times,* November 8, 2011.

239 **Going back to multibillion-dollar profits**   Zachary A. Goldfarb, "Wall Street's Resurgent Prosperity Frustrates Its Claims and Obama's," *The Washington Post,* November 7, 2011.

239 **A foreclosure assembly line**   "Only 1 in 4 Got Mortgage Relief," *The Wall Street Journal,* February 28, 2011.

239 **Found themselves stuck**   "Banks Amass Glut of Homes, Chilling Sales," *The New York Times,* May 23, 2011.

239 **Banks agreed in February 2012**   Nelson D. Schwartz and Sheila Dewan, "States Negotiate $26 Billion Agreement for Homeowners," *The New York Times,* February 9, 2012, and Nelson D. Schwartz and Julie Creswell, "Mortgage Plan Gives Billions to Homeowners, but with Exceptions," *The New York Times,* February 10, 2012.

240 **Only 894,000 were ultimately helped**   Zachary A. Goldfarb, "Obama's Efforts to Aid Homeowners, Boost Housing Market, Fall Far Short of Goal," *The Washington Post,* October 23, 2011; "Home Lending Revamp Planned," *The Wall Street Journal,* October 24, 2011.

240 **Compounded the problem by moving slowly**   Annie Lowrey, "Treasury Faulted in Effort to Relive Homeowners," *The New York Times,* April 12, 2012.

240 **The banking lobby succeeded**   Stephen Labaton, "Ailing Banks Still Field Strong Lobby at Capitol," *The New York Times,* June 5, 2009.

240 **"Hard to believe"**   Senator Richard Durbin, interview with Ray Hanania, WJJG, Chicago, April 27, 2009.

241 **The experts have come up with ideas**   Floyd Norris, "Time to Accelerate

the House Recovery," *The New York Times*, December 2, 2011; Ezra Klein, "Mass Refinancing: The 'Biggest Thing' Obama Can Do Without Congress," *The Washington Post,* January 10, 2012; "President to Offer Way for Easing Home Debt," *The New York Times,* January 25, 2012.

241 **Give a shot in the arm to the economy**   Lawrence Summers, "Why the Housing Burden Stalls America's Economic Recovery," *Financial Times,* October 23, 2011, http://www.ft.com; Paul Krugman, "It's Not a Banking Problem," *The New York Times* blog, May 13, 2011, http://krugman.blogs.nytimes.com.

241 **"We won't come back big time until"**   Warren Buffett, interview transcript, PBS, *Charlie Rose,* August 17, 2011, http://www.cnbc.com.

CHAPTER 15: OFFSHORING THE DREAM

242 **"Wal-Mart and China have"**   Excerpt of interview of Gary Gereffi for the *Frontline* program "Is Wal-Mart Good for America?," September 9, 2004, http://www.pbs.org/frontline.

242 **"Over the past 8 years"**   Dan Slane, "On the U.S.-China Relationship & Manufacturing," presentation, Ohio State University, October 25, 2010, http://www.omi.osu.edu.

243 **Rubbermaid made them**   "America's Most Admired Company—It's Rubbermaid," *Fortune,* February 7, 1994.

243 **"A lot of this stuff"**   Excerpt of interview of Larry Ptak for the *Frontline* program "Is Wal-Mart Good for America?," June 16, 2004, http://www.pbs.org/frontline.

243 **" 'We're shutting it down' "**   Excerpt of interview of Harry Frank for the *Frontline* program "Is Wal-Mart Good for America?," June 16, 2004.

243 **"They're from all over"**   Excerpt of interview of Scott Mihalic for the *Frontline* program "Is Wal-Mart Good for America?," June 16, 2004, http://www.pbs.org/frontline.

244 **"You could have bought a home for nothing"**   Larry Ptak, interview, June 16, 2010.

244 **Rubbermaid's most important customer**   Excerpt of interview of Stanley Gault for the *Frontline* program "Is Wal-Mart Good for America?," http://www.pbs.org/frontline.

245 **Can also cut a supplier to ribbons**   "Rubbermaid Shares Plunge as Rising Raw Material Prices Cut Profits," Bloomberg Business News-AP, *Milwaukee Journal Sentinel,* September 5, 1996.

245 **Rubbermaid was intent**   Excerpt of interview of Wolfgang Schmitt for the *Frontline* program "Is Wal-Mart Good for America?," June 17, 2004, http://www.pbs.org/frontline.

245 **"We're just not gonna take it"**   Excerpt of interview of Carol Troyer for the *Frontline* program "Is Wal-Mart Good for America?," June 3, 2004, http://www.pbs.org/frontline.

246 **"You don't *understand*"**   Excerpt of interview of John Mariotti for the *Frontline* program "Is Wal-Mart Good for America?," March 25, 2004.

246 **"Signs of the decline of Rubbermaid"**   Ibid.

246 **Pivotal shift of power in American business**   In a series of studies on U.S. job losses to China, Robert E. Scott, senior economist at the Economic Policy Institute, calculated a loss of 2.4 million jobs from 2001 to 2008, another 500,000 jobs in 2010, and a cumulative job loss of 3.5 million to 3.6 million from the 1990s through 2010. Robert E. Scott, "Unfair China Trade Costs Local Jobs: 2.4 Million Jobs Lost, Thousands Displaced in Every U.S. Congressional District," EPI Briefing Paper 260, March 23, 2010, Economic Policy Institute, http://www.epi.org; Scott, "Rising China Trade Deficit Will Cost One-Half Million U.S. Jobs in 2010," EPI Briefing Paper 283, September 20, 2010, Economic Policy Institute, http://www.epi.org. Per Scott interview, January 21, 2011, cumulative job losses are 3.5 million to 3.6 million from 1990s to end of 2010.

246 **Time for Wal-Mart to build muscle**   "Walmart 2011 Annual Report," April 18, 2011, 4, http://www.walmartstores.com.

247 **Cut America's overall inflation**   Global Insight, "The Price Impact of Wal-Mart: An Update Through 2006," February 4, 2007, http://www.ihsglobalinsight.com.

247 **"In the nineteenth century"**   Excerpt of interview of Nelson Lichtenstein for the *Frontline* program "Is Wal-Mart Good for America?," June 9, 2004.

248 **"It tells me the sales price"**   Excerpt of interview of Linda Dillman for the *Frontline* program "Is Wal-Mart Good for America?," September 17, 2004, http://www.pbs.org/frontline.

248 **"A can of 9Lives cat food"**   Jon Lehman, interview, October 7, 2004.

249 **"Wal-Mart, as an efficiency machine"**   Gary Gereffi, interview excerpt from *Frontline*, "Is Wal-Mart Good for America?"

249 **"The push system involved manufacturers"**   Excerpt of interview of Edna Bonacich for the *Frontline* program "Is Wal-Mart Good for America?," June 9, 2004, http://www.pbs.org/frontline.

250 **"Buyers who overdrive"**   Wolfgang Schmitt, interview excerpt from *Frontline*, "Is Wal-Mart Good for America?"

250 **"It's very one-sided"**   Excerpt of interview of Jon Lehman for the *Frontline* program "Is Wal-Mart Good for America?," October 7, 2004, http://www.pbs.org/frontline.

250 **Its "opening price point"**   Bob Ortega, *In Sam We Trust: The Untold Story of Sam Walton and Wal-Mart, the World's Most Powerful Retailer* (New York: Random House, 1998), 54–59.

250 **"The heart of Wal-Mart's pricing strategy"**   Lehman, interview, "Is Wal-Mart Good for America?"

251 **"China, practically speaking, is *it*"**   Excerpt of interview of Bill Nichol for the *Frontline* program "Is Wal-Mart Good for America?," September 16, 2004, http://www.pbs.org/frontline.

252 **"We will open those facilities"**   Ibid.

252 **"They were selling at prices"** Excerpt of interview of Ray Strutz for the *Frontline* program "Is Wal-Mart Good for America?," June 6, 2004, http://www.pbs.org/frontline.

252 **That put a crunch on the Thomson plant** Excerpt of interview of Roy Wunsch for the *Frontline* program "Is Wal-Mart Good for America?," June 14, 2004, http://www.pbs.org/frontline.

253 **Shenzhen shot up** Orville Schell, *Mandate of Heaven: The Legacy of Tiananmen Square and the Next Generation of China's Leaders* (New York: Simon & Schuster, 1994), 331–57.

254 **"A joint venture"** Gary Gereffi, interview excerpt from *Frontline,* "Is Wal-Mart Good for America?"

255 **"Wal-Mart . . . are very shrewd people"** Excerpt of interview of Kenneth Chan for the *Frontline* program "Is Wal-Mart Good for America?," July 26, 2004, http://www.pbs.org/frontline.

255 **"There's always going to be"** Ibid.

256 **"I saw this as a store manager"** Jon Lehman, interview excerpt from *Frontline,* "Is Wal-Mart Good for America?"

257 **"Wal-Mart sources a huge"** Kenneth K. T. Tse, general manager, Yantian Port Terminal, Shenzhen, interview, May 14, 2004.

257 **"Wal-Mart is providing a gateway"** Gary Gereffi, interview excerpt from *Frontline,* "Is Wal-Mart Good for America?"

258 **More than $30 billion** Excerpt of interview of Ray Bracy for the *Frontline* program "Is Wal-Mart Good for America?," November 16, 2004, http://www.pbs.org/frontline.

258 **"They're all carrying Chinese cargo"** Excerpt of interview of Yvonne Smith for the *Frontline* program "Is Wal-Mart Good for America?," June 8, 2004, http://www.pbs.org/frontline.

259 **Apple's longtime CEO, Steve Jobs** Governor Mitch Daniels, "Republican Address to the Nation," January 24, 2012; press release, Office of House Speaker John Boehner, http://www.speaker.gov.

259 **Apple overlooked sweatshop conditions** Charles Duhigg and Keith Bradsher, "How the U.S. Lost Out on iPhone Work," *The New York Times,* January 22, 2012; Charles Duhigg and David Barboza, "In China, Human Costs Are Built into an iPad," *The New York Times,* January 26, 2012; Paul Krugman, "Jobs, Jobs and Cars," *The New York Times,* January 25, 2012.

259 **Illegal labor practices, confirmed** Jessica E. Vascellaro, "Audit Faults Apple Supplier," *The Wall Street Journal,* March 30, 2012. Auditors from the Fair Labor Association found that Foxcomm, or Hon Hai Precision Industry Company, as it is formally known, has been working its employes *an average of more than sixty hours* a week, in violation not only of Apple's stated standards, but of China's legal limit of forty hours per week with a maximum of thirty-six hours. Apple pledged to shorten working hours and raise pay inside Chinese plants making its products, as reported by Charles Duhigg and Steven Greenhouse, "Electronic Giant Vowing Reforms in China Plants," *The New York Times,* March 30, 2012.

259 **"The speed and flexibility"** Charles Duhigg and Keith Bradsher, "How the U.S. Lost Out on iPhone Work," *The New York Times,* January 22, 2012; Charles Duhigg and David Barboza, "In China, Human Costs Are Built into an iPad," *The New York Times,* January 26, 2012; Paul Krugman, "Jobs, Jobs and Cars," *The New York Times,* January 25, 2012.

260 **America's record $273 billion trade deficit** U.S. Census Bureau, "U.S. Trade in Goods with China," June 6, 2011, http://www.census.gov.

260 *Bought $1.928 trillion more* in goods Scott, interview, January 21, 2011.

260 **Topping $3.2 trillion** Trade imbalance: Prestowitz, *Betrayal of American Prosperity,* 142. Financial reserves: "China Says It's Unable to Easily Aid Europe," *The New York Times,* December 5, 2011.

260 **"Open China's markets"** President Clinton, remarks, "House Passage of Permanent Normal Trade Relations with China," May 24, 2000, http:// Clinton6.nara.gov.

260 **"Help export American values"** Eric Schmitt, "Opening to China: Overview: Senate Votes to Lift Curbs on U.S. Trade with China; Strong Bipartisan Support," *The New York Times,* September 20, 2000.

261 **"The potential is explosive"** "Final Passage of Bill to Normalize U.S. Ties Is Approved, 83 to 15," *The New York Times,* September 20, 2000; "Rallying Round the China Bill, Hungrily," *The New York Times,* May 21, 2000.

261 **"The most dynamic international market"** "Opening to China: Overview," *The New York Times,* September 20, 2000.

261 **Trade deficit with China was already $83 billion** U.S. Census Bureau, "Trade in Goods with China," accessed April 11, 2012, http://www.census .gov/foreign-trade/balance/c5700.html.

261 **"They looked at China like a super-Mexico"** Alan Tonelson, interview, January 12, 2011.

261 **Adding to the U.S. trade deficits** Alan Tonelson, "Wake Up Call: What a Tangled Web," U.S. Business and Industry Council Educational Foundation, December 3, 2009, http://www.americaneconomicalert.org.

261 **$172 billion** Alan Tonelson, email, January 11, 2011. The data showed $596 billion in exports, $768 billion in imports.

262 **"Argument is that trade deficits don't matter"** Tonelson, interview, January 12, 2011.

262 **In the last twenty years** Scott, interview, January 21, 2011.

262 **Think Scott has understated** Mike Wessel, interview, January 19, 2011.

262 **Dispute the notion** David Ricardo, *On the Principles of Political Economy and Taxation* (London: John Murray, 1817).

263 **"Putting these jobs overseas is"** Jagdish Bhagwati, "Why Your Job Isn't Moving to Bangalore," *The New York Times,* February 15, 2004.

263 **"Trade policy or trade flows"** Excerpt of interview of Brink Lindsey for the *Frontline* program "Is Wal-Mart Good for America?," October 7, 2004, http://www.pbs.org/frontline.

263 **Dispute the old orthodox argument** Prestowitz, *Betrayal of American Prosperity,* 2.

264 "A shift in productive capability"   Ralph Gomory, testimony, House Committee on Science and Technology, June 12, 2007, http://science.house .gov.

264 He challenged the contention   "An Elder Challenges Outsourcing's Orthodoxy," *The New York Times,* September 9, 2004.

264 "It is dead wrong"   Paul A. Samuelson, "Where Ricardo and Mill Rebut and Confirm Arguments of Mainstream Economists Supporting Globalization," *Journal of Economic Perspectives* 18, no. 3 (Summer 2004); "An Elder Challenges Outsourcing's Orthodoxy."

264 Ignoring the "drastic change"   Samuelson, "Ricardo and Mill."

265 "Most people have been losers from trade"   Excerpt of interview of Larry Mishel for the Frontline program "Is Wal-Mart Good for America?," September 9, 2004, http://www.pbs.org/frontline.

265 On track for a reasonable retirement   Mike Kendall, interview, June 19, 2010; Ron Wright, interview, June 24, 2010.

266 "They brought us groceries, paid our electric"   Sylvian Greene, interview, June 27, 2010.

266 "It's the unpredictability that gets to you"   Don and Ginny Lingle, interview, July 4, 2010.

266 "After I lost my Rubbermaid job"   Pam Constantino, interview, July 11, 2010.

267 Most were making less than before   "Working Displacement: 2007–2009," Bureau of Labor Statistics, August 26, 2010, http://www.bls.gov, table 7.

267 Added 2.4 million employees to their overseas workforces   U.S. Bureau of Economic Analysis, "Summary Estimates for Multinational Companies: Employment, Sales, and Capital Expenditures for 2009," April 18, 2011, table 1 shows that overseas employment by U.S. multinationals rose from 7.9 million to 10.3 million and their domestic employment fell from 24.0 million to 21.1 million from 1999 to 2009, http://www.commerce .gov.

267 Very different track records since 1990   Michael Spence and Sandile Hlatshwayo, "The Evolving Structure of the American Economy and the Employment Challenge," working paper, Council on Foreign Relations, March 2011, http://www.cfr.org.

268 "You could say, as many do"   Andy Grove, "How America Can Create Jobs," *Bloomberg BusinessWeek,* July 1, 2010, http://www.businesweek.com.

CHAPTER 16: HOLLOWING OUT HIGH-END JOBS

269 "Merchants have no country"   Thomas Jefferson to Horatio G. Spafford, March 17, 1814, in *The Writings of Thomas Jefferson* (Washington, DC: Taylor & Maury, 1854), 334.

269 **"What we are trying to do"** Prestowitz, *Betrayal of American Prosperity,* (NY: Free Press, 2010) 213.

269 **"In this new era of globalization"** Gomory, testimony, House Committee on Science and Technology.

270 **Masses of high-skill, high-wage, high-tech jobs** President Bill Clinton, "Technology for America's Economic Growth," press release, White House Briefing Room, February 22, 1993; Clinton in campaign debate, "Transcript of First TV Debate Among Bush, Clinton and Perot: The 1992 Campaign," *The New York Times,* October 12, 1992.

270 **"Going digital"** William A. Niskanen and Robert E. Litan, *Going Digital! A Guide to Policy in the Digital Age* (Washington, DC: Brookings Institution Press, 1998).

270 **Americans' increasing dependence** Bhagwati, "Why Your Job Isn't Moving to Bangalore."

270 **"You could think of it"** "Know What? Knowledge Will Power Nations in the New World Order," Associated Press, July 23, 1989.

271 **This category was set up** Clyde Prestowitz, email, December 10, 2011.

271 **America's deficit in advanced technology trade** U.S. Census Bureau, Bureau of Economic Analysis, "U.S. International Trade in Goods and Services, December 2011," Exhibit 16 and Exhibit 16a, February 10, January 13, 2012, http://www.census.gov/foreigntrade/Press-Release/current_press_release/ft900.pdf.

271 **$94.2 billion high-tech trade deficit** Ibid.

271 **China's steep upward leap** Alan Tonelson, interview excerpt from *Frontline,* "Is Wal-Mart Good for America?"

272 **"It is a fallacy"** Prestowitz, *Betrayal of American Prosperity,* 11.

272 **The Chinese had shown their mastery** Tonelson, interview excerpt from *Frontline,* "Is Wal-Mart Good for America?"

272 **Hardest-hit sector was computers** Robert Scott, "Unfair China Trade Costs Local Jobs," EPI Briefing Paper, March 23, 2010, Economic Policy Institute, http://www.epi.org; TechAmerica, "Cyberstates 2010," http://www.techamericafoundation.org.

272 **"We're now calling it *Skeletal Valley*"** Scott, interview, January 21, 2011.

272 **Even the service sector** Scott, "Unfair China Trade Costs Local Jobs."

273 **Roughly 2.8 million jobs in finance, IT, HR** "Offshoring of Back Office Jobs Is Accelerating," Hackett Group, January 6, 2009, http://www.thehackettgroup.com; and "How Offshoring Could Prolong the Jobless Recovery," Hackett Group, ThomasNet News, January 18, 2011, http://www.news.thomasnet.

273 **"Millions of skilled workers"** Alan Blinder, testimony, House Committee on Science and Technology, June 12, 2007, http://science.house.gov.

274 **"U.S. high-tech industry is *coming unglued*"** Prestowitz, *Betrayal of American Prosperity,* 30–31; Richard McCormack, "The Plight of Manufacturing," in *Manufacturing a Better Future for America,* ed. Richard McCormack

(Washington, DC: Alliance for American Manufacturing, 2009); President's Council of Advisors on Science and Technology, "Sustaining the Nation's Innovation Ecosystems, Information Technology Manufacturing and Competitiveness," January 16, 2004, http://www.whitehouse.gov.

274 **At least 1,160 high-end research installations** Prestowitz, *Betrayal of American Prosperity,* 36.

274 **"China was much more clever"** Steve Lohr, "Maybe Japan Was Just a Warm-Up," *The New York Times,* January 23, 2011.

274 **By 2005, GE had twenty-seven labs in China** Jeffrey Garten, "The High-Tech Threat from China-America Inc. Is Rushing Beijing Ahead by Sharing R&D Treasures," *BusinessWeek,* January 31, 2005.

275 **GE disclosed a joint venture** General Electric, "GE to Invest More than $2 Billion in R&D, Technology and Financial Services Partnerships in China," Business Wire, November 9, 2010, http://www.businesswire/com; "GE Venture Will Share Jet Technology with China," *The New York Times,* January 17, 2011.

275 **General Motors broke ground** General Motors, "GM Breaks Ground on Advanced Technical Center in Shanghai," July 7, 2010, http://media.gm.com.

275 **Microsoft, already spending $300 million** "Microsoft to Spend $1 Bn on R&D in China," Reuters, November 13, 2008; Microsoft, "Microsoft Opens World-Class Innovation and Technology Service Park in Shanghai," March 31, 2010, http://www.microsoft.com.

275 **Applied Materials of Silicon Valley** Keith Bradsher, "China Drawing High-Tech Research from U.S.," *The New York Times,* March 17, 2010.

275 **"China has a carrot and stick strategy"** Clyde Prestowitz, email, December 10, 2011.

276 **"A blueprint for technology theft"** James McGregor, "China's Drive for 'Indigenous Innovation,' " U.S. Chamber of Commerce, July 28, 2010, http://www.uschamber.com.

276 **"Indigenous innovation"** "Obama Pushes Hu on Rights, but Stresses Ties to China," *The New York Times,* January 20, 2011.

276 **"A technology powerhouse"** McGregor, "China's Drive for 'Indigenous Innovation.' "

276 **U.S. companies have become integrated** U.S. International Trade Commission, "Certain Passenger Vehicle and Light Truck Tires from China," Publication 4085, July 2009, http://www.usitc.gov.

276 **"That kind of thing is"** Prestowitz, interview, January 11, 2011.

277 **"It costs $1 billion more per factory"** "Intel Chief: Obama (Still) Driving US off Cliff," *The Register,* August 25, 2010, http://www.theregister.co.uk.

277 **"U.S. companies are understandably seeking"** Garten, "The High-Tech Threat from China-America Inc."

278 **Described his firm as "agnostic"** "EDS CEO Says No Problem," ITBusiness, April 23, 2008, http://www.itbusiness.ca.

278 **"Intel can be a totally successful company"** Friedman, "Tuning In."

278 **"Strategy of becoming a Chinese company"** Prestowitz, *Betrayal of American Prosperity*, 213.

278 **"What's good for our country"** "Armed Forces: Engine Charlie," *Time,* October 6, 1961.

278 **"The interests of companies and countries have diverged"** Gomory, testimony, House Committee on Science and Technology.

279 **Summarizing the impact** James Hagerty, "U.S. Loses High-Tech Jobs as R&D Shifts Toward Asia," *The Wall Street Journal,* January 18, 2012.

279 **IBM cut its American workforce by 30 percent** Lee Conrad, Alliance@ IBM/CWA Local 2071, interview, January 25, 2011.

280 **Close behind IBM** "U.S. Tech Firms Continue to Grow in India," Livemint.com, September 10, 2010, http://www.livemint.com.

280 **Computer giant Hewlett-Packard** Dan Rather Reports, "Help Wanted! (Not Here)," HDNet, January 18, 2011, http://www.hd.net/programs/danrather.

280 **Accounting firm Deloitte** "Deloitte to Treble Headcount in India," Diligent Media Corp., November 28, 2009, http://www.dnaindia.com.

280 **American IT outsourcing firms** Ron Hira, interview, January 7, 2011.

280 **Even Perot Systems** "Perot Systems, Founded by an Offshoring Foe, Increases Offshoring," *ComputerWorld,* February 12, 2009, http://www.computerworld.com.

280 **India has burst upon** "The Other Elephant," *The Economist,* November 4, 2010, http://www.economist.com.

280 **India has largely leapfrogged over manufacturing** "Information Economy Report 2010," United Nations Conference on Trade and Development, October 14, 2010, http://unctad.org, 49–40, figures III.4 and III.5. The report estimated global exports in IT services and business processing at $92 billion to $96 billion and India's share at 35 percent, but it said these figures underestimate the overall global IT offshoring market. NASSCOM, India's National Association of Software and Service Companies, put India's exports in this field at $50 billion in the executive summary of its Strategic Review 2010, "Global Sourcing Trends," http://epi.nasscom.in/upload/SR10/ExecutiveSummary.pdf.

281 **"The Indian firms had a disruptive business model"** Hira, interview, January 7, 2011.

281 **"Cross border job shifting"** IBM Directors' Presentations on Offshoring, internal IBM document, March 13, 2003.

282 **"Hiring over There"** "Cutting Here, Hiring over There," *The New York Times,* June 24, 2005.

282 **Job reductions would save IBM $1.8 billion** "Amid Layoffs, IBM Scours the Globe for IT Talent," CRN TechWeb, September 23, 2005, http://www.crn.com.

282 **The cuts were being rolled out in modest batches** "IBM Quietly Cuts Thousands of Jobs," CBS, January 27, 2009.

282 **IBM had fired another five thousand employees** Steve Lohr, "Piecemeal Layoffs Avoid Warning Laws," *The New York Times,* March 6, 2009;

Steve Lohr, "Tallying I.B.M.'s Layoff Numbers," *The New York Times,* March 30, 2009; William Bulkeley, "IBM to Cut U.S. Jobs, Expand in India," *The Wall Street Journal,* March 26, 2009.

283 **"They used to bring the people"** Tom Midgley, interview, January 30, 2011.

283 **"I was responsible"** Kristine Serrano, interview, January 29, 2011.

284 **Serrano was offended** Ibid.

284 **Cutting-edge R&D** "IBM and Globalisation: Hungry Tiger, Dancing Elephant—How India Is Changing IBM's World," *The Economist,* April 4, 2007, http://www.economist.com.

285 **"We will triple our investment in India"** Samuel J. Palmisano, remarks, IBM press release and speech text, June 6, 2006.

285 **"New levels of cost competitiveness"** IBM Global Services paper, IBM Global Briefing, Bangalore, India, June 6, 2006.

285 **"It's like a slap in the face"** "NYC Hit by Nerd Job Rob; City $$ for Indian Hires," *New York Post,* June 28, 2009.

286 **IBM decided to patent its offshoring blueprint** U.S. patent application no. 11/324,958 for "Outsourcing of Services" from Bryan L. Behrman et al., patent assignee: International Business Machines Corp., Armonk, NY, publication date July 12, 2007.

286 **Help clients achieve "50% of resources in China"** U.S. patent application no.11/860,336 for "Method and System for Strategic Global Resource Sourcing," from Ching-Hua Chen-Ritzo et al., patent assignee: International Business Machines Corp., Armonk, NY, publication date March 26, 2009.

286 **"Downright unpatriotic"** "IBM Files for Patent on Offshoring Jobs," *Times Herald-Record,* March 30, 2009; "IBM Drops Patent Application for Outsourcing Offshore Jobs," *Times Herald-Record,* March 31, 2009.

287 **"Task by task, function by function"** David Streitfeld, "Office of Tomorrow Has an Address in India," *Los Angeles Times,* August 29, 2004.

287 **Offshoring today involves brainpower jobs** Marla Dickerson, "Offshoring Trend Casting a Wider Net," *Los Angeles Times,* January 4, 2004.

287 **Shot up exponentially since 1990** "Information Economy Report 2010," United Nations Conference on Trade and Development, http://www.unctad .org.

287 **"They told all the workers"** Lee Conrad, interview, January 24, 2011.

288 **83 percent cited outsourcing** "Americans Sour on Trade," *The Wall Street Journal,* October 2, 2010.

288 **"Job cuts at home, big hiring overseas"** Hackett Group, "Offshoring of Back Office Jobs Is Accelerating," January 6, 2009; "New Data: 2.8 Million Business-Support Jobs Eliminated Since 2000," November 15, 2010, and "How Offshoring Could Prolong the Jobless Recovery," January, 18, 2011, http://news.thomasnet.com/IMT/archives/2011/01/how-offshoring-trend -could-prolong-jobless-recovery-hackett-group.html.

288 **The big Wall Street banks** Pankaj Mishra & Shruti Sabharwal, "Citi, Bofa & JPMorgan to Outsource $5 Bn of IT and Back Office Projects to

India," *Economic Times,* Times of India Group, February 14, 2011, http://economictimes.indiatimes.com.

288 **At home, the big banks were firing**   "Profits Falling, Banks Confront a Leaner Future," *The New York Times,* August 29, 2011.

288 **"How Offshoring Could Prolong the Jobless Recovery"**   "How Offshoring Could Prolong the Jobless Recovery," Hackett Group, January 18, 2011, http://www.thehackettgroup.com; "New Data: 2.8 Million Business-Support Jobs Eliminated Since 2000," Hackett Group, November 15, 2010, http://www.thehackettgroup.com.

289 **That "corresponds to about 30–40 million jobs"**   Alan S. Blinder, "Offshoring: Big Deal, or Business as Usual?" CEPS Working Paper No.149, Center for Economic Policy Studies, June 2007, http://www.princeton.edu.

CHAPTER 17: THE SKILLS GAP MYTH

290 **"We have seen numerous"**   William Branigin, "White-Collar Visas: Back Door to Cheap Labor?" *The Washington Post,* October 21, 1995.

290 **"These are not Einsteins"**   Bruce Morrison, interview, January 24, 2011.

290 **"We find neither an inadequate supply"**   William Butz, Terrence K. Kelly, David M. Adamson, et al., "Will the Scientific and Technology Workforce Meet the Requirements of the Federal Government?" Rand Corporation, 2004, http://www.rand.org.

291 **To recruit hot new talent**   "American-Made: The Impact of Immigrant Entrepreneurs and Professionals in U.S. Competitiveness," National Venture Capital Association, 2006, http://www.nvca.org.

291 **"It makes no sense to"**   "Bill Gates to Congress: Let Us Hire More Foreigners," CNET News, March 12, 2006, http://news.cnet.com.

292 **No ironclad protections for Americans**   Morrison, interview, January 24, 2011.

293 **Senior AIG executives summoned 250**   Linda Kilcrease, "Problems with the H-1B Visa Expansion and T-Visas," web post, January 8, 2008, accessed January 17, 2011. http://www.zazona.comLibrary/BrainSavers/Problems_Kilcrease.htm, and Kilcrease, letter to editor, "H-1B Visa: A Bad Idea," Cnet, 2009, accessed April 21, 2012.

293 **"After we were seated"**   Douglas Crouse, "Competition from Abroad," *The Daily Record,* Morris County, New Jersey, May 2, 2000. http://www.programmersguild.org/archives/lib/abuse/drm20000502aig.htm.

293 **Americans were being replaced by H-1B**   Kilcrease, "Problems with the H-1B Visa Expansion."

293 **Did not bring in any special skills**   William Branigan, "White Collar Visas: Back Door for Cheap Labor," *The Washington Post*, October 21, 1995.

293 **"This profitable company boasted**   Kilcrease, "Problems with the H-1B Visa Expansion."

294 **One-third of its 46,000-member workforce**   "Quota Quickly Filled on Visas for High-Tech Guest Workers," *The New York Times,* April 5, 2007.

294 **Foreign worker tide kept rising** "Flaws in Guest Worker Programs Add to US Unemployment Misery," *International Business Times News,* November 21, 2010.

294 **Or multinational temp agencies** Ron Hira and Anil Hira, *Outsourcing America: The True Cost of Shipping Jobs Overseas and What Can Be Done About It,* 2nd. ed. (New York: Amacom, 2008) 54–59, 158–160. "Outsourcers Are Criticized on Visa Use," *The New York Times,* March 31, 2011.

295 **"Tata has about 18,000 people in the U.S."** Infosys financial statements, Hira, interview, January 7, 2011.

295 **Its H-1B trade made Desai** "Forbes 400," Forbes.com, September 30, 2009, http://www.forbes.com; see also http://www.syntelinc.com.

295 **Fraudulent visa applications** Senator Charles Schumer, debate on Emergency Border Security Supplemental Appropriations Act, *Congressional Record* S6997, August 12, 2010, http://www.gpo.gov.

295 **"Willfully underpaid its Indian computer programmers"** Robert Reich, testimony, Senate Judiciary Subcommittee on Immigration, September 28, 1995, http://www.dol.gov/oasam/programs/history/reich/congress/092895rr.htm.

295 **"Pervasive cheating"** Office of the Inspector General, "Foreign Labor Certification Programs: The System Is Broken and Needs to Be Fixed," U.S. Department of Labor, May 22, 1996, http://www.oig.dol.gov.

295 **Improperly firing American workers** Reich, testimony, Senate Judiciary Subcommittee on Immigration.

295 **"We have seen numerous instances"** Branigin, "White-Collar Visas."

296 **"It is a subsidy"** Paul Donnelly, "H-1B Is Just Another Gov't. Subsidy," *ComputerWorld,* July 22, 2002, http://www.computerworld.com.

296 **Estimated that one million or more** Paul Almeida, interview, January 16, 2011.

296 **Approved 828,677 H-1B visas** U.S. Department of Homeland Security, "Characteristics of H-1B Specialty Occupation Workers," April 15, 2010, Table 1, http://www.uscis.gov.

297 **"If I had known in 1990"** Morrison, interview, January 24, 2011.

297 **India has "been viewed as"** Som Mittal, "At Last Washington's Anti-Outsourcing Rhetoric Cools," *Mercury News* (San Jose, CA), December 12, 2010.

297 **Indian firms are saving U.S. corporations** "Global Sourcing Trends," Strategic Review 2010, executive summary, NASSCOM.

298 **"Pfizer adopted Corporate Procedure 117"** Pfizer, "Contingent Worker Procedure," Corporate Procedure #117, November 3, 2007, http://kalamazoocontractoradministration.pfizer.com.

298 **Pfizer signed up two Indian staffing agencies** "Pfizer to Outsource Some Computer Services," *The Day* (New London, CT), June 23, 2005.

298 **When the first Indian IT specialists arrived** Lee Howard, interview, January 27, 2011.

299 **"Everybody was scared to death"** Former Pfizer systems analyst (name withheld on request), interview, January 31, 2011.

299 **"Five years ago"** Howard, interview, January 27, 2011; Lee Howard, "Pfizer to Ax IT Contractors, *The Day,* November 2, 3008.

299 **"These contracting companies"** Pfizer systems analyst, interview, January 31, 2011.

300 **Pfizer maintained** Senator Christopher J. Dodd and Representative Joseph Courtney, letter to Pfizer CEO Jeff Kindler, November 3, 2008.

300 **Pfizer contended that these were not** Bruce Morrison, email, April 15, 2012, and interview, April 16, 2012.

300 **"Pfizer would have had no involvement"** Anthony J. Principi, Pfizer senior vice president, letter to Senator Christopher J. Dodd and Representative Joseph Courtney, November 6, 2008.

300 **Requiring U.S. firms** Senator Charles Grassley, prepared statement, Senate Immigration Subcommittee Hearing, July 26, 2011, Office of Senator Grassley, http://www.grassley.senate.gov; Paul Almeida, interview, January 6, 2011.

301 **"Program is riddled with loopholes"** Office of Senator Charles Grassley, press release, "Grassley, Durbin Say GAO Report Highlights Need for Major Reform of the H-1B Visa Program," January 31, 2011, http://www.grassley .senate.gov.

301 **"The myth of a desperate software labor shortage"** Norman Matloff, testimony to House Judiciary Subcommittee on Immigration, April 21, 1998, http://judiciary.house.gov/about/subimmigration.html.

301 **Rejected high-tech industry claims** Butz et al., "Will the Scientific and Technology Workforce Meet the Requirements of the Federal Government?"

302 **Offshoring strategies were causing** B. Lindsay Lowell, Harold Salzman, Hamutal Bernstein, et al., "Steady as She Goes? Three Generations of Students Through the Science and Engineering Pipeline," Institute for the Study of International Migration at Georgetown University, Rutgers University, and the Urban Institute, October 2009, http://policy.rutgers.edu/ faculty/salzman/steadyasshegoes.pdf.

302 **"A glorified international temp agency"** "Border Bill Aims at Indian Companies," *The New York Times,* August 6, 2011.

303 **"Erode cost arbitrage"** *Congressional Record,* S6997–S6998, August 12, 2010, http://www.gpo.gov.

303 **One potentially helpful step** "Highly Skilled May Wait Less for Visas," *The New York Times,* November 29, 2011.

PART 5: OBSTACLES TO A FIX

307 **"The people's business"** Evan Bayh, press statement at Purdue University, February 15, 2010, http://bayh.senate.gov.

307 **"Strident partisanship"** Evan Bayh, "Why I'm Leaving the Senate," *The New York Times,* February 21, 2010.

CHAPTER 18: THE MISSING MIDDLE

309 **"Over the past thirty years"** Nolan McCarthy, Keith T. Poole, and Howard Rosenthal, *Polarized America: The Dance of Ideology and Unequal Riches* (Cambridge, MA: Massachusetts Institute of Technology Press, 2006), 1–3.

309 **"It's the incredible shrinking middle"** Senator John Breaux, quoted in "Congress—Mr. In-Between," *National Journal,* December 16, 1995.

309 **"There are still times when"** Tom Mann, interview, January 7, 2010.

310 **"Just one or two determined senators"** Bayh, "Why I Am Leaving the Senate."

310 **"This type of social interaction"** Ibid.

311 **The last straw** Bayh, press statement.

311 **"The best way to address"** "Senate Rejects Plan to Create Commission on the Deficit," *The Washington Post,* January 27, 2010; Mike Allen, "Why Washington Is Broken?" Politico, January 26, 2010, http://www.politico.com.

311 **"It's impossible to avoid"** Fred Hiatt, "McConnell's Cynical Flip," *The Washington Post,* February 1, 2010.

312 **The debate in each case was** Nicholas D. Kristof, "The Wrong Side of History," *The New York Times,* November 19, 2009.

312 **In the Senate, 13 Republicans** John D. Morris, "Congress Passes Bill on Medicare," *The New York Times,* July 29, 1965.

313 **GOP opposition was monolithic in 2010** "Senate Passes Health Care Overhaul on Party-Line Vote," *The New York Times,* December 25, 2009; "Congress Sends White House Landmark Health Overhaul," *The New York Times,* March 22, 2010.

313 **Health reform proposed by Republican Richard Nixon** "Nixon Offers Health Insurance Program," *The New York Times,* February 7, 1974.

313 **Senator Joe Lieberman of Connecticut** "Lieberman Gets Ex-Party to Shift on Health Plan," *The New York Times,* December 15, 2009.

313 **Eisenhower regularly shared drinks** Harry McPherson, interview, April 2, 2010.

314 **"I am now a Keynesian"** "Nixon Reportedly Says He Is Now a Keynesian," *The New York Times,* January 7, 1971.

314 **When Johnson was in the worst jams** McPherson, interview, April 2, 2010.

314 **The most productive legislative records** Sarah A. Binder, "The Dynamics of Legislative Gridlock, 1947–1996," *American Political Science Review* 93, no. 3 (September 1999).

315 **"Shame, Shame, Shame"** Bill D. Moyers, "What a Real President Was Like," Outlook, *The Washington Post,* November 13, 1988.

315 **He worked on Dirksen's pride in America** Lyndon B. Johnson, *The Vantage Point: Perspectives of the Presidency, 1963–1969* (New York: Holt, Rinehart & Winston, 1974), 157–58.

315 **"There is no way on earth that"** Harry McPherson, interview, August 8, 2010.

316 **Democrats fell all over themselves** E. W. Kenworthy, "Dirksen Shaped

Victory for Civil Rights Forces in Fight to Bring Measure to Vote," *The New York Times,* June 20, 1964.

316 **"Pull to the center"** Johnson, *Vantage Point,* 102–03.

317 **"I think we just delivered"** Moyers, "Real President."

318 **Up from just 4 Senate seats to 20** "Members and Seniority 88th Congress, 2nd Session," *CQ Almanac 1964* (Washington, DC: Congressional Quarterly, 1965), 27–32; Directory of Representatives, U.S. House of Representatives, May 27, 2011, http://www.house.gov.

319 **The parties have deserted the center** McCarty, Poole, and Rosenthal, *Polarized America,* 1.

319 **See the widening gulf** Keith Poole and Howard Rosenthal, "Two Dimensional Animated Gif for the 46th to 105th Congresses (House and Senate Simultaneously)" (Athens: University of Georgia, May 12, 2011), http://www.voteview.com/animate.htm.

319 **"This sense of the tribe"** Mann, interview, January 7, 2010.

320 **"This is the sharpest, most rancorous"** Norman Ornstein, interview, January 7, 2010.

320 **"Nobody goes there anymore"** David M. Herszenhorn, "In Health Vote, a New Vitriol," *The New York Times,* December 24, 2009.

320 **"Partisan polarization"** Binder, "Dynamics of Legislative Gridlock."

321 **"Republicans began using filibusters"** Ornstein, interview, January 7, 2010.

321 **Senator Strom Thurmond** "Carolinian Sets Talking Record," *The New York Times,* August 30, 1957.

322 **"You have *tyranny of the minority*"** Senator Tom Udall, interview, November 18, 2011.

322 **"The silent filibuster"** Thomas E. Mann and Norman J. Ornstein, *The Broken Branch* (New York: Oxford University Press, 2008), 81–82.

322 **Originally, personal holds** Norman Ornstein, "Our Broken Senate," *The American* (American Enterprise Institute), March–April 2008.

322 **"A hold is a hostage-taking weapon"** Ornstein, interview, January 7, 2010.

322 **"The use of delaying tactics"** Mann, interview, January 7, 2010.

323 **"Condemned to death-by-filibuster"** Barbara Sinclair, testimony to the Senate Rules Committee, July 28, 2010.

323 **Senate has become such a bottleneck** Tom Udall, Senate floor speech, *Congressional Record,* January 27, 2011, http://www.gpo.gov.

323 **These procedures have evolved** Senator Jeff Merkley, "Why 'Supermajority' No Longer Works in the Senate," *The Washington Post,* November 6, 2011.

323 **Filibuster came into being by mistake** Sarah A. Binder, testimony to the Senate Rules Committee, April 22, 2010.

324 **To bar filibusters on the procedural motion** "Senate Limits 'Holds,' Keeps Filibuster," Weekly Report, *CQ Weekly,* January 31, 2011.

324 **"We want to force a talking filibuster"** Udall, interview, November 18, 2011.

325 **The two trends overlap almost perfectly** McCarty, Poole, and Rosenthal, *Polarized America*, 2–8; Keith T. Poole and Howard Rosenthal, "The Political Economy of American Income Inequality," voteviewblog, November 23, 2011, http://voteview.com.

325 **Litmus tests: The Minimum Wage** Bartels, *Unequal Democracy*, 5, 27.

326 **Below the real value** "Congress Passes Increase in the Minimum Wage," *The New York Times,* May 25, 2007; Doug Hall, "Increasing the Minimum Wage Is Smart for Families and the Economy," Economic Policy Institute, May 19, 2011, http://www.epi.org.

326 **Twelve states passed state minimum wages** McCarty, Poole, and Rosenthal, *Polarized America,* 169–71. In 2005, Washington State had the highest legal minimum wage: $7.35 an hour.

326 **Eight of them** Catherine Rampell, "Wage Floor Is Increasing in 8 States in New Year," *The New York Times,* December 23, 2011.

326 **Bush made the big changes in 2002** Bartels, *Unequal Democracy,* 197.

326 **Gridlock was the ally of the wealthy** "Estate Tax Will Return Next Year, but Few Will Pay It," *The New York Times,* December 17, 2010.

327 **"The fight over estate tax repeal"** Bartels, *Unequal Democracy,* 197.

CHAPTER 19: THE RISE OF
THE RADICAL RIGHT, 1964–2010

328 **"Let me now . . . warn you"** George Washington, Farewell Address, September 19, 1796, http://www.access.gpo.gov/congress/senate/farewell/sd106–21.pdf.

328 **"The GOP's evolution"** Hacker and Pierson, *Winner-Take-All Politics,* 264.

328 **"Zero-sum politics"** Robert Gates, speech, "Brent Scowcroft: Soldier, Scholar and Statesman," Atlantic Council, December 12, 2011, http://www.acus.org.

329 **"We are radicals working to overturn"** "The New Right—'Revolutionaries' Out After the 'Lunch-Pail' Vote," *National Journal,* January 21, 1978, updated February 7, 2011; Thomas J. McIntyre, *The Fear Brokers* (New York: Pilgrim Press, 1979), 67; James Canaway, "Righting Reagan's Revolution," *The Washington Post,* March 22, 1983.

329 **"I don't want to abolish government"** Mara Liasson, "Conservative Advocate," *Morning Edition,* National Public Radio, May 25, 2011, http://www.npr.org.

330 **"The Right's ideology [is] vehemently antistatist"** Donald T. Critchlow, *The Conservative Ascendancy: How the GOP Right Made Political History* (Cambridge, MA: Harvard University Press, 2007), 2.

330 **The Republican Party's steady (if interrupted) march** Hacker and Pierson, *Winner-Take-All Politics,* 293. Their term is "more conservative."

330 **There are many brands of conservatism** Andrew Kohut, Carroll Doherty, Michael Dimock, et al., "Beyond Red vs. Blue: Political Typology,"

Pew Research Center for the People & the Press, May 4, 2011, http://www
.people-press.org.

331 **"Siren song of socialism"** "Ike's Medical Plan a Puzzle to Democrats;
Goldwater Terms It Dime-Store New Deal," *Chicago Tribune,* May 6, 1960.

331 **Goldwater lashed out at Ike's budget** "Republicans: The Backward
Look," *Time,* April 22, 1957.

331 **Goldwater struck themes that are echoed** Critchlow, *Conservative Ascendancy,* 43–50.

332 **His fervent anticommunism** Nicol C. Rae, *The Decline and Fall of the
Liberal Republicans from 1952 to the Present* (Oxford: Oxford University Press,
1989), 55–70.

332 **"More dangerous to our country than *Sputnik*"** "Reuther's Profit-
Sharing Proposal Hits Rough Going at UAW Session," *Chicago Tribune,* January 23, 1958.

332 **"What has been frightening here"** Richard Rovere, *The Goldwater Caper*
(New York: Harcourt, Brace & World, 1965), 88.

332 **"Extremism in the defense of liberty is no vice"** Barry Goldwater,
"Goldwater's 1964 Acceptance Speech," *The Washington Post* online, www
.washingtonpost.com.

332 **An image of rampant extremism** Critchlow, *Conservative Ascendancy,*
70–72.

332 **The finale of the Goldwater campaign** Lou Cannon, *Reagan* (New York:
G. P. Putnam's Sons, 1982), 13–14.

333 **Paul Weyrich** Canaway, "Righting Reagan's Revolution."

333 **Helped gear up the New Right** "The Heritage Foundation Mourns Loss
of Founding President Paul Weyrich," Heritage Foundation, December 18,
2008, http://www.heritage.org.

334 **Wealthy individuals such as David and Charles Koch** W. John Moore,
"Wichita Pipeline," *National Journal,* May 16, 1992.

334 **"Government is not the solution"** Lou Cannon, "Reagan Announces,
Urges Strength at Home, Abroad," *The Washington Post,* November 15, 1979.

334 **Abolish entire cabinet departments** Doug Kneeland, "A Summary of
Reagan's Positions on the Major Issues of This Year's Campaign," *The New
York Times,* July 16, 1980.

334 **Reagan disappointed the hard-core Right** Hedrick Smith, "Reagan
Loyalists Are Worrying About Their Champion's Loyalty," *The New York
Times,* November 20, 1980.

334 **Stop Reagan's nomination of Sandra Day O'Connor** Jane Mayer, "Politics '84—Nurturing Conservatives: New Right Tends a New Generation,"
The Wall Street Journal, December 4, 1984.

335 **"Starve the Beast"** Bruce Bartlett, " 'Starve the Beast': Origins and Development of a Budgetary Metaphor," *Independent Review* 12, no. 1 (Summer
2007).

335 **"Phony war on spending"** David A. Stockman, *The Triumph of Politics:
Why the Reagan Revolution Failed* (New York: Harper & Row, 1986), 454.

335 **"No Reagan Revolution"** Hedrick Smith, *The Power Game: How Washington Works* (New York: Random House, 1988), 654.

335 **Gingrich personified the confrontational politics** Newt Gingrich, speech, June 24, 1978, cited in "The Long March of Newt Gingrich," PBS *Frontline,* January 16, 1996, http://www.pbs.org.

336 **Getting into high-profile scraps** Smith, *Power Game,* 141–43.

336 **"Newt had this vision of how"** Norman Ornstein, interview, January 7, 2010.

336 **Gingrich built a formidable political machine** "House Republicans Elect Gingrich of Georgia as Whip," *The New York Times,* March 23, 1989.

336 **"This war has to be fought"** Sheryl Gay Stolberg, "Gingrich Stuck to Caustic Path in Ethics Battles," *The New York Times,* January 26, 2012.

337 **It took a titanic effort by Clinton** David E. Rosenbaum, "House Passes Budget Plan, Backing Clinton by 218–216 After Hectic Maneuvering," *The New York Times,* August 6, 1993.

337 **The Senate deadlocked, 50–50** David E. Rosenbaum, "Clinton Wins Approval of His Budget Plan as Gore Votes to Break Senate Deadlock," *The New York Times,* August 7, 1993.

337 **More than half the bills (56 percent) died** Binder, "Dynamics of Legislative Gridlock."

337 *Least productive sessions in half a century* Ibid.

337 **"Perhaps the worst congress"** "Perhaps the Worst Congress," *The Washington Post,* October 7, 1994.

337 **To generate public disgust with Congress** Ornstein, interview, January 7, 2010.

338 **Right-wing commentator Rush Limbaugh** "F.C.C. Votes Down Fairness Doctrine in a 4–0 Decision," *The New York Times,* August 5, 1987.

338 **Pollster Frank Luntz** "Call-in Political Talk Radio: Background, Content, Audiences, Portrayal in Mainstream Media" (Philadelphia: Annenberg Public Policy Center, University of Pennsylvania, August 7, 1996), http://www.annenbergpublicpolicycenter.org; *U.S. News & World Report,* May 1993; *Talk Daily,* August 1995.

338 **Limbaugh's importance** "Republicans Get a Pep Talk from Rush Limbaugh," *The New York Times,* December 12, 1994; Linda Killian, *The Freshmen: What Happened to the Republican Revolution?* (Boulder, CO: Westview Press, 1998), 26.

338 **"Contract with America"** The account that follows comes principally from the author's reporting and interviews reflected in the transcript of Hedrick Smith Productions, *The People and the Power Game,* PBS, September 3 and 10, 1996, www.hedricksmith.com.

338 **A confrontation with President Clinton** "President Vetoes Stopgap Budget; Shutdown Looms," *The New York Times,* November 14, 1995.

339 **A 51 percent majority blamed the Republicans** "As Standoff Ends, Clinton Is Seeking High Ground," *The New York Times,* November 21, 1995.

339 "The tax collector for the welfare state" Richard Reeves, "The Republicans," *The New York Times Magazine,* September 9, 1984.

339 Senate Republicans had tired Smith, *The People and the Power Game.*

339 Gingrich had to back down "Clinton Meets Challenge by Offering Budget Plan; Crucial Talks Begin Soon," *The New York Times,* January 7, 1996.

339 Target No. 1 was Pennsylvania's Arlen Specter Peter Ross Range, "Thunder from the Right," *The New York Times Magazine,* February 8, 1981.

340 Specter the defector Martin Tolchin, "The Washington Priorities of a Philadelphia Pragmatist," *The New York Times,* April 8, 1984.

340 "If we beat Specter" James Dao, "Conservative Takes on Moderate G.O.P. Senator in Pennsylvania," *The New York Times,* April 3, 2004.

340 "Not far right, he's far out" Ibid.

340 "Since my election in 1980" "Specter Statement on His Decision to Switch Parties," *The New York Times,* April 28, 2009.

341 Toomey won Specter's old Senate seat "Toomey at Helm of a Republican Wave in Pennsylvania," *The New York Times,* November 3, 2010; "Senate Tea Party Caucus Holds First Meeting Without Some Who Had Embraced Banner," *The Washington Post,* January 28, 2011.

341 "Ideological cleansing" Dana Milbank, "I'll Miss You, Sen. Apostasy," *The Washington Post,* May 23, 2010.

341 Cannibalism—"eating or defeating your own" "Specter Farewell Speech Slams GOP 'Cannibalism,' " Associated Press, December 22, 2010, http://www.delcotimes.com.

342 A $1.2 trillion stimulus Ryan Lizza, "Inside the Crisis: Larry Summers and the White House Economic Team," *The New Yorker,* October 12, 2009.

342 A supersized stimulus of $1.5 trillion to $2.4 trillion Paul Krugman, "The Obama Gap," *The New York Times,* January 9, 2009; Baker, *False Profits,* 2.

342 Could "spook markets" Larry Summers, "Executive Summary of Economic Policy Work," memo to President-Elect Barack Obama, December 15, 2008, http://s3.documentcloud.org/documents/285065/summers-12-15-08-memo.pdf.

342 He told Obama Ryan Lizza, "The Obama Memos: The Making of a Post-Post-Partisan Presidency," *The New Yorker,* January 30, 2012.

343 "All you capitalists" *Squawk Box,* CNBC, February 19, 2009, http://www.cnbc.com.

343 Big-time right-wing political donors Jane Mayer, "Covert Operations: The Billionaire Brothers Who Are Waging a War Against Obama," *The New Yorker,* August 30, 2010.

343 Far to the right of average Americans "Poll Finds Tea Party Backers Wealthier and More Educated," *The New York Times,* April 14, 2010; "Tea Party Supporters: Who They Are and What They Believe," CBS News, April 14, 2010; polling data, http://s3.amazonaws.com/nytdocs/docs/312/312.pdf.

344 In the Republican primaries "Tea Party Set to Win Enough Races for

Wide Influence," *The New York Times,* October 15, 2010; "Where Tea Party Candidates Are Running," *The New York Times,* October 15, 2010.

345 **House Republicans cut millions** "House Republicans Vote to Cut Millions from Food Safety Funds," *The Washington Post,* June 17, 2011.

345 **"They are more rigid"** Ornstein, interview, May 25, 2011.

345 **"An infantile form of conservatism"** Matt Bai, "Establishment Republicans Look at These Guys and Say, 'You're Nuts!' " *The New York Times Magazine,* October 16, 2011.

345 **"Some revenue in the mix"** President Barack Obama, news conference, White House transcript, June 29, 2011, http://www.whitehouse.gov.

346 **"Come on, you and I"** Paul Kane, "President, Speaker Motivated by 'Big Deal,' " *The Washington Post,* July 10, 2011.

346 **Reduce the national debt by $4 trillion** Carl Hulse, "A Lofty Vision vs. Realpolitik," *The New York Times,* July 11, 2011; "Boehner Says Obama 'Not Serious' About Deficit," CBS News, *Face the Nation,* May 15, 2011; Kane, "President, Speaker Motivated by 'Big Deal.' " Matt Bai, "The Game Is Called Chicken," *The New York Times Magazine,* April 1, 2012.

346 **The risk was** Kane, "President, Speaker Motivated by 'Big Deal.' "

346 **Boehner had to back out** Ibid.; David A. Fahrenthold and Paul Kane, "Eric Cantor Emerges a Key Player in Debt Negotiations," *The Washington Post,* July 11, 2011.

346 **"The Mother of All No-Brainers"** David Brooks, "The Mother of All No-Brainers," *The New York Times,* July 5, 2011.

347 **In this final push, their grand bargain** Bai, "The Game Is Called Chicken," and Peter Wallstein, Lori Montgomery, and Scott Wilson, "He Promised Change in Washington. Then the Debt Deal Collapsed. So Obama Changed Course," *The Washington Post*, March 18, 2012.

347 *Lowest level in sixty years* Senator Daniel K. Inouye, "Domestic Discretionary Spending Flat Since 2001; Not Responsible for Growing Debt," press release, Senate Committee on Appropriations, June 30, 2011, http://appropriations.senate.gov.

347 *Third lowest overall tax rates* "U.S. Is One of the Least Taxed Developed Countries," Citizens for Tax Justice, June 30, 2011, www.ctj.org/pdf/oecd201101.pdf.

347 **Millionaires when elected** "Tea Party House Members Even Wealthier than Other GOP Lawmakers," Center for Responsive Politics, January 4, 2012, www.opensecrets.org.

347 **"On balance, they're rich"** "Freshmen in 112th Congress Exceedingly Wealthy Despite Struggling Economy," Center for Responsive Politics, March 9, 2011, http://www.opensecrets.org.

348 **Has a large crop of millionaires** "Congressional Members' Personal Wealth Expands Despite Sour National Economy," OpenSecrets.org, November 17, 2010, http://www.opensecrets.org.

348 **Wealth in Congress has shot up** Eric Lichtblau, "Economic Slide Took a Detour on Capitol Hill," *The New York Times,* December 27, 2011.

348 **Cantor is a multimillionaire** Kate Andrews, "Eric Cantor's Climb Up

the Hill," September 2007, *Richmond* magazine.com, http://www.richmond magazine.com.

348 **Worth about $5 million** Eric Cantor, Financial Disclosure Statement, May 13, 2011, Legislative Resource Center, U.S. House of Representatives, http://pfds.opensecrets.org/N00013131_2010.pdf.

348 **More than $2 million in campaign donations** Alec MacGillis, "In Cantor, Hedge Funds and Private Equity Firms Have Voice at Debt Ceiling Negotiations," *The Washington Post,* July 25, 2011.

348 **"Hypnotizing" influence** Deval Patrick, "How Grover Norquist Hypnotized the GOP," *The Washington Post,* June 30, 2011.

349 **The de facto leader of** Steve Kroft, "The Pledge: Grover Norquist's Hold on the GOP," CBS News, *60 Minutes,* November 20, 2011. Alexander Bolton, "Reid Says Republican Lawmakers 'Being Led Like Puppets' by Grover Norquist," *The Hill,* November 1, 2011.

349 **across-the-board reductions** Grover Norquist, testimony, National Commission on Fiscal Responsibility and Reform, June 30, 2010. Although Norquist framed his proposal as a freeze in discretionary spending, by his freezing program budgets at fiscal year 2007 levels, he is actually advocating reducing all programs from their already higher levels of fiscal year 2011. http://www.fiscalcommission.gov/meetings/public-forum/3/Grover _Norquist_6_30_2010.pdf.

349 **Oppose virtually all government** Norquist, testimony, National Commission, June 30, 2010. "Who Is Grover Norquist?" Americans for Tax Reform, July 7, 2011, http://www.atr.org; Rick Henderson and Steven Hayward, "Happy Warrior," *Reason* magazine, February 1997; Robert Dreyfuss, "Grover Norquist: 'Field Marshal' of the Bush Plan," *The Nation,* May 14, 2001, 11–16.

349 **"No sacred cows"** Americans for Tax Reform, letter to Speaker John Boehner and Senate minority leader Mitch McConnell, "Conservative Leaders Call on Congress to Consider Defense Spending Cuts: Coalition Asks Republican Leaders to Restrain All Federal Outlays, Reject the Practice of Protecting Sacred Cows," November 30, 2010. See also press release on letter, http://s3.amazonaws.com/atrfiles/files/files/11302010pr_Defense%20 Letter(2).pdf.

349 **Signing a pledge** "Who Is Grover Norquist?"

349 **No congressional Republican** Ibid., accessed April 9, 2012.

349 **"We will make it"** Patrick, "How Grover Norquist Hypnotized the GOP."

350 **Just as Grover Norquist had predicted** "House Passes Deal to Raise Debt Cap and Defuse Crisis," *The New York Times,* August 2, 2011.

350 **"It is an unhappy fact"** David Bromwich, "Obama: His Words and His Deeds," *New York Review of Books,* July 14, 2011.

350 **Appalled at the "irresponsible actions"** Chuck Hagel, interview, *Financial Times Video,* August 31, 2011. http://video.ft.com/v/1138459180001/ Former-Republican-senator-criticises-party.

351 **"I find it frustrating"** Jennifer Steinhauer, "Snowe Opts Not to Seek Re-election in Maine," *The New York Times,* February 29, 2012.

351 **"Lugar was knocked off"** Monica Davey, "Lugar Loses Primary Challenge

in Indiana," *The New York Times,* May 8, 2012; Kirk Johnson, "Leader of '76 Insurgency Is Now the Target of One," *The New York Times,* May 22, 2012.

351 **"It's not honorable to kowtow"**   David Brooks, "The Possum Republicans," *The New York Times,* February 28, 2012.

351 **"Today's Republican Party"**   Mann and Ornstein, *It's Even Worse Than It Looks,* 102.

352 **"Bringing the Republican Party"**   Ibid.

CHAPTER 20: THE HIGH COST
OF IMPERIAL OVERSTRETCH

353 **"To amass military power"**   President Dwight Eisenhower, State of the Union Address, February 2, 1953, http://www.eisenhowermemorial.org.

353 **"The total amount"**   Christopher A. Preble, *The Power Problem: How American Military Dominance Makes Us Less Safe, Less Prosperous, and Less Free* (Ithaca, NY: Cornell University Press, 2009), 3.

353 **"The hell that was Anbar Province"**   Matthew Hoh, "Measuring Quick Sand," *HuffPost World,* June 9, 2011, http://www.huffingtonpost.com.

354 **Twenty-one thousand more U.S. troops**   President Barack Obama, remarks, "A New Strategy for Afghanistan and Pakistan," March 27, 2009, http://www.whitehouse.gov; Bob Woodward, *Obama's Wars* (New York: Simon & Schuster, 2010), 95–98, 113.

354 **Win support among the tribes**   Karen DeYoung, "U.S. Official Resigns over Afghan War," *The Washington Post,* October 27, 2009.

354 **There was not one insurgency**   Ibid.

355 **America was widely perceived as the occupier**   Matthew Hoh, resignation letter to Ambassador Nancy J. Powell, director general of the United States Foreign Service, September 10, 2009, http://www.washingtonpost .com.

355 **"The people we are fighting"**   Matthew Hoh, media press conference, ABC News, October 27, 2009, http://abcnews.go.com.

355 **"I have lost understanding"**   Hoh, resignation letter.

356 **The initial withdrawal**   President Barack Obama, remarks, "The Way Forward in Afghanistan," June 22, 2011, http://www.whitehouse.gov.

356 **"If we're going to cut programs"**   House Clerk records, final vote results for roll call 373, May 26, 2011, show vote of 215–204 against the measure (207 Republicans and 8 Democrats against; 26 Republicans and 178 Democrats in favor), http://clerk.house.gov/evs/2011/roll373.xml.

356 **Forced to make "deeply painful cuts"**   Michael Cooper, "Mayors See End to Wars a Fix for Struggling Cities," *The New York Times,* June 18, 2011.

356 **"We can no longer"**   "Cost of Wars a Rising Issue as Obama Weighs Troop Levels," *The New York Times,* June 22, 2011.

357 **Appropriated $1.4 trillion in funds**   Amy Belasco, "The Cost of Iraq, Afghanistan, and Other Global War on Terror Operations Since 9/11," Congressional Research Service, March 29, 2011, fpc.state.gov.

357 **Totaled the costs of the war through fiscal year 2015**   Eisenhower
Study Group, "The Costs of War Since 2001: Iraq, Afghanistan, and
Pakistan." (Providence, RI: Watson Institute for International Studies,
Brown University, June 2011), table 5. From their total estimated cost of
$3.668 trillion, I have subtracted $155 billion listed as projected Pentagon
war spending for fiscal years 2016–2020 because U.S. military engagement
in that period is highly problematic. That gives a total of $3.513 trillion.
For simplicity, I have also combined cost for fiscal year 2012 with previous
years.

358 **A more realistic "moderate" estimate . . . would be**   Ibid. Here, I have
given original Eisenhower Study Group estimate. Also, see Daniel Trotta,
"Cost of War at Least $3.7 Trillion and Counting," *Reuters*, June 29, 2011.

358 **Fired his top economic adviser**   Lawrence Lindsey, "What the Iraq War
Will Cost the U.S.," CNNMoney.com/*Fortune,* January 11, 2008, http://
money.cnn.com; Secretary Donald Rumsfeld, media stakeout, transcript,
U.S. Department of Defense, January 19, 2003, http://www.defense.gov;
Bruce Bartlett, "The Cost of War," Forbes.com, November 26, 2009, http://
www.forbes.com.

358 **Pentagon estimated the Afghan war**   James Dao, "The War Budget:
U.S. Is Expecting to Spend $1 Billion a Month on War," *The New York Times,*
November 12, 2001.

358 **"History shows that wars"**   Bartlett, "Cost of War."

358 **Unfunded wars drag on**   William A. Niskanen and Benjamin Friedman,
comment on Senator Al Franken's pay for war resolution, November 4, 2006,
http://www.franken.senate.gov.

359 **"The mission is"**   President George W. Bush, remarks, "Welcoming Aid
Workers Rescued from Afghanistan," November 26, 20001, http://
georgewbush-whitehouse.archives.gov.

359 **"Some very important lessons in Vietnam"**   President George W. Bush,
press conference, October 11, 2001, http://georgewbush-whitehouse.archives
.gov.

359 **"Our military should be used to fight"**   President George W. Bush,
roundtable interview with foreign press, July 17, 2001, Briefing Room,
http://georgewbush-whitehouse.archives.gov.

359 **"We know that true peace"**   President George W. Bush, "President Out-
lines War Effort," Virginia Military Institute, April 17, 2002, http://
georgewbush-whitehouse.archives.gov.

360 **Al-Qaeda and its Arab recruits**   General David McKiernan, briefing for
Vice President–Elect Joseph Biden, December 2008, cited in Woodward,
Obama's Wars, 71.

360 **"The mistaken mission creep in Afghanistan"**   Robert Blackwill,
quoted in David Sanger, "Rethinking the Afghanistan War's What-Ifs," *The
New York Times Magazine,* July 31, 2010.

361 **"No matter how long it takes"**   President George W. Bush, speech, Bagram Air Base, Afghanistan, December 15, 2008, http://georgewbush-
whitehouse.archives.gov.

361 **Obama committed twenty-one thousand more troops** Obama, "New Strategy for Afghanistan and Pakistan."

361 **Failure to send in more troops** General Stanley A. McChrystal, memo, "Commander's Initial Assessment," NATO International Security Assistance Force, Afghanistan, August 30, 2009, http://media.washingtonpost.com/wp-srv/politics/documents/Assessment_Redacted_092109.pdf.

362 **Wanted *defeat* written into Obama's official orders** Woodward, *Obama's Wars,* 144–45.

362 **A bone of contention in** "President Obama's Final Orders for Afghanistan Pakistan Strategy, or Terms Sheet," November 29, 2009, in Woodward, *Obama's Wars,* 385–86.

362 **Obama did agree** Obama, "The Way Forward."

362 **"Inflicted enormous losses"** Joshua Partlow, "In Letter, Petraeus Offers Optimistic Assessment of Afghan War," *The Washington Post,* January 26, 2011.

362 **"Very hard, but it is doable"** Carlotta Gall, "Petraeus Confident as He Leaves Afghanistan," *The New York Times,* July 11, 2011.

362 **Pregnant parallels** Rufus Phillips, "Déjà Vu All Over Again: Are We Repeating Vietnam?" *World Affairs,* September–October 2010, http://www.worldaffairsjournal.org.

363 **"It rhymes"** Mark Twain, in Kurt Andersen, *Reset: How This Crisis Can Restore Our Values and Renew America* (New York: Random House, 2009), 25.

363 **But the Afghan government** Phillips, "Déjà Vu."

363 **Ambassador Richard Holbrooke** Richard Holbrooke, interview, December 15, 2009.

364 **The war is more political than military** Ambassador Karl W. Eikenberry, classified cable to Secretary of State Hillary Clinton, November 6, 2009; Eric Schmitt, "U.S. Envoy's Cables Show Worries on Afghan Plans," *The New York Times,* January 26, 2010.

365 **Disillusioned with Karzai** Elisabeth Bumiller and Mark Landler, "U.S. Envoy Urges Caution on Forces for Afghanistan," *The New York Times,* November 12, 2009.

365 **Crooked Afghan cops** T. Christian Miller, *ProPublica,* Mark Hosenball and Ron Moreau, *Newsweek,* "$6 Billion Later, Afghan Cops Aren't Ready to Serve," March 20, 2010, http://www.propublica.org.

365 **Desertions and resignations** "U.S. General Cites Goals to Train Afghan Forces," *The New York Times,* August 23, 2010.

365 **"Rapidly growing systemic homicide threat"** Matthew Rosenberg, "Afghan Soldiers Step Up Killings of Allied Forces," *The New York Times,* January 20, 2012.

366 **U.S. Marines urinating on the dead bodies** Graham Bowley and Matthew Rosenberg, "Video Inflames a Delicate Moment for U.S. in Afghanistan," *The New York Times,* January 12, 2012.

366 **NATO forces mistakenly burned Korans** Sangar Rahimi and Alissa J. Rubin, "Koran Burning in NATO Error Incites Afghans," *The New York Times,* February 22, 2012.

366 **Two dozen Afghans** Alissa J. Rubin and Sharifullah Sahak, "Koran Burnings Resume in Afghanistan Despite U.S. Apology," *The New York Times,* February 25, 2012.

366 **Two U.S. advisory officers were killed** Matthew Rosenberg and Thom Shanker,"Afghan Uproar Casts Shadows on U.S. Pullout," *The New York Times,* February 27, 2012.

366 **President Karzai responded to widespread** Rod Nordland and Matthew Rosenberg, "Karzai Calls on U.S. to Pull Back as Taliban Cancels Talks," *The New York Times*, March 15, 2012.

366 **"Under the spell of the Taliban"** Ray Rivera, "Afghan Army Attracts Few Where Fear Reigns," *The New York Times,* September 6, 2011.

366 **"50 percent of the people"** Partlow, "In Letter, Petraeus Offers Optimistic Assessment."

366 **"The Taliban are coming back"** Jill Abramson, "Mission Unfinished," *The New York Times,* Sunday section, "The Reckoning," September 11, 2011.

367 **"We have *never once gotten it right"*** Robert M. Gates, speech at U.S. Military Academy at West Point, NY, February 25, 2011 (emphasis added), http://www.defense.gov.

368 **"Empire of Bases" that** Chalmers Johnson, *The Sorrows of Empire: Militarism, Secrecy, and the End of the Republic* (New York: Metropolitan Books, 2004), 151–85; Chalmers Johnson, "America's Empire of Bases: Militarism, Secrecy and the End of the Republic," TomDispatch.com, January 15, 2004, http://www.tomdispatch.com.

368 **More than 580,000 personnel** The Pentagon listed 406,518 military personnel: "Department of Defense: Active Duty Military Personnel Strengths by Regional Area and by Country (309a)," Statistical Information Analysis Division, U.S. Department of Defense, September 30, 2011, http://siadapp.dmdc.osd.mil/personnel/MILITARY/history/hst1109.pdf. In addition, the Pentagon reported 175,045 defense contractors: "Contractor Support of U.S. Operations in the USCENTCOM Area of Responsibility, Iraq, and Afghanistan," October 17, 2011, Office of the Under Secretary of Defense Acquisition, Technology and Logistics, U.S. Department of Defense, http://www.acq.osd.mil/log/PS/docs/5A_paper/5A_October_2011_final.doc.

368 **Listed 611 U.S. overseas** The Pentagon's official report lists 611 overseas bases, but just like the defense budget, which did not include appropriations for the wars in Afghanistan and Iraq, the base structure report does not include bases and military installations in war zones. "Base Structure Report: Fiscal Year 2011 Baseline," Office of Deputy Undersecretary of Defense for Installations and Environment, U.S. Department of Defense, http://www.acq.osd.mil/ie/download/bsr/bsr2011baseline.pdf.

368 **Hot war zones—then 411 in Afghanistan** Nick Turse, "Empire of Bases 2.0," CBS News Opinion, January 10, 2011, http:www.cbsnews.com.

368 **"No other military in world history"** Tom Kane, "Global U.S. Troop Deployment, 1950–2005," 10, Heritage Foundation, May 24, 2006, http://www.heritage.org.

368 **Simply maintaining those bases** Deputy Undersecretary of Defense Dorothy Robyn, cited in Christine Anh and Sukjong Hong, "Bring War Dollars Home by Shutting Down Bases," Institute for Policy Studies, March 31, 2011, http://www.ips-dc.org.

369 **"There was no corner of the known world"** Joseph Schumpeter, *Imperialism and Social Classes: Two Essays* (Cleveland: Meridian Books, 1951), 51.

369 **Rumsfeld made plans to bring seventy thousand troops home** Donald H. Rumsfeld, testimony, Senate Armed Services Committee, September 23, 2004, http://www.defense.gov.

369 **"America stands alone"** President William Clinton, Second Inaugural Address, January 20, 1997, http://www.gpo.gov.

369 **"The survival of liberty"** President George W. Bush, Second Inaugural Address, January 20, 2005, http://www.whitehouse.gov.

370 **In its defense doctrine** Preble, *Power Problem,* 29.

370 **"America has underwritten global security"** Obama, "The Way Forward."

370 **"America cannot act alone"** President Barack Obama, Nobel Prize speech, Oslo, Norway, December 10, 2009, http://www.whitehouse.gov.

370 **With a monopoly of atomic weapons** Kennedy, *Great Powers,* 357–59.

370 **"Reagan severed the connection"** Andrew J. Bacevich, *The Limits of Power: The End of American Exceptionalism* (New York: Henry Holt & Co., 2008), 28–30, 36–40.

371 **The nation's pre-recession global trade deficits** Census Bureau, "Trade in Goods with World, Seasonally Adjusted," accessed April 11, 2012, shows U.S. global trade deficit of $808.8 billion in 2007 and $828.0 billion in 2006, http://www.census.gov/foreign-trade/balance/c0004.html.

371 **A doubling of the overall defense budget** Thomas Christie and Pierre M. Sprey, letter to Erskine Bowles, co-chair, National Commission on Fiscal Responsibility and Reform, November 15, 2010; Winslow Wheeler, "Ignorance Is Not Bliss," *Defense Monitor,* March 2011, www.cdi.org.

371 **To nearly $1 trillion a year** Winslow Wheeler, "U.S. Security Total Budget," Center for Defense Information, email, August 22, 2011, http://www.cdi.org.

371 **Calculated that U.S. defense spending** Preble, *Power Problem;* Christie and Sprey, letter to Erskine Bowles.

371 **"It has been a common dilemma"** Kennedy, *Great Powers,* 533.

372 **America's challenge** Ibid., 514–15.

373 **"To amass military power"** Eisenhower, State of the Union Address, February 2, 1953.

373 **"We pay for a single destroyer"** President Dwight Eisenhower, "The Chance for Peace," speech to American Society of Newspaper Editors, April 16, 1953.

373 **"Instead of fighting this war"** Barack Obama, campaign speech, Charleston, WV, March 20, 2008, http://www.cfr.org.

373 **"That is enough"** Hillary Clinton, campaign speech, George Washington University, Washington, DC, March 15, 2008, http://www.presidency.ucsb.edu.

374 **"Afghanistan is no longer a war"** Leslie Gelb, "Mission Accomplished," *The Wall Street Journal,* May 9, 2011.

374 **The Arc of Danger** Congressional Research Service, "State, Foreign Operations, and Related Programs: FY2012 Budget and Appropriations," November 23, 2011, fpc.state.gov; Walter Pincus, "U.S. Military Presence Will Continue in Iraq," *The Washington Post,* November 21, 2011; Daniel Froomkin, "Massive U.S. Embassy Will Expand Further as Soldiers Leave," *HuffPost World,* September 16, 2011, http://www.huffingtonpost.com.

374 **"The smallest footprint necessary"** Thom Shanker and Charlie Savage, "After Bin Laden, U.S. Reassesses Afghan Strategy," *The New York Times,* May 10, 2011.

CHAPTER 21: RECLAIMING THE DREAM

379 **"A free people ought"** Alfred E. Eckes, Jr., *Opening America's Market: U.S. Foreign Trade Policy Since 1776* (Chapel Hill: University of North Carolina Press, 1992), 2.

379 **"Today, our most important task"** Susan Hockfield, "Manufacturing a Recovery," *The New York Times,* August 29, 2011.

379 **"The social contract"** Leslie H. Gelb, "What Germany's Economy Can Teach Obama," *The Daily Beast,* June 5, 2011, http://www.thedailybeast.com.

380 **A dramatic increase** Two-thirds of Americans see "sharp conflicts" between rich and poor, a jump of nearly 20 percent in just two years. See "Rising Share of Americans See Conflict Between Rich and Poor," Pew Research Center.

380 **Advocating a comeback for manufacturing** Michael A. Fletcher and David Nakamura, "For Factories, 2012 Brings a Happier Tune," *The Washington Post,* February 16, 2012.

381 **A domestic Marshall Plan** Horizon Project, "Report and Recommendations."

381 **"Job creation must be the number one objective"** Grove, "How America Can Create Jobs." Grove was co-founder of Intel in 1979, CEO 1987–1997, and chairman 1997–1998.

381 **Spence has documented how global competition** Michael Spence and Sandile Hlatshwayo, "The Evolving Structure of the American Economy and the Employment Challenge," working paper, Council on Foreign Relations, March 2011, 1, 4–5, 12–13, 31–32. http://www.cfr.org.

382 **America needs "to devote public funding"** Michael Spence, "The Impact of Globalization on Income and Employment: The Downside of Integrating Markets," *Foreign Affairs* 90, no. 4 (July–August 2011).

382 **"They should promote such manufactories"** George Washington, cited in Eckes, *Opening America's Market,* 2.

383 **"Manufactures are now as necessary"** Thomas Jefferson, letter to Benjamin Austin, January 1, 1816, *The Writings of Thomas Jefferson,* vol. vi, edited by

H. A. Washington. (New York: Riker, Thorne & Co., Washington: Taylor & Maury, 1855), 520–23. http://books.google.com/books?id=NDg-AAAAYAAJ &lpg=PA520&ots=w3Damr1zCP&dq=To%20Benjamin%20Austin%2C %20Esq.Monticello%2C%20January%209%2C%201816&pg=PR1#v= onepage&q&f=false.

383 **American history is replete with examples** For a broad, detailed discussion, see Prestowitz, *Betrayal of American Prosperity,* 50–61, 76–78.

383 **In 1842, Congress awarded Samuel F. B. Morse** Office of the Clerk, U.S. House of Representatives, "House History: Electronic Technology in the House of Representatives: 'What Hath God Wrought': House of Representatives and the Telegraph." http://artandhistory.house.gov/house_history/ technology/telegraph.aspx.

384 **Reagan administration put political pressure on** Clyde Prestowitz, email, December 10, 2011.

384 **To create "precompetitive" technologies** Prestowitz, *Betrayal of American Prosperity,* 103–09.

384 **So there was ample precedent** "Obama Advisor Bloom to Depart," *The Wall Street Journal,* August 9, 2011.

385 **"Virtually everything Jobs has developed"** Prestowitz, *Betrayal of American Prosperity,* 287.

385 **"We invented products and then made them"** Susan Hockfield, "Manufacturing a Recovery," *The New York Times,* August 11, 2011.

386 **"We broke the chain of experience"** Grove, "How America Can Create Jobs."

386 **The German economy has grown faster** David Leonhardt, "The German Example," *The New York Times,* June 8, 2011; Robert Reich, "The Limping Middle Class," *The New York Times,* Sunday Review, September 4, 2011.

386 **Germany generated $2 trillion in trade surpluses** German Office of Federal Statistics, "Foreign Trade Data," Statistisches Bundesamt, Deutschland, 2011, http://www.destatis.de.

386 **The United States racked up $6 trillion in trade deficits** U.S. Census Bureau, "U.S. Trade in Goods and Services, Balance of Payment Basis," Foreign Trade Division, June 9, 2011, www.census.gov.

387 **The German model shows** Steven Rattner, "The Secrets of Germany's Success," *Foreign Affairs* 90, no. 4 (July–August 2011).

387 **Marquee brands and precision machine tools** Census Bureau, "U.S. Trade"; and German Office of Federal Statistics, "Foreign Trade Data."

387 **"It's because we stuck to manufacturing"** Marcus Walker, "Is Germany Turning into the Strong Silent Type?" *The Wall Street Journal,* July 27, 2011.

387 **"The social contract"** Gelb, "What Germany's Economy Can Teach Obama."

387 **"German unions also agreed"** Harold Meyerson, "Two Cheers for Germany," *The Washington Post,* June 28, 2011; Nicholas Kulish, "Defying Others, Germany Finds Economic Success," *The New York Times,* August 13, 2010; John Schmitt, "Labor Market Policy in the Great Recession: Some

Lessons from Denmark and Germany," Center for Economic and Policy Research, May 2011, http://www.cepr.net.

387 **German companies shortened everyone's workweek** Rattner, "Germany's Success."

388 **A long-term structural jobs problem** Horizon Project, "Report and Recommendations."

388 **Modernize America's outdated transportation networks** Building America's Future Educational Fund, "Falling Apart and Falling Behind: Transportation Infrastructure Report 2011," 5, www.bafuture.org.

388 **Backing from such traditional political adversaries** Office of Senator John F. Kerry, "U.S. Chamber, AFL-CIO Urge Infrastructure Bank, BUILD Act Creates Jobs, Strengthens Competitiveness," March 15, 2011, http://kerry.senate.gov.

389 **The United States has fallen from No. 1** World Economic Forum, "The Global Competitiveness Report 2011," table 6, http://www3.weforum.org/docs/WEF_GCR_2010–11.pdf.

389 **An estimated cost of $115 billion** Building America's Future, "Falling Apart," 11, 16–35.

389 **It will "never be cheaper"** Daniel Alpert, Robert Hockett, and Nouriel Roubini, "The Way Forward," New America Foundation, October 2011, 15–16, http://www.newamerica.net.

390 **A win-win for all sides** Ibid., 17–18.

390 **Put five million young people to work** Leo Hindery, Jr., and Leo W. Gerard, "A Vision for Economic Renewal: An American Jobs Agenda," *Huffington Post,* July 22, 2011, http://www.huffingtonpost.com.

390 **A "gathering storm"** National Academy of Sciences, National Academy of Engineering, and Institute of Medicine, *Rising Above the Gathering Storm: Energizing and Employing America for a Brighter Economic Future* (Washington, D.C.: National Academy Press, 2007); *Rising Above the Gathering Storm, Revisited: Rapidly Approaching Category 5* (Washington, D.C.: National Academy Press, 2010), 2, 5.

390 **Scientists date the American slide** Evan Osnos, "Green Giant—Beijing," *The New Yorker,* December 21, 2009. Osnos's statistics come from the American Association for the Advancement of Science.

391 **The United States fell to No. 4** Robert D. Atkinson and Scott M. Andes, "The Atlantic Century II: Benchmarking EU and U.S. Innovation and Competitiveness," Information Technology and Innovation Foundation, July 2011, http://www.itif.org.

391 **China in 2008 surpassed the United States** Alan L. Porter, Nils C. Newman, Xiao-Yin Jin, et al., "High Tech Indicators: Technology-Based Competitiveness of 33 Nations" (Atlanta, GA: Technology Policy and Assessment Center, Georgia Tech University, 2008), http://www.tpac.gatech.edu.

391 **Ranked the United States fifth** "U.S. Falls to 5th in Global Competitiveness, Survey Shows," Associated Press, September 7, 2011.

391 **The trends in patents**   National Academy of Sciences, *Gathering Storm, Revisited.*

391 **The United States will soon be importing**   Rob Atkinson, Michael Shellenberger, Ted Nordhaus, et al., "Rising Tigers, Sleeping Giant: Asian Nations Set to Dominate the Clean Energy Race by Out-Investing the United States," Breakthrough Institute and Information Technology and Innovation Foundation, November 2009, http://www.thebreakthrough.org.

391 **It will take dramatically expanding government funding**   National Academy of Sciences, *Gathering Storm,* appendix E, recommendations called for $13 billion a year in government spending for a decade, starting in 2007.

391 **Obama provided a kick start**   President Barack Obama, remarks, National Academy of Sciences, April 27, 2009; "Fact Sheet: A Historic Commitment to Research and Education," April 27, 2009, http://www.white house.gov.

392 **Obama put $400 million**   Matthew L. Wald, "Energy Firms Aided by U.S. Find Backers," *The New York Times,* February 2, 2011.

392 **Government has to be much smarter**   "FBI Raids Solar-Panel Maker," *The Wall Street Journal,* September 9, 2011; "In Rush to Assist a Solar Company, U.S. Missed Signs," *The New York Times,* September 22, 2011; "Rich Subsidies Powering Solar and Wind Projects," *The New York Times,* November 12, 2011.

392 **"Many bought into the idea"**   Jeffrey R. Immelt, "An American Renewal," Detroit Economic Club, June 26, 2009; Steve Lohr, "G.E. Goes with What It Knows: Making Stuff," *The New York Times,* December 4, 2010.

392 **"Without an industrial base"**   Richard McCormack, "The Plight of American Manufacturing," *American Prospect,* December 21, 2009, http://prospect.org.

393 **"You cannot survive as a nation"**   Leo Hindery, Jr., interview, June 28, 2011.

393 **Fifty-nine thousand factories were shut down**   U.S. Bureau of Labor Statistics, *Quarterly Census of Employment & Wages (QCEW) Database,* accessed January 20, 2012, http://www.bls.gov.

393 **"Close a manufacturing plant"**   McCormack, "Plight of American Manufacturing."

393 **Booz Allen Hamilton predicted**   Booz Allen Hamilton, "The Green Jobs Study," U.S. Green Building Council, November 12, 2009, http://www.booz allen.com.

394 **More modest job growth**   "Clean Power, Green Jobs," Union of Concerned Scientists, March 2009, http://www.ucsusa.org; Robert Pollin, James Heintz, and Heidi Garrett-Peltier, "The Economic Benefits of Investing in Clean Energy," Center for American Progress, June 2009, http://www.americanprogress.org; Steven Greenhouse, "Millions of Jobs of a Different Collar," *The New York Times,* March 23, 2008.

394 **The test is whether**   Grove, "How America Can Create Jobs."

394 **The Alliance for American Manufacturing**   Hindery and Gerard, "Vision for Economic Renewal."

394 **The alliance wants the government** "Our Plan," Alliance for American Manufacturing, August 15, 2011, http://www.americanmanufacturing.org.

394 **Two recent high-profile cases** David Barboza, "Bridge Comes to San Francisco with a Made-in-China Label," *The New York Times,* June 26, 2011; Annys Shin, "As Chinese Workers Build the Martin Luther King Memorial, a Union Investigates," *The Washington Post,* November 23, 2010.

395 **George W. Bush tax cuts** Fieldhouse and Pollack, "Tenth Anniversary of the Bush-Era Tax Cuts." Thomas L. Hungerford, "Changes in the Distribution of Income Among Tax Filers Between 1996 and 2006: The Role of Labor Income, Capital Income, and Tax Policy," Congressional Research Service, December 29, 2011, fpc.state.gov. Edmund L. Andrews, "Tax Cuts Offer Most for Very Rich, Study Says," *The New York Times,* January 8, 2007.

395 **Large majorities of the public favor** Bruce Bartlett, "23 Polls Say People Support Higher Taxes to Reduce the Deficit," Capital Gains and Games, August 10, 2011, http://www.capitalgainsandgames.com; "Poll Shows Americans Oppose Entitlement Cuts to Deal with Debt Problem," *The Washington Post,* April 20, 2011; CNN poll, August 5–7, 2011; Gallup poll, August 10, 2011.

395 **An alternative idea is to** Fieldhouse and Pollack, "Bush-Era Tax Cuts."

395 **Estimated the tax loss to** Charles Rossotti, former IRS commissioner, interview, October 27, 2003.

395 **"They are very decent people"** Warren Buffett, "Stop Coddling the Super-Rich," *The New York Times,* August 15, 2011.

396 **Close the exemption in the payroll tax** "Warren Buffett Tells Charlie Rose Why Congress Should Stop 'Coddling' the Super-Rich," *Charlie Rose.*

396 **Solving the funding shortfall for Social Security** Larry Mishel, interview, July 7, 2010.

396 **A majority of Americans** Fifty-four percent said capital gains should be taxed at the 35 percent rate or higher. Allison Kopicki, "Partisan Split over Tax Policies," *The New York Times,* January 24, 2012. Romney's tax rate: Nicholas Confessore and David Kocieniewski, "For Romneys, Friendly Code Reduces Taxes," *The New York Times,* January 25, 2002.

396 **Gains are heavily concentrated at the top** Robert Lenzner, "The Top 0.1% of the Nation Earn Half of All Capital Gains," *Forbes,* November 20, 2011.

397 **Citizens for Tax Justice examined the records** Robert S. McIntyre, Matthew Gardner, Rebecca J. Wilkins, et al., "Corporate Taxpayers & Corporate Tax Dodgers 2008–10," Citizens for Tax Justice and Institute on Taxation and Economic Policy, November 2011, http://www.ctj.org; John McKinnon, "Business Roundtable: We Pay Enough Taxes, Thank You," *The Wall Street Journal Washington Wire,* April 14, 2011.

397 **Others cashed in heavily on loopholes** Aviva Aron-Dine, "Well-Designed, Fiscally Responsible Corporate Tax Reform Could Benefit the Economy," Center on Budget and Policy Priorities, June 4, 2008, http://www.cbpp.org.

397 **The multinationals that have been most successful** McIntyre, "Corporate Tax Dodgers."

397 **Companies that pay roughly 35 percent**   Catherine Rampell, "Winners and Losers Under the U.S. Corporate Tax Code," *The New York Times Online,* January 27, 2011; Binyamin Appelbaum, "Corporate Taxes: More Winners and Losers," *The New York Times Online,* January 27, 2011; "Analysis: 12 Corporations Pay Effective Tax Rate of Negative 1.5% on $171 Billion in Profits: Reap $62.4 Billion in Tax Subsidies," Citizens for Tax Justice, June 1, 2011, http://www.ctj.org.

398 **"Double Irish with a Dutch sandwich"**   Charles Duhigg and David Kocienieski, "How Apple Sidesteps Billions in Taxes," *The New York Times,* April 29, 2012.

398 **Paid only $3.3 billion in taxes on $34.2 billion in profits**   Ibid.

398 **"Check the Box"**   Vanessa Houlder, Megan Murphy, and Jeff Gerth, "Tax Wars: The Accidental Billion-Dollar Break," *FT.Com Financial Times,* September 27, 2011.

399 **They lobby Congress for a "tax holiday"**   David Kocieniewski, "Companies Push for Tax Break on Foreign Cash," *The New York Times,* June 19, 2011; Linnley Browning, "A One-Time Tax Break Saved 843 U.S. Corporations $265 Billion," *The New York Times,* June 24, 2008. Dhammika Dharmapala, C. Fritz Foley, and Kristin J. Forbes, "Watch What I Do, Not What I Say: The Unintended Consequences of the Homeland Investment Act," *Journal of Finance,* April 27, 2010, http://www.nber.org.

399 **Want tax reform to require proof**   Hindery and Gerard, "Vision for Economic Renewal."

400 **Jobs advocates want ironclad provisions**   Kocieniewski, "Companies Push for Tax Break"; Dan Eggen, "The Influence Industry: Companies Lobbying for Tax Holiday on Overseas Money," *The Washington Post,* April 27, 2011; Mike Zapler, "Big Biz: How About a Tax Holiday?" *Politico,* March 4, 2011, http://www.politico.com.

400 **China manipulates the value**   Currency data from Peterson Institute for International Economics, in press release, Alliance for American Manufacturing, "Ending China's Currency Manipulation Would Create Over 2 Million Jobs," June 17, 2011.

400 **Widespread intellectual piracy**   "Ballmer Bares China Travails," *The Wall Street Journal,* May 26, 2011; "Piracy: China Still in the Game," ABC News, November 16, 2010; "Special Report: Warren Buffett's China Car Deal Could Backfire," Reuters, March 9, 2011.

400 **A major national intelligence report**   "Foreign Spies Stealing U.S. Economic Secrets in Cyberspace: Report to Congress on Foreign Economic Collection and Industrial Espionage, 2009–2011," Office of the National Counterintelligence Executive, October 2011, accessed January 27, 2012, http://www.dni.gov.

401 **Violating rules of the World Trade Organization**   "Intel Chief: Obama (Still) Driving US off Cliff," *The Register,* August 25, 2010, http://www.theregister.co.uk; Clyde Prestowitz, interview, January 11, 2011.

401 **The United States would gain 2.25 million jobs**   Robert E. Scott, "The

Benefits of Revaluation," EPI Briefing Paper, June 17, 2011, Economic Policy Institute, http://www.epi.org.

401 **Gain another 2.1 million full-time jobs** "China: Effects of Intellectual Property Infringement and Indigenous Innovation Policies on the U.S. Economy," U.S. International Trade Commission, May 2011, http://www.usitc .gov.

401 **"China's currency manipulation"** Office of Senator Robert B. Casey, Jr., press release, "China's Currency Manipulation Undermines U.S. Manufacturing Base by Making U.S.-Made Goods More Expensive Relative to Foreign Goods," January 17, 2011.

402 **Accused China of violating free trade rules** Keith Bradsher, "In Victory for the West, W.T.O. Orders China to Stop Export Taxes on Minerals," *The New York Times,* January 30, 2012.

402 **$450 billion in projected defense cuts** President Barack Obama, remarks, U.S. Department of Defense, January 3, 2012; Secretary of Defense Leon Panetta, "Sustaining Global Leadership: Priorities for 21st Century Defense," January 2012.

403 **Another $500 billion in cuts** Congressional Budget Office, "Final Sequestration Report for Fiscal Year 2012," January 12, 2012, http://www.cbo .gov.

403 **$1 trillion can be cut** Lawrence J. Korb, "Why Panetta's Pentagon Cuts Are Easier Than You Think," Snapshot, *Foreign Affairs,* January 4, 2012; Winslow Wheeler, email, December 2, 2011; Christie and Sprey, letter to Erskine Bowles.

403 **2007 level of $470 billion a year** Wheeler, email.

403 **That level would still enable** Christie and Sprey, letter to Erskine Bowles; Winslow Wheeler, "Ignorance Is Not Bliss," *The Hill,* March 9, 2011, http:// www.thehill.com.

403 **Cost the nation more than $3.5 trillion** Eisenhower Study Group, "The Costs of War Since 2001: Iraq, Afghanistan, and Pakistan" (Providence, RI: Watson Institute for International Studies, Brown University, June 2011), table 5. From their total cost of $3.688 trillion, I have dropped war costs of $155 billion for fiscal years 2016–2020, since America's actual involvement in war during those years is problematic, http://costsofwar.org. Daniel Trotta, "Cost of War at Least $3.7 Trillion and Counting," Reuters, June 29, 2011.

403 **Cutback of $1 trillion** Fareed Zakaria, "Why Defense Spending Should Be Cut," *The Washington Post,* August 3, 2011.

404 **The "gross mismanagement"** Vice Admiral Norb Ryan, Jr., "Another Burden for Our War Fighters," *Washington Times,* November 23, 2011.

404 **McCain issued a savage critique** Senator John McCain, remarks on the "military-industrial-congressional" complex, December 15, 2011, http:// mccain.senate.gov.

404 **"Every gun that is made"** President Dwight Eisenhower, speech, "A Chance for Peace," April 16, 1953, http://millercenter.org/president/speeches/ detail/3357.

404 **"Instead of fighting this war"**   Barack Obama, campaign speech, Charleston, WV, March 20, 2008, http://www.cfr.org.

404 **A faster draw-down of U.S. forces**   Leslie Gelb, "Mission Accomplished," *The Wall Street Journal,* May 9, 2011.

405 **Proposed $750 billion in defense cuts**   Zakaria, "Why Defense Spending Should Be Cut."

405 **It's a catch-22**   "U.S. Refinancing Effort Casts Wider Net to Aid Underwater Owners," *The New York Times,* November 30, 2011.

406 **The agreement in February 2012**   Nelson D. Schwartz and Julie Creswell, "Mortgage Plan Gives Billions to Homeowners, but with Exceptions," *The New York Times,* February 10, 2012.

406 **"No compensation, no amount of money"**   Barack Obama, cited in ibid.

406 **"Residential mortgage market is wholly inadequate"**   William C. Dudley, "Securing the Recovery and Building for the Future," speech, West Point, NY, November 17, 2011, http://www.newyorkfed.org; Floyd Norris, "To Revive Economy, Rescue Housing," *The New York Times,* December 2, 2011.

406 **Smart economists have suggested multiple ways**   Ezra Klein, "Mass Refinancing: The 'Biggest Thing' Obama Can Do Without Congress," *The Washington Post,* January 10, 2012.

407 **Government buy up near worthless second mortgages**   Alpert, Hockett, and Roubini, "The Way Forward."

407 **Convert many of these homes into rentals**   Dudley, "Securing the Recovery."

407 **Offer loan guarantees**   "Obama Proposes Mortgage Relief," *The Washington Post,* February 2, 2012.

408 **Measures to slow Medicare cost growth**   Centers for Medicare and Medicaid Services, "Affordable Care Act Update: Implementing Medicare Cost Savings," August 2010, www.cms.gov.

408 **Eliminate the anticipated Social Security shortfall**   Thomas Geoghegan, "Get Radical: Raise Social Security," *The New York Times,* June 20, 2011; Andrew Fieldhouse, Economic Policy Institute, email, August 22, 2011.

408 **Our economy is projected to grow by 60 percent**   Lawrence Mishel, "We're Not Broke, Nor Will We Be," EPI Briefing Paper, May 19, 2011, Economic Policy Institute, http://www.epi.org.

CHAPTER 22: POLITICS: A GRASSROOTS RESPONSE

410 **"There is a disconnection"**   Gardner, "American Experiment."

410 **"Either democracy must be renewed"**   Phillips, *Wealth and Democracy,* 422.

411 **Government "of the 1%"**   Stiglitz, "Inequality."

411 **"Selling the country to the highest bidder"**   McCain, CNN AllPolitics.

412 **Public discontent**   "Rising Share of Americans See Conflict Between Rich and Poor," Pew Research Center.

412 **Confidence in government** "Disapproval Rate for Congress at Record 82% After Debt Talks," *The New York Times,* August 5, 2011.

412 **Special interests have too much influence** "Alienated Nation: Americans Complain of Government Disconnect," CBS News poll, June 28, 2011, http://www.cbsnews.com.

412 **"We don't have representative government anymore"** Stanley B. Greenberg, "Why Voters Tune Out Democrats," *The New York Times,* Sunday Review, July 30, 2011.

412 **Senators were "vastly more responsive to affluent constituents"** Bartels, *Unequal Democracy,* 253.

412 **Politicians had disregarded the views of middle-class voters** Martin Gilens, "Inequality and Democratic Responsiveness," special issue, *Public Opinion Quarterly* 69, no. 5 (2005): 778–96, www.princeton.edu.

413 **Dissatisfaction with both parties** Neil King, Jr., "Antsy Voters Look for a Third Way," *The Wall Street Journal,* November 26–27, 2011.

413 **"There is just so much unrest"** Ibid.

413 **By early 2012, Americans Elect** Ezra Klein, "Save American Politics: Kill the Primary," *The Washington Post,* March 17, 2012. Krissah Thompson, "Group Seeks Middle Option for 2012 Ballot," *The Washington Post,* November 25, 2011.

414 **Bloomberg, seemed to cast himself as a centrist contender** Mayor Michael R. Bloomberg, remarks on economic growth, Brooklyn Navy Yard, December 8, 2010, http://www.nyc.gov.

414 **Another sign of rising protest against political extremism** Liz Halloran, "New 'No Labels' Movement Seeks Bipartisanship," NPR, December 13, 2010. http://www.npr.org/blogs/itsallpolitics/2010/12/13/132033081/new-no-labels-movement-seeks-bipartisanship.

414 **To counteract "this kind of hyper-partisanship"** *The Diane Rehm Show,* "Prospects for a Less-Polarized Nation," National Public Radio, December 16, 2010, http://thedianerehmshow.org.

414 **Its leaders . . . want to break party control** William A. Galston and Elaine C. Kamarck, "The Still-Vital Center: Moderates, Democrats, and the Renewal of American Politics," Third Way, February 2011, http://www.thirdway.org.

415 **"The problem is the party system itself"** Rehm, "Less-Polarized Nation."

415 **Open primaries . . . push candidates** Galston and Kamarck, "Still-Vital Center," 4, Table 1.

415 **The parties wound up with less of a lock** Ibid.

416 **Favor more moderate candidates** FairVote, "Congressional and Presidential Primaries: Open, Closed, Semi-Closed, and 'Top Two,' " accessed February 1, 2012, http://www.fairvote.org.

416 **To increase American voter turnout** U.S. Census Bureau, "Participation in Elections for President and U.S. Representatives, 1932–2010," Statistical Abstract of the United States: 2012, table 397, www.census.gov/compendia/statab/2012/tables/12s0397.pdf.

416 **An estimated 2.2 million Americans** The Pew Center on the States,

"Upgrading Democracy: Improving America's Elections by Modernizing States' Voter Registration Systems," November 2010. http://www.pewcenter onthestates.org/uloadedFiles/Upgrading_Democracy_report.pdf.

416 **Maine, Minnesota, and Wisconsin** Mann and Ornstein, *It's Even Worse Than It Looks,* 136.

416 **In America, 25 percent of eligible voters** Ibid, 140.

416 **About thirty countries have compulsory voting** William A. Galston, "Telling Americans to Vote, Or Else," *The New York Times*, November 6, 2011. http://www.newyorktimes.com/2011/11/06/opinion/sunday/telling-americans-to-vote-or-else?pagewanted=all.

417 **"The way to gain votes"** Norman Ornstein, "Vote—or Else," *The New York Times,* August 10, 2006.

417 **"Corrupted by the process"** John McCain, *ABC This Week,* October 3, 1999.

417 **The Supreme Court . . . ruled** Adam Liptak, "Justices, 5–4, Reject Corporate Spending Limit," *The New York Times,* January 21, 2010.

418 **In Iowa's Republican caucuses** Nicholas Confessore and Jim Rutenberg, "Group's Ads Rip at Gingrich as Romney Stands Clear," *The New York Times,* December 30, 2011.

418 **In South Carolina, the pro-Gingrich** Trip Gabriel and Nicholas Confessore, "PAC Ads to Attack Romney as Predatory Capitalist," *The New York Times,* January 8, 2012.

418 **"The Super-PACs are plainly an avenue"** Mann and Ornstein, *It's Even Worse,* 154.

418 **Super-PACs had raised $160 million** Center for Responsive Politics, "Super-PACs," Open Secrets. http://www.opensecrets.org/pacs/superpacs.php.

418 **A small group of billionaire would-be kingmakers** Nicholas Confessore, Michael Luo, and Mike McIntire, "In G.O.P. Race, a New Breed of Superdonor," *The New York Times,* February 22, 2012; Dan Eggen and T.W. Farnam, "The Men Behind the GOP's Millions," *The Washington Post,* February 22, 2012. Monica Langley, "Texas Billionaire Doles Out Election's Biggest Checks," *The Wall Street Journal,* March 22, 2012. *Journal* chart shows that by late March 2012, three donors provided more than one-fifth of all the Super-PAC funding to date: the Adelsons, with $15 million, Howard Simmons and Contran, with $14.4 million, and Robert Perry, with $6.6 million.

418 **record-breaking $1.8 billion presidential election** Federal Election Commission, new release, "2008 Presidential Campaign Financial Activity Summarized: Receipts Nearly Double 2004 Total," June 8, 2009. http://www.fec.gov/press/press2009/20090608PresStat.shtml.

418 **Charles and David Koch, billionaire owners** Amanda Terkel and Ryan Grim, "Koch Brothers, Allies Pledge $100 Million at Private Meeting to Beat Obama," *HuffPost Politics,* February 3, 2012. http://www.huffingtonpost.com/2012/02/03/koch-brothers-100-million-obama_n_1250828.html.

419 **American Crossroads and Crossroads GPS** Jim Rutenberg and Jeff Zeleny, " 'Super PAC,' Eyeing General Election, Aims Blitz at Obama," *The*

New York Times, April 8, 2012; T. W. Farnam, "Mystery Donor Gives $10 Million for Attack Ads," *The Washington Post,* April 14, 2012.

419 **Initially, President Obama had rejected**   Jeff Zeleny and Jim Rutenberg, "Obama Yields in Marshaling of 'Super PAC,' " *The New York Times,* February 6, 2012.

419 **Fred Wertheimer of Democracy 21**   Fred Wertheimer, "Super PACs Can Be Thwarted," *The Washington Post,* April 9, 2012.

420 **"The loss of civic faith"**   Gardner, "American Experiment."

421 **Business outspent labor 97 to 1**   "Lobbying Database," Center for Responsive Politics, based on data from Senate Office of Public Records, January 31, 2011, http://www.opensecrets.org; Drutman, *The Business of America Is Lobbying,* online doctoral thesis, 3–6.

421 **"hands off my Medicare"**   "S.C. Senator Is a Voice of Reform Opposition," *The Washington Post,* July 28, 2009; Paul Krugman, "Health Care Realities," *The New York Times,* July 31, 2009.

421 **94 percent had actually benefited**   Suzanne Mettler, "Our Hidden Government Benefits," *The New York Times,* September 20, 2011.

424 **"Housing debt is at the heart"**   Floyd Norris, "To Revive Economy, Rescue Housing," *The New York Times,* December 2, 2011.

424 **It cuts consumer demand**   Mark Lasky and Andrew Gisselquist, "Housing Wealth and Consumer Spending," Congressional Budget Office, January 2007, 7, http://www.cbo.gov; Binyamin Appelbaum, "Gloom Grips Consumers, and It May Be Home Prices," *The New York Times,* October 18, 2011.

424 **Cost the U.S. economy**   Karl E. Case, John M. Quigley, and Robert J. Shiller, "Wealth Effects Revisited 1978–2009" (New Haven, CT: Cowles Foundation, Yale University, February 2011), 30–37, http://cowles.econ.yale.edu.

424 **"Consumer spending"**   Livingston, "It's Consumer Spending, Stupid."

425 **In Israel**   "Protests Grow in Israel, with 250,000 Marching," *The New York Times,* August 6, 2011.

425 **Israelis threw up tent cities**   "Protests Force Israel to Confront Wealth Gap," *The New York Times,* August 11, 2011.

426 **"The consumer will feel the government's decision"**   "Israeli Cabinet Approves Tax Plan Following Social Protests," Bloomberg, October 30, 2011, http://www.bloomberg.com.

BIBLIOGRAPHY

BOOKS

Bacevich, Andrew J. *The Limits of Power: The End of American Exceptionalism.* New York: Henry Holt & Co., 2008.

Baker, Dean. *False Profits: Recovering from the Bubble Economy.* San Francisco: Berrett-Koehler, 2010.

Bartels, Larry M. *Unequal Democracy: The Political Economy of the New Gilded Age.* New York: Russell Sage Foundation; Princeton, NJ: Princeton University Press, 2008.

Birnbaum, Jeffrey H. *The Lobbyists: How Business Gets Its Way in Washington.* New York: Times Books, 1992.

Bitner, Richard. *Confessions of a Subprime Lender: An Insider's Tale of Greed, Fraud, and Ignorance.* Hoboken, NJ: John Wiley & Sons, 2008.

Bivens, Josh. *Failure by Design: The Story Behind America's Broken Economy.* Ithaca, NY: Cornell University Press, 2011.

Blair, Anne E. *Lodge in Vietnam: A Patriot Abroad.* New Haven, CT: Yale University Press, 1995.

Bogle, John C. *The Battle for the Soul of Capitalism.* New Haven, CT: Yale University Press, 2005.

Branch, Taylor. *Parting the Waters: America in the King Years 1954–63.* New York: Simon & Schuster, 1988.

———. *Pillar of Fire: America in the King Years 1963–65.* New York: Simon & Schuster, 1998.

Cannon, Lou. *President Reagan: The Role of a Lifetime.* New York: Simon & Schuster, 1991.

———. *Reagan.* New York: G. P. Putnam's Sons, 1982.

Cappelli, Peter, *The New Deal at Work.* Boston: Harvard Business School Press, 1999.

Chandler, Alfred D. Jr. *The Visible Hand: The Managerial Revolution in American Business.* Cambridge, Massachusetts: Harvard University Press, 1977.

Carlson, Clayborne, David J. Garrow, Bill Kovach, and Carol Polsgrove, comps. *Reporting Civil Rights,* parts 1 and 2. New York: Literary Classics of the United States, 2003.

Clifford, Clark. *Counsel to the President: A Memoir.* New York: Random House, 1991.

Critchlow, Donald T. *The Conservative Ascendancy: How the GOP Right Made Political History.* Cambridge, MA: Harvard University Press, 2007.

Cronin, Thomas E., ed. *Rethinking the Presidency.* Boston: Little, Brown, 1982.

Dallek, Robert. *Flawed Giant: Lyndon Johnson and His Times.* New York: Oxford University Press, 1998.

———. *Lone Star Rising: Lyndon Johnson and His Times.* New York: Oxford University Press, 1991.

De Graaf, John, David Wann, and Thomas Naylor. *Affluenza: The All-Consuming Epidemic.* San Francisco: Berrett-Koehler, 2001.

Deming, W. Edwards, *Out of the Crisis.* Cambridge, Massachusetts: MIT Center for Advanced Engineering Study, 1986.

Dine, Philip M. *State of the Unions: How Labor Can Strengthen the Middle Class, Improve Our Economy, and Regain Political Influence.* New York: McGraw-Hill, 2008.

Dionne, E. J. *Why Americans Hate Politics.* New York: Simon & Schuster, 1991.

Dobbs, Lou. *War on the Middle Class: How the Government, Big Business, and Special Interest Groups Are Waging War on the American Dream and How to Fight Back.* New York: Penguin Group, 2006.

Drutman, Lee Jared. *The Business of America Is Lobbying: The Expansion of Corporate Political Activity and the Future of American Pluralism.* Online Ph.D. thesis. Berkeley: University of California, Berkeley, fall 2010.

Edsall, Thomas Byrne. *The New Politics of Inequality.* New York: W. W. Norton & Co., 1995.

Fein, Bruce. *American Empire Before the Fall.* Washington, DC: Campaign for Liberty, 2010.

Fiorina, Morris P., with Samuel J. Abrams. *Disconnect: The Breakdown of Representation in American Politics.* Norman, Oklahoma: University of Oklahoma Press, 2009.

Fleckenstein, William A., with Frederick Sheehan. *Greenspan's Bubbles: The Age of Ignorance at the Federal Reserve.* New York: McGraw-Hill, 2008.

Frank, Robert. *Richistan: A Journey Through the American Wealth Boom and the Lives of the New Rich.* New York: Crown Publishing Group, 2007.

Frank, Robert H. *Falling Behind: How Rising Inequality Harms the Middle Class.* Berkeley: University of California Press, 2007.

Frank, Thomas. *What's the Matter with Kansas? How Conservatives Won the Heart of America.* New York: Henry Holt & Co., 2004.

Fraser, Steve. *Wall Street: American's Dream Palace.* New Haven, CT: Yale University Press, 2008.

Friedman, Thomas L. *The World Is Flat: A Brief History of the Twenty-first Century.* New York: Farrar, Straus & Giroux, 2005.

Galbraith, John Kenneth. *The New Industrial State.* New York: New American Library, Signet, 1967.

Gates, William H., Sr., and Chuck Collins. *Wealth and Our Commonwealth: Why America Should Tax Accumulated Fortunes.* Boston: Beacon Press, 2002.

Gillespie, Ed, and Bob Schellhas, eds. *Contract with America.* New York: Times Books, 1994.

Goodwin, Doris Kearns. *Lyndon Johnson and the American Dream.* New York: St. Martin's Griffin, 2003.

Gould, Lewis. *Grand Old Party: A History of the Republicans.* New York: Random House, 2003.

Gramlich, Edward M. *Subprime Mortgages: America's Latest Boom and Bust.* Washington, DC: Urban Institute Press, 2007.

Grant, James. *Mr. Market Miscalculates: The Bubble Years and Beyond.* Mt. Jackson, VA: Axios Press, 2008.

Greenhouse, Steven. *The Big Squeeze: Tough Times for the American Worker.* New York: Anchor Books, 2008.

Greenstein, Fred. *The Hidden-Hand Presidency: Eisenhower as Leader.* New York: Basic Books, 1982.

Greider, William. *Who Will Tell the People? The Betrayal of American Democracy.* New York: Simon & Schuster, 1992.

Hacker, Jacob S. *The Great Risk Shift: The New Economic Insecurity and the Decline of the American Dream.* New York: Oxford University Press, 2008.

———, and Paul Pierson. *Winner-Take-All Politics: How Washington Made the Rich Richer and Turned Its Back on the Middle Class.* New York: Simon & Schuster, 2010.

Halberstam, David. *The Children.* New York: Fawcett, 1998.

———. *The Making of a Quagmire: America and Vietnam During the Kennedy Era.* Plymouth, UK: Rowman & Littlefield, 2007.

Harwood, John, and Gerald F. Seib. *Pennsylvania Avenue: Profiles in Backroom Power: Making Washington Work Again.* New York: Random House, 2008.

Haskins, Ron, and Isabel Sawhill, *Creating an Opportunity Society*. Washington: Brookings Institution Press, 2009.

Heymann, Jody. *The Widening Gap: Why America's Working Families Are in Jeopardy and What Can Be Done About It.* New York: Basic Books, 2000.

Hira, Ron, and Anil Hira. *Outsourcing America: The True Cost of Shipping Jobs Overseas and What Can Be Done About It.* 2nd ed. New York: Amacom, 2008.

Isaacs, Julia B., Isabel V. Sawhill, and Ron Haskins. *Economic Mobility: Getting Ahead or Losing Ground in America.* Washington, DC: Brookings Institution, 2008.

Johnson, Lyndon Baines. *The Vantage Point: Perspectives of the Presidency 1963–1969.* New York: Holt, Rinehart & Winston, 1971.

Johnson, Simon, and James Kwak. *13 Bankers: The Wall Street Takeover and the Financial Meltdown.* New York: Pantheon Books, 2010.

Johnston, David Cay. *Perfectly Legal: The Covert Campaign to Rig Our Tax System to Benefit the Super Rich—and Cheat Everybody Else.* New York: Penguin Group, 2003.

Judt, Tony. *Ill Fares the Land.* New York: Penguin Group, 2010.

Karnow, Stanley. *Vietnam: A History.* Middlesex, UK: Penguin Books, 1997.

Kennedy, Paul M. *The Rise and Fall of the Great Powers.* New York: Random House, 1987.

Keynes, John Maynard, *The General Theory of Employment, Interest and Money*. London: MacMillan & Co., 1954.

Killian, Linda. *The Freshmen: What Happened to the Republican Revolution?* Boulder, CO: Westview Press, 1998.

Kinsley, Michael. *Creative Capitalism: A Conversation with Bill Gates, Warren Buffett and other Economic Leaders*. New York: Simon & Schuster, 2008.

Kochan, Thomas A., *Restoring the American Dream: A Working Families' Agenda for America*. Cambridge, Massachusetts: MIT Press, 2005.

Kotz, Nick. *Judgment Days: Lyndon Baines Johnson, Martin Luther King Jr. and the Laws That Changed America*. New York: Houghton Mifflin, 2005.

Kristof, Nicholas D., and Sheryl WuDunn. *China Wakes: The Struggle for the Soul of a Rising Power*. New York: Vintage Books, 1995.

Krugman, Paul. *The Conscience of a Liberal*. New York: W. W. Norton & Co., 2007.

Levitt, Arthur. *Take On the Street: What Wall Street and Corporate America Don't Want You to Know*. New York: Pantheon Books, 2002.

Lewis, Anthony. *Portrait of a Decade: The Second American Revolution*. New York: Random House, 1964.

Lewis, John. *Walking with the Wind: A Memoir of the Movement*. New York: Simon & Schuster, 1998.

Lewis, Michael. *The Big Short: Inside the Doomsday Machine*. New York: W. W. Norton & Co., 2010.

Lorsch, Jay W., with Elizabeth MacIver. *Pawns or Potentaties: The Reality of America's Corporate Boards*. Boston: Harvard Business School Press, 1989.

MacArthur, John R. *The Selling of "Free Trade": NAFTA, Washington, and the Subversion of American Democracy*. Berkeley: University of California Press, 2001.

Maier, Charles S. *Among Empires: American Ascendancy and Its Predecessors*. Cambridge, MA: Harvard University Press, 2006.

Mann, Thomas E., and Norman J. Ornstein. *The Broken Branch: How Congress Is Failing America and How to Get It Back*. New York: Oxford University Press, 2008.

————*It's Even Worse Than It Looks: How the American Constitutional System Collided with the New Politics of Extremism*. New York: Basic Books, 2012.

McCarty, Nolan, Keith T. Poole, and Howard Rosenthal. *Polarized America: The Dance of Ideology and Unequal Riches*. Cambridge, MA: Massachusetts Institute of Technology Press, 2008.

McCormack, Richard, ed. *Manufacturing a Better Future for America*. Washington, DC: Alliance for American Manufacturing, 2009.

McIntyre, Thomas J. *The Fear Brokers*. Philadelphia: Pilgrim Press, 1979.

McNamara, Robert S. *In Retrospect: The Tragedy and Lessons of Vietnam*. New York: Random House, 1995.

McPherson, Harry. *A Political Education: A Washington Memoir*. Austin: University of Texas Press, 1995.

Mishel, Lawrence, Jared Bernstein, and Sylvia Allegretto. *The State of Working America, 2006/2007*. Ithaca, NY: Cornell University Press, 2007.

Mishel, Lawrence, Jared Bernstein, and Heidi Shierholz. *The State of Working America, 2008/2009.* Ithaca, NY: Cornell University Press, 2009.

Morgenson, Gretchen, and Joshua Rosner. *Reckless Endangerment: How Outsized Ambition, Greed, and Corruption Led to Economic Armageddon.* New York: Times Books, 2011.

Murray, Charles. *Coming Apart: The State of White America, 1960–2010.* New York: Crown Forum, 2012.

Nace, Ted. *Gangs of America: The Rise of Corporate Power and the Disabling of Democracy.* San Francisco: Berrett-Koehler, 2003.

National Academy of Sciences, National Academy of Engineering, and Institute of Medicine. *Rising Above the Gathering Storm: Energizing and Employing America for a Brighter Economic Future.* Washington, DC: National Academy Press, 2007.

———. *Rising Above the Gathering Storm Revisited: Rapidly Approaching Category 5.* Washington, DC: National Academy Press, 2010.

Ornstein, Norman, and Thomas Mann, eds. *The Permanent Campaign and Its Future.* Washington, DC: American Enterprise Institute and Brookings Institution, 2000.

Ortega, Bob. *In Sam We Trust: The Untold Story of Sam Walton and Wal-Mart, the World's Most Powerful Retailer.* New York: Random House, 1998.

Page, Benjamin I., and Lawrence R. Jacobs. *Class War? What Americans Really Think About Economic Inequality.* Chicago: University of Chicago Press, 2009.

Phillips, Kevin. *Bad Money: Reckless Finance, Failed Politics, and the Global Crisis of American Capitalism.* New York: Penguin Group, 2009.

———. *The Emerging Republican Majority.* New Rochelle, NY: Arlington House, 1969.

———. *Post-Conservative America: People, Politics, and Ideology in a Time of Crisis.* New York: Vintage Books, 1983.

———. *Wealth and Democracy: A Political History of the American Rich.* New York: Broadway Books, 2002.

Phillips, Rufus. *Why Vietnam Matters: An Eyewitness Account of Lessons Not Learned.* Annapolis, MD: Naval Institute Press, 2008.

Preble, Christopher A. *The Power Problem: How American Military Dominance Makes Us Less Safe, Less Prosperous, and Less Free.* Ithaca, NY: Cornell University Press, 2009.

Prestowitz, Clyde. *The Betrayal of American Prosperity: Free Market Delusions, America's Decline, and How We Must Compete in the Post-Dollar Era.* New York: Free Press, 2010.

Rae, Nicol C. *The Decline and Fall of the Liberal Republicans from 1952 to the Present.* New York: Oxford University Press, 1989.

Rauch, Jonathan. *Demosclerosis: The Silent Killer of American Government.* New York: Times Books, 1994.

Reeves, Richard. *President Kennedy: Proof of Power.* New York: Simon & Schuster, 1993.

Reich, Robert. *Supercapitalism: The Transformation of Business, Democracy, and Everyday Life.* New York: Alfred A. Knopf, 2007.

Roberts, Gene, and Hank Klibanoff. *The Race Beat: The Press, the Civil Rights Struggle, and the Awakening of a Nation.* New York: Afred A. Knopf, 2006.

Rossotti, Charles O. *Many Unhappy Returns: One Man's Quest to Turn Around the Most Unpopular Organization in America.* Boston: Harvard Business School Press, 2005.

Rothkopf, David. *Superclass: The Global Power Elite and the World They Are Making.* New York: Farrar, Straus & Giroux, 2008.

Scammon, Richard M., and Ben J. Wattenberg. *The Real Majority: An Extraordinary Examination of the American Electorate.* New York: Coward-McCann, 1970.

Schattschneider, E. E. *Party Government: American Government in Action.* New York: Rinehart & Co., 1942.

————. *The Semisovereign People: A Realist's View of Democracy in America.* New York: Holt, Rinehart & Winston, 1960.

Schell, Orville. *Mandate of Heaven: The Legacy of Tiananmen Square and the Next Generation of China's Leaders.* New York: Simon & Schuster, 1995.

Schoenbaum, Thomas J. *Waging Peace & War: Dean Rusk in the Truman, Kennedy & Johnson Years.* New York: Simon & Schuster, 1988.

Schultz, Ellen E. *Retirement Heist: How Companies Plunder and Profit from the Nest Eggs of American Workers.* New York: Portfolio/Penguin, 2011.

Shabecoff, Philip. *A Fierce Green Fire: The American Environmental Movement.* Rev. ed. Washington, DC: Island Press, 2003.

Shiller, Robert J. *Irrational Exuberance.* 2nd ed. New York: Broadway Books, 2005.

Shulman, Beth. *The Betrayal of Work: How Low-Wage Jobs Fail 30 Million Americans.* New York: The New Press, 2005.

Smith, Hedrick. *The Power Game: How Washington Works.* New York: Random House, 1988.

————. *Rethinking America: Innovative Strategies and Partnerships in Business and Education.* New York: Random House, 1995.

Stiglitz, Joseph E. *Freefall: America, Free Markets, and the Sinking of the World Economy.* New York: W. W. Norton & Co., 2010.

————. *Globalization and Its Discontents.* New York: W. W. Norton & Co., 2003.

Toynbee, Arnold J. *A Study of History.* Abridgment of vols. 1–6 by D. C. Somervell. New York and London: Oxford University Press, 1947.

————*A Study of History.* Abridgment of vols. 7–10 by D. C. Somervell. New York and London: Oxford University Press, 1957.

Uchitelle, Louis. *The Disposable American: Layoffs and Their Consequences.* New York: Alfred A. Knopf, 2006.

Useem, Michael. *Investor Capitalism: How Money Managers Are Changing the Face of Corporate America.* New York: Basic Books, 1996.

Vogel, David. *Fluctuating Fortunes: The Political Power of Business in America.* New York: Basic Books, 1989.

Warren, Elizabeth, and Amelia Warren Tyagi. *The Two-Income Trap: Why Middle-Class Parents Are Going Broke.* New York: Basic Books 2003.

Wicker, Tom. *One of Us: Richard Nixon and the American Dream.* New York: Random House, 1991.

Wilkinson, Richard, and Kate Pickett. *The Spirit Level: Why Greater Equality Makes Societies Stronger*. New York: Bloomsbury Press, 2009.

Woodward, Bob. *Obama's Wars*. New York: Simon & Schuster, 2010.

Young, Andrew. *An Easy Burden: The Civil Rights Movement and the Transformation of America*. New York: HarperCollins, 1996.

————, and Kabir Sehdal. *Walk in My Shoes: Conversations Between a Civil Rights Legend and His Godson on the Journey Ahead*. New York: Palgrave Macmillan, 2010.

LIST OF IMPORTANT ARTICLES, PAPERS, AND STUDIES

Aaronson, Daniel, and Bkhashkar Mazumder. "Intergenerational Economic Mobility in the U.S., 1940 to 2000." Federal Reserve Bank of Chicago, Chicago, February 2007.

Aghion, Philippe, Eve Caroli, and Cecilia García-Peñalosa. "Inequality and Economic Growth: The Perspective of the New Growth Theories." *Journal of Economic Literature* 37, no. 4 (December 1999): 1615–60.

Alpert, Daniel, Robert Hockett, and Nouriel Roubini. "The Way Forward." New America Foundation, Washington, DC, October 2011.

Aron-Dine, Aviva. "Well-Designed, Fiscally Responsible Corporate Tax Reform Could Benefit the Economy." Center on Budget and Policy Priorities, Washington, DC, June 4, 2008.

Aron-Dine, Aviva, and Isaac Shapiro. "Share of National Income Going to Wages and Salaries at Record Low in 2006." Center on Budget and Policy Priorities, Washington, DC, March 29, 2007.

Atkinson, Robert D., and Scott M. Andes. "The Atlantic Century II: Benchmarking EU and U.S. Innovation and Competitiveness." Information Technology and Innovation Foundation, Washington, DC, July 2011.

Atkinson, Rob, Michael Shellenberger, Ted Nordhaus, et al. "Rising Tigers, Sleeping Giant: Asian Nations Set to Dominate the Clean Energy Race by Out-Investing the United States." Breakthrough Institute; Information Technology and Innovation Foundation, Washington, DC, November 2009.

Baker, Dean. "The Productivity to Paycheck Gap: What the Data Show." Center for Economic and Policy Research, Washington, DC, April 2007.

Bakija, Jon, Adam Cole, and Bradley T. Heim. "Jobs and Income Growth of Top Earners and the Causes of Changing Income Inequality: Evidence from U.S. Tax Return Data." Research paper, School of Public and Environmental Affairs, Indiana University, Bloomington, November 2010.

Bartlett, Bruce. " 'Starve the Beast': Origin and Development of a Budgetary Metaphor." *Independent Review* 12, no. 1 (Summer 2007).

Bebchuk, Lucian A., Alma Cohen, and Holger Spamann. "The Wages of Failure: Executive Compensation at Bear Stearns and Lehman 2000–2008." Discussion Paper No. 657, John M. Olin Center for Law, Economics, and Business, Harvard University, Cambridge, MA, February 2010.

Binder, Sarah A. "The Dynamics of Legislative Gridlock, 1947–1996." *American Political Science Review* 93, no. 3 (September 1999).

Blackwill, Robert D. "Plan B in Afghanistan." *Foreign Affairs* 90, no. 1 (January–February 2011).

Building America's Future Educational Fund. "Falling Apart and Falling Behind: Transportation Infrastructure Report 2011." http://www.bafuture.org.

Butz, William, Terrence K. Kelly, David M. Adamson, et al. "Will the Scientific and Technology Workforce Meet the Requirements of the Federal Government?" Rand Corporation, 2004.

Case, Karl E., and Robert J. Shiller. "Is There a Housing Bubble?" *Brookings Papers on Economic Activity* 2, no. 2 (2003): 299–342.

Case, Karl E., John M. Quigley, and Robert J. Shiller. "Wealth Effects Revisited 1978–2009." Cowles Foundation for Research in Economics, Yale University, New Haven, CT, February 2011.

Cassidy, John. "The Greed Cycle." *The New Yorker,* September 23, 2002.

Congressional Research Service. "State, Foreign Operations, and Related Programs: FY2012 Budget and Appropriations." CRS Report for Congress, Washington, DC, November 23, 2011.

Dew-Becker, Ian, and Robert J. Gordon. "Where Did the Productivity Growth Go? Inflation Dynamics and the Distribution of Income." *Brookings Papers on Economic Activity* 2 (2005).

Eisenhower Study Group. "The Costs of War Since 2001: Iraq, Afghanistan, and Pakistan." Watson Institute for International Studies, Brown University, Providence, RI, June 2011.

Fieldhouse, Andrew, and Ethan Pollack. "Tenth Anniversary of the Bush-Era Tax Cuts." Economic Policy Institute, Washington, DC, June 1, 2011.

Foster, John Bellamy, and Hannah Holleman. "The Financial Power Elite." *Monthly Review* 62, no. 1 (May 2010).

Frydman, Carola, and Raven E. Saks. "Executive Compensation: A New View from a Long-Term Perspective, 1936–2005." Working Paper No. 14145, National Bureau of Economic Research, Cambridge, MA, June 2008.

Gandhi, Sima J. "Audit the Tax Code: Doing What Works for Tax Expenditures." Center for American Progress, Washington, DC, April 2010.

Gilens, Martin. "Inequality and Democratic Reponsiveness." Special issue, *Public Opinion Quarterly* 69, no. 5 (2005): 778–96.

Gramlich, Edward M. "Booms and Busts: The Case of Subprime Mortgages." Lecture, Federal Reserve Bank of Kansas City symposium, Jackson Hole, Wyoming, August 30–September 1, 2007, 105–13.

Greenspan, Alan. "Activism," *International Finance* 14, no. 1 (Spring 2011).

Hacker, Jacob S., and Paul Pierson. "Abandoning the Middle: The Bush Tax Cuts and the Limits of Democratic Control." *Perspectives on Politics* 3, no. 1 (March 2005): 33–53.

Heidkamp, Marie, Nicole Corre, and Carl E. Van Horn. "The New Unemployables." Issue Brief 25, Sloan Center on Aging & Work, Boston College, Chestnut Hill, MA, November 2010.

Hindery, Leo, Jr., and Leo W. Gerard. "A Vision for Economic Renewal: An American Jobs Agenda." *Huffington Post,* July 22, 2011.

International Trade Commission. "China: Effects of Intellectual Property Infringement and Indigenous Innovation Policies on the U.S. Economy." U.S. Department of Commerce, Washington, DC, May 2011.

Jensen, Michael C., and Kevin Murphy. "Performance Pay and Top-Management Incentives." *Journal of Political Economy* 98, no. 2 (April 1990).

Jensen, Michael C., and William H. Meckling. "Theory of the Firm: Managerial Behavior, Agency Costs and Ownership Structure." *Journal of Financial Economics* 3, no. 4 (October 1976).

Johnson, Simon. "The Quiet Coup." *The Atlantic,* May 2009.

Jones, David R. "Party Polarization and Legislative Gridlock." *Political Research Quarterly* 54, no. 1 (March 2001).

Kane, Tom. "Global U.S. Troop Deployment, 1950–2005." Center for Data Analysis, Heritage Foundation, Washington, DC, May 24, 2006.

Katzman, Kenneth. "Afghanistan: Politics, Elections and Government Performance." Congressional Research Service, Washington, DC, May 5, 2011.

———. "Afghanistan: Post-Taliban Governance, Security, and U.S. Policy." Congressional Research Service, Washington, DC, May 11, 2010.

Krepinovich, Andrew. "The Pentagon's Wasting Assets." *Foreign Affairs* 88, no. 4 (July–August 2009).

Lasky, Mark, and Andrew Gisselquist. "Housing Wealth and Consumer Spending." Congressional Budget Office, Washington, DC, January 2007.

Lawless, Robert M. "The Paradox of Consumer Credit." *University of Illinois Law Review* 2007, no. 1 (December 15, 2006).

———, Angela Littwin, Katherine M. Porter, et al. "Did Bankruptcy Reform Fail? An Empirical Study of Consumer Debtors." *American Bankruptcy Law Journal* 82 (October 15, 2008).

Levy, Frank, and Peter Temin. "Inequality and Institutions in 20th Century America." Working Paper Series, Department of Economics, Massachusetts Institute of Technology, Cambridge, MA, June 27, 2007.

Lizza, Ryan. "Inside the Crisis: Larry Summers and the White House Economic Team." *The New Yorker,* October 12, 2009.

———. "The Obama Memos: The Making of a Post-Post-Partisan Presidency." *The New Yorker*, January 30, 2012.

LoPucki, Lynn M., and William C. Whitford. "Corporate Governance in the Bankruptcy Reorganization of Large, Publicly Held Companies." *University of Pennsylvania Law Review* 141, no. 3 (January 1993).

Lorsch, Jay, and Rakesh Khurana. "The Pay Problem." *Harvard Magazine,* May–June 2010.

Lowell, B. Lindsay, Harold Salzman, Hamutal Bernstein, et al. "Steady as She Goes? Three Generations of Students Through the Science and Engineering Pipeline." Paper, Institute for the Study of International Migration at Georgetown University, Rutgers University, and the Urban Institute, October 2009.

Mazumder, Bkhashkar. "Fortunate Sons: New Estimates of Intergenerational Mobility in the United States Using Social Security Data." Federal Reserve Bank of Chicago, Chicago, July 6, 2004.

McCormack, Richard. "The Plight of American Manufacturing." *American Prospect,* December 21, 2009.

McIntyre, Robert S., Matthew Gardner, Rebecca J. Wilkins, et al. "Corporate Taxpayers & Corporate Tax Dodgers 2008–10." Citizens for Tax Justice; Institute on Taxation and Economic Policy, Washington, DC, November 2011.

Munnell, Alicia, Anthony Webb, and Francesca Golub-Sass. "The National Retirement Risk Index: After the Crash." Issue Brief No. 9–22, Center for Retirement Research at Boston College, Chestnut Hill, MA, October 2009.

Munnell, Alicia, Anthony Webb, Francesca Golub-Sass, and Dan Muldoon. "Long Term Care Costs and the National Retirement Risk Index." Issue Brief No. 9–7, Center for Retirement Research at Boston College, Chestnut Hill, MA, March 2009.

Nathan, Richard P. "A Retrospective on Richard M. Nixon's Domestic Policies." *Presidential Studies Quarterly* 26, no. 1 (Winter 1996).

Norton, Michael I., and Dan Ariely. "Building a Better America—One Wealth Quintile at a Time." *Perspectives on Psychological Science* 6, no. 1 (2011).

Organisation for Economic Co-operation and Development. "An Overview of Growing Income Inequalities in OECD Countries: Main Findings." In *Divided We Stand: Why Inequality Keeps Rising,* OECD, Paris, France. Accessed December 6, 2011. http://www.oecd.org/dataoecd/40/12/49170449.pdf.

Palley, Thomas I. "America's Exhausted Paradigm: Macroeonomic Causes of the Financial Crisis and Great Recession." New America Foundation, Washington, DC, June 2009.

Palmisano, Samuel J. "The Globally Integrated Enterprise." *Foreign Affairs* 85, no. 3 (May–June 2006).

Pew Research Center. "Inside the Middle Class: Bad Times Hit the Good Life." Report, Pew Social & Demographic Trends, Pew Research Center, Washington, DC, April 9, 2008.

Phillips, Rufus. "Déjà Vu All Over Again: Are We Repeating Vietnam?" *World Affairs,* September–October 2010.

Piketty, Thomas, and Emmanuel Saez. "How Progressive Is the U.S. Federal Tax System? A Historical and International Perspective." National Bureau of Economic Research, Washington, DC, July 2006.

Poole, Keith T. "The Decline and Rise of Party Polarization in Congress During the Twentieth Century." *Extensions*, Fall 2005.

———, and Howard Rosenthal. "The Political Economy of American Income Inequality." Voteviewblog, November 23, 2011.

Powell, Lewis F., Jr. "Attack on American Free Enterprise System." Memorandum, U.S. Chamber of Commerce, Washington, DC, August 23, 1971.

Rattner, Steven. "The Secrets of Germany's Success." *Foreign Affairs* 90, no. 4 (July–August 2011).

Repetti, James R. "Democracy, Taxes, and Wealth." Research Paper No. 2001–03, Boston College Law School, Newton, MA, June 14, 2001.

Saez, Emmanuel. "Striking It Richer: The Evolution of Top Incomes in the United States." *Pathways,* Winter 2008, 6–7, Stanford Center on Poverty and Inequality, Stanford, CA.

———. "Striking It Richer: The Evolution of Top Incomes in the United States (Updated with 2008 Estimate)." July 17, 2010, *Pathways Magazine*, Stanford Center on Poverty and Inequality, Stanford, CA, winter 2008, 6–7.

———. "Striking It Richer: The Evolution of Top Incomes in the United States (Updated with 2009 and 2010 Estimates)." March 2, 2012. Stanford Center on Poverty and Inequality, Stanford, CA.

Samuelson, Paul A. "Where Ricardo and Mill Rebut and Confirm Arguments of Mainstream Economists Supporting Globalization." *Journal of Economic Perspectives* 18, no. 2 (Summer 2004).

Sanger, David. "Rethinking the Afghanistan War—What-Ifs." *The New York Times Magazine,* July 31, 2010.

Schmitt, John. "Labor Market Policy in the Great Recession: Some Lessons from Denmark and Germany." Center for Economic and Policy Research, Washington, DC, May 2011.

Scott, Robert E. "The Benefits of Revaluation." EPI Briefing Paper. Economic Policy Institute, Washington, DC, June 17, 2011.

———. "Unfair China Trade Costs Local Jobs: 2.4 Million Jobs Lost, Thousands Displaced in Every U.S. Congressional District." EPI Briefing Paper. Economic Policy Institute, Washington, DC, March 23, 2010.

Shiller, Robert J. "Household Reactions to Changes in Housing Wealth." Discussion Paper 1459, Cowles Foundation, Yale University, New Haven, CT, April 2004.

Spence, Michael. "The Impact of Globalization on Income and Employment: The Downside of Integrating Markets." *Foreign Affairs* 90, no. 4 (July–August 2011).

———, and Sandile Hlatshwayo. "The Evolving Structure of the American Economy and the Employment Challenge." Working paper, Council on Foreign Relations, Washington, DC, March 2011.

Stillman, Sarah. "The Invisible Army: Workers Hired into the War Zone." *The New Yorker,* June 6, 2011.

Summers, Larry. "Executive Summary of Economic Policy Work." Memo to President-Elect Barack Obama, December 15, 2008. http://s3.documentcloud .org/documents/285065/summers-12-15-08-memo.pdf.

VanDerhei, Jack. "Evaluation of the Adequacy and Structure of U.S. Voluntary Retirement Plans, with Special Emphasis on 401(k) Plans." *Benefits Quarterly,* Third Quarter 2010.

———. "401(k) Plan Asset Allocation, Account Balances, and Loan Activity in 2009." EBRI Issue Brief No. 350, Employee Benefits Research Institute, Washington, DC, November 2010.

———. "Measuring Retirement Income Adequacy: Calculating Realistic Income Replacement Rates." EBRI Issue Brief No. 297, Employee Benefits Research Institute, Washington, DC, September 2006.

———. "A Post-Crisis Assessment of Retirement Income Adequacy for Baby

Boomers and Gen Xers." EBRI Issue Brief No. 354, Employee Benefits Research Institute, Washington, DC, November 15, 2010.

Waterhouse, Benjamin C. "Reviving the 'Voice of Business': American Employers' Associations in Economic Crisis, 1970–1975." Working paper, Business History Conference, St. Louis, MO, April 2, 2011.

Whitaker, John C. "Nixon's Domestic Policy: Both Liberal and Bold in Retrospect." *Presidential Studies Quarterly* 26, no. 1 (Winter 1996).

INDEX

Abrahams, Albert, 13
Abrams, Frank, 37
Ackerman, Peter, 413
activism. *See* citizen action
Adams, John, 383
Adams, John Quincy, 383
Adelson, Sheldon and Miriam, 418
adjustable-rate mortgages, 224, 227,
   233–34
Advanced Research Projects Agency
   (ARPA-E), 391–92
Advanced Technology Products, 271
Aetna, 398
Affordable Care Act of 2010, 312–13, 342,
   408
Afghanistan War, 353–56, 373–74; Afghan
   nationalism in, 364–66; al-Qaeda in,
   354, 359–60; as civil war, 354–55; costs
   of, 355–60, 403, 511n, 521n;
   counterinsurgency strategy in, 360–61,
   367; mission creep in, 359–64;
   scheduled drawdowns in, 356, 365, 403,
   404; U.S. bases in, 368
AFL-CIO, 15–17, 38, 129–30, 388
Aghion, Philippe, xvi
AIG, 292–95
Aiken, George, 312, 318
air controllers strike of 1981, 49
airline industry, 18
Air Transportation Stabilization Board,
   160
Ajaye, Robert, 285
Akerson, Dan, xxvi
Allen, Robert, 57

Alliance for American Manufacturing, 381,
   392, 394
Almeida, Paul, 296
Alpert, Daniel, 407
al-Qaeda, 354–55, 359–60, 364, 374
American Crossroads, 419
American Dream, xvi–xvii, 66–67; citizen
   reclamation of, xix, xxv–xxviii, 377,
   379–80, 410–13, 420–26; home
   ownership in, 192, 198, 204, 221,
   226–27; Metlife Study of, 81, 89–90,
   462n; postwar expansion of, xviii,
   xxiii–xxiv; stakeholder capitalism in, 45,
   110–11; unraveling of, xix–xx, 12, 65–80,
   83–97; virtuous circle of growth in, xiv,
   xxiii–xxvi, 35–42, 45, 51–52, 62, 380
American Enterprise Institute, 11, 334
Americans Elect, 413–14
Americans for Tax Reform, 348–49
Ameriquest, 201, 236
Amin, Sunny, 285
anti-unionism, 16, 49
Apple, 115, 259, 398–400, 492n
Applied Materials, 275
Arab Spring, 425–26
Aristotle, xi
Armey, Dick, 144
Aronson, Arnold, 99
the aspiring middle class, 408–9
AT&T, 57, 87
Auble, Dan, 347–48
Augustine, Norman, 391
auto industry bailout, xxvi, 384
Aviation Consumer Action Project, 33

Bacevich, Andrew, 370
Bain Capital, 56–57
Baker, Dean, 221, 229
Baker, James A., III, 334–35
Baker, Russell, 25
Baker, William, 31
Ballas, Jerry, 51
banking. *See* financial sector
Banking Act of 1933, 146–47
Bank of America, 239, 288
bankruptcy: of company pension plans,
    155, 157–69, 237, 475n, 476n;
    Congressional reforms of, 18–19,
    163–65; corporate restructuring under,
    162–65, 167, 476n; executive payoffs in,
    167; home mortgage modifications for,
    240–41; legal fees from, 167; personal
    filings for, 90–97; protected assets under,
    90, 92
Bankruptcy Abuse Prevention and
    Consumer Protection Act, 95
bar codes, 248–49
Barrett, Craig, 279, 391
Barshefsky, Charlene, 260
Bartels, Larry M., 125, 135, 152, 327, 412,
    447n
Bartlett, Bruce, 138, 358
Bartz, Carol, 77
"bathtub" conservatism, 329–30
The Battle for the Soul of Capitalism (Bogle), 117
Baucus, Max, 320
Bayh, Birch, 310
Bayh, Evan, 307, 310–11, 320
Bear Stearns, 114, 148, 223, 236
Bechtolscheim, Andreas von, 291
Belt, Bradley, 166
Benna, Ted, 170, 186–87
Bentham, Jeremy, 420
Bergman, Lowell, 94
Bergstein, C. Fred, 274
Bernanke, Ben, 233, 236
The Betrayal of American Prosperity
    (Prestowitz), 274
Bhagwati, Jagdish, 262–64, 270
big-box retailers, 246–47. *See also*
    Wal-Mart
The Big Short (Lewis), 200, 487n
Billionaireville, 102–3
Binder, Sarah, 320, 337
bin Laden, Osama, 359, 361, 373–74
bipartisanship and compromise, xxiv–xxv,
    8–11, 313–19, 325
Bitner, Richard, 232–33
B-1 visa program, 299, 302
Black, William, 233, 236

Blackwill, Robert, 360
Blankfein, Lloyd C., 234–35
Blattmachr, Jonathan, 106
Blinder, Alan, 273, 289
Bloomberg, Michael, 389, 414
BMW, 387
boards of directors, 60–61, 116. *See also*
    Corporate America
Boehner, John, 341, 345–47, 348
Boeing, 57, 397
Bogle, John C. (Jack), 116–17, 182–83,
    185–86, 190, 216
Bonacich, Edna, 249
bond-rating agencies, 222, 233, 235–36
Bonfire of the Vanities (Wolfe), 110, 142
Bork, Robert, 340
Born, Brooksley, 145–46
Boutwell, Alberg, 28
Bowles, Erskine, 405
Breaux, John, 309
Brennan, Ed, 57
Brin, Sergey, 291
The Broken Branch (Mann and Ornstein),
    323
Bromwich, David, 350
Brooks, David, 346, 351
Brown, Scott, 320
Brown v. Board of Education, 3, 26
Buckley, William, 6
Buffett, Warren, 47; on derivatives, 145; on
    the housing market, 241; on stock
    options, 119; on taxing policies, 107,
    138, 395–96
Bull Moose Party, 414
bundling, 132
Burke, James, 110
Burr, Aaron, 323
Burry, Mike, 234
Bush, George H. W., 403
Bush, George W., 131; airline loan policies
    of, 160; bank bailout program of,
    148–50, 239–40, 384, 405; Chinese
    trade agreements of, 260; defense
    doctrine of, 359–61, 369–70; defense
    spending under, 355–56, 358, 370–71,
    403; financial sector influence on, 143,
    145; on income inequality, 98, 104;
    labor policies of, 160; mortgage policies
    of, 198, 228; on offshoring practices,
    273–74; ownership society policies of,
    88–89, 192, 198, 226–27; Republican
    Party of, 330; SEC management under,
    115–16; Social Security policies of, 407;
    tax cuts of, 21, 107–8, 123, 126–40,
    326–27, 395, 399, 468n, 471n; War on

Terror of, 353–74. *See also* Afghanistan War; Iraq War
business. *See* Corporate America
business investment tax credit, 10–11
Business Roundtable, 11–12; campaign funding by, 469n; on labor law reform, 16; on shareholder group power, 134–35; on tax cuts, 128–30, 139; on trade with China, 260
"buy American" programs, 394
Byrd, Kahlil, 413

Calio, Nick, 128–29
campaign financing: bundling in, 132; by business groups, 130, 132–33, 143, 348, 469–70n, 474n; *Citizens United v. Federal Election System* decision in, 133, 143, 417–20; power associated with, 411, 417–20; public opinion on, 474n; reforms of, 419–20; with soft money, 132–33, 421; Super-PACs in, 418–20, 524n
Cantor, Eric, 346–47, 348
capital gains taxes, 21, 106–7, 139, 395–96
Capitalism and Freedom (Friedman), 49
Carson, Rachel, 30
Carter, Jimmy, and Congress, xix, 13–22; austerity message of, 370; reform agenda of, 14–15, 17, 224; tax policies of, 20–22
Case, Clifford, 312, 318
Cassidy, John, 113
Castellani, John, 134–35
caste society, 70–72
Cathcart, Ronald, 231
Cato Institute, 11, 334
Cayne, James, 114
Center for Auto Safety, 33
Center for Responsive Politics, 130, 133, 347–48, 447n, 450n, 469n, 470–71n, 473n
Center for the Study of Responsive Law, 33
CENTO, 368
CEOs, 49–50; appointment of corporate boards by, 60–61; Business Roundtable and, 11–12; cheating on stock options of, 16–17; compensation and stock options of, 56, 58–63, 100, 109–20, 134–35, 396; Dunlap's wedge economics as, 45, 47–57; of failed mortgage banks, 237–39; fraud prosecutions of, 238–39; lobbying activities of, 129, 139; options as "managerial heroin," 117–18; predatory capitalism of, 45, 47–49, 108–10; structural layoffs by, 57–59; union-busting tactics of, 63

Chafee, Lincoln, 340
Chambers, John, 269, 278
Champy, James, 280
Chan, Kenneth, 255
cheap money policies, 225–27
China, 377; cheap labor in, xxvi, 259–60, 270, 492n; currency manipulation of, 400–401; financial leverage of, 260; high-tech industry in, 271–79, 391; illegal labor practices in, 259, 492n; impact on U.S. high-tech industry base, 271–75; indigenous innovation policy of, 275–76; intellectual piracy of, 400–401; job loss to, 262–67; manufacturing in, 242–68, 386, 394; profits earned in, 255–56; Shenzhen's role in, 253–54, 256–58; subsidies and tax breaks in, 276–77, 401; unfair trade practices of, 400–402; U.S. trade with, 258–62, 271–73; Wal-Mart's role in, 251–58. *See also* offshore economy
Christ, Charlie, 414
Christian Coalition, 334
Chrysler, xxvi, 384
Circleville, OH, 66–69
Cisco, 293, 294
Citigroup, 98–99, 238, 239, 288
citizen action: decline of, xviii; jobs and fairness demands in, 422–24; lobbying in, 421–22; need for revival of, xix, xxvii–xxviii, 377, 379–80, 410–13, 420–26; in the 1960s and 1970s, 23–34, 412; volunteering for, 425–26
Citizens United v. Federal Election System, 417–20
Civil Aeronautics Board, 33
Civilian Conservation Corps, 390
Civil Rights Act of 1964, 314–17
civil rights movement, 24; Birmingham project of, 26–28; desegregation of schools in, 3, 26; Goldwater's opposition to, 332; March on Washington of 1963 of, 24–26, 28–30; voting rights campaigns of, 30, 317
class divide, xiv–xvi, 380, 515n; economic inequality in, xiv–xvi, 98–120; educational opportunity and, 71–72, 104–6; Nixon on, 40–41; political inequality in, xviii, xxvii, 151–52, 411–12, 420; reduced mobility in, 70–74, 76–77. *See also* the middle class; the 1 percent
Clean Air Act, 31
clean energy, 391, 393–94
Clean Water Act, 9, 31

Clinton, Bill, xx; budget bill in 1993, 337; budget surplus of, 129; Chinese trade promotion of, 260–61, 270–71; defense spending of, 403; economic growth under, 137; financial sector influence on, 143, 145; foreign policies of, 359; health care plan of, 337; high-tech industry policies of, 270, 271, 294; mortgage policies of, 198, 226–27; Republican warfare against, 322, 336–39; showdown with Congress 1995, 337–38; tax policies of, 112–13, 128, 337
Clinton, Hillary, 373
Coastal Zone Management Act, 31
Coburn, Tom, 481n
Cold War legacy, 368, 372–73, 404–5
college attendance, 72, 77, 105–6, 459n
Collins, Susan, 320
Com, Chuck, 350
commercial banks, 146–47, 148, 473n
commoditization, 273
Commodity Futures Trading Commission, 145–46
Common Cause, 129–30
compensation/pay: of CEOs, 58–63, 109–20; by stock options, 109, 111–20, 396; for failure, 113–14; pay restraint ethics in, 109–10; peer benchmarking in, 60–61; shareholder power over, 134–35; through stock options, 109, 111–20, 396; of two-income families, 76–77; of the workforce, 72–77, 459n
compromise and bipartisanship, xxiv–xxv, 8–11, 313–19, 325
compulsory voting, 416–17
Conable, Barber, 20, 171
Congress. See U.S. Congress
Congressional Budget Office, 448n
Congress Watch, 32–33
Conner, Brian, 173
Connor, Eugene (Bull), 26–28
Conrad, Lee, 286–88
conservative movement. See New Right
Constantino, Pam, 266–67
Consumer Federation of America, 32
Consumer Financial Protection Bureau, 96, 149–51, 313
consumer movement, 14–15, 24, 32–34
Consumer Product Safety Administration, 9
contingent workers, 74–75
Contract with America, 338–39
Contran Corporation, 418
Cooper, John Sherman, 312, 318
Cooper Tire & Rubber, 276
Coors, Joseph, 333–34

Corporate America: campaign contributions by, 130, 132–33, 469–70n; care for the workforce in, 35–40, 45, 48–50, 54–55, 86, 380–81; conservatism of, 330–31; exploitation and predatory capitalism of, 47–48, 50–57, 108–20; globalized mindset of, 278–80; idle capital of, 136–37; jobless recoveries of, xxiii–xxiv, 79–80, 288–89, 460n; laissez-faire philosophy of, xxii, 217–18, 331; legislative agenda of 1978 of, 18–22, 163–65, 171; lobbying activities by, 13–22, 126–30, 139–40; Nixon-era regulations on, 7–11; offshore jobs of, 262–68, 491n, 494n; Powell memorandum to, xiii–xiv, 5–8, 11–12; shareholder value in, 45, 49, 56–60, 112, 117; Super-PACs of, 418–20, 510n; taxes on, 10–11, 21, 107, 112–13, 139, 397–400; wedge economics of, xxii–xxiii, 47–64. See also CEOs; financial sector; lobbying; offshore economy; the social contract
Cortes, Ernie, xviii, 152
Costco, 86
Council on Union-Free Environment, 16
counterinsurgency strategy, 360–61, 366
counterterrorism strategy, 360
Countrywide, 114, 201, 223, 236, 238, 489n
Courtney, Joe, 300
Cova, Freddy, 205
Cowan, Jonathan, 414
Crabb, Winson, xx, 174–77
Crash of 1929, xv, 146
credit card debt, 93–95
crisis politics, xxiv–xxv
Critchlow, David, 330
Crossroads GPS, 419
Crystal, Graef, 113
CVS Caremark, 397

Dahl, Robert A., 141
Dale, Ed, 10–11
Daniels, Mitch, 259, 358
Davidowitch, Greg, 157, 163
Davis, Michele, 127
debit cards, 93–94
debt: of American consumers, 91–95; deficit spending in, 335, 358; financial sector leveraging of, 142–43; in the housing sector, 216–26, 233–35, 407, 424; of the U.S. government, 127, 335, 345–47, 357–58, 397; from wars against al-Qaeda, 355–60

debtor in possession (DIP), 164–65
defense. *See* military overreach
Defense Advanced Research Projects
  Agency (DARPA), 392
defined benefit pensions, 158–59, 475n
"Déjà Vu All Over Again" (Phillips),
  362–63
Dell Computer, 279–80
Democratic Party, 317–18, 330, 352;
  Carter and, xix, 13–22; Clinton budget
  and, 337; Senators quitting in
  frustration, 307, 310–11, 320
Deng Xiaoping, 253
Department of Veterans Affairs, 334
Depository Institutions Deregulation and
  Monetary Control Act of 1980, 224
deregulation, 18, 146–49, 217–18,
  223–28, 473n
derivatives trading, 145–46, 148, 150,
  234–35
Desai, Bharat, 295
Detroit bailout, xxvi, 384
digital economy. *See* high-technology
  industry
Digital Equipment, 57
Dillman, Linda, 248
Dirksen, Everett, 310, 312, 314–16
Dodd, Chris, 300
Dodd-Frank Wall Street Reform and
  Consumer Protection Act of 2010,
  149–51
Dole, Bob, 144, 338–39
domestic Marshall Plan proposal, xxv–
  xxvii, 380–86, 402–3
Dow Chemical, 10
downsizing, 45. *See also* predatory
  capitalism
Dudley, William C., 406
Dunlap, Al, xx, 45, 47–57, 64, 111, 113
Dunlap, Marsha, 53–54
DuPont, 397
Durbin, Richard, 240–41, 300–301, 303

Earth Day 1970, 30–31
Eastern Establishment conservatism,
  330–31
economic espionage, 400–401
economic inequality, xiv–xvi, 98–120, 377;
  Congressional gridlock in, 309–27;
  dimensions of, 72–74, 100–103;
  globalization in, xvii, xx–xxi, 61;
  interaction with political inequality of,
  xix–xx; middle-class insecurity in,
  83–97, 405–9; military overreach in,

355–60, 370–74; minimum wage levels
  in, 17, 325–27; offshore jobs in, 262–68;
  in other advanced economies, 61–62;
  reduced economic mobility in, 70–74,
  76–77; slow economic growth linked to,
  xvi, xxiii–xxiv, 41–42, 136–37; wedge
  economics in, xxii–xxiii, 47–64,
  73–74, 77–80. *See also* Corporate
  America
Economic Insecurity Index, 84
Edsall, Thomas, 5, 14
education, 104–6; class divisions in access
  to, 71–72; earning potential from, 77,
  105–6, 459n; housing costs related
  to, 77
Edwards, Mickey, 415
Eikenberry, Karl, 364, 365
Eisenhower, Dwight, xxv, 313–14; defense
  spending under, 403, 404; economic
  growth under, 137; interstate highway
  project of, 383, 388; mainstream
  conservatism of, 331; on military power,
  353, 372–73; tax policies of, 41
Eisenhower Study Group, 357–58
Eisman, Steve, 234
Eisner, Michael, 112
electoral system, 414–17. *See also* campaign
  financing
Ellison, Larry, 98, 103, 111–12
Employee benefits, 401(k) plans, 171–89;
  burden shift, 81–90; GM-UAW Treaty
  of Detroit, 38–40, 62; health benefits,
  84–86; impact of corporate bankruptcies
  on, 155–69; lifetime pensions, 155–62,
  166, 168–69; national proposals,
  190–91; Nebraska's plan 189–90
Employee Retirement Income Security Act
  (ERISA), 9, 159, 166
Endangered Species Act, 31
environmental movement, 24, 30–32
Environmental Protection Agency (EPA),
  8–10, 31, 334
equity stripping, 218–20, 226, 407
estate tax, 139–40, 325–27
ExxonMobil, 397

fairness, 423–24
Fairness Doctrine in broadcasting, 338
fair trade practices, 400–402
Falwell, Jerry, 334
family life, 76–77, 234–35, 485n
Fannie Mae (Federal National Mortgage
  Association), 198, 232–33, 241, 406
Fasten Your Financial Seatbelt (Scott), 187

Federal Aviation Administration, 33
Federal Communications Commission, 338
Federal Deposit Insurance Corporation (FDIC), 199
Federal Insecticide, Fungicide, and Rodenticide Act, 31
Federal Reserve, 222–23, 225–28, 485n
Federal Retirement Board, 190
Federal Trade Commission, 9
Fields, Bill, 245–46
the filibuster, 16–17, 311, 320–24
Financial Accounting Standards Board (FASB), 118–20
financial insecurity: lost saftey nets and, 83–90; personal bankruptcies and, 90–97
financial sector, 141–52; bank tax proposal for, 149; bond rating agencies in, 222, 233, 235–36; campaign donations of, 143, 348, 474n; debt leveraging in, 142–43; deregulation of, 146–48, 149, 223–28, 473n; derivative trading in, 145–46, 148, 150, 234–35; Dodd-Frank reforms of, 149–52; expansion and growth of, 142, 472n; fees and transaction costs in, 183, 424; government oversight of, 143–44; housing-related debt owned by, 220–41; legislation deregulating, 223–27; mutual funds in, 171–72, 183, 190–91; offshoring of IT work by, 288–89; political lobbying and power of, 141–52, 240–41, 421–22; predatory lending of, 192–215; profits of, 405; regulation of, xxii, 217–18, 240; secondary mortgage market in, 216–18, 221–25, 233–35; stock index funds in, 183; synthetic derivatives in, 222; taxpayer bailout of, 142–43, 148–50, 239–40, 345, 384, 405; "Too Big to Fail" in, 147–48, 151; Volcker Rule on, 150–51. See also hedge funds
Fitch Rating, 235
floating-rate mortgages, 210–14
Food and Drug Administration, 33
Ford, Gerald, 9, 14, 31, 334
Ford, Henry, 35–36
Ford Motor Corporation, xxvi, 36, 278
foreclosures, 193, 239–40, 266, 405
foreign body shops. See imported workers
Fort, Vincent, 129
401(k) plans, 19–20, 86–88, 160–62, 170–91, 408; deficit of, 184–91;

employer contributions to, 172–73, 181–82, 408; financial sector gains from, 171–72, 183, 190–91; impact of market losses on, 174, 175, 181–83, 187–88; individual management and yield disparities of, 173–80; original goal of, 171, 187; participation rates in, 173, 180, 184–85; taxes on, 175; track record of, 178–79, 182–83, 188–90
Foxcomm, 259, 492n
Fragoso, Luis, 231–32
Frank, Barney, 134–35
Frank, Harry, 243
Frank, Robert, 98, 102–3
Fraser, Douglas, 17
Freddie Mac (Federal Home Loan Mortgage Corporation), 198, 241, 406
Freeman, Richard B., 270
Free enterprise system, 5–7
free market strategy, 6, 377; de facto government spending in, 385; of the high-tech industry, 270–71; laissez-faire economics of, xxii, 217–18, 331, 380; of offshore manufacturing, 262–68
Friedman, Benjamin, 358
Friedman, Karen, 190
Friedman, Milton, 6, 49–50, 112, 295–96
Friedman, Thomas, 278
Fuld, Richard, 114
future strategies: business commitments in, 380–81; buying American in, 394; campaign financing reforms in, 419–20; citizen activism in, xxvii–xxviii, 377, 379–80, 410–13, 420–26; clean energy projects in, 391, 393–94; confronting Chinese trade practices in, 400–402; defense spending cuts in, 402–5; domestic Marshall Plan proposal of, xxv–xxvii, 380–86, 402–3; housing and fairness in, 405–7, 423–24; improving the tax code in, 395–400, 423–24; innovation and invention in, 390–92; manufacturing renaissance in, 392–94; Medicare and Social Security in, 407–8; public-private partnerships in, 388–90; rebuilding the political center in, 413–20; reform of the primary system in, 415–16; the safety net in, 405–9; transportation infrastructure in, 388–90

Gaddafi, Muammar, 369
Galbraith, John Kenneth, 109–10
Galvin, Bob, xx, 48–49
Gang of Six, 126–30, 139–40

Gardner, John, xi, xxviii, 410, 411, 420
Garten, Jeffrey, 147–48, 277
Gates, Bill, 138, 291, 297
Gates, Melinda, 138
Gates, Robert, 328, 362, 363, 367
Gault, Stanley, 244–45
Gavin, Bob, 56–57
Geithner, Tim, 143, 149, 150, 240
Gelb, Leslie, 374
General Electric, 58–59, 87–88, 274–75, 397
General Motors, xxvi, 33, 384; offshore research labs of, 275; structural layoffs at, 57; Treaty of Detroit of, 38–40, 62
Gephardt, Dick, 144
Gerard, Leo, 390
Gereffi, Gary, 242, 249, 254, 257
German economy, xxi–xxii, 74, 104, 379, 386–88, 447n
Gerstner, Lou, 57, 282
Ghilarducci, Teresa, 170, 188, 190
Ghoshal, Sumantra, 49–50
Gilded Age, xv, 100, 142
Gilens, Martin, 135, 412
Gilinger, Robin, 167–68
Gingrich, Newt, xx; as Speaker of the House, 335–39, 381; Contract with America of, 338–39, 341, 407; GOPAC of, 336, 418; Republican Party of, 330; proposal to privatize Medicare, 338–39; showdown with Clinton, 338–39
givebacks, 159–60, 165, 166–68, 476n
Glass-Steagall Act of 1933, 146–48, 149, 473n
globalization, xvii, xx–xxi, 61, 74, 377; commoditization of production in, 273; fair trade practices in, 400–402; German response to, xxi–xxii, 74, 104, 379, 386–88, 447n; of the high-tech industry, 269–89; nontradable sector under, 267–68, 381–82; offshoring of manufacturing jobs in, 262–68; tradable sector under, 268, 381. See also free market strategy; offshore economy
Glos, Michael, 387
GMAC, 239
Goldman Sachs, 143, 234–35
Goldwater, Barry, xiv, 6, 316–17; anti-union rhetoric of, 16, 49, 332; civil rights opposition of, 332; conservatism of, 329–33
Gomory, Ralph, 263–64, 269, 278–79
GOPAC, 336, 418
Gordon Gekko (character), 110

Gore, Al, 337
Gott, Ed, 10
government of the U.S. See U.S. government
Graetz, Michael, 130
Graham, Lindsey, 401
Gramlich, Edward, 224, 228
Grant, James, 218–19
Grassley, Chuck, 300–301, 303
grassroots democracy. See citizen action
Grayson, Mark, 261
the Great Compression, 41–42, 62, 325
Great Depression, xv, 38, 229, 331, 390
Great Recession (of 2008–?), xxii, 81–82, 461n; auto industry bailout in, xxvi, 384; impact on 401(k) plans of, 174, 181–82; jobless recovery of, xxiii–xxiv, 79–80, 288–89, 460n; loss of middle-class wealth during, 83, 216–41; offshore jobs and, 288–89; slow recovery of, 136–37; subprime mortgage crisis in, 192–215; tax policies during, 126; "Too Big to Fail" in, 147–48, 151; Wall Street bailout of, 142–43, 148–50, 239–40, 248–50, 344, 384, 405; Wall Street bank practices in, 57
Greenberg, Stanley, 412
Greenberger, Michael, 150
green cards, 303
Greene, Sylvian and Lois, 265–66
Greenhouse, Linda, 3
Greenhouse, Steven, 39–40
Greenspan, Alan, 143, 144–45, 471n; on diversifying risk, 222–23; on Glass-Steagall, 146–47; on home equity extraction, 219–20; on the housing market, 225–29, 233, 237; on idle capital, 136–37; on market deregulation, 217–18; on offshore production and job loss, 262–63; on sub-prime and exotic mortgages, 226–27; on superbanks, 147–48
gridlock in Congress, 307, 309–27; civil rights legislation and, 314–20; on the deficit, 311, 347; economic impact of, 324–27; under Gingrich's leadership, 336–38; on Obama's health care bill, 312–13, 319–20; on rule reform, 323–24; Senate filibuster impact on, 16–17, 311, 320–24; Senate resignations due to, 307, 310–11, 320, 350–51
Grove, Andy, xx, 268, 291, 381, 385–86, 392, 515n
Guardado, Armando, 205

Guardado, Eliseo, xx, 192, 204–6, 215, 240
Gulf War of 1991, 358

Hacker, Jacob, 81, 84, 88, 105, 131, 328
Hall, John, 286
Hamilton, Alexander, 383
Hamilton, Brooks, 87, 172, 176–77, 179, 185, 189
Harkin, Tom, 324
Harlow, Bryce, 5
Hart, Peter, 413
Hartwick, Thomas, 274
Hatch, Orrin, 16–17, 351
health care: Medicare for, 178–79, 184, 312–13; Obama's legislation on, 312–13, 342, 408; private insurance for, 84–86; public insurance for, 313
Health Research Group, 33
hedge funds: derivative trading of, 145–46, 148, 150; Goldman Sachs and, 233–35; managers' tax rates, 101–2, 106–7; secondary mortgage market in, 233–35, 447n
Heinz, John, 339
Heller, Bre, xx, 193–202, 212, 215, 222
Heritage Foundation, 11, 333–34
Hewlett-Packard, 279–80
Hiatt, Fred, 311
H-1B visa program, 291–303
high-technology industry, 269–89, 497n; clean energy technology in, 391, 393–94; future innovation and invention in, 390–94; government investment in, 384–85; importing of foreign workers by, 283–84, 290–303; offshore lures of, 276–77, 280–81, 286; technology theft in, 275–76; trade deficit in, 271–73
Highway Safety Administration, 33
Hindery, Leo, Jr., 390, 393, 399
Hira, Ron, 281, 295
Hockett, Robert, 407
Hockfield, Susan, 379, 385–86
Hoh, Matthew, 353–56, 364
Holbrooke, Richard, 363
Home Depot, 397
home equity loans, 218–20, 226, 407
Homegate Mortgage, 212–14
Honda, 384
Horizon Project, 381, 388, 393. See also domestic Marshall Plan proposal
housing boom and bust, 236–41; broker

fraud in, 231–33, 237–39, 472n, 475n; cheap money policies in, 225–27; Federal Reserve policies for, 219–20; 225–28, 233, 237; foreclosures in, 193, 239–40, 266, 406; future options for, 405–7, 423–24; home equity borrowing in, 218–20; inflated prices (bubble) in, 76–77, 103, 225–29; Justice Department on, 237–39; loss of equity in, 220, 484n; sub-prime mortgage lending for, 192–215, 226–27, 481n; warnings of, 228–29. See also mortgage market
Howard, Lee, 298–99
Hubbard, Glenn, 406
Huffington, Arianna, 349
Hughes, Mike, 66, 67–69, 252
Hu Jintao, 276
Humana, 398
Humphrey, Hubert, 317
Hussein, Saddam, 354, 358, 364
Hutchison, Kay Bailey, 389
Hyman, Edward, 83–84

IBM, 278–88, 397; imported foreign workers at, 293, 294; marketing of offshore services of, 284–85; offshoring blueprint patents of, 286–87; structural layoffs at, 57, 279, 282–84; training of (foreign) replacements in, 283–84
Immelt, Jeffrey, xxvi, 87, 385, 392
imperial wars. See military overreach
imported workers, 290–303; cheap labor of, 292, 293, 295–96; foreign management of, 297–300; H-1B visa program for, 291–94; layoffs of American workers for, 295–99; numbers of, 296–97; recruitment of, 291; reform proposals for, 300–303; skills gap rationale for, 291, 297, 301–2
In Defense of Globalization (Bhagwati), 263
independent contractors, 74–75
independent mortgage brokers, 199–201, 222
index funds, 183
India, 269, 273, 377, 497n; business lures of, 280–81, 286; cost competitiveness of, 281, 285; IBM in, 279–88; IT companies in U.S., 280–81, 295–96, 301–3; IT exports of, 294–95, 297–303, 497n
IndyMac Bank, 236
inequality. See economic inequality; political inequality
inflation, 247, 407–8

Infosys, 281, 294–95, 298
infrastructure proposals, 388–90
innovation and invention, 390–92
In Search of Excellence (Peters and
    Waterman), 37
insider power. *See* lobbying
Intel, xx, 268, 276–77, 278, 293, 381
International Accounting Standards Board,
    120
International Association of Machinists and
    Aerospace Workers, 158
inventory stuffing, 55–56
investment banks, 146–47, 148, 473n
Iraq War, 353–54, 360, 364, 373; costs of,
    355–60, 403, 511n, 521n; mission creep
    in, 358–59; U.S. bases in, 368; U.S.
    embassy costs in, 374
Irrational Exuberance (Shiller), 229
Isaacs, Julia, 71
Israeli demonstrations, 425–26; economic
    reforms, 425–26
It's Even Worse Than It Looks (Mann and
    Ornstein), 323

Jacobs, Lawrence R., 125
Jacobs, Sy, 200
Jacobson, Nancy, 414
Javits, Jacob, 312, 318
Jefferson, Thomas, 141, 269, 383
Jensen, Michael C., 112, 117
jobless recoveries, xxiii–xxiv, 79–80,
    288–89, 460n
jobs. *See* organized labor; the workforce
Jobs, Steve, 115, 259, 385
Johnson, Chalmers, 368
Johnson, Lyndon, 8, 29–30, 312–17,
    332
Johnson, Simon, 141, 144, 223, 228
Jones, Reginald, 11, 59
Jones, Walter, 356
JPMorgan Chase, 237, 239, 288
junk mortgages. *See* sub-prime mortgage
    lending

Karzai, Hamid, 354, 360, 365–66
Katz, Lawrence, 70
Katzenberg, Jeffrey, 418
Keillor, Garrison, 60
Keller, Kathryn, 192–93, 203–4
Kendall, Mike, 265
Kennedy, Edward, 18
Kennedy, John F., 10, 29, 41, 137, 314
Kennedy, Paul, 371–72

Kennedy, Robert, Jr., 31
Kerry, John, 374, 389
Khan, Mahmood, 366
Khosla, Vinod, 291
Khurana, Rakesh, 60, 117
Kidner, Rich, 184–85
Kilcrease, Linda, 293–94
Killinger, Kerry, 196–98, 230, 232, 237,
    238, 481n, 486n
Kindler, Jeffrey, 299–300
King, Martin Luther, Jr., xx, xxvii, 23,
    26–30, 394
Kleinfeld, Klaus, 379, 387
knoweldge economy, 270. *See also* high-
    technology industry
Knowland, William, 314
Koch, David and Charles, 334, 418
Kolchinsky, Eric, 236
Korb, Lawrence, 403
Korean War, 358
Kosch, Diane, 207–9
Kristol, Bill, 345
Kristol, Irving, 6
Krueger, Alan, xv, 137
Krugman, Paul, 35, 36, 42, 60, 151, 229,
    342, 385
Krushchev, Nikita, 40
K Street. *See* lobbying
Kuchel, Thomas, 312
Kumar, Jeya, 302–3

labor. *See* organized labor
Lacker, Jeffrey, 151
laissez-faire philosophy, xxii, 217–18, 331,
    380
Lake Wobegon syndrome, 60
Landrum-Griffin Act of 1959, 15
Lannoye, Lee, 197, 199, 203
Lawless, Robert, 92–93, 95, 96
Leen, David, 214
Lehman, Jon, 85, 248, 250–51, 255–56
Lehman Brothers, 114, 148, 223, 236
Leonhardt, David, 137
Levin, Carl, 238, 481n
Levine, David I., 72
Levitt, Arthur, 21, 118–20
Lewis, John, 25, 30
Lewis, Michael, 200, 487n
Lichtenstein, Nelson, 247
Lieberman, Joe, 119, 313
Limbaugh, Rush, xvii, 338
Lincoln, Abraham, xiii, xxv, 383, 388
Lincoln, Blanche, 150
Lindsey, Brink, 263

Lindsey, Lawrence, 228
Lingle, Don and Ginny, 266
Litan, Robert, 270
Liveris, Andrew, xxvi, 385
Livingston, James, 137, 424
L-1 visa program, 294–95, 299, 302
lobbying, xviii–xix, 411, 421–22;
    campaign spending in, 130, 132–33,
    411, 417–20, 469–70n, 474n; by
    Corporate America, xviii–xix, 11–12,
    21–22, 133–35, 141–52, 447n; Gang of
    Six domination of, 128; impact on the
    95th Congress (1978) of, 13–22; liberal
    opposition to, 129–33; on the mortgage
    market, 240–41; on tax cuts, 107–8,
    123, 125–40, 397, 399
Long Beach Mortgage Company, 194–204,
    207–9, 230–31, 234, 481n
Long Term Capital Management, 145–46
Lorsch, Jay, 60, 117
Lott, Trent, 144
Loughridge, Mark, 282
Lower Richistan, 102
low income. See the poor
Lugar, Richard, 351, 374
Luntz, Frank, 338
Lynch, Tom, 281–82

Madison, James, 383
Mahidra Satyam, 298
Maier, Charles, xx
Majid, Munshi Abdul, 366
Make It in America (Liveris), xxvi
Manchin, Joe, III, 356
Mankiw, Gregory, 263
Mann, Tom, 309, 319, 322–23, 351–52,
    418
Mansfield, Mike, 321, 323
manufacturing: in China, xxvi, 242–68,
    386; employment decline in U.S.,
    78–79; EPA regulations on, 9–10;
    erosion of U.S. high tech industrial base,
    273–76; in Germany, 386–88; push and
    pull production in, 249–50; return of
    U.S. jobs in, xxvi–xxvii, 392–94;
    Wal-Mart impact on, 243–52, 257–58.
    See also offshore economy
March on Washington of 1963, 24–26,
    28–30
Marine Mammal Protection Act, 31
market strategy. See free market strategy
Marquette Nat. Bank of Minneapolis v. First of
    Omaha Service Corp., 93–94

Marshall, Ray, 16–17
Marshall Plan proposal, xxv–xxvii, 380–86,
    402–3
Matloff, Norman, 301
McCain, John: on campaign financing, xviii,
    411, 417; on defense spending, 404; on
    G. W. Bush's tax policies, 131, 139
McCarty, Nolan, 309, 325
McChrystal, Stanley A., 361–63
McConnell, Mitch, 311
McCormack, Richard, 392–93
McCurdy, Dave, 261
McGire, William, 115–16
McGovern, George, 9
McGurn, Patrick, 115
McKiernan, David, 360
McKinnon, Mark, 414
McPherson, Harry, 315–16
Mean Business (Dunlap), 50
Meany, George, 16
Meckling, William H., 112
Medicare, 107, 178–79, 312–13; future
    options for, 407–8; New Right's assault
    on, 329–30, 335, 338–39, 349;
    privatization schemes for, 89
megabanks, 147–48, 151
Mehta, Shailesh, 94
Melrose, Ken, 110–11
Merck, 397
Merkley, Jeff, 324
Merrill Lynch, 148
"Method for Identifying Human-Resource
    Work Content to Outsource Offshore"
    (IBM), 286–87
MetLife Study of the American Dream, 81,
    89–90, 462n
Microsoft, 75, 275, 293, 294, 298
the middle class, 66–67; debt and
    bankruptcies of, 90–97; definition of,
    434n; economic insecurity of, xvi–xvii,
    xxii; education of, 105–6; impact of
    benefit shift on, 81–90; impact of 401(k)
    plans on, 172–88; in Germany, xxi–xxii,
    74, 379, 386–88, 447n; under
    globalization, xx–xxi; labor's
    contributions to, 37–40; loss of pensions
    of, 155, 157–69, 237, 475n, 476n; loss
    of safety nets of, 83–90, 405–9; lost
    wealth of, 64, 73–74, 77–80, 83,
    216–41, 484n; Misery Index of, 83–84;
    as the new poor, 65–80; overseas job loss,
    263–65, 287–89, 296–97; pay rates of,
    xxiii; political activism of, 23–34, 412;
    political marginalization of, xvii–xix,

xxvii, 151–52, 411–12, 420; postwar
prosperity of, xiv–xv, xx, xxiii–xxiv,
35–42, 73, 325; reduced mobility of,
70–74, 76–77; revival of civic activism
of, xix, xxv–xxviii, 377, 379–80,
410–13, 420–26; stagnation of living
standards of, 69–70, 72–74; sub-prime
mortgages and, 209–10, 227; tax rates
on, 106–8, 395; unstable retirement
plans of, 174–79, 185–91, 478n;
winners and losers of, 81–83. *See also*
American Dream
Middle Richistan, 102
Midgeley, Tom, 283
Mihalic, Scott, 243–44
Milbank, Dana, 341
military overreach, 353–74; Arc of Danger
threats in, 363, 367, 374; Cold War
legacy of, 368–70, 372–73, 405; costs
of, 355–60, 370–74, 402–5, 511n,
521n; drone aircraft in, 361; empire of
military bases in, 368–69, 374, 404–5,
513n; future options on, 402–5; guns *vs.*
butter debates on, 356, 370, 373, 404,
510n; imperial nature of, 367–74;
mission creep in, 358–64; nation
building mission in, 369–70; terrorism
as reasons for, 354, 359–60, 364;
Vietnam War analogy of, 362–64
the minimum wage, 16, 17, 325–27
Mining Enforcement Safety
Administration, 9
Minow, Nell, 51
Misery Index, 83–84
Mishel, Larry, 76, 105–6, 264–65
Mittal, Som, 297
mobility, 70–74, 76–77
mobilization of the middle class. *See* citizen
action
Mohaqeq, Muhammad, 366
Monroe, James, 383
Moody's, 235–36
Moonves, Leslie, 77
Moore, Stephen, 125, 128, 340
Moral Majority, 333, 334
Morgan, Chuck, 27
Morgenson, Gretchen, 216, 224
Morin, Rich, 81
Morrison, Bruce, 290, 292, 296–97
Morrow, Lance, 65
Morse, Samuel F. B., 383
Mortgage Bankers Association, 233
mortgage market, 236–41; adjustable-rate
mortgages in, 202–4, 224, 227, 230–31,

233–34; deregulation of, 223–28;
diversification of risk in, 222–23; equity
stripping in, 218–20, 226, 407;
foreclosures in, 193, 239–40, 266, 406;
future options in, 405–7; negative
amortization practices in, 224; Obama's
refinancing program in, 240–41; 100
percent financing in, 224; secondary
mortgage market in, 216–18, 221–25,
233–35; sub-prime mortgages in,
192–215, 226–27, 237–39, 489n;
traditional mortgages in, 222, 486n;
warnings of crisis in, 228–29
Motorola University, 48–49
movement conservatism. *See* New Right
Moyers, Bill, 315, 317
Mozilo, Angelo, 114, 238, 489n
Mr. Smith Goes to Washington, 321
Munnell, Alicia, 178–81, 188–90, 478n
Murphy, Thomas, 11
Murray, Charles, xv
Muskie, Edmund, 9
mutual funds, 171–72, 183, 190–91

Nader, Ralph, 14–15, 32–34, 129–30
Nardelli, Bob, 113–14
National Association of Manufacturers, 12,
16–17, 128–29
National Association of Wholesaler-
Distributors, 128–29
National Federation of Independent
Business, 12, 128–29
National Highway Safety Administration, 9
National Restaurant Association, 128–29
National Retirement Risk Index (NRRI),
478n
National Review, 6
National Semiconductor, 173–77
National Traffic and Motor Vehicle Safety
Act of 1966, 34
National Transportation Safety Board, 33
NATO, 368
Nebraska's retirement savings plan, 189–90
negative amortization practices, 224
Netanyahu, Benjamin, 426
New Century, 236
New Deal, 38, 331, 390
New Economy. *See* economic inequality
New Mortgage Game, 193–215, 216–41
The New Politics of Inequality (Edsall), 14
New Poor. *See* the poor
New Power Game, xxiv–xxv. *See also*
political inequality

New Right, 6, 316–20, 328–52; attack on
Specter of, 339–41; blocking of Clinton
by, 322, 336–39; blocking of Obama by,
341–43, 349–50; cutting of government
programs by, 344–45, 349; Gingrich's
role in, 335–39; Goldwater conservatism
in, 330–33; ideological purity of, 330,
332–33, 341, 351–52; 1994
Congressional elections of, 337–38;
Norquist's influence on, 329, 348–50,
509n; Reagan's role in, 333, 334–35;
religious fundamentalism and, 334;
Super-PACs of, 418–20, 524n; talk radio
and, 338; tax policies of, 329–30, 335,
345–47, 350; Tea Party of, xviii, xxvii–
xxviii, 329, 343–52; Weyrich's
organization of, 333–34. See also
Goldwater, Barry
new technology. See globalization
Ngo, John, 209
Nichol, Bill, 251–52
Nicskanen, William, 270
the 99 percent, xiv–xvi, 425
Niskanen, William, 358
Nixon, Richard, 35; anti-business policies
of, 5–11, 18; on classless society, 40–41;
consensus politics of, 314; defense
spending of, 403; environmental policies
of, 8–10, 31–32; mainstream
conservatism of, 331; regulatory stories
of, 7–11; Republican Party of, 330;
Southern strategy of, 317–18; tax
policies of, 10–11; Watergate scandal
of, 15
Noise Pollution and Abatement Act, 31
No Labels, 413, 414
nonpartisan primary elections, 415–16
nontradable sector, 267–68, 381, 392
Norquist, Grover, 329, 348–50, 509n
Norris, Bob, 212–14

Obama, Barack: Afghanistan War of,
354–56, 361–62, 404; auto industry
bailout by, xxvi, 384; China trade policies
of, 276; defense spending proposals of,
402–5; deficit reduction policies of,
311, 346; economic stimulus policies of,
82, 341–42; financial sector influence
on, 143–44, 145, 149, 342; on global
security, 370; health care legislation of,
312–13, 342, 408; housing policies of,
240–41; on the Iraq War, 373; on the
peace dividend, 404–5; postpartisan vision
of, 341; Republican obstructionism of,

341–43, 349–50; science and technology
policies of, 391–92; Social Security tax
cuts by, 108; on Super-PACs, 419; tax
policies of, 82, 138–40, 324, 326–27,
344–47; Tea Party rhetoric on, 344
Obey, David, 65
Occupational Safety and Health
Administration (OSHA), 9, 334
Occupy Wall Street, xviii, xxviii, 425
O'Connor, Sandra Day, 335
offshore economy, xxii, xxiv, 48–49, 63, 67,
80, 242–68, 386; CEO comments on,
52–55, 278–79, 284–285, 381–82, 387
392–94; cheap labor in, xxvi, 259–60,
270, 492n; under Sunbeam CEO Al
Dunlap, 52–56; high-tech industry in,
269–89, 497n; job loss to, 79, 262–68,
288–89, 491n, 494n; large-scale
shipping for, 256–59; profits from,
255–56; service industry in, 272–73; tax
breaks and government subsidies of,
276–77, 280–81, 286, 398–400;
technology theft in, 275–76; trade
deficit from, 258–62, 276, 386–87;
Wal-Mart's role in, 244–58. See also
China; India
oil dependence, 370
Omidyar, Pierre, 291
O'Neill, Pat, 155, 157–61, 166–69
O'Neill, Paul, 126, 127
O'Neill, Steve, xx
O'Neill, Tip, 14–15, 336
the 1 percent, xiv–xvi, 98–120; access to
education in, 105–6; annual average
income of, 74, 458n, 463n; capital gains
of, 106–7, 395–96; economic gains of,
xv, 100–102; estate taxes on, 139–40,
326–27; inherited wealth of, 111;
lifestyles and consumption of, 98–99,
102–3; payroll taxes of, 396, 408;
political power of, 411–13; Super-PACs
of, 418–20, 510n; tax cuts for, 20–22,
106–8, 347, 395–97, 423–24
100 percent financing practices, 224
"One Recession, Two Americas" (Taylor and
Morin), 81–82
onshoring. See imported workers
Option ARM mortgages, 209–14, 227,
230–31
Oracle, 293
Organisation for Economic Co-operation
and Development (OECD), 61–62
organized labor, xxii, 15–17, 24, 63; auto
industry bailout and, xxvi, 384; under
bankruptcy reforms, 19; bankrupt

pension plans of, 155, 157–69, 474n;
campaign financing by, 132, 133;
conservative policies against, 16, 49,
332; employee share ownership programs
for, 159–60; in Germany, 387–88;
givebacks and compromises by, 74,
159–60, 165–68, 476n; on G.W. Bush's
tax cuts, 129–30; lobbying power of,
131–33; pension negotiations of,
158–59, 475n; the social contract of,
37–40, 49–50; Treaty of Detroit,
38–40, 62
Ornstein, Norman: on the filibuster,
320–23; on Gingrich, 336; on
mandatory voting, 417; on the New
Right, 345, 351–52; on Super-PACs,
418
Otellini, Paul, 277
Oxley, Art, 52–53

Pacific Railroad Act of 1862, 383
Packard, David, 110
PACs (political action committees),
132–33
Page, Benjamin I., 125
Palmer, Robert, 57
Palmisano, Sam, 282, 284–85
Pandit, Vikram, 62
Panetta, Leon, 403
Panic of 1893, xv
part-time workers, 74–75
patent awards, 391
Patient Protection and Affordable Care Act
of 2010, 312–13, 342, 408
Patrick, Deval, 348
Paul, Rand, 318
Paulson, Henry, 143, 148
Paulson, John, 101–2, 234
Paulson, John A., 418
payroll taxes, 107, 108, 396, 408
the peace dividend, 404–5
peace movement, 24
peer benchmarking, 60–61
Pension Benefit Guaranty Corporation
(PBGC), 161, 166, 186
pension plans: bankruptcy of, 155,
157–69, 237, 476n; as defined benefit
plans, 158–59, 475n; employer
contributions to, 172; government safety
net for, 161, 166; as moneymakers, 87,
161–62, 171; Pat O'Neill and, 155–61,
166–69; replacement by 401(k) plans of,
19–20, 86–88, 160–62, 170–73, 408
permatemps, 74–75, 297–98

Perot, Ross, 184, 280, 413, 414
Perot Systems, 184–85, 280
Perry, Rick, 418
Perry, Robert J., 418
Peters, Thomas, 37
Petraeus, David, 362–63
Pew Research Center, 81–82, 83
Pfizer, 297–300
phantom filibusters, 322–24
Phillips, Kevin, 76, 142, 410
Phillips, Rufus, 362–63
Pierson, Paul, 105, 131, 328
piggyback loans, 203–4
Piketty, Thomas, 101–2, 453n
Pinto, Mark R., 275
the plutocracy, 98–102. See also the
1 percent
Polarized America (McCarty, Poole,
Rosenthal), 319, 325
political inequality, xvii–xix, 377; citizen
activism in response to, xix, xxvii–xxviii,
377, 379–80, 410–13, 420–26;
Congress listening to affluent, 125,
133–34, 141, 411–12; interaction with
economic inequality of, xix–xx;
middle-class powerlessness in, xviii,
xxvii, 151–52, 411–12, 420; rebuilding
the political center in, 413–20; role of
party extremism in, 330, 332–33, 341,
351–52, 411; unequal democracy,
151–52. See also lobbying
political parties: compromise and
bipartisanship of, 8–11, 313–19, 325;
electoral domination by, 413–20;
ideological purity of, xxiv–xxv, 330,
332–33, 341, 351–52; missing middle
in, 307–27; partisan polarization in,
307–13, 319–20; political realignment
in, 316–19; soft money of, 132–33, 421;
third-party movements in, 413–14;
Washington's warning against, 328. See
also Democratic Party; Republican
Party
pollution, 30–32
Poole, Keith T., 309, 319, 325
the poor, 408–9; the former middle class as,
65–80; poverty line of, 70, 448n
populist demands. See citizen action
Port of Long Beach, 258–59
post–World War II prosperity, xiv–xv, xx,
xxiii–xxiv, 35–42, 73; the Great
Compression of, 41–42, 62, 325; social
contract in, 35–40, 77–80; tax policies
of, 41–42
poverty line, 70, 448n

Powell, Lewis, xiii, 3, 5, 59
Powell Memorandum, xiii–xiv, 3, 5–8,
    11–12, 16, 132
The Power Game: How Washington Works
    (Smith), xix
Preble, Christopher, 353, 371
predatory capitalism, 47–48; inventory
    stuffing as, 55–56; subprime mortgages
    as, 197–200, 211–15; workforce policies
    of, 50–56. *See also* wedge economics
prepayment penalties, 214
Prestowitz, Clyde, 263, 272, 274–77,
    385
Price, Michael, 48, 49, 64
primary election system, 415–16
Prince, Charles, 236
Providian Financial, 94
Ptak, Larry, 243–44
Public Citizen, 32, 129–30
Public Interest, 6
public opinion: on capital gains taxes, 396;
    Congress's ignoring of, 125, 133–35,
    141, 411, 412–13; on financial sector
    campaign contributions, 474n; on G. W.
    Bush's tax policies, 127, 129, 135, 471n;
    on Obama's tax policies, 138; on offshore
    jobs, 288–89; on political power,
    151–52, 412; on the social safety net,
    408; on Social Security and Medicare,
    407
public-private partnerships, 388–90
pull production, 249–50
push production, 249–50

racial contexts: income and, 70, 71–72;
    segregation and, 3, 26–28. *See also* civil
    rights movement
radical right. *See* New Right
railroad industry, 18
Ramirez, Thomas, 231–32
Ranieri, Lewis, 225
Rattner, Steve, 387
Ray, Hugh, 164–65
Rayburn, Sam, 313–14
Raynes, Sylvain R., 234
RCA-Thomson, 66–67, 252
Reagan, Ronald, xix; defense spending
    policies of, 370, 403; domestic spending
    policies of, 340; 401(k) plan policies of,
    19–20, 171, 186; new Gilded Age
    under, 100; New Right disappointed in,
    334–35; New Right politics of, 332–35;
    pro-business policies of, 224–25,
    384–85; Republican Party of, 330;

research cuts by, 390–91; Supreme Court
    nominees of, 335, 340; tax policies of,
    21, 107–8, 128, 326, 335, 348–49, 395;
    union-busting policies of, 16, 49
real estate mortgage investment conduit
    (REMIC), 225
Reardon, Sean, 71
recession of 1990, 79
recession of 2001, 79, 225–26, 229
Recession of 2008–?. *See* Great Recession
reclamation of the American Dream, xix,
    xxv–xxviii, 379
recovery of 2002–03, 79
Reed, John, 146, 150
Reich, Robert, 42, 290, 295–96
Reid, Harry, 349
Rell, M. Jodi, 342
Rendell, Ed, 389
Repetti, James R., 136
Republican Party: Bipartisanship with
    Johnson, 314–15; centrists and
    moderates in, 315–16, 318–19, 320,
    339–40; Class of 1944 in House, 337,
    345; conservative movement in, 6,
    316–20, 328–52; Eastern Establishment
    of, 330–31; party evolution, 329;
    purging of RINOs, 339–41; resignations
    of centrists of, 307, 310–11, 320,
    350–51; Southern strength in, 318–19.
    See also New Right
response to inequality. *See* reclamation of
    the American Dream
Restore Our Future, 418
retirement, 174–79, 188–91; actual
    financial needs in, 184–86; of the
    boomer generation, 177–90, 478n;
    federal plan for, 189–91; 401(k) plans
    for, 19–20, 86–88, 160–62, 170–91,
    408; health care costs in, 178–79, 184;
    National Retirement Risk Index on,
    478n; national shortfall in, 185–89;
    official age for, 188; pension plans for,
    155, 157–69, 476n. *See also* Medicare;
    Social Security
Reuther, Walter, 39, 332
Reynolds, Bob, 172
Ricardo, David, 136, 263–64
Richistan (Frank), 102–3
right to work states, 63
right wing. *See* New Right
RINO moderates, 339–40
Rios, Brian, 205
The Rise and Fall of the Great Powers
    (P. Kennedy), 371–72
Rittenmeyer, Ron, 278

Roach, Stephen, 47, 56, 64, 79, 229
Roaring Twenties, 100, 142
robber baron era, xv, 100
Robertson, Pat, 334
robo-signing, 239–40
Robyn, Dorothy, 368
Rogoff, Kenneth, 424
Roman Empire, 368
Romer, Christina, 342
Romney, Mitt, 56–57, 381, 396, 418
Roosevelt, Franklin D., 38, 331, 390
Roosevelt, Theodore, xv, xxv, 388, 414
Rosenthal, Howard, 309, 319, 325
Rossiter, Gene, 86
Rossotti, Charles, 395
Rotella, Steve, 238
Roubini, Nouriel, 407
Rove, Karl, 123, 126, 348–49, 419
Rovere, Richard, 332
Royal Bank of Scotland, 234, 235
Rubbermaid, 242–44, 265–67
Rubin, Robert, 143, 145, 147–48
Ruckelshaus, William, 9–10, 23, 32
Rumsfeld, Donald, 369
Russell, Richard, 315
The Russians (Smith), xix
Ryan, Norb, Jr., 404
Ryan, Paul, 89
Rybak, R. T., 356

Saez, Emmanuel, 100–102, 448n, 463n
Safe Drinking Water Act, 31
safety net losses, 83–90; for the aspiring
    middle class, 408–9; Congressional
    gridlock and, 324–27; future protections
    for, 405–9; of health insurance, 84–86;
    New Right and, 329–30; of pension
    plans, 19–20, 86–88, 157–69; of
    retirement security, 177–91, 478n
Salisbury, Harrison, 27
Saltonstall, Leverett, 312, 318
Samuelson, Paul, 264
San Francisco–Oakland Bay Bridge project,
    394
Santelli, Rick, 343
Santorum, Rick, 381, 418
Satyam, 294–95, 298
Sawhill, Isabel V., 65, 71
Scaife, Richard Mellon, 333–34
Schacht, Henry, 56–57
Schlademan, Dan, 86
Schmitt, Wolfgang, 245–46, 250
Schneider, David, 232, 238
Scholl, Pam, 66–69, 91–92, 95, 252

Schultz, Ellen, 87–88
Schumer, Charles, 302–3, 401
Schumpeter, Joseph, 368
Schurenberg, Eric, 170, 187–88
Schwarzenegger, Arnold, 342, 389
Scott, Hugh, 312, 318, 339
Scott, Lee, 59
Scott, Robert, 262, 272–73, 401, 491n
Scott, Thomas C., 187
Scott Paper Company, 50–51
Sears, Roebuck, 57
SEATO, 368
secondary mortgage market, 216–18,
    221–25, 233–35
Secondary Mortgage Market Enhancement
    Act of 1984, 224–25
Securities and Exchange Commission
    (SEC), 115–16
segregation, 3, 26–28
Sematch, 384
serial downsizers, 45
Serrano, Kristine, 283–84
service economy, 392; as nontradable sector,
    267–68, 381–82; offshoring of, 272–73
Service Employees International Union
    (SEIU), 129
Shapiro, Irving, 11
shareholders: on CEO compensation,
    62–63; cheating by CEO stock options
    of, 116–17; power of, 63, 134–35; shift
    of wealth to, 64
shareholder value, 45, 49, 56–60, 112,
    117
Shiller, Robert J., 226, 229
Shrontz, Frank, 57
Shuttlesworth, Fred, 25
silent filibusters, 322–24
Silent Spring (Carson), 30
Simmons, Harold C., 418
Simons, James, 101
Simpson, Alan, 405
Sinegal, Jim, 86
Singer, Paul, 418
skill-based technological change (SBTC),
    104
the skills gap, 290–303
Slane, Dan, 242
Sloan, Allan, 57
Smith, Adam, 136
Smith, Greg, 234–35
Smith, Margaret Chase, 312
Smith, Yvonne, 258–59
Snow, John, 228
Snowe, Olympia, 320, 340, 350–51
social conservatism, 331

the social contract, xxii, 35–40; corporate rewriting of, 12, 83–90; decline of, 77–80; Friedman's argument against, 49–50; in Germany, xxii, 74, 379, 386–88; Treaty of Detroit on, 38–40, 62. *See also* safety net losses

social responsibility. *See* citizen action

Social Security, 107, 178; covering shortfall of, 407–9; different tax levels on, 107; future options for, 407–8; New Right's assault on, 329–32, 335, 349; Obama's tax cuts for, 108; official retirement age for, 188; privatization schemes for, 89

soft money, 132–33, 421

Solyndra, 392

Soros, George, 101

Sotello, Lili, 206–7, 231

Southern Christian Leadership Project, 26. *See also* civil rights movement

Specter, Arlen, 339–41

Spence, Michael, 267–68, 381–82, 385

Sprayregen, James M., 157, 163, 165, 167

stakeholder capitalism, 45, 110–11

Standard & Poor's, 235

Stempel, Robert, 57

STEM (science, technology, engineering, and mathematics) workers, 290, 291, 301–2

Stewart, Jimmy, 321

Stiglitz, Joseph, 235, 342, 385, 411

stimulus spending, xxv–xxvii, 79, 82, 341–42

stock index funds, 183

Stockman, David, 335

stock options, 109, 111–20; CEOs cheating on, 114–16; critiques of, 116–17, 119–20; employee-share programs of, 159–60, 174; government regulation of, 118–20; John Bogle, 116–17; pay for performance basis of, 112–13; payoffs for failure, 113–14; political battle over, 118–20; price manipulation of, 114–16; shareholder criticism of, 116–17; tax proposals for, 396

Stone, Oliver, 110

"Strike it Richer" (Saez), 100–101

structural layoffs, 57–59, 78–79; of imported workers, 293, 295–99; for outsourcing, 279, 282–84

Strutz, Ray, 252

A Study of History (Toynbee), xi–xii

sub-prime mortgage lending, 192–215, 226–27; broker fraud in, 194–95, 205, 208–9, 231–33, 237–39, 486n, 489n;

floating-rate mortgages in, 210–14; hidden fees in, 211–14; independent brokers in, 199–201, 212–14, 222, 231–32; middle-class buyers of, 209–10; penalties and settlements for, 237–39; predatory practices in, 202–7; quality control of, 207–8; Senate investigation of, 232–33, 481n

Sullivan, Anna, 189

Summers, Larry, 77, 143–44, 145, 342

Sunbeam, 52–56, 64

superbanks, 147–51

Super-PACs, 132–33, 418–20, 524n

super-rich. *See* the 1 percent

supertax proposal, 396

Supreme Court. *See* U.S. Supreme Court

Sweeney, John, 129

Syntel, 293–95

synthetic derivatives, 222

Taft-Hartley Act of 1947, 15

Taliban. *See* Afghanistan War

talk radio, 338

Target, 397

Tata Consulting, 281, 294–95

taxes/tax code: of advanced economies, 347; on capital gains, 21, 106–7, 139, 395–96; on corporations, 10–11, 21, 107, 112–13, 139, 397–400, 423; economic growth and, 41–42, 136–37; economic theory on, 136–37; fight of 2010 on, 138–40, 324, 326–27, 345–47; on 401(k) cash-outs, 174–77; on 401(k) plans, 19–20, 86–88, 160–62, 170–91; future options for, 395–400; G. W. Bush's cuts of, 21, 107–8, 123, 126–40, 326–27, 395, 399, 468n, 471n; lobbyist impact on, 107–8, 123, 125–40, 397; loopholes and shelters in, 395, 397–400, 423–24; New Right's assault on, 329–30, 335, 345–47, 350; Nixon's policies on, 10–11; Obama's policies on, 82, 138–40, 324, 326–27, 344–47; on offshore operations, 276–77, 280–81, 286, 398–400; on the 1 percent, 20–22, 106–8, 347, 423–24; payroll taxes in, 107, 108, 396, 408; of the postwar prosperity years, 41–42; Reagan's policies on, 21, 107–8, 128, 326, 335, 348–49, 395; real estate mortgage investment conduit (REMIC) in, 225; rebate programs in, 130; on stock options, 116–17; supertax proposal for, 396; tax cutting trend in, 20–22,

106–8, 123; Tea Party approach to,
345–47; of temporary workers, 75
Tax Relief Coalition, 126–30, 139–40
Taylor, Paul, 81–82
Tea Party, xviii, xxvii–xxviii, 329, 343–52;
on defense cuts, 373, 405; demographics
of, 343–44; 2010 elections and, 343,
344; Goldwater's influence on, 331–32;
on government programs, 344–45, 349,
402; lobbying power of, 421–22;
millionaires club of, 347–48; origins of,
343; in primary elections, 351–52; on
taxes, 345–47
technological change. See globalization
Templeton, John, 229
temporary workers, 74–75
Tepper, David, 101
Terboss, John, xx, 211–15
Thibeau, Gil, 173–76
Thiel, Peter, 418
think tanks, 11–12
Third Way, 413, 414–16
Thurmond, Strom, 321
Tilton, Glenn, 165, 166
Tomlinson, Harry, 218–19
Tonelson, Alan, 261–62, 272
"Too Big to Fail," 147–48, 151
Toomey, Pat, 340–41
Toynbee, Arnold J., xi–xii, xxvii, 109,
377
Toyota, 384
tradable sector, 268, 381
Trade Adjustment Assistance program,
402
trade associations, 12
trade deficits, xx–xxii, xxvi, 387, 447n; on
Chinese manufactured goods, 258–62,
276; on high-tech goods, 271–73
Train, Russell, 31
transportation infrastructure proposals,
388–90
Treaty of Detroit, 38–40, 62
Trotman, Alex, 278
Troyer, Carol, 245–46
trucking industry, 18
Trumka, Rich, xvii
Turner, Ted, 138
Twain, Mark, 363
Two Americas, xii–xiii, 81–83, 461n;
interplay of economics and politics in,
xix–xx; origins of, xiii–xiv, 13–22;
skill-based technological change in,
104
2/28 ARM mortgages, 202–4, 227,
233–35

The Two-Income Trap (Warren and Tyagi),
76–77, 94
Tyagi, Amelia Warren, 76–77, 94

Udall, Tom, 321–22, 324
the ultra-rich, 74, 102, 106–7. See also the
1 percent
unemployment, 78; following the Great
Recession of 2008–?, 79–80, 137, 460n;
as long-term, 70, 79
Unequal Democracy (Bartels), 447n
unions. See organized labor
United Airlines, 155, 158–61, 164–68
United Auto Workers, xxvi, 38–40, 62,
159, 332
United Electrical Workers, 39
United Steelworkers, 39, 159
United Technologies, 397
Unsafe at Any Speed (Nader), 33
Upper Richistan, 102–3
U.S. Business and Industry Council, 381
U.S. Census Bureau, 448n
U.S. Chamber of Commerce, 12, 128–29; on
China's indigenous innovation policy, 275;
on labor law reform, 16–17; on the Powell
Memorandum, 6–7; on public-private
infrastructure partnerships, 388–90
U.S. Conference of Mayors, 356
U.S. Congress: campaign costs of, 143, 411,
417–20, 474n; civil rights legislation of,
28–30; compromise and bipartisanship
in, 8–11, 313–19; consumer safety
legislation of, 34; defense spending of,
356, 373–74, 510n; on the deficit, 311,
347; Dodd-Frank banking reforms of,
149–51; on economic inequality, xvi;
environmental legislation of, 31; gridlock
of, 307, 309–27, 336–38; ignoring public
opinion, 125, 133–35, 141, 411, 412;
Medicare bill in, 312–13; millionaires in,
347–48; mortgage rate legislation of,
198; nonpartisan primaries for, 415–16;
Obama's health care bill in, 312–13,
319–20; reform agenda of 1978 of,
13–22, 163–65, 170–73; revolving door
with K Street of, 144; rule reform in,
323–24; Senate filibuster power in,
16–17, 311, 320–24; social interaction
in, 310–11, 320; Social Security policies
of, 407; tax cut legislation of, 125–40,
324, 326–27, 345–47; Tea Party
members of, xxvii–xxviii, 344–49;
unresponsiveness to public opinion of,
135, 411, 412–13. See also lobbying

U.S. government: "buy American" policies of, 394; domestic Marshall Plan proposal for, xxv–xxvii, 380–82, 402–3; kick-starting of innovation by, 390–92; public-private infrastructure projects of, 388–90; stimulus spending by, xxv–xxvii, 79, 82, 341–42; support of American industry by, 382–86, 392

U.S. Steel, 10

U.S. Supreme Court: *Brown v. Board of Education* decision of, 3, 26; *Citizens United v. Federal Election System* decision of, 417–20; *Marquette Nat. Bank of Minneapolis v. First of Omaha Service Corp.*, 93–94; Reagan's nominees to, 335, 340

usury law, 224

Vagelos, Roy, 391

Vanasek, James, 481n, 486n

VanDerhai, Jack, 178

Van Dongen, Dirk, 123, 126–30, 139–40

Van Horn, Carl, 70

Verizon, 87

Vietnam War, 24, 332, 358, 362–64

Villaraigosa, Antonio, 356

virtuous circle of growth, xiv, xxiii–xxvi, 35–42, 380, 405–6; demolition by wedge economics of, 51–52, 62, 77–80; Henry Ford's role in, 35–36; organized labor's contributions to, 37–40; stakeholder capitalism in, 45, 110–11

Vogel, David, 34

Voinovich, George, 340

Volcker, Paul, 60, 150–51

Volcker Rule, 150–51

volunteers, 425–26

voter turnout, 416–17

Voting Rights Act of 1965, 30, 317

Votocracy, 413

Wahl, Jack, 54–55

Wall Street. *See* financial sector

Wall Street (film), 110

Wal-Mart: anti-union policies of, 63; CEO compensation at, 59, 86; economic power of, 244–52, 255, 491n; employee turnover at, 86; growth of, 247; health insurance coverage at, 85–86; informational efficiency of, 248–50; offshore production for, 244–46; offshoring pressures from, 251–52; pricing strategy of, 250–51; profits of,

255–56; Shenzhen operation of, 253–54, 256–58; tax rate on, 397

Walton, Sam, 102, 246–47, 255

Walton family, 102–3

Warner, Mark, 389

War on Terror. *See* Afghanistan War; Iraq War

Warren, Elizabeth, 19, 76–77, 149; on corporate bankruptcy, 163; on personal debt and bankruptcy, 90–91, 93, 94

wars. *See* military overreach

Warsaw Pact, 369

Washington, George, xxv, 379, 382

Washington Mutual Bank (WaMu), 223; broker fraud in, 194–95, 205, 208–9, 230–32, 486n; collapse of, 236–37; exotic loans of, 201–2; FDIC prosecution of, 238; Killinger as CEO of, 196–98, 230–32, 236–9; Long Beach Mortgage subsidiary of, 194–204, 207–10, 230–31, 234, 481n; Option ARM loan of, 209–14, 230–31; President's Club of, 232; Senate investigation of, 232–33, 238, 481n; sub-prime mortgage business of, 194–204, 207–9, 230–31, 234, 481n, 486n

watchdog organizations, 33

Watergate scandal, 15

Waterman, Robert, Jr., 37

Watson, Tom, Jr., 282

wealth gap. *See* economic inequality

Webb, Anthony, 185–86

wedge economics, xxii–xxiii, 47–64; appointment of corporate boards in, 60–61; CEO compensation in, 56, 58–63; Dunlap's practice of, xx, 45, 47–57; middle-class stagnation under, 65–74; rewriting of the social contract in, 12, 83–90; separation of wages from productivity growth, 74–75; shareholder value in, 45, 49, 56–60, 112, 117; structural layoffs in, 57–59, 63, 78–79; wage freezes in, 61

Weill, Sandy, 112, 147–48

Weisbrot, Mark, 229

Welch, Jack, 58–59

Wells Fargo, 238, 397

Wertheimer, Fred, 419

Wessel, Mike, 262

Weyrich, Paul, 329, 333–35

Wheeler, Winslow, 371, 403

Willis, Earl, 37

Wilson, Charlie "Engine," 39, 109, 278

Wilson, Woodrow, 326

Winning Our Future, 418

Wipro, 281, 294–95
Wolfe, Tom, 110, 142
women in the workforce, 76–77
women's movement, 24
the workforce: compensation of, 73, 75–76,
 458n; contingent sector of, 74–75; at
 failed mortgage banks, 237; future
 expansion of, 381–82; gender factors in,
 76–77; in Germany, xxi–xxii, 74, 379,
 386–88, 447n; job creation in, 137,
 422–23; in manufacturing, 78–79,
 393–94; nontradable sector of, 267–68;
 offshore high-tech industry and, 269–89,
 497n; offshore job loss in, 79, 262–68,
 288–89, 477n, 480n; offshore
 manufacturing and, xxii, xxiv, 48–49,
 52–56, 63, 79, 262–68, 491n, 494n;
 under predatory capitalism, 50–58;
 productivity of, 73, 76, 264, 458n;
 retraining programs for, 402; return of
 U.S. jobs in, xxvi–xxvii; skills gap myth
 of, 291, 297, 301–2; the social contract
 of, xxii, 12, 35–40, 45, 48–50, 54–55,
 77–80; stagnant pay scales of, 65–74;
 STEM workers in, 290, 291, 301–2;
structural layoffs of, 57–59, 78–79, 279,
 282–84, 293, 295–99; turnover rates of,
 86; unemployment rates in, 70, 78,
 79–80, 137, 460n; wealth gap of, 61–62,
 73–74, 77–80. See also the middle class;
 organized labor
"Workforce Sourcing Optimizer" (IBM),
 286–87
World Trade Organization, 402
Wray, David, 187
Wright, Jim, 336
Wright, Ron, 265
Wriston, Walter, 11
Wunsch, Roy, 66, 252

Yang, Jerry, 291
Yermack, David, 115
Young, Andrew, 27–28
Young, Stephen, 113
YSP (yield spread premium) fees, 211–14
the yuan, 400

the zero decade (2000–09), 83

ABOUT THE AUTHOR

Hedrick Smith is a bestselling author, Pulitzer Prize–winning reporter, and Emmy Award–winning producer. His books *The Russians* (1976) and *The Power Game* (1988) were critically acclaimed bestsellers and are widely used in college courses today. As a reporter at *The New York Times,* Smith shared a Pulitzer for the *Pentagon Papers* series and won a Pulitzer for his international reporting from Russia in 1971–1974. Smith's prime-time specials for PBS have won several awards for examining systemic problems in modern America and offering insightful, prescriptive solutions.